TO Peter & Lianne,
Love,
Jim

CRIME

A publication of the
Center for Self-Governance

JAMES Q. WILSON
AND JOAN PETERSILIA

EDITORS

Institute for Contemporary Studies
San Francisco, California

Publication of this volume was made possible through the generosity of the Lynde and Harry Bradley Foundation and the Rand Corporation.

© 1995 Institute for Contemporary Studies

This book is a publication of the Center for Self-Governance, dedicated to the study of self-governing institutions. The Center is affiliated with the Institute for Contemporary Studies, a nonpartisan, nonprofit, public policy research organization. The analyses, conclusions, and opinions expressed in ICS Press publications are those of the authors and not necessarily those of the Institute or of its officers, its directors, or others associated with, or funding, its work.

Inquiries, book orders, and catalog requests should be addressed to ICS Press, 720 Market Street, San Francisco, CA 94102. (415) 981-5353. Fax (415) 986-4878. To order, call toll free (800) 326-0263.

Crime was edited at ICS Press by Tracy Clagett, and the cover was designed by Debbie Reece. The index was prepared by Shirley Kessel. The book was set in Garamond type by ComCom, an R. R. Donnelley & Sons Company, and printed and bound by Haddon Craftsmen, Inc., an R. R. Donnelley & Sons Company.

0 9 8 7 6 5 4 3 2 1

Library of Congress Cataloging-in-Publication Data
Crime / edited by James Q. Wilson and Joan Petersilia.
    p. cm.
    "A publication of the Center for Self-Governance"—Prelim. p.
    Includes bibliographical references (p.   ) and index.
    ISBN 1-55815-427-2 (cloth : acid-free paper).—ISBN
1-55815-417-5 (pbk. : acid-free paper)
    1. Crime—United States. 2. Crime prevention—United States.
I. Wilson, James Q. II. Petersilia, Joan. III. Center for Self-
Governance.
HV6789.C68 1995
364.973—dc20
                                                              94-33070
                                                              CIP

Dedicated to the memory of Richard J. Herrnstein, scholar, colleague, friend

CONTENTS

Foreword   *Robert B. Hawkins, Jr.*   xiii

Editors' Note   xvii

I   Introduction

1   Introduction   3
James Q. Wilson and Joan Petersilia

II   Crime and the Criminal

2   Crime in International Perspective   11
James Lynch

Choosing the Appropriate Object of Comparison □ Choosing
the Appropriate Method of Comparison □ Conventional
Wisdom: The United States Is the Most Crime-ridden of
Modern Industrialized Nations □ Illuminating the
Differences □ Conventional Wisdom: The United States Has
the Most Punitive Sentencing Policies of Any Industrialized
Democracy □ Conclusion

3   Criminogenic Traits   39
R. J. Herrnstein

The Stages of a Criminal Life □ The Psychology of Criminal
Behavior □ The Biology of Criminality □ Females, Males,
and Supermales □ A Case History □ The Causes of Criminal
Behavior

4   Biomedical Factors in Crime   65
Patricia A. Brennan, Sarnoff A. Mednick, and
Jan Volavka

Historical and Political Considerations □ Genetic Factors □
Perinatal and Neurodevelopmental Factors □
Neuropsychological Factors □ Neurological Factors □
Neurochemical Factors □ Psychophysiological Factors □
Biosocial Interactions □ Summary: Biomedical Factors and
Crime □ Policy Implications □ Concluding Thoughts on
Historical and Political Considerations

5   Juvenile Crime and Juvenile Justice   91
Peter W. Greenwood

Trends in Juvenile Crime □ Possible Explanations for Recent
Trends in Juvenile Arrests □ The Juvenile Justice System □
The Effectiveness of Juvenile Corrections Programs and
Placements □ The Case for Early Prevention

III   The Social Context of Crime

6   The Family   121
Travis Hirschi

The Family in Criminology □ Child-Rearing Practices and
Delinquency □ Other Family Activities Relevant to
Delinquency □ Structure and Functions of the Family □
Policy Implications □ Conclusion

7   The Schools   141
Jackson Toby

Statistical Reports of Everyday School Violence □ How
Disorder Fuels Everyday School Violence □ An Ounce of
Prevention □ What Can Be Done? □ Alternative Strategies for
Coping with School Violence

8   The Labor Market   171
Richard B. Freeman

The Facts □ Labor Market Incentives and Crime: Statistical
Studies □ The Effect of Labor Market Incentives on Crime:
Ethnographic Studies □ The Effect of Crime on Labor Market
Outcomes □ Earnings from Crime □ Conclusion

9   The Community   193
Robert J. Sampson

The Social Ecological Model of Crime □ Community Social
Disorganization □ The Ecological Concentration of Race and
Poverty □ Effects of Crime on Social and Economic
Organization □ Limitations of the Community Approach □
Public Policy Implications: Changing Places, Not People □
Conclusion

10   Street Gang Cycles   217
Malcolm W. Klein

Cycles and Definitions □ Examples of Asian, Drug, and
Entrepreneurial Gangs □ The Problem of Cycles □ Varieties
of Cycles □ Cycles and Recent Changes □ Cycles,
Cohesiveness, and Control

11   The Media   237
Edward Donnerstein and Daniel Linz

Violence in American Society □ The American Public's View
of Mass Media Violence □ Defining Violence in the Mass
Media □ Variables Contributing to the Media Violence and
Aggression Relationship □ Measuring the Amount of Violence
on Television □ The Relationship between Television
Violence and Aggressive Behavior □ The Effect of Television
Violence on Violent Crime □ The Twenty-two-Year New York
State Studies □ Theories of Media Violence and Aggression □
The Television and Film Industry View of the Research □
The Government and the Problem of Television Violence

IV   Crime Control Strategies

12   Gun Control   267
Philip J. Cook and Mark H. Moore

Gun Ownership, Use, and Misuse □ Instrumentality and
Availability □ The Values at Stake □ Alternative Gun Control
Policies □ Conclusion: What's to Be Done?

13   Alcohol and Other Drugs   295
David Boyum and Mark A. R. Kleiman

The Drugs-Crime Connections □ Drug Abuse Control
Policies □ Summary of Policy Implications

14   The Police   327

Lawrence W. Sherman

How Many Police Do We Need? □ Community Policing:
Police as Security Guards □ Problem Solving: Police as Public
Health Agents □ Tough Choices for Crime Prevention

15   The Physical Environment   349

Charles Murray

Defensible Space Theory □ Can the Creation of Defensible
Space Reduce Crime? Fear of Crime? □ The Community, the
Physical Environment, and Crime □ Situational Crime
Prevention □ Conclusion

16   Prosecution and Sentencing   363

Brian Forst

Typical Case Dispositions □ Variation in Screening and
Plea-Bargaining Practices □ Factors Associated with
Conviction and Incarceration □ Unbridled Prosecutorial
Discretion? □ The Exercise of Discretion in Sentencing □
Incentives of Prosecutors and Judges □ Structuring the
Exercise of Prosecutorial Discretion □ Structuring More
Consistent Sentencing Policies □ How Punitive *Should*
Sentences Be? □ Alternatives to Incarceration □ Directions
for Further Reform: The Effective Use of Information □ Where
from Here?

17   Prisons   387

Alfred Blumstein

Escalating Prison Populations □ Responses to the Population
Growth □ Some Projections for the Future □ Developing a
Rational Strategy for the Use of Prisons

18   Community Corrections   421

Todd R. Clear and Anthony A. Braga

The Changing Context of Community Corrections □ Changes
in Offenders under Supervision □ Changes in Supervision
Programming □ The Effectiveness of Corrections in the
Community □ Removing Offenders from Community
Supervision □ Challenges for Corrections in the Community

19   The Federal Role in Crime Control   445
John J. DiIulio, Jr., Steven K. Smith, and
Aaron J. Saiger
Political and Intellectual Barriers ☐ Administrative Barriers ☐
Conclusion

V   Reflections

20   Investing in Criminal Justice Research   465
Alfred Blumstein and Joan Petersilia
The Federal Research Program on Crime and Criminal
Justice ☐ Structure for a Criminal Justice Research Program ☐
Commitment to a New and Significant Research Program

21   Crime and Public Policy   489
James Q. Wilson
Our Two Crime Problems ☐ The Characteristics of Repeat
Offenders ☐ Prevention, Deterrence, and Western Values ☐
Controlling the Streets ☐ Prison ☐ Attacking the Causes ☐
Conclusions

Notes and References   511
Contributors   615
Index   619

FOREWORD

The American public's concern about crime is not new. But it has reached unprecedented proportions, as we recoil from the randomness and brutality of the criminal activity that afflicts our nation—and particularly our cities—today. Crime is a widespread problem that leaves few Americans and no communities untouched. For many of the poorest and least powerful of our citizens, however, protecting themselves and their families from violent crime is virtually a full-time preoccupation.

Through the work of our Center for Self-Governance, which supports community-building efforts in some of the nation's worst government housing projects, we at the Institute for Contemporary Studies have become more aware than ever that self-governance and the strong civil society that nurtures it are deeply threatened if citizens cannot count on a reasonable level of safety in their homes and persons. For this reason we proudly publish *Crime*. It will stand as a major contribution to the knowledge that is necessary if we are to find effective ways to lessen the menace of crime in our society.

In the face of rising public anxiety, the pressure on policy makers to "do something" about crime is strong—with the result that extensive and costly programs, with deep ramifications for our society, have often been put in place without real evidence of whether or not they will work. Too much policy has been made according to what we wish or believe rather than on the basis of what is known. The financial and social costs of ill-framed crime policy make it imperative that we find a way to understand the consequences and relative merits of our policy choices.

More than a decade ago, ICS Press published James Q. Wilson's *Crime and Public Policy,* which became an essential guide for policy makers. As the crime problems of the 1990s defined themselves, it became clear that a major update of that work was needed. The result is a new book: *Crime.* In compiling this volume, Wilson and his coeditor, Joan Petersilia, set out to bring the discussion begun in *Crime and Public Policy* into the present. This they have done with stunning success.

Wilson and Petersilia called upon twenty-six of the most respected scholars in the field of crime research to contribute new essays on the current state of research on crime and criminal justice. The book that the editors and contributors have written vastly surpasses the earlier volume in its scope and summarizes research on issues of urgent current concern—including "hot button" topics such as gun control and innate causes of criminal behavior. Many of the original subjects have been given updated treatment, but fully half the chapters in *Crime* add *new* subjects and new authors to the book. *Crime* represents some of the best scholarship on crime and criminal justice. No other volume provides this inclusive and authoritative account of what crime researchers know today. The authors explode a number of unhelpful myths about the origins and control of crime and hold up signposts pointing toward practical policy reforms. As Wilson and Petersilia write in their Introduction, "What we can understand, we can often improve."

Crime was written by leading experts in the field. But it is not just *for* experts. The book is intended to become the standard source for academic students of criminology and policy studies, for community leaders, for policy makers at all levels of government—local, state, and national—and for members of the general public actively interested in encouraging the creation of effective policy on crime. Not least, it will be valuable to members of the media for general background information—and to interdisciplinary scholars whose work needs to be informed by the best thinking in criminology.

For a new student of the subject or for the nonspecialist reader, the book contains unsettling revelations—on gangs, for example, or the biological wellsprings of criminal behavior. And some readers who hold strong ideological views of crime and justice will not like what they learn from these pages—that the war on drugs has contributed to the early release of violent offenders; or that there is good evidence that the viewing of violent, especially sexually violent, "entertainment" is associated with violent behavior; or that legalizing some drugs, marijuana, for example, would tend to reduce crime. That these chapters present their evidence objectively, however, does not mean that they lack a point of view. The authors and volume editors do not indulge what they see as wrong turns in our efforts to oppose predatory crime. And they propose a different focus for our national spending in pursuit of crime control—that we should stop committing large amounts of our national treasure blindly to "cures" we only *hope* will work and invest, instead, in furtherance of basic research into the causes, prevention, and control of crime—that is, the kinds of research embodied in this volume.

This book summarizes, then, the best available evidence on crime and crime control, but—more important—it considers how scientific knowledge can be used to design better crime control strategies. Success in dealing with crime will require wise choices by policy makers—particularly in Washington but in our communities, too. If we will take the lessons of *Crime* seriously, there is much that we can do as self-governing individuals in the community—keeping our families strong, working for safety in our schools, and supporting effective policing and correctional strategies. All of us can be empowered if we read these chapters and use what we learn from Wilson, Petersilia, and their contributors. Guided by this book, all of us can choose better strategies to curb violence and the fear of crime.

Robert B. Hawkins, Jr.
President
Institute for Contemporary Studies

EDITORS' NOTE

In September 1994, as this book was going to press, Richard J. Herrnstein, a contributor, died after a long battle with cancer. Dick was a scholar of immense erudition, breadth, and courage. His contributions to the understanding of behavior, criminal and noncriminal, have been great. He will be missed.

CRIME

INTRODUCTION

I

JAMES Q. WILSON AND JOAN PETERSILIA

INTRODUCTION

The essays in this book were written in order to show how social science research might help us understand and control crime. In 1983, one of us (Wilson) edited *Crime and Public Policy,* a collection having a similar purpose. Since then, the rates of some crimes have increased and the rates of others have decreased, but popular concern about crime has greatly increased. It seemed appropriate, therefore, to ask the leading scholars in this field to take a fresh look at crime and criminal justice. The result is this book, one that is much longer than its predecessor, a fact that reflects both an increase in our knowledge about certain topics and the inclusion of certain topics not treated at all in 1983.

The choice of new subjects reflects in part heightened public concern over certain aspects of the crime problem: juvenile crime, urban gangs, the challenge of supervising probationers and parolees in the community, and the role of television in producing violence. But the choice also reflects the availability of important research that did not exist, or did not exist to nearly the same degree, eleven years ago. And so we have chapters comparing the American experience with crime and punishment with that of other industrialized nations, reviewing our growing knowledge of biomedical factors in criminality, and explaining how neighborhood conditions may affect crime rates. One topic—the impact on crime of drugs, alcohol, and firearms—that was covered in a single chapter in 1983 is now discussed in two much longer chapters, reflecting both the heightened importance of these topics and our much greater knowledge of them in 1994.

The chapters that in this volume treat the same topics as were covered in 1983—the ones on the police, prosecutors, prisons, schools, families, and the physical environment—have been completely revised and updated. The additions and revisions are so extensive that this is not a "revised edition" of an older book; it is a wholly new book, and so we have given it a new title to distinguish it from its predecessor.

We believe that research findings can help policy makers; in fact, Alfred Blumstein and Petersilia discuss in the next-to-last chapter how such findings have already shaped some important policies and suggest ways by which this shaping might be expanded. But we are under no illusion that, when it comes to crime, science can save us. Every society has crime, and almost every one today has rising rates of crime. The universality of crime—and the near universality of its growth—suggest that understanding crime is tantamount to understanding some of the deepest mysteries of human nature and the greatest complexities of human society. Social science has made a beginning on this, but it has a very long way to go.

There are two great mistakes one can make in thinking about crime. The first is to assume that we already know what the problem is and how to solve it; all we need is "action." The second is to doubt that intellectuals can tell us anything at all of value; reducing crime, therefore, ought to be left entirely to cops on the beat and judges on the bench.

People of almost all political persuasions—liberals, conservatives, and libertarians—are likely to make the first mistake, though they differ in what they think we know. Many liberals think they know that unemployment, inadequate schooling, and the availability of guns are the big causes of crime. If so, they should carefully read the essays by Richard B. Freeman, Jackson Toby, and Philip J. Cook and Mark H. Moore. Many conservatives think that putting more cops on the street and imposing tougher sentences will make a big difference; if so, they should study the chapters by Lawrence W. Sherman, Brian Forst, Alfred Blumstein, and Todd R. Clear and Anthony A. Braga. Many libertarians think that legalizing (or at least decriminalizing) drugs will reduce street crime; if so, they had better ponder the chapter by David Boyum and Mark A. R. Kleiman.

People who think of themselves as nonideological pragmatists often make the second mistake. Forget this "ivory tower" research, they say, and get more cops on the street and take the handcuffs off the judges. If that is their view, they will be surprised to find how greatly police officers, judges, and correctional officials are already influenced by research and how much *more* guidance from research many of them would like to have. The wide gap between "the field" and "the ivory tower" that once may have existed in criminal justice exists no more; though there are skeptics within both groups, there is today an unprecedented level of collaboration between practitioners and researchers. Many of the ideas that we take for granted—the concept of the career criminal, the value of problem-oriented policing, the use of house arrest and other methods of intensive supervision—were developed by practitioners and researchers working in partnership.

There is one aspect of the crime problem with which many readers will be almost totally unfamiliar, and that is the role of various genetic and biomedical factors in criminality. And some who are familiar with these findings are apprehensive about them. Is science telling us that people are "born criminals" who should be treated that way from birth and for whom no hope exists? Not at all. The chapters by R. J. Herrnstein and by Patricia A. Brennan, Sarnoff A. Mednick, and Jan Volavka not only summarize the very powerful evidence implicating genetic and biomedical factors in criminality, they show how these factors interact with the environment and suggest ways by which this interaction can be modified by appropriate care. (The chapter by Travis Hirschi on the family contains many important lessons in this regard.) No reader should be surprised by any of this; it is almost impossible to imagine any important aspect of human behavior—athletic or musical ability, personality and mental health—that is not under the joint and complex control of our biological endowment, our social experiences, and sundry accidents and diseases. What we can understand, we can often improve. This has been the lesson learned from biomedical research in mental illness, substance abuse, and learning disabilities; it may in time be the lesson of research on delinquency and criminality.

Before turning to any of the chapters that follow, the reader should understand what we mean by "crime" and how it is measured. By "crime" we mean what the average person thinks of as predatory or street crime—muggings, murders, assaults, rapes, robberies, burglaries, and other thefts. This is not a book about white collar or organized crime or about political or commercial corruption. These are all important subjects, but they are beyond the scope of this volume. An entire book could be produced on any one of these other topics, and we hope that many will be.

Crime is measured in the United States (and in many other democratic nations) in one of two ways: police reports and victim surveys. In this country, police reports are compiled by the Federal Bureau of Investigation in an annual report called *Uniform Crime Reports* (UCR). The UCR tells us what crimes have been reported by people to the police and then reported by the police to the FBI. A victim survey is a survey of households in which people are asked whether they have been a victim of a crime during the preceding few months. An annual victim survey has been conducted in the United States each year since 1973 that involves questioning about 160,000 people located in some 84,000 households.

These two sources of data often produce different results. For many offenses, the National Crime Victimization Survey (NCVS) shows more crimes being committed than does the UCR, since many victims don't bother to report crimes to the police and (sometimes) a police department does not accurately report to the FBI even the crimes it hears about. But there are some offenses—homicide and assaults—in which the police count more crimes than does the NCVS. Homicide victims (obviously) cannot answer a survey.

Some assault victims—especially those who were assaulted by their spouse or the person they are living with—will tell the police about the assault when it first happens but are reluctant to tell surveyors about it after tempers have cooled or when they worry about reprisals if their report is overheard.

There are other differences as well. Among them are these:

- The UCR will count crimes reported by people (the homeless, those confined to institutions) and by many businesses that are not reached by the victim survey.

- The UCR counts every separate crime report; the NCVS will not count repeated instances of the same crime happening to the same person. If a woman is beaten up five times by her husband and calls the police each time, that is counted as five assaults in the UCR. But when (and if!) she reports these beatings to the NCVS, they are counted as one victimization.

- The NCVS relies on victims' memories of things that may have occurred some months ago. Many of us are not very good at remembering things, even crimes, or at remembering whether they happened to us this year or last. It also relies on somebody in the household reporting crimes committed against other members of that household, and so more errors may creep in.

- The NCVS is based on a random sample of all American households, and so, like any opinion poll, it is subject to some degree of sampling error.

These and other factors help explain why news accounts of "the crime rate" may differ depending on whether they are based on the UCR or the NCVS. During the 1980s, the UCR often reported rates of rape and assault as increasing whereas the NCVS reported the rates of these offenses as declining. (Perhaps rape and assault victims were more willing to report their victimization to the police as the decade wore on.) But the UCR and the NCVS are in general agreement that, over the decade (though not always in every particular year), burglary and larceny declined in the United States and that, during the second half of the 1980s, there was an upward trend in auto theft and robbery.

In the chapters that follow, the authors usually specify which crime rate—the UCR rate or the NCVS rate—they are using. When they don't, it is usually safe to assume that both sources suggest comparable trends. (A caution to the reader of newspapers: Don't pay much attention to news stories that report a sudden increase or decrease in crime during a single year. There is a lot of more-or-less random fluctuation in these numbers for any single year. Look at *trends* that last for three to five years.)

In selecting the authors for these chapters, the editors did not look for people who were in agreement with the editors on matters of analysis or policy; indeed, the editors are not necessarily in agreement on these matters themselves. We searched instead for the best available scholars. This book, therefore, does not represent a single point of view. It does represent, however, examples of some of the best scholarship on crime and criminal justice. We are not aware of any other book that provides as inclusive and as authoritative an account of the research findings on these topics.

We hope this book will stimulate discussion and clarify issues for policy makers, community leaders, and students of crime and criminal justice. Some readers may want to apply some of the findings reported here. But far more important than programs to be embraced are the methods to be learned: We want this book to teach people how to think about crime and policies proposed for its reduction. In this field, nothing is as easy as it sometimes seems.

The final chapter (by Wilson) tries to make that clear. It was written after the other chapters had been submitted and was informed by his perusal of them. But it is not intended to be a summary of them, and it was not reviewed or approved by the other authors. It is his personal statement of what he has learned from reading this book. Each reader is invited to make his or her own statement.

CRIME AND
THE CRIMINAL

II

JAMES LYNCH

CRIME IN INTERNATIONAL PERSPECTIVE

2

Conventional wisdom has it that the United States is both the most crime-ridden and the most punitive of industrialized nations. This chapter reexamines the conventional wisdom and finds it too simple to be useful. The United States has higher levels of lethal violence than other nations but similar or lower levels of minor violence and property crime than nations normally considered more civil. Similarly, prison use in the United States is not radically different from that in other industrialized nations for serious violence; but the propensity to incarcerate and time served in the United States is greater than in other nations for property and drug offenses.

Cross-national comparisons are often used to inform debates about crime and justice in the United States (Koppel 1992; Maurer 1991; Trebach and Inciardi 1993). Other nations, and particularly those similar to the United States in culture and level of development, are used as standards to which the United States should aspire. These comparisons are useful mirrors for evaluating our public policy and searching for ways to improve it. The danger of using cross-national comparisons for these purposes is that they are difficult to do well. The "foreign-ness" of culture, laws, and practices in other nations makes it easy to misrepresent policies and outcomes, and thereby the relative condition of nations. This misinformation distorts rather than informs policy debates by focusing attention on mythical problems or by overstating those that do exist.

While cross-national comparisons should be made, we must be aware of the limitations of these comparisons. In an effort to serve both of these ends, this paper examines the conventional wisdom on crime and justice in the United States. Beliefs that the United States is the most crime-ridden and the most punitive of industrialized nations are based upon casual cross-national comparisons of the United States with other nations. More rigorous comparisons are made both to illuminate the most common problems with these comparisons and to see if the conventional wisdom can withstand this type of scrutiny.

Choosing the Appropriate Object of Comparison

Most of the issues in cross-national comparisons are unique to the subject being addressed. As we will see in the following sections, the pitfalls common to comparisons of crime are different from those affecting studies of responses to crime. Nonetheless, some issues are common to all cross-national comparisons. Principal among these universal problems is the choice of appropriate nations to compare. Almost any comparison can be enlightening. For the purposes of evaluating or advocating policy, however, comparisons of very similar nations are more useful than comparisons of those very dissimilar (MacCoun et al. 1993). Such comparisons generate both heat and light. They generate the heat necessary for improvement because it is more difficult to attribute observed differences between nations to some fundamental cultural (or equally immutable) difference and, thereby, dismiss them. Comparisons of similar nations also generate more light in that they suggest that successful policies can be transplanted and may even suggest how or under what conditions.

For purposes of informing criminal justice policy, nations are similar to the extent that their criminal justice systems operate in similar environments. These environments are defined in large part by those institutions of social control that are less formal than the criminal justice system and that employ less coercive force. These less coercive institutions include family, community, schools and work. The role of the criminal justice system is to intervene when and where these more major institutions of social control breakdown (Bittner 1968 and 1973). The major burden of social control is carried by these less coercive institutions. The relative effectiveness of these institutions will determine the task confronting the criminal justice system in a particular country. Where these institutions are weak or in flux then intervention by the justice system will be both prevalent and severe.[1]

The second major component of the environment is the political and legal institutions operating in a particular nation. These arrangements shape the types of responses that criminal justice agencies make to the exigencies presented by the relative effectiveness of the less coercive institutions of social control. For example, the response of criminal justice agencies in democratic nations to breakdowns in major institutions of social control will be different from the response in nondemocratic societies. Presumably, agencies in democracies will be less likely to engage in overt, broad-based, and prolonged coercion than will those in nondemocratic nations. In addition, the specific division of labor and the procedures followed on a daily basis within the criminal justice system will also be influenced by the legal culture of the nation. Police in common law nations, for example, may be more restrained from intruding into the lives of the citizenry than police in civil code countries, but when they do intrude the police have broader powers to detain than they would in nations with code traditions (Langbien 1979; Lynch 1988).

Nations that are more similar to the United States on these three dimensions will provide much more useful points of comparison than countries that are less similar. Using this schema, nations such as England and Wales, Australia and Canada would be the best points of comparison because they have similar levels of participation in the major institutions of social control as does the United States; they are democracies; and they have common law legal traditions. France, Germany, and the Netherlands would be less similar and therefore less useful in that they have somewhat higher rates of participation in less coercive institutions of social control and do not have common law legal traditions. Switzerland and Sweden would be even less similar still because of their very high levels of participation in less coercive institutions, very high levels of democracy, and the lack of a common law legal tradition.

Choosing the Appropriate Method of Comparison

As with objects of comparison any method of comparison can be enlightening, but some are more appropriate for policy research than others. Cross-national studies of crime and criminal justice issues have customarily employed two different methodologies—comparative case studies and quantitative models. The former compare two or several nations on a particular policy or issue.[2] They offer a great deal of descriptive information on the nation and the policy. Comparisons are made qualitatively or on the basis of simple statistics. The latter method employs samples of twenty or thirty or more nations. Very little descriptive information is provided on policies or practices in the sampled nations. Formal models are used to understand differences in policies or outcomes across nations. These models are tested using very sophisticated multi-variate techniques.[3]

These two methods are complimentary, and each contributes to our understanding of cross-national differences in policies and outcomes. At this time and for the purposes of informing policy debates, however, comparative case studies hold the most promise and will be emphasized in the discussions that follow. If, as noted above, it is the very foreignness of nations that complicates cross-national studies, then the most important attribute of a study is to "get things right"—that is, policies and outcomes are accurately characterized in and across nations (MacCoun et al. 1993). Comparative case studies have a better chance of doing that than studies employing large samples of nations. This is especially the case with studies of prison populations, for reasons that are presented later in this chapter.

Even when policies and outcomes are understood and accurately characterized across nations, these models are quite fragile and potentially misleading. First, measures of policies and outcomes are based on highly aggregated data such as national means or other measures of central tendency. The distribution of crime or sentences in two nations can be very different, but the measures of central tendency can be the same, thereby obscuring the differences. Second, the results of these models are highly dependent upon the group of nations included as well as the variables in the model. Since sample sizes are small (usually ranging from eighteen to thirty-four) including or excluding even a few nations can radically change the results obtained. Similarly, adding or deleting a single variable or employing a different measure for a concept can alter the results. Again, this is aggravated by small samples in that only a few predictors can be included in any models and researchers must choose carefully. Third, usually only simple direct effects models can be tested, again because of sample size limitations. This limits a priori the information that can be gleaned from these studies. These problems affect much of the quantitative modeling in the social sciences, but they are particularly severe in cross-national studies because the level of aggregation is very high and the samples are very small.

Finally, although nation-level quantitative models may contribute to testing theories, they are not as appropriate for informing policy. Theory building requires the identification of principles that hold across all or a specific set of nations. Policy makers are usually more concerned about conditions in their nation or some similar nation than they are about general principles that may or may not adhere in their nation. Quantitative models often do not provide the information necessary to determine if the principles pertain to a specific nation. Similarly, it is often sufficient in theory building to identify relationships or principles that are not due to sampling error. The strength of that relationship or its impact on the outcome is less important. In formulating policy the question of how much difference it makes is central. We will see in subsequent sections that many of the "significant" relationships found with quantitative models have little effect on crime rates or other outcomes.

With these two limits on our review, we will now turn to two pieces of common wisdom that have emerged from cross-national comparisons—that the United States is the most crime-ridden nation in the world and that it is also the most punitive of industrialized nations.

Conventional Wisdom: The United States Is the Most Crime-ridden of Modern Industrialized Nations

The basis for this bit of conventional wisdom is not clear. It may be that the country is suffering from its Wild West or gangster movie image. Certainly, there have been spectacular crimes, such as those involving the murder of tourists in Florida, that have attracted a great deal of attention. Also the extremely high homicide rate in the United States may be a major contributor to the image of the country as the most crime-ridden of developed nations. But homicide is not coincident with crime in general, indeed it is a very rare event even in the United States. Moreover, anecdotes are weak evidence.

There are better sources of evidence available in the form of new and improved statistical systems designed to measure the prevalence of crime cross-nationally. These statistical series have routinized the collection of information on a broad range of crimes in a manner that avoids some of the most common errors in anecdotal observation. While these systems have their limitations (which will be discussed below), they can provide a useful test of the common wisdom, if they are used with an appreciation of their strengths and weaknesses.[4]

Determining the Prevalence of Crime Cross-nationally

There are two major sources of statistical data on crime incidence cross-nationally—police statistics and victimization surveys. Police statistics are compiled internationally by Interpol (Interpol 1988), the United Nations (Kalish 1988), and a number of independent researchers (Gurr 1977; Archer and Gartner 1984; Bennett and Lynch 1990).[5] Victim survey data are routinely collected independently by a number of nations (Kaiser, Kury, and Albrecht 1991) and the International Crime Survey (ICS) has been conducted in as many as thirty-three different jurisdictions (van Dijk, Mayhew and Killias 1990; van Dijk and Mayhew 1993). Each of these data sources can tell us something about the relative prevalence of crime across nations. Each also has its own set of distortions that can result in misleading comparisons across nations. It is important to use each source of data for that which it does best.

Cross-national Comparisons: Simple and Complex

From the perspective of police statistics, the United States has much higher rates of serious violence than other industrialized democracies, even those nations most similar in terms of the environment of the criminal justice system. As Table 2.1 shows, the homicide rate in the United States is more than twice that of the next-highest country—Canada—and many times that in other common law countries such as England and Wales. The same is generally true for robbery.

With respect to serious property crime, however, the United States is considerably lower than other similar nations. The burglary rate in Australia is 40 percent higher than that in the United States, in Canada 12 percent higher, and in England and Wales 30 percent greater. Even Sweden and the Netherlands, which enjoy the reputation of low crime countries, have burglary rates 35 percent and 84 percent greater than the U.S. rate. Among the industrialized democracies we compared, only France and Switzerland have lower rates of burglary than the United States. The picture is much the same for auto theft. Among the nations most institutionally similar to the United States, Australia and England and Wales have higher rates of auto theft. The nations more dissimilar to the United States are evenly split between those with substantially higher rates (France and Sweden) and those with lower rates (Germany and the Netherlands).

The view from victim surveys is similar in many respects to that from police statistics and different in others. United States respondents report the highest levels of violent crime,[6] but these levels are not significantly different from those in some countries most institutionally similar to the United States, such as Australia and Canada (Table 2.2). Indeed, the differences between the United States and other nations in terms of the prevalence of violence generally is much less in the victim surveys than in the police statistics. In

TABLE 2.1
Rates of Crime Reported by the Police per 100,00 Population by Nation and Offense, Interpol, 1984

Nation	Homicide	Robbery	Burglary	Auto theft
USA	7.9	205.4	1,263.7	437.1
Australia	3.4[a]	83.6	1,754.3	584.7
Canada	2.7	92.8	1,420.6	304.9
England & Wales[b]	1.1	44.6	1,639.7	656.6
W. Germany	1.5	45.8	1,554.1	118.0
France	2.3	105.6	809.8	483.4
Netherlands	1.2	52.9	2,328.7	155.9
Sweden	1.4	44.1	1,708.8	460.0
Switzerland	1.1	24.2	276.8	NA[c]

NA = not applicable.
a. This figure includes attempted homicide as well as completed homicide.
b. These data are for 1983.
c. These data were not reported because they include bicycle theft as well as motor vehicle theft.
SOURCE: Carol Kalish, *International Crime Rates* (Washington, D.C.: Bureau of Justice Statistics, 1988), 3.

TABLE 2.2
Crime Rates by Type of Crime and Nation, 1988, 1992

	Type of crime		
	Total violence	Serious violence	Property crime
USA	6.7	3.9	10.7
Canada	5.5	3.4	9.8
Australia	6.1	3.9	12.4
England	3.7	2.0	9.0
W. Germany	3.9	2.7	5.7
France	2.4	1.9	8.4
Netherlands	4.6	2.9	7.1
Sweden	3.0	1.7	7.3
Switzerland	1.7	1.2	5.5

SOURCE: International Crime Survey.

contrast, the differences between the United States and other nations with respect to property crime in the victim surveys are in the opposite direction of those found in the police statistics. The prevalence of property crime is fairly similar in common law countries. It is somewhat greater in Australia than in the United States and somewhat less in England and Canada. Germany, the Netherlands, and Sweden, however (which have higher rates of serious property crime than the United States according to police statistics), have substantially lower rates of property crime in victim surveys.

These two sets of findings are consistent if we assume (1) that the police statistics accurately characterize very serious violence and several classes of serious property crime and (2) that the victim surveys better represent lesser violence and most larcenies. This type of interpretation is supported by the fact that when comparisons of violence are restricted to more serious violence such as robbery the differences between the United States and other nations (even common law nations) using victim statistics begin to resemble those from the police statistics (van Dijk and Mayhew 1993, 19). The same is true when we restrict property crime to motor vehicle theft (van Dijk and Mayhew 1993, 11). As we will see in the following section, there is a limit to the extent to which data from police statistics can and should be consistent with those from victim surveys (Biderman and Lynch 1991). It is important to demonstrate that the two sources are reasonably consistent where they should be and that anomalies between them are comprehensible. It is equally important to recognize that overall they tap two very different components of the crime problem.

Limitations of Existing Data

One of the major problems in comparing statistics is ensuring that the systems in each country include a large proportion of criminal acts and that the range of crimes is the same in each nation. Given comparable scope, it is important that these statistical systems classify and count crime incidents in a similar fashion. Some systems are sample-based and therefore suffer from sampling error and cannot be easily used to estimate the prevalence of rare crimes, such as rape. Finally, some data systems are highly aggregated and therefore inflexible, so that they cannot be easily used to understand cross-national differences in crime prevalence.

Problems of scope.   Both available police statistics and victim surveys focus on a fairly narrow range of common law crimes such as homicide, sexual assault, other types of assault, robbery, and theft. While there is some attention to fraud or drug crimes, most white collar and victimless crimes are excluded from these data systems by design. Hence, there are no compendia of international data on a large component of behavior that many people consider criminal.

Police statistics, of course, exclude crimes that do not come to the attention of the police. In some crime classes—for example, homicide—this omission is trivial (Riedel 1990), while in others—for example, larceny—a substantial proportion of crimes will be excluded.[7] For purposes of cross-national comparisons, however, the absolute number of crimes excluded is of less concern than the constancy of that exclusion across nations. Valid cross-national comparisons of police statistics can be made, if approximately the same proportion of each type of crime is reported to the police in each of the nations compared.

The best evidence that we have about differences in reporting to the police across nations suggests that the proportion of crime not reported to the police varies considerably across nations and types of crime. Van Dijk and Mayhew (1993) indicate that reporting of crimes in the ICS to the police varied from a low of 31 percent in Spain to a high of 62 percent in Scotland.[8] This variability across nations is different for different types of crime. Virtually all of the motor vehicle thefts in the ICS were reported to the police in every country, and the same is true for burglaries involving forcible entry. The cross-national variability of reporting to the police is much greater for theft, vandalism, threats, assaults, and even robbery. This suggests that cross-national comparisons using police statistics are best done for extreme violence, such as homicide, burglary with forcible entry, and motor vehicle theft.

Victimization surveys include crimes that are recognized as such by the respondent whether they are reported to the police or not. They do not include homicide, for obvious reasons.

Police statistics include reported crimes against commercial establishments while victimization surveys do not, unless the crimes against commercial establishments involve injuries to employees or theft of an employee's property.[9] Consequently, victimization surveys will also underestimate the total level of crime in a nation. This may not pose a problem, if one is interested in the victimization of individuals and not total crime in a society. This could distort comparisons based on police statistics, however, if the volume of commercial enterprises varies considerably across nations. Crime rates that use police statistics in the numerator and population in the denominator will be higher in a nation with a large number of commercial enter prises than in another with fewer commercial establishments, when the risk to private citizens is the same. For some classes of property crime the effect of commercial crime on cross-national comparisons is not trivial. According to the FBI (1989) the gross burglary rate in the United States was 1,314 per hundred thousand population in 1988. In England and Wales, the rate was 1,628 per hundred thousand (Home Office 1989). When commercial burglaries were excluded the U.S. rate was 880 and the British rate was 878. Comparing the gross burglary rates, the risk in England and Wales is 24 percent higher than it is in the United States. Risk based on the noncommercial rates is essentially the same. If commercial crimes were uniformly identified in police statistics, commercial and noncommercial rates could be computed and used as appropriate. Unfortunately, this is not the case. Commercial burglaries are identified, but this is not true for most larcenies or motor vehicle thefts.

Problems in classification and counting.   The principal classification decision made in these systems is that which places an eligible crime into a subclass, such as homicide. The pertinent rules define the attributes of an event that requires it to be counted in a particular subclass. These rules can vary substantially across nations. In the United States, for example, attempted murder is reported as aggravated assault in the *Uniform Crime Reports* (UCR), while in England and Australia attempted murder is included with other homicides.

The common response to this variability in classification rules is to define classes of crime that are extremely broad and can, thereby, accommodate great differences in classification rules. The disadvantage of this approach is that the resulting crime classes are large and heterogeneous. Two nations can have the same number of thefts, but the type of theft events in the two countries can be quite different. Ninety percent of the thefts in one can involve forcible entry while only 20 percent of the thefts in the second nation are burglaries. Although these nations are radically different in terms of their crime problem, they would appear the same in police statistics.

Even when crime classes are fairly narrow and similarly defined across nations there can be intra-class variations that can distort comparisons. For example, in 1988 the FBI reported 542,968 robberies, of which 33 percent involved firearms (FBI 1989). In the same year, the British Home Office reported 34,137 robberies, of which 8.6 percent involved firearms (Home Office 1989). While all of the events in the two nations may have included the attributes necessary to be classified as robbery—force or threat and theft—

the robberies in the United States involved more force, as indicated by the more extensive use of weapons. On this basis one could argue that robberies in England and Wales are not comparable to those in the United States. Given the current state of police statistics, there is not much that can be done about this type of intra-class variation.

The importance of crime classification for cross-national comparisons cannot be overstated. As we will see in a later section, the differences in the mix of crime across nations is much greater than the differences in the level of criminal activity. Crime-specific comparisons across nations will tell us much more than comparisons of total crime. These crime-specific comparisons, however, are predicated on the assumption that crime classification is uniform across nations. Very little of the detailed work necessary to support that assumption has been done.[10]

Since victim survey data are collected on an incident basis rather than as aggregated counts (as most police statistics are), obtaining comparable crime classifications is less problematic than it is with police data. As long as the attributes necessary for crime classification are included in the survey, they can be used to classify crime events. Victimization surveys done under the auspices of individual nations or by individual researchers differ widely with regard to the information included on each crime reported (Kaiser, Kury, and Albrecht 1991; Block 1992). More recently, efforts to standardize the content of crime surveys were undertaken with the International Crime Survey (ICS) (van Dijk, Mayhew, and Killias 1990; del Frate, van Zvekic, and van Dijk 1993). Given this common core of information, it should be possible to obtain a common crime classification across nations.

Flexibility.   Most national police data systems and all international compendia of police data are based on aggregated counts of crime occurring in a jurisdiction. These counts cannot be disaggregated in ways that would help us understand cross-national differences in rates. For example, we may know the gross rate of robbery in the United States and Germany but we cannot compute rates separately for men and women or for racial or ethnic minorities. Victim survey data, on the other hand, are collected on an incident basis, so that crimes can be distinguished by characteristics of the victim, the place of occurrence, and many other characteristics of the event.

Samples and censuses.   Victim surveys employ probability samples of the resident population, while most police statistics purport to be censuses of crimes reported to the police.[11] As a result, we must take sampling error into account when comparing victimization data cross-nationally. More important, the small sample sizes in the ICS will limit the extent to which we can use the very detailed information included in the survey. For example, with samples that average about 2,000 per nation, it is impossible to create very detailed crime classes because there will not be enough cases in the class to provide reliable estimates of prevalence. As with police statistics, we are forced to use broad and potentially heterogeneous crime classes that can defeat the purpose of crime-specific comparisons.

What Do I Use When?

We are fortunate to have two reasonably comprehensive sources of data on crime internationally that can be used to establish the position of the United States relative to other countries with regard to crime. Police and victim statistics are complementary in that each measures best a component of the crime problem that the other does not (Biderman and Lynch 1991). Police statistics should be used for comparing those classes of crime that are known to be well reported to the police and that are consistently well reported across nations. This includes homicide, motor vehicle theft, and burglaries involving forcible entry. Victim surveys should be used for comparing classes of crime that are not well reported to the police. These classes include most larcenies other than motor vehicle theft and more minor forms of violence. In addition, police statistics should be used to assess differences in rare classes of crime such as homicide or rape (if other reporting errors are not too severe) that either cannot be assessed in victim surveys or are seriously affected by sampling error. Victim surveys, on the other hand, can be used to explore the reasons for cross-national differences in crime because they are collected on an incident basis and can be aggregated and disaggregated more than available police data. We should compare and contrast these different sources of data to increase both our understanding of crime and the strengths of these data.

Is There Really More Crime in the United States?

When the various data sources are used with appropriate consideration of their error structure, the picture emerging from international crime statistics both supports and contradicts the common wisdom that the United States is the most crime-ridden of industrialized democracies. The risk of lethally violent crime is much higher in the United States than in other nations, even those most institutionally similar. The risk of minor violence, however, is not greater in the United States than it is in other common law countries. This risk *is* greater than the risk of minor violence in less similar countries such as Germany or France. In contrast, the United States has lower rates of serious property crime than other similar nations and even lower rates than many countries considered civil or safe. The victim survey data suggest that the prevalence of minor property crime is about the same in the United States as in other common law countries, but greater in the common law countries than in other industrialized democracies.

Illuminating the Differences

Some analyses have been done to explain these differences in cross-national crime rates. These analyses have examined the effects of various factors believed to affect either the motivation or the opportunity to commit crime (Nettler 1978; Cohen and Felson 1979; Clarke and Cornish 1986). Studies that emphasize criminal motivation examine the relative size of crime-prone populations such as the young, persons living in urban areas, or the unemployed. Other studies have examined the effect of the social organization of nations, such as the level of inequality or the depth of social safety nets. Studies emphasizing opportunity have examined the influence of the availability of crime targets or the instruments and situations that permit potential offenders to act on their motives. These have included the volume of property and its portability, the availability of necessary instruments (such as weapons), or appropriate settings—for example, rate of activity out of the home and the prevalence of vulnerable housing structures. Some of these studies have addressed the two aspects of crime where the United States tends to have higher offense rates than other similar nations—lethal violence and minor theft.

Homicide

There have been a few cross-national comparisons of homicide that have held age and other factors constant (Fingerhut and Kleinman 1990). These studies indicate that the differences between the United States and other nations in the risk of homicide do not disappear when age-specific rather than gross rates are used. The differences between the United States and other nations remain quite large even when comparisons are restricted to the most violence-prone groups—fifteen- to twenty-four-year olds.

Other studies have shown that differentiating homicides into those committed with a firearm and those using other means substantially changes the position of the United States relative to other countries. Fingerhut and Kleinman (1990) find that a much higher percentage of homicides in the United States are committed with firearms than in any other nation, including those nations most institutionally similar to the United States. Sloan et al. (1988) found that the difference between homicide rates in Seattle and Vancouver were due almost entirely to differences in the rate of homicides with firearms. Sproule and Kennett (1990) found that the rate of homicide in the United States is roughly twice that of Canada for homicide by means other than firearms and also for homicides with firearms other than handguns. The U.S. rate of homicides with handguns is 14.6 times that of Canada. The gross homicide rate in the United States for 1988 was 7.4 per hundred thousand population, while the gross rates in England and Wales were 1.31 for the same year. When homicides due to firearms are excluded from the rates, the

British rate is 1.22 per hundred thousand and the United States rate is 2.92 per hundred thousand. [12] When gross rates are used, citizens in the United States are 5.6 times more likely to be victims of homicide than citizens of England and Wales. When firearms are excluded, persons in the United States are only 2.4 times as likely to be victims of homicide as persons in England and Wales. The evidence is mounting that firearms and especially handguns are an important determinant of the high homicide rates in the United States relative to other, institutionally similar nations, indeed nations with otherwise comparable levels of violence overall.

The central role of firearms in producing the relatively high rates of homicide in the United States has led to calls for national policies to reduce the availability of guns. These findings cannot be used to support availability reduction policies until there is some evidence that those motivated to kill will not simply choose other weapons to accomplish their ends. Studies of opportunity reduction for suicide (Clarke and Mayhew 1988) suggest that displacement is not great. Killias (1993) and Sproule and Kennett (1990) infer that displacement will not be substantial from the fact that nations with low or reduced availability of firearms do not have high rates of homicides with other weapons. This inference may not be warranted, however, since these same cross-section patterns could be attributed to factors other than gun availability that keep all forms of homicide low in nations with regulation of firearms. Longitudinal data would be more appropriate to make this point. Sproule and Kennett (1989) used longitudinal data to evaluate the effects of handgun restrictions on homicides with handguns in Canada. They observed a slight displacement effect. At this point the preponderance of the evidence seems to suggest that displacement will not be substantial.

Property Crime

Analyses of the ICS have been done to understand observed differences in crime across nations (van Dijk, Mayhew, and Killias 1990; van Dijk and Mayhew 1993). These studies have identified differences in the composition and social organization of nations that are associated with higher rates of criminal victimization both within and across nations. Within nations they have found almost uniformly

1. that the young are at greater risk than the old
2. that those in large urban areas are more at risk than persons in smaller places
3. that those with higher income are more at risk than those with lower income [13]
4. that those who engage in activity out of the home more frequently are more often victimized than those who stay home

Some regularities have also been observed between nations. These are mostly relationships between opportunity factors and levels of crime. There is a persistent relationship, for example, between car ownership and levels of motor vehicle theft—the higher the ownership the higher the rate of theft. Similar correlations have been observed for the proportion of the population living in detached, semidetached, and terrace houses (attached row houses). The greater the proportion of the population residing in attached housing the greater the risk of burglary (van Dijk, Mayhew, and Killias 1990).

These very interesting data on individual and national factors have not been combined in models or even simple standardizations to determine the effect of individual risk factors on cross-national differences in rates. If, for example, we computed age-specific rates for all nations and then forced the age distribution in each nation to conform to that of the United States, we would be able to determine the effect of differing age distributions on observed differences between the United States and these nations. It is possible that nations will not differ in the distribution of factors related to risk within nations. Consequently, these factors cannot explain cross-national differences. Similarly, correlations observed at the national level may be statistically significant but may explain little of the difference in the level of crime across nations.

The few standardizations that have been done suggest that many of the factors affecting risk within countries or factors that correlate with differences in the level of crime across nations have little effect on cross-national differences in property crime rates. Van Dijk, Mayhew, and Killias (1990) report that standardizing motor vehicle rates for vehicle ownership had very little effect on differences in motor vehicle theft. Similar results occurred when burglary rates were adjusted for differences in the distribution of the population across different types of housing. Standardization of property crime rates in the 1988 ICS by age and urban residence also had little impact on cross-national differences.[14]

Standardization by income, however, has a sizable effect on cross-national differences in property crime rates. When income-specific victimization rates in each nation are multiplied by the income distribution found in the United States, the rates of property crime in these other nations become substantially more like that of the United States. The average change in the rate of property crime across the seven nations examined is 19 percent. The property crime rate in England and Wales increased by 27.8 percent, in Germany by 26.8 percent, in France by 26.3 percent, and in Switzerland by 30.8 percent. In almost every case, the difference between the standardized and unstandardized rates was due to the facts that the United States had a greater proportion of the population in higher income groups and that these groups had higher property victimization rates in each nation. It is interesting to note that the two common law nations that were essentially the same as the United States in terms of the unadjusted property crime rate were not much affected by the income standardization. This provides further support for the importance of income distributions for property crime rates. (See Table 2.3.)

It is not clear exactly what this effect of income distributions means. One interpretation is that the income distribution reflects the availability of property to steal. The United States, Australia, and Canada have similarly high property crime rates because these nations have more people with more property than other industrialized democracies. Income, and therefore property for taking, is held by a smaller proportion of the population in other nations. More work is required to interpret these initial findings.[15]

Making Better Comparisons

Newly available data on the prevalence of crime cross-nationally and some of the analyses of these data can make cross-national comparisons more useful for informing policy. First, these data indicate that the United States is not the most crime-ridden of industrial democracies. The fact that the United States does not differ from other common law nations with respect to minor violence and serious property crime casts doubt on global indictments of the United States as having a criminal culture. The United States stands alone, separate from even other common law countries, not in the prevalence of violence but in its lethality. Differences between the United States and other nations are crime-specific, and the search for understanding and remedies should be equally specific. It is unlikely that explanations for such specific differences will operate at the level of culture.

Second, the difference between the relative position of the United States and other nations with respect to homicide when firearm use is held constant

TABLE 2.3
Five-Year Prevalence Rates per 100 Population, 1983–1988: Original and Standardized on U.S. Income Distribution

Nation	Property crime rates		
	Unadjusted	Adjusted	Percentage change
USA	41.13	41.13	0
Australia	37.95	37.65	−00.77
Canada	37.85	38.23	01.00
England & Wales	30.48	38.96	27.83
Germany	39.92	50.62	26.79
France	36.81	46.49	26.30
Netherlands	45.43	54.71	20.43
Switzerland	29.21	38.23	30.88
Average percentage change			18.92

SOURCE: International Crime Survey, 1988.

clearly indicates that more attention must be given to reducing the availability of firearms. While it may be impossible to eliminate firearms once they are widely available in a nation, it seems that from the standpoint of reducing homicide, it is worth trying. Third, much more work should be done with the ICS and other victim surveys to inform cross-national differences in property crime rates. Specific attention should be given to elaborating the effects of income distributions on cross-national crime rates.

The work in this area tells us even more clearly that the information that we have on hand to study cross-national differences in crime is not adequate. Incident-level police data on well-reported crimes and especially lethal violence is essential. More information on the offender and the victim would be useful both in police records and in victim surveys. This information should include factors related to the social marginality of victims, such as their race (or ethnicity), participation in the labor force and educational institutions, family structure, and citizenship status. Without these data it is difficult to test many of the arguments concerning the role of heterogeneity in producing the higher violence rates in the United States.

The utility of victim surveys for understanding crimes not well reported to the police would be greatly enhanced if the samples employed in the ICS could be increased. Currently, the samples sizes are too small to take full advantage of the very detailed information that the surveys offer. Our understanding of cross-national differences in minor theft would be increased if more information were gathered in the ICS pertaining to the volume of property in households and to its the use and storage. Interpreting the effects of income distributions noted above would be simplified if the surveys included measures of the volume of goods available in households that was independent of income. Finally, more information on the geographical areas in which crimes occur would be useful in both police and victim survey data.

Conventional Wisdom: The United States Has the Most Punitive Sentencing Policies of Any Industrialized Democracy

The common wisdom about the punitiveness of U.S. sentencing policy is based largely on comparisons of incarceration rates across nations. Many studies have shown that the United States has a higher per capita incarceration rate than any nation other than the (then) Soviet Union and South Africa (Doleschal 1977; Waller and Chan 1975; Maurer 1991). As in the case of cross-national comparisons of crime rates, it is important to characterize accurately the nature of punishment cross-nationally. It is equally important to determine whether the observed differences are the result of more punitive sentencing policies or some other factors. Most cross-national comparisons do neither.

Accurately Characterizing Punishment Cross-nationally

Punishment here refers to sanctions imposed by the state in response to violations of the criminal law. Describing punishment policies cross-nationally is difficult in part because sanctions can be administered at so many points. Police officers can punish by taking you into custody or giving you a warning or a citation. The prosecutor's decision to prosecute or not can be construed as a form of punishment. Judges can punish at sentencing. Prison and parole officials can punish through classification, decisions regarding good time or early release, decisions regarding institutional discipline, and revocation decisions. Few nations document all of these decision points well and in a manner that facilitates cross-national comparison. As a result, comparisons of punishment policies focus on the sentencing decision and beyond. This focus quickly leads to an examination of incarceration largely because this is generally the most severe form of punishment allowed by the state and because the availability and comparability of data are greater here than at other stages in the postconviction process. Hence, the comparison of punishment policy becomes a comparison of prison use (Young and Brown 1993).

Conceptual Ambiguity

Even with the focus narrowed to incarceration, good comparisons are difficult because the concept remains ill-defined. Incarceration can be defined as taking a person into custody and requiring him or her to reside in a particular, secure setting. "Secure" here means that the person is not free to come and go. Certainly, a traditional prison will fall within this definition. It is less clear whether community-based facilities fall in this category—or mental hospitals or court-ordered drug treatment facilities or internal exile. Nations differ widely in the mix of facilities used for incarceration, and the decision as to which to include or exclude can be very consequential.[16] It is important, therefore, to establish that the concept of incarceration is equivalently defined across the countries being compared. Young and Brown (1993) maintain that these differences between incarceration and imprisonment do not affect cross-national comparisons substantially. It is likely, however, that offense-specific comparisons can be affected while the import for total rates of imprisonment will not be large.

A second conceptual ambiguity in most comparative studies of prison use is the failure to distinguish the propensity to incarcerate from the length of time served. Both of these decisions are important dimensions of punishment policy, but they can be quite distinct. Nations can have the same incarceration rates—that is, the same number of persons in prison per capita on a given day—yet have very different imprisonment policies. One nation may use incarceration frequently for any given offense but impose very short sentences. Another nation can impose very long prison terms but use that sanction sparingly for any given offense. While comparisons of incarceration rates are useful, it would be much more informative for policy purposes to distinguish the prevalence of incarceration from the length of sentences imposed.

The treatment of pretrial detention is also problematic. While pretrial detention is not a sentence, it is certainly custody and can affect sentencing. Judges can take time served before trial into consideration at sentencing, so that an offender is sentenced to time served pretrial. Absent the pretrial detention, the convicted person would have been sentenced to custody. Since the person is never in custody serving a sentence, he or she will not appear in incarceration rates. To the extent that countries have very different practices regarding the use and duration of pretrial detention, these differences will distort cross-national comparisons. This information is not easily retrievable from correctional data systems cross-nationally. Lynch et al. (forthcoming) found that the proportion of the prison population that were detainees as opposed to prisoners was essentially the same in the United States and England and Wales for 1991. Young and Brown (1993) report levels of detention use similar to those in the United States for England and Wales, West Germany, Scotland, and Norway in 1987. Use of detention in Australia was about 25 percent less than in the United States. This suggests that pretrial detention practices are roughly the same in some of the nations most institutionally similar to the United States and will not confound comparisons based on sentenced populations.

Differences in the age of adult jurisdiction can also influence cross-national comparisons of imprisonment. Most comparisons of imprisonment are based upon the adult prison population. The age of adult jurisdiction can vary both within and across nations. In the United States and Canada, for example, the generally agreed-upon age of adult jurisdiction is eighteen, while in England and Wales it is seventeen. Within the United States, however, some states begin adult jurisdiction at sixteen. Moreover, the increased use of offense-specific waivers further blurs the lower age limit of adult jurisdiction. Young and Brown (1993) maintain that differences in age of jurisdiction do not amount to much. This assessment would seem appropriate for both total and offense-specific comparisons because the age distribution of offenders should not vary much by offense, while the use of mental hospitals will be more pronounced in some offenses than in others.

Finally, the fact that many decision makers have control over the time actually served in prison complicates the determination of length of stay. Most industrialized democracies have some forms of sentence reduction after admission—such as good time, or early release—that can substantially alter the sentence imposed by the court. There is some evidence that these practices differ across nations (Farrington and Langan 1992). These decisions must be taken into account in determining length of stay in custody.

Data Availability

Once the concept of incarceration is defined equivalently across nations, those who wish to compare incarceration policies must ensure that the statistics they use include all of the jurisdictions responsible for custody. In a country like England this is a simple matter, since the entire correctional system is administered by the Home Office. It is more complicated in federal systems such as those of the United States and Canada, where responsibility for custody is distributed across federal, state or province, and local levels of government.

In the United States, the federal government has responsibility for persons convicted of violating federal laws. The state has custody of persons convicted of violating state laws and of persons whose sentence generally exceeds one year. Local jails (usually administered at the county level) have responsibility for detainees and sentenced prisoners with sentences under one year. State institutions house about two-thirds of the imprisoned population, jails about one-quarter, and federal institutions the remainder. Omitting any jurisdiction will result in an underestimate of the U.S. prison population. Until recently the data available on the state prison population in the United States were more readily available than information on jails. Consequently researchers would include U.S. prison statistics but would fail to include, or would include less precisely, data on jails. This selective inclusion led not only to underestimates of the prevalence of incarceration but also to inaccurate estimates of sentence length. Since persons in jail serve less time in custody by definition than persons in prison, excluding jail populations would result in inappropriately high estimates of time served in custody.

Computational Complexity

Even the computation of incarceration rates can introduce distortions into cross-national comparisons. The most common method for computing imprisonment rates is to divide the number of persons in prison by some at-risk population such as the number of adults in the population or the number of arrested persons. This is commonly referred to as a stock rate. This approach is preferred largely because data for prisoners in custody are believed to be most accurate, and they are certainly more readily available than admissions or release data in many countries. However, since the probability of an offender being in prison on a given day is a function of the length of his sentence, stock statistics tend to over-represent the more serious offenders with longer sentences. Serious offenders with long sentences also accumulate in prison populations and, therefore stock studies overestimate the propensity to incarcerate in those countries with higher rates of serious crime. In contrast, flow studies using annual *admissions* over some at-risk population, such as adults in the population or arrested persons in that year, are not affected by the accumulation of more serious offenders. This is not to say that length of sentence is not an important dimension of punitiveness but, as I argued earlier, that, for reasons of clarity, it should be treated separately. Flow designs permit the separation of the propensity to incarcerate from the length of sentence served and, thereby, provide a clearer picture of both dimensions of punishment. [17]

When flow rates are used to assess the propensity to imprison, other methods must be used to compute the length of time served in custody. [18] The particular choice of computational method can have substantial effects on cross-national comparisons. The usual way of estimating time served in custody for a particular offense involves using the experience of persons released in a given year, that is, exiting cohorts. This can be misleading because these cohorts under-represent inmates with long sentences (Shryock and Siegel 1973). This can lead to the ironic situation in which a nation that is increasing the length of time served can actually appear to be shortening sentences. [19] Life tables and other techniques, such as ratios of stock to flow rates, that take account of long term prisoners may yield very different estimates of time served.

Standardizing for Factors Other Than Punitiveness

One of the major criticisms of comparisons of imprisonment rates that are used to support statements about relative punitiveness is that they fail to account for differences in the level and nature of crime and criminals in a society. This is crucial because greater punitiveness requires that a more severe sanction be imposed in response to a similar provocation. Unless one is willing to assume that crime and criminals are equally prevalent or similar across nations, comparisons of per capita incarceration rates have little to tell us about the relative punitiveness of sentencing policies. Following this logic, the United States should have higher per capita incarceration rates because it has higher per capita crime rates and more serious crimes. If other nations were confronted with a similar crime problem, they would have the same per capita imprisonment rates.

Accounting for different levels of crime.   The best way to inform this debate is to compare incarceration rates for fairly specific types of crime—for example, homicide—that take account of the differences in the incidence of that crime across nations. Crime-specific comparisons are better than total rates because they increase the comparability of the type of provocations confronted by each sentencing system. Rates based on total incarcerations and total crimes can confound differences in the nature of crime with the relative punitiveness of sentencing policy. Nations with higher levels of homicide, for example, can have higher levels of incarceration without being more punitive. If comparisons are made on the basis of homicides, specifically, then the effect of the mix of crimes in society is reduced.[20] Moreover, if rates are based upon the number of homicides, the number of arrests for homicide, or the number of convictions for homicide, rather than population, then the effect of the volume of crime on incarceration will be held constant.[21]

Accounting for different types of crime.   Crime-specific comparisons go a long way toward standardizing the provocation to which the criminal justice system responds. As I noted earlier in this chapter, commonly used crime classes, however, can include very different types of events. Robberies in the United States, for example, involve firearms to a much greater extent than events classified as robbery in England and Wales (see the earlier section "Problems in Classification and Counting"). The United States could imprison convicted robbers at a much higher rate than England and Wales without being more punitive. If firearms use was taken into account as an aggravating circumstance, the two nations may not be different in their response to the crime. This type of intra-class variation in the severity of the crime is not easily accounted for, because most statistical systems classify crime events by charge or crime type without specifying additional aggravating or mitigating circumstances.

Accounting for different types of offenders.   The prior criminal history of convicted persons can affect the type of sentences received (see Chapter 16 in this volume). Persons with prior involvement in serious crime receive more severe sentences than those with less prior criminal involvement. If offenders in one nation have more extensive and serious criminal histories than offenders in another nation, then sentences in the first nation can be more severe than those in the other without being more punitive. There is not a great deal of information on the distribution of criminal histories among convicted persons cross-nationally. The available information suggests that in general fewer prisoners in the United States have prior convictions for criminal offenses than do inmates in England and Wales (Lynch et al forthcoming; Lynch 1993a). Approximately 60 percent of the inmates in both nations claimed to have a prior sentence to custody as an adult, but only 11 percent of the British inmates claim no prior record while 22 percent of the United States prison population have no prior record of juvenile or adult custody (Lynch et al. forthcoming; Dodd and Hunter 1992).

Comparing the Level and Length of Incarceration

The foregoing discussion describes several of the most prevalent problems encountered in using cross-national comparisons of imprisonment to assess the relative punitiveness of sentencing policies. Some of these problems cannot be easily addressed with available information. Others can be. The picture of the relative punitiveness of the United States changes when (1) both the prevalence of incarceration and the time served are evaluated and (2) the extent and nature of crime is taken into account.

The prevalence of incarceration.   In 1988 I compared the United States, Canada, England and Wales, and West Germany using both stock and flow incarceration rates for specific offenses as well as population-based and arrest-based rates (Lynch 1988). This comparison also included both the jail and prison populations in the United States and federal and provincial prisoners in Canada. When arrest-based as opposed to population-based rates are used, the difference between the United States and other nations is reduced substantially.

On the basis of the customary measure of prison use—population-based stock rates—I found that the United States was much more likely to incarcerate for violent offenses than either England or West Germany. In the case of homicide, the United States incarcerated at 7.5 times the rate of Great Britain and 5.3 times that of Germany. The relative propensity to incarcerate was similar for robbery, where the rate for the United States was 8.7 times that of England and 4.7 times that of Germany. Differences in the rates were somewhat less for property crime. For burglary, the English rate was approximately one-half that of the United States. In the larceny/theft category, which combines burglary, larceny and motor vehicle theft, the incarceration rate for the United States was roughly twice that of Germany and England. (See Table 2.4.)

When flow rates based upon arrest were used, the probability of incarceration given arrest was roughly the same for violent offenses in the United States, England, and Canada, although England had a somewhat lower rate for homicide. Essentially the same was true for burglary and for the more inclusive class of property crime—larceny/theft. With the exception of homicide, the rates for both violent and property crime were still considerably lower in West Germany than they are in other countries. The rate for robbery

TABLE 2.4
Arrest-based Incarceration Rates by Country and Offense

Offense	Country			
	1982 USA	1983 England	1980 Canada	1984 West Germany
Homicide	.738	.636	na[a]	.816
Robbery	.394	.388	.435	.085
Burglary	.236	.219	.175	na[b]
Larceny/Theft	.107	.093	.119	.019

na = not available.
a. Data on admissions to provincial institutions were not readily available on a national basis.
b. Germany does not report data on a class of crime exactly the same as burglary. Burglary is included in the Larceny/Theft class.

was approximately one-fifth of that in the United States, England, and Canada. For the larceny/thefts, the incarceration rate in Germany was one-sixth of that in the United States and Canada and one-fifth of that in England.

Farrington and Langan (1992) compared the use of incarceration in the United States and England and Wales on the basis of court data. Their results were different, but consistent with those in Lynch (1988). The probability of incarceration given conviction was not radically different across nations for violent crimes, but it was substantially different for property crimes. The probability of being sentenced to prison or jail for homicide was .86 in England[22] and .98 in the United States, and for robbery it was .87 and .88 respectively. In contrast, a person found guilty of burglary in the United States had a .74 probability of a custodial sentence but only a .40 chance in England and Wales.

Time served.   I compared the United States, England and Wales, Canada, Australia, and West Germany in terms of the length of imposed sentences and actual length of stay for specific offenses (Lynch 1993a). Again efforts were made to include all components of the custody population in Canada and the United States. I found that the length of sentences imposed for these offenses was much longer in the United States than in the other nations. The mean sentence imposed in the United States was longer than sentences in other countries for similar offenses. The "mean" sentence imposed for homicide in the United States is 1.12 times that imposed in West Germany. The mean sentence imposed in the United States for robbery is 1.29 times that in West Germany, 1.58 times that in England and Wales, and 2.26 times the sentence imposed in Canada. For burglary, the mean sentence imposed in the United States is 2.17 times the sentence levied in England and Wales and 3.51 times that imposed in Canada. For the combined larceny/theft category used in West Germany, the mean U.S. sentence is 2.37 times that imposed in England and Wales, 3.1 times that in West Germany, and 3.29 times the sentence levied in Canada.

When comparisons were made on the basis of the average time actually served, however, the differences between the United States and these other nations were reduced considerably, especially for violence. The mean time served for homicide is greater in Canada (57 months) than it is in the United States (50.5 months without adjusting for the jail population and 42.5 months when jail adjustments are made). The average time served for homicide in England and Wales (43.0 months) is not very different from that served in the United States. The average time served for robbery in the United States and Canada is approximately the same, 20.9 and 23.6 months respectively, when the jail population is included. The mean sentence for robbery is higher in the United States (30 months) than in Canada when only the prison population is used. Time served for robbery is much lower in England and Wales (15.8 months) than in the other countries. (See Table 2.5.)

The large differences in time served between the United States and these

TABLE 2.5
Mean Time Served in Custody by Nation and Offense, Exiting Cohort
Method (in months)

Nation	Offense[a]			
	Homicide	Robbery	Burglary	Theft[b]
Canada (1986)	57.2	23.6	5.23	2.0
England & Wales (1986)	43.0[c]	15.86	6.72	4.65
United States, prison only (1983)	50.5[c]	30.14	16.06	12.1
United States, prison and jail (1983)	42.5	20.9	10.56	7.01

a. These means were computed from data grouped in large class intervals. Intra-class variation in sentence length may produce differences between these estimates and those based on less aggregated data.
b. Theft refers to larceny only and does not include burglary and motor vehicle theft.
c. See David Farrington and Patrick Langan, "Changes in Crime and Punishment in England and Wales and America in the 1980s," *Justice Quarterly* 9, no. 1 (1992): 6–46. These estimates of time served are lower than those obtained by Farrington and Langan largely because of differing assumptions about the end interval for time served and the treatment of persons receiving life sentences and death sentences. The relative differences between the countries are in the same direction and of approximately the same magnitude.

other countries occurs for property crimes—burglary and larceny. The length of time served for burglary in the United States is 16.2 months (for prisons only) or 10.6 months (for combined jail and prison populations), while burglars in Canada serve 5.3 months and in England 6.8 months. For larcenies (excluding motor vehicle theft) the average time spent in the United States is between 7.01 months and 12.5 months. In Canada, the average time served is 2 months and in England it is 4.65 months. (See Tables 2.6 and 2.7.)

The differences that I observed using exiting cohorts were consistent with those obtained using life tables and stock/flow ratios. There was no appreciable difference in time served for homicide in the United States and England and Wales, but length of stay for homicide was about 14 percent longer in the United States than in Australia. For robbery, the expected length

TABLE 2.6
Expected Sentence by Nation and Offense, Life
Table Method (in months)

Nation	Offense	
	Homicide	Robbery
England & Wales (1986)	80.4	27.3
United States (1983)	76.2	44.8
Australia (1987)	64.3	23.9

TABLE 2.7
Estimates of Time Served by Nation and Offense, Stock/Flow Ratio
Method

	Offense			
Nation	Homicide	Robbery	Burglary	Theft[a]
England & Wales (1983)	5.86	1.19	.57	.71
United States (1982)	5.06	2.04	.86	.96
West Germany (1984)	4.75	3.30	na	1.27

NOTES: na = not available. Adjustments were made to the jail correction used to estimate the flow rates in James P. Lynch, "A Comparison of Prison Use in England and Wales, Canada, the United States, and West Germany: A Limited Test of the Punitiveness Hypothesis," *Journal of Criminal Law and Criminology* 79, no. 1 (1988): 180–217.
a. Theft includes larceny, burglary, and motor vehicle theft.

of stay in the United States is considerably more than that in either Australia or England and Wales. Convicted robbers in England and Wales can expect to spend an average of 27 months in custody and those in Australia will spend 24 months in custody on average. In the United States, convicted robbers can expect to spend approximately 45 months in custody. The stock/flow ratio method allowed for the inclusion of comparisons between England and Wales, the United States, and West Germany. The stock/flow ratio for homicide was somewhat higher for England and Wales than for the United States and West Germany, and the U.S. ratio was slightly higher than that of Germany. In the case of robbery, the estimate of time served for England and Wales is only 58 percent of that in the United States and 36 percent of that served in West Germany. Moreover, the estimate of time served for robbery in West Germany is 1.6 times that in the United States. The pattern is similar for the large larceny/theft class. The time served for this crime is lowest in England and Wales, somewhat greater in the United States, and greatest in West Germany. Time served in England and Wales is only 74 percent of that served in the United States, while time in custody in West Germany is 32 percent greater than that served in the United States.

Farrington and Langan (1992) also found that the length of stay for homicide does not differ much between the United States and England and Wales. Time served in the United States, however, is substantially longer for robbery than it is in England, and the difference is even greater for burglary. The ratio of time served in the United States to time served in England and Wales is 1.87 for robbery and 2.27 for burglary in 1987.

The special case of drug offenses.   In order to maximize coverage within nations and comparability across countries, virtually all of the cross-national studies of prison use have compared nations on their response to serious common law crimes and specifically crimes similar to UCR Index crimes. Many of the most dramatic changes in prison use, however, seem to be occurring in the area of drug offenses. This is certainly true in the United States, where the proportion of the state prison population in custody for drug crimes increased from 8 percent in 1986 to 22 percent in 1991.

Comparisons of prison use for drug offenses are complicated by the breadth and the heterogeneity of drug crime classifications cross-nationally and the ambiguity of the line between treatment and imprisonment in any given nation. These problems are aggravated by the fact that statistical systems that document responses to drug offenses are not as well established as those for the common law crimes. Nonetheless, some rough comparisons can be made between the response to drug crimes in England and Wales and that in the United States. In 1990, the probability of incarceration (at the state, local, or federal level) given arrest for drug offenses in the United States was .119. [23] The comparable figure in England and Wales was approximately .055 (Home Office 1992). [24] In terms of the length of stay for persons admitted for drug offenses, there is some evidence that time served in custody is longer in the United States than it is in England and Wales. In 1990, the stock/flow ratio for drug offenses was approximately 1.84 in the United States and 1.21 in England and Wales. Lynch et al. (forthcoming) found that a much larger proportion of inmates sentenced for drug offenses in the U.S. received sentences in excess of ten years than inmates serving sentences in England and Wales. Twenty-six percent of inmates sentenced for drug offenses in the United States had sentences in excess of ten years while only 8 percent of persons serving sentences for drug crimes in England and Wales had such sentences. While these data are fragile, they do suggest that the United States is substantially more punitive than at least one other similar nation in its response to drug offending.

Is the United States Really More Punitive?

Although the common wisdom holds that the United States is the most punitive of industrialized democracies, the picture emerging from this discussion is more complex. The United States has the highest per capita rates of incarceration of any industrialized democracy. This is prima facie evidence for punitiveness. When this stock rate is decomposed into the propensity to incarcerate and the length of stay and when account is taken of the level and type of crime in a nation, however, the relative punitiveness of the United States becomes less clear. The propensity to incarcerate and the length of time served for homicide is not radically different in the United States and other institutionally similar countries. Indeed, there is some evidence that other nations may require longer terms in custody for homicide. Within violent crimes, as the level of violence decreases the disparity between the United States and other common law countries increases with respect to time served, but not the propensity to incarcerate. In the case of property crime, it is clear that the United States incarcerates more and for longer periods than other similar nations. The same appears to be true for drug offenses. The United States, then, is not universally more punitive than other industrialized democracies, but it does seem to be more punitive with respect to property crime and drug offenses. As the type of property crime becomes less severe the disparity between the United States and other common law nations increases both with respect to the propensity to incarcerate and the length of time served.

If other similar nations are useful standards then these cross-national comparisons suggest that the United States should reduce both the propensity to use incarceration and the length of time served for lesser property offenses (and perhaps drugs).[25] The use of incarceration for extreme violence in the United States is not very different from that in other nations and need not change. The relative position of the United States and other similar nations with regard to moderate violence is not clear. The United States seems to impose longer sentences for crimes such as robbery, but this may be due to more extensive use of weapons in the United States. More work must be done in this area.

These findings also have implications for efforts to reduce prison populations. It is clear from these studies that the United States will have larger prison populations than other institutionally similar nations largely because of the relatively high levels of lethal violence. Even if sentencing policies were similar in the United States and England, for example, the high rates of serious violence in the United States would produce higher per capita rates of incarceration. This is a point often missed in studies of prison use that control for total crime in a society. At the same time, reasonably large reductions in the prison population could be achieved by reducing the use of incarceration and the length of time served for property crime (and possibly drug offenses) to the level of nations like England or Canada.[26]

Conclusion

Cross-national comparisons of crime and responses to it figure prominently in debates about criminal justice policy. Unfortunately these comparisons are often done without sufficient attention to the complexities involved. This chapter has described some of that complexity. It has also described some of the recently available data that can be used to make appropriately complex comparisons and thereby dispel some of the misinformation created by those that are more casual. Finally, these data have been used to test the common wisdom that the United States is both the most crime-ridden and most punitive of industrialized democracies. I have attempted to show that the differences between the United States and other nations in these areas are less extreme than commonly believed and are more crime-specific. Hopefully this kind of specificity in cross-national comparison will refocus the policy debate from vague and general prescriptions to more particular suggestions for improvement and for further investigation.

R. J. HERRNSTEIN

CRIMINOGENIC TRAITS

Who commits crime? Our picture of the typical offender depends on how broad a brush we use to paint the answer. With too fine a brush, only the accidents of single lifetimes become salient—a harsh parent, an evil influence, a bad break or two that tipped the balance the wrong way. We may look at this picture and say that there is no typical offender, only atypical ones, each atypical in his or her own way. At the other extreme, with too broad a brush, only the general sociological forces emerge—poverty, inequality, oppression, racism, and the like. In this picture, an offender is typical only to the extent that he or she has been buffeted by those social forces. But between these two levels of description lies evidence showing offenders to be, on the average, something other than a random sampling of the population at large or of the populations subjected to the sociological forces. The focus of this chapter is on this intermediate level of description, where we seek the distinguishing individual traits of the average offender. These are the *criminogenic* traits referred to in the chapter's title.

To the extent that this intermediate level differs from the two on either side of it, the traits of the typical offender cannot be assumed to be caused either by how he or she was treated by society—by the educational system, by the job market, by the political system, by the law—or by accidental circumstances having led the offender astray. Social institutions, families, friends, even random events, matter, but they do not tell the whole story about the average criminal life. This chapter shows that the average offender is psychologically atypical in various respects, not necessarily to a pathological degree, but enough so that the normal prohibitions against crime are relatively ineffective. In designing public policy, we must bear in mind that a society that successfully keeps 80 to 90 percent of its population on the right side of the law may find that it needs other measures to deter the remaining 10 to 20 percent, for reasons that have more to do with individual criminogenic traits than with defects in policy.

The Stages of a Criminal Life

Some people find it hard to imagine criminogenic traits at all, independent of social forces. Aren't crimes, they say, crimes only because society says so? The answer is yes, but that does not mean that everyone is equally likely to violate the social and legal constraints on our behavior. Whatever else criminal behavior may be, it is distinctive in being illegal. The very fact that it is illegal may affect different people differently, depending on their psychological makeup. For example, in the nineteenth century, when the use of opium and morphine was legal, the typical addict was an upper or middle class, middle-aged woman. After the drugs became controlled substances and their use illegal, their price skyrocketed; but the typical opiate addict became a young, lower class man, someone who could afford it less than a middle or upper class woman.[1] Making it illegal evidently deterred the earlier population of users; the current population of illegal users differs from the earlier one in its individual characteristics as well as in its sociological ones.

The most serious crimes are, in addition, not just arbitrarily so. They are not like the consumption of opium, which is illegal now but was routinely recommended by physicians a century ago. Most serious crimes are activities that no human society has ever tolerated. Rape, murder, robbery, arson, and theft are among the crimes that are criminal because they strike most people in most societies as sufficiently wrong to warrant restraint by the weighty arm of the law. Virtually by definition, acts that most people are disposed to do are not going to fall into this category of *male in se*—crimes that are wrong in themselves. It should come as no surprise that the small minority of people who kill, steal, rape, or burn for their own evil purposes are unlike the rest of us.

The typical offender today, like the typical addict, is a young male, probably between the ages of fifteen and twenty-four. Age and sex are, in fact, among the most predictive variables we know of for criminal behavior, but there are other distinctive factors, which the chapter will consider in due course. Age and sex, as criminogenic variables, serve to illustrate what is meant by saying that offenders are not a random selection of the population: the average person is not a young male, but the average criminal is. Later in the chapter, sex as a criminogenic variable is considered further. Here, I comment briefly on adolescence as criminogenic.

Many youngsters, especially males, break the law during their teens and early twenties, but most of them quit soon thereafter. Younger than that, boys may be boys, but they are too small, too much under the control of grown-ups, and not interested enough in sex, money, mayhem, and fast cars to wreak much damage. Older, the processes of socialization, or a regular paycheck, tame most of them. This tells us that the typical offender is young not just because habitual criminals are active in their late teens and early twenties but because a few crimes are committed at this age by many people who will not be habitually criminal at other times of their lives.[2]

For example, almost all male college undergraduates (a population which, we hope, is not distinctive for its criminal tendencies) admit (or boast about) committing a few crimes—underage drinking, falsifying drivers' licenses, driving while intoxicated, illegally using controlled substances, shoplifting, and various other manifestations of adolescence.[3] A much smaller proportion of the general population starts offending even earlier than in mid-adolescence and continues doing so at high rates until well into adulthood. But even though some low level of occasional criminality during male adolescence is the rule more than the exception, most of the personally threatening crime around us is committed by a small fraction of the population. What is this small fraction like?

One way to find out is from longitudinal studies, which pick a sample of people at one point in their lives, then follow them long enough to see who breaks the law, how they break it, and how much they do so. Or, alternatively, they may pick a sample of offenders, and then try, retrospectively, to reconstruct the events or characteristics that foreshadowed the criminal behavior.

Longitudinal studies tell us that juvenile offenders are at risk to become adult offenders. And vice versa: adult offenders are likely to have been juvenile offenders. In a large sample of men born in Philadelphia, for example, then followed in a longitudinal study that covered several decades, the ones who had been arrested as juveniles were more than four times as likely to be arrested as adults as the ones not arrested as juveniles. Similarly, those arrested as adults were almost three times as likely to have been arrested as juveniles as the men who had not been arrested as adults.[4] Although the precise ratios vary, the pattern is firmly established in other longitudinal studies.[5]

It would an overstatement to say "once a criminal always a criminal," but it would be closer to the truth than to deny the evidence of a unifying and long-enduring pattern of encounters with the law for most serious offenders. We cannot, however, accept this unifying pattern uncritically, for it is possible that being labeled a criminal by the criminal justice system marks a person for further arrests and convictions and that that, rather than any personal trait, explains the apparent continuity of criminal lives. Or, perhaps, a person who has been caught breaking the law resigns himself to a life of crime, believing that the odds of a happy, law-abiding life have become hopelessly stacked against him.

These alternative explanations probably have some validity; but they cannot fully, or even nearly, account for the enduring patterns of behavior suggested by the evidence. Even among males who have never been arrested or convicted, those who characterize themselves (on anonymous questionnaires) as offenders in youth are more likely to do so in adulthood than those who did not do so earlier, and those who so describe themselves in adulthood were likewise more likely to have done so as youngsters.[6]

Longitudinal studies uncover other traces of the continuity of criminal behavior. The probability of first arrests is smaller than that of second arrests, which, in turn, is smaller than that of third arrests, and so on. In the Philadelphia study mentioned earlier, about 35 percent of the men had a first arrest. Among these men, about 54 percent had a second arrest. The trend continues upward: for men arrested six times, about 80 percent had a seventh arrest.[7] Other studies have found the risks of arrest rising even higher for those with long arrest records. The average seriousness of the crime similarly rises with each successive arrest.[8]

If each arrest *reduced* the risk of further arrests, we could conclude that encounters with the criminal justice system deterred further offending, or at least that criminals learn to become shrewder about their crimes after they've been caught a few times. What does the reverse trend, which is so strongly present in the data, mean? One possibility is that encounters with the criminal justice system literally increase a person's tendency to break the law or decrease his ability to get away with it. But a simpler explanation is that each successive arrest isolates a population at increasingly high risk for being arrested, so that by the time a person has been arrested, say, eight or nine or ten times, he (or, infrequently, she) falls into a category of people whose behavior is so strongly tipped toward whatever it is that gets one arrested that future arrests are almost certain. What is it that gets one arrested? Perhaps part of it is that each successive arrest isolates a less competent group of offenders, one that is more likely to get caught for its crimes. But it would be extremely odd if breaking the law were not at least one of the factors that get a person arrested.

The rising risk of arrest and the increasing gravity of the offenses suggest that within the population as a whole is a subpopulation of repeating, perhaps close to incorrigible, serious offenders. Each successive arrest draws an ever tighter loop around this highly criminal population, by filtering out the people with weaker tendencies to break the law and get arrested. The 5 to 7 percent of the population falling into the category of habitual offenders is responsible for no less than half of all arrests or police contacts. For example, 70 percent of all convictions by 1981 of English men born in 1953 were of the 5.5 percent who had six or more convictions.[9] Comparable concentrations of crime have turned up in Scandinavian statistics as well.[10] Everything points toward there being a small (in percentage terms) population of chronic offenders who are committing most of the serious crime that has inflated the crime statistics, frightened people off our streets, and filled up the prisons since 1960.[11] The sharp concentration of crime among a relatively small fraction of the population has been used to argue for selective detention and incapacitation,[12] but here I note it simply as a fact about who breaks the law.

For more insight into who these chronically criminal people are, we turn to one of the leading contemporary studies, still under way and already invaluable to students of criminal behavior. The Cambridge Study of Delinquent Development started in 1961–62 with a survey of 411 boys, ages eight to nine, living in working class neighborhoods in London within a one-mile radius of a research office that had been established for the study. The sample comprised all the boys of their age attending six local primary schools (399) plus, in order to make the group more representative cognitively, a dozen boys from a local school for the educationally subnormal. Eighty-eight percent of the boys were whites whose parents had been raised in Great Britain; 3 percent were blacks with at least one parent from the West Indies or Africa; the rest of the sample included a smattering of other ethnic and national backgrounds. Compared with the British population at this time, the sample was disproportionately working class, white, and urban.

A deluge of publications—by the original director, Donald West, and his successor, David Farrington, and their associates—continues to flow from this sample of youngsters as they have grown into adulthood.[13] At this writing, the sample has been interviewed eight times, starting at the age of eight, most recently at thirty-two. It has been repeatedly tested psychologically. The families have been visited by social workers and interviewed. The boys' schoolteachers at several grade levels filled out questionnaires. Their classmates were asked for ratings of the boys—for their popularity, aggressiveness, and other behavioral traits. Official police and court records for the boys and their families have been obtained, along with self-reports of criminal and noncriminal behavior. Data were assembled on school performance, employment, sexual experiences, and family life. The follow-up has been singularly effective. Every man from the original 411 was accounted for at the age of thirty-two. Eight had died; of the 403 still alive, almost 94 percent have been interviewed or have responded to questionnaires.

By the age of thirty-two, the sample had suffered 683 convictions of 153 of the men, for crimes more serious than petty violations of law. Although only 12 percent of the convictions were for violent offenses, a third of the men convicted for any crime had at least one conviction for a violent crime. Twenty-two of the men had 9 or more convictions. Almost one-half of the offenses ever committed by all 411 men were the work of this most chronically criminal 5 percent of the men. The serious offenders had started breaking the law early and often, and were still at it in their early thirties. The signs of chronic adult criminal behavior were already in evidence before the boys reached the age of ten. This, along with other information, is presented in Figure 3.1.

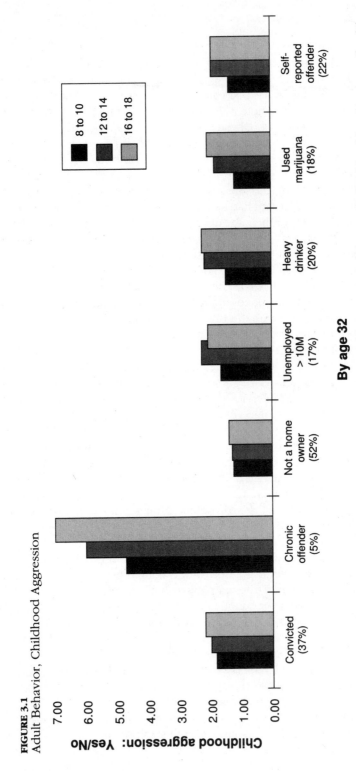

FIGURE 3.1
Adult Behavior, Childhood Aggression

By age 32

NOTE: The horizontal scale lays out categories of adult behavior in the Cambridge Study of Delinquent Development, and the percentages of the adult sample who manifested the behaviors. The vertical scale is the ratio of those engaging in the adult behaviors who were rated as aggressive in childhood divided by those who were not rated as aggressive.

SOURCE: David P. Farrington, "Childhood Aggression and Adult Violence: Early Precursor and Later Life Outcomes," in *The Development and Treatment of Childhood Aggression*, ed. D. J. Repler and K. H. Rubin (Hillsdale, N.J.: Erlbaum, 1991), 5–29.

Consider the second group of three columns in Figure 3.1, pertaining to the 5 percent who were chronic offenders by the age of thirty-two. These men were almost five times as likely to have been rated as aggressive between the ages of eight and ten as to have been rated as nonaggressive.[14] That ratio is plotted as the first of the three columns in this group. Those who would become adult chronic offenders were six times as large a proportion of those rated aggressive between the ages of twelve and fourteen as those rated nonaggressive. The ratio increased further, to seven to one, when they were between sixteen and eighteen. Chronic adult offenders, in other words, are disproportionately recruited from the population of children and teenagers who are aggressive early in life. The figure shows several other adult behaviors that were similarly foreshadowed by aggressiveness in childhood—whether they were ever (that is, by the age of thirty-two) convicted at all (first group of three columns), whether they had been unemployed for more than ten months (fourth group of columns), and whether they described themselves as heavy drinkers (fifth group) or as offenders (final group).[15]

Among these categories, childhood aggression is least predictive of not owning a home (third group of three columns); but even here, the predictiveness reaches statistical significance. Presumably home ownership measures, not only economic resources, but something about rootedness in the community. The men who do not develop this rootedness were disproportionately aggressive in childhood. We may take it as self-evident that the most deviant behavior was the chronic offending of the most criminal 5 percent, which was best predicted by childhood aggression; the least deviant behavior in the figure—the 52 percent who do not own their own homes—is least well predicted. But, across the board, childhood aggression is predictive of adult antisocial or criminal behavior. The generally rising heights of the columns say that the older the boy is, the more predictive his childhood aggressiveness was of his adult antisocial or asocial behavior.

Aggression was not the only childhood behavior that foreshadowed later criminality. Figure 3.2 looks at the fifty-seven men in the sample who, by the age of thirty-two, had at least one conviction for burglary. Because most habitual offenders commit a variety of crimes, the convicted burglars turn out to have been engaging in other crimes as well.[16] The figure shows whether, by the age of fourteen, these men had manifested various signs of antisocial or unconventional behavior, such as sheer troublesomeness, thievery, bullying, and so on. The ratio in the figure is obtained by dividing into the proportion of burglars who engaged in the childhood activity the proportion of nonburglars who had. Thus, the ratio of over eight for sexual activity says that over eight times as many of those who were convicted of burglary by the age of thirty-two had been sexually active by the age of fourteen, compared with those who were not convicted.[17] The five childhood behaviors that are most strongly associated with becoming an adult burglar are sexual activity,

FIGURE 3.2
Childhood Asociality, Adult Burglary

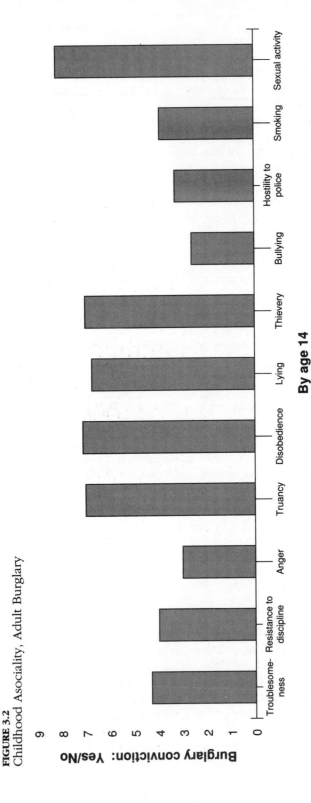

By age 14

NOTE: The horizontal scale lays out categories of behavior at the age of fourteen for the boys in the Cambridge Study of Delinquent Development. The vertical scale is the ratio of those engaging in the boyhood behaviors who had a conviction for burglary by the age of thirty-two divided by those who had no burglary conviction.

SOURCE: David P. Farrington, "Explaining the Beginning, Progress, and Ending of Antisocial Behavior from Birth to Adulthood," *Facts, Frameworks, and Forecasts*, ed. Joan McCard (New Brunswick, N.J.: Transaction, 1992), 253–86.

disobedience, truancy, thievery, and lying. Less predictive are childhood anger and bullying. But all of the plotted ratios in the Figure are significantly above one, indicating their association with adult burglary.[18]

The Cambridge study leaves little doubt that adult criminal behavior is part of a broader category of uncivil or antisocial behavior that reaches back to childhood. A sample of over 200 American boys pushes the foreshadowing of such behavior still earlier into childhood.[19] These boys[20] were recruited from two school districts in an unidentified small metropolitan area when they were between ten and sixteen years old, then followed up for five years. They were questioned about their behavior, delinquent and otherwise. Their parents, peers, teachers, and others who knew them were also interviewed.

The mothers were questioned about the boys prior to the first interviews. How hard had the boys been to raise? mothers were asked. Were they problem children; were the mothers ever worried about their sons' behavior or adjustment, and why? The answers provided various measures of psychological trouble reaching back into the boys' second year of life and afterward. Mothers were also asked about their (and their spouses') parental styles. Besides the answers the mothers gave, the interviewers were trained to take note of the way the mothers and sons behaved with each other.

From official records and self-reports a picture could be drawn of the boys' delinquency, the seriousness of their offenses, and the frequency of offenses up to the latest point in the survey, when they were between fifteen and twenty-one years old. The survey ranged widely enough to show whether, in addition to offending, the boys pursued "the delinquent lifestyle," as it has been called—use of alcohol and drugs, frequent fighting, or otherwise raising hell. The study does not give us a full picture of lifetime criminality, because it terminates so early in the boys' lives, but it shows the precursors of at least the beginnings of criminal behavior in adolescence and early adulthood. Inasmuch as we know that almost all chronic adult offenders were in some kind of trouble by late adolescence, we can assume that the variables in this study foreshadow chronic criminality to some extent.

The boys who were hardest to raise between the ages of one and five started offending earlier than the boys who were easier to raise. They were likely to be arrested younger, and they committed more, and more serious, crime. Boys who were hard to raise when they were toddlers were more than four times as likely to be multiple offenders as boys who were easy to raise. Their thefts were of larger amounts; their aggressions were more severe; and the variety of their criminal offenses, more diverse. The boys who were identified as aggressive, hyperactive, impulsive, and lacking in attention span when they were between ten and sixteen years old were more likely to have been problem children between one and five years old. Thus, troublesomeness in infancy unfolded into hyperactive aggressiveness and impulsiveness in childhood, thence into delinquency and crime in the teens.

The sequence is not rigid or unvarying, inasmuch as it often varies in one respect or another from boy to boy, but it is a prototypical pattern, observed with at least statistical regularity. In this particular study, not much effect on later delinquency could be traced to parental behavior, although one has turned up in other studies.[21] For example, in the Cambridge study, among the five major predictors of chronic offending that were available when the boys were not yet ten years old, one was parenting that was inconsistent, indifferent, or harsh, along with troublesome childhood behavior, low tested intelligence, poor economic conditions, and parents with criminal records.[22]

Troublesome toddlerhood as a predictor of later delinquency was unearthed only in mothers' memories both in the Cambridge study and in the American study just described. It may therefore be suspect. After all, a mother with an uncontrollable adolescent son may simply be misremembering the boy's infancy as being more difficult than it actually was. This interpretation is refuted by yet another major, and still ongoing, longitudinal study, involving over 1,000 boys and girls born in 1972 and 1973 in a small city in New Zealand, almost all of whom were of European ancestry. Several dozen physiological and psychological measures were obtained when the children were three years old, supplemented by data available from records back to their births.[23] Ratings and objective assessments of the children for various kinds of psychological difficulty—from interviews and questionnaires administered to the children, to parents, and to teachers—were repeatedly obtained until they were thirteen years old, at which point it was possible to state which children had developed a psychological disorder and which ones had not. The disorders have themselves been broken down further into antisocial disorders or "other" disorders (for example, anxiety, phobias, depression). The early precursors of these disorders can be extracted. In addition, the boys and girls have been asked for self-reports of their behavior, including delinquent behavior, at the age of fifteen. Police records are also available.

Boys were more than twice as likely to develop psychological difficulties as girls. But antisocial boys were four times as large a proportion of the boys as antisocial girls were of the girls, while being only 1.67 times as likely as girls to suffer from other disorders. The early predictors of antisocial disorders in later childhood were essentially the same for boys as for girls, except that boys were generally at greater psychological risk. At the age of three, the statistically significant precursors of antisocial disorder at the age of eleven included poor motor control, low scores on the Peabody Picture Vocabulary Test (a measure of general cognitive ability), hyperactivity and inattentiveness,[24] and being rated as "difficult to manage." At the age of five, the precursors included low IQ scores, problems with sleep, and a high frequency of "bad" behavior. The parents' ratings of their children at the age of three or five were among the best predictors of antisocial disorder at the age of eleven, but their ratings were echoed in the results of various objective indexes of behavior.

Psychological disorders—both antisocial and otherwise—at the age of eleven were predicting both self-reported crimes and contacts with the police by the age of fifteen. For the children with two or more police contacts—the clear recidivists, in other words—antisocial disorder was by far more predictive than other disorders, or than no disorders at all.

Most of the children identified as having antisocial disorders at eleven were *not* demonstrably delinquent at fifteen. However, most of the delinquents at age fifteen were identifiable from variables gathered in their preschool years. This is a recurrent pattern in the technical literature. Most individuals with the early precursors of criminal behavior do not become serious offenders, but most (albeit not all) serious offenders have shown the precursors earlier in life. How shall we interpret this?

For one thing, the pattern suggests that we do not know all of the precursors. There may be signs in early life or in the individual's background that would, if we knew about them, make the predictions more accurate. It's not hard to believe that our knowledge is incomplete, but another explanation is also doubtless correct to some degree. To the extent that offending depends on events that arise later on in life, it is going to be unpredictable from early precursors. One study, for example, suggests that later offending is dependent to a degree on prior offending per se, as if the breaking of the law somehow disinhibits additional acts of crime.[25] More obviously, circumstances not yet taking their toll on an individual—such as success or failure in school or at work—affect whether or not his or her predisposing traits will show up in criminal behavior.

The Psychology of Criminal Behavior

From longitudinal and other kinds of studies, we know a great deal about the psychological makeup of offenders. We do not know about every offender, to be sure, nor about every kind of offender, but, in the aggregate, it is clear that the typical offender is not only a young male, but a young male with a particular configuration of psychological traits. Here are some highlights of this enormous empirical literature.

Intelligence

After sex and age, the single most firmly established psychological fact about the population of offenders is that the distribution of their IQ scores differs from that of the population at large.[26] Instead of averaging 100, as the general population does, offenders average about eight points lower. Since the general population includes the lower-than-average population of offenders, the population of nonoffenders alone must average someplace above 100, in order to get the general average down to 100. The IQ gap between offenders and nonoffenders must therefore be more than eight points; an informed guess puts it at about ten points. More serious or more chronic offenders generally have lower scores than more casual offenders.[27] The relationship between IQ and repeat offending is found with IQ scores obtained even in the offender's childhood, as young as four years old.[28] However, it stands to reason (and is supported by the data) that the population of offenders lacks not only high-scoring individuals, but very low-scoring ones as well, people whose scores are so low that they have trouble mustering the competence to commit most crimes.[29] Moreover, a sufficiently low IQ is usually enough to exempt a person from criminal prosecution, no matter what he or she did.[30]

The gap between offenders and nonoffenders is typically larger on verbal than on performance (that is, nonverbal) intelligence tests.[31] The more powerful predictive power of verbal ability for later criminal behavior may already be evident in measures of linguistic development taken as early as age three, according to one Swedish study.[32] It has been suggested that verbal intelligence is especially relevant because the essential cognitive difference between offenders and nonoffenders is the one in general intelligence or "g"; it is well known that verbal scores are more dependent on g than performance scores.[33] Another interpretation, not necessarily inconsistent with the foregoing, is that verbal intelligence scores do better at measuring the capacity for internalizing the prohibitions that help deter crime in nonoffenders.[34] Still another interpretation is that low verbal ability is more of a disadvantage in school and in the legal job market than low performance ability, and that the frustrations of failure lead to crime.[35] Multiple offenders, as distinguished from offenders in general, also have significant deficits in logical reasoning ability per se.[36] Whatever the reason for these patterns of differences, the methodological implications are clear: the rare study that fails to find much of an association between IQ and offending may have used nonverbal scores or scores that, for one reason or another, minimize individual differences in g.

The association between crime and IQ has been apparent since testing began in earnest. The test data just confirmed what was already long known. Deficient intelligence was accepted as a preeminent distinguishing feature of the most serious offenders within the evolving discipline of forensic psychiatry throughout the eighteenth and nineteenth centuries.[37] The British physician Charles Goring mentioned a lack of intelligence as one of the key traits of the prison population that he described in a landmark of modern criminology early in the twentieth century.[38] H. H. Goddard, an early leader in both modern criminology and the use of intelligence tests, concluded that a large fraction of convicts were intellectually subnormal.[39] However, by the mid-1930s, criminologists were beginning to discount IQ as a factor in criminal behavior.[40] They could not doubt that convict populations generally earned lower-than-average scores, because the numbers were overpoweringly clear; but they had concluded that the numbers said nothing about a real difference in *intelligence* between offenders and nonoffenders. They were skeptical about whether the convicts in prisons were truly representative of offenders in general; and they were dubious, at best, about what tests measured: Weren't tests just measuring socioeconomic status by other means, and weren't they biased against the people from the lower socioeconomic classes or the minority groups who were most likely to break the law for other reasons? By the 1960s, the association between intelligence and crime had all but disappeared from criminology textbooks. If it was mentioned at all, it was to criticize or denounce.

Public commentary on crime has remained stuck where criminology was in the 1960s. In the meantime, most criminologists now accept not just the fact that there is an IQ gap between offenders and nonoffenders, but that the gap is genuinely a gap in average intellectual level or, as it is sometimes called, "academic competence." The tables began to turn with a major review of the literature published in 1977 by two respected criminologists, Travis Hirschi and Michael Hindelang.[41] Subsequent work has supported their conclusion that a difference in tested intelligence is among the prime discoveries of criminology.

Not only is there a gap in IQ between offenders and nonoffenders, but a disproportionately large fraction of all crime is committed by people toward the low end of the scale of intelligence. For example, in a twenty-year longitudinal study of over 500 boys in a community in Sweden, 30 percent of all arrests of the men by the age of thirty were of the 6 percent with IQs below 77 (at the age of ten), and 80 percent were of those with IQs below 100.[42] Criminology textbooks now routinely report the correlation between crime and intelligence.[43] Some questions of interpretation are still open, but they are narrower than they used to be because the correlation itself is no longer in dispute.[44]

What happened to shift opinion about IQ? The answer is largely a matter of the evidence. IQ has proved to be a stronger predictor of criminal behavior than socioeconomic status (SES) or paternal education, and at least as strong as race.[45] Hence, the argument that IQ is just a cryptic measure of SES or race stumbles. IQ remains predictive within populations that are racially or socioeconomically homogeneous, as in some of the longitudinal studies I summarized.[46] Test scores are *not* predictively biased against blacks or against people low in SES,[47] contrary to the assumption that criminologists freely made in the 1960s.

Critics argue that offenders whose IQs we know are unrepresentative of the true criminal population. The smart ones presumably slipped through the net. I assume, in fact, that this is correct to some degree. If intelligence has anything to do with a person's general competence, then smart criminals should get arrested less often because they pick smarter crimes or because they execute their crimes more skillfully.[48] But how much of a bias does this introduce into the data? Not much, seems to be the answer. The crimes we can trace to the millions of offenders that do pass through the criminal justice system and get their IQs measured or estimated account for much of the crime around us, particularly the serious predatory crime.[49] There is no evidence for any other large population of offenders, and there is barely enough crime left unaccounted for, for them to be committing. Not many, if any, Professor Moriartys are out there, brilliantly and busily committing crimes for which they are never caught.

The IQs of uncaught offenders are not measurably different from the ones who get caught, as far as we can tell from the data in hand. For example, in the New Zealand study, when caught and uncaught offenders were equated for the seriousness of the offenses they disclosed on a questionnaire, their average IQ scores did not differ significantly.[50] If caught offenders are not as bright as offenders who are not caught, then there should have been a difference in IQ scores between these groups. In general, an IQ gap separates offenders and nonoffenders among self-described offenders who haven't been caught yet, showing that the gap in the official statistics is not just a result of differential arrest rates.[51] Differential arrests, assuming they exist, are evidently a minor factor in the aggregate data. Among those who have criminal records, there is still a significant negative correlation between IQ and frequency of offending.[52]

Moreover, a high IQ appears to protect a person from offending, even if the other precursors are present. For example, one study followed a sample of almost 1,500 boys born in Copenhagen, Denmark, between 1936 and 1938.[53] Sons whose fathers had a prison record were almost six times as likely to have a prison record themselves (by the time they were thirty-four to thirty-six) as the sons of men who had no police record of any sort. Having a convicted father, then, establishes a high risk of conviction for their sons. Among these high-risk sons, the ones who had no police contacts at all had IQ scores one standard deviation higher than the sons who had police contacts. Among the low-risk sons, the offenders and nonoffenders had about the same IQ scores. Overall, the offenders among the sons were about seven IQ points below the nonoffenders.[54]

The protective power of elevated intelligence also shows up in the New Zealand study. Boys and girls were divided into high and low risk for delinquency on the basis of their behavior by the age of five. High-risk children were more than twice as likely to become delinquent by the age of thirteen or fifteen as low-risk children. The high-risk boys or girls who did *not* become delinquent were the ones with the higher IQs. This was also true for the low-risk boys and girls: the nondelinquents had higher IQs than the delinquents.[55]

Children growing up in troubled circumstances on Kauai in the Hawaiian chain confirm the pattern. Several hundred children were followed in a longitudinal study for several decades.[56] Some of the children were identified by their second birthday as being "vulnerable" to behavioral disorders or delinquency. These were children suffering from two or more of the following circumstances: they were being raised in troubled or impoverished families; had alcoholic, psychologically disturbed, or unschooled (eight years or less of schooling) parents; had experienced prenatal or perinatal physiological stress. Two-thirds of these children succumbed to delinquency or other psychological disturbances. But how about the other third, the ones who grew up without becoming delinquents or disturbed psychologically? Prominent among the protective factors were higher intellectual ability scores than the average for the vulnerable group. [57]

Personality and Temperament

As certain as it is that low IQ scores are a predisposing factor for offending and other kinds of antisocial behavior, it is also certain that other psychological factors are involved. By the age of thirty, approximately 5 percent of the Hawaiian sample had adult criminal records. [58] These were people who, by the age of ten, had already been disproportionately notable for their temper tantrums, aggression and bullying tendencies, irritability, and dishonesty, besides their low IQs. Among those who had been otherwise vulnerable but had not succumbed to criminal behavior, childhood personality was diagnostic. To have survived the risks, a child was likely to have been affectionate, cuddly, easygoing, even-tempered, and likable, to use the very words applied to them already in infancy. At twenty months, they were alert, active, and responsive, according to pediatricians and psychologists who examined the sample. A child with a sunny disposition, one that evoked affectionate and friendly responses from adults, was to a degree protected from the risks he or she was being exposed to. In the Cambridge study, the boys who did not become criminal had similar traits. Being shy in childhood, especially if not combined with aggressiveness, is also something of a shield from later offending. [59]

In one form or another, these results echo innumerable others. Breaking the law is part of a more general disposition toward unsociable or actively antisocial behavior that, in many cases, begins to emerge in the pre-toddler stage. [60] As usual, however, many more children show the tendencies than become offenders; of those who become offenders, the signs were likely to have been present early in life. [61] When offenders and nonoffenders are equated for IQ, they remain distinctly different in personality or temperament. [62]

In trying to pinpoint what these personality or temperamental differences are, however, we run into an embarrassment of riches. In discussing intellectual differences, measurement converges on IQ tests. But, for personality and temperament, there is no comparably standard measurement. This is partly because personality or temperament is inherently more complex than intelligence. For intelligence, factor analysis uncovers a single major factor, g, which accounts for at least 50 percent of all the variation in

IQ among individuals. Anything that measures g is likely to look a lot like an IQ test, and almost anything that plausibly measures intelligence will be saturated with g. But, as far as we know, personality or temperament is a multidimensional pie that can be cut into a bewildering array of slices. For the same reason, English contains thousands of words describing personality and temperament, but barely a dozen or so describing intellect. Because of all the ways there are to measure personality and temperament (many of which are not very reliable), the data give the impression of less consistency in the link between these traits and criminal behavior than I believe there really is. [63]

Among the nonintellectual childhood precursors of criminal behavior one runs into repeatedly in the technical literature are restlessness; aggressiveness; resistance to discipline; hyperactivity; attention deficits; an appetite for risk, excitement, and danger; impulsiveness; coldness; shallow emotional attachments to other people (including one's family); a lack of commitment to social or religious mores; "problem behavior" or "troublesomeness"; dishonesty; and a precocious tendency to experiment with sex and drugs. In extrem form, this is a list that suggests a psychiatric disorder called antisocial personality. Offender populations indeed appear to include a disproportionate number of people with the disorder, as well as large numbers with less extreme manifestations of the symptoms. [64] Antisocial personality almost never shows up in adulthood (barring brain injury or disease) without having been foreshadowed by antisocial behavior in childhood. [65]

Some personality tests ask people to answer lists of questions about their beliefs, wishes, preferences, habits, fears, and self-perceptions. These "inventories," as they are often called, consistently show that the typical offender, particularly the typical serious offender, is high in antisocial tendencies and low in sociability. [66] That is to say, a serious offender is likely to give patterns of responses similar to those given by people who have been found to be antisocial or unsociable by other means. Less consistently, but still notably, personality tests find offenders to be impulsive. [67] They are likely to be impatient and to do poorly with requests for restraint, with situations that require deferring gratification, with tasks that are better performed slowly and methodically.

One of the precursors of offending is doing even worse in school than would be predicted by the lower-than-average IQ. This shows that the precursors include something besides IQ. To do well in school, it helps to have decent IQ scores, verbal scores especially, to accept social mores, to be able to control one's impulses, to maintain attention, or just to sit still for more than a moment or two. Just about every precursor of criminal behavior is, in other words, at odds with what is needed to do well in school. Moreover, doing poorly in school may well be among the causes of later offending, as a person is drawn into a search for illegal gratification to compensate for the frustrations and failures in school and for a dawning recognition that legal pursuits are likewise going to be unsatisfying. Not surprisingly, some evidence suggests that poor school performance predicts criminal behavior better than IQ per se.[68]

The Biology of Criminality

Some theorists criticize the search for the psychological characteristics of chronic offenders.[69] Doing so, they imply, is like the wise men describing the elephant, each sedulously describing the trunk or the tail or the tusks or the ears, but all missing the beast. Instead, they suggest, we should be looking at the propensity for breaking the law, "criminality," as a trait in its own right. This is not unlike the approach in this chapter.

Yet, there are good pragmatic reasons for teasing out the specific psychological correlates. For one thing, there are established ways for measuring them. Insofar as "criminality" differs from the behavior of breaking the law, it is not obvious how to measure it.[70] For another, we know something about the origins of intelligence, personality, and temperament. The evidence for a substantial heritability for IQ is no longer seriously in doubt.[71] Personality has likewise been shown to have significant genetic involvement, although probably less so than IQ.[72] Inasmuch as criminal behavior is associated with intelligence and personality, and inasmuch as personality and intelligence have genetic influences on them, then it follows logically, as night follows day, that criminal behavior has genetic ingredients.[73]

However ironclad the logic, it is reassuring to have it confirmed by data. In some of the longitudinal studies we mentioned, the criminal behavior (or other forms of antisocial behavior) of parents is one of the primary risk factors for criminal behavior in their children. It may seem that this is more readily explained environmentally than genetically, but it is also true for children who are raised in adoptive homes by foster parents who are not offenders.[74] Adopted children resemble their natural parents in their offending more than they resemble their foster parents. The more serious an offender a biological parent is, the greater the risks of crime in his or her adopted-away child. The more serious the offending of the adopted offspring, the more likely it is that there is an offender among the natural parents.

The data on adopted children resonate with the data on twins. If one twin is an offender, his or her co-twin is at risk for being one, too. If the twins are identical, then the correlation between them is significantly larger than if they are fraternal.[75] Since identical twins share all their genes, while fraternal twins share about one half,[76] a difference between fraternals and identicals in the correlation is evidence for a genetic ingredient in offending. The evidence has frequently been disputed on the grounds that it is the greater similarity of environments for identical twins that makes them resemble each other in antisociality, rather than all the genes they share. As a general argument against twin studies, this one has been largely refuted. The greater similarity among identical twins in personality and in intelligence is evidently caused primarily by their greater genetic overlap, not because they are treated similarly or share a family environment.[77] One of the more unexpected discoveries of human behavior genetics of the past decade has been that the family environment develops psychological differences among the children growing up in it, rather than resemblances.[78] Identical twins, in other words, resemble each other psychologically so much, not because of the family environment, but in spite of it.

On the other hand, recent data seem to indicate that this general finding may need to be qualified for criminal activities specifically. Lawbreaking activities are somewhat contagious, as anyone who has witnessed the looting and vandalizing mobs in urban riots should realize. On a microscopic scale, something similar may go on within families. Siblings (including twins) influence each other's tendency to break the law. If one sibling uses illegal drugs or commits other crimes, the chance that the other one will as well depends on how close a relationship and on how many mutual friends the siblings have.[79] One plausible (though not the only) interpretation is that siblings reinforce or inhibit each other's behavioral dispositions toward criminal behavior, the more so the closer their relationship with each other.[80]

Let us summarize by saying that the cognitive and personality *dispositions* toward antisocial behavior may be less influenced by the family environment than the acting out of the behavior itself. But this is not the same as saying that only the environment matters in determining behavior, as distinguished from dispositions. In adoption data, blood relatives act criminally in similar ways even though they have not shared a family environment.

Some commentators argue that behavior is too ephemeral to have genetic roots. This argument arises in a misunderstanding of how inheritance works,[81] but perhaps such critics will be helped by the evidence of physical correlates of criminal behavior. No one doubts that physical traits may have genetic influences on them.

It has been shown repeatedly that offender populations are moderately atypical in physique. They are more likely to be mesomorphic (i.e., muscular, large-boned) and less likely to be ectomorphic (i.e., tall, linear bodies) than the population at large.[82] Even among childhood delinquents, who are disproportionately nonectomorphic mesomorphs (i.e., chunky, large-boned, and muscular), the ones who go on to adult criminal behavior are still more disproportionately nonectomorphic mesomorphs.[83] Why? One reason is that physique is correlated with personality and temperament, and that nonectomorphic mesomorphs are likely to have the traits associated with offending in higher frequency than the population at large. Another may be that children like this are generally more effective in acting out their frustrations and desires than delicately built children. Yet another may be the stereotypic expectations of people, based on their appearance. A strong-looking, large-boned youngster may simply look tougher to adults and his or her peers. He or she then learns to live up to the expectations, and vice versa for a delicate-looking youngster. Many chunky people, of course, do not become criminals, but the elevation of the risk among them is easy to substantiate, if not to interpret.

A growing scientific literature is replete with other evidence of correlations between offending or antisocial behavior and physical traits. I will run through a few of them, but note, first, that most of these correlations are *weaker* than the correlations with psychological traits. It has been shown that offenders have, on the average, lower heart rates than nonoffenders, and lower nervous system responsiveness to sudden stimuli. Their brain waves are more likely to have had atypical patterns in childhood.[84] Neurological, biochemical, and metabolic abnormalities, some of which may be caused by abuse, injury, or disease, rather than genes, turn up disproportionately in offenders who are especially brutal or violent.[85] An expected correlation has not been clearly substantiated: although a good many studies show some weak association between male hormones and criminal behavior or antisociality, many do not.[86]

An association between criminal behavior and hormones was expected because few variables correlate as strongly with criminal behavior as sex, in our society and in every other one for which data are available. The changing woman's role in America has just barely narrowed the huge disproportion between male and female crime.[87] The next section further discusses the sex difference in offending; it is noted here as yet another example of a physical variable that correlates with criminal behavior.

Females, Males, and Supermales

The disproportion in offending across the sexes varies with the crime, but it ranges from barely two to one for certain property offenses and vagrancy to well over fifty to one for overtly violent crimes.[88] Men outnumber women in prisons by more than twenty to one and in jails by almost ten to one.[89] As a rule, the more heinous the crime or more chronic the criminal, the greater the disproportion between males and females. The only major category of crime with an excess of female perpetrators is prostitution, which may say more about sexual behavior and about a criminal justice system that considers the seller of a commodity more culpable than the buyer than it does about criminal tendencies. While some have argued that the disproportionate antisocial behavior of males is a result of culture and learning pure and simple, by far the majority of experts grant that it has some genetic foundation. The sheer universality of the difference across time and place makes the purely cultural explanation implausible on its face. Yet, it has not been easy to pinpoint wherein the fundamental psychological differences reside, beyond noting that it is more likely to be in something that distinguishes the typical personalities of males and females than in their intelligence. The average female offender is more deviant psychologically than the average male offender, for a given level of criminal behavior.

Whatever differentiating genetic factor makes men more likely to be antisocial than women, it must ultimately arise in the chromosome pair that determines genetic sex. This pair is called XX in women and XY in men, referring to what the chromosomes look like microscopically. If one Y chromosome increases the tendency toward offending, it seems plausible that two should increase it more. Thus, it is not surprising that the discovery of XYY males in the 1960s prompted talk of "supermales" who were supposedly prone to frighteningly violent criminal behavior. The picture of an XYY male conjured up in the popular media looked like Boris Karloff playing Frankenstein's monster. This was certainly overdrawn, but now the pendulum has swung too far back. It has become commonplace to deny any correlation at all between the XYY syndrome and criminal behavior.[90] In fact, there is a clear elevation of criminal behavior among the tiny population of XYY males. But the crime is, as far as has been shown in aggregate studies, usually (but not always; see the case history that follows) fairly ordinary, not excessively or preternaturally violent.[91]

At the least the extra Y chromosome reduces IQ, and thereby elevates the risk of criminality. However, studies of other species have shown that the level of aggression displayed by males can be traced to genes on the Y chromosome.[92] It therefore remains possible that an extra Y chromosome does something to personality and temperament to increase the tendency to break the law, as well as to IQ. The practical significance of the XYY syndrome is negligible, since it is so rare (probably fewer than 1 per 1,000 men). The theoretical significance is not small. Here is a genetic contributor to crime that is not hereditary, in the sense that it does not run in families; it pops up randomly across social classes and races, as far as is known. It increases the risk of criminal incarceration by a factor of about ten: the proportion of XYY male prisoners is about 1 per 100. The XYY syndrome is thus a natural experiment separating genetic from environmental factors, and the results of this experiment show decisively that criminal behavior can have genetic roots.

There is, in short, a scientific consensus that criminal and antisocial behavior have genetic, as well as environmental, sources. The disagreements among experts concern the size of the genetic factor. Some say it is negligible; others, that it may account for as much as 50 percent or more of the variance in criminal behavior. I will make no attempt to set a figure on the heritability of criminality or criminal behavior. For the purposes of this essay, it is enough to show that individual traits play a significant role in criminal behavior. For that proposition, it seems to me, there can be no doubt.

A Case History

The case of Arthur Shawcross, a serial killer currently serving a 250-year sentence, illustrates the power of criminogenic traits. Ordinarily, case histories are of limited value beyond describing the cases themselves. But when the individual's criminal history is as egregious as Shawcross's has been, then it could help identify the variables that have large effects on the kinds of criminal behavior involved in the case. We have the benefit of detailed forensic/psychiatric accounts of this frighteningly dangerous person.[93]

Shawcross is in prison for murdering eleven adult females. The crimes were committed in and around Rochester, New York, in the late 1980s, where, in his early forties, he had been released on parole after having been in prison for fifteen years for the manslaughter of two children. He had been released early for the two manslaughters because he was considered a model prisoner. Mutilated bodies of women started being found in the Rochester area within months of his release. When confronted by police, Shawcross confessed to the killings, blaming them on a hatred for his mother and on incestuous impulses toward a younger sister. He also blamed feelings of sexual inadequacy and uncontrollable rages. Shawcross told the interviewing psychiatrist that he had always felt so different from the rest of his family that he believed himself to have been a "doorstep baby," a foundling left to be raised by strangers.

For being a foundling, there is no substantiation. Shawcross was the eldest of four children born into a stable family, rooted in a small community in New York State named after his forebears (Shawcross Corners) and still populated by relatives. He was raised on land owned by his family, in a house built by his father. His father had stable employment throughout his working life; his three siblings suffer no known psychopathology or criminality. There are no other known instances in his immediate family of criminal violence or mental illness. Nor is there any evidence that he was abused, neglected, or unloved in childhood.

Shawcross's mother is unable to account for her eldest child's bitter hostility toward her, describing him as having been a good and beautiful baby. Nor is she able to account for the behavioral troubles that started turning up when Shawcross was six years old. He began running away from home and cutting himself off from other children and his parents. When he was seven, he was referred to a mental health clinic for having threatened other children on a school bus with an iron pipe. Descriptions of Arthur at this time characterize him as hostile, untruthful, unreliable, unable to form an identification with either parent or to internalize moral standards. He was, however, also described as a well-dressed, neat, and clean child, further testifying to the evident desire of his parents to take care of him.

He lost interest in school in the second grade; by fourth grade, he was failing to get promoted. He quit school by the ninth grade. Before he was ten, his mother recalls, he was stealing money from his teachers. Family members and acquaintances remember the teenage Arthur to be strange, moody, hostile, dishonest, and dull. Out of school and on his own, he had trouble holding a job and was prone toward injuries at work. [94] Each of his first three wives described him similarly—angry, trigger-tempered, moody, taciturn, and adrift in his own world. When he talked to his wives, it was frequently about his resentment of his mother and alienation from his father, and about his sense of not belonging in his family. He occasionally noted that he even looked different from his relatives, and one of his wives concurred (see later discussion for relevance).

He started getting into trouble with the law soon after leaving school, getting convicted for several burglaries and for arson in the space of a few years. An examining prison physician after one of the arson convictions cautioned about what he considered to be Shawcross's homicidal inclinations. Nevertheless, he was placed on probation for the burglaries and arsons, during which time Shawcross was arrested for killing an eight-year-old child. He eventually confessed to two child killings while he had been on probation. These crimes finally caused him to be imprisoned for an extended period.

What can we say about this person, described in an early parole report as a "psychosexual maniac," one "whose inner workings are probably completely beyond comprehension?" When he was released after serving fifteen years of his sentence for the child slayings, a local parole officer wrote, "At the risk of being dramatic, the writer considers this man to be possibly the most dangerous individual to have been released to this community in many years." [95] A few weeks later, a woman complained to the parole office that Shawcross had robbed her and had made unwelcome sexual advances. Within seven months (at the latest), he started killing women.

Shawcross had none of the socioeconomic or home life disadvantages often blamed for criminal behavior. His family was not poor and suffered no alcoholism; he is not a member of a minority group; he had the benefit of professional counseling early in life; and he probably had abundant wholesome role models. His personal history does contain several circumstantial factors that could, conceivably, have been involved in his descent into crime. Twice during adolescence, he sustained head injuries bad enough to leave permanent traces of a healed skull fracture and of scar tissue over his brain, but not bad enough to result in seizure disorders. The brain injuries are medically classified as "mild." In addition, he served thirteen months in a combat unit in Vietnam, which he characterized (without independent confirmation) to his wives as brutal and traumatic, involving not only killings but cannibalism.

A recent medical assessment of him found no evidence of post-traumatic stress disorder nor of any identifiable psychosis. The primary criminogenic traits are evidently found elsewhere in the accounts of this case. Shawcross's full-scale IQ is 95; his verbal IQ, which is generally more predictive of criminal behavior, is 88. His personality is similarly inclined toward the criminogenic. Clinical evaluation characterizes him as quick to anger, intolerant of frustration, deficient in abstract thinking, and as having an antisocial personality with "episodic acting out" and "a truly amazing failure to look at what (he is) doing."[96]

He is a large man—six feet tall and 250 pounds—as is typical of the XYY syndrome that was first diagnosed at his latest arrest. This may account in part for his atypical appearance in his family, but it had evidently never been suspected until it came to light in his trial for the recent murders. The syndrome was dismissed in court as being of no relevance. It may be immaterial legally, but hardly to our understanding of his behavior. The lower-than-average IQ, the distortions of personality and temperament, and perhaps even the sense of not belonging to his biological family, are all more readily understood in the context of a chromosomal anomaly that may have a broad range of physical and psychological consequences.

In addition to the XYY syndrome, Shawcross has now been found to suffer from a possibly genetic metabolic disorder[97] that is often associated with psychiatric, as well as physiological, symptoms. An elevated risk of episodic violence is one of the symptoms of this disease.

In summary, a lifelong tendency toward antisocial behavior; alienation from his family and community; a verbal IQ well below average; brain trauma; an extra Y chromosome; a psychiatrically relevant metabolic disorder; and, according to his own account, harrowing experiences of brutality as a soldier in Vietnam constitute an extraordinary aggregation of circumstantial and risk factors for criminal behavior. That the person who suffered from this incalculably improbable collection of risks developed into an offender of comparably incalculable dangerousness is less mystifying than the bald facts of his crimes suggest.

It has become almost a cliché to say that criminal dangerousness is, to all intents and purposes, virtually unpredictable.[98] Most of the youngsters who show one or another of the statistical precursors of criminal behavior do not, in fact, become criminals. Also, most of the people judged dangerous by the criminal justice system[99] do not commit further violent crimes.[100] But the cliché of unpredictability is wrong. Most of the people at risk for offending are only slightly at risk. They may, for example, have low verbal IQs, but not the antisocial personality traits that are associated with criminal behavior; they may be nonectomorphic mesomorphs with high IQs and shy, nonaggressive personalities. They may have the impulsiveness of the typical offender, but not the cruelty nor the emotional detachment from friends and family. They may have been convicted for a crime, but have no other known risk factor for future offending. We need only assume that the likelihood of committing crimes rises in an orderly fashion with the number and intensity of the risk factors that a person has to make sense of the large number of "false alarms" in the literature on criminal dangerousness. As the risk factors move further out into the tail of the distribution of dangerousness, the risk of offending similarly rises. Arthur Shawcross is a living example of the principle. His risks were extreme, and when he succumbed to them, his crimes were extreme, too.

The Causes of Criminal Behavior

The chapter started with a question, Who commits crime? which I have attempted to answer in a limited way, at the individual level and in the probabilistic terms that the data provide. Age, sex, intelligence, personality, and a history of previous criminal or antisocial behavior are among the overlapping individual variables that affect the probability that a person will break the law.

Now let us to turn to a different question: What causes crime? I am asked this question in one form or another by nonspecialists more often than the one I tried to answer, but it is too hard for me.[101] My purpose in this final section is to make the case that the question is not only hard but ill-framed.

Criminal behavior is behavior. It is not necessary to prove that human behavior is multiply determined, for it is obvious. Nothing we do, not even coughing or sneezing, has just one governing antecedent condition. The more complex the set of antecedent conditions, the less sense it makes to frame questions about behavior in terms of causes. We will never be able to say what caused Arthur Shawcross to murder no fewer than thirteen people, let alone to have predicted in advance that he would do so; but we can say why he was more likely to have done so than almost anyone else. And even with the benefit of all that science can tell us about the variables that predispose people toward crime, we may not be able to say whether someone at his high risk for criminal behavior will murder one or two or ten people or content himself with assaults, batteries, muggings, arsons, and rapes. Accidents, situations, and social forces do, after all, take their toll. They modulate the criminogenic factors that have been reviewed here.

Let us assume that a behavior occurs because there is an occasion for it and because it has some probability of earning a currently desired consequence. It also has a cost, both current and deferred. The consequence may be economic—for example, money or goods in a burglary—or more personal and idiosyncratic—for example, seeing a building go up in flames or wreaking revenge for old grievances, as in the case of Shawcross. The costs, too, have a calculus of their own. They comprise a mixture of the objective risks of getting caught and the subjective penalties of conscience. The people who commit a lot of crime are, simply, people for whom the positive side of the ledger sufficiently outweighs the negative side and who have the opportunity for breaking the law. Their appetites for the fruits of crime may be very strong or their perceptions of the risk of getting caught and of feeling the sting of conscience, very small.

The risk factors that turn up at the intermediate level of analysis in this chapter exemplify the personal and idiosyncratic elements in the consequences and costs of criminal behavior. They concern people's appetites for violence and cruelty, their capacity for internalizing abstract rules of conduct, their degree of present-orientation, their anger at society, their sexual impulses, their attitudes toward conventional morality. None of these things causes crime, for each can only operate in contexts that provide opportunities for getting the desired consequences and that minimize paying the costs of punishment. But then, the opportunities do not cause crime either. One cannot mug an elderly person on a dark street if dark streets contain no elderly persons, but we are not likely to say that muggings are caused by elderly persons venturing out of their homes at night.

If talking about causes of crime is misguided, so is talking about public policy in terms of causes (more familiarly, "root causes"). Just as the data push us to see criminal behavior within the framework of risk factors, so they should push public policy. The evidence about individual precursors of criminal behavior reach back, not only to childhood and infancy, but to parental traits as well. Within the constraints of due process and of a decent regard for individual freedom and privacy, society needs to consider taking heed of the evidence concerning criminogenic traits—and of how these traits vary from person to person—when it is seeking ways to solve the problem of crime.

PATRICIA A. BRENNAN, SARNOFF A. MEDNICK, AND JAN VOLAVKA

BIOMEDICAL FACTORS IN CRIME

4

Recent scientific investigations have established strong links between biological factors and many behavioral disorders. However, regardless of empirical support, the suggestion that *biological factors may influence criminal behavior* is likely to be met with strong protests and resistance.

Historical and Political Considerations

One obvious reason for resistance to the concept of biological influence is historical context. The first modern biological theory of criminality put forth by Cesare Lombroso was disturbingly consistent with the notions of social Darwinism. Lombroso's theory stated that criminals were inferior throwbacks to a more primitive stage in human development—reproductions of the physical, psychological, and behavioral characteristics of remote ancestors. In social Darwinism (the historical application of Charles Darwin's views on evolution to the planning of social and political systems), ideas such as this were used to rationalize European imperialism as well as American racist social policies. During the Holocaust, Nazi theoreticians considered the physical characteristics of the Jews as important landmarks confirming their sub-human and therefore inferior nature. Given this history, it is not surprising that biological studies of crime are viewed with suspicion and protest.

A second reason for the lack of acceptance of biological influences on crime is the changes it may require in our consideration of free will and criminal responsibility. Criminals are held culpable for their actions and punished on the basis of the assumption that their behavior resulted from their own free will. We assume that criminal acts are voluntary acts of behavior under the control of the individual who commits them. In cases where individuals are not exercising free will, where a mental disease or defect impairs their ability to understand right from wrong, they are not held legally responsible. It is thought by some that if we were to determine that biological factors influenced people's criminal outcomes, then to some degree these individuals may not be held responsible for their criminal acts. This is often challenged, especially in cases of heinous crimes. The public's desire for retribution is particularly strong in such instances, regardless of the biological background of the offender. Biological research on crime forces us to face this moral and ethical dilemma. (Rearing in an unstable family will also influence criminal outcomes. It is not clear why this nonbiological determinant would not also free such individuals from responsibility for their criminal acts!)

Related to the issue of free will and responsibility is the idea of "crime as destiny." Treatment specialists and criminal justice system personnel have an investment in the notion that criminal behavior can be changed and in some cases prevented. Whereas social and cognitive factors are seen as treatable, biological factors are often seen as completely predetermined and impossible to fix. Therefore, these professionals resist the consideration of potential biological bases of crime.

The notion of crime as destiny is rooted in the historical "either/or" context of research on crime causation. In this context, the acceptance of biological causes of crime has been perceived as a direct contradiction to the belief that environmental factors play a significant role in criminal outcome. This is the underpinning of the nature-versus-nurture debate. Scientists who put forth biological theories are seen as dismissing the importance of society's or the environment's role in crime causation. In fact, such a dismissal is not inherent in the biological study of crime. Almost all biomedical researchers realize that biological factors alone cannot account for all criminal outcomes, just as they realize that social factors alone cannot account for all criminal outcomes. The current challenge in crime research is for biological and social researchers to integrate their theories and methodologies in order to assess the combined and interactive role of biological and social influences on criminal outcome. This move from the either/or approach to the "combined" approach is evident in several recent studies of biosocial interactions and crime.

Biosocial or combined models of crime causation have important implications for prevention and intervention. If a biological factor leads to criminal outcome only in a certain environmental circumstance, then prevention programs can target the biologically vulnerable and change their environment before the criminal behavior ensues. Certain biological factors in particular social environments could also be targeted in prevention or intervention strategies. Radical medical interventions are not the only intervention strategies suggested by research evidence linking biomedical factors and crime.

This point can be made more clearly by a presentation of the research evidence in this area of study.

In this chapter we provide a review of biomedical research on criminal outcome. We will review studies concerning genetic, perinatal, neurodevelopmental, neuropsychological, neurophysiological, and neurochemical factors, as well as biosocial interactions. We will then suggest policy recommendations based upon this empirical evidence. Our primary focus will be on adult criminal behavior. However, it should be noted that criminals often engage in other deviant behaviors such as alcohol abuse, truancy, and reckless driving. Biological factors may predispose these individuals to a variety of behaviors including criminal acts.

Genetic Factors

The empirical investigation of genetic influences on crime has been focused in three distinct methodologies. The first, *family studies,* provides valuable information about increased risk for criminal behavior found among family members of affected individuals. Family studies provide few conclusions about genetic etiology, however, because members of families share environments as well as genes. A second approach, *the study of twins,* offers a somewhat better separation of genetic and environmental effects. The twin studies compare monozygotic (MZ) twins, who are genetically identical, with fraternal, same-sex, dizygotic (DZ) twins who have no more genes in common than do other siblings. The research design assumes that the effect of hereditary factors is demonstrated if the MZ twins have more similar outcomes (concordance for deviance) than DZ twins. In almost all studies, the twins are reared together, and the method assumes that the environmental influences upon MZ twins are no different from those upon DZ twins. The possibility exists, however, that environmental influences treat MZ pairs more similarly than DZ pairs. A third approach, *the adoption study,* to a large extent overcomes the possibility of confounding genetic and environmental factors which limit inferences from the results of twin studies. In this method, the deviant outcomes of adopted children (separated early in life from their biological parents) are compared with the outcomes of their adoptive parents and their biological parents. Similarity in outcome between adoptees and biological parents indicates a genetic effect. In addition, with the application of cross-fostering analysis, relative contributions to deviance from the genetic family and from the family of rearing may be compared, and interactions between genetic and environmental factors may be examined.

Family Studies

Family studies of criminality and antisocial behavior have consistently revealed a relationship between parental and offspring criminality.[1] In the classic study by Robins, a father's criminal behavior was the single best predictor of antisocial behavior in a child.[2] As we have previously mentioned, very little can be concluded in terms of genetics from such family data alone. The parents have a major influence on the child's environment as well as on his genetic makeup; family studies cannot disentangle these hereditary and environmental influences.

Twin Studies

Historically, twin studies have used the measure of pairwise concordance to reflect heritability of criminal behavior. When both members of a twin pair are criminals, that twin pair is said to be *con*cordant. If one member of a twin pair is criminal and the other member is not criminal, that twin pair is labeled *dis*cordant. The percentage of concordant twin pairs in the sample of twins is the "pairwise concordant rate" for that sample. In the first twin-criminality study, the German psychiatrist Johannes Lange found 77 percent pairwise concordance for criminality for his MZ twins and 12 percent pairwise concordance for his DZ twins. Lange concluded that "heredity plays a preponderant part among the causes of crime."[3] Subsequent studies of twins (until 1961 there were eight in all) tended to confirm the direction, but not the extent, of Lange's results.

Some of these eight previously reviewed twin studies[4] (presented in Table 4.1) suffer from the fact that their sampling was rather haphazard. Some were carried out in Germany or Japan during a period of Fascism. They report too high a proportion of MZ twins. Most were selected samples from prisons, a setting in which concordant MZ pairs are more likely to be brought to the attention of the investigator. Twinship is usually easier to detect in the case of identical twins, especially if they end up in the same prison. All of these factors tend to inflate MZ concordance rates in nonsystematic studies.

The Table 4.1 twin studies also share another methodological weakness—they all report pairwise concordance rates rather than proband concordance rates for all the individuals studied. As defined earlier, pairwise concordance rates directly reflect the percentage of concordant twin pairs in the ascertained sample. This rate has been shown to be biased in that concordant twin pairs are more likely than discordant twin pairs to be located in a selected sample. This bias can be avoided by determining the concordance rate according to the individual rather than the twin pair. The most appropriate measure for this rate is the proband concordance rate, which is equal to the conditional probability of one twin's being criminal when it is known that the other is criminal, where each individual in the twin pair is independently ascertained.[5]

A twin study carried out by Christiansen minimizes the methodological problems discussed in the preceding paragraphs. In this pilot study, he studied all twins (3,586 twin pairs) born in a well-defined area of Denmark

TABLE 4.1

Twin Studies of Antisocial Behavior: Monozygotic and Same-Sex Dizygotic Twins Only

Study	Location	Monozygotic		Dizygotic	
		Number of pairs	Pairwise concordance rate (%)	Number of pairs	Pairwise concordance rate (%)
Lange[a]	Bavaria	13	77.0	17	12
Legras[b]	Holland	4	100.0	5	20
Rosanoff[c]	U.S.A.	37	68.0	28	18
Stumpfl[d]	Germany	18	61.0	19	37
Kranz[e]	Prussia	32	66.0	43	54
Borgstrom[f]	Finland	4	75.0	5	40
Slater[g]	England	2	50.0	10	33
Yoshimasu[h]	Japan	28	61.0	18	11
All studies		138	67.2	145	31.0

NOTE: Pairwise concordance rates for "all studies" are calculated by dividing the total number of concordant pairs across the studies.

a. J. Lange, *Verbrechen als Schisgal* (Baltimore: Williams and Wilkins).

b. A. M. Legras, *Psychese en Criminalitet bij Twellingen* (Utrecht: Kemink en Zonn, 1932).

c. A. J. Rosanoff, L. M. Handy, and F. A. Rosanoff, "Criminality and Delinquency in Twins," *Journal of Criminal Law and Criminology* 24 (1934): 923–34.

d. F. Stumpfl, *Die Ursprunge des Verberchens: Dargestellt am Lebenslauf von Zwillingen* (Leipzig: Georg Thieme, 1936).

e. H. Kranz, *Lebensschicksale Kriminellen Zwillinge* (Berlin: Julius Springer, 1936).

f. C. A. Borgstrom, *Eine Serie von Kriminellen Zwillingen* (Archiv fur Rassenbiologie, 1939).

g. E. Slater, "The Incidence of Mental Disorder," *Annals of Eugenics* 6 (1953): 172.

h. See L. T. Yeudall and D. Fromm-Aach, Neuropsychological Impairments in Various Psychopathological Populations," in *Hemisphere Assymetries of Function and Psychopathology*, ed. J. Gruzelier and P. Flor-Henry (New York: Elsevier, 1979).

between 1881 and 1910. He used a national, complete criminality register to ascertain their criminal histories. Proband concordance rates were reported as well as pairwise concordance rates. Proband concordance rates were 52 percent for MZ and 22 percent for DZ twins. The MZ concordance rate in this unselected twin population was lower than in previous studies. Nevertheless, the MZ rate was 2.3 times as high as the DZ rate; such a difference is consistent with a genetic influence in criminal behavior.[6]

A study by Dalgaard and Kringlen based on a sample of 139 Norwegian male-male twins reported 41 percent proband concordance for MZ twins and 25.8 percent proband concordance for DZ twins.[7] Though the differences between MZ and DZ twins were smaller than in previous reported studies, they were in the same direction. It is important to note that the Dalgaard-Kringlen twin sample seems to have been drawn relatively heavily from lower socioeconomic groups: that is, individuals in the sample have a "less-than-normal degree of education, they are to a lesser degree married; and frequency of alcoholism seems higher in this group than in the general population" (Dalgaard and Kringlen 1976, 221). In Christiansen's larger Danish twin investigation, MZ-DZ concordance differences were considerably lowered in subgroups characterized by these sorts of variables. It would seem to have been prudent for Dalgaard and Kringlen to sample additional segments of the Norwegian twin register in order to attempt to overcome these social class and deviance over-representations.

All of the aforementioned twin studies found higher concordance rates for criminality in MZ twins than in DZ twins. This suggests that the greater number of shared characteristics of MZ twins result in greater similarity in criminal behavior than do the smaller number of shared characteristics of DZ twins. It is important to note, however, that MZ twins are not only more similar genetically but also may experience more similar environments than DZ twins. It has also been found that when twin pairs socially influence each other's antisocial behavior, the influence is greater for MZ twins than for DZ twins.[8]

New methods of statistical modeling have been suggested as useful tools in differentiating the effects of heredity and social environment in twin studies of criminality. In a recent twin study of self-reported delinquency, Rowe utilized a biometrical modeling approach to examine the role of genetic, common environmental, and specific environmental factors on the development of delinquent behavior. In this approach the data are fitted to different hypothesized models (using a statistical package called LISREL—for "linear structural relationships") in order to determine which models most closely resemble the actual data. Rowe discovered that only those models which contained a genetic component fit well with the data. A purely environmental model containing both common and specific environmental components was rejected.[9]

Rowe's twin study revealed both the utility and the limitations of current biometrical models in twin research. While this method allows for a separation of some genetic and environmental factors, it is difficult to conceive of a model which could account for all of the possible genetic and environmental similarities which may exist among twins. Unless all the pertinent variables are included in the model, it is not possible to determine which are more important than others in influencing criminal behavior. Specifically, the omission of certain common environmental factors for MZ twins may result in the premature conclusion that genetic factors play a predominant role in the etiology of criminal behavior.

The use of more appropriate proband concordance rates and newer statistical modeling procedures has enhanced the utility of the twin method in genetic research. Nevertheless, some may still question this method because of the possible influence of the greater interpair environmental similarity of MZ twins. One type of twin study that circumvents this criticism is the study of identical twins reared apart. Christiansen reported on eight cases studies of identical twins reared apart. Four of these eight twin pairs were found to be concordant for registered criminality, providing evidence for heritable influences. [10] Only one study to date has moved beyond the case study approach in its examination of antisocial outcomes for identical twins reared apart. In this study, thirty-two sets of MZ twins had been separated at birth and reared apart. Zygosity (MZ versus DZ status) was assessed through blood samples, which result in only a 0.1 percent chance of misdetermination. Self-reports of antisocial acts were ascertained from these subjects in adulthood, and significant heritabilities were noted for these reports of antisocial behavior. [11] The results of this study are consistent with the case studies reported by Christiansen, and suggest that the examination of twins reared apart may be an important research strategy for our future understanding of the genetics of crime.

Adoption Studies

The study of adoptions also clearly separates environmental from genetic influences; if adopted children with criminal biological parents were found to commit more crimes than appropriate controls, this would suggest a genetic influence in antisocial behavior. Crowe found just such a suggestion of genetic influence in an adoption study examining fifty-two offspring born to incarcerated female offenders in Iowa. Seven of those fifty-two adoptees were convicted as adults in comparison with one adoptee conviction in a well-matched control group. Similarly, six of the offspring of criminal mothers were diagnosed as having an antisocial personality, in comparison with only one adoptee in the control group. Crowe also reported an interaction between genetic and environmental factors such that adoptees who had *both* a criminal mother *and* spent a longer time in temporary placement were found to have the highest rates of conviction. [12]

In a separate Iowa adoption study, Cadoret et al. compared the rates of alcoholism and antisocial personality in two groups of adoptees: those with antisocial biologic family members, and those with alcoholic biologic family members. The authors reported that approximately one-third of the adoptees in each of these groups could be diagnosed with antisocial personality disorder. [13] These rates were significantly higher than the rate of antisocial personality in a matched control group, suggesting a genetic influence in antisocial behavior. It seems likely that the explanation for the high rate of antisocial behavior in adoptees with *alcoholic* biological families is the fact that many of the alcoholic family members were also antisocial. When biological relatives' antisocial diagnoses were controlled, the authors found that the rate of antisocial personality in this group of adoptees was not significantly elevated over the rate for normal controls.

Cadoret et al. reported a replication of the above findings with a separate group of adoptees in Iowa. Whereas the first study diagnosed the adoptees through structured personal interviews with the subjects themselves, this second study based the adoptee diagnosis on information gathered only by phone interviews with the adoptive parents.[14] Although the results of the second study replicated the first, the method of data collection in the latter study is of questionable validity.

Bohman, in a large adoption study in Sweden, also examined the possible genetic influences in alcoholism and criminality. The criminal behavior and alcohol abuse of 2,324 adoptees and their biological parents was assessed through national registers. Results revealed that male adoptees whose biological fathers were registered for criminal behavior alone (no alcohol abuse) were not more criminal than male adoptees whose biological fathers had no record of criminal behavior (12.5 percent versus 12.0 percent). As a result of this finding, Bohman concluded that there is no genetic influence in criminality.[15] This conclusion, however, is based on a limited view of the available data. Bohman was careful to separate out the alcohol abuse and the criminality in the biological fathers in this analysis. He did not, however, distinguish between registrations for criminality alone and criminality plus alcohol abuse in the sons. If one separates these two groups, it is discovered that there are significantly more "criminal only" sons of "criminal only" biological fathers than there are "criminal only" sons of other fathers in the study—8.9 percent versus 4.9 percent.

In a later study of the Swedish adoption cohort, Bohman et al. recognized and expanded on this distinction between adoptees who were registered for criminality only and those registered for both criminality and alcohol abuse. They discovered that the adoptees who were registered for criminality only were likely to have committed property crimes, whereas those who were registered for both criminality and alcohol abuse were more likely to have committed more serious, violent crimes.[16] It is interesting to note that the genetic influence was found to be significant in the case of the property criminals, but *not* in the case of the alcoholic or violent criminals.

Further studies of the Swedish cohort have revealed important findings about sex differences in the genetic transmission of property crime.[17] It is widely known that men have more social and environmental pressures toward criminal behavior than women. It is reasonable to hypothesize then that those females who *do* become antisocial may have a stronger genetic predisposition toward this behavior than the males who become antisocial. This hypothesis was supported by Sigvardsson, et al., who found that the female adoptee property criminals in their cohort had a much higher percentage of biological parents who were property criminals than did the males (50 percent versus 21 percent.[18]

A register of all nonfamilial adoptions in Denmark in the years 1924–1947 has been established in Copenhagen at the Psykologisk Institute by a group of American and Danish investigators headed by Kety et al.[19] There are 14,427 adoptions recorded, including information on the adoptee and his or her biological and adoptive parents. Three completed investigations on antisocial behavior utilized information from this Danish adoption register. In the first, Schulsinger selected fifty-seven psychopaths from psychiatric registers and police files and compared them with fifty-seven nonpsychopath control adoptees matched for sex, age, social class, neighborhood of rearing, and age of transfer to the adoptive family. He found that five of the psychopathic adoptees had psychopathic biological fathers. In contrast only one of the control adoptees had a psychopathic biological father.[20] Although the numbers are small, the direction of the findings supports the hypothesis of heredity as an etiological factor in psychopathy.

Using the same adoption register, Mednick et al. compared the court conviction histories of all 14,427 adoptees, their biological mothers and fathers, and their adoptive mothers and fathers.[21] The conviction rates of the completely identified members of this cohort are shown in Figure 4.1. The rates for biological fathers and their adopted-away sons were considerably higher than those for adoptive fathers and sons. Most of the criminal adoptive fathers were one-time offenders, while male adoptees and their biological fathers were more heavily recidivistic. The conviction rates of the women in this study were lower than those of the men but followed the same pattern. In view of the low conviction rates for women, the analyses in the study concentrated on male adoptees.

The size of this population permitted the segregation of subgroups of

FIGURE 4.1
Conviction Rates of Completely Identified Members of Adoptee Families

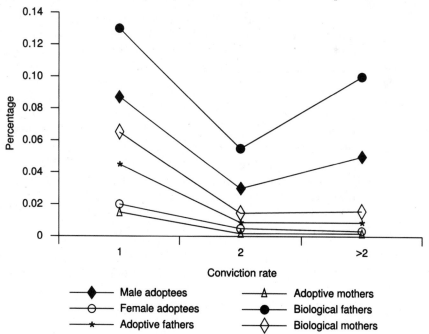

adoptees with certain combinations of convicted and nonconvicted biological and adoptive parents in a design analogous to the cross-fostering model used in behavior genetics. If neither the biological nor the adoptive parents were convicted, 13.5 percent of the sons were convicted. If the adoptive parents were convicted and the biological parents were not, this figure rose only to 14.7 percent. However, if the adoptive parents were not convicted and the biological parents were, 20.0 percent of the sons were convicted. If the adoptive parents as well as the biological parents were convicted, 24.5 percent of the sons were convicted. These data favor the assumption of a partial genetic etiology.

It is important to note that Mednick et al. found that these significant relationships between biological parent convictions and adoptee son convictions existed only for property offenses, not for violent offenses. [22] These results paralleled those of the Swedish adoption studies, which found a significant genetic influence for property crimes rather than violent crimes or alcohol abuse. [23]

The Mednick et al. study further replicated the Swedish findings on sex differences. [24] The Danish adoption study revealed that the relation between biological *mother* convictions and adoptee convictions was significantly stronger than that between biological *father* convictions and adoptee convictions. A more recent examination of the data more closely replicated the Swedish finding (Sigvardsson et al. 1982) in that female criminal adoptees were found to have a higher percentage of criminal biological parents than male criminal adoptees. [25]

Perhaps the most important finding of Mednick et al. is one that has not been reported in other adoption studies; that finding concerns genetic influences on recidivism. [26] Figure 4.2 shows how chronic offenders, other offenders (one or two convictions) and nonoffenders were distributed as a function of amount of crime in biological parents. Note that the proportion of chronic adoptee offenders increased as a function of recidivism in the biological parents.

Another way of expressing this concentration of crime is that the chronic male adoptee offenders with biological parents having three or more offenses numbered only thirty-seven. They made up 1 percent of the 3,718 adoptees in Figure 6.2, but they were responsible for 30 percent of the total male adoptee convictions. The mean number of convictions for the chronic adoptee increased sharply as a function of biological parent recidivism. These results suggested not only that a genetic factor is more important for property than for violent crimes but that this genetic factor also plays a very significant role in repeat offending.

In considering the results of adoption studies one must keep in mind potential problems such as limited generalizability, selective placement, and parental labeling of the child. Our consideration of selective placement and

FIGURE 4.2

Male Adoptee and Biological Parent Criminal Convictions

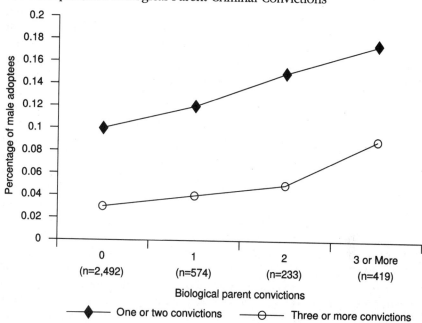

parental labeling in the Danish adoption study points out the need to attend to them as potential confounds. Nevertheless, even when these potential pitfalls were controlled, the results of the Danish adoption study remained significant. Both the Danish and Swedish adoption studies, however, still suffer from limited generalizability. Specific findings concerning the relative heritability of violent and property offending have not been replicated outside of Scandinavia. It is possible that the lack of findings for genetic heritability of violent crime are a reflection of the low base rate of criminal violence in Scandinavian countries. Adoption studies in countries with higher rates of violence need to be undertaken to rule out this methodological confound. Nevertheless, the research evidence to date supports the contention that a genetic basis exists for property offending, but not for violent offending.

Summary

Review of the family, twin, and adoption studies reveals strong evidence that a part of the cause of criminal behavior may stem from the genetic transmission of specific biological characteristics from parent to child. The characteristics transmitted by a criminal biological parent are effective in increasing risk for property crimes.

Perinatal and Neurodevelopmental Factors

There has been one analysis of the Danish adoption cohort that found biological parents' characteristics associated with adoptee *violence*. If one biological parent (typically the father) was frequently convicted and the other biological parent (typically the mother) was admitted to a hospital with an antisocial psychiatric diagnosis, then the adopted-away son was more likely to evidence violent offending. [27] This may be a genetic effect or it may be a result of the biological (antisocial) mothers' poor health habits during pregnancy (alcohol consumption, drug use, poor nutrition) which changed the development of the fetus's brain. There is some substantiating evidence for this second hypothesis from the research literature linking perinatal factors and criminal outcome.

In 1861 W. J. Little observed that "the act of birth does occasionally imprint upon the nervous and muscular systems of the nascent infantile organism very serious and peculiar evils." However, it was not until 1934 that Rosanoff and his coworkers suggested that some types of adult behavioral deviance might be a consequence of perinatal events. Several researchers since then have found increased rates of perinatal problems in the histories of acting out, aggressive, and criminal individuals. Pasamanick, Rodgers, and Lilienfield studied the effect of obstetrical complications on behavior disorders in children. They found a significant relationship between such behavior disorders and prematurity, neonatal seizures, and pregnancy complications. Mungas noted a similar relationship between perinatal factors and violence in a sample of neuropsychiatric patients. Litt studied perinatal disturbances in a birth cohort of 1,944 individuals in Denmark born between January 1, 1936 and September 30, 1938. He discovered that perinatal trauma predicted impulsive criminal offenses in adulthood. [28]

Not all researchers have noted a significant relationship between perinatal factors and antisocial outcome. In a recent retrospective study, perinatal and medical histories were found to be similar for delinquent offenders and controls. [29] In the context of prospective study of 5,966 males in Finland, low birthweight and premature delivery were studied as risk factors for adult crime. Neither of these perinatal complications significantly predicted to criminal outcome. [30]

Mixed results in this area of research may be explained by a closer examination of the types of perinatal problems and antisocial outcomes that were assessed. Delivery complications appear to be more predictive of later criminal behavior than pregnancy problems or low birthweight. [31] In addition, the relationship between perinatal factors and antisocial behavior may be particular to violent offending, rather than property or other less serious types of offending. In 1977, Lewis and Shanok reported no differences between delinquents' and nondelinquents' perinatal histories.[32] Later they compared nonincarcerated delinquents with incarcerated delinquents (who were more violent), and discovered a positive relationship between more serious offending and perinatal difficulties.[33] Kandel and Mednick compared the differential effects of delivery complications on violent and property offending in young adulthood. They found that violent offenders, especially recidivistic violent offenders, had experienced significantly more delivery complications than controls or property offenders.[34] Studies that have failed to show a relationship between perinatal problems and antisocial outcome have not examined offenders according to specific types of crimes committed.

The social environment may also play an important role in determining the effects of perinatal complications on criminal outcome. In a prospective longitudinal study in Kauai, Werner found that the effects of perinatal stress on delinquent outcome were strongest for children exposed to a disruptive family environment. A disruptive family environment was defined by Werner as separation from the mother, marital discord, absence of the father, illegitimacy of the child or parental mental health problems.[35]

As noted above, previous research has not found evidence for a relationship between composite measures of pregnancy complications and criminal outcome. Perinatal complications are hypothesized to be related to criminal outcome through the mediating factor of brain dysfunction. Delivery complications may damage the brain through anoxia or physical injury (as in forceps extraction). Pregnancy complications may result in disruptions in fetal neural development and therefore result in brain dysfunction as well. Why then, do we not find a relationship between composite measures of pregnancy complications and criminal outcome? One possible explanation is methodological. Measures of pregnancy complications are subjective and often retrospective; measures of delivery complications are more objective and therefore more reliable. There is one pregnancy complication measure, however, that can be reliably and objectively measured. This is a count of small aberrations in external physical characteristics known as minor physical anomalies (MPAs). As an example of how such MPAs occur, consider the fetal development of the ears. In fetal life, the ears begin low on the neck of the fetus and slowly drift upwards into their proper position. If a noxious event or substance impinges itself on the fetus, the development may be slowed or stopped and the ears' drift upward may end prematurely, resulting in low-seated ears—an observable MPA. The same agents that cause the formation of externally visible MPAs may also alter critical central nervous system development. The presence of many MPAs suggests repeated interference with neurological development.

Preliminary evidence exists for a relationship between MPAs and violent offending. A longitudinal study of 129 males examined the relationship between MPAs measured at age twelve and criminal arrests through the age of twenty-one. Although this study found no relationship between MPAs and property offending, MPAs were found to be significantly related to violent criminal arrest. The relationship was especially strong in the case of recidivistic violent offending.[36] Although this study is impaired by several limitations including a nonrepresentative sample and a small number of violent offenders, it does tentatively support the hypothesis that disruptions in fetal neurodevelopment are related to criminal outcome.

Summary

Evidence has been reviewed which indicates that delivery complications are often found to be related to adult offending. The offending associated with these perinatal events tends to be violent. Perhaps the perinatal brain damage acts to reduce inhibitory control of aggressive responses. The results for perinatal complications are consistent with those that have related abnormalities in brain structure and function to criminal outcome.

Neuropsychological Factors

One indirect method of measuring brain functioning is through the use of neuropsychological tests. Neuropsychological tests are designed to measure discrete neurological damage or dysfunction in particular areas of the brain.[37] One of the basic principles of neuropsychology is the notion that certain functions are localized within certain areas of the brain, or lateralized to one or the other side of the brain. Evidence concerning localization and lateralization has been inferred from the test performance of patients with lesions that are localized in certain parts of the brain. If an individual performs poorly on a particular neuropsychological test, this performance is assumed to reflect dysfunction in the relevant brain area. Neuropsychological tests are noninvasive and relatively inexpensive to administer (compared with brain scans), and therefore are useful tools for research. Evidence from previous studies reveals that the specific brain areas relevant to criminal outcome are the frontal lobes and the frontal and temporal regions of the left hemisphere.

Frontal Lobe Dysfunction

Individuals who suffer damage to the frontal cortex are characterized by argumentativeness, lack of concern for consequences of behavior, impulsivity, distractibility, emotional lability (volatility), and aggression.[38] Limited neuropsychological evidence exists for a relationship between frontal lobe dysfunction and adult criminal violence.[39] One study of violent and nonviolent subjects utilizing the Luria-Nebraska Neuropsychological battery found that violent subjects were significantly more impaired on tasks that reflect frontal lobe functioning.[40] Another study that compared violent criminals with controls on the Halstead-Reitan Neuropsychological Test Battery yielded similar results.[41] The results of this latter study may be affected by selection bias, however, as the criminals were obtained from a clinical population suspected of having neuropsychological impairments.

Frontal lobe dysfunction may be particular to violent crime and to adult offenders. Studies examining male delinquents[42] and psychopaths[43] have failed to find increased frontal lobe dysfunction in these groups when compared with control subjects.

Left Fronto-temporal Dysfunction

Several researchers have theorized that criminals may evidence more left hemisphere dysfunction than noncriminals.[44] Specifically, these theorists hypothesized disruption of left frontal and temporal cortical-limbic systems. In support of these theories, detailed and extensive neuropsychological testing has revealed evidence for left fronto-temporal locus of damage in a wide variety of criminal groups including criminal psychopaths, adult male violent criminals, sex offenders, and adolescents with conduct disorder.[45]

The findings for left hemisphere dysfunction are consistent with the extensive literature that links low verbal IQ to delinquency and criminal behavior.[46] Verbal IQ deficits tend to be linked to left hemisphere dysfunction, while performance IQ deficits are linked to right hemisphere dysfunction.

Implications

Research finds evidence of increased levels of left hemisphere dysfunction in criminals and increased frontal lobe deficits in violent offenders. However, this should not be interpreted as an identification of certain criminals who have "clinically significant" brain damage. Instead, groups of criminals *as a whole* tend to show more dysfunction than groups of noncriminals. This important point has implications for the utility of neuropsychological measures as predictors of future aggression. Neuropsychological deficits cannot reliably be used as "biological markers" of who will be violent in the future.

A second important point to be made about the relationship between neuropsychological deficits and crime is that the research to date has been cross-sectional, and therefore cannot answer the question of causality. The origins of neuropsychological deficits and their role in the maintenance of criminal behavior is unclear. These impairments may cause aggressive behavior, or they may be consequences of injuries suffered as a result of aggressive behavior, or they may be epiphenomena related to aggression through some unexplained third variable (for example, child abuse). One prospective study of the effect of adolescent neuropsychological functioning on adult criminal outcome is now under way;[47] but until it and similar studies are completed, the issue of causality remains uncertain.

A third important consideration of the neuropsychological research on crime concerns the fact that neuropsychological measures are *indirect* measures of brain dysfunction. These measures vary in the degree to which they are sensitive to dysfunction. In addition, the ability of neuropsychological tests to localize dysfunction is not absolute, as several brain areas may be involved in one specific form of information processing. The indirect and imprecise nature of neuropsychological tests limits the information that can be obtained from such measures. More direct measures of brain structure and function—brain-imaging techniques—may hold more promise for future research linking brain dysfunction and criminal behavior.

Neurological Factors

Several brain-imaging techniques have been used to study central nervous system structure and function in antisocial adults. We will limit our review to computerized tomography (CT), regional cerebral blood flow (RCBF), and positron emission tomography (PET) studies of adult criminal offenders. While CT scans measure brain structure, RCBF and PET scans provide information on brain function. Table 4.2 presents the studies to date that have utilized these measures with adult criminal offenders. The findings from these studies suggest some specificity of brain dysfunction. All significant differences concern the frontal and temporal areas of the brain. Frontal dysfunction tends to be found in violent offenders, including rapists. Temporal and frontal dysfunction are often noted in sexual offenders. Evidence for lateralization in these studies is weak. It should be noted that there have been a small number of studies completed in this area, and that many of those that have been completed come from the same laboratories. In addition, the use of normal control comparisons in these studies has been infrequent. Findings from this area of research should be considered preliminary.

Summary

Results from brain imaging and neuropsychological studies converge on the finding that frontal lobe dysfunction may be related to criminal offending. There are several ways in which this type of neurological deficit could predispose an individual to criminal behavior. In terms of neurophysiology, reduced frontal functioning could result in a loss of inhibition exerted by the frontal cortex onto subcortical structures that play a role in the facilitation of aggression.[48] In terms of personality effects, frontal lobe damage has been associated with impulsivity and poor social judgment, and these factors in

TABLE 4.2

Overview of Brain-Imaging Studies and Criminal Groups

Study	Subjects	Technique	Results
Graber[a]	3 pedophiles 3 rapists	CBF	Reduced CBF in pedophiles
Hucker[b]	39 pedophiles 14 property offenders	CT	Temporal horn dilation in pedophiles
Volkow & Tancredi[c]	4 violent 4 controls	PET	Left temporal dysfunction and hypofrontality in violent
Langevin[d]	18 murders 21 assaulters 16 property offenders	CT	No significant differences
Hendricks[e]	16 pedophiles 16 controls	CBF	Reduced CBF in frontal areas in pedophiles
Hucker[f]	22 sadistic sex assaulters 21 nonsadistic sex assaulters 36 property offenders	CT	Right temporal abnormalities in sadists
Langevin[g]	91 incest offenders 36 property offenders	CT	Temporal lobe abnormalities for violent within incest group
Langevin[h]	84 pedophiles 32 property offenders	CT	No significant differences
Wright[i]	18 pedophiles 12 incest offenders 34 rapists	CT	Smaller left frontal and temporal areas in sex offenders
Raine and Lenz[j]	22 murderers 22 controls	PET	Selective prefontal dysfunction in murderers

a. B. Graber et al., "Brain Damage among Mentally Disordered Offenders," *Journal of Forensic Science* 27 (1982): 125–34.

b. S. Hucker et al., "Neuropsychological Impairment in Pedophiles," *Canadian Journal of Behavioral Science* 18 (1986): 440–48.

c. N. D. Volkow and L. Tancredi, "Neural Substrates of Violent Behavior: A Preliminary Study with Position Emission Tomography," *British Journal of Psychiatry* 151 (1987): 668–73.

d. R. Langevin et al., "Brain Damage, Diagnosis, and Substance Abuse among Violent Offenders," *Behavioral Sciences and the Law* 5 (1987): 77–94.

e. S. E. Hendricks, et al., "Brain Structure and Function in Sexual Molesters of Children and Adolescents," *Journal of Clinical Psychiatry* 49 (1988): 108–12.

f. S. Hucker et al., "Cerebral Damage and Dysfunction in Sexually Aggressive Men," *Annals of Sex Research* 1 (1988): 33–47.

g. R. Langevin et al., "Neuropsychological Impairment in Incest Offenders," *Annals of Sex Research* 1 (1988): 401–15.

h. R. Langevin et al., "Studies of Brain Damage and Dysfunction in Sex Offenders," *Annals of Sex Research* 2 (1989a): 163–79.

i. P. Wright et al., "Brain Density and Symmetry in Pedophilic and Sexually Aggressive Offenders," *Annals of Sex Research* 3 (1990): 319–28.

j. A. Raine and T. Lencz, "The Neuronatomy of Electrodermal Activity," in *Electrodermal Activity: From Physiology to Psychology*, ed. J. C. Roy (New York: Plenum, 1993).

turn could predispose to aggressive actions.[49] In terms of cognitive effects, frontal dysfunction may be related to poor concentration and decreased planning abilities, which could result in academic failure and employment failure, and a push toward a criminal career. And in terms of social deficits, the loss of concept formation and problem-solving skills associated with frontal lobe impairment[50] may result in a reduced ability to formulate nonaggressive solutions to social conflicts. It is important to note that these *predispositions* toward crime do not *predetermine* a criminal outcome, but they are associated with significantly increased risk of criminal behavior. A criminal outcome may require other environmental, psychological, and social factors that enhance this disposition.

Neurochemical Factors

Thoughts, behavior, and emotions are mediated by the transmissions of electrical impulses between neurons, the cells of the nervous system. Gaps that exist between neurons are called synapses, and communication between neurons requires the passage of electrical impulses across these synapses. Neurotransmitters are chemicals stored in neurons and released to stimulate adjoining neurons to allow for the transmission of an electrical impulse across the synapse. Neurotransmitters such as dopamine, norepinephrine, and serotonin therefore form the basis for information processing and communication within the brain; and as a result they underlie all types of behavior, including sensation, perception, learning and memory, and—more controversially—antisocial behavior. Given that an up-to-date comprehensive review is currently available on the relationship between neurochemistry and aggression[51] we will simply summarize major findings here.

Scerbo and Raine have recently completed a comprehensive meta-analysis of twenty-nine studies assessing neurotransmitters in antisocial populations. Results of this meta-analysis revealed reduced serotonin in antisocials, especially those with a history of alcohol abuse, borderline personality disorder, and violence.[52] A link between serotonin and violence is also suggested by recent research that has found high levels of manganese in hair samples of violent criminals.[53] The neurotoxic effects of manganese include a depletion of serotonergic activity.[54] Our recent review of neurochemistry and violence suggests that the relationship between serotonergic dysfunction and antisocial behavior may be mediated by the trait of *impulsiveness*.[55] Support for this contention is found in studies that have linked reduced serotonergic activity to both suicidal behavior and aggressiveness[56] and in a recent study that linked reduced serotonergic function to impulsive aggression.[57] We have discovered that the relationship between serotonergic dysfunction and aggression seems to be specific to certain populations (such as alcoholics) and to certain types of aggression. To date the specific origins and nature of the serotonergic dysfunction are not well understood.

In their meta-analysis concerning neurotransmitters, Scerbo and Raine noted that the relationship between norepinephrine and antisocial behavior was equivocal.[58] Whereas some studies suggest a relative *in*crease in norepinephrine for antisocial individuals, other studies suggest a relative *de*crease in norepinephrine for antisocial individuals. We have also noted this inconsistency in the findings for norepinephrine in antisocial populations.[59] We suggest that norepinephrine dysfunction may be reflected by irritability or hyperarousal rather than overt aggression.

Psychophysiological Factors

Neurochemical factors and psychophysiological factors are strongly interrelated. Both serotonin and norepinephrine are related to skin conductance responses,[60] and norepinephrine is correlated with heart rate.[61] In the study of criminal behavior, psychophysiological research has several distinct advantages over neurochemical research. First, concepts in psychophysiology more easily map onto broader concepts such as arousal, learning, emotion, and cognition. Second, temporal resolution is high in psychophysiological responses. Measures of heart rate and skin conductance are sensitive to momentary changes in the environment, and reactivity is relatively easy to assess with such measures. Third, physiological recordings are noninvasive in comparison with neurotransmitter assays that require a spinal tap or the withdrawal of blood. The most commonly used psychophysiological measures in the study of criminals have been skin conductance; heart rate; and electrical patterns in the brain, revealed in electroencephalograms (EEGs). A majority of the research studies that have examined the psychophysiology of antisocial individuals have focused on psychopathic individuals.[62] Therefore, our review of this literature will include studies on both psychopaths and adult criminal offenders.

Skin Conductance Arousal

No unique, one-to-one relationships between psychophysiological measures and specific emotions have been established.[63] Nevertheless, because skin conductance measures reflect sympathetic autonomic nervous system activity, they can be interpreted as measures of stress reactions and emotional arousal. Emotional underarousal is theorized to be one underlying cause of criminal behavior. Criminals are hypothesized to be biologically underaroused. One consequence of this underarousal is a lack of fear, which allows them to more easily initiate risky or dangerous behaviors including acts of crime and aggression. Biological underarousal may also lead to stimulation-seeking behaviors such as gang involvement and criminal activity that, in turn, raise their arousal to more optimal, "normal" levels.

Skin conductance measures correspond to the electrical activity of the skin. Skin conductance responses are quantitative changes in electrical activity, whereas skin conductance *levels* are simply absolute levels of electrical activity in the absence of skin conductance responses. These levels of electrical activity can be interpreted as a reflection of arousal. A review of skin conductance studies and arousal found that psychopaths have reduced skin conductance levels when compared with matched controls.[64] The studies that have been carried out since 1978, however, reveal equivocal findings for a relationship between skin conductance arousal and antisocial behavior. Several studies have shown nonsignificant differences for such antisocial groups as psychopathic gamblers,[65] criminals,[66] psychopaths,[67] and conduct-disordered adolescents.[68] The studies that have found significant differences in skin conductance activity for antisocial groups suggest that autonomic arousal measured in childhood may prospectively predict to later criminal outcome,[69] and that low autonomic arousal may especially characterize covert crimes or crimes of evasion.[70]

Skin Conductance Orienting

Individual differences in the size of skin conductance responses to orienting stimuli are interpreted as a reflection of degree of attentional processing.[71] Studies undertaken prior to Hare's review[72] in 1978 revealed no differences in skin conductance response to neutral or orienting tones. Those studies undertaken since 1978 that have found significantly reduced skin conductance orienting responses for antisocial individuals have noted these findings either prospectively[73] or in offender groups with schizoid or schizotypal features.[74] These findings suggest that developmental age and concomitant disorders are important factors to assess in the examination of skin conductance reactivity and crime.

Skin Conductance Responses to Aversive Stimuli

Hare noted that substantial research evidence existed for the psychopath's tendency for reduced skin conductance responses to aversive stimuli.[75] However, six of the eight studies reported in the literature since 1978 have revealed nonsignificant differences for this measure.[76] Nonsignificant differences are noted for both psychopathic and nonpsychopathic criminal groups.

Skin Conductance Half-recovery Time

Mednick has previously presented a theory which suggests how autonomic nervous system (ANS) responsiveness may play a role in the social learning of law-abiding behavior. Briefly stated, this theory suggests that faster ANS recovery (or half-recovery times) should be associated with greater reinforcement and increased learning of the inhibition of antisocial responses. Slow ANS recovery, on the other hand, should be associated with poor learning of the inhibition of antisocial responses.[77]

Mednick cited support for this theory of learning from several completed studies of skin conductance half-recovery time with antisocial individuals. In support of Mednick's theory, research completed since 1978 has revealed consistent findings for longer half-recovery times to environment stimuli in antisocial groups.[78] While the empirical data are supportive of Mednick's theory, an alternative explanation of these findings has also been offered.[79] Mednick's theory is based on the assumption that ANS recovery time reflects fear dissipation. However, long skin conductance half-recovery time may also be interpreted as a reflection of shutting out of environmental stimuli, or reduced attention to the environment. Given this interpretation, the skin conductance half-recovery findings may reflect reduced attentional processes in criminal groups.

Skin Conductance and Classical Conditioning

Classical conditioning studies using skin conductance measures consistently suggest that criminals are poor conditioners.[80] In a classical conditioning paradigm, a neutral tone (or conditioned stimulus, CS) is presented to the subject, followed a few seconds later by either a loud tone or an electric shock (unconditioned stimulus, UCS). After several pairings of the CS and UCS, the skin conductance response to the CS is measured. Higher skin conductance responses are interpreted to reflect better conditioning to punishment. Several variations of the classical conditioning paradigm have been used in studies of antisocial behavior, and the results of these studies have been uniformly consistent. Antisocial individuals tend to be poor conditioners when compared with normal control groups.

Resting Heart Rate

Heart rate, like skin conductance, is thought to be a biological measure of arousal. One would hypothesize, therefore, that criminals would have lower resting heart rates than noncriminals. Although resting heart rate has been found to be strongly related to delinquency, there is very little research evidence linking this psychophysiological measure to adult criminal or psychopathic behavior.[81] Most of the studies using adults have focused on more serious criminal offenders or psychopaths. Resting heart rate may be more related to petty crime and nonviolent crime. Future research on nonserious adult offenders is required to better explain the discrepancy between adolescent and adult findings.

EEG Studies

EEG reflects the electrical activity of the brain and is recorded from electrodes placed at different locations on the scalp. EEG is thought to reflect activity in the cortex (cortical arousal). It should be noted, however, that localization to one area of the scalp may not reflect localization to one area of the brain. Spatial resolution of EEG is far inferior to brain-imaging techniques. EEG frequency is interpreted as reflecting differing levels of cortical arousal from lowest to highest as follows: delta, theta, alpha, and beta. Individuals with a predominance of theta or slow alpha activity would be viewed as relatively less aroused than individuals with a predominance of fast alpha and beta activity.

A large number of studies have been completed on EEG measures and antisocial outcome. Reviews of these studies can be found in work by Volavka and by Venables.[82] These reviews conclude that there is strong evidence for EEG abnormalities in criminal offenders, and especially violent offenders. They also suggest that the prevalence of EEG abnormalities in violent individuals ranges from 25 percent to 50 percent, with the comparative rate of EEG abnormalities in normal populations ranging from 5 percent to 20 percent. However, these studies used clinical judgment to determine "abnormalities" rather than computer scoring with established criteria.

Most studies involving computer-scored EEG measures and crime report slowing of the EEG frequency within the alpha range.[83] Two prospective studies have revealed that this alpha slowing is evident many years before the onset of criminal offending. In one of these studies, EEG measures collected on 129 males at age twelve were predictive of their criminal arrests at age eighteen.[84] Specifically, high levels of slow alpha activity were found to be related to recidivistic thievery in this sample. This finding was replicated in a larger sample of 571 subjects in Sweden.[85] EEG measures obtained during childhood were predictive of criminal arrest twelve years later. Slowing of alpha frequency was again noted in property offenders in this sample. Slowing of arousal may be interpreted to reflect a low level of arousal that might lead to difficulty in learning law-abiding behavior.

Studies by Mednick and his colleagues utilized computer scoring of EEG, which is more reliable than clinical judgment measures used in previous studies in this area. These studies were also prospective and longitudinal in design, and therefore could determine temporal order of crime and EEG abnormalities. These studies also included control groups, and are more the exception than the rule in the area of EEG research.[86] As Volavka and Venables have noted, in separate articles, most EEG studies are compromised by the lack of adequate control groups, a lack of reliable criteria for defining "abnormality, a lack of theoretical bases, an inability to determine causality, and a lack of attention to environmental factors that may mediate the relationship between cortical arousal and violent criminal outcome.[87]

Summary

Psychophysiological studies have noted relatively slow autonomic system recovery and poor conditioning in criminal groups when compared with controls. In addition, low skin conductance arousal and slow EEG alpha activity have been found to predict prospectively to adult criminal outcome.

Biosocial Interactions

Relatively few investigations have been completed on biosocial interactions and the outcome of criminal behavior.[88] Several studies, however, have noted interactions between biological factors and more adverse social environments in predicting violent or recidivistic crime. In line with this general finding, a recent study from our laboratory suggests that biological effects of perinatal damage may be particularly relevant for the development of criminal behavior in rejecting social environments. This study utilized a cohort of 4,260 Danish males to examine the effect of delivery complications and maternal rejection on violent criminal outcome. In this study, a significant interaction was noted for delivery complications and maternal rejection. The biological effects of delivery complications did not result in violent outcomes unless they were combined with a social environment of maternal rejection. It was only those subjects with *both* higher numbers of delivery complications *and* more rejecting mothers who evidenced increased rates of arrest for criminal violence. Studies of biosocial interactions suggest that such biological deficits can be compensated for by consistent upbringing, and may be potentiated by adverse social environments.

Summary: Biomedical Factors and Crime

Genetics

Criminal behavior in parents increases the likelihood of nonviolent crime in the offspring. This relationship is due, in part, to genetic transmission of criminogenic characteristics. This genetic effect is stronger for females and is especially important for recidivistic crime.

Perinatal Factors

Delivery complications are associated with juvenile and adult violent crime. The effect of delivery complications on crime is stronger in more unstable families.

Neuropsychological and Neurological Factors

Frontal lobe dysfunction has been found to be associated with adult violent crime. Left hemisphere fronto-temporal dysfunction is related to a wide variety of antisocial outcomes.

Neurochemical Factors

Reduced cerebrospinal fluid 5-hydroxyindoleacetic acid (a metabolite of serotonin) levels have been found in individuals exhibiting impulsive aggression, especially those with a history of alcohol abuse.

Psychophysiology

Antisocial individuals evidence reliably reduced levels of autonomic reactiveness and poor conditioning of autonomic responses. Prospective studies reveal a relationship between EEG slow alpha activity in childhood and arrests for property crimes in adulthood.

Biosocial Interactions

Biological factors have been found to be especially likely to predict criminal outcome when combined with adverse social environments.

Policy Implications

This review has demonstrated that biological factors influence certain types of criminal behavior. These biological influences do not occur in a vacuum—the social context often interacts with the biological predisposition in predicting the eventual outcome of criminal behavior. What are the implications of this knowledge for public policy?

One obvious implication is the suggestion of prevention strategies that may reduce the outcome of criminal behavior. To exemplify this point, consider the finding that perinatal factors may interact with unstable family environments in predicting antisocial outcome. One prevention strategy suggested by this finding would be the provision of intensive prenatal health care to mothers, including education on nutrition and on alcohol and drug use during pregnancy and earlier hospitalization to facilitate trouble-free deliveries. This prevention program could be focused on socially vulnerable families. The focus of this program would be to change the biological factor in potentially adverse social environments. The flip side of this approach would be to change or strengthen the social environment for those children who may be biologically vulnerable. Children who have suffered from perinatal complications could be targeted for parent-training interventions or school enrichment programs that would help to ameliorate the effects of their biological deficits. Such prevention programs may prevent criminal offending.

Findings concerning the psychophysiological responses of antisocial individuals to punishment also have implications for society's intervention strategies with criminals. Antisocial individuals have been found to be less responsive to punishment than are controls. Rehabilitation through criminal justice system punishment may be an unrealistic goal for some criminals. The continued research of biological factors may suggest treatments that would better affect rehabilitation for these individuals. These treatments need not be drastic or invasive. Current biological research suggests that treatment as benign as increased nutritional supplements for prisoners may reduce their future rates of aggression.[89]

Concluding Thoughts on Historical and Political Considerations

Historically, social scientists in the field of criminal behavior have viewed studies of biology and crime with suspicion. This suspicion was in evidence when the XYY chromosome episode surfaced in the early 1970s. Males usually have two sex chromosomes, one X and one Y. Sandberg's discovery of a man with an extra Y (male) chromosome suggested the possibility of individuals with exaggerated masculinity, aggression, and violence. Indeed, following Sandberg's discovery, chromosome studies were completed in some institutions for mentally ill offenders. The results seemed to suggest that XYY men were especially violent. The popular press began to develop the image of XYY men as huge hulks of super-maleness, spurred on to violent acts by their extra Y chromosome. However, a review of the scientific literature on XYY chromosomes and crime revealed inconsistent results and arbitrarily defined small samples.[90] A large population study was therefore planned to make a sound empirical test of the relationship between XYY chromosomes and violent outcome.

Several social scientists protested the XYY research plans. For example, Sarbin and Miller made it clear that they were opposed to the possibility of "internal causality" (their term) in the etiology of crime. They labeled the XYY research "demonism revisited" referring back to the persecution of the witches. They implied that it was immoral, or at least scientifically unethical, even to consider investigating the possibility that a biological, internal characteristic might increase the likelihood that an individual would commit a crime.[91] Despite these objections, this large-scale population study of XYY men was undertaken and completed. The results of this study revealed a relationship between criminal convictions and the presence of the XYY chromosome.[92] In addition, the XYY men in this study self-reported an increased rate of acts of domestic violence compared with controls.[93] These XYY men did not differ from the controls, however, in *official* criminal arrests and convictions for *violent* crime. This lack of a finding for official rates of violence was used by social scientists as further "proof" that biological factors were not to be the concern of criminological researchers. These scientists stated that the proper study of crime should be restricted to social, economic, and political variables.

We find several reasons not to accept this view:

1. Attempts to control scientific inquiry have always proved fruitless. Even heavily authoritarian governments have failed to blot out the spirit of free inquiry.

2. Even with the dominance of a focus on socio-environmental variables for many years, our treatments for criminal offenders cannot be described as especially effective.

3. There is a fear that biological causes must be treated with radical medical interventions such as heavy psychopharmacological agents or even psychosurgery. This is simply not true. The preferred treatments may not even be biological. Negative outcomes for children with biological risk can be partially or even completed prevented by appropriate environmental intervention.

4. Understanding of the interaction of genetic and environmental factors in the causes of crime may lead to the improvement of treatment and prevention. Partial genetic etiology does not in the least imply pessimism regarding treatment or prevention. Quite the contrary! Several genetically based conditions are treated very successfully by environmental intervention.

PETER W. GREENWOOD

JUVENILE CRIME AND JUVENILE JUSTICE

Somewhere between 30 percent and 40 percent of all boys growing up in urban areas in the United States will be arrested before their eighteenth birthday. Most of those arrested will not be arrested again. For those that are, each successive arrest will place them at a higher level of risk until after five or six arrests they will have more than a 90 percent chance of being arrested again. Those who reach the five-arrest milestone have been labeled by criminologist Marvin Wolfgang as chronic offenders: the 6 percent of all boys who account for more than 50 percent of all arrests. [1]

Most criminal careers begin in the juvenile years. Most chronic adult offenders have had multiple contacts with the juvenile justice system, a legal innovation of this country that has been both hailed as one of the greatest social inventions of modern times and attacked for failing to protect either the legal rights of juvenile offenders or the public on whom they prey.

Although a variety of interest groups are continually lobbying for changes in the juvenile law, or in the way the system operates, political attacks upon the court appear to increase during periods of increasing crime rates. We appear to be in such a period now. Once again, the call to "get tough on juvenile delinquents" can be heard throughout the land. Editorial writers and politicians rail against "increasing juvenile lawlessness" and the apparent breakdown in family values. Everyone seems to know a story about a fourteen-year-old killer, or an exemplary student gunned down on the way home from basketball practice. A number of states have recently enacted, or are currently considering, new laws to restrict the access of juveniles to handguns and to lower the age threshold at which juveniles can be tried in adult courts. Other critics urge the elimination of all distinctions between juveniles and adults when it comes to their responsibility for serious crimes, including distinctions in imposition of the death penalty.

From the general media one can get the impression that juveniles have come to represent an increasing threat of criminal violence in many communities. Rather than the earlier image of penny-ante thefts and joyriding, the current perception of juvenile crime is that of gang-related drive-by shootings, the gratuitous killing of even cooperative victims, and intimidation of witnesses. Not only are juveniles perceived as committing more violence, but the popular media also convey the impression that their violence is becoming more calloused. Many juvenile killings appear to take place without any rational cause or purpose. It is this latter characteristic that has caused some observers to question the whole concept of rehabilitation upon which the juvenile justice system is presumably based. Another concern expressed by many observers is that, in the name of rehabilitation or protecting the interests of the minor, hardened young criminals are let off much more leniently than they would be if they were treated as adults.

Many criticisms of the juvenile court are based on the presumption that the primary goal of the court is to rehabilitate juvenile offenders, no matter what the risk to society. Incapacitation, deterrence, and accountability are seldom recognized as principles that guide current dispositions of the juvenile court.

Still other critics fault the court for shortchanging juveniles in terms of the basic procedural protections that are guaranteed to adult criminals by the Bill of Rights. In many states, there is no right to bail for juveniles, or right to a jury trial. In many areas a majority of juvenile offenders waive their right to counsel without ever speaking to a lawyer or supportive adult. Some critics believe that these omitted protections represent an unfair shifting of the balance away from the rights of the individual toward the interests of the state.

Even among those who can agree that it is appropriate for juvenile courts to order some youth to be placed out of their homes, there is considerable debate over where the programs in which the juveniles are placed should be located and who should run them. Some states continue to place most of their committed juveniles in large, secure institutions, where they are effectively cut off from community contacts and influences. Other states have moved aggressively to eliminate or downscale the size of their institutions while putting as many youth as possible in small community-based programs. Another wrinkle in the where-to-place issue involves the role of private providers in running such programs. In some states, a majority of committed youth are placed in programs run by private agencies, whereas in others private placements are the exception rather than the rule.

Although there is still a good deal of debate among academics and researchers concerning which types of treatment programs are most effective, there are some clear favorites among politicians. Juvenile boot camps are clearly the innovation of the moment—although their effectiveness is yet to be demonstrated—apparently because they satisfy political desires to appear both tough and compassionate, without spending a lot of money.

Another issue that is getting increasing attention is the need for more aggressive early intervention in the lives of youth who are showing early signs of potential delinquency or risk. Although juveniles account for only a small proportion of the total population, older juveniles have the highest arrest rates of any age group. Furthermore, studies of criminal careers have demonstrated that one of the best predictors of sustained and serious adult criminality is the age of initiation and seriousness of the delinquent career. A number of experiments are currently underway to determine what kinds of programs might prove effective as early interventions for high-risk youth, although there has been little discussion of how such programs might be paid for. Furthermore, at the same time that advocates are arguing for more opportunities and services for high-risk youth, public investment in such services appears to be on the decline. [2]

The next section of this chapter describes recent trends in juvenile crime rates with regard to both volume and seriousness. Subsequent sections summarize studies regarding the juvenile justice system's handling and disposition of cases, the effectiveness of programs for juvenile offenders, and the need for greater public investment in delinquency prevention efforts. The most difficult aspect of any examination of the juvenile justice system is maintaining the perspective that the subjects being dealt with are both children and criminals at the same time, with all the limitations and vulnerabilities which the first label implies, and all of the problems and risks implied by the second. Reconciling these competing realities is clearly the most demanding task confronted by juvenile justice policy makers.

Trends in Juvenile Crime

Is juvenile crime on the rise? Are juvenile crimes becoming more serious? Recent coverage provided by the news media gives the strong impression that many communities have much to fear from an an increasing threat of juvenile criminal violence. Not only does it seem that juveniles are committing more violence, but the image in the popular media is one of violence that is becoming more calloused and gratuitous. There seems to be no rational motive for many juvenile killings. Stories about juveniles killing helpless old ladies or innocent bystanders have become a common occurrence in most big city newspapers. It is this characteristic of hardened malice that has caused many to question the concept of protecting and rehabilitating youth upon which the juvenile justice system has historically been based. This section will attempt to reconcile the available data with these common perceptions.

Sources of Information on Juvenile Crime Trends

Stories about outrageous juvenile crimes always seem to draw public attention: the twelve-year-old who shoots a candy store owner for no apparent reason; the two fourteen-year-olds who beat an old woman to death in the course of a burglary; the two young men who killed Michael Jordan's father; the teenage taggers who spray their graffiti on every available target, no matter what countermeasures are taken by the community; the car full of gangbangers who fire a volley of shots into a crowd of school children from a passing automobile. These are the kinds of headlines that produce editorials and legislation designed to crack down on the "juvenile hoodlums" involved in these outrageous acts.

While many media stories may give the impression that both the amount and seriousness of juvenile crime are on the rise, we have only the most rudimentary of measures to tell whether or not this is true. The most widely cited measure of crime, the FBI's *Uniform Crime Reports* (UCR), tells us nothing about the level of juvenile crime because it contains no information about the characteristics of offenders. The only sources of information on juvenile crime rates are are indirect: arrest rates and surveys of victims or high-risk youth.

Arrest rates are probably the best measure for monitoring nationwide trends in juvenile offending, although these data also reflect the shifting priorities of both the public and the police. If the public's consciousness about certain types of crime is raised, as it has been recently for so-called date rapes and child abuse, then the likelihood that any particular offense of that nature will be reported is likely to increase. On the other hand, if police resources become so strained in dealing with violent crimes or drug selling that they are unable to engage in preventive patrol or respond to calls about suspicious groups of youth, then the number of youth arrested for minor types of property crimes and antisocial behavior will probably decline, even though the number of crimes has not changed.

Victim surveys are not very useful for tracking juvenile crimes because they rely on victims' perceptions of whether offenders are over or under eighteen years of age. These perceptions are often not very reliable; and, furthermore, victims can give age estimates only for those crimes where their assailant is seen, not for most property crimes where the offender is unlikely to be observed.

Self-reporting surveys of youth, in theory, could provide a valuable means of assessing changes in delinquent behavior over time, if they were implemented in a systematic fashion. However, the self-reporting surveys that have been conducted to date are so varied in their methods, and their geographic and age group focus, that they provide little basis for estimating changes in prevalence and offending rates between age cohorts.[3]

Age-Specific Arrest Rates and Crimes Attributable to Juveniles

Although crime is still a young man's game, with arrest rates peaking in the mid- to late teens, there are considerably fewer young men around now than there were just a few years ago. Between 1980 and 1990, the total U.S. population increased by 9.5 percent while the number of juveniles between the ages of ten and seventeen declined by 10.2 percent. The figures in Table 5.1 show how the juvenile population and the fraction of arrests they accounted for declined over the past decade. In 1980, juveniles between the ages of ten and seventeen represented 14 percent of the total U.S. population but accounted for 41 percent of all arrests for property crimes included in the FBI's Uniform Crime Reporting Index[4] and 22 percent of all arrests for the four violent crimes included in the Index.[5] By 1990, this age group had shrunk to just 11 percent of the total population and accounted for only 32 percent of all Index property crime arrests and just 16 percent of all Index violent crime arrests. Clearly, over the decade, juveniles accounted for a disproportionate but diminishing share of arrests for serious felonies. Furthermore, since juveniles are more likely than adults to commit their crimes in groups, they probably account for an even smaller percentage of actual offenses than they do arrests.

However, the declining proportion of juveniles within the general population hides some very significant changes in their rates of arrest, defined as the number of juveniles arrested divided by their number within the general population. These data are presented in Table 5.2, with the arrests stated in terms of arrests per 100,000 juveniles aged ten through seventeen. Between 1980 and 1985, while the arrest rate for adults (for all Index felonies) was decreasing by 3 percent, the arrest rate for juveniles fell by 14 percent—more than four times as rapidly. Then between 1985 and 1990, while the adult arrest rate for Index crimes increased by 15 percent, the juvenile index arrest rate increased by only 9 percent.

Unfortunately, more of the decline in juvenile arrest rates is accounted for by property offenses than by violent offenses. By 1990 the juvenile arrest rate for violent offenses had climbed back up to what it was in 1980, while the arrest rate for property offenses was about 6 percent lower. Further

TABLE 5.1
Percentage of Total Population and Index Felony Arrests
Accounted for by Juveniles Aged 10–17

	1980	1985	1990
Total U.S. population	14	12	11
Violent Index felonies	22	17	16
Property Index felonies	41	34	32

TABLE 5.2
Arrest Rates for Juveniles Aged 10–17

	1980	1985	1990
Index violent felonies	393.6	334.3	392.8
Index property felonies	2,887.2	2,491.0	2,689.3
All Index felonies	3,280.8	2,825.3	3,082.1

NOTE: Only some jurisdictions, covering about half of the total U.S. population, report their arrests to the FBI, broken down by age. In calculating age-specific arrest rates from these figures, it has been assumed that the age distribution in those jurisdictions reporting is the same as that for the country as a whole.

evidence that the involvement of juveniles in violent crimes has recently been growing much more rapidly than their involvement in property crimes is provided by trends in their arrest rates for homicide. In 1980, juveniles accounted for just 10 percent of all arrests for homicide. By 1990, juveniles accounted for 13.6 percent of all homicide arrests. Between 1984 and 1992 the number of juveniles arrested for homicide, who were *under the age of fifteen,* increased by 50 percent.

A recent analysis of data for fifteen major California cities revealed that arrest rates for homicide were increasing faster for juveniles than for any other age group. Between 1980 and 1990, the homicide arrest rate for juveniles ten through seventeen years of age in California increased 65 percent, from thirty-one to fifty-one arrests per 100,000 (juveniles). The next largest increase was registered by young adults between the ages of eighteen and twenty-four with an increase of only 6 percent, from 77 to 81. During that same time period, arrest rates for all other age groups declined.[6]

Clearly, the rise in juvenile homicide arrest rates provides significant substantiation for the common perception that juvenile crime is becoming more serious. However, the diminishing number of juveniles and the small percentage of total crime that is attributable to this age group raises the question of why they are being singled out for so much concern. One part of the answer is clearly the attention being given to the subject by the media and elected officials. People are hearing more about gratuitous juvenile violence than they used to, even if they are not experiencing it themselves. Another reason may be that the popular media are often careless in distinguishing juveniles from those over eighteen years of age. Since so many young adults and gang members continue to dress and act like teenagers, adult offenders may often be mistaken for juveniles, when in fact they are not. Another reason for heightened public concern with juveniles may be the probability that members of our increasing older population, who do not have contact with children in their homes, are more likely to be frightened or disturbed by the boisterous and possibly disrespectful behavior of the teenagers who hang out in shopping malls and on the street. In other words, youth may appear more threatening and difficult to understand to those who do not have any of their own currently living with them.

Possible Explanations for Recent Trends in Juvenile Arrests

The decreasing juvenile arrest rates for all types of crime, from 1980 through 1985, and then the sharp reversal and increases through 1990 are similar to trends observed in reported crime rates and adult arrests, but not to those for surveys of victims, which have remained fairly flat. Whether there was in fact a real dip in offending during the first half of the decade, or only changes in reporting rates by citizens and police, is difficult to say. There does not appear to have been any similar trend in those factors that are thought to be the primary causes of delinquent behavior, other than the changing patterns of drug use that characterized the 1980s. The increasing prevalence of cocaine use, primarily among young adults, that began in the mid-1980s, and the heavy involvement of juveniles in the street-level marketing of this drug, may account for the shift away from juvenile property offending and the increase in violence.

The risk factors that contribute to juvenile delinquency and violence are fairly well known. They include: alcoholism, drug use, or mental health problems among parents; abuse, neglect, and inadequate or inconsistent parenting; criminogenic neighborhoods; problems in school; inadequate bonding with prosocial community institutions; involvement with delinquent peers; and poverty. Over the past two decades an increasing proportion of children have been and are continuing to be raised in single parent and impoverished households. With the rise in drug use, primarily among adults, that occurred in the 1970s and early 1980s, a higher proportion of youth were also being raised by parents who had drug problems of their own.

Both of these newer factors would suggest a rise in all forms of delinquency, not just violence alone. The more rapid rise in juvenile arrest rates for violent offenses, as opposed to property crime, may be accounted for by the heavy involvement of youth in selling drugs.[7] Anecdotal evidence from interviews with youth participating in a variety of correctional programs suggests that drug selling has replaced theft as the primary source of illegal income for many juveniles.

An increasing involvement in street-level drug selling; the increased availability and lethality of firearms; and the glorification of violence in movies, videos, and rap music are all factors that are consistent with increasing violent crimes but not property crimes among the young. Other factors that many believe contribute to higher delinquency rates include: diminishing blue collar employment opportunities in inner cities; increasing animosity and tensions between recent immigrants and those with whom they compete for the declining number of low-skilled urban jobs, and low income housing; and the decline of the public schools. If these really are primary causal factors, then recent increases in youth violence appear to be due, at least in part, to economic, demographic, and social trends over which individual families and youth have little control.

Counterbalancing their disproportional involvement in committing violent offenses, juveniles are also disproportionately represented as victims. The annual risk of victimization by violent crime peaks at age sixteen to nineteen for both sexes and declines substantially with age thereafter.[8] In 1992, there were 2,428 murder victims under the age of eighteen; 662 were under the age of four. In 1989, it was estimated that at least 1,200 and perhaps as many as 5,000 children died as a result of maltreatment from their guardians, and over 160,000 children were seriously harmed.[9] Between 1980 and 1988, the number of incidents of child maltreatment reported to authorities increased more than 100 percent, from 1.1 million to 2.4 million. Since victimization surveys show low reporting rates for incidents of child abuse and maltreatment, it is not clear how much of this increase is due to higher reporting rates (as increased sensitivity to the problem and mandatory reporting requirements took effect) as opposed to increases in the true level of maltreatment. Rates of reported abuse, both physical and sexual, are six times higher for children in families with incomes under $15,000 per year than for children from higher income families[10] although, again, some of this difference may be due to differences in reporting rates between income groups, with lower income groups more likely to be affected by mandatory reporting requirements.

Drug Use and Delinquency

Surveys show that experimentation with marijuana and other illicit drugs has declined among the general teenage population over the past decade, and that the perceived likelihood of potential harm from drug use has risen significantly.[11] Even among samples of juvenile arrestees, drug tests reveal far lower prevalence of drug use among juveniles than for adults, particularly for drugs other than marijuana. However, among juvenile offenders who are released from corrections programs, drug use and involvement in drug selling remain two of the primary risk factors.

Experimentation with alcohol or marijuana is usually preceded by minor delinquency, use of tobacco, and early sexual involvement. The earlier the age of onset and the higher the frequency of these behaviors, the more likely the use of drugs, the higher the frequency of drug use, and the greater the likelihood of escalation to hard drugs. The onset of regular substance abuse increases the likelihood of more serious and more frequent delinquent acts.[12]

Crime Reduction Potential

Clearly, the significance of juvenile crime does not end at the age of majority. Studies of criminal careers demonstrate that the juvenile record is one of the best predictors of adult criminality.[13] The earlier and more serious the involvement, the more likely the behavior will continue into adulthood, and the more serious it is likely to be. What also appears fairly obvious is that special attention devoted to curbing the criminal activities of juvenile offenders is not likely to have much observable effect on public safety unless it affects their propensity to continue their criminal behavior into their adult years.

The Juvenile Justice System

The juvenile court was founded at the turn of this century as a specialized institution for dealing with dependent, neglected, and delinquent minors. At that time, American cities were being flooded by poor immigrants from Europe, whose values, behavior, and childrearing practices were both alien and frightening to middle class moralists.

The original guiding principle of the juvenile court was *parens patriae,* a medieval English doctrine that allowed the Crown to supplant natural family relations whenever a child's welfare was at stake—in other words, to become a substitute parent. The procedures of the court were purposefully informal, and its intentions were presumed to be benign. Fact-finding focused on the minor's underlying problems and special needs rather than on the specific acts which brought him or her before the court. Dispositions were intended to reflect the "best interests" of the child, which were assumed to be the same as the public's.

The new court represented one aspect of a broad progressive movement to accommodate urban institutions to an increasingly industrial-immigrant population, and to incorporate then-recent discoveries in the behavioral, social, and medical sciences into the rearing of children. The juvenile court was also part of another philosophical movement that has been termed "the revolt against formalism." The new juvenile procedures reflected the ultimate pragmatic philosophy—"It's all right if it works."[14]

In juvenile court, children were not charged with specific crimes. The central language of the criminal law—"accusation," "proof," "guilt," "punishment"—was dropped in favor of terms reflecting the social worker's vocabulary—"needs," "treatment," "protection," "guidance." It did not matter whether a child came into the court because of neglect or an act of delinquency. In all cases, the court's intervention, guidance, and supervision were presumed to be required and benevolent.

Juvenile courts have come a long way over the course of this century. Social scientists and juvenile advocates have demonstrated that the "benign" intentions of the court can be just as punitive and onerous as the sanctions inflicted by the criminal courts, often for much less serious behavior. From an early stance of complete informality, the court now accords juveniles most of the procedural protections available to adults, at least in theory if not always in practice, the two primary exceptions being the right to a jury trial and bail.

In spite of these reforms, or perhaps encouraged by them, juvenile law activists continue to advocate further expansion of procedural protections, the current objective being the right to a jury trial. In somewhat the same vein, there is a youth advocacy lobby that argues for reducing the amount of juvenile court intervention in delinquents' lives. Diversion, deinstitutionalization, and community treatment are the current battle cries of this group, which argues that formal sanctions and institutionalized treatment only aggravate delinquent tendencies and that youth are better served by returning them to their own communities. In the 1990s, this group has added fiscal retrenchment as another reason for reducing the use of training schools and detention centers.[15]

But the most numerous critics of the juvenile court take it to task for failing to protect the public from predatory juvenile criminals in deference to what is seen as its naive concern for protecting these minors' "best interests." The views of this group are articulated most forcefully by police and prosecutors, who generally support tougher, more adult-like sanctions for serious or repeat juvenile offenders, and much longer terms. Reform recommendations from this group range from decreasing the age jurisdiction of juvenile courts, from eighteen years of age to sixteen, to increased waiver of serious juvenile cases to the adult court and mandatory or at least longer sentences for violent juvenile offenders.

However, the juvenile court is an easier target to criticize than to reform. Juvenile justice continues to remain a troublesome public policy issue because of the competing social objectives it involves and because our basic knowledge about how to reform troublesome youth is so deficient. Other obstacles to change include: the system's heavy reliance on informal discretionary decision making, necessitated by its voluminous caseload; the confidentiality that protects its case records from outside scrutiny and the lack of quantitative data on its operations; the unfamiliarity of most state legislators with actual juvenile court practices and policies; and a shortage of community-based programs and services to deal with the problems of delinquency-prone youth.

Does the system coddle juvenile offenders? Does the juvenile system get in the way of protecting the public? How effective is the juvenile justice system compared with the adult criminal justice system? Are programs run by private providers more effective than those run by public agencies? This section describes the policies, practices, and programs of the juvenile justice system, and some of the major reforms that have been proposed by its critics.

The Operation of the Juvenile Court

In most states, the dividing line between the juvenile and adult systems is the eighteenth birthday, although a few use the seventeenth, sixteenth, or nineteenth birth date for this purpose. Crimes committed before that birthday fall within the jurisdiction of juvenile courts. Crimes committed after it are subject to criminal penalties and procedures. Almost all states provide for some procedure by which cases involving serious felonies (such as homicide, rape, and aggravated assault) and older juveniles (typically sixteen- and seventeen-year-olds) can be transferred to adult criminal courts. In some jurisdictions motions for such transfers can be initiated by the prosecutor. In others, they have been made presumptive, with juveniles so waived retaining the right to "fitness hearings" at which their attorneys can argue why such a transfer should not be made.

Originally, four basic characteristics distinguished the juvenile court system from the criminal courts: informality in procedures and decorum; a separate detention center for juveniles; contributory delinquency statutes that encouraged the judge to punish adults, primarily parents, who actively contributed to the delinquency of juveniles; and probation.

Today these distinguishing features are considerably blurred. The informality is largely gone. In many jurisdictions juveniles sit through proceedings with their counsel just like any adult defendant in criminal court unless they have waived that right. Unfortunately, there are jurisdictions in which juveniles routinely waive that right without ever consulting with a lawyer, or any other supportive adult.[16]

Juvenile hearings proceed along much the same lines as criminal trials. The rules of evidence and rights of the parties are about the same, except that juveniles in most states still do not have the right to a jury trial or to bail. Parents are no longer held accountable for the delinquency of their children, and in most states cannot even be compelled to participate in delinquency proceedings. Even the liability of parents for the acts of their children in civil tort litigation has been severely restricted by statute.

The separate detention centers remain. Separateness, in fact, is now the principal distinguishing characteristic of the juvenile system: separate detention, separate records, separate probation officers, separate judges, even separate funding agencies for program development and research.[17]

And finally, probation has seeped over into the adult court. The distinguishing feature about probation in the juvenile court is its role in screening arrests made by the police. Originally, the prosecutor had no role in a juvenile hearing. A delinquency case was completely handled by a probation officer. Then, as the appellate courts became more demanding about due process considerations in juvenile proceedings, and granted juveniles the right to counsel, prosecutors were brought into the process to represent the interests of the state. In most states, probation still screens all juvenile arrests and decides in which ones the prosecutor should be asked to file a petition. However, several states have eliminated this function (Washington is one), and many prosecutors would like to see it discarded completely.

The principal features that currently distinguish juvenile delinquency proceedings from those in criminal courts can be summarized as follows:

1. *Absence of legal guilt.* Legally, juveniles are not found guilty of crimes but are "found to be delinquent because they have committed a crime." The difference is one of responsibility. The juvenile is not held legally responsible for his acts. Juvenile status, like insanity, is a defense against criminal responsibility. It is not an absolute defense because of the possibility of waiver to criminal court.

2. *Treatment rather than punishment.* Whatever action the court takes following a finding of delinquency is done in the name of treatment or community protection, not punishment as is the case for adult felony offenders. Many states do not include accountability as one of the guiding principles upon which their treatment is based.

3. *Absence of public scrutiny.* Juvenile proceedings and records are generally closed to the public. What goes on in court is presumed to be only the business of the juvenile and his family—a position that clearly has its roots in the early child-saving mission of the court. In some states; however, hearings for serious juvenile offenders are being opened to the public and the press.

4. *Needs and amenability to treatment deduced from social history, prior behavior, and clinical diagnosis.* This presumption is used to justify the wide discretionary powers granted to probation officers in screening petitions, to the court in deciding fitness and making dispositions, and to juvenile corrections in deciding when a ward can safely be released.

5. *Long-term incarceration not required.* Terms of confinement for juveniles are in theory shorter than those for adults. However, the early release policies adopted for adult offenders in many states, to deal with prison overcrowding, have often resulted in adults serving less time than juveniles for similar offenses.

6. *Separateness.* The juvenile system is kept separate from the adult criminal system at every point: from detention at arrest to the officials who handle the case in court, and in subsequent placements.

7. *Speed and flexibility.* Delinquency cases are disposed of more quickly than comparable adult criminal cases, and the juvenile court judge has a broader range of disposition alternatives.

Current Criticisms

In most states, interest in the juvenile justice system, on the part of elected officials and the public, is highly sporadic and is usually prompted by media-supported perceptions that the juvenile crime rate is getting out of hand or that juvenile offenders are being coddled by an antiquated system designed to serve truants and runaways rather than remorseless killers. We are currently in the midst of such a period of renewed attention. The last such period occurred in the late 1970s and early 1980s when juvenile arrest rates were increasing rapidly and juveniles represented a much larger proportion of total arrests than they do today. The current attention appears to be driven by concerns about increases in the severity of juvenile crime rather than its absolute volume.

Many of the criticisms currently being leveled against the juvenile justice system appear to ignore the fact that the systems in most states are a far cry from the earliest versions. Current juvenile courts have far less power to address and far less interest in dealing with the truant and runaway status offenders who made up the bulk of juvenile caseloads in earlier times. Just like criminal courts, juvenile courts have had to focus their attention and resources on the most serious offenders, with whom the public is most concerned.

Some criticisms ignore basic differences in the character of juvenile and adult crimes. Victimization data indicate that within any given crime category, crimes committed by juveniles tend to be less serious than those committed by adults. For instance, juveniles involved in robberies are less likely to be armed with a gun or to seriously injure their victims.[18] The property losses from crimes committed by juveniles are also likely to be less than from those committed by adults. And, as I have mentioned before, juvenile crimes are more likely to involve multiple offenders than are crimes by adults. A comparison of average disposition patterns between juvenile and adult criminal courts ignores the fact that the juvenile court must dispose of a much higher percentage of less serious cases, involving either minor offenses or real first-time offenders.

In 1981, the Rand Corporation was hired by the California legislature to take a careful look at the juvenile crime problem in that state, and how juvenile offenders were being dealt with. The study included an analysis of case disposition patterns in several sites as well as analyses of the juvenile arrest patterns we have already described. Not surprisingly, that study[19] found a high correlation between, on the one hand, the seriousness of the charges and the youth's prior record and, on the other, the disposition of the case. Less serious cases were more likely to result in dismissal or informal handling. The more serious cases were more likely to result in the filing of a petition, a finding of delinquency, and an out-of-home placement. A comparison of case outcomes between samples of older juveniles and young adults revealed that when aggravating factors were present (such as lengthy prior record, gun use, or violent prior) juveniles were as likely to be convicted and sentenced to state time as the young adults.[20]

An analysis of more than 1.4 million juvenile cases brought before the juvenile courts of ten states (Alabama, Arizona, California, Maryland, Mississippi, Nebraska, Ohio, Pennsylvania, Utah, and Virginia) during the period of 1985 through 1989 revealed the following:[21]

- Violent offenses represented only 7 percent of the caseload.

- The juvenile violent offense case rate (expressed as the number of juvenile cases involving violent offenses divided by the population) increased by 18 percent from 1985 through 1989.

- In 1989, 76 percent of violent juvenile cases were petitioned, compared with a petition rate of 50 percent for nonviolent juvenile cases. The petition rate for juvenile homicide and robbery cases was 90 percent. By way of comparison, in California in 1989 only 69 percent of all violent felony adult arrests resulted in the filing of a complaint. [22]

Table 5.3 compares the pattern of outcomes for the sample of 1989 juvenile cases involving violent offenses with outcomes for adult cases involving violence in California's criminal courts for that same year. California is about average among states in its sentence severity and prison population levels.

From these figures it does not appear that the outcomes of violent juvenile cases are substantially more lenient than cases involving violent California adults. Furthermore, a study, conducted by the *Los Angeles Times*, [23] of times actually served revealed that juveniles placed in the California Youth Authority currently serve longer terms than adults committed to prison for similar offenses. The number of months served by each group for various violent offenses is shown in Table 5.4.

It is not clear whether the relationship between juvenile and adult sanction severity depicted by the studies described here, involving only a few states, would be found in many others. However, these findings should

TABLE 5.3
Outcomes of Juvenile and Adult Cases Involving Violent
Offenses (percentage of all cases)

Disposition	Juvenile	Adult
Dismissed	27	26
Probation	33	9
Jail or jail and probation	NA	52
Placement or state institution	30	13
Waiver	3	NA
Other	5	NA

NA = not applicable.

TABLE 5.4
Average Times Served by Juveniles and
Adults for Various Offenses

Offense	Juveniles	Adults
Homicide	60	41
Kidnapping	49	42
Robbery	30	25
Assault	29	21

refute the automatic presumption that juvenile offenders are consistently treated more leniently than adults.

Suggested Procedural Reforms

In spite of the consistent evidence cited above, that the juvenile justice system is no more lenient with serious offenders than its criminal counterpart, many commentators continue to proclaim that juvenile offenders get off with a "slap on the wrist." A typical example of this type of misleading and inaccurate rhetoric is a *Wall Street Journal* editorial following the 1993 arrest of two juveniles in the killing of a British tourist in Florida and the arrest of two eighteen-year-olds for the killing of Michael Jordan's father. The editorial says, "The current system is essentially a license to kill. No matter how awful the crime, violent youngsters rarely get more than a suspension or year or two in jail."[24] All those juveniles doing thirty months for robbery and sixty months for homicide in California would probably beg to differ with this opinion.

Aside from the more general calls for increasing toughness or abolishing specialized juvenile courts all together, the four areas of potential reform that are currently receiving the most attention are

1. widening or expanding the criteria under which juveniles can be waived to criminal courts
2. providing greater procedural protections to juveniles
3. reducing the number of "free rides" or "diversions" received by repeat juvenile offenders before some significant intervention and/or sanction is imposed
4. removing some of the confidentiality restrictions on juvenile court records

Waiver Criteria

Most state juvenile codes contain a set of criteria and procedures for waiving the juvenile court's jurisdiction over a serious case and transferring the matter into regular criminal courts. The criteria vary from specific offense categories and age ranges to general criteria. In some states, the "fitness" or "waiver" hearings are held in juvenile court. In others, fitness hearings for juveniles who meet specified criteria are held in criminal courts, to determine in which court the proceedings should take place.

Many states are now considering a variety of proposals intended to increase the number of youth waived to the criminal courts. Colorado legislators recently passed a law which provides for fourteen- to seventeen-year-olds charged with certain violent felonies to be tried as adults and, if convicted, to serve their time in new intermediate prisons. California legislators are considering a proposal to reduce the minimum age for waiver from the sixteenth to the fourteenth birthday. One of the factors that is motivating this proposal is a concern that the California Youth Authority can hold a juvenile only up until his or her twenty-first birthday and that this might not be long enough for some of the worst fourteen- or fifteen-year-olds.

In spite of this continuing pressure to expand the use of waiver, the number of youth actually waived appears to have held fairly constant through the last half of the 1980s, and several studies have found that youth who were waived were not, on the average, treated any more severely than those who were not.

Increasing Procedural Protections

Some of those who would like to see more juvenile offenders treated like adults are less concerned with their sanctions than with their rights. Barry Field, for one, has criticized the procedures by which many juveniles voluntarily waive their right to counsel without ever consulting a lawyer or supportive adult. He would make such consultations mandatory before the right to counsel could be waived.[25] Professor Feld also questions the trend of the juvenile court toward increasing punitiveness, based on the seriousness of the charged offense, without also granting juveniles the right to jury trials.[26]

Decreasing Free Rides and Increasing Accountability

For the majority of juvenile offenders who do not repeat after one or two arrests, station house adjustment and informal diversion appear to be wise and prudent actions. For the small percentage who do repeat, time and time again, this lenience appears to be seriously misguided. Simple common sense would suggest that repeated diversions lead determined offenders to believe that they will not be punished. Clinical studies of responses to punishment suggest that initial low levels of punishment and gradual escalation desensitize subjects and make them less likely to respond.[27]

Some jurisdictions have responded to these concerns by attempting to develop and impose a sequence of sanctions that will ensure that no offenders get off with just a free ride. The state of Washington provides an example of how a state can modify its juvenile laws to bring more accountability to juvenile proceedings and to more explicitly balance the competing interests of public protection and reformation of juvenile offenders. Between 1913 and 1977, Washington's juvenile code, like that of most other states, was based on the twin concepts of "in loco parentis" and "the best interests of the child." The 1977 revision, which was sponsored by the King County prosecutor, was designed to provide greater due process protection to juveniles and more protection to the community against serious juvenile crime. One key aspect of the revised law is a presumptive sentencing framework that ties dispositions to the seriousness of the current offense and the juvenile's prior criminal history.

The Washington juvenile law eliminates the role of probation officers in screening petitions and places filing decisions completely in the hands of the prosecutor. The police bring juvenile cases directly to the prosecutor, who screens them for legal sufficiency without consideration of prior record. Legally, sufficient cases must be either filed or diverted, a decision which is based on the seriousness of the current offense and prior record. A diversion agreement involves a written contract between the juvenile and the diversionary unit whereby the juvenile agrees to fulfill certain conditions in lieu of prosecution. In theory these conditions are supposed to be the same as would be imposed following conviction. The primary advantage of diversion to the juvenile is the avoidance of a formal conviction record. However, if the juvenile is subsequently charged with another offense, prior diversions can be counted a part of his or her prior record.

The code's sentencing scheme is semideterminate or presumptive in nature. It is based on the concept that accountability for an offense should be determined primarily by the seriousness of the offense, the age of the offender, the offender's prior criminal history, and the recency of that history.[28]

Reducing the Confidentiality of Juvenile Proceedings

Juvenile court records were traditionally sealed and offenders' names kept out of the papers in the belief that this confidentiality was required to enhance the court's efforts to identify the roots or antecedents of each juvenile's problems and that disclosure of the juvenile record might unfairly penalize defendants for their youthful indiscretions. However, along with increasing concerns about juvenile crime came concerns about protecting the public from youthful predators and holding the juvenile court more accountable for punishing youth. A number of states have now relaxed their restriction on what can be reported about juvenile cases in the press, and most states have some procedure for ensuring that criminal courts and prosecutors have access to juvenile records, at least for some specified window period lasting for several years after the youth becomes an adult.

Finally, while the "get tough on juveniles" efforts get most of the press, a group of individuals and organizations continue to work for what were the original goals of the federal Office of Juvenile Justice and Delinquency Prevention (OJJDP): reducing or eliminating the use of large training schools, removing juveniles from adult jails and police lockups, reducing the use of detention through improved screening for risk, and increasing the number and variety of community-based alternatives. The group includes Ira

Schwartz, a former director of OJJDP who now heads the Center for the Study of Youth Policy, [29] Barry Krisberg, president of the criminal justice advocacy and research organization National Council on Crime and Delinquency (NCCD), [30] and the Edna McConnell Clark Foundation. With the assistance of these individuals and organizations, a number of states and local jurisdictions have revamped their juvenile justice systems, reducing the use of unnecessary confinement and increasing the variety of community-based options. Utah, Pennsylvania, Oklahoma, Florida, Alabama, and Maryland have been among the leaders in instituting such reforms.

The Effectiveness of Juvenile Corrections Programs and Placements

Juvenile courts are granted considerable procedural leeway and provided with a variety of dispositional alternatives in the belief that these concessions allow them to be more effective in rehabilitating and protecting the youth who come before them. Therefore, one primary measure of the juvenile justice system is its effectiveness in protecting the youth who come before it and decreasing the likelihood of their committing future crimes. Unfortunately, there is no clear-cut evidence that allows us to compare the effectiveness of juvenile programs with those available for adults. The evidence is even quite limited for comparing different types of juvenile programs against each other. This section summarizes recent reviews and evaluations of specific treatment modalities.

Types of Programs and Facilities

Since the disposition of juvenile cases in most states is still supposed to be tailored to the individual needs and circumstances of each juvenile, it should come as no surprise that a wide variety of programs have been developed to meet these needs. For those juveniles whose crimes or records are not very serious, and whose families are sufficiently supportive that the youth can continue to reside in their homes, there are a variety of programs such as informal or formal probation, intensive supervision, tracking and in-home supervision by private agencies, mentoring programs, after-school or all-day programs in which a youth reports to the program site for part of the day and then returns home, and community service. Some judges and probation departments have established special programs to seek out and develop unique community services and contacts that might be of help with particular youth and their families.

For those youth who must be placed out of their homes but who do not represent such a risk that they must be removed from the community, many jurisdictions provide or contract for a wide variety of group homes, foster care, and other community living situations. Placements in such facilities are typically in the range of six to twenty-four months, depending on the program and seriousness of the youth's offense. For those youth who represent a more serious risk to the community, or who cannot function appropriately in an open setting, most states provide a continuum of increasingly restrictive settings ranging from isolated wilderness camps and ranches to very securely fenced and locked facilities. In some jurisdictions, youths are committed to detention centers for punitive or allegedly protective purposes.

The big issues that divide the field are the extent to which residential placements are necessary, the best settings for such placements, and the most effective way to run them. Up until the early 1970s, the typical residential placement for juvenile delinquents in most states consisted of small community group homes or large congregate training schools. A significant departure from this pattern occurred in 1971 when Jerry Miller, head of the Department of Youth Services (DYS) in Massachusetts, abruptly removed most of the youth who were residing in that state's training schools and placed them in a variety of small community-based institutions and programs. Those youth that did require secure care were placed in a number of small (typically twenty- to thirty-bed) facilities. To this day, the Massachusetts system continues to operate with only a fraction of the secure beds utilized in many other states and with the majority of its youth in a variety of small, privately operated programs. Over the last decade a number of other states (Utah, Pennsylvania, Maryland, Florida) have adopted similar reforms in their systems.

An evaluation of the Massachusetts reforms, which compared outcomes for samples of youth committed to DYS before and after the reforms occurred, found higher average recidivism rates for the postreform youth which were partially explained by a decrease in less serious offenders being committed to DYS. However, in those parts of the state where the new models were most successfully implemented, postreform recidivism rates appeared to be lower.[31] A more recent attempt to evaluate the Massachusetts model[32] compared recidivism rates for all youth released by the Massachusetts DYS in 1985 with those reported for several other states (California, Pennsylvania, Utah, Florida, and Wisconsin) and found the Massachusetts rates to be among the lowest, according to several different indicators of postrelease failure (rearrest, reconviction, reincarceration). The 1985 Massachusetts release cohort also had lower recidivism rates than the groups studied earlier by Coates et al.[33] However, the significance of these comparisons is obscured by systematic differences in the characteristics of youth committed to state programs, across the states, and by differences in the reporting by juvenile police and court contacts.

The primary criticisms leveled against traditional training schools have been that they offered sterile and unimaginative programs, were inappropriate places to run rehabilitative programs, and fostered abuse and mistreatment of their charges.[34] At this point, the debate still goes on. A number of comparisons that set out to demonstrate that small community-based programs were more effective than traditional training schools failed to do so.[35] Yet, several recent meta-analyses purport to demonstrate that particular types of treatment programs, primarily those employing cognitive/behavioral techniques, are more effective when run in community rather than institutional settings.[36]

Many states have used these results as the basis for shifting more of their youth to privately run, community-based programs. National surveys of juveniles in custody have found that between 1975 and 1986 the number of commitments to private programs increased by 122 percent, while commitments to public programs declined by 7 percent.[37] However, many states, most prominently California, remain steadfast in their reliance on large, secure training schools. California alone accounts for 20 percent of the youth locked up in the entire nation. Institutional populations in the badly overcrowded California Youth Authority range from 700 or 800 in institutions serving younger youth to over 1,500 in those serving older populations.

It is difficult to tell whether the shift to community programs has resulted in less abuse or mistreatment of confined youth, because of major efforts to cut down on mistreatment of youth in all types of programs that were underway at the same time as the deinstitutionalization movement began to have its effects. What is clear is that community programs appear to offer a much wider variety of settings and methods. Part of the reason for this difference may be due to the fact that community-based programs are more likely to be run by private (usually nonprofit) providers, rather than by the county or state. Nationwide, about 40 percent of delinquent youth placed out of their homes are in privately run placements. In some states, (Massachusetts, Pennsylvania, Maryland, and Florida) the private sector also runs a variety of secure programs for even the most serious youth. In addition to offering a greater variety in programming, surveys show that privately run programs offer more treatment services, compared with publicly run programs, and are less likely to be overcrowded.[38]

What Works

Although academics continue to debate what types of treatment, if any, are more effective than simple custody or outright release, politicians seem to have some clear favorites. Juvenile boot camps are definitely in, apparently satisfying the need to be both humanitarian and tough.

Few if any corrections practitioners believe that strict discipline and harsh living conditions on their own will lead to lasting behavioral changes. However, many are prepared to accept that techniques for harnessing peer pressure and group spirit may contribute to rehabilitative goals. Therefore, most boot camp or short-term challenge programs attempt to strike a balance between rigorous exercise and strict discipline on the one hand and behavioral training and skill building efforts on the other. Many also include long-term aftercare and intensive follow-up supervision when youth are returned to the community,[39] a programming technique that has recently received favorable comment by several experts in the field.[40] However, a recent evaluation of intensive aftercare programs in Detroit and Pittsburgh that failed to find any significant impacts of the experimental program on postrelease recidivism, drug use, or involvement in school or work, raises serious questions about the value of such supervisory and advocacy efforts without the availability of more structured programming.[41]

Most evaluations focus on a particular program or variations of a particular strategy, such as using college student volunteers to develop and enforce performance contracts with juvenile probationers, compared to the traditional methods that have been used in that site. In reviewing the results of many such evaluations, researchers combine similar methods into broader categories (such as intensive supervision, behavior modification, vocational education, or life skills training) for the purposes of comparing alternative methods. In the 1970s a series of reviews concluded that the available evidence was insufficient to support the claim that any one particular form of treatment was more effective than any other, including no treatment at all.[42] More recently, a number of critics have argued that these earlier reviews failed to take into account the therapeutic integrity of the experimental treatment, or the quality of its implementation. Several recent meta-analyses have attempted to control for these factors.

A meta-analysis of eighty recent evaluations by Andrews et al.[43] concluded that appropriate correctional services could reduce recidivism by as much as 50 percent. Appropriate services were defined as those that target high-risk individuals; address criminogenic needs, such as substance abuse or anger management; and use styles and modes of treatment (for example, cognitive and behavioral) that are matched with client needs and learning styles. A meta-analysis of more than 400 juvenile program evaluations by Mark Lipsey[44] found that behavioral, skill-oriented and multi-modal methods produced the largest effects and that positive effects were larger in community rather than institutional settings. The mean effect of treatment in this study, in comparison with untreated control groups, was to reduce recidivism rates by five percentage points—say from 50 percent to 45 percent.

There are several differences between these two studies which favor the Lipsey analysis as the basis for estimating the potential impacts that might result from improved juvenile correctional programming. First, the Lipsey study was restricted to just juvenile programs while the Andrews study included programs treating both juveniles and adults. Second, the Lipsey study attempted to be comprehensive in its selection of evaluations while the Andrews study used a small, select sample. Finally, the Lipsey study compared programs across a number of objective categories while the Andrews study applied a somewhat subjective theoretical classification scheme that could have been biased by the coders' knowledge of the outcomes for individual evaluations. Furthermore, Lipsey's observation, that most program and experimental evaluations lack sufficient statistical power (sample size) to detect the mean effect size observed in his analysis, helps explain why so many individual evaluations fail to detect the significant positive effects that are observed in some meta-analyses.

At this point it is difficult to say what if any effect program evaluations have on correctional programming. Most state juvenile systems, like those for adults, are struggling with reduced budgets to handle an increasingly more difficult and dangerous population. Community-based interventions for less serious offenders are often sacrificed to meet the custodial needs of those who are seen to represent more of a risk to the community, while here and there a few states continue to experiment with alternative forms of community programming. What can be said is that some changes in correctional programming techniques can produce modest, but still valuable, reductions in recidivism rates for juvenile offenders, but not wholesale changes in the basic pattern of criminal career development and transition from juvenile to adult crime. Remember, in many of the evaluations contained in the meta-analyses just described, recidivism rates for subjects in the experimental programs were compared with control samples that received no treatment at all. The effect sizes that are observed in such comparisons are not what we can expect when we compare two different forms of intervention of approximately the same intensity.[45]

The Case for Early Prevention

Given the clear connections between juvenile delinquency and adult crime, there are two basic approaches that might be taken in attempting to reduce the number of juvenile offenders who go on to become adult criminals: increase the effectiveness of correctional programs for juvenile offenders, or decrease the number of youth who become delinquent. The evidence presented in the preceding section revealed that prospects for the former approach are modest at best. This section will examine the prospects for the preventive approach.

Everybody likes *prevention*. Police, prosecutors, and corrections officials are all in favor of it, until it comes to putting up resources, or knowing how to do it. Historically, delinquency prevention has been the most widely endorsed and underfunded approach to dealing with crime. Despite the interest and the availability of a number of promising models, there have been only a relatively few serious attempts to test the effectiveness of alternative strategies and little in the way of sustained programmatic support. Many of the delinquency prevention programs that were funded in the 1960s and 1970s were faulted for creaming subjects and only working with relatively low-risk youth. More recent crime prevention efforts have focused on attempting to achieve fairly quick short-term effects with community-based approaches.[46] Much of our recent knowledge about prevention comes from a number of experimental programs that have focused on attempting to delay or reduce experimentation with drug use or improving the parenting skills of families with hard-to-manage children. For all the lip service paid to prevention, there is still very little hard evidence regarding techniques that work, or their expected payoff.

Correlates

In order to think seriously about delinquency prevention, it is necessary to understand how patterns of delinquency develop. A consistent finding across all of several recent epidemiological studies is that the best predictors of future delinquency are past involvement in delinquency, the presence of other related problem behaviors (drug or alcohol use, problems at school, truancy, early sexual experience), and association with delinquent peers.[47] Youth who come from impoverished homes; homes with only one parent or guardian present; homes in which one or both parents exhibit some kind of problem behavior such as substance abuse, alcoholism, or mental illness; or homes in which the parents exhibit poor parenting practices are more likely to become delinquent than those who do not.

It is not clear to what extent poverty itself is causal. Conditions of poverty, homelessness, or unemployment are indicators or correlates for some degree of social incompetence. Therefore, we might expect to find more incompetent parenting among poorer families. This is not to say that one leads to the other, or that some families do not become impoverished or homeless through simple bad luck. It just says that families who share one characteristic are more likely to share the others, through the potentially common underlying cause of social incompetence.

Since the late 1970s, structural changes in the U.S. economy and demographic changes in society have caused a substantial and broad-based deterioration in the economic position of young adults aged twenty-five to thirty-four, who are the primary means of economic support for the majority of children. A combination of declining real earnings and rising levels of unemployment has pushed a large percentage of families into poverty.[48] Between 1973 and 1990 the median inflation-adjusted income of families with children headed by a parent under thirty years of age dropped by 32 percent. In 1991 about 23 percent of families headed by an adult aged twenty-five to thirty-four had incomes below the poverty line. For whites, the percentage was 18.6; for blacks it was 46.0; and for Hispanics it was 38.0.

Not only is the percentage of youth being raised in poverty on the

increase, but these youth are increasingly being concentrated in impoverished and underclass neighborhoods characterized by a high degree of social
disorganization and high rates of crime and drug abuse. During the 1970s
there was a 75 percent increase in the number of census tracts with concentrated poverty, and a 331 percent increase in the number of "underclass"
neighborhoods. By 1980, more than half of all neighborhoods classified as
poor in 1970 had become underclass. [49]

However, poor parenting explains delinquency, not the shift from property offending to violence that we have seen over the past decade. One of the
reasons which may explain why we are currently seeing more violence
among youth may be the connection between youth poverty and child
abuse. Poverty has been shown to substantially increase the risk of child
abuse, and reported cases of child abuse have been rising sharply over the
past decade, along with the number of children being raised below the
poverty line. A disproportionately high percentage of youthful violent offenders appear to have been victims of abuse or neglect themselves. Other
possible explanations for the rise in youth violence may be the increase in
availability and firepower of handguns, the increasing violence of the media,
and increase in gang activity in many urban neighborhoods.

Causal Theories

Over the past half century, delinquency theorists have developed a number
of increasingly complex causal models to explain the involvement of youth
in delinquent activities. *Strain* theorists believe that delinquency occurs primarily among lower class youth who are frustrated by their inability to satisfy
needs and aspirations through legitimate needs. *Control* theorists argue that
most individuals experience the strain or frustration of not being able to
satisfy their needs and desires and would be tempted to use delinquent
means were it not for the restraining influences exerted by their bonds with
conventional community institutions such as their family, school, and church.
Social learning theorists assume neither a constant motivation for delinquency nor a constant socializing influence by the community. Rather, they
view the decision to engage in conforming or delinquent behavior as the
result of differential social reinforcement, the net effect of all the perceived
rewards and punishments associated with a particular pattern of behavior.

Most of the current leading theorists favor integrated or interactional
models which combine the effects of strain, control, social learning, and
other theories based on inherited physiological or psychological characteristics. Many also believe that the chain of causality between primary factors
(such as substance abuse or association with delinquent peers) is not unidirectional or consistent over time. Not only will the weakening of bonds
increase delinquency, but participation in delinquent acts is also likely to
reduce the strength of bonds to conventional institutions. As youth mature,

the influence of parental bonding declines while that of peers is likely to increase.

Promising Approaches

It is now generally accepted that in order to be effective, delinquency prevention efforts must target some of the specific risk factors that are contributing to the delinquency rather than simply providing resources or improving general skills.[50] Some risks can be identified on the basis of family characteristics before a youth is born. A recent review of early intervention programs dealing with high-risk youth and their families found that interventions that targeted multiple family and child-related risk factors were more likely to produce long-term positive effects on delinquent and antisocial behavior.[51] The most successful intervention approaches involved home visits, the provision of parenting information, emotional support to the parents, and early childhood education for children from one to five years of age.

A ten-year follow-up of youth from the Syracuse Family Development Research Project found that only 6 percent of the experimental subjects had juvenile records compared with 22 percent of the controls; and only one of the experimental subjects was a chronic delinquent compared with five of the controls.[52] Long-term follow-up of participants in the Perry Preschool program in Yipsilanti, Michigan, which also involved a family support component, showed that the program not only improved later school performance but significantly reduced reported arrests, over a twenty-year period.[53]

Moving from early childhood to adolescence, researchers have shown that families employing ineffective or inappropriate parenting practices can be identified through a three-step series of school record checks, telephone interviews, and home visits.[54] Once such families have been identified, a number of organizations offer parent training classes that have been shown to reduce subsequent delinquent behavior among disruptive youth.[55]

Denise Gottfredson conducted evaluations of school-based delinquency prevention programs and identified several program characteristics associated with reduced rates of delinquent behavior, including: involvement of staff, students, and community members in planning the program; schoolwide organizational changes to support project goals; improvements in career education; and special services or case management for high-risk youth.[56] School-based drug prevention programs that help adolescents identify and develop strategies for dealing with social pressures to use drugs have been shown to reduce or delay initiation, but the effects wear off without follow-up booster sessions.[57] An evaluation of a non–school-based skills development program by Jones and Offord found that assigning full-time workers to a variety of recreational, arts, and skill development programs in a public housing project resulted in significant reductions in antisocial behavior.[58]

The prevention approaches I have described all share the common characteristic that they try to change the attitudes, skills, and/or behavior of high-risk youth or their families. However, a recent study by a National Academy of Sciences panel suggests that the high rate of violence among American youth is produced by a combination of political, social, economic, and individual psychological factors. [59] Ours is a society that clearly condones and even romanticizes certain types of violence. Youth are bombarded with violence in the movies, on television, and in the music that is tailored to their taste. Guns are much more widely available in the United States than in any other industrialized country. Other potentially contributing factors may include: high school dropout and youth unemployment rates in many areas of our cities that leave young men with extensive time on their hands and limited opportunities to engage in productive activities; a flourishing drug trade that actively recruits ambitious young men to become street-level dealers and encourages them to use violence to protect their turf and settle their disputes; the heavy media promotion and social acceptability of alcohol use, which has been shown to increase the likelihood of violence in many settings; and the spread of gang culture in many urban areas, which encourages youth to participate in acts of senseless violence in order to prove themselves to fellow gang members and demonstrate their loyalty to their neighborhood.

The complex and multidimensional aspects of youth violence make it virtually impossible to establish direct causal relationships for many of these exogenous factors, since they are not subject to direct policy control or experimental manipulation. Furthermore, research efforts aimed at investigating these relationships are hampered by the lack of systematically collected victimization data for individual jurisdictions and by increasing restrictions on the ability to conduct even anonymous school-based surveys of children regarding their involvement in high-risk behaviors without first securing active parental consent—a requirement which eliminates all but the most lavishly funded projects.

Yet each of these potentially causal or aggravating factors suggests a number of possible violence prevention efforts such as various strategies for reducing access to handguns, or enhanced efforts to reduce teenage drinking and reducing the exposure of youth to violence in the media. The interrelationships among the many causal factors is much too complex to predict the impact of programs designed to address any one of them alone. We are just beginning to see the development and testing of multifaceted, community-based violence prevention efforts, spurred on primarily by the interests of the public health profession, which has identified firearms as one of the leading causes of premature death in this country.

Granted, there are some juveniles who need to be placed in restrictive settings to protect the community. However, the ultimate choice in youth violence prevention is not just whether some fifteen-year-old mugger should serve an additional year, at a cost to the public of about $40,000 per year, but whether that same $40,000 might be used to hire two staff to run after-school recreational programs for hundreds of youth, or to hire two caseworkers to work with forty high-risk youth and their families. Although the evidence regarding these issues is still fairly weak, the prevention literature cited in this chapter suggests that some of these latter investments might be more effective in preventing future youth violence than is simply lengthening the terms of those offenders who happen to get caught.

III

THE
SOCIAL CONTEXT
OF CRIME

TRAVIS HIRSCHI

THE FAMILY

In the realm of crime, husbands and wives, parents and children, brothers and sisters tend to resemble one another. The criminal records of parents and siblings are among the best predictors of one's own trouble with the law. Even more so than is true for individuals, a small portion of families accounts for a large portion of crime. These facts are not much in dispute. What is in dispute is their meaning, the role of the family in producing them.

This dispute itself stems from long-standing and fundamental disagreement on the origins of crime. Is crime inherited, acquired, or invented? The answer we give to this question determines our view of the role of the family in crime causation and public policy.

If crime is inherited, parents and children and siblings will resemble one another in the ways indicated because the family is, after all, a biological entity. From the biologist's point of view, family structure and child-rearing practices may appear to be important causes of crime, but they are in all likelihood themselves genetically determined, such that modification of family structure or practice would have little or no effect on the crime rate.[1] If crime is inherited, appropriate policy will tend toward identification of those at high risk for crime in order to intensify preventive treatment, or to discourage them from reproducing themselves in unusual numbers. It will not see strengthening of the family or improvement of family child-rearing techniques as worthwhile activities.

If crime is invented, if it is a device available to children as soon as they are capable of anticipating the immediate consequences of their acts, the family will play a central role in causation and policy. In this view, parents, children, and siblings resemble one another with respect to crime because faulty child-rearing practices tend to be concentrated in weak families. If crime is invented, policy should focus on strengthening families currently unable or unwilling to control the natural behavior of their children. The invention perspective thus puts the family at the heart of the matter. Children (all children) enter the world capable of crime. They do not inherit crime (although they may inherit general properties indirectly conducive to such behavior). Nor need they learn crime. Crime presupposes no knowledge or skill that is not routinely available to all. What children must learn is self-control, the ability to resist temptations of the moment in favor of long-term projects or prospects. The teaching of self-control (socialization) is a major function of the family, and proper research and policy will therefore, from this perspective, concentrate on child-rearing practice and family structure to understand crime and reduce its frequency.[2]

For many reasons, modern social science tends to reject inheritance and invention in favor of acquisition, the idea that crime is learned. From a learning perspective, the family is either irrelevant to crime or a force positively producing it. Academic versions of learning theory lean toward the idea that the family is basically neutral with respect to crime. Differences in criminality between families are a consequence of inadvertent differences in exposure to criminal influences outside the family (to gangs, peer groups, or the juvenile justice system). Similarities in the criminal behavior of parents, children, and siblings are a consequence of their immersion in a common culture or neighborhood environment. Children can be saved from crime by physically removing them from crime-producing environments. There is no point in worrying about the structure or workings of the family itself.

In practitioner versions of this perspective, the family is an unwitting but important positive source of crime.

> The $1 billion Family Preservation and Support Program . . . does not try to keep families together no matter what. Substantial resources are devoted to making sure that children are protected from danger. That's critical, because millions of children are forced to witness violence between their parents every year—and the consequences can be devastating. Just as charity and learning begin at home, so does violence. Some children learn to be aggressive toward others; others learn to be passive when they are being abused. Both are tragedies.[3]

The policy implications of the social work version of learning theory are virtually opposite to those provided by invention theory. If crime requires learning, if it is produced by exposure to stressful influences, the way to prevent crime is to remove the child from the setting in which such learning occurs, in this case, the family. Preservation and support of the family are not the goals of policy. Nor, in this view, should they be. Families are settings in which criminal violence against spouses and children teaches children criminal violence. Because families are the source of the problem, they should be weakened or destroyed whenever it is determined that their net effects are negative.[4]

Learning theories of crime reflect the optimistic view of human nature dominant in modern social science. In this view, individuals are naturally resilient and resourceful, and thrive best when least encumbered by external constraints. Institutions such as the family are arbitrary arrangements that limit the natural horizons and useful independence of individuals. Some degree of family breakdown is thus prerequisite to the individualism and rationalism of modern society. Whatever the functions of the family, they have been or will be assumed by more efficient institutions; and, nostalgia to the contrary notwithstanding, we are all mostly better off as a result.[5]

By the same token, the invention or control theory of crime is a child of the view that culture is neither arbitrary nor accidental but has its origins in choice and human nature. Institutions are human creations based on analysis and experience. Universal institutions, such as the family, presuppose countless observations and decisions under immensely various conditions. It would be strange indeed were the products of these processes inconsistent with basic human needs and the long-term values of the community. Put another way, invention theory assumes that in the absence of institutional restraints, individuals will tend to follow their own short-term interests to the detriment of others and eventually themselves.

Finding evidence that would allow us to choose between these perspectives as they relate to crime is not easy. Consistent with its image of the individual, the learning perspective is especially adaptive and resilient. Consistent with its image of institutions, the invention perspective is stubbornly resistent to change. Given the complications of the matter, it seems wise to focus here on the contrast between these perspectives and set aside the question of biology.[6]

The Family in Criminology

For a long time, criminologists tended to accept the assumption that the family was irrelevant to crime (or the assumption that crime and progress have the same causes). Nothing in the statistics seemed to argue otherwise. At least until the 1960s, the crime rate did not appear to reflect the steady weakening of the family assumed by many students of the subject.[7] On the contrary, until the 1960s, economic prosperity and freedom from restrictive institutions appeared to be driving the crime rate toward zero. Statistics directly relevant to the relation between family factors and crime were interpreted as telling a similar story: Offenders from weak or broken families were heavily over-represented in the criminal justice system, but this said everything about the system and nothing about families or offenders![8] As a result, the criminological significance of the major indicator of family weakness, the broken home, remained the focus of considerable skepticism:

> No other term in the history of criminological thought has been so much overworked, misused, and discredited as this. For many years, universally proclaimed as the most obvious explanation of both juvenile delinquency and adult crime, it is now often regarded as the "black sheep" in the otherwise respectable family of criminological theories, and most writers shamefacedly turn their backs to it.[9]

Given this state of affairs, the obvious place to look for the origins of what little crime remained was in the workings of institutions that had taken over the functions of the family—the school and neighborhood peer group.

Gradually, however, the family gained a more prominent place in discussions of delinquency and crime. The marked increases in crime during the 1960s and 1970s ran parallel to indicators of family breakdown, and careful examination of the families of delinquents provided a picture contrary to the idea that family functioning was irrelevant to their behavior. Eventually, in fact, some social scientists came to accept the firm and long-standing view of the general public that defective upbringing or neglect in the family is the primary cause of crime.

Child-Rearing Practices and Delinquency

Research on the connection between child-rearing practices and delinquency has produced consistent results. The nature of these results was anticipated by Sheldon and Eleanor Glueck in their famous *Unraveling Juvenile Delinquency*, published in 1950. The Gluecks reported that they were able to predict delinquency from an early age using five factors of family background: discipline of the boy by the father, supervision of the boy by the mother, affection of the father for the boy, affection of the mother for the boy, and cohesiveness of the family.[10]

More than thirty years later, coming at the child-rearing question from a very different angle, Gerald Patterson and his colleagues at the Oregon Social Learning Center reached conclusions remarkably similar to those reported by the Gluecks. Asking themselves what parents must do to teach the child not to use force and fraud, Patterson and his colleagues came up with a simple scheme. To rear a nondelinquent child, parents must (1) monitor the child's behavior; (2) recognize deviant behavior when it occurs; and (3) punish such behavior. All that is required to activate this system is affection for or investment in the child. The parent who cares for the child will watch his behavior, see him doing things he should not do, and correct him. Presto! A socialized, decent human being.

Where might this simple system go wrong? Obviously, it can go wrong at any one of four places. The parents may not care for the child (in which case none of the other conditions would be met); the parents, even if they care, may not have the time or energy to monitor the child's behavior; the parents, even if they care and monitor, may not see anything wrong with the child's behavior; finally, even if everything else is in place, the parents may not have the means or inclination to punish the child. So, what may appear at first glance to be nonproblematic turns out to be problematic indeed. Many things can go wrong. According to the Oregon group, in the homes of problem children many things have gone wrong: "Parents of stealers" do not interpret stealing as "deviant"; they "do not track; they do not punish; and they do not care."[11]

The generality of these conditions has been confirmed by a recent survey of the research literature by Rolf Loeber and Magda Stouthamer-Loeber.[12] Although Loeber and Stouthamer-Loeber organize the results of their review around a set of paradigms, it is easy to see the relation between their paradigms and the dimensions identified by Patterson and the Gluecks.

Research based on the *neglect* paradigm focuses on measures of supervision and the amount of interaction between parent and child. In juvenile court statistics, neglect is a common parental failing, a primary indicator of family inadequacy. Neglected children are highly likely to be delinquent. Being relatively common and highly criminogenic, neglect is a major factor in delinquency.

The *conflict* paradigm deals with the adequacy of parental discipline or punishment, and mutual rejection of parent and child. As is now expected, the data on discipline and punishment produce mixed results. Even when parents behave as a child-rearing model says they should behave, such behavior will often coincide with inappropriate behavior on the part of the child—leaving the statistical impression that the attempt to discipline or punish has backfired. To complicate matters further, conflict and rejection may in fact follow from unsuccessful attempts at correction. Such complications, and the results of research, do not show discipline or punishment to be inappropriate. They do, however, remind us that conclusions drawn from such research may require considerable qualification. To say that punishment prevents delinquency may be no more meaningful than to say that abuse causes it.

Because abuse is a criminal form of punishment, and an important concept separating the invention and acquisition perspectives, a word or two should be said about it here. In the Gluecks' data, collected in the 1930s, physical punishment of the child by his parents was fairly common. Two-thirds of the fathers of delinquents and one-third of the fathers of nondelinquents used physical punishment. Nevertheless, the Gluecks characterized the discipline of delinquents by their fathers as "overstrict" in only one-quarter of the cases where information was available, and they characterized the discipline of nondelinquents as "overstrict" in less than one-tenth of the cases. It seems clear, then, that the Gluecks, no fans of physical punishment, were not inclined to see such punishment as "abuse." There is further evidence along the same lines. The Gluecks report that only one-sixth of the fathers of delinquents were hostile or rejective toward their sons, compared with the more than two-fifths characterized as indifferent toward them. In a situation where physical punishment was fairly common, the Gluecks saw much more neglect than hostility, and their data do not reveal a noticeable difference between neglect and hostility in their effects on delinquency.

An article by Cathy Spatz Widom, published in *Science* in 1989, seems consistent with this picture. Widom followed a sample of neglected and abused children identified from juvenile and adult court records and a sample of controls matched on age, race, sex, and socioeconomic status. The first thing to note in Widom's data is the numerical preponderance of neglect over abuse cases. She reports finding 609 neglect cases and 76 "physical only" abuse cases. Children without proper parental care or guardianship are much more common in juvenile and criminal court records than children who have suffered "unnecessarily severe" physical or corporal punishment. The second thing to note is that differences in subsequent criminality between abuse and neglect cases are small. The increase in the likelihood of subsequent criminal behavior that comes from neglect is essentially the same as the increase that comes from physical abuse. These two facts combined lead to the conclusion that neglect is more important than abuse as a cause of crime. Indeed, in Widom's data, neglect accounts for 4.67 violent offenses for every violent offense accounted for by physical abuse.[13]

All of this, it seems to me, is heavy evidence against the acquisition, or violence-begets-violence, hypothesis. There is more.

The paradigm Loeber and Stouthamer-Loeber label *deviant behavior and attitudes* focuses on parental behavior that encourages delinquency by positive example or by failure to respond negatively to clearly deviant behavior on the part of the child. The facts in this area are clear, and we have met them before: Children whose parents have records of criminal or other forms of deviant behavior are much more likely to be delinquent than children from law-abiding or conforming families. The question of their meaning remains unanswered. They are not, it should be noted, irrelevant to the child abuse question. Because such abuse is a crime, it is not immediately obvious that the connection between abuse and crime is anything more than the connection between crime and crime. In fact, analysis suggests that it is not. In the Widom data, abuse and neglect predict general delinquency and adult crime as well as they predict violent crime. This is a standard finding of research. Variables that predict one type of crime predict other types of crime as well.[14] Contrary to the evidence, the "cycle of violence" hypothesis asserts that violence begets violence, which is also an assertion that violent offenders can be separated from nonviolent offenders. To my knowledge, efforts to locate violent offenders as distinct from offenders in general have met with little success.[15]

Taken together, the complex results of current research and treatment efforts provide support for a simple child-rearing model. This model makes sense of the strong effects of parental supervision, parental rejection, and parent-child involvement. It also in principle explains the effects on delin- quency of adolescent employment (which is positively correlated with delin- quency), parental criminality, large family size, single parenthood, and mother's employment. With respect to the latter variables, the argument is straightforward: family structure (elements such as number of parents or number of children) has its effects on delinquency through its effects on the ability (or willingness) of parents to monitor their children's behavior and to recognize and correct misbehavior when it occurs.[16]

This argument has been tested directly in a recent reanalysis of the Gluecks' data. Robert Sampson and John Laub show that parental discipline, mother's supervision, parental rejection, and attachment of the child to the parent do indeed account for the effects on official delinquency status of such background factors as residential mobility, family disruption, mother's em- ployment, family socioeconomic status, and parental deviance. Of the back- ground factors examined, only family size and crowding had an effect on official delinquency over and above their effects on the variables included in our child-rearing model.

In contrast, "all of the family process [child-rearing] variables maintain significant effects on delinquency"[17] when the background or family struc- ture variables are taken into account by statistical adjustment. The pattern of findings did not change when parent- teacher- and self-report measures of delinquency were substituted for the official measure.

Preliminary Conclusions

Three general conclusions would appear to follow from these findings.

1. Inadequate child-rearing practices are strong predictors of involvement in delinquent behavior. Because delinquent acts are themselves only part of a large class of deviant or imprudent behaviors, adequate child rearing appears to protect the child from a multitude of difficulties, from accidents to school dropout, from drugs to unmarried pregnancy, from theft to vandalism to violence. A single cause has many wondrous effects.

2. Difficulties produced by adverse objective conditions (divorce, poverty, mobility) may be compensated for by proper attention to internal pro- cesses. Families can rise above their circumstances and save their children from crime and delinquency.

3: Some aspects of family structure and practice appear to have an impact on delinquency in their own right, over and above their influence on the child's level of self-control or socialization. We may thus add to "child rearing" or socialization a number of other lessons, as described in the next section, from research on the impact of families on delinquency.

Other Family Activities Relevant to Delinquency

The family may reduce the likelihood of delinquency by restricting its children's activity, by maintaining actual physical surveillance of them, and by knowing their whereabouts when they are out of sight. Parental supervision may be essential to proper socialization, but it is effective in preventing delinquency even when it has no long-term impact on behavior. Children who must be home at reasonable hours and who must account to their parents for their friends and activities are less likely than others to be delinquent. Indeed, according to the Gluecks' data, the best predictor of delinquency, however measured, was the adequacy of supervision by the mother. Because delinquency reaches its peak in middle to late adolescence, when the child is still normally under the control of the family, variation in levels of family supervision is potentially a major source of variation in criminal as well as delinquent acts.

The family may reduce the likelihood of delinquency by commanding the love, respect, or dependence of its members. There is a strong tendency among delinquency researchers and theorists, especially in the United States, to assume that parents, whatever their class or status, oppose delinquency on the part of their children. Consistent with this assumption, in most studies attachment of the child to the parent is an important predictor of nondelinquency. Attachment presumably facilitates supervision and discipline, but it also appears to deter delinquency independent of its indirect effects on socialization or self-control. Children closely tied to their parents will refrain from acts that jeopardize the relationship, whatever the legal status of such acts. Because illegal acts entail additional embarrassment and inconvenience to the parents, such acts will be especially avoided by children concerned about the parents' good opinion.

The family may reduce crime by guarding the home, by protecting it from potential thieves, vandals, and burglars. Criminological theory traditionally focused on offenders rather than offenses and assumed that offenders were powerfully motivated to commit their crimes, especially "serious" crimes. Once the focus shifted to criminal events it became evident that offenders were not all that skillful, motivated, or dangerous. In fact, it soon became plain that familial institutions may play a role in crime control beyond watching their own members, that they can do much by merely protecting their own property. Further, it became clear that to do so effectively they need not brandish weapons or cower behind closed doors. The mere presence of a family member in the house or on the property is enough to deter the typical offender interested in burglary or theft. As a result, a major predictor of the burglary rate in an area is the proportion of homes occupied during the day, a proportion clearly affected by family practices and structure.[18]

The family may reduce delinquency by protecting its members from physical harm, and from the advances of unwanted suitors, molesters, and rapists. Deterring potential burglars is one thing, deterring those interested in sex with or revenge on family members is another. Lone women and women-only families are at unusual risk from male predators, both inside and outside the home. The situation described by Judith Blake in Jamaica must exist at least in attenuated form in many households whose defense can enlist no adult males:

> One of the most important and effective ways of protecting young girls from sexual exploitation is for male relatives to be ready and able to retaliate if such exploitation occurs. Whether this condition prevails depends heavily on the organization of the family. . . . Among lower-class Jamaicans, however, a father is as likely as not to be absent from the family picture. Brothers may be merely half-brothers, or living elsewhere. . . . The sexual exploitation of young girls therefore both results from family organization and contributes to it. Men are provided with a far wider range of sexual partners than there would be if girls were protected. Thus, there are fewer pressures on the man to form a permanent liaison. Moreover, once a woman has a child or two, her desirability can always be weighted by men against that of the childless young girl. Thus, because young girls are in many ways unprotected from male advances, older women are unprotected from the competition of young girls.[19]

Finally, the family may reduce delinquency by acting as an advocate for the child, as a probation or parole agency willing to guarantee the good conduct of its members. At all levels of the criminal justice system, community or family ties are taken into account in processing decisions. The individual with no family to vouch for him is likely to penetrate the system further than the person whose family is willing to take responsibility for his conduct. It is sometimes said, in fact, that the criminal justice system tends to avoid intervention whenever it has an excuse for doing so. A stable family obviously concerned for or dependent on the offender's welfare makes a very good excuse indeed. As a consequence, even those who belittle the family's role in crime agree that weak families contribute far more than their share of those detained or imprisoned by the state:

> In a sample of state prisoners interviewed by researchers at the Rand Corporation, 56 percent came from broken homes and lived with a single

parent during adolescence. Only 29 percent of male and 19 percent of female wards of the California Youth Authority in 1980 came from "unbroken" homes. In a sample of institutionalized juvenile serious offenders . . . in Chicago, less than a quarter had been living with both natural parents.[20]

All of this rightly suggests that strong families deeply involved in child rearing are unlikely to run into trouble with the criminal justice system, at least into trouble they cannot handle themselves.

We know what the family can and must do to prevent delinquency, and we know how objective states of the family affect its ability to carry out its child-rearing tasks. This knowledge can take us in one of two directions. Not surprisingly, our two perspectives describe these alternatives in very different ways. According to learning theory, the unwanted consequences of structural difficulties may be reduced by modifying the process to counteract them. Because family problems are evidence of an inadequate or uninformed response to objective conditions, they can be resolved by teaching people how to deal with them, and by providing them with the means for doing so. There is, then, nothing wrong with the family or families that cannot be remedied by individual reason and effort:

> Considerable research on the effect of broken homes and discord on children has been summarized in review articles. . . . The reviews usually minimize the importance of the relation between broken homes and children's behavior problems and stress marital discord as a stronger factor.[21]

> If we wish seriously to address the ways in which the stresses on single parent families may generate behavioral problems, we will need to start by acknowledging that such stresses are not part of the natural order of things. We will accomplish more by way of preventing delinquency if we worry less about the decline of traditional family forms and more about the quality of work and public supports available to parents, in whatever sort of family they may be found.[22]

> But in the end, regeneration in a free society must come from within.[23]

> It has become customary to distinguish criminogenic factors present in families which are structurally normal from those present in families whose structure deviates from the norm. While accepting this distinction we have to make it clear that our growing awareness of the preponderance of psychological over purely structural, i.e., basically external, factors is increasingly leading to a state of affairs where this latter category becomes rather empty and meaningless.[24]

Learning theorists start with the view that the family is not essential to, and may actually impede, the realization of human values. The data show, on the contrary, that weak families are less able to socialize and otherwise protect their members from crime. Reacting to this evidence, learning theorists maintain the position that there is nothing in the institution of the family that cannot be provided as well by other means. The cause of family breakdown is the unhappiness of individuals. Unhappiness in some individuals (parents) creates unhappiness in others (children). Therefore, everyone is better off, at least in the long run, when families that are a source of potential or actual unhappiness are not created in the first place or are dissolved by divorce or separation. Better to be illegitimate than witness to an unhappy or discordant marriage. Whatever problems tend to accompany single parenthood under current conditions may be relieved by provision of technical assistance and financial support.

In the view of invention or control theory, there is something profoundly wrong with such logic. It negates the consequences of family weakness by merely assuming otherwise. It does not appreciate distinctions between thoughts and deeds, between velleities and authentic, energizing desires. People in weak families may know of a better life, but they may also see no point in forgoing the certain pleasures of today for the unknown and uncertain pleasures of the future. Indeed, when the family is weak, when individuals are freed from its constraints, ambition, interest, and forethought are not the consequences. On the contrary, when the family is weak, interest in the future is also weak.

To choose between these views it is necessary to look again at the connection between family structure and child-rearing practices. Is child rearing in weak families inadequate because they lack resources and knowledge, or is it inadequate because they lack the will to do otherwise?

Structure and Functions of the Family

The traditional functions of the family were reproduction, maintenance, socialization, and placement of the young.[25] So defined, the family plays a central role in the transmission of wealth, traditions, and values. As a consequence, it has been a target of unremitting attack from those opposed to current arrangements, whatever their particular quarrel with the status quo.[26] Given the family's centrality in this ongoing quarrel, it is sometimes hard to distinguish hope from reality. It may be true that the traditional functions of the family need not be performed by a single institution, and that none of them requires the family for its performance. Children may be born outside of families, nourished and tended by people other than their biological parents, and trained and educated by a variety of adults and peers. They may also find for themselves sexual arrangements and occupations consistent with their interests and talents. But none of this should be mistaken for evidence that the family no longer performs its traditional functions, or that it does so in an inferior way.

The family, for present purposes, consists of two parents, who are husband and wife, and their children. Families are strong to the extent all members are present and the bonds among them are intense and durable. So defined, the family is not normally associated directly with crime but is associated with moral issues, with divorce, desertion, illegitimacy, adultery, and promiscuity. Because the family is to morality as the state is to crime, the connection between the family and crime is dependent on the connection between morality and crime. If immorality and crime are the same thing, the family is central to the crime problem. If immorality and crime are independent, the family is logically irrelevant to the latter. Social scientists sometimes assert that moral issues have little or nothing in common with the criminal acts of interest to the state (such as rape, robbery, assault, theft), that the family and crime exist in separate domains. [27] But the assumption of independence is so frequently encountered in social science, and is so often contrary to the facts, that we are entitled to initial skepticism. If it turns out that immorality and crime are the same thing, the role of the family in crime control would be seen in a new light, to say the least.

Morality and the Family

The several moral problems of the family appear to revolve around threats to its structure or survival, the most serious of which is unmarried parenthood, the situation in which the child does not have two parents responsible for his or her welfare. The primary and most threatening form of unmarried parenthood is of course illegitimacy, where "the child is brought into the world without a man—and one man at that—assuming the role of sociological father." [28] The threat of illegitimacy is neither recent nor merely theoretical. The Glueck study mentioned earlier was based on 500 delinquent and 500 nondelinquent boys born between 1924 and 1935, well before the sexual revolution. According to the Gluecks, almost two in five of the marriages of the delinquents' parents and three in ten of the marriages of the nondelinquents' parents were "forced" by premarital pregnancy. [29] At about the same time, a researcher determined by ingenious means that as many as 30 percent of marriages in Provo, Utah, the heart of Mormonism, also involved premarital pregnancy. [30]

These figures suggest that premarital sex is not particularly threatening to families strong enough to require marriage in the face of potential resistance. In the Gluecks' study, in fact, only one in twenty-five of the boys (delinquent and nondelinquent) was illegitimate. Some sixty years after the Gluecks' sample was born, rates of premarital pregnancy in the United States as a whole were virtually identical to those experienced by the mothers of the Gluecks' delinquents (in 1988, two in five women were not married when they became pregnant with their first child). [31] By 1988, however, almost three in ten women giving birth to their first child remained unmarried at the time. In reporting this statistic, the Census Bureau analyst offered the view that illegitimacy "may reflect the opinion of some women that they may be better off in the long run by relying more on the support of their parents and relatives for financial and emotional assistance than by entering a potentially unstable marriage undertaken solely to prevent an out-of-wedlock birth."[32] There is better reason to believe that this decision reflects the declining strength of the family. Because many families have lost the power to force marriage, the risk of illegitimacy has increased for all families in the community.

Because legitimacy is enforced in the first instance by the families of the child's parents, illegitimacy is a long-term as well as immediate threat to the family: illegitimate (or unattached) children will tend to bear or father illegitimate children for the very reason that their "families" lack the power to require marriage or acceptance of responsibility.[33] Illegitimacy also weakens the general community by depriving it of the interlocking alliances of families automatically produced by marriage.

Desertion and divorce are akin to illegitimacy in that they too tend to remove the father from the scene or to weaken the link between him and his children. From this perspective, a major reason for the traditional condemnation of adultery and promiscuity was that they threatened the family by increasing the risk of unmarried parenthood.

Current data on illegitimacy, desertion, and divorce, and on extramarital and premarital sexual activity suggest that the decline in the centrality or relative share of the family in reproduction continues. More and more children are born outside of families and more and more can expect at some time to live in a family broken by divorce or desertion. In historical perspective, it seems, everyone is now relatively free to behave in ways inconsistent with or potentially damaging to the preservation of the family.

As the family loses control of reproduction, it also loses in some measure its role in the maintenance, placement, and socialization of children. By maintenance is meant provision of food, clothing, and shelter, and protection from disease and injury. In modern, affluent societies, minimum maintenance may be nonproblematic, at least for the bulk of the population. There is, in principle, food, clothing, and even shelter enough for all. But this does not mean that family structure is irrelevant to maintenance of the young. On the contrary, poverty is a frequent and major consequence of unmarried parenthood,[34] and accidents and injury are also more common in weak or disordered families.[35]

It deserves mention that if poverty were a major cause of crime, if relatively poor people tended to turn to crime as an economic or psychological escape, weak families would be important in crime for this reason alone. The evidence, however, suggests that poverty is not a major cause of crime. On the contrary, well-to-do juveniles and rich countries appear to have problems with crime that escape their less affluent fellows.

As we have seen, placement in marriage is problematic among structurally weak families. If families cannot guarantee married parenthood for their children, they are unlikely to have much say in their children's eventual choice of mates. When structural weakness is compounded by poverty, such families will also be especially unlikely to have much say in their children's educations or occupations.[36]

The inability of a family to place its daughters in marriage puts it at considerable risk of illegitimate birth. The inability of the family to guarantee the responsible behavior of its sons exposes other families to the same risk. The placement and reproduction functions of the family are thus intimately related.

Ironically, as the risk of illegitimacy rises, the willingness to engage in behavior that makes illegitimacy likely also increases. Pearl Buck captured the psychology of this situation as it applies to males: ". . . it is one of the benefits of the soldier's life—his seed springs up behind him and others must tend it!"[37] Boys in a position to have sex without consequences are likely to do so. But how explain the girls left to tend their illegitimate children? Girls in weak families face a relatively problematic and uncertain future. The boys in their lives are like soldiers, more or less free to ignore the consequences of their acts. Girls caught in these circumstances will thus have little reason themselves to delay or avoid premarital sex. Unmarried parenthood may be seen as an unfortunate consequence of sexual activity, but the likelihood of such an outcome may not be greatly reduced by delay.

In a better designed world, weak families could compensate for their weakness in maintenance, placement, and legitimate reproduction by emphasizing the socialization of their children, by seeing to it that by dint of hard work and delayed gratification they freed themselves from the cycles of illegitimacy and poverty. In this world, it does not seem to work that way. When the father was explicitly responsible for the education of his children, he was routinely awarded custody of the children in the case of divorce. Now the mother typically gets the children, presumably because she is better able to provide those aspects of education that cannot be provided by the school.

What does she (the unmarried mother) do with this opportunity? Clearly, whatever she may wish to do, the odds are stacked against her. Her children are "more likely to drop out of high school and less likely to attend college than children from intact families."[38] Interestingly enough, anecdotal evidence suggests that the unmarried mother tends to take a combative stance toward the school, seeing it as a conspiracy of sorts against her and her children. If so, this is presumably exactly what she should not do if her interest is in socializing the child to adult standards. If the long-term interests of the child are her primary concern, she would be well advised to cooperate with the school, and to encourage her children to do the same. Otherwise, they are going to be on their own at an early age, and their socialization, such as it is, is going to take place elsewhere.

For the time being, then, it seems reasonable to conclude that structurally weak families have difficulty performing the traditional functions of the family, and are therefore more likely to be exposed to its traditional moral problems. What is the connection between these moral problems and crime?

Moral problems and criminal behavior. Child rearing takes lots of hard work over an extended period of time. Within our scheme, the goal of such work is to reproduce the family, to produce a healthy, educated child capable of making a good marriage and a good living. Obviously, none of these things is going to happen if crime or immorality intervenes, if the son ends up in prison or the daughter ends up an unmarried parent.

And when are they most likely to intervene? When the family is weak. The logic of the unmarried mother is thus irreproachable: Nothing is likely to come of her efforts to advance the long-term interests of her children. She should therefore seize the moment and get what she can from life without undue concern for the uncertain future of those about her. In fact, if she is clever, she may in effect stage the failure of her children, arranging as it were the premature end of their educational careers and the beginning of their lives as independent adults. So, family weakness causes immorality and crime, which cause or perpetuate family weakness. Crime and immorality have the same causes and consequences and are thus the same thing. They are the same thing from other perspectives as well.

The Concept of Self-Control

Criminal acts are among a large group of acts in which the actor appears to ignore long-term negative consequences in favor of immediate benefits. This group of acts includes use of dangerous drugs (whether legal or illegal), reckless driving, promiscuous sex, truancy, job quitting, divorce, rape, robbery, embezzlement, sexual harassment, and school dropout. All of these acts tend to be engaged in by the same people, and differences in this tendency remain relatively stable over long periods of time. For several reasons, it seems reasonable to label this dimension of difference *self-control.* Those with high levels of self-control will tend to avoid all of the acts in question; those with low levels of self-control will tend to engage in all of them. And how is self-control produced? By conscientious application of the child-rearing model previously described.[39]

So, from the perspective of causation and meaning, the moral problems that plague the family are indistinguishable from crimes. The distinction between them is a political distinction built on ideas of responsibility for their control. The family worries about divorce and job quitting and unmarried pregnancy and the state about theft and vandalism and violence; but they are all species of a tendency to neglect long-term considerations in favor of the here and now, a tendency that is itself rooted in family weakness. The idea that short-sightedness and the traditional family somehow go together and the corollary idea that crime is a species of aggression or ambition are thus utterly inconsistent with the evidence.

Relevant Research

As typically described in the literature, research on the connection between broken homes and delinquency does not seem to support the view that family structure has consequences of the magnitude suggested. However, these descriptions often have more to do with the embarrassment of the reporter than with the facts in question. At the time the broken home was being dismissed by criminologists, it was generally believed that police, court, and prison data were biased and invalid measures of criminal activity. The heavy over-representation of children from broken homes in arrest, conviction, and prison statistics could thus be dismissed as evidence of a "selection principle" (see note 8). An immense amount of research later, we know better. The major determinant of arrest, conviction, and imprisonment is the behavior of the offender. We have not, however, gone back and corrected our interpretive mistakes but have continued to treat family disruption as a "black sheep" in the otherwise respectable family of criminological research.

Today, differences between adolescents from broken and unbroken homes remain small and occasionally nonexistent in studies relying for their measure of delinquency on self-reports of offenders. These "results," too, often neglect what we know. We know that delinquents and children from single parent families are underrepresented in general population samples, and especially in school-based samples. (Children from single parent families are more likely to drop out of school. Delinquents are much less likely than nondelinquents to participate in surveys, even when they are nominally available.)[40] Still, for reasons mentioned, we should expect single parenthood to predict trouble with the law better than it predicts delinquent behavior. This causes no problem for our demoralization thesis. From the perspective of the parent, eventual imprisonment of her children presumably carries greater weight than the delinquent acts they commit in secret during adolescence.

There are further reasons to be unashamed of our interest in this topic. At the neighborhood or community level, rates of family disruption (measured by percentage of single-headed families or the divorce rate) are major predictors of the crime rate. Indeed, according to Robert Sampson, such measures survive controls for traditional indicators of social disorganization at the community level (such as poverty, age structure, or urbanization), and go a long way toward explaining race differences in violent crime and victimization at this level. Sampson's explanation of this fact focuses on supervision and the resources available to families with strong bonds to the local community, an explanation fully consistent with the demoralization argument advanced here.[41]

The connection between family disruption and delinquency is not restricted to particular times or places. Farrington reports from a London sample that parental "separation before age 10 predicted both juvenile and adult convictions . . . and predicted convictions up to age 32 independently of all other variables."[42] In a study comparing Anglo, Mexican American, and Mexican families in the Southwest, Rosenquist and Megargee report finding greater marital instability among the families of delinquents in all three cultures.[43] Analyses of recently collected data agree in essential respects with data collected some sixty years ago.[44]

Given the varied and numerous consequences of low self-control, it seems inappropriate and misleading to restrict attention to any one of its many manifestations. A condition that measurably increases the likelihood of accidents, truancy, incorrigibility, suspension, smoking, drinking, drug use, dropout, theft, arrest, incarceration, unmarried parenthood, divorce, and chronic unemployment merits attention even though its statistical impact on any one of its consequences may be relatively small. The evidence suggests that all of the "outcomes" listed are to some degree consequences of family disruption.[45]

A systematic investigation of effects of family structure on crime cannot ignore a second variable of equal or superior importance to family disruption—the number of children in the family. Research consistently shows that the larger the number of children in the family, the greater the likelihood that each of them will be delinquent. In the Sampson and Laub analysis of the Gluecks' data, the family size effect is so strong that it survives statistical controls for family child-rearing processes.[46] With a different body of data, I reached a similar conclusion: "In addition to its effects on deviant behavior through verbal ability, supervision, and attachment, number of children in the family has an effect on deviant behavior unexplained by the variables available to our analysis."[47] In the study from which I quote, I concluded that size of family predicts delinquency because it is itself an indicator of self-control. Nothing we have seen in discussion of the effects of family weakness would seem to require modification of that hypothesis. A large number of children reflects and causes demoralization, even among otherwise strong families. What is the major cause of demoralization? Inability to influence the future. What does the making of many children guarantee? Limited ability to provide for their maintenance, socialization, or placement. The resources of the family may be strained by too many children as well as by too few adults. Consistent with this argument, number of siblings or size of family is also an all-purpose indicator, predicting delinquency and drug use, as well as school performance and attainment.

Policy Implications

Knowing what is wrong is one thing. Knowing how to fix it is another. And knowing whom to give the job to is something else again. We know that weak families have trouble supervising and disciplining their children. It follows that we can reduce delinquency by strengthening the family and/or by improving the quality of family child-rearing practices. Previous discussion suggests concentration on the form, size, and stability of the family unit. There should be two parents for every child; the number of children should be small (one, two, or three); the bonds between husband and wife and between parents and children should be strong and durable. These may be goals difficult to achieve, but they are probably no more difficult than many now pursued by the criminal justice system. Further, because they are favored by almost everyone, policy can focus with relative confidence on the task of accomplishing them. How? By adopting direct means to reduce the number of weak families, a goal that probably commands even broader support.

In my view, the teenage mother is not the problem.[48] The Gluecks' data show no connection between the age of parents at marriage and the delinquency of their children. The problem is the mother without a husband. Her children are likely to be delinquent, and she is likely to have more of them. She should thus be seen as a golden opportunity in the fight against crime, an opportunity superior in value to early identification of the fabled career criminal. Unlike the career criminal, she *can* be identified early in her career and *can* be effectively treated using techniques of persuasion and prevention well within the bounds of morality and good sense.

She is also the best source of information about the identity of her child's father. He should be the object of an aggressive and determined search. At a minimum, he should be apprised of his responsibilities to the mother and the child, and his Social Security number added to the birth certificate. As noted by Theda Skocpol and William Julius Wilson, he could then be assessed a tax for the direct support of his children, a tax that would "make it unattractive for [him] to father and abandon multiple families, [and which] might well encourage stable marriages."[49] Because the weak link in the structure of the family will always be that between father and child, all efforts to strengthen this link should be supported.

Disruptive behavior shows itself at an early age. So early, in fact, that it is possible to identify parents and children with problems in time to avert delinquency through improved child-rearing practices. Richard Tremblay and his colleagues report "relatively strong indications" that a family intervention program based on the Oregon Social Learning Center child-rearing model reduced physical aggression and delinquency and improved school adjustment in a sample of kindergarten boys in Montreal. Indeed, there appears to be a growing consensus that "parent-management training programs . . . are the most promising forms of intervention" in the delinquency area.[50]

To the extent such treatment programs are based on experimental designs (as is the Tremblay study), they show an effect of family child-rearing practices on crime that is independent of biology; socioeconomic conditions; and, for that matter, family structure. To this extent, they answer in an effective way the claim that the family is merely a conduit for the influence of biological inheritance or broader social context. They answer in an equally effective way the idea that family-based explanations of delinquency are devoid of practical or policy significance.

Whatever the focus of family policy, as far as possible, the police should not be involved. They, or those who speak for them, tend to see family problems as unbefitting officers trained to deal with real criminals and serious crimes.[51] As a result, their employment limits the range of issues that can be addressed, and increases the likelihood that those addressed will not receive the undivided attention of those addressing them.

As far as possible, the social service system should not be involved in family policy. Workers in this system, or those who speak for them, persistently misperceive the problem, saddling strong families with the sins of weak families (for example, child abuse), and promoting child-rearing practices at best orthogonal (that is, unconnected) to the practices suggested by research on delinquency.[52] As in other realms of treatment, the obvious candidates for the job are elementary teachers and successful parents, people whose experiences and records of accomplishment are directly relevant to the child-rearing task.

Conclusion

One way, perhaps the usual way, of thinking about the family and crime has been to imagine an unmarried teenage mother, with all the handicaps that implies, facing the awesome task of child rearing. In this image, a family fails to form, and fifteen years later the reverberations are felt in the juvenile justice system. In this image, things will get worse before they get better, because we have yet to suffer the full consequences of current family weakness. In this image, things will get progressively worse, because family weakness fosters further family weakness.

For several reasons, this image appears to be excessively gloomy. For one, the crime rate has been reasonably stable for some time now, with the National Crime Survey in fact reporting remarkable declines in burglary and household larceny over a twelve- to fourteen-year period from the early 1980s to 1994. For another, this image ignores its own argument for the resilience of the family and its consistency with basic human needs. As with crime, people are born with the capacity to invent families. One-sixth of the Gluecks' 500 delinquents came from "cohesive" families. By the time they were in their early thirties, more than half of these delinquents had formed families worthy of that description.[53] Fifty percent of the Gluecks' delinquents came from two-parent families; when they were in their early thirties, almost three-quarters of their own children were living in two-parent families.[54] Finally, this image neglects its own arguments about the concentration of crime in weak families and the interchangeability of criminal and moral problems. Beyond the important connection between mother and child, there are also connections between mothers and fathers and brothers and sisters. If our teenage girl's unmarried state tells us something about the future of her child, it tells us at least as much about her child's father and about her own brothers and sisters. Put more simply, current levels of family weakness tell us a great deal about current levels of crime and delinquency. There is reason to hope that they may tell us less about the future.

But we should not allow ourselves to end on this note. There are indeed grounds for optimism. Most children turn out okay whatever their family circumstances. Most would vote for a strong and stable family if given the opportunity. But these facts should not be allowed to obscure the fact that some family circumstances are better than others. The optimistic approach, much favored by those concerned with the dire consequences of negative stereotypes, would emphasize the success rate of an airline that manages to complete 95 percent of its flights without death or serious injury. A responsible approach would point out that this level of safety is unacceptable, that we can, and therefore should, do better.

JACKSON TOBY

THE SCHOOLS

In January 1989, an alcoholic drifter named Patrick Purdy walked onto the playground of the Cleveland Elementary School in Stockton, California, and, without warning, began spraying bullets from his AK-47 assault rifle. Five children died and twenty-nine persons were wounded, some critically.[1] In January 1992, two students at Thomas Jefferson High School in Brooklyn, New York, were fatally shot by an angry fifteen-year-old classmate.[2] In April 1993, three teenagers armed with a baseball bat, a billy club, and a buck knife invaded an American government class at Dartmouth High School, in Dartmouth, Massachusetts, a small town six miles southwest of New Bedford. They were looking for a boy they had fought with the previous Sunday. When sixteen-year-old Jason Robinson stood up and asked why they were looking for his friend, one of the youths fatally stabbed him in the stomach.[3] Also in 1993, on the day before Thanksgiving, at 10:30 A.M., three masked intruders interrupted a mathematics class being taught by Evan Wagshul at Brooklyn Technical High School. They repeatedly punched and kicked the teacher, although two of his students came to his aid.[4]

School violence is often blamed on a violence-prone society. Some urban schools *are* located—as Thomas Jefferson High School is—in slum neighborhoods where drug sellers routinely kill one another, as well as innocent bystanders, on the streets surrounding the school. More than fifty Thomas Jefferson students died in the five years from 1989 to 1994, most of them in the neighborhood, a few in the school itself. Some violence erupts inside schools like Thomas Jefferson when intruders import neighborhood violence to the schools or when students, themselves products of the neighborhood, carry knives and guns to school "to protect themselves."

But some violent incidents in schools—like those in Stockton, California, and in Dartmouth, Massachusetts, which received so much media attention and aroused great parental concern about public education—did not occur in particularly violent communities. In order to see school violence in perspective, one must begin by recognizing that not all incidents of school violence are created equal. The most frightening cases of school violence, those of insanely furious armed intruders like Patrick Purdy, are, like floods or tornadoes, not easy to predict or to prevent. Some dramatically violent acts that occur at schools cannot be blamed on anything the schools did or failed to do. Such *extraordinary* cases of school violence differ from *everyday* school violence: fights between individual students, one student forcing another to surrender lunch money or jewelry, a group of students beating up a disliked classmate in the boys' toilet. Mundane nonlethal, everyday school violence is more common in big-city schools than in suburban and rural ones, but it can be found in these schools as well.

This chapter is concerned with everyday school violence: its frequency, its causes, and measures that may bring it under more effective control. Although I will be discussing violence in American public schools, everyday school violence is not a uniquely American phenomenon; the newspapers of developed countries like Great Britain, France, and Sweden report school violence that sounds oddly familiar. And scattered cases of school violence have occurred in Japan and China.[5]

Statistical Reports of Everyday School Violence

Partly in response to alarming newspaper, magazine, and television reports of violence and vandalism in American public schools—not just occasionally or in the central cities, but chronically and all over the United States—the Ninety-third Congress decided in 1974 to require the Department of Health, Education, and Welfare to conduct a survey to determine the extent and seriousness of school crime.[6] Was school violence really getting worse?

In January 1978, the National Institute of Education published a 350-page report to Congress, *Violent Schools—Safe Schools,* which detailed the findings of an elaborate study.[7] Principals in 4,014 schools in large cities, smaller cities, suburban areas, and rural areas filled out questionnaires. Then 31,373 students and 23,895 teachers in 642 junior and senior high schools throughout the country were questioned about their experiences with school crime—in particular, about whether they themselves were victimized and, if so, how. From among the 31,373 students who filled out anonymous questionnaires, 6,283 were selected randomly for individual interviews on the same subject. Discrepancies between questionnaire reports of victimization and interview reports of victimization were probed to find out exactly what respondents meant when they answered that they had been attacked, had been robbed, or had had property stolen from their desks or lockers. Finally, intensive field studies were conducted in 10 schools that had experienced especially serious crime problems in the past and had made some progress in overcoming them.

On the issue of whether or not school violence was increasing, the report could give only a tentative answer. The Safe School Study (a survey) was conducted for the first and only time in 1976 and had no comparable studies with which to compare its results. Nevertheless, the authors of the report concluded on the basis of fragmentary evidence that crime and disruption was "considerably more serious than it was fifteen years ago, and about the same as it was five years ago."[8] I and three colleagues analyzed crime data from the National Crime Survey by place of occurrence, which included "schools," and concluded, as the Safe School Study had, that the *recent* trend of school violence was flat.[9] Even so, while school violence may not have been increasing overall, the Safe School Study suggested that in some schools it had already reached levels high enough to threaten the educational process.

The Safe School Study has not been the only attempt to throw light on the violence problem in American public schools. Two other national surveys of school violence, one based on data collected at about the same time as the Safe School study, the other in 1989,[10] were based on a few questions about school victimizations in the interview schedule of the National Crime Survey—too few questions to throw light on why some schools seemed unable to control violent students. A third national survey of school violence, the most recent, was part of a series of studies dealing with the American teacher, sponsored by the Metropolitan Life Insurance Company and conducted by Louis Harris and Associates; this survey contained slightly more than 700 secondary school student-respondents.[11] The picture of crime and violence in public secondary schools that emerged from these four studies placed the sensational media stories of school homicides in the broader context of everyday school violence.

The data for *Violent Schools—Safe Schools,* collected nearly twenty years ago, remain illuminating because of their scope: interviews with students and teachers in a large sample of schools (642) that probed a broad range of factors in the school milieu that might explain the emergence of school violence. The Safe School Study was not concerned with mischief or with foul language—although it mentioned in passing that a majority of American junior high school teachers (and about a third of senior high school teachers) were sworn at by their students or were the target of obscene gestures within the month preceding the survey. The report was concerned principally with illegal acts and with the fear those acts aroused. On both the questionnaires and in personal interviews, students were asked questions designed to provide an estimate of the amount of theft and violence in public secondary schools:

In [the previous month] did anyone steal things of yours from your desk, locker, or other place at school?

Did anyone take money or things directly from you by force, weapons, or threats at school in [the previous month]?

At school in [the previous month] did anyone physically attack and hurt you?

Eleven percent of secondary school students reported in personal interviews having something worth more than a dollar stolen from them in the past month. A fifth of these nonviolent thefts involved property worth ten dollars or more. One-half of one percent of secondary school students reported being *robbed* in a month's time—that is, having property taken from them by force, weapons, or threats. One out of nine of these robberies resulted in physical injuries to the victims. Students also told of being assaulted. One and one-third percent of secondary school students reported being attacked over the course of a month, and two-fifths of these were physically injured. (Only 14 percent of the assaults, however, resulted in injuries serious enough to require medical attention.)

These percentages were based on face-to-face interviews with students. When samples of students were asked the same questions by means of anonymous questionnaires, the estimates of victimization were about twice as high overall, and in the case of robbery four times as high. (Table 7.1 is based on student questionnaires rather than on interviews.) Methodological studies conducted by the school-crime researchers convinced them that the interview results were more valid than the questionnaire results for estimating the extent of victimization; it appeared that some students might have had difficulty reading and understanding the questionnaire.

The report also contained data on the victimization of teachers, which were derived from questionnaires similar to those filled out by students. (There were no teacher interviews, perhaps because teachers were presumed more capable of understanding the questions and replying appropriately.) Table 7.2 shows that an appreciable proportion of teachers reported property stolen, but only a tiny proportion of teachers reported robberies and assaults.

Tables 7.1 and 7.2 show that school crime was a problem of national scope, although crimes against students were a somewhat different problem from crimes against teachers and the problem was at its most serious in the central cities. Violence directed at teachers was more common in the inner cities of large metropolitan areas than in small cities, suburbs, or rural areas. Robberies of teachers were three times as common in inner city schools as in

TABLE 7.1
Students Victimized in Public Schools over a One-Month Period in 1976

Size of community (population)	By larcenies of more than $1		By assaults		By robberies of more than $1	
	In junior high schools (%)	In senior high schools (%)	In junior high schools (%)	In senior high schools (%)	In junior high schools (%)	In senior high schools (%)
500,000 or more	14.8	14.9	8.5	3.7	5.7	2.8
	(56)	(59)	(56)	(59)	(56)	(59)
100,000–499,999	18.0	16.8	7.8	2.7	3.6	1.9
	(45)	(36)	(45)	(36)	(45)	(36)
50,000–99,999	18.0	15.3	7.7	2.9	3.8	1.3
	(23)	(31)	(23)	(31)	(23)	(31)
10,000–49,999	15.5	15.8	6.8	2.7	3.3	1.4
	(94)	(74)	(94)	(74)	(94)	(74)
2,500–9,999	16.1	14.6	7.4	3.1	3.5	1.4
	(41)	(47)	(41)	(47)	(41)	(47)
Under 2,500	15.8	14.2	6.2	3.5	3.8	2.0
	(42)	(53)	(42)	(53)	(42)	(53)
All communities	16.0	15.2	7.3	3.1	3.9	1.8
	(301)	(300)	(301)	(300)	(301)	(300)

NOTE: Numbers in parentheses refer to the number of schools on the basis of which the average percentage of personal victimization was calculated for each cell.
SOURCE: Special tabulation of data from United States Department of Health, Education, and Welfare, *Violent Schools—Safe Schools: The Safe School Study Report to the Congress* (Washington, D.C.: U.S. Government Printing Office, 1978).

TABLE 7.2
Teachers Victimized in Public Schools over a Two-Month Period in 1976

Size of community (population)	By larcenies		By assaults		By robberies	
	In junior high schools (%)	In senior high schools (%)	In junior high schools (%)	In senior high schools (%)	In junior high schools (%)	In senior high schools (%)
500,000 or more	31.4 (56)	21.6 (59)	2.1 (56)	1.4 (59)	1.4 (56)	1.1 (59)
100,000–499,999	24.5 (45)	22.8 (36)	1.1 (45)	1.0 (36)	0.7 (45)	0.9 (36)
50,000–99,999	21.0 (23)	19.3 (31)	0.2 (23)	0.3 (31)	0.3 (23)	0.4 (31)
10,000–49,999	20.8 (94)	16.5 (75)	0.6 (94)	0.3 (75)	0.5 (94)	0.4 (75)
2,500–9,999	16.9 (41)	19.1 (47)	0.3 (41)	0.2 (47)	0.4 (41)	0.4 (47)
Under 2,500	15.9 (42)	18.5 (53)	0.2 (42)	0.2 (53)	0.0 (42)	0.4 (53)
All communities	22.1 (301)	19.3 (301)	0.8 (301)	0.5 (301)	0.6 (301)	0.6 (301)

NOTE: Numbers in parentheses refer to the number of schools on the basis of which the average percentage of personal victimization was calculated for each cell.
SOURCE: Special tabulation of data from United States Department of Health, Education, and Welfare, *Violent Schools—Safe Schools: The Safe School Study Report to the Congress* (Washington, D.C.: U.S. Government Printing Office, 1978).

rural schools, and assaults were nine times as common. Even in big-city secondary schools, fewer than 2 percent of the teachers surveyed cited assaults by students within the past month; but threats were more frequent. Some 36 percent of inner city junior high school teachers reported that students threatened to hurt them, as did 24 percent of inner city high schoo! teachers. Understandably, many teachers said they were afraid of their students.

Violence against teachers (assaults, rapes, and robberies) was rarer than violence against students. It was an appreciable problem only in a handful of inner city schools. Presumably, though, even a small incidence of violence against teachers carries enormous symbolic weight.[12] It suggests that teachers are not in control of the school where such violence occurs.

In another segment of the Safe School Study, principals were questioned about a variety of crimes against the school as a community: trespassing, breaking and entering, theft of school property, vandalism, and the like. On the basis of these reports as well as data collected by the National Center for Education Statistics in a survey of vandalism, *Violent Schools—Safe Schools* estimated the monetary cost of replacing damaged or stolen property at $200 million per year. Vandalism, called "malicious mischief" by the legal system, is a nuisance in most schools, not a major threat to the educational process. But vandalism of school property, especially major vandalism and fire setting, is a precursor of school violence because its existence suggests that a wide range of misbehavior will go unpunished.

On one issue there may have been substantial change from the mid-1970s to the 1990s. The Safe School Study showed that *students,* although not teachers, were twice as likely to be assaulted or robbed in junior high schools as in senior high schools. The later studies, however, portrayed the high schools as at least as violent as the junior high schools. The 1989 School Crime Supplement to the National Crime Survey showed about the same percentages of violent victimizations in the junior high school and the senior high school grades.[13] The Louis Harris–MetLife Survey, which contained more detailed questions about types of violence and was conducted in 1993, showed that big-city high schools had more serious violence problems than big-city junior high schools.[14] Not only did urban high school students report a higher rate of victimization than junior high school students for four of the seven types of victimization asked about—three of the types of violence quite serious violence, as Table 7.3 shows. In addition, the Louis Harris–MetLife Survey asked respondents to tell about their *own* misbehavior, the only national study of school crime to do so. As Table 7.4 reveals, urban high schools students were *much* more likely to report engaging in violent behavior than junior high school students on every one of the eight items in the survey, including threatening a teacher. Although both the rates of self-reported violence in Table 7.4 and the rates of violent victimization in Table 7.3 seem rather high, the actual rates are even higher in the most violent

TABLE 7.3
Violent Victimizations Reported by Junior High School Students and Senior High School Students, 1993

	Victims	
Violent acts	High school students (%)	Junior high school students (%)
Verbally insulted you	66	66
Threatened you	39	28
Pushed, shoved, grabbed, or slapped you	38	39
Kicked, bit, or hit you with a fist	25	20
Threatened you with a knife or gun	15	4
Stole something from you	38	35
Used a knife or fired a gun at you	5	0

SOURCE: Louis Harris and Associates, *The Metropolitan Life Survey of the American Teacher 1993: Violence in America's Public Schools* (New York: Metropolitan Life Insurance Company, 1993).

TABLE 7.4
Self-Reported Violence and Theft by Junior High School Students and Senior High School Students, 1993

	Self-reporters	
Violent acts	High school students (%)	Junior high school students (%)
Verbally insulted someone	69	58
Threatened another student	38	23
Pushed, shoved, grabbed, or slapped someone	62	45
Kicked, bit, or hit someone with a fist	42	29
Threatened someone with a knife or gun	15	3
Stole something	32	9
Used a knife or fired a gun at someone	2	1
Threatened a teacher	23	3
Student base (number of individuals)	293	431

SOURCE: Louis Harris and Associates, *The Metropolitan Life Survey of the American Teacher 1993: Violence in America's Public Schools* (New York: Metropolitan Life Insurance Company, 1993).

demographic categories. The data in Tables 7.3 and 7.4 were for *all* junior and senior high school students, including females. From other tabulations not reproduced here, it is known that male students are more likely to be both the perpetrators and the victims of school violence. Consequently, excluding the female students from Table 7.4 would have revealed an even higher rate of high school violence.

Of course, student misbehavior varies from serious violence to minor altercations and thefts. The 1976 Safe School Study and an analysis of the qualitative narratives dealing with school crime in the National Crime Survey both showed that much school crime is fights between students that stop as soon as teachers loom into view, graffiti scrawled secretly on toilet walls, and minor crime such as the theft of the unattended property of students and teachers, rather than violent attacks or robberies.[15] But schools differ in the mix of nonviolent and violent crime; in some schools violence was appreciable—and frightening to both students and teachers. What apparently happens is that what would have been furtive larcenies in a well-ordered school can become robberies when the school authorities do not appear to be in control, just as angry words can turn into blows or stabbings. Under conditions of weak control, students are tempted to employ force or the threat of force to get property they want or to hurt someone they dislike. Consequently, student-on-student shakedowns (robberies) and attacks occur—infrequently in most schools, fairly often in some inner city schools.

Variability of school violence from one school to another is much more important than whether school violence is now quantitatively somewhat worse on the average than it was in 1976 or about the same. Because the Safe School survey sampled students and teachers from a large number of schools (642), it made possible a comparison of the fears and the attitudes of teachers and students in the most violent urban schools with fears and attitudes in the majority of schools, which were relatively safe. Such an analysis can throw light both on the causes of everyday school violence and on the effect of such violence on the educational process.

How Disorder Fuels Everyday School Violence

It may seem obvious that violence is a threat to the educational process, but violence is only the tip of the iceberg. Under the surface is disorder. Disorder in inner city schools takes many forms. Some students arrive an hour or more late, explaining that they were needed at home to baby-sit, to market, or to translate for their foreign-born mothers. Others come to school on time, are recorded present in the homeroom where daily absences are officially determined, and then seek out their friends for sociability or mischief. But a school in which students wander the halls during times when they are supposed to be in class, where candy wrappers and empty soft-drink cans have been discarded in the corridors, and where graffiti can be seen on most walls is disorderly. And disorder invites youngsters to test further and further the limits of acceptable behavior. One connection between the inability of school authorities to maintain order and an increasing rate of violence is that, among students with little faith in the usefulness of the education they are supposed to be getting, challenging rules is part of the fun. When they succeed in littering or in writing on walls, they feel encouraged to challenge other, more sacred, rules like the prohibition against assaulting fellow students and even teachers.

The relationship between disorder and violence is a general one and not peculiar to *school* violence. James Q. Wilson and George Kelling have been pointing out for many years that neighborhoods ordinarily become vulnerable to the violent street crime that arouses so much fear among city dwellers only *after* they have first become disorderly. According to Professor Wilson, in "disorderly" neighborhoods conventional expectations about proper conduct in public places are violated, and property is allowed to get run down or broken. Wilson believes that the informal community controls effective in preventing crime cannot survive in a neighborhood where residents believe that nobody cares.

> Many residents will think that crime, especially violent crime, is on the rise, and they will modify their behavior accordingly. They will use the streets less often, and when on the streets will stay apart from their fellows. . . . For some residents, this growing atomization will matter little, because the neighborhood is not their "home" but "the place where they live." But it will matter greatly to other people, whose lives derive meaning and satisfaction from local attachments rather than from worldly affairs; for them, the neighborhood will cease to exist except for a few reliable friends whom they arrange to meet.

> Such an area is vulnerable to criminal invasion. Though it is not inevitable, it is more likely that here, rather than in places where people are confident they can regulate public behavior by informal controls, drugs will change hands, prostitutes will solicit, and cars will be stripped. Drunks will be robbed by boys who do it as a lark, and the prostitutes' customers will be robbed by men who do it purposefully and perhaps violently. Muggings will occur.[16]

Persuasive as Wilson's thesis is with regard to *neighborhood* crime rates, it seems even more relevant to *school* crime rates because school clienteles are semisocialized youngsters. Given these clienteles, what is remarkable is not that some schools are disorderly but that so many are safe and conducive to learning. A Martian sociologist might well conclude that, given the difficulty of maintaining order when large numbers of children are taught by small numbers of adults, modern educational systems on Planet Earth have ignored obvious dangers. Two social trends have made school order more precarious than it used to be. One trend has been the increasing proportion of youngsters enrolled in school who lack a stake in behavioral conformity to school rules. The second trend is the concomitant weakening of the authority of teachers and other adults over children in school buildings. I shall discuss these trends separately.

Lack of a Stake in Conformity to School Rules

Probably the most important single reason that increasing proportions of youngsters lack a stake in behavioral conformity to school rules is that more of them now than formerly do not want to be in school at all. Why increasing proportions? It has long been true that some children become rebellious as a result of their failure to learn what schools are designed to teach them; some families do not provide enough encouragement, support, and preschool training to give their children a good chance at competitive success. [17] It has also long been true that some peer groups develop goals unrelated to or opposed to academic achievement; children in school are exposed not only to the official curriculum but to the tutelage of their schoolmates, who are more numerous than adult teachers. What has changed is that modern societies are now insisting on more and more years of education for all children. In former generations children who hated school dropped out; now they are more likely to remain enrolled but without a stake in behavioral conformity.

Why do they stay? Partly for legal reasons. All modern societies have raised the age of compulsory school attendance. These formal legal requirement are not the whole story. Dropout prevention programs are part of the informal pressure on youngsters to remain enrolled in school at least until high school graduation. True, many enrolled youngsters are convinced, as adults are, that they need all the education they can get to work at satisfying jobs in an increasingly complex economy and to vote intelligently. But some don't buy into this adult ideology; they feel like prisoners. Obviously, such youngsters don't respect the rules or the rule enforcers as much as students who regard education as an opportunity.

Keeping more children in school who do not want to be there interferes with traditional learning as well as with school order. Consequently, functional illiteracy has spread to more students, resulting not necessarily in the formal withdrawal from school of marginal students but, more usually, in "internal" dropouts. Such students used to be described as "lazy," and they were given poor grades for "conduct." It is perhaps not surprising that the public schools have had great difficulty providing satisfaction, not to mention success, to students whose aptitudes or attitudes do not permit them to function within the range of traditional standards of academic performance. One response of schools is to "dumb down" the curriculum with undemanding courses that increase the proportion of entertainment to work. Despite this effort to be "relevant," most students uninterested in traditional education do not get much satisfaction out of intellectually weak courses and do not develop a stake in conformity to school rules.

The proportion of students with little stake in conformity varies from school to school, although the proportion is larger, on the average, in big-city school systems than in rural or suburban school systems. But the overall trend has been to greater proportions of rebellious students because greater proportions of students are staying in school without being convinced that further education is worthwhile. This trend makes for disorder, but it would not be sufficient to produce disorder in the absence of another trend: that toward weakened social and cultural controls of adults over all students.

Weakening of Social and Cultural Controls over Students

Historically, the development of American public education increasingly separated the school from students' families and neighborhoods. Even the one-room schoolhouse of rural America represented separation of the educational process from the family. But the consolidated school districts in nonmetropolitan areas and the jumbo schools of the inner city carried separation much further. Large schools developed because the bigger the school, the lower was the per capita cost of education; the more feasible it was to hire teachers with academic specialties like art, music, drama, or advanced mathematics; and the more likely it was that teachers and administrators could operate according to professional standards instead of in response to local sensitivities—for example, in teaching biological evolution or in designing a sex education curriculum. But the unintended consequence of large schools, which operated efficiently by bureaucratic and professional standards, was to make them relatively autonomous; they could ignore the local community.

The disadvantage of the separation of school and community was that students developed distinctive subcultures only tangentially related to education. Thus, in data collected during the 1950s Professor James Coleman found that American high school students seemed more preoccupied with athletics and personal popularity than with intellectual achievement. [18] Students were doing their own thing, and their thing was not the same as what teachers and principals were mainly concerned about. Even in the 1950s, student subcultures at school promoted misbehavior; in New York and other large cities, fights between members of street gangs from different neighborhoods sometimes broke out in secondary schools. [19] Presumably, if parents had been more closely involved in the educational process, they would have strengthened the influence of teachers. However, Soviet achievements in space during the 1950s drew more attention to academic performance than to school crime and misbehavior. Insofar as community adults were brought into schools as teacher aides, they were introduced not to help control student misbehavior but to improve academic performance.

Until the 1960s and 1970s, school administrators did not sufficiently appreciate the potential for disorder when many hundreds of young people come together for congregate instruction. Principals did not like to call in police, preferring to organize their own disciplinary procedures. They did not believe in security guards, preferring to use teachers to monitor behavior in the halls and lunchrooms. They did not tell school architects about the need for what has come to be called "defensible space," and as a result schools were built with too many ways to gain entrance from the outside and too many rooms and corridors where surveillance was difficult. Above all, principals did not consider that they would lose control over potential student misbehavior when parents were kept far away, not knowing how their children were behaving. The focus of PTAs was on the curriculum, and it was the better-educated, middle class parents who tended to join such groups. In short, the isolation of the school from the local community always meant that, if a large enough proportion of students misbehaved, teachers and principals could not maintain order.

Then the civil rights revolution spread to public schools. At the same time that increasing proportions of school children had less stake in behavioral conformity to adult rules, adults were becoming increasingly sensitive to the rights of children. A generation ago it was possible for principals to rule schools autocratically, to suspend or expel students without much regard for procedural niceties. Injustices occurred; children were pushed out of schools because they antagonized teachers and principals. But this arbitrariness enabled school administrators to control the situation when serious misbehavior occurred. Student assaults on teachers were punished so swiftly that such attacks were almost unthinkable. Even disrespectful language was unusual. Today, as a result of greater concern for the rights of children, school officials are required to observe due process in handling student discipline. [20] Hearings are necessary. Charges must be specified. Witnesses must confirm suspicions. Appeals are provided for. Greater due process for students accused of misbehavior gives unruly students better protection against teachers and principals; unfortunately, it also gives well-behaved students less protection from their classmates.

Related to the extension of civil rights in the school setting was another effect of the civil rights revolution: the decreased ability of schools to get help with discipline problems from the juvenile courts. Like the schools themselves, the juvenile courts have become more attentive to children's rights. Juvenile courts today are less willing to exile children to a correctional Siberia than they used to be. More than twenty-five years ago the Supreme Court ruled that children could not be sent to juvenile prisons for "rehabilitation" unless proof existed that they had *done* something for which imprisonment was appropriate. The 1967 *Gault* decision dramatically changed juvenile court procedures. For example, formal hearings with youngsters represented by attorneys became common practice for serious offenses that might result in incarceration.

Furthermore, a number of state legislatures restricted the discretion of juvenile court judges. In New York and New Jersey, for example, juvenile court judges may not commit a youngster to correctional institutions for status offenses, that is, for behavior that would not be a crime if done by adults. For example, truancy or ungovernable behavior in school or at home are not grounds for incarceration in New York and New Jersey. The differentiation of juvenile delinquents from persons in need of supervision (PINS in New York nomenclature, JINS in New Jersey) may have been needed. However, one consequence of this reform is that the public schools can less easily persuade juvenile courts to help with school discipline problems that threaten the educational process. In some cases the juvenile court judge cannot incarcerate because the behavior is a status offense rather than "delinquency." To a juvenile court judge, the student who called his history teacher an asshole is not a candidate for incarceration in a juvenile correctional institution. In other cases the alleged behavior, such as slapping or punching a teacher, is indeed delinquency; but many judges will not commit a youngster to a correctional institution for this kind of behavior because they have to deal with what they perceive as worse juvenile violence on the streets.

Increased attention to civil rights for students, including students accused of violence, was also an unintended consequence of compulsory school attendance laws. The Supreme Court held in *Goss v. Lopez* not only that school children were entitled to due process when accused by school authorities of misbehavior but that greater due process protections were required for students in danger of suspension for more than ten days or for expulsion than for students threatened with less severe disciplinary penalties. The Court held also that the state, in enacting a compulsory school attendance law, incurred an *obligation* to educate children up until the age specified in the law, which implied greater attention to due process for youngsters still subject to compulsory attendance laws than for youngsters beyond their scope. Boards of education interpreted these requirements to mean that formal hearings were necessary for youngsters in danger of losing the educational benefits the law entitled them to receive. Such hearings were to be conducted at a higher administrative level than the school itself, and the principals had to document the cases and produce witnesses who could be cross-examined.

Social changes that separated secondary schools from effective family and neighborhood influences and that made it burdensome for school administrators to expel students guilty of violent behavior or to suspend them for more than ten days partially explain the reduced ability of teachers and principals to maintain order in the schools. *Social* changes were not the entire explanation, however. *Cultural* changes have also undermined order. There was a time when the judgments of teachers were unquestioned. No more. Reduced respect for teachers is part of fundamental cultural changes by which many authority figures—parents, police, government officials—have come to have less prestige. In the case of teachers, the general demythologizing was amplified by special ideological criticism. Best-selling books portrayed teachers, especially middle class teachers, as the villains of education, insensitive, authoritarian, and even racist.[21]

The erosion of teacher authority was part of the reason for the decline of homework in public secondary schools. When teachers could depend on all but a handful of students to turn in required written homework, they could assign homework and mean it. The slackers could be disciplined. But in public secondary schools where teachers could no longer count on a majority of students doing their homework, assigning it became a meaningless ritual, and many teachers gave up. Researchers found that private and parochial high school sophomores reported doing, on the average, at least two hours more of homework per week than public school sophomores. [22] Many teachers felt they lacked authority to induce students to do what they did not want to do: to attend classes regularly, to keep quiet so that orderly recitations could proceed, to refrain from annoying a disliked classmate.

Understandably, teachers in disorderly schools get discouraged. It is difficult to teach a lesson that depends on material taught yesterday or last week when only a few students can be counted on to be in class regularly. Eventually, these circumstances lead teachers to stop putting forth the considerable effort required to educate. Some quit teaching for other jobs; some get teaching positions in private or parochial schools at a cut in pay; some take early retirement; some hold on grimly, taking as many days off as they are entitled to, including not only sick days but days in which to escape from pressure (known in the business as "mental health days").

Teacher absences are both a symptom of disorder in the school and a cause of further disorder. Schools whose students present serious academic and behavior problems find substitute teachers difficult to recruit. A substitute's pay is not sufficient compensation for the strain of trying to maintain order in an unruly class—not to mention the fear of possible violence in the school or in its surrounding neighborhood and the anticipation that one's car may be vandalized in the school parking lot. If substitutes cannot be found, students will have to be given "study periods," which are misnamed. When substitutes *are* found, neither they nor the students in the class expect much learning to take place.

Enrolled students not interested in learning undermine the motivation of those more committed to obtaining an education. Students, both black and white, who are committed to learning transfer out of troubled public institutions to private or parochial schools, or they find a friend or relative to live with in the catchment area of a more attractive school. This siphoning out of the better-behaved, more industrious students makes the problem of controlling the remaining students more difficult. Class cutting increases, and students wander through the halls in increasing numbers. In the classrooms, teachers struggle for the attention of students. Students talk with one another; they engage in playful and not so playful fights; they leave repeatedly to visit the toilet or to get drinks of water. Some are inattentive because they are intoxicated; they become defiant or abusive when the teacher tries to quiet them. Only a quixotic teacher expects students to take home books and study assigned lessons. In such an atmosphere, violence directed at both students and teachers periodically erupts.

Many burned-out teachers feel that it is too late to start over in a new field, so they remain in disorderly, violent schools; but they are ineffective. [23] Some idealistic teachers remain also. A charismatic teacher may still be able to control a class. But the erosion of teacher authority means that *run-of-the-mill* teachers are less effective at preventing disorderly behavior in their classes, in hallways, and in lunchrooms. What has changed is that the *role* of teacher no longer commands the automatic respect of students and their parents, as it once did. Consequently, less forceful, less experienced, or less effective teachers cannot rely on the authority of the role to help them maintain control. They are on their own in a sense that the previous generation of teachers was not.[24]

The public thinks of teachers primarily as educators, not as agents of control. Teachers themselves tend to downplay their disciplinary role. Some object to hall or cafeteria duty on the grounds that they are not policemen. If pressed, however, teachers will agree that control of the class is a prerequisite for education. Teachers who abdicate control cannot teach effectively. The Safe School survey asked teachers, "In May how many times did you hesitate to confront misbehaving students for fear of your own safety?" The response categories on the questionnaires were, "Never," "Once or twice," "A few times," and "Many times." For those who can remember the days when teachers were on a pedestal, the results of the survey were surprising: 28 percent of teachers in cities of half a million population or more said that they hesitated to confront misbehaving students at least once in the month before the survey. Smaller percentages of teachers in other locations were afraid to confront misbehaving students: 18 percent in schools in smaller cities, 11 percent in suburban schools, and 7 percent in rural schools.[25] Since violence against teachers was found to be greatest in the big-city schools and least in the rural schools, the Safe School Study inferred that teachers' fears were realistic.

Whatever the reasons for individual teachers' reluctance to admonish misbehaving students, including the desire to be popular, this reluctance implies at least partial abandonment of their disciplinary role. When teachers see student misbehavior and turn away to avoid the necessity of a confrontation, adult control over students diminishes at school, thereby encouraging student misbehavior that might not otherwise occur. In short, teachers' reluctance to admonish misbehaving students may be partly the *cause* of the high level of disorder in some schools as well as its effect. The *formal* controls that have developed in big-city schools—uniformed security guards, for example—are a partial result of the breakdown of *informal* social controls over students, such as the expression of teacher approval or disapproval. Informal controls still work quite well in the smaller schools of smaller communities.

The complexity of the issue of teacher authority suggests that calls for "stricter discipline" in the schools—including the use of corporal punishment—may be confusing effects and causes. True, student violence is rare in rural schools and parochial schools; and corporal punishment is common in rural schools and legendary in parochial schools. The Safe School Study revealed that 42 percent of rural secondary schools used spanking as a disciplinary measure as against 17 percent of the big-city schools.[26] But spanking does not create an orderly atmosphere. The legitimacy of teacher authority in rural schools makes for an orderly atmosphere and incidentally makes corporal punishment feasible. Corporal punishment can be used by teachers and principals to discipline students only in schools that are already under informal control; the meaning of a spanking in such schools is similar to the meaning of a spanking in a well-functioning family.

In a tough urban school where a spanking is interpreted by students as akin to police brutality, attempting to use force courts violent retaliation from students and their parents. Even a whiff of force may precipitate a counter-attack. The Safe School report, *Violent Schools—Safe Schools,* recounts a story of a principal in an inner city high school who, during a fire drill, attempted to direct a new student down a particular flight of stairs by grabbing his arm from behind and pushing him. The student "turned and hit the principal in the eye, breaking his glasses and bruising his face around the eye."[27] The teachers in the school and the principal himself decided in retrospect that he had violated a cardinal rule: Don't put hands on students.

When students care what teachers think of them, spanking, although not necessary, serves as a symbol of teachers' disapproval. When students feel indifferent to or contemptuous toward their teachers, classroom control becomes precarious even with security guards around. A 1984 national survey of teacher attitudes threw incidental light on student respect for teachers and for schoolwork.[28] Teachers were asked whether eight "things that some people have said are problems in the public schools" were very serious, somewhat serious, not very serious, or not at all serious "in the public school where you teach." Sixty-six percent of all teachers said that "students' lack of interest in their classes" was very serious or somewhat serious; 40 percent said that "lack of discipline" was very serious or somewhat serious in their schools. Higher percentages of the teachers in big-city schools regarded these as serious problems. The same survey asked teachers to react to the statement, "As a teacher I feel respected in today's society." More than half the respondents disagreed with the statement, and the disagreement was even stronger in the big cities. The statement did not distinguish between respect from students and respect from members of society at large. However, it seems reasonable to infer that students are a salient part of society for teachers and that teachers were responding at least partially in terms of lack of respect from their own students.

Students' lack of interest in schoolwork and their disrespect for teachers may well have contributed to the drop in teacher morale in recent years, which in turn decreased teacher motivation to attempt to control student misbehavior. Schools are not self-policing. Teachers used to be willing peace keepers, not only in classrooms, but in halls, on stairs, in schoolyards: wherever they had occasion to interact with students. For example, a teacher who saw a student in the hall who should have been in class would ask to see a pass. This meant that a student who cut a class could not wander the halls with impunity, looking for friends to visit with or something to steal. He (or she) ran the risk of being apprehended by a passing teacher and being sent to the principal's office. When teachers became less willing to be peace keepers in the school, one possible consequence was the collapse of order. At its worst, this can mean a school controlled by the students themselves, which is the way the researchers participating in the Safe School study described one urban junior high school.

> Each individual teacher, in effect, was on his or her own, and the extent to which the teachers were able to control their own classrooms determined not only their own success but also their own safety. Teachers would lock themselves and their classes into their rooms, opening the doors only for class changes and to eject unruly students. Students who were put out of class were supposed to report to the principal's office but in fact roamed the halls at will. The school's corridors, the gym, the playground, and the bathrooms were essentially under the control of the students. The principal and his assistants, who were also elderly, remained in the administrative offices throughout the day and responded only when problems actually were brought to them by the teachers.[29]

An Ounce of Prevention

In the Safe School Study most of the ethnographic accounts were of extremely disorderly schools. One account, however, was a description of an *orderly* primary school. The way it achieved that pervasive order shows that, even in face of social forces making for disorder, islands of order are possible. The "Dawson" School (a pseudonym), an all black school in the central city of a large metropolitan area, is located in a community with high unemployment that had been "the scene of intense and explosive urban rioting 10 years before, with large sections burned out and abandoned." The field observer characterized its neighborhood as "tightly knit" and "down but not out." Nevertheless, the neighborhood presented problems for the school; for example, every morning broken bottles littered the areas immediately adjacent to the building where older boys had thrown them the night before, presumably after a drinking party. On one occasion a young boy cut his foot badly on the glass. The ethnographic field notes of the observer shows how Dawson managed to forestall rule-violative behavior:

> An example of the "nip-in-the-bud" approach to discipline, as practiced and developed over the years, occurred when a child around 7 threw a piece of orange at another child in the cafeteria. The initial response was from the volunteer aide, a neighborhood mother, who removed him from the room and scolded him severely. Next the lunchroom supervisor, a staff member employed by the school but also from the neighborhood, took him to the main office and spent about 10 minutes explaining to him

how potentially serious this offense had been. Following this, the school secretary phoned his home and explained the situation to his mother, asking her to come in and to pick him up. The boy did not return to class but spent the hour sitting in the outer office. When the mother arrived, she also scolded the boy at length, while several of the office staff reiterated the incident to the boy and to his mother. The boy was sent home and appeared to be thoroughly ashamed and embarrassed. The school secretary, in remarking on the incident, indicated that "making such a fuss" was their standard approach whenever any child "got out of line." You'd be amazed, one teacher said, "how soon they get their heads straight if you catch them young enough." All teachers who were asked about the approach supported it, citing that it gave primary control of discipline back to them and to the parents, rather than setting up the front office as the sole source of discipline. . . .

No children move around the school alone. Aides in every classroom and in the major corridors observe any individual movements, say, to the restrooms and retrieve children who "disappear." Whenever groups of students move from class to class or to the gym, lunch, or elsewhere, they are moved in double-file lines by a teacher and an aide. The children are taught to respond to the direction of any adult in the building, since only grownups with legitimate reason for access are permitted inside. [30]

The formula developed by the Dawson School for achieving an orderly atmosphere worked partly because Dawson, a primary school, had younger, more tractable students than disorderly urban high schools and partly because Dawson, with 526 pupils, was much less anonymous than some of the schools studied by the field staff. Teachers and staff members had a better chance not only to know students personally at Dawson but to know who was a student and who an intruder from the neighborhood. But some credit has to go to a conscious policy of the principal, the teachers, and the parents: keep control at all times. Dawson's formula for order paralleled the measures that criminologist Travis Hirschi found that effective families use to prevent their kids from becoming delinquent. [31] According to Professor Hirschi, most parents care about their children, but caring is not enough to prevent delinquency. Parents must take three actions in order to produce well-behaved children:

1. They must monitor their children's behavior in order to know what they are doing and with whom. A child who is not supervised cannot be controlled.

2. They must identify their children's rule-violative behavior when it occurs rather than rationalizing the misbehavior.

3. They must punish misbehavior. Correcting misbehavior may include spanking, but the critical factor is not the form that the correcting process takes but the fact that parents express strong disapproval.

What Can Be Done?

How can school disorder, the precursor of school violence, be ameliorated?
The usual recommendation is costly new federal programs because the federal government has greater financial resources than the states. For example,
Keith Geiger, president of the National Education Association, to which two
million American teachers belong, called a press conference in January 1992
to demand that the federal government *do* something about school violence.[32] Mr. Geiger suggested that Congress appropriate $100 million for grants
to local school districts to develop programs to curb violence, drug trafficking, and gang activity. Probably, grants to hire additional security guards and
to install metal detectors in the high crime schools of central cities were not
the preventive programs that Mr. Geiger had in mind, but President Clinton
and the Congress seem more likely to favor security measures in urban
schools—even though they are certain to cost a lot more than $100 million.

Security guards and metal detectors *are* useful, especially in inner city
schools where invading predators from surrounding neighborhoods contribute to disorder, violence, and nonviolent theft. Unless intruders can be kept
out of schools, or apprehended swiftly after getting in, the safety of schools
in the central city cannot be taken for granted. But would additional security
guards help much to deter violence perpetrated by students against their
classmates and teachers and, by sheer visibility, promote a more orderly
atmosphere? Probably not. A security program cannot be the *main* instrument for coping with violence caused by students, because there can never
be enough security guards to patrol large junior or senior high schools thoroughly or to screen all of the students in a school for weapons every day.
From a research point of view it is difficult to assess the effect of security
measures on school violence in the absence of controlled experiments: when
security guards are introduced into a school that school already has a school
crime problem. As the report of the Safe School Study put it:

> Security personnel do not cause crime, but crime causes schools to hire
> security personnel, and our multivariate analysis cannot distinguish be-
> tween these two explanations.[33]

Dealing with *student* sources of everyday school violence requires coping with the submerged part of the violence iceberg: disorder. The two issues
that must be addressed to cope with student sources of disorder—a concentration in some schools of unwilling students with no stake in conformity, and
flabby adult control over student misbehavior—require new public policies
rather than massive infusions of scarce resources for security guards or new
technology.

How to Ensure a Critical Mass of Willing Students

Everyday school violence is difficult to avoid in big-city school systems because of the demographic character of central cities. They have large welfare populations characterized by individual and social pathologies: substance abuse, physical and mental illness, criminality. Among the parents in such populations, encouraging their children to do well in school is rarely a priority. Yet without parental encouragement students are unlikely to commit themselves to academic effort. And without this commitment teacher approval and disapproval will not be able to control student behavior.

But all schools contain some unwilling students; the more important reason for the school violence problem of big cities is a natural process of mutual selection that results in a piling up of uninterested students in some schools and of students more committed to learning in others. On the average, the level of violence in big-city high schools is not so different from the level of violence in suburban high schools. But averages misleadingly ignore variability. Violence tends to be concentrated in a small number of out-of-control schools, whereas some academically or artistically selective high schools—like the Bronx High School of Science or Boston Latin School—are not only safe but educationally outstanding. [34] The competition to attend safe and academically meritorious schools takes place in middle-level schools also, schools not usually considered the jewels of the public high school system. Thus, in New York City, which has about 125 high schools, Aviation High School and the Murry Bertraum High School for Business Careers are swamped with applicants; the two schools enroll large numbers of black and Hispanic students whose goals are jobs in the aviation industry or jobs in business. [35]

The competition for admission to the selective schools means that the schools with good reputations, usually deservedly so, attract students whose subsequent performance enhances those academic and behavioral reputations. Exactly the same competitive process works with teachers. Although the most violent schools need the most experienced teachers in order to deal as effectively as possible with student misbehavior, teachers, like students, prefer to be in the academically and behaviorally better schools. Since teachers are unionized and their unions have detailed contract provisions dealing with seniority rights, their seniority entitles them to have first choice when vacancies appear in other schools in the system. Thus, the most experienced and most effective teachers tend to teach in schools with less need for their experience, leaving the least experienced and least committed teachers in the most ungovernable schools.

In a free society it is extremely difficult to prevent students and teachers from voting with their feet, that is, from exercising their choice of more attractive high schools within big-city school systems when they are allowed to choose. Programs of school choice, which have become very popular in recent years, formalize what is already going on informally.

Urban school districts have tried a variety of strategies to avoid the downward spiral that eventuates in violent schools in which education is impossible. None has worked because none has recognized the precondition for a successful high school: a critical mass of willing students. How does an urban school district ensure a critical mass of willing students in every high school? By insisting that educational achievement is the primary mission of schools. Such a policy implies that the small minority of high school students who lack the slightest interest in learning anything except how to drive their teachers into another profession would have to mend their ways in order to remain enrolled.

Taking high school education seriously means that it is not enough for a youngster to be on the high school rolls and show up occasionally. Dropout prevention is not an end in itself; a youngster who does not pay attention in class and do homework *ought* to drop out. The policy in every high school, including inner city high schools with traditionally high dropout rates, should be that students have to be studious in order to receive the public subsidy involved in a high school education. Those who balk at giving prospective dropouts a choice between a more onerous school experience than they now have and leaving school altogether should keep in mind that students would make the choice in consultation with parents or other relatives. Most families, even demoralized ones, would urge children to stay in school when offered a clear choice.

Unfortunately, many families today don't get a clear choice because the schools their children attend unprotestingly accept tardiness, class cutting, inattention in class, and truancy. A child can drop out of such a school psychologically, unbeknownst to the family, because enrollment doesn't even mean regular attendance. In effect, prospective dropouts choose whether to fool around inside of school or outside of school. In effect, internal dropouts turn school into a recreation center. That is why making schools tougher academically, with substantial amounts of homework, might have the paradoxical effect of persuading a higher proportion of families to encourage their children to choose of their own volition to try to learn. Education, unlike imprisonment, which can be imposed on the unwilling, requires cooperation between teachers and learners. However much we may *wish* to educate even unwilling students, the American effort to universalize high school education has shown that it is not *possible* to stuff much in the way of English composition, literature, history, geography, and mathematics into the heads of unwilling students.

Consider why Japanese high schools are so much safer than ours. In Japan school is a full-time, six-days-a-week, ten-months-a-year task for young people, although *compulsory* education ends at the completion of junior high school. Students are expected to study extremely hard by American standards, because they and their parents believe that their futures depend on graduating not merely from high school but from a *good* high school. Prestigious high schools select entering students by competitive examinations; on the basis of these examinations, students are admitted or rejected by the high schools of their choice. Few Japanese youngsters fail to go to high school, and few leave it to enter the labor force. These few, however, are expected to (and do) find jobs, although not very good ones. In Japan, adults and children alike understand that educational achievement leads to occupational success. That is one reason why 94 percent of Japanese junior high school graduates attend high school and 90 percent of them complete it.[36]

Partly because of a rather homogeneous culture that values education but also because Japanese high school students *choose* to attend or not to attend high school, discipline problems are rare in Japanese high schools, although not so rare in Japanese *junior* high schools, as will be pointed out later. Without the help of security guards or of metal detectors, which are never seen in schools in Japan, Japanese high school teachers are firmly in control; they are not afraid to admonish students who start to misbehave, because the overwhelming majority of students will respond deferentially. Japanese high school teachers know that voluntary students care about the grades that they receive at school and also about the favorable or unfavorable attitudes of teachers. (After all, teachers not only give grades; they write letters of recommendation.)

What Japan has done is to *persuade* students that education pays. We could do the same. Certainly, some students will not be persuaded and will leave school, and we should provide opportunities for them to return when and if they realize that they made a mistake. A voluntary high school program is the best alternative to shooting ourselves in the foot by keeping internal dropouts in school.[38]

Even in states that made high school attendance voluntary, violent incidents would still occur. It is almost impossible for security guards to prevent a pathologically enraged student or intruder from attacking school children, as happened at Thomas Jefferson High School in Brooklyn and at the Cleveland Elementary School in Stockton, California. But all high schools would have less *everyday* violence; and the decline in everyday violence would be most dramatic in inner city high schools. The cost of making American high schools safer for education would not be a mass exodus from the high schools: adolescents cast adrift on the streets with no job skills and with enormous potential to increase the crime problem. Most American high school students believe, as Japanese high school students do, that at least a high school education is necessary for a satisfying and well-paid job or to prepare for college.

Teenagers go to school because they have been convinced by their parents, their friends, and the general culture that it is a good idea. By the time youngsters reach the age of fifteen, compulsory attendance laws will do little to persuade those who have not accepted this idea to participate in a meaningful way in the educational process. Conversely, students who consider school valuable to their future lives, including students in inner city schools, will not only stay in school; they can also be required to be studious—to attend regularly, to do homework, to pay attention in class. If the small minority of students who victimize their schoolmates and interfere with the learning process refuse to accept these restrictions on their accustomed freedom and drop out, their places might well be taken by students who now attend parochial or private secular schools. In Hawaii, for example, where a tenth of the state's secondary school students are enrolled in private schools, and where the public secondary schools have a reputation for low academic performance and sporadic violence, a voluntary approach might well improve the educational climate in public high schools sufficiently to lure back some private school students.[39]

Actually, the numbers of fifteen-, sixteen-, and seventeen-year-old students leaving voluntary public high schools would probably be in the tens of thousands and not, as some might assume, in the hundreds of thousands. I base this estimate on an analysis of census data on school enrollment in states with varying ages of compulsory attendance. There were only small differences in the enrollment of sixteen- and seventeen-year-olds between states with low ages of compulsory school attendance and those with high ages, as Table 7.5 shows. Compulsory attendance laws are a minor factor in enrollment and very likely a less important factor in actual attendance.

At present, we coerce the attendance of a handful of unwilling students at the price of promoting a climate of violence and fear in many public high schools, especially in big cities.[40] This in turn makes it especially difficult for public schools to rival private schools in educational accomplishment.[41] If the option of leaving were offered to high school students who are not ready to learn, some disruptive youngsters would leave—until they became ready to accept the discipline that real education requires—and teachers and

TABLE 7.5
White Males Enrolled in School by Age and Compulsory Attendance Requirement, 1970 (percentage)

| | Compulsory attendance required by state law | | |
Age	To age 15 or under (five states)	To age 18 (four states)	Difference
14	94.6	97.1	2.5
15	93.7	96.5	2.8
16	90.2	94.9	4.7
17	85.8	90.1	4.3
18	70.3	71.3	1.0

SOURCE: United States Bureau of the Census, *Census of Population* 1 (Washington, D.C.: U.S. Government Printing Office, 1973), chap. D, parts 5, 13, 20, 21, 37, 39, 46, 49.

school administrators would exercise better control over high school students who remained. In *Goss v. Lopez*, the Supreme Court held that in enacting a compulsory school attendance law, a state incurred an *obligation* to educate children until the age specified in the law was reached.[42] Although this ruling did not render impossible the expulsion of disruptive or violent students subject to compulsory attendance, it made it very difficult. As a result, many schools in central cities have tended to abandon expulsion as the ultimate enforcer of strict discipline.[43] Thus, a consequence of making high school attendance optional will be that high school students who assault fellow students can be forced to choose between adopting acceptable behavior or leaving school. Although younger students would continue to be protected from expulsion, younger students with behavior problems are better candidates for reform through counseling than are older ones.

Past experience with varying ages of compulsory attendance in different states provide empirical evidence that a policy of voluntary high school attendance can in fact improve educational climates of troubled schools. The National Center for Education Statistics collected data on school crime from the fifty states in the fall semester of 1974–75.[44] Researchers tallied incidents serious enough to result in reports to the police and computed rates per thousand enrolled students for each state. (See Table 7.6.) Higher compul-

TABLE 7.6
Referral of School Crimes to the Police by Age of Compulsory School Attendance in the State, 1974–75

Age of Compulsory School Attendance	Average number of referrals per 1,000 enrolled students		
	In elementary schools	In secondary schools	Difference
15 or under (Arkansas, Louisiana, Maine, Mississippi, Washington)	3.1	8.0	4.9
16 (36 states and the District of Columbia)	3.2	10.5	7.3
17 (Nevada, New Mexico, Pennsylvania, Texas, Virginia)	3.8	11.6	7.8
18[a] (Hawaii, Ohio, Oregon, Utah)	4.8	20.1	15.3

a.Because there are so few states in the 18 age group, extreme values for one of them greatly influence the average. Hawaii, for example, had by far the highest rate of school crime on both the elementary and secondary levels. If Hawaii were excluded from the average and the remaining eight states with compulsory ages of school attendance of 17 or higher were averaged, the result would be 4.0 for elementary schools and 11.4 for secondary schools, with a difference of 7.4.
SOURCE: Computed from data published in United States Department of Health, Education, and Welfare, *Violent Schools—Safe Schools: The Safe School Study Report to the Congress* (Washington, D.C.: U.S. Government Printing Office, 1978), appendix B, 6.

sory attendance ages went hand in hand with higher rates of secondary school crime: in the five states with a compulsory attendance age of fifteen or less, the average offense rate per thousand secondary school students (reported to the police) was 8.0; in the thirty-six states and the District of Columbia with a compulsory age of sixteen, it was 10.5; in the five states with a compulsory age of seventeen, it was 11.6; while the four states with a compulsory age of eighteen had an average of 20.1. As would be expected, corresponding rates of elementary school crime differed only marginally among states with different ages of compulsory school attendance. What is most convincing about the information in Table 7.6 are the differences between the rates of primary and secondary school disruption in the four groups of states. Crude though these data are—states vary in urbanization, ethnic composition, and economic development—they suggest that the higher the age of compulsory attendance, the more high school disruption and violence.

Even so, the notion of allowing tens of thousands of youngsters to leave school, even temporarily, is daunting. If youngsters are put out of the schools and into the streets, won't they turn to crime? After all, they will have little chance of obtaining employment without experience or education. In fact, although truants and dropouts have a higher crime rate than high school graduates, the usual inference that dropping out of school *leads* to involuntary unemployment and eventually to criminality seems to be incorrect.[45] There are two excellent longitudinal studies that followed students carefully throughout their high school years and beyond, gathering data covering the entire time period.[46] In one study, official arrest records and self-reported crimes were monitored; in the other, only self-reported offenses. The studies were conducted independently—one in California, the other in the nation as a whole—yet the results were identical. In both cases, the higher delinquency rate of the dropouts was found to *precede* their dropping out of school. In the national study the rate remained at the same high level after the students dropped out of school; in the California study, delinquency actually declined somewhat after the students left. Although dropouts committed more crimes than students who remained in school, they did not *increase* their crime rate after dropping out. Furthermore, dropouts did not appear to be seriously disadvantaged in the labor market compared with high school graduates who did not go on to college.

Apparently, characteristics that lead to higher-than-average delinquency rates manifest themselves while students are still enrolled in school.[47] To put it another way, American society would probably not experience a crime epidemic even if large numbers of youngsters responded to the lower age of compulsory school attendance by dropping out. This conclusion is also compatible with the fact that arrests of juvenile offenders are not appreciably greater during the summer vacation or other holiday periods than when schools are in session. In short, the impact of compulsory attendance laws on antisocial youngsters has been exaggerated. Even if delinquent students attended school regularly, which few do, the school day is short enough to leave time and energy for plenty of crime.

But even the violence-prone would not inevitably drop out. In the present situation, neither the students who make schools disorderly nor their parents realize how little education can be obtained merely by remaining enrolled, coming to school occasionally, and putting forth negligible academic effort. In disorderly schools, youngsters tend to be pitifully unaware of just how little educational benefit they are obtaining from their presence in the school building. One finding of a study of minority students in San Francisco public schools uncovered a startling discrepancy between the objective inadequacies of student performance in reading and other basic skills and the students' awareness of these handicaps.[48] Youngsters who were barely literate, who attended school irregularly, and who never studied, nevertheless believed that they could attend college and become doctors and lawyers. By establishing high classroom standards and then insisting that studious behavior is necessary, society would clarify the choice presented to youngsters in the public schools. This clarification of the meaning of school already occurs in selective private and public schools where education is taken seriously; it was clear, for example, in Dunbar High School, an all black high school in Washington, D.C., where from the years 1870 to 1955 black children were selected for their aspirations rather than for their abilities, were made to work hard, and in a majority of cases went on to college.[49] Given a choice between meaningful education and no education, most students will prefer an academically demanding school to dropping out. There were few dropouts from Dunbar.

Outweighing the social disadvantage of a possible increase in the dropout rate would be a reduction in the rate of everyday violence in all high schools, including public high schools now too dangerous for meaningful education to take place in them. With a greater proportion of students sensitive to teacher attitudes, teachers would no longer be afraid to admonish misbehaving students. Teachers rather than security guards make for an orderly school, but they do not exercise their responsibilities in schools containing students so uninterested in the educational process that they are capable of assaulting their teachers as well as fellow students.

What about junior high schools and intermediate schools? The higher academic and behavioral standards that voluntary enrollment will make possible in high schools will seep down into lower secondary schools. Once all high schools in a state have become voluntary—and are thereby able to raise their academic and behavioral standards—junior high school students will face the problem of getting accepted at the high school of their choice (as they face it now in Japan). Teachers will be able to say to junior high school students, truthfully, "If you do not learn what you are supposed to learn in junior high school, you will cut yourself off from later educational opportunities."

This will not eliminate junior high school violence, but it will reduce it.

The Japanese experience is instructive. Although Japanese junior high schools have much more school violence than Japanese senior high schools, *most* Japanese junior high school students are too busy preparing for the examinations for high school admission to engage in disciplinary infractions.

If high school attendance became voluntary in the United States, a majority of the age cohort would attend, a greater proportion in some communities than in others but a majority in American society as a whole. Teacher morale would improve; students would have a greater stake in conformity; they would respond better to their teachers and work harder. Academic achievement would increase overall in American society, but it would improve most in those inner city high schools where today serious education is an endangered species.

How to Strengthen Adult Control over Student Misbehavior

The United States cannot bring back the one-room schoolhouse. Formal education will continue in bureaucratic school systems that permit only limited influence from parents and local communities. What can be done, however, is to increase the psychological presence—and more rarely the physical presence—of adults in high school classrooms. For instance, school boards should encourage community adults to come into high schools, not as teachers, not as aides, not as counselors, not as security guards, but as full-time students. This has actually occurred.[50] At Chicago's DuSable High School, an all black school close to a notorious public housing project, dropouts regarded by current students as middle-aged hungered for a second chance at a high school education. A thirty-nine-year-old father of six children; a twenty-nine-year-old mother of a fourteen-year-old son, who, like his mother was a freshman at DuSable; and a thirty-nine-year-old mother of five children—all had come to believe that dropping out a decade or two earlier had been a terrible mistake. Some of these adult students were embarrassed to meet their children in the hallways; some of their children were embarrassed that their parents are schoolmates; some of the teachers at the high school were initially skeptical about mixing teenagers and adults in classes. But everyone at DuSable High School agreed that the adult students lent seriousness to the educational atmosphere and became role models for younger students.

These adult students were in school not to reduce school violence but to make themselves more literate and therefore more employable. But an incidental byproduct of their involvement in classwork must inevitably have been improved order. For example, it is less easy to cut classes or skip school altogether when your mother or even your neighbor is attending the school. The principal at DuSable High School observed one mother marching her son off to gym class, which he had intended to cut. Unfortunately, most school systems are dubious about adult students and relegate them to special adult school programs or G.E.D. classes. Such separate programs will continue to enroll most of the high school dropouts who later decide they want a high school diploma; work, child-care responsibilities, and inflexible school regulations will keep all but the most determined in these age-segregated programs.

But educational policies should not *prevent* persons over 21 from reenrolling in high school. The age limit for high school enrollment should be raised from 21, the usual age at present, to 100. Encouraging even a handful of adult dropouts to return to regular high school classes would help maintain order. Teachers who have an adult student or two in their classes are not alone with a horde of teenagers. They have adult allies during the inevitable confrontations with misbehaving students. Whether the adult students express support for the teacher explicitly or not, the implicit message of their presence is that community adults stand squarely behind teachers, and this knowledge bolsters the will of teachers to maintain order. Inner city high schools have most to gain by actively seeking to enroll adult students because they have more serious order problems than rural or suburban schools. They also are able to find suitable adult students relatively easily because illiterate dropouts from previous generations are concentrated in inner city neighborhoods.

Recruiting adult students can strengthen teacher control in an individual high school. Professor James Rosenbaum of Northwestern University has suggested an institutional change: linking high schools and employers more directly, as is done in Japan.[51] Professor Rosenbaum's comparative study of the transition to work of Japanese and American high school students showed that the failure of American employers to pay much attention to the grades high school graduates receive undermines teacher authority. Here is how Professor Rosenbaum put it:

> Since employers ignore grades, it is not surprising that many work-bound students lack motivation to improve them. While some students work hard in school because of personal standards or parental pressure or real interest in a particular subject, students who lack these motivations have little incentive since schoolwork doesn't affect the jobs they will get after graduation, and it is difficult for them to see how it could affect job possibilities ten years later. . . .
>
> While employers ask why teachers don't exert their authority in the classroom, they unwittingly undermine teachers' authority over work-bound students. Grades are the main direct sanction that teachers control. When students see that grades don't affect the jobs they will get, teacher authority is severely crippled.[52]

Grades do count for some high school students: those who want to apply to selective colleges and know that the transcripts of their high school records will affect their admission or rejection. In high schools with a high proportion of such students, who want good grades and care what teachers think of them, teachers are in control. What Professor Rosenbaum has suggested is that students planning to go directly into the work force after high school (as well as students not aiming for selective colleges) could also be controlled better by teachers—if employers paid attention to high school performance. This would require a change in the way employers hire young workers in entry-level jobs. But the only cost it would entail would be the cost of spreading the message to employers: the better job opportunities should go to the high school graduates with the better grades. Teacher approval and disapproval would become a force to be reckoned with in every American high school, including what are currently considered the worse inner city high schools, as soon as jobs came to depend on academic performance.

Alternative Strategies for Coping with School Violence

Other strategies for dealing with school violence exist: teaching school children conflict resolution skills, attempting to reduce bullying,[53] sending violent students to alternative schools, improving "classroom management"[54] or achieving curriculum reform. I assume that these approaches cannot address everyday school violence successfully because they do not try to *make every high school in an urban school district safe*. Across-the-board safety is most likely to be achievable by empowering high school teachers. Two measures that I have suggested are voluntary high school attendance to give students a greater stake in conformity and increasing the psychological presence of adult "guardians" in high schools.

In America, public education has traditionally functioned as a social escalator, carrying talented children from poorer families into higher-paying business or professional careers.[55] Particularly in the slum neighborhoods of central cities, public schools in former days offered prospects of a bright future for intelligent, diligent children with academic aptitude. Most public schools still offer this opportunity to enrolled students. Partly because of school violence, however, even able and motivated youngsters cannot learn in some schools what they need to know in order to escape from poverty. Children enrolled in such schools (that are not really schools) will remain at the bottom of the socioeconomic heap, trapped by schools that offer no real hope. The approach suggested in this chapter is designed to improve all schools, including inner city schools, until they reach minimum standards of safety and education. In this way, children from the worst neighborhoods of the inner cities will retain a chance for social mobility through educational achievement.

RICHARD B. FREEMAN

THE LABOR
MARKET

The question that has traditionally motivated analyses of crime and the labor market has been the effect of unemployment on crime. Many people believe that joblessness is the key determinant of crime, and have sought to establish a significant crime-unemployment trade-off. Studies through the mid-1980s found that higher unemployment was associated with greater occurrence of crime, though the unemployment-crime link was statistically looser than the link between measures of deterrence (such as the severity of criminal sentences or chances of being caught) and crime, and was more closely aligned to property crimes than to violent crimes.[1] Most important, although the rate of unemployment drifted upward from the 1950s to the 1990s, even the largest estimated effects of unemployment on crime suggest that it contributed little to the rising trend in crime.

Developments in the 1980s–1990s raise a broader set of issues regarding the link between the job market and crime.[2] The high rate of crime in the 1980s despite increased incarceration directs attention at potential increases in economic incentives to commit crime. Perhaps the widely heralded increase in earnings inequality and the fall in the real earnings of the less skilled men who commit most crimes gave young men a job market "push" into crime. Perhaps the growth of the illegal drug business raised the returns to crime compared with those from work. At the minimum, the massive incarceration of criminals in the 1980s has brought the issue of crime from the periphery to the center of discussions of poverty and the underclass.

In this chapter I examine evidence and studies regarding the effect of labor market incentives on crime, the reverse effect of criminal activity on labor market outcomes, and the financial payoff to crime. There are two bottom-line questions: (1) What part, if any, of the high rate of criminal activity among young men results from the deteriorating job market for less skilled workers? and (2) How does crime affect the long run economic position of those who commit crimes? Before turning to these questions, I review the basic facts on the criminal participation of young men and incarceration that make crime important to understanding the economics of the American "underclass."

The Facts

In 1993 the number of men incarcerated in the United States was 1.9 percent the number in the labor force. The number of men on probation or parole relative to the male labor force was approximately 4.7 percent,[3] so that the number of men "under supervision of the criminal justice system" was 6.6 percent of the male workforce—one man incarcerated, probated, or paroled for every twelve men in the workforce. This was nearly as many men as were unemployed in that year. At extant growth rates, the number under supervision will exceed the number unemployed in 1994–1995.

No, I have not made an error. These figures do not refer to young men or to minority men. They refer to all men. For men aged eighteen to thirty-four, the ratio of those incarcerated to the labor force was 3.1 percent; the number under supervision of the criminal justice system was 11 percent of the workforce in 1993. For all black men, the ratios to the workforce are 8.8 percent incarcerated, and 25.3 percent under supervision relative to the workforce. For black men aged eighteen to thirty-four, the ratios to the workforce are 12.7 percent incarcerated and 36.7 percent under supervision.[4] Since a disproportionate number of prisoners are high school dropouts, the proportion of less educated men, especially young men, who were incarcerated, probated, or paroled, was even greater (Freeman 1992).

High though these figures are, they understate the extent to which American men are involved in criminal activity. Not everyone who commits crimes is caught by the police, and not everyone caught is convicted of crime. The magnitude of involvement in crime is such that analysts who once dismissed criminal behavior as a peripheral issue to employment or poverty can do so no longer. No other advanced society has as large a proportion of its potentially productive workforce involved in illegitimate activities, nor as large a proportion incarcerated.

Trends

The most striking trend in crime statistics in the 1980s was the growth of the prison and jail population. From 1980 to 1991 the number of persons incarcerated rose at an exponential rate, with no sign of deceleration (Figure 8.1)

FIGURE 8.1

Prison and Jail Population in the United States, 1947–1992

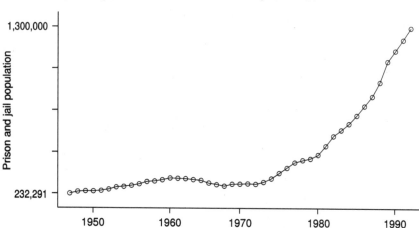

SOURCES: Bureau of Justice Statistics, *Sourcebook of Criminal Justice Statistics 1991* (Washington, D.C.: United States Department of Justice, 1992), 611, 636. Darrell K. Gilliard and Allen J. Beck, *Prisoners in 1993*, Bureau of Justice Statistics Bulletin, NCJ-147036 (Washington, D.C.: U.S. Department of Justice, June 1994). Estimates of jail population before 1983 based on prison population.

The average annual increase in the jail and prison population was 8.5 percent. Had nothing else changed, the imprisonment trend should have greatly reduced the crime rate. It removed men with a high propensity to commit crime from society and increased the risk to potential criminals that they would end up in jail or prison.

The standard administrative measure of crime, the Justice Department's Crime Index, obtained from police departments around the country, does not show the expected drop in crime. The Uniform Crime Rate, reflected in the FBI's *Uniform Crime Reports* (UCR) and defined as the number of Uniform Crime Reporting Index crimes per 100,000 persons,[5] at best stabilized in the 1980s (Figure 8.2). It fell from 1980 to 1984, then increased through 1991 to approach its 1980 peak level before dropping modestly in 1992. By contrast, the rate of criminal victimizations, defined as the number of times people report they or their family were victims of crime on the annual National Crime Victimization Survey, dropped over the same period (Figure 8.3), creating a problem of data inconsistency.

The victimization figures differ markedly from the Uniform Crime Rate in level as well as trend.[6] Because individuals do not report all crimes to the police, reported victimizations range from 2.4 to 4.1 times the police data on crimes. In 1973, 32 percent of victimizations were reported to the police. In 1991, 38 percent of victimizations were reported to the police. A large proportion of the difference in volume of crime between the administrative data

FIGURE 8.2
Uniform Crime Reporting Index per 100,000, 1947–1992

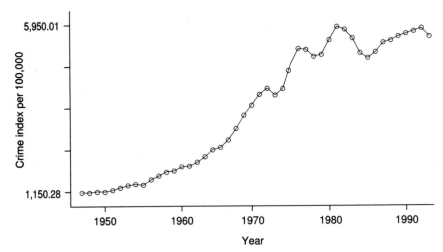

SOURCES: Federal Bureau of Investigation, *Crime in the United States* (Washington, D.C.: United States Department of Justice, various years). Bureau of Justice Statistics, *Sourcebook of Criminal Justice Statistics 1991*, (Washington, D.C.: U.S. Department of Justice, 1992), 372. Current statistics from the U.S. Department of Justice, Bureau of Justice Statistics.

FIGURE 8.3
Victimizations per 100,000, 1973–1992

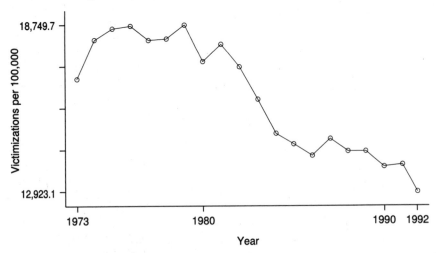

SOURCE: Bureau of Justice Statistics, *Criminal Victimization 1992*, NCJ-144776 (Washington, D.C.: United States Department of Justice, October 1993).

and victimization survey is for crimes that are difficult to measure or report, such as rapes or larceny.

Several factors explain the difference in trends between the two sets of data. Some of the trend in the Uniform Crime Rate is due to an increase in the proportion of crimes that individuals report to the police. Boggess and Bound (1993) estimate that increased reporting accounts for about one quarter of the difference in trend. Perhaps another quarter of the difference in trend is the increase in victimless drug crimes, which individuals do not report. This still leaves a sizable difference in trend. Should one put greater weight on the administrative UCR data or on the survey data on victimization in assessing the trend in crime? One way to judge which data might be more accurate is to examine changes in crimes that are well measured, such as murder or automobile thefts. Murder rates roughly stabilized in the 1980s, rising for teenagers while falling for adults. Auto thefts rose in the period. The change in these crimes suggests that the stability in the UCR rate may give a better fix on what is happening to crime levels than the falling rate in the victimization survey.

Increased Propensity for Crime

As noted earlier, the rough doubling in the prison and jail population in the 1980s should, all else the same, have greatly reduced crime because of the incapacitation of criminals. It produced, in addition, an upward trend in the proportion of crimes that resulted in prison sentences (following a decline from the mid-1960s to the late 1970s) (Langan 1991) that should have further reduced crime through the deterrent effect. The different trends in the UCR and victimization rates notwithstanding, the 1980s levels of both statistics differ so much from the levels that massive incarceration should have produced that they tell the same story about criminal behavior: namely that the *propensity for crime* among noninstitutionalized men increased immensely in the 1980s.

Figure 8.4 demonstrates the increased propensity for crime in the UCR data. It plots the annual relation between the proportion of the adult male population confined to prison or jail and index crimes per man in the non-institutional population.[7] If the propensity for crime in the noninstitutional male population were constant, the increased confinement would reduce crime through incapacitation or deterrence, producing downward-sloping confinement-crime (CC) curves. The greater the rate of criminal activity of those sent to jail or prison and the greater the deterrent effect of jail or prison on future crimes, the more steeply sloped will be the CC curve.

The curve joining the percentage confined and crimes per man in the figure is not, however, downward-sloping. It is a straight line, because the increased confinement of the population in the 1980s was accompanied by a roughly constant number of crimes per adult male. The three hypothetical

FIGURE 8.4

Crimes and Confined Population per Adult Male, 1977–1992

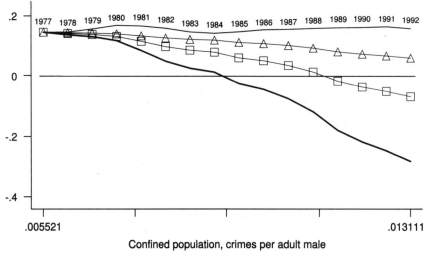

Confined population, crimes per adult male

— YEAR —   Actual crimes per adult male

——△——   Hypothetical crimes per adult male, assuming 10 crimes per confined individual

——□——   Hypothetical crimes per adult male, assuming 25 crimes per confined individual

————   Hypothetical crimes per adult male, assuming 50 crimes per confined individual

SOURCES: Federal Bureau of Investigation, *Crime in the United States* (Washington, D.C.: United States Department of Justice, various years). Bureau of Justice Statistics, *Sourcebook of Criminal Justice Statistics 1991* (Washington D.C.: U.S. Department of Justice, 1992), 372, 611, 636. Current statistics from Darrell K. Gilliard and Allen J. Beck, *Prisoners in 1993*, Bureau of Justice Statistics Bulletin, NCJ-147036 (Washington, D.C.: U.S. Department of Justice, June 1994). Estimates of jail population before 1983 based on prison population. Population figures from *Economic Report of the President* (Washington, D.C.: U.S. Government Printing Office, February 1993).

CC curves in the figure show what "should" have happened to the rate of crimes per adult male as a result of increased incapacitation of criminals. These curves take 1978 as a starting year and calculate hypothetical crime rates by subtracting from the number of crimes in each succeeding year different estimates of the change in crime resulting from the growth of the prison and jail population since 1978. The changes in crime are obtained from conservative estimates of the number of crimes each additional confinee would have committed had he been free,[8] and ignore deterrent effects that should have begun operating in the mid- to late 1980s and the changing age structure of the male population,[9] both of which would further add to the expected drop in crime. By construction, the hypothetical CC curves slope downward. The gap between the actual and the hypothetical CC curves measures the increased propensity for crime among the noninstitutional male population from the base 1978 year.

Figure 8.5 shows actual CC curves for reported victimizations committed per adult male and hypothetical curves calculated in a similar manner to

FIGURE 8.5

Victimizations and Confined Population per Adult Male, 1977–1992

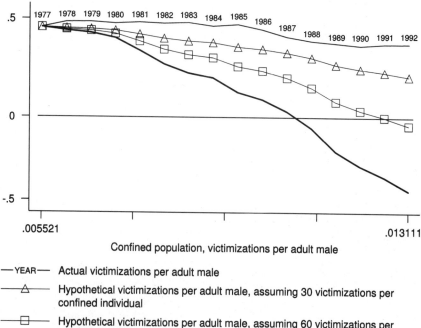

Confined population, victimizations per adult male

——YEAR—— Actual victimizations per adult male

——△—— Hypothetical victimizations per adult male, assuming 30 victimizations per confined individual

——□—— Hypothetical victimizations per adult male, assuming 60 victimizations per confined individual

———— Hypothetical victimizations per adult male, assuming 100 victimizations per confined individual

SOURCES: Bureau of Justice Statistics, *Criminal Victimization 1992*, NCJ-144776 (Washington, D.C.: United States Department of Justice, October 1993). BJS, *Sourcebook of Criminal Justice Statistics 1991* (Washington, D.C.: U.S. Department of Justice, 1992), 611, 636. Darrell K. Gilliard and Allen J. Beck, *Prisoners in 1993*, Bureau of Justice Statistics Bulletin, NCJ-147036 (Washington, D.C.: U.S. Department of Justice, June 1994). Estimates of jail population before 1983 based on prison population. Population figures from *Economic Report of the President* (Washington, D.C.: U.S. Government Printing Office, February 1993).

those in Figure 8.4. The actual CC has a negative slope, reflecting the drop in victimizations. In calculating hypothetical CCs in this figure, I assume a greater number of crimes per person confined than I did in Figure 8.4 because the volume of victimizations exceeds the volume of index crimes, though my estimates are still moderate ones. The hypothetical CC curves show a much more pronounced negative slope than the actual CC curve. The gap between the curves shows an increased propensity for crime comparable to that in Figure 8.4.

The bottom line is that *the propensity of the noninstitutional population to commit crime rose sharply in the 1980s.*

How might we explain this increase? The economist is naturally drawn to a job market explanation. Given the well-documented growth of earnings inequality and fall in the job opportunities for less skilled young men in this period, and the increased criminal opportunities due to the growth of demand for drugs, the economist finds appealing the notion that the increased propensity for crime is a rational response to increased job market incentives to commit crime. What is appealing, however, need not be true or, if true, may be difficult to prove. To see how much weight we might reasonably give to an earnings explanation of the rising crime propensity, I turn next to extant studies of the effect of economic incentives on crime.

Labor Market Incentives and Crime: Statistical Studies

Social science analyses of the effect of the labor market on crime take several forms: time series studies that compare the crime rate with labor market variables over time; cross-area studies that compare crime and economic characteristics across cities or states; and individual studies that compare crime and economic characteristics across people. In addition, there are longitudinal studies that follow the same area or individual over time, as economic opportunities change, and studies based on social experiments, in which the experimenter manipulates opportunities.

Studies of crime and the job market through the mid-1980s, which focused largely on unemployment, have been reviewed and summarized in detail in Freeman (1983) and Chiricos (1987). Building on those reviews for the earlier period, I concentrate here on ensuing work, and the "trend" in research results. Rather than updating the scorecard of findings, I direct attention to specific studies that are either particularly innovative or particularly convincing.

Time Series Studies

Time series data allow us to examine the effect of the business cycle on crime and to answer the question of what might happen to crime levels if overall job prospects improved or worsened on a short-term basis. For this reason, analysts often use time series data to examine the effect of unemployment on crime. But time series analyses suffer from a myriad of problems that make many social scientists leery of their results. Variables tend to move together over time, providing little independent variation from which to infer relations, and often suffer from a tendency for the unexplained part of the dependent variable to be correlated from one year to the next. All too often, addition of further observations or of another explanatory variable, or choice of statistical technique, substantively changes results.

Time series studies through the mid-1980s showed that the overall crime rate and the rates of particular crimes, such as burglary, were positively related to unemployment. But the estimated effect of unemployment was moderate and, as noted, incapable of explaining much of the upward trend in crime. Figure 8.6 shows a modest positive relation between the number of index crimes per adult male and unemployment in each year from 1948 to 1992, dominated by the upward trend in crime, so that any given unemployment rate is associated with very different crime rates over time. A linea: regression of the crime rate per 100,000 in the population on a trend and the rate of unemployment gives a positive coefficient on the unemployment rate with a moderate standard error (that is, crime rate and unemployment rate are correlated). But the same regression with the crime rate per 100,000 adult men as in the figure (rather than per the entire population) gives a statistically insignificant positive coefficient on the unemployment rate.

Higher-tech statistical models—in which the *change* in a crime rate is regressed on the *change* in unemployment and the *change* in unemployment one year earlier—tell a more complex story about the relation between crime and unemployment. Calculations for the United Kingdom show that changes in the unemployment rate are associated with changes in crime in the same direction, consistent with the notion that unemployment raises crime, while changes in unemployment a year earlier have essentially no effect on crime (Hale and Sabbagh 1991). But calculations for the United States show that changes in unemployment this year are associated with changes in crime in the opposite direction (an increase in unemployment reduces crime!), while

FIGURE 8.6
Crimes per Adult Male and Unemployment, 1948–1992

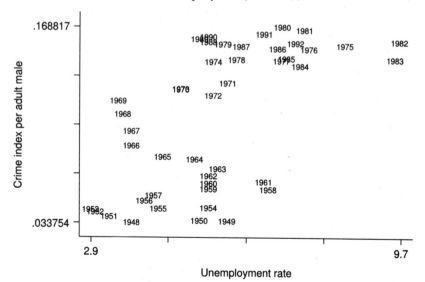

SOURCES: Federal Bureau of Investigation, *Crime in the United States* (Washington, D.C.: United States Department of Justice, various years). Bureau of Justice Statistics, *Sourcebook of Criminal Justice Statistics 1991* (Washington, D.C.: U.S. Department of Justice, 1992), 372. Current statistics from the Bureau of Justice Statistics. Population and unemployment figures from *Economic Report of the President* (Washington, D.C.: U.S. Government Printing Office, February 1993).

the past year's change in the unemployment rate has the more plausible effect of changing crime in the same direction (Land, Cantor, and Russell 1994). Analysts have interpreted the negative relation between changes in current unemployment and crime as reflecting a reduction in criminal opportunities in a sluggish economy (when unemployment is high, there may be less to burgle and more people home watching their property) while interpreting the positive effect between changes in last year's unemployment and crime as reflecting the increase in criminal motivation due to joblessness. The net of the two effects varies by crime, is close to zero in several calculations, but shows that higher unemployment is associated with reductions in motor vehicle thefts.

The time series results are, however, sensitive to the model and time period covered. Using a model with several explanatory variables over the period 1933–1985 Cappel and Sykes report a positive effect of contemporaneous unemployment rates on crime rates for the United States. As a check on the robustness of the time series relations, I regressed changes in burglary rates on changes in unemployment rates and on changes in unemployment rates in the previous year, for the years from 1948 to 1993. I obtained a negative coefficient on the contemporaneous change in unemployment and a positive coefficient on the previous year's change, mimicking Land, Cantor, and Russell (1994). However, the coefficient on the contemporaneous change in unemployment was insignificant, while the coefficient on the lagged change in unemployment was large and significant, implying that higher rates of unemployment are positively associated with crime.

All in all, I would not weigh heavily the time series evidence. The same problems that plague time series analyses of wages, interest rates, and unemployment plague time series analyses of crime. Differences in years covered or in the model chosen or in the particular measures used affect results substantively. The safest conclusion is that the time series are not a robust way to determine the job market–crime link. For more reliable results of how economic incentives may affect crime, I turn to evidence across areas and individuals.

Cross-section Area Studies

Studies of crime and the job market that use cross-section area data compare crime rates in areas with greater or lesser jobless problems or where the earnings of crime-prone groups or income inequality are particularly low or high. These studies are free from collinearity or serial correlation. But they suffer from their own set of inference problems. Areas may differ in labor market conditions and crime for reasons having to do with the features of the population that are not measured, producing spurious correlations or hiding true ones. In some 1960s cross-section studies, for instance, crime was inversely related to the percentage of nonwhites in the area. At face value, this would imply that nonwhites are less likely to be criminals than whites, or that areas of black concentration are subject to less crime than areas of white concentration—both of which fly in the face of individual data on who commits crime, on who are the victims of crime, and on the locus of crime among neighborhoods in a city. Rapid changes in the characteristics of areas, for instance a sudden boom or bust or change in demographic mix, may also give misleading inferences if crime (or other dependent variables) changes more gradually.

Still, cross-area studies are a natural way to examine the effects on crime of economic variables, such as income inequality or rates of poverty, that are likely to characterize the area for extended periods. At the minimum, these data can answer such questions as, Is crime higher in areas with higher levels of income inequality or in areas with higher rates of poverty?

The majority of cross-area studies show a link between labor market factors and crime. In my 1983 review, I classified four of fifteen cross-area studies as giving significant effects for unemployment and an additional seven as giving positive but "weak" results. Summarizing forty-two studies, including several for Canada or the United Kingdom, Chiricos reports coefficients on unemployment that were positive but insignificant in 51 percent of the cases and positive and significant in 14 percent of cases in pre-1970s data and that were positive but insignificant in 44 percent and positive and significant in 48 percent of the cases in 1970s data (Chiricos 1987, table 3, results for all crimes). Some of the cited studies use similar data (though processing it with different models), so that the results are not truly "independent." Some studies have larger samples and more precise estimates than others, so that simple counts of signs and significance of coefficients is also not ideal. Still, even absent a definite mega-statistical analysis of these results, it is clear that the cross-area data support a positive unemployment-crime link.

Not all the work since those reviews has yielded statistically significant coefficients on unemployment, but nothing has arisen to overturn their conclusion.[10] As an exemplar study that extends the analysis to the 1980s, consider Lee's study of crime in fifty-eight standard metropolitan statistical areas (SMSAs) from 1976 to 1989. He estimated the effect of economic variables on a set of crime rates using three statistical models: a cross-section model that compares economic incentives and crime among cities; a fixed effects model where city dummy variables eliminate unmeasured city effects; and a model that allows for last period's unemployment to affect this year's crime rate. All three models gave a positive crime-unemployment link. In the cross-section analysis the overall crime and most specific crimes were positively associated with unemployment. In the fixed effects model the total crime rate, property crime rate, burglary, and motor vehicle theft rates were positively related to unemployment, while murder, rape, and some other crime rates were not positively related to unemployment. The models which explored different time patterns of unemployment-crime effects confirmed the positive link between the variables. The magnitude of the link is, however, modest: Lee (1993) estimates that a one point increase in the unemployment rate raises property crimes by 1.1 percent to 1.4 percent. This contrasts with a coefficient of variation in property crimes across SMSAs of roughly 30 percent.

Results with respect to other labor market variables are also supportive of the notion that economic incentives affect crime rates. Some studies use the income of the population in an area and the percentage of families in poverty to measure the potential gain and opportunity cost of crime. Others include a Gini coefficient or other measure of inequality to capture both the gain and opportunity costs in a single term. The reviews by Freeman (1983) or Chiricos (1987) show that variables measuring inequality/poverty across areas are associated with differing crime rates across cities. Land, McCall, and Cohen (1990) find that even homicide rates tend to be higher in cities with greater inequality. In his analysis of 127 SMSAs in 1979 and 1969, Lee obtained a significant positive relation between crime and inequality measured as the difference between the household income of the ninth decile and the first decile divided by the median household income, calculated from the Census of Populations for 1970 and 1980 (Lee 1993). His model included numerous other controls, such as the percentage of an SMSA that was black, population density, and region of the country. Figure 8.7 gives the scatter plot between property crimes and inequality that underlies his work for 1979.

To what extent, if at all, can these cross-section findings explain the rising crime participation among adult men? From 1979 to 1990 the ratio of the difference between the ninth decile and tenth decile of household incomes divided by the median in the United States rose by about twelve percentage points. [11] Given the magnitude of Lee's estimated relation between crime and inequality, this change would have induced a 10 percent increase in the crime rate. This goes part of the way to explaining why the Uniform Crime Reporting Index did not fall, despite rising incarcerations.

But two aspects of Lee's analysis raise doubts about this inference. First, Lee finds that most of the inequality effect operated through a link between crime and income at the ninth decile: crime was more responsive to the income of the upper parts of the distribution than to income in the lower part of the distribution. This is troublesome because the rise of inequality took the form largely of falling real income in the lower part of the distribution. Second, he reports that changes in crime rates across the SMSAs from 1969 to 1979 were unrelated to changes in income inequality. Perhaps the cross-section pattern shown in Figure 8.7 is due to omitted area characteristics, and thus disappears when the analysis treats changes in variables. Alternatively, perhaps measures of changes in inequality among cities are subject to such huge measurement error that we should discount the results that show change over time.

In sum, cross-section evidence continues to support a positive link between unemployment and crime and suggest that inequality may be an

FIGURE 8.7
Property Crime versus Income Inequality in 127 Metropolitan Areas in the
United States, 1979

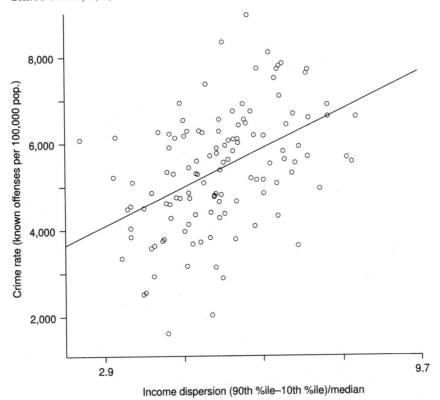

SOURCE: David Sang-Yoon Lee, "An Empirical Investigation of the Economic Incentives for Criminal Behavior" (B.A. thesis in economics, Harvard University, March 1993).

important contributor to crime. But there is enough statistical frailty in extant
estimates to leave a door open to doubt about how helpful the cross-section
inequality results will be in explaining the rising propensity to crime that
characterized the 1980s.

Individual Comparisons

Studies that compare the economic circumstances of individuals who commit
crimes with those who do not commit crimes, or the criminal behavior of the
same person in different economic circumstances, potentially offer the best
way to assess how the job market affects crime. The main reason for this
is that these studies focus on the people who are in fact making the
crime decision and on their particular circumstances. Some studies use
records on arrests or on prisoners. Arrest or prisoner data accurately measure

the characteristics of arrestees or prisoners, but do not provide information on criminals who have not been caught nor on the characteristics of non-criminals. Other studies use self-reported criminal activity on household surveys. Survey data in which people self-report crime cover all criminal activity, whether the crime was solved or not, and include people who did not commit crime. But people may incorrectly self-report crime: black youths, in particular, understate their criminal involvement (Hindelang, Hirschi, and Weiss 1981).

The strongest evidence that economic incentives are important in determining the crime rate comes from studies of individuals. At a descriptive level, these studies find that criminals are disproportionately from the groups whose incomes and employment opportunities have been low and falling: young, less educated men, often with low scores on the Armed Forces Qualifying Test (AFQT) or other standard tests. The evidence also shows that those who end up in jail or under arrest are more likely to be jobless or to have low incomes than other groups. Two studies of the Philadelphia birth cohort of 1945 (Wolfgang, Figlio, and Sellin 1972) found positive relations between unemployment and crime. Tauchen, Witte, and Griesinger (1993) report that youths who were employed for a larger percentage of a year were less likely to be arrested than those employed for a smaller percentage of a year; Thornberry and Christenson (1984) report a substantial contemporaneous positive relation of unemployment and crime. In the 1980 National Bureau of Economic Research (NBER) survey of inner city black youth, 30 percent of those who committed a crime held a job at the time of the survey compared with 46 percent of those who had not committed a crime (Freeman 1987).

While this evidence makes it clear that the population of criminals overlaps with the population at the bottom of the increasingly unequal income distribution in the United States, it does not establish a causal link from the labor market to crime. The data may, after all, simply reflect the fact that the criminal population consists of people who are unable to succeed in society because of "personal characteristics." That is, the cause of both the poor labor market record and criminal activity may be a third variable having to do with the specific attributes of the individuals. If this were the case, improved labor market conditions would have little or no effect on the criminal's life of crime, although we would always find poor work records among criminals. Moreover, though it is hard to argue that wages have fallen among low skilled workers because they engage in more crime than in the past, criminals may have higher *joblessness* than noncriminals because they rejected jobs in favor of unemployment—a status that enabled them to engage more readily in crime.

There are three ways in which researchers use information on individuals to surmount these problems and make plausible inferences about causality. One is to look at the same person in different periods. Farrington et al. (1986) compared the timing of criminal activity among young men in the

United Kingdom. The question is whether these men were more likely to commit a crime when they were unemployed or when they held a job. Consider, for example, someone who is unemployed for six months and employed for six months in a year and who commits four crimes. If the person commits all the crimes while unemployed, it is reasonable to conclude that unemployment is associated with crime, not with some unobserved personal characteristic of the individual. By contrast, if the person commits the crimes as frequently when employed as when unemployed, we would reject the notion that his unemployment caused the crime. Farrington et al. find that crime rates are higher during periods of unemployment than during periods of employment. This does not "prove" that the unemployment caused the crimes, but points in that direction.

A second way to link crime to economic incentives with data on individuals is to examine the relation of the individuals' criminal behavior to characteristics of the area in which they live. The rate of unemployment or level of income in that area is presumably independent of the characteristics of the individual, and thus a good indicator of outside labor market incentives that might induce illegal activity. Analysis of the link between criminal behavior and characteristics of the county in which a youth resides in the National Longitudinal Survey of Youth (NLSY) shows no relation between crime and unemployment and a positive relation between crime and the income level in the county (Lee 1993). Good, Pirog-Good, and Sickles (1986) find an insignificant negative relation between the monthly area unemployment rate and crime in a sample of 300 youths enrolled in a Youth Service Center in Philadelphia. Trumbull finds a negative coefficient on area unemployment in a sample of 2,200 ex-offenders from North Carolina. These findings conflict with the results from the area studies, which find a positive relation between area crime and area unemployment. No one has explored the reason for this divergence in results.

The third way to use individual data to infer causal links between economic factors and crime is to estimate labor supply relations between criminal participation and actual or predicted wages and criminal wages or perceptions of the attractiveness of crime. This form of analysis is infrequent because most data sets do not contain information on criminal behavior or perceptions of returns or risks. An exception is the 1980 National Bureau of Economic Research Inner City Youth Survey that included a special crime module designed to allow researchers to probe the economic model of criminal behavior (Freeman and Holzer 1986). Viscusi used these data to estimate the effects of personal objective factors and of perceptions of the return to crime on participation. He found that youths who believed that they "make more on the street than on a legitimate job" were far more likely to engage in crime than others and that estimated difference in income from crime and from legitimate work also significantly affected crime behavior (Viscusi 1986). His study does not "prove" that these economic factors motivated crime. Perhaps those who commit crime feel it necessary to justify such by reporting that crime was lucrative. Still, this evidence supports that interpretation.

In a similar vein, Grogger (1994b) estimated the effect of "potential" wages on criminal participation in the NLSY. He obtained a significant negative relation that implied that, roughly, a 10 percent decrease in the real wages of youths would increase their crime rate by nearly 10 percent. Applying this estimate to the observed drop in the real wages of young men, he predicts a 23 percent increase in crime due to falling wages from the mid-1970s through the period 1985–1988, which he notes is roughly equal to the 18 percent increase in the index arrest rate for young males over that period. Grogger's estimates are imbedded in a highly structured economic model and may very well be sensitive to alternative specifications, so I would not take them as "truth" but rather would see them as another piece of imperfect individual level evidence on the role of economic factors in crime behavior.

The Effect of Labor Market Incentives on Crime: Ethnographic Studies

Ethnographic studies of crime provide qualitative information on the way individuals view the opportunities and constraints in their local community and their perceptions of the factors that underlie the choice of crime or work, or both. By viewing events through the eyes of participants, ethnographic research can bring the decision to engage in crime "up close and personal" and help us interpret statistical evidence.

The findings of recent ethnographic studies on youth gangs and crime provide strong support for a job market interpretation of the decision of young men to engage in crime. Jeff Fagan, who directed a major multi-site ethnographic study of youth gangs reports that "Gangs in South Central Los Angeles, Chicago, and Detroit changed in recent years from ethnic enterprises organized around turf, ethnicity, conflict, and natural group processes to business organisations with monetary and material goals. Money became the driving force and organizational principal for these groups. . . . [This] almost ideological emphasis on money . . . [by gangs is] a dramatic shift from the gangs of ten and twenty-five years ago" (Fagan 1992, chap. 9; 23, 25–26).

Here I summarize some of the conclusions from specific ethnographic studies that back up Fagan's conclusion about the economic factors in gang and crime activity:

> All . . . agreed money was the primary focal point within their gangs. Virtually all criminal activities are oriented toward this end." (Vigil and Yun [1990], on Vietnamese gangs, 156). A dominant . . . is their intense desire to obtain money for themselves." (Vigil, Yun, and Long 1992, 49)

The "gang as a business" albeit its illegal status, is a fact of life for many inner-city youths throughout America today. More and more young men are turning to the gang to make a living." (Padilla [1992], on Puerto Rican gangs in Chicago)

Gangs moved beyond the scavenger stage . . . [to become] corporate gangs. (Taylor [1990, 112], on black gangs in Detroit)

Kids . . . are drawn to the underground economy because of the opportunities that exist there. They know the work is hard and dangerous; there is no such thing as a quick dollar. (Williams 1989, 132)

Making money is their main motive. (Chin [1990, 137], on Chinese gangs in New York)

Those who had joined a gang most often gave as their reason the belief that it would provide them with an environment that would increase their chances of securing money. (Jankowski 1991, 60)

The conclusion that gangs survive and grow because of the financial rewards they gain for their members suggests that the resurgence of gangs is due largely to their potential to cash in on new illicit opportunities.[12] Ethnographers also report that many crime-prone youths disdain the types of low wage work available to them: "Simply wanting to work may not be enough, it is the type of work and wage they are willing to accept" (Quicker, Galesi, and Batani-Khalfani, 4, 19). This observation is consistent with the economists' reservation wage–job mismatch story of inner city joblessness (Holzer 1986).

Taken together, the statistical and ethnographic evidence present a consistent story, one that supports the notion that crime responds to economic incentives.

The Effect of Crime on Labor Market Outcomes

As the number of men incarcerated or involved in crime has risen, attention has shifted from the effect of the labor market on crime to the reverse link—the effect of crime on labor market outcomes. How does crime affect current employment and earnings? How does it affect future employment and earnings?

Data on work and crime activity by individuals in the same period provides a way to answer the first question. As summarized earlier, the general finding in studies of individuals is that crime and joblessness go together. It is easy, however, to exaggerate the strength of the relation. Many people commit crimes while employed. In the NLSY the difference in the employment rate of young men who admit to committing crimes (but were not arrested or convicted or sent to jail) and those who did not so admit is rather low. In 1979 and 1980, 59 percent of those who were out of school and unemployed said they committed a crime, compared with 53 percent of those out of school and employed.[13] Tabulating the data the other way, of those who admitted committing crimes, 72 percent had a job, compared with 76 percent of out of school young men who did not have a job. Many young men hold jobs for short spells, and may move back and forth between legitimate and illegitimate earnings activities, as well as making money from crime and legitimate work at the same time. The big difference in employment rates between those who commit crimes and those who do not is found for young men who later go to jail for their crimes.

To determine which way the relation between crime and employment actually runs, Thornberry and Christenson estimated structural path models in which they sought to identify both the crime → unemployment and the unemployment → crime links. They found evidence for both (Thornberry and Christenson 1984). While this is a plausible finding, I am leery of reading much into it. Absent knowledge of what in fact influenced the individual's decision, which the data do not provide, any division of the relation between the variables is likely to depend critically on the particular structural model used to make the estimates.

Interpreting the causal link between criminal activity in one year and future labor market outcomes is much easier. Since the criminal activity precedes the outcomes, it is difficult to argue that this reflects the influence of job market opportunities on crime. It is easy, by contrast, to interpret any relation as reflecting the effect of crime today on future employment or earnings performance. Many employers eschew hiring persons with a criminal record (Finn and Fontaine 1985). Some jobs legally exclude ex-offenders (Dale 1976). On the supply side, individuals engaged in crime today are likely to build up criminal skills at the expense of legitimate skills, so that todays' crime will alter the relative rewards from legal and illegal activity in the future.

In any case, studies of the effect of criminal activity on future job market outcomes in longitudinal survey data give clear results. Persons whose criminal behavior leads them into prison have markedly lower employment rates in the future than those who do not commit crimes or those whose offenses are more modest (Freeman 1992; Hagan and Palloni 1988; Sampson and Laub 1994; Ferguson 1994). My estimates show that a prison record has a substantial quantitative adverse effect on future employment: in the NLSY a young man incarcerated in 1979 worked about 25 percent less in the ensuing eight years than a young man who had not gone to prison. In 1987, for example, respondents averaged forty-four weeks of work over the year, whereas those who had been incarcerated in 1979 averaged thirty-two weeks of work. Part of this is due to the greater likelihood that these youths were in jail during some of the ensuing years. Sampson and Laub estimate a model that indicates that the effect of jail on job stability underlies much of recidivism. In the 1980

NBER survey I found that the monthly employment record of an individual deteriorates relative to that of others after a spell of prison.

By contrast, other involvement with the criminal justice system has much less, if any, long-term deleterious effect on employment. Grogger (1994a) reports only short-term effects of arrests on future employment using data for California. In the NLSY and two other data sets I found that anything short of probation has no discernible effects on future employment of youths (Freeman 1992). Sampson and Laub interpret the strong effect of incarceration but not of committing crimes per se on future employment as supporting a developmental model of criminal activity. They suggest that a labelling theory in which individual behavior is affected by their social label may help explain this result (Sampson and Laub 1994).

The effect of imprisonment on future employment can be decomposed into two separable effects. The first is recidivism: persons who are incarcerated have a high recidivist rate and thus will be absent from the job market in many future years. The Department of Justice's 1983 follow-up of prisoners released in 1983 found that 63 percent were arrested within three years of their release and that 41 percent were reincarcerated. In a longitudinal sample that follows Georgia prison releases for seventeen years, Needels finds that 61 percent were reincarcerated, and that the releasees averaged 15 percent of ensuing years in prison and nearly 30 percent of ensuing years under supervision of the criminal justice system. The second effect is that when they are out of prison, ex-offenders work much less than "otherwise comparable" men (Needels 1993).

Earnings from Crime

The reader will undoubtedly have noticed one missing element in my review of the statistical studies of the effect of economic factors on crime. Conceptually, the crime decision depends on how the earnings from crime (adjusted for the various risks of crime) compare with the earnings from legal activity. But most studies report estimates of the effect of criminal behavior on unemployment, earnings inequality, or predicted earnings rather than on the earnings from crime—*Hamlet* without the Prince, as it were.

The main reason is that few surveys ask about criminal earnings, and those that do may not obtain accurate estimates. Criminals are generally "self-employed"—a group for whom it is difficult to obtain good data on earnings for *legal* activities. One must distinguish between gross and net earnings, and must determine the time the self-employed actually work to obtain an average wage rate comparable to wage rates in the job market. In contrast to workers paid a fixed wage per hour (or month) the self-employed are likely to have their hourly pay vary with the amount of time they work. Commit one burglary when you see a good chance and you do well per hour.

Commit lots of burglaries and you are likely to move down the marginal returns curve, reducing average earnings.

To the extent that criminal earnings and legitimate earnings are positively correlated, the lack of a good measure of illegal earnings will bias *downward* the estimated effects of job market factors on criminal behavior. The reason for this is that measures of legal opportunities will pick up both their posited negative effect on crime and the positive effect of correlated illegal opportunities.

Not surprisingly, given the data problem, there is disagreement on how much men make from crime and thus on the net payoff to criminal activity. In a 1992 study, I reported estimates of earnings from crime from several surveys. The 1989 Boston Youth Survey showed sharply falling hourly earnings with numbers of crimes and relatively modest annual earnings of $3,008 for sixteen- to twenty-four-year-olds who report crime income. The 1980 NBER survey also showed modest annual earnings from crime (Viscusi 1986). A 1990 survey of seven drug runners in Oakland estimated that hourly pay was $7.92. My conclusion from these scattered figures is that the hourly earnings exceed the hourly earnings the youths could make in legitimate work (which is consistent with the youths' assessment, as well, on the Boston Youth Survey that asked if they can make more on the street or in legitimate work). At the same time, annual earnings from crime are modest, possibly because the marginal earnings fall sharply.

For adult criminals, my calculations for prisoners in the 1986 Justice Department Inmate Survey who said all of their income came from crime was that they earned $24,775 per year. Reuter (1990) reports that drug dealers earned $2,000 a month net in his sample for Washington, D.C., which he transformed into a $30.00 hourly rate of pay. Using the Rand Inmate Survey on numbers of crimes and various estimates of how much those crimes could garner, Wilson and Abrahamse estimated that criminal earnings for burglary/theft, robbery, swindling are modest, below the earnings these criminals could make at work, and find that only auto theft is potentially profitable. They also report that criminals estimated their take from crime to be much higher than those crimes could plausibly have yielded, raising serious doubts about self-reported incomes from crime (Wilson and Abrahamse 1992).

All told, the quality of data on criminal earnings is too weak for any strong claims about the long-term economic payoff to crime.

Conclusion

As the proportion of American men engaged in crime and incarcerated for criminal activity has risen, it has become increasingly important to understand the causes and consequences of criminal activity in addressing poverty as well as crime problems. While extant research leaves open many important questions, it has shown several important things about the link between the job market and crime:

1. In the 1980s and early 1990s the United States developed a large, relatively permanent group of young male offenders and ex-offenders, who for the most part are unlikely to be productive members of the workforce in the foreseeable future.
2. There is a general positive relation between joblessness and crime, which appears most strongly in comparisons of unemployment rates and crime rates across areas.
3. Labor market incentives beyond joblessness—the wages from legitimate work or measures of inequality—affect crime and potentially contributed to the rising propensity of noninstitutionalized men to commit crime in the 1980s.
4. Incarceration reduces an individual's economic outcomes over the long run. This implies that the future costs of crime to an individual exceed the opportunity cost of devoting less time to legitimate activity today.

Although research has not yielded sufficiently strong results to predict reliably how much crime might fall if the job market for crime-prone groups improved substantively, the limited estimates we have are consistent with an expectation that such effects would not be negligible.

ROBERT J. SAMPSON

THE
COMMUNITY

Public discourse on crime policy has been dominated in the past decade by proposals requiring ever greater penetration of official control—especially more police, more prisons, and longer mandatory sentences. Recent public health approaches have challenged this emphasis on reactive strategies by the criminal justice system, advocating instead crime prevention (Prothrow-Stith 1991; Reiss and Roth 1993). In thinking about the prevention of crime, policy makers have turned to programs that attempt to change individuals (for example, Head Start, job training) or families (for example, training in child-rearing skills, conflict resolution).

Although individual- and family-level prevention are welcome partners in crime control, there is another target of intervention that has been widely neglected in public policy circles—the *community*. This level of social inquiry asks how community structures and cultures produce differential rates of crime. For example, what characteristics of communities are associated with high rates of violence? Are communities safe or unsafe because of the persons who reside in them or because of community properties themselves? Perhaps most important, by changing communities can we bring about changes in crime rates?

As implied by these questions, the goal of community-level research is not to explain individual involvement in criminal behavior but to identify characteristics of neighborhoods, cities, or even regions that lead to high rates of criminality. A community-level perspective also makes it possible to point out how federal, state, and local governmental policies not directly concerned with crime policy may nonetheless bear on crime rates. In particular, not enough attention has been paid to "noncrime" public policies—

especially on housing, families, and child development—and how they influence the link between crime and the community.

In an attempt to address this imbalance, I describe in this chapter a sociological perspective on crime and the social organization of communities. My first goal is to review the major findings produced by research on the characteristics of communities that foster high (or low) rates of crime. I thus begin by highlighting continuities running throughout recent community-level research.[1] I also consider the reciprocal effect of crime on the social organization of communities. I then turn to the implications of this approach for urban crime policy.

The Social Ecological Model of Crime

Research conducted in Chicago earlier this century provided the impetus for modern American studies of the social ecology of crime. In their classic work *Juvenile Delinquency and Urban Areas* (1942) Shaw and McKay argued that low economic status, ethnic heterogeneity, and residential instability led to the disruption of local community social organization, which in turn accounted for variations in crime and delinquency. In their revised edition (1969), Shaw and McKay also demonstrated that high rates of delinquency in Chicago persisted in certain areas over many years, regardless of population turnover. More than any other, this finding led them to question individualistic explanations of delinquency and focus on the processes by which criminal patterns of behavior were transmitted across generations in areas of poverty, instability, and weak social controls (see also Bursik 1988).

After a hiatus in ecological research during the middle of this century, the past two decades have witnessed a sharp increase in research focused on variations in urban crime rates.[2] Although many factors have been studied, the following stand out.

Poverty and Inequality

Not surprisingly, a large number of recent neighborhood-based studies of crime have emphasized poverty or economic inequality. Unlike the work of Shaw and McKay, however, the majority of these have attempted to estimate the explanatory role of economic structure independent of other factors such as population composition. Overall, the results have been mixed—some studies show a direct relationship between poverty and violence (for example, Block 1979; Curry and Spergel 1988), whereas others show a weak or insignificant independent relationship (Messner and Tardiff 1986; Sampson 1985 and 1986).

Interestingly, some evidence suggests that the effect of poverty is conditional on neighborhood contexts of mobility. For example, in an evaluation of Shaw and McKay's (1969) theory, Smith and Jarjoura (1988) discovered a significant interaction between mobility and low income in explaining violence across fifty-seven neighborhoods in three cities. Mobility was positively associated with violent crime rates in poorer neighborhoods but not in more affluent areas. The main effects of mobility and income were not significant when this interaction term was in the model. Smith and Jarjoura concluded that communities characterized by rapid population turnover *and* high levels of poverty have significantly higher violent crime rates than mobile areas that are more affluent, or poor areas that are stable.

Mobility and Community Change

Consistent with this finding, one of the fundamental claims made by Shaw and McKay (1969) was that population turnover had negative consequences for the social control of delinquency. A high rate of mobility, especially in areas of decreasing population, was inferred to increase institutional disruption and weaken community controls. The research on mobility is not as extensive as that on economic status, but it has been revealing. For example, Block's (1979, 50) study of Chicago revealed large negative correlations between residential stability and the violent crimes of homicide, robbery, and aggravated assault. Victimization data from the National Crime Survey also show that residential mobility has significant positive effects on rates of violent crime (Sampson 1985). Even after adjusting for other neighborhood-level factors, rates of violent victimization for residents of high mobility neighborhoods are at least double those of residents in low mobility areas (Sampson 1985, 30; 1986, 44). And as noted above, Smith and Jarjoura (1988) found a positive effect of residential mobility on robbery and assault victimization in low income neighborhoods.

Taylor and Covington's (1988) study of poverty, instability, and violent crime (murder and aggravated assault) paints a similar picture. These authors examined ecological changes in economic status and family status for 277 Baltimore city neighborhoods in the period 1970–1980. Taylor and Covington (1988, 561) hypothesized that neighborhoods experiencing declines in relative economic status and stability should also experience increases in violence. In support of this notion, they found that the increasing entrenchment of urban poverty among disadvantaged minority areas was linked to increases in violence. Especially in neighborhood contexts of poverty, then, residential instability appears to have important consequences for violence.

Heterogeneity and Racial Composition

Although ethnic heterogeneity was accorded a central role in early ecological research (see, for example, Kornhauser 1978), in their writings Shaw and McKay (1969, 153) referred mostly to population composition. This is not surprising, because their data showed that delinquency rates were higher in predominantly black and foreign-born areas than in areas of maximum heterogeneity. For example, in Shaw and McKay's data (1969, 155) the delinquency rate in areas with over 70 percent black/foreign-born was more than double the rate in areas of maximum heterogeneity (for example, 50–59 percent black/foreign-born).

Later research on violence has also focused on racial composition. A consistent finding has been that the percentage of blacks in a neighborhood is positively and strongly related to rates of violence. Block (1979) showed that rates of violence had significant and large correlations with the black percentage of population, as did Messner and Tardiff (1986), Sampson (1985), Roncek (1981), and Smith and Jarjoura (1988). The dispute arises over the *independent* effect of racial composition on rates of violence. Specifically, several studies report a sharply attenuated effect of neighborhood racial composition on rates of violence once family structure and socioeconomic factors are accounted for (see, for example, Block 1979; Messner and Tardiff 1986; Sampson 1985). Thus, while percentage black is a significant correlate of violent crime rates, it is questionable whether neighborhood racial composition has unique explanatory power.

Housing and Population Density

Though infrequently studied, the potential role that the physical structure and density of housing may play in understanding patterns of violent crime has been highlighted in recent research. Roncek (1981) found that the percentage of units in multi-unit housing structures was a consistent and strong predictor of block-level variations in violent crime in Cleveland and San Diego. Land area in acres, population size, and the percentage of primary individual households also had significant effects on violence despite age and race composition. As Roncek (1981, 88) summarizes, "the most dangerous city blocks are relatively large in population and area with high concentrations of primary individuals and apartment housing." In a similar vein, Schuerman and Kobrin (1986, 97) found that increases in multiplex dwellings and renter-occupied housing were major predictors of increases in crime rates in Los Angeles neighborhoods.

Roncek argues that such findings are consistent with the idea of *anonymity* because primary individual households and high proportions of multi-unit structures increase the number of residents who do not know one another. For example, as the number of households sharing common living space increases, residents are less able to recognize their neighbors, to be concerned for them, or to engage in guardianship behaviors (Roncek 1981, 88). These arguments were supported in studies of violent victimization using neighborhood characteristics data and the National Crime Survey (Sampson 1985). Several studies also report a significant and large association between population density and violent crime despite controlling for a host of social and economic variables (see Sampson and Lauritsen 1994). Housing and population density thus appear to increase the level of violent crime regardless of compositional factors.

Family Structure

Several recent studies have examined the community-level consequences of family "disruption" (such as divorce rates or female-headed families with children), largely ignored in early ecological research. Family disruption has been posited to facilitate crime by decreasing networks of informal social control such as observing or questioning strangers, watching over one another's property, and assuming responsibility for supervision of general youth activities (see, for example, Sampson and Groves 1989; Taylor, Gottfredson, and Brower 1984). This conceptualization focuses on the community-wide effects of family structure and does not require that it is the children of divorced or separated parents that are engaging in crime. For instance, youth in stable family areas, regardless of their own family situation, have more controls placed on their leisure time activities, particularly with peer groups (Sullivan 1989, 178). Neighborhood family structure thus influences whether neighborhood youth are provided the opportunity to form a peer control system free of supervision by adults.

Felson and Cohen (1980) also note the potential influence of family structure not just on the control of offenders but on the control of criminal targets and opportunities. They argue that traditional theories of crime emphasize the criminal motivation of offenders without considering adequately the circumstances in which criminal acts occur. Predatory crime requires the convergence in time and space of offenders, suitable targets, and the absence of effective guardianship. The spatial and temporal structure of family activity patterns plays an important role in determining the rate at which motivated offenders encounter criminal opportunities. For example, singles and those who live alone are more likely to be out alone (going to work, restaurants, clubs) than married persons and are thus more vulnerable to personal crimes of violence (such as rape and robbery).

The salience of family structure has been supported by studies reporting a large and positive relationship between measures of family disruption (usually the population percentage of female-headed families or the divorce rate) and rates of violence. For example, Sampson (1985, 1986) found that rates of victimization were two to three times higher among residents of neighborhoods with high levels of family disruption than in neighborhoods with low levels, regardless of alternative predictors of violent victimization such as percentage black and poverty. In fact, the percentage of female-headed families helped to explain in large part the relationship between percentage black and violence. That is, percentage black and percentage female-headed families were positively and significantly related, but when percentage female-headed families was controlled, percentage black was not significantly related to violent victimization.

Similarly, Messner and Tardiff (1986) found that when percentage divorced and percentage poverty were controlled, the relationship between percentage black and homicide rates was insignificant. Smith and Jarjoura (1988) also report that family structure, especially percentage single parent families, helps account for the association between race and violent crime: racial composition was not significantly related to rates of violent crime when percentage single parent families was controlled.

Community Social Disorganization

Although the empirical evidence reviewed in the preceding sections clearly points to a number of neighborhood-level correlates of crime rates, it does not answer what is potentially the most important question: *Why* does community structure matter? Put differently, what are the mechanisms and social processes that help explain why factors such as family disruption, residential mobility, and poverty lead to increases in crime and violence? It is to these questions that criminologists have increasingly turned their attention, especially those working in the Chicago-school tradition of social disorganization theory.

In general, social disorganization may be defined as the *inability of a community structure to realize the common values of its residents and maintain effective social controls* (Sampson and Groves 1989). The social organizational approach views local communities and neighborhoods as a complex system of friendship, kinship, and acquaintanceship networks, and formal and informal associational ties rooted in family life and ongoing socialization processes (for further elaboration see Bursik 1988). From this view, both social organization and social *dis*organization are inextricably tied to systemic networks that facilitate or inhibit social control.[3] When formulated in this way, social disorganization is analytically separable not only from the processes that may lead to it (for example, poverty, residential mobility) but from the degree of criminal behavior that may be a result. This conceptualization also goes beyond the traditional account of community as a strictly geographical phenomenon by focusing on social networks of residents.

A major dimension of social disorganization is the ability of a community to supervise and control teenage peer groups—especially gangs. It is well documented that delinquency is primarily a group phenomenon (Thrasher 1963; Shaw and McKay 1969; Reiss 1986); and, hence, the capacity of the community to control group-level dynamics is a key theoretical mechanism linking community characteristics with crime. Moreover, the majority of gangs develop from unsupervised, spontaneous play groups (Thrasher 1963,

25). Shaw and McKay (1969) thus argued that residents of cohesive communities were better able to control the teenage behaviors that set the context for gang violence. Examples of such controls include the supervision of leisure-time youth activities, intervention in street-corner congregation (Thrasher 1963, 339; Shaw and McKay 1969, 176–85), and challenging youth "who seem to be up to no good" (Skogan 1986, 217; Taylor, Gottfredson, and Brower 1984, 326). Socially disorganized communities with extensive street-corner peer groups are also expected to have higher rates of adult violence, especially among younger adults who still have ties to youth gangs (Thrasher 1963).

A second dimension of community social organization is the density of local friendship and acquaintanceship networks. Systemic theory holds that locality-based social networks constitute the core social fabric of human ecological communities (Bursik 1988). When residents form local social ties their capacity for community social control is increased, because they are better able to recognize strangers and are more apt to engage in guardianship behavior against victimization (Taylor, Gottfredson, and Brower 1984, 307; Skogan 1986, 216). The greater the density and multiplexity of interpersonal networks in a community, the greater the constraint on deviant behavior within the network.

As I have previously argued (Sampson 1992), the social networks among adults and children in a community are particularly important in fostering the capacity for collective socialization and supervision. Central to this argument is the concept of *social capital*. As Coleman (1988, 98) argues, social capital is created when relations among persons facilitate action, "making possible the achievements of certain ends that in its absence would not be possible." By contrast, physical capital is embodied in observable material form, and human capital is embodied in the skills and knowledge acquired by an individual. Social capital is less tangible, for it is a social good embodied in the structure of social networks (Coleman 1990, 304).

Coleman's notion of social capital can be linked with social disorganization theory in a straightforward manner—lack of social capital is one of the primary features of socially disorganized communities (see also Sampson 1992; Putnam 1993). The theoretical task is to identify the characteristics of communities that facilitate the availability of social capital to families and children. One of the most important factors, according to Coleman (1990, 318–20), is the *closure* (that is, connectedness) of social networks among families and children in a community. In a system involving parents and children, communities characterized by an extensive set of obligations, expectations, and social networks connecting the adults are better able to facilitate the control and supervision of children.

The notion of social capital thus helps us to understand parent-child relations that extend beyond the household. For example, when closure is present through the relationship of a child to two adults whose relationship transcends the household (through friendship, for example, or work-related acquaintanceship), the adults have the potential to "observe the child's actions in different circumstances, talk to each other about the child, compare notes, and establish norms" (Coleman 1990, 593). This form of relation can also provide reinforcement for disciplining the child, as is found when parents in communities with dense social networks and high stability assume responsibility for the supervision of youth that are not their own (Coleman 1990, 320; Sampson and Groves 1989). Hence, closure of local networks can provide the child with norms and sanctions that could not be brought about by a single adult alone, or even married-couple families in isolation.

Another structural component of social organization is the density and the rate of participation in voluntary associations and local organizations. Community organizations reflect the structural embodiment of local community solidarity, and thus the instability and isolation of community institutions are key factors underlying the structural dimension of social disorganization. Kornhauser (1978, 79) argues that when the links among community institutions are weak, the capacity of a community to defend its local interests is weakened. Shaw and McKay (1969, 184–85), and more recently Taylor, Gottfredson, and Brower (1984) and Simcha-Fagan and Schwartz (1986, 688), have also argued that a weak community organizational base attenuates local social control functions. Similarly, Bursik and Grasmick (1993) highlight the importance of public control, which they define as the capacity of local community organizations to obtain extra-local resources (such as police and fire services and block grants) that help sustain neighborhood organization and crime control.

Empirical Evidence

Although it is difficult to study the intervening mechanisms of social disorganization, a new generation of research has emerged in the past decade that attempts to measure directly the theory's structural dimensions. For example, Taylor, Gottfredson, and Brower (1984) examined variations in violent crime (such as mugging, assault, murder, rape) across sixty-three street blocks in Baltimore. Based on interviews with 687 household respondents, Taylor, Gottfredson, and Brower constructed block-level measures of the proportion of respondents who belonged to an organization to which co-residents also belonged, and the proportion of respondents who felt responsible for what happened in the area surrounding their home. Both dimensions of informal social control were significantly and negatively related to rates of violence, exclusive of other ecological factors (1984, 316, 320). These results support the social disorganization hypothesis that organizational participation and informal social control of public space depress rates of criminal violence in urban areas.

Simcha-Fagan and Schwartz (1986) collected rich survey-based information on 553 residents of twelve different neighborhoods in New York City. Although the number of neighborhoods was small, the investigators found a significant negative relationship between the rate of self-reported delinquency and rates of organizational participation by local residents. A limited multivariate analysis provided further support for this pattern—"level of organizational participation and residential stability have unique effects in predicting survey-reported delinquency" (Simcha-Fagan and Schwartz 1986, 683).

In a third study conducted in Great Britain in 1982 and 1984, Sampson and Groves (1989) showed that the prevalence of unsupervised teenage peer groups in a community had the largest effect on rates of robbery and violence by strangers. The density of local friendship networks also had a significant negative effect on robbery rates, while the level of organizational participation by residents had significant inverse effects on both robbery and stranger violence (1989, 789). Central to present concerns, variations in these structural dimensions of community social (dis)organization transmitted in large part the effects of community socioeconomic status, residential mobility, ethnic heterogeneity, and family disruption in a theoretically consistent manner. In particular, socioeconomic status was significantly related to increased levels of organizational participation.

Taken together, the research of Taylor, Gottfredson, and Brower (1984), Simcha-Fagan and Schwartz (1986), and Sampson and Groves (1989) supports the notion that communities characterized by (a) anonymity and sparse acquaintanceship networks among residents, (b) unsupervised teenage peer groups and attenuated control of public space, and (c) a weak organizational base and low social participation in local activities face an increased risk of crime and violence. There is further evidence, although limited, that these dimensions of social organization are undermined by antecedent conditions of poverty, family disruption, and residential instability. Along with research on gang delinquency that points to the salience of informal and formal community structures in controlling the formation of youth gangs, the data suggest that structural elements of social disorganization have relevance for explaining rates of urban violence.

The Ecological Concentration of Race and Poverty

A community-level perspective also reveals the extent to which race, urban poverty, and social disorganization are intertwined. Although approximately 70 percent of all poor non-Hispanic whites lived in nonpoverty areas in the ten largest U.S. central cities in 1980, only 16 percent of poor blacks did. Moreover, whereas less than 7 percent of poor whites lived in extreme poverty or ghetto areas, 38 percent of poor blacks lived in such areas (Wilson 1987). This trend of ecological inequality by race has continued into the 1990s.

The combination of urban poverty and family disruption concentrated by race is particularly severe. Sampson and Wilson (1994) searched for cities where the proportion of blacks living in poverty was equal to or less than that for whites, and where the proportion of black families with children headed by a single parent was equal to or less than that for white families. Although it is known that the average national rate of family disruption and poverty among blacks is higher than that for whites, in not one city over 100,000 population in the United States do blacks live in ecological equality to whites when it comes to these basic features of economic and family organization. Accordingly, racial differences in poverty and family disruption are so strong that the "worst" urban contexts in which whites reside are considerably better off than the average context of black communities (Sampson and Wilson 1994).

In short, differential ecological distributions by race lead to the systematic confounding of correlations between community contexts and crime with correlations between race and crime. Analogous to research on urban poverty, comparisons between poor whites and poor blacks are confounded with the fact that poor whites reside in areas which are ecologically and economically very different from those of poor blacks. This means that observed relationships involving race are likely to reflect unmeasured advantages in the ecological niches that poor whites occupy (see Wilson 1987, 58–60). For example, regardless of whether or not a black juvenile is raised in an intact or single parent family, or in a rich or poor home, he or she is not likely to grow up in a community context similar to whites' with regard to family structure and the concentration of poverty. Hence the returns on a black family's educational and economic resources in terms of neighborhood environment are usually much less than those of a white family with similar resources.

Effects of Crime on Social and Economic Organization

It is important to recognize as well that crime and its consequences (such as fear) may themselves have important reciprocal effects on community structure. Skogan (1991) has recently provided an insightful overview of some of the feedback processes that may further increase levels of crime. These include

- physical and psychological withdrawal from community life
- weakening of the informal social control processes that inhibit crime

- decline in the organizational life and mobilization capacity of the neighborhood
- deteriorating business conditions
- importation and domestic production of delinquency and deviance
- further dramatic changes in the composition of the population.

For example, if people shun their neighbors and local facilities out of fear of crime, fewer opportunities exist for local networks and organizations to take hold. Relatedly, street crime may be accompanied by residential out-migration and business relocation from inner city areas. As a result, crime itself can lead to simultaneous demographic "collapse" and a weakening of the informal control structures and mobilization capacity of communities, which in turn fuels further crime.

Although the number of empirical studies is relatively small, the evidence is rather consistent that crime does in fact undermine the social and economic fabric of urban areas. One of the most important findings is that crime generates fear of strangers and a general alienation from participation in community life (Skogan 1986 and 1991; Rosenbaum 1991). Besides weakening neighborhood social organization, high crime rates and concerns about safety may trigger population out-migration. For example, Bursik (1986) found that delinquency rates are not only one of the outcomes of urban change, they are an important part of the *process* of urban change. Studying Chicago neighborhoods, Bursik (1986, 73) observes that "although changes in racial composition cause increases in the delinquency rate, this effect is not nearly as great as the effect that increases in the delinquency rate have in minority groups being stranded in the community." In a study of forty neighborhoods in eight cities, Skogan (1991) also found that high rates of crime and disorder were associated with higher rates of fear, neighborhood dissatisfaction, and intentions to move out. And in a study of Dallas neighborhoods, Katzman (1980, 278) found that high rates of property crime were linked to out-migration.

These general trends are observed at the city level as well. In a study of the nation's fifty-five largest cities, Sampson and Wooldredge (1986) reported that crime rates were negatively related to population change from 1970 to 1980, especially nonwhite population change. Crime rates had significant lagged effects on net migration patterns as well. That is, net of fertility and mortality differences, serious crime led to decreases in central city populations and thereby migration to suburbs (see also Frey 1979). Sampson and Wooldredge's findings persisted despite controls for the effects of other important factors in population migration such as region, per capita tax rate, employment, racial composition, manufacturing base, population density, and poverty.

Evidence on relocation decisions by businesses as a function of crime rates is extremely scarce. However, one study of sixty-two manufacturing firms that moved from New York City to New Jersey does shed light on the matter. When asked for reasons why they moved, many of the surveyed manufacturing firms cited perceived safety concerns. For example, 9 percent claimed crime was the single most important reason for moving, while 21 percent cited crime as one among several other reasons. Less than 5 percent said that a lower crime rate was the most important reason for moving to New Jersey rather than the outer boroughs of New York City, but 19 percent did say that less crime was one of the factors increasing the desirability of New Jersey relative to alternatives in New York. The report concluded that "Security, taxes, 'quality of life' issues, and image problems all contribute to a marketability gap which places many outer borough locations at a competitive disadvantage when compared to New Jersey" (Interface 1985, iv). Hence, while business decisions appear to be less sensitive to crime rates than do residential ones, they are not immune from the social disorganization, fear, and social incivilities associated with street violence.

Although the empirical base is limited, the overall picture painted by prior research on the effects of crime is one of considerable population abandonment of urban neighborhoods, business relocation to the suburbs, loss of economic revenue, a decrease in economic status and property values, and escalating levels of fear in central cities. Moreover, many cities—especially in the North and Midwest—have not only lost population but have become increasingly poorer and racially isolated in recent decades (Wilson 1987). An important part of this racially selective decline in population and economic status apparently stems from variations in serious crime. As Skogan (1991) has emphasized, crime is a salient event that has important symbolic consequences for perceptions of the inhabitability and civility of city life. By undermining social and economic organization, crime generates a reciprocal, feedback effect that leads to even further increases in crime. Breaking the cycle of violence in communities is thus crucial to a general strategy for urban policy.

Limitations of the Community Approach

Like any complex phenomenon, research on communities and crime is plagued by numerous problems. Among an assortment of limitations, the use of varying and sometimes highly aggregated units of analysis, potentially biased sources of information on violence (for example, official data), feedback or reciprocal effects from crime itself, widely varying analytical techniques, and high correlations among social variables all hinder the attempt to draw inferences about the unique explanatory power of community characteristics.

Furthermore, prior research has mostly inferred the existence of intervening social processes, even though the correlation of crime with community characteristics is consistent with many different theoretical perspectives. For example, studies typically show that percentage black, poverty, and family disruption predict rates of crime. While useful as a preliminary test, this strategy does not go much beyond the steps taken by Shaw and McKay over forty years ago. As Kornhauser (1978, 82) argues, most criminological theories take as their point of departure the same independent variables (such as socioeconomic status). The variables that *intervene* between community structure and violence are at issue, and to test adequately competing theories one must establish the relationship to violence of the interpretive variables each theory implies.

Unfortunately, previous macro-level research has relied primarily on census data that rarely provide measures for the social variables hypothesized to mediate the relationship between community structure and violence. Some studies have examined quantitative dimensions of informal social control (see, for example, Maccoby, Johnson, and Church 1958; Simcha-Fagan and Schwartz 1986), but they have been limited to a few communities, precluding comprehensive multivariate analysis and generalization. Reliance on census data has also meant that culture is commonly ignored even though a key element of macro-level explanation is how community cultures and value systems produce differential rates of crime. Consequently, empirical examination of between-community differences in social disorganization and other community-level processes have been rarely undertaken (see Taylor, Gottfredson, and Brower 1984; Sampson and Groves 1989).

Another problem in community research is that an apparent ecological or structural effect may in fact arise from individual-level causal processes. For example, an observed result such as the correlation of median income or percentage black with violence rates may simply represent the aggregation of relationships occurring at lower levels of social structure and not a manifestation of processes taking place at the level of the community as a whole. Even though rates of crime may not be used to make inferences about individuals, individuals surely commit the crimes that constitute the rates.

Consider further the basic facts on delinquency. Research has consistently demonstrated the early onset of delinquency and its long-term stability (Glueck and Glueck 1950; Robins 1966). These general differences among individuals that are stable over time have direct implications for an ecological study of crime. Antisocial children tend to fight, steal, become truant, drop out of school, drift in and out of unemployment, live in lower class areas and go on to commit adult crime. The causal nature of the relationship between achieved adult characteristics (such as employment status) and adult crime is thus fraught with methodological difficulties. In fact, in *Deviant Children Grown Up*, Lee Robins (1966) offered the provocative hypothesis that antisocial behavior predicts class status more efficiently than class status predicts antisocial behavior.

If area differences in violence rates result from the characteristics of individuals selectively located in those communities (Kornhauser 1978), the findings derived from community-level research must be questioned. Is the correlation of concentrated poverty with violence caused by an aggregation of individual-level effects of class, by a genuine community-level effect, or simply by a differential selection of individuals into communities based on prior (for example, prior antisocial) behavior? Or is it that common third factors cause individuals to both commit violence and perform poorly in the occupational sphere? And if violent and antisocial tendencies are formed at early (preteen) ages, what plausible roles can community labor markets and economic stratification play in understanding violence?

Simply put, community-level research is not immune to questions concerning the level at which causal relations operate. The level at which a causal relation occurs is a complex issue that is not solved simply by the nature of how variables are measured or the unit for which they are measured. To make matters more complicated, the concrete actions of individuals also feed back to shape the collective environment (Tienda 1991). Thus the unit of analysis does not define the level of causal explanation, and the information contained in aggregate data is not necessarily generated by macrosociological processes.

Perhaps most disturbing, there seems to be a consensus in evaluation research that community crime prevention programs have achieved only limited success (see Bursik and Grasmick 1993, 148–75; Rosenbaum 1991). The most common crime prevention approach has been the so-called neighborhood watch, where attempts are made to increase residents' participation in local efforts at social control (for example community meetings or neighborhood patrols). More ambitious interventions have tried to increase social interaction among neighbors and instill concern for the public welfare of local residents (see Greenberg, Rohe, and Williams 1985). There have also been even more general efforts to change neighborhood opportunity structures, such as the classic Chicago Area Project patterned after Shaw and McKay's (1942) theory. Yet evaluations of these programs are for the most part pessimistic about concrete reductions in crime (Rosenbaum 1991; Bursik and Grasmick 1993; Greenberg, Rohe, and Williams 1985).

Although disappointing results from evaluation research could mean that neighborhood-level theories are wrong, another possibility is that programs were not implemented correctly. We know, for example, that community crime prevention is especially hard to implement in the areas that need it the most—poor, unstable neighborhoods with high crime rates. Participation levels also tend to fall off quickly once interventions are removed. On the other hand, efforts to reduce crime are more likely to succeed if they are embedded in more comprehensive programs for neighborhood stabilization that local residents support. That is, "one shot" interventions that are externally imposed and simply try to reduce crime in the short run without confronting other key aspects of the neighborhood are, not surprisingly, highly susceptible to failure. Whether the poor track record of community interventions (similar, I should note, to the poor track record of individual interventions) is due to a failure of theory or a programmatic failure of implementation is thus unknown. It is also possible that neighborhood-level interventions have attempted to pull the wrong levers of change.

A confluence of factors—selective decisions to live in different communities, misspecification due to population composition effects, overlap among ecological variables, a static conceptualization of community structure, the early onset of many forms of violence, indirect measurement of community characteristics, and weak intervention results—clearly suggest caution in the interpretation of community-level research. Nevertheless, I believe not only that a community-level perspective improves our understanding of the etiology of crime and violence but that it expands our conceptual apparatus to think about fresh policies for the public agenda on crime.[4] Indeed, what seem most promising are policies that embed a concern for crime reduction in larger, more systemic efforts to improve the social organizational capacities of the neighborhood. The following section builds on this idea.

Public Policy Implications: Changing Places, Not People

Having outlined both the strengths and weaknesses of a community-level perspective on crime and social organization, I now examine eight policy-related implications that attempt to move beyond past efforts. I focus primarily on community-level correlates of crime reviewed earlier that are related, both directly and indirectly, to the policy decisions of public officials. For the most part these are policy domains that focus on crime prevention and the enhancement of community social organization from *other* than criminal justice agencies. Initiatives that rely on the police, prisons, and other agencies of social control have been reviewed at length many times, and hence I do not cover them here except as they interface with community-level efforts. For example, I do not cover the traditional literature on neighborhood watch and community crime prevention (see Rosenbaum 1991; Bursik and Grasmick 1993). Rather, my strategy is to begin discussion with alternative neighborhood-level policies most directly related to crime, and then build toward more comprehensive strategies that attack "root causes" of crime but that are still amenable to public policy.

1. Identify Neighborhood "Hot Spots" for Crime

One area of promise is simple yet powerful. Research has long demonstrated that crimes are not randomly distributed in space. Rather, they are disproportionately concentrated in certain neighborhoods and "places" (for example, taverns, parking lots). Ecologically oriented criminologists have dubbed these areas "hot spots" of crime. (See "The Police," Chapter 14 in this volume and Sherman, Gartin, and Buerger 1989.) Drawing on community theory and advances in computer mapping technology, the argument is that policing strategies can be more effective if they are implemented using information on ecological hot spots (see also Reiss and Roth 1993, 17). In Chicago, for example, Block (1991) has pioneered the use of what is termed an "early warning system" for gang homicides. By plotting each homicide incident and using sophisticated mapping and statistical clustering procedures, the early warning system allows police to identify potential neighborhood crisis areas at high risk for suffering a spurt of gang violence (Block 1991). With rapid dissemination of information, police can intervene in hot spots to quell emerging trouble. Places may also be modified or watched so as to reduce the opportunities for crime to occur. Sherman and colleagues (Chapter 14 in this volume; Sherman, Gartin, and Buerger 1989, 48) have considered "place" interventions based on hot spot data such as differential patrol allocations by place, selective revocation of bar licenses, and removal of vacant crack houses.

The idea of hot spots suggests a neighborhood-level response that in the end may be much more effective than policies that simply target individuals or even families. By proactively responding to neighborhoods and places that disproportionately generate crimes, policing strategies can more efficiently stave off epidemics of crime and its spatial diffusion.

2. Reduce Social Disorder and Physical "Incivilities"

Both the logic of social disorganization theory and the extant evidence suggest that "incivilities" such as broken windows, trash, public drinking, and prostitution increase fear of crime (Wilson and Kelling 1982; Skogan 1986 and 1991). Incivilities and signs of disorder are expected to increase not just fear but crime itself, because potential offenders recognize such deterioration and assume that residents are so indifferent to what goes on in their neighborhood that they will not be motivated to confront strangers, intervene in a crime, or call the police. Moreover, it is difficult if not impossible to successfully raise children and inculcate prosocial attitudes in a context of rampant fear and social disorder. As one step in fostering a climate of safety, public order, and hopefully social organization, policy should consider collective strategies in the community that might:

- clean up graffiti, trash, needles, vials, and the like
- stagger bar closing times and enact strict zoning/licensing

- picket public drinking, drug use, prostitution, and other objectionable activities
- organize walking groups for adults in public areas

There is limited evidence on these strategies, although various neighbor-hood-based cleanup interventions have been found to increase perceptions of safety (Rosenbaum 1991). An interesting study was also conducted by the Police Foundation where a specially trained group of officers performed a variety of disorder reduction tasks within a Newark experimental area (Skogan 1991). The results were mixed, but they did indicate that recorded crime was lower under conditions of aggressive field interrogations. The implications for general citizen involvement are broader—the community must take partial responsibility for stemming the spiral of decay. The optimal strategies are those that involve both police and the community in the planning and execution of crime control measures (for example, community policing that focuses on reduction of incivilities).

3. Build Informal Social Control and Social Capital

As described earlier, a major dimension of social organization is the ability of a community to supervise and control teenage peer groups. Communities characterized by an extensive set of obligations, expectations, and social networks connecting the adults are better able to facilitate this task. For example, when the parents' friends or acquaintances are the parents of their children's friends, the adults have the potential to observe the child's actions in different circumstances, talk to one another about the child, compare notes, and establish norms (see Coleman 1990). This form of relation can provide reinforcement for inculcating positive youth outcomes, as found when parents in communities with dense social networks and high stability assume responsibility for the supervision of youth that are not their own. Closure of local networks provides the child with social capital of a collective nature (as in, it takes a whole village to raise a child). Social capital is thus a social good that is created when relations among persons facilitate action. One can extend this model to closure among networks involving parents and teachers, religious and recreational leaders, businesses that serve youth, and even agents of criminal justice (Sampson 1992).

Programs that might foster informal social controls and social capital (hence increasing social organization) include:

- organized supervision of leisure-time youth activities
- observation/reduction of street-corner congregation

- staggered school-closing times to reduce peer control systems
- parent surveillance/involvement in after-school and nighttime youth programs (recreational or educational)
- adult-youth mentoring systems and adult acquaintanceship

The key here is to increase positive connections among youth and adults in the community. Stricter sanctions such as curfews for adolescents in public areas may also be necessary, but the preceding focus is on *informal* social controls that arise naturally from ongoing social interactions.

4. Promote Housing-based Neighborhood Stabilization

A more general option for enhancing social organization is to focus on joint public/private intervention programs to help stabilize and revitalize rapidly deteriorating inner city neighborhoods. My focus is primarily on investment in the *physical* structure of declining but still reachable communities. As noted earlier, a long history of community-based research shows that population instability and housing decay are linked to crime and social problems among youth (see also Sampson and Lauritsen 1994). The implication is that community-based policy interventions may help to reverse the tide of social disintegration in concentrated poverty areas. Among several, these policies might include:

- resident management of public housing
- tenant buy-outs
- rehabilitation of existing low income housing
- strict code enforcement
- low income housing tax credits

For example, inner city neighborhoods have suffered disproportionately from severe population and housing loss of the sort that is disruptive of the social and institutional order. Bursik (1989) has shown that the planned construction of new public housing projects in Chicago's poor communities in the 1970s was associated with increased rates of population turnover, which in turn were related to increases in crime independent of racial composition. More generally, Skogan (1986, 206) has noted how urban renewal and forced migration contributed to the wholesale uprooting of many urban black communities, especially the extent to which freeway networks driven through the hearts of many cities in the 1950s destroyed viable low income communities. For example, in Atlanta one in six residents, the great majority of whom were poor blacks, were dislocated through urban renewal (Logan and Molotch 1987, 114). Nationwide, fully 20 percent of all central city housing units occupied by blacks were lost in the period 1960–1970 alone. Recognizing these patterns, housing policies should focus more on stabilization of existing areas—especially those dominated by single family homes.

Municipal code enforcement and local governmental policies toward neighborhood deterioration are also relevant. In *Making the Second Ghetto* Hirsch (1983) documents how lax enforcement of city housing codes played a major role in accelerating the deterioration of inner city Chicago neighborhoods. More recently, Daley and Meislen (1988) have argued that inadequate city policies on code enforcement and repair of city properties contributed to the systematic decline of New York City's housing stock and, in some cases, entire neighborhoods. When considered with the practices of redlining and disinvestment by banks and "blockbusting" by real estate agents (Skogan 1986), local policies toward code enforcement—which on the surface are far removed from crime—have nonetheless contributed to crime through neighborhood deterioration, forced migration, and instability.

In short, the hope is that by acting to reduce population flight, residential anonymity, and housing deterioration, neighborhood stabilization and ultimately a more cohesive environment for youth socialization will emerge. This general strategy is quite compatible with that of Community Development Corporations (CDCs). Although CDCs focus on more comprehensive economic development, there are recent examples that such interventions are viable and in fact have stabilizing effects on communities. For example, Bethel New Life in Chicago, Banana Kelly in New York, New City in Newark, Mission Housing in San Francisco, and several other CDC efforts are revitalizing previously declining areas and building social stability and hopefully safer neighborhoods in the process (Sullivan 1993).

5. De-concentrate Poverty: Scattered Site New Housing

This strategy is linked to promoting housing-based stabilization, but it is more focused on certain forms of segregation. As Wilson (1987) shows, the social transformation of the inner city has resulted in a disproportionate concentration and segregation of the most disadvantaged segments of the urban black population—especially poor, female-headed families with children. The social transformation of the inner city in recent decades has been fueled by macrostructural economic changes related to the de-industrialization of central cities where disadvantaged minorities are concentrated. Some of these changes are the shift from goods-producing to service-producing industries; increasing polarization of the labor market into low wage and high wage sectors; and relocation of manufacturing out of the inner city. The exodus of middle and upper income black families from the inner city has also removed an important social buffer that could potentially deflect the full impact of prolonged joblessness and industrial transformation. Consistent with a social organizational approach, this thesis is based on the assumption that the basic institutions of a neighborhood (such as churches, schools, stores, recreational facilities) are more likely to remain viable if the core of their support comes from more economically stable families (Wilson 1987, 56).

Of course, an understanding of concentration effects must also recognize the negative consequences of policy decisions to concentrate minorities and the poor in public housing. Opposition from organized community groups to the building of public housing in "their" neighborhoods, de facto federal policy to tolerate segregation against blacks in urban housing markets, and decisions by local governments to neglect the rehabilitation of existing residential units have led to massive, segregated housing projects which have become ghettos for the minorities and disadvantaged (Massey and Denton 1993).

Although a community-level intervention cannot change the macrostructural economy and declining industrial base in urban America, the ecological concentration of poverty and racial segregation can be addressed by housing policies. Building on strategy Number 4, two key approaches seem to be:

• dispersing of concentrated public housing

• scattered site, new, low income housing

The evidence that dispersion policies and scattered site housing can work is small but still persuasive (Massey and Denton 1993). For example, the Chicago Housing Authority is embarking on a plan to "scatter" (on a voluntary basis) some 355 units of the Cabrini Green housing project across the city as a means to break down the severe segregation that presently exists. There is also quasi-experimental evidence that offering inner city mothers on welfare the opportunity to relocate to more thriving neighborhoods improved the social outcomes of both the mothers and their children (Rosenbaum and Popkin 1991). These results suggest the positive outcomes of housing policies that encourage (but do not require) increased integration among classes and races.

6. Maintain and Build the Municipal Service Base

Decisions about the provision of city municipal services for public health and fire safety—decisions presumably made with little if any thought to crime and violence—appear to have been salient in the social disintegration of poor communities. As Wallace and Wallace (1990) argue on the basis of an analysis of the "planned shrinkage" of New York City fire and health services in recent decades: "The consequences of withdrawing municipal services from poor neighborhoods, the resulting outbreaks of contagious urban decay and forced migration which shred essential social networks and cause social disintegration, have become a highly significant contributor to decline in public health among the poor" (1990, 427). The loss of social integration and networks from planned shrinkage of services may increase behavioral patterns of violence which may themselves cause further social disintegration (1990, 427). This pattern of destabilizing feedback (see Skogan 1986) appears central to an understanding of the role of governmental policies in fostering the downward spiral of low income, high crime areas. Housing and community-based policies should thus be coordinated with local policies regarding fire, sanitation, and other municipal services.

7. Integrate Community with Child Development/Health Policy

Although often neglected in policy discussions, a substantial connection between structural disadvantage and childhood development has been demonstrated by research. One link comes in the form of physical abuse and maltreatment. In a study of twenty subareas and ninety-three census tracts within a city, Garbarino and Crouter (1978) found that poverty, residential mobility, and single parent households accounted for over 50 percent of the variation in rates of child abuse. A recent analysis by Coulton et al. (1994) of conditions in Cleveland showed that children who live in neighborhoods characterized by poverty, population turnover, and the concentration of female-headed families are at highest risk of abuse. The influence of concentrated poverty extended to adolescent risk factors as well, including the teen birth rate, delinquency, and high school dropout rate. In an observation similar to Shaw and McKay's (1942), they suggest that child maltreatment is a manifestation of community social disorganization and that its occurrence is related to the same underlying social conditions that foster other urban problems (1994, 1).

Additional evidence consistent with social disorganization theory is found in a series of studies by Wallace and Wallace of community-level variations in low birthweight babies and infant mortality. Wallace and Wallace (1990) document the strong upsurge in infant mortality and low birthweight in the late 1970s in New York City, especially in devastated areas of the Bronx. In particular, they found that poverty, overcrowded housing, and rapid population change were the main predictors of increased rates of low birthweight starting in 1974. Community instability coupled with concentrated poverty predicted increased infant mortality above and beyond what was expected based on migration patterns.

There is thus evidence that concentrated urban poverty and social disorganization combine to increase child abuse/neglect, low birthweight, cognitive impairment, and other adjustment problems, which in turn constitute risk factors for later crime and violence. In particular, recent data suggest that child neglect and physical abuse are prime risk factors for long-term patterns of violence among adults (Widom 1989). For these reasons, community-based interventions are needed to foster *prenatal health care, infant/ child health,* and support programs for *prosocial family management* (through, for example, child-rearing skills; conflict resolution). Community-level interventions of this sort appear promising, and may prove even more important in the long run than housing-based policies (see Sampson 1992).

8. Increase Community Power/Organizational Base

Stable interlocking organizations form a major linchpin of community solidarity and effective social control. When local organizations are unstable and isolated, and when the vertical links of community institutions to the outside are weak, the capacity of a community to defend its local interests is thus weakened. As Bursik and Grasmick (1993 and 1994) argue along similar lines, *public control* refers to the regulatory capacities that develop from the networks among neighborhoods and between neighborhoods and public/ private agencies. More specifically, this dimension "refers to the ability to secure public and private goods and services that are allocated by groups and agencies located outside of the neighborhood" (1994, 19). It follows that interventions promoting public control might:

- enhance community "empowerment"
- increase local involvement in community organizations
- promote the vertical integration of local institutions with City Hall and other extralocal resources
- promote collective action and awareness of local power

Although it cannot be said that massive changes will result from this type of mobilization, success at the margins produces cumulative changes that may ultimately promote a more stable and long-lasting social organization (Bursik and Grasmick 1994).

Conclusion

What seem to be "noncrime" policies—for example, where or if to build a housing project, enforcement of municipal codes, reduction in essential municipal services, rehabilitation of existing residential units; the dispersal of the ghetto poor; building social capital among adults and youth—may have important effects on crime. As detailed above, residential instability and the concentration of poor, female-headed families with children appear to have been shaped by planned governmental policies at local, state, and federal levels. This conceptualization diverges from the natural market assumptions of the early social ecologists, such as Shaw and McKay (1942), by considering the role of political decisions in shaping local community structure.

Crime also generates a reciprocal feedback effect by undermining social and economic organization, which in turn leads to further increases in crime. Even decisions to relocate businesses appear to be shaped in part by the corrosive impact of serious crime on the quality of life for workers and customers alike. Hence policies on urban development can ill afford to ignore the symbolic and economic consequences of crime for the habitability, civility, and economic vitality of city life.

On the positive side, the implication of this chapter's community-level perspective is that policy-manipulable options may help reverse the tide of community social disorganization in concentrated poverty areas. Indeed, the unique value of a community-level perspective is that it cautions against a simple "kinds of people" analysis by suggesting a focus on how social characteristics of collectivities are interrelated with crime. On the basis of the theory and research reviewed in this chapter (see also Sampson and Lauritsen 1994), it seems that policy makers should pay special attention to integrating crime-targeted interventions (such as early warning systems, "hot spot" identification, and reduction of social disorder) with more general policies that address:

• the interaction of concentrated urban poverty with other structural features of urban areas (such as population loss and family disruption)

• mediating processes of social organization (such as density of friendship and acquaintanceship, intergenerational ties and age integration, control of street-corner peer groups, and organizational participation and mobilization)

• the political economy of place, especially how concentrated poverty is influenced by public policies regarding housing and municipal services

• the effects of concentrated poverty on child, adolescent, and consequently adult developmental outcomes

• the reciprocal relationship between crime and urban socioeconomic development.

Only then can we expect a more lasting effect of neighborhood-based interventions on the reduction of crime and disorder.

Overall, the community-level approach proposed in this chapter points to simultaneous investment in the *physical capital* and *social capital* of local communities. Ultimately, however, much of this investment must come from communities themselves—that is, residents must come together and join forces with the criminal justice system to establish and maintain social order. Consistent with social disorganization theory, this strategy relies on a vision of urban America based on shared values for a safe and healthy environment—not on divisive policies that separate by race and class.

MALCOLM W. KLEIN

STREET GANG CYCLES

10

Are we doomed to an ever escalating pattern of gangs and gang violence in America? As noted later in this chapter, a country with a few score gang-involved cities has now become a country with at least 800 gang cities. We're approaching a figure of 10,000 street gangs, and half a million gang members. Understanding this escalation requires knowledge of gangs, of course, but also knowledge of cycles in gang activity. Contributing to that understanding is the charge of this chapter.

Comprehensive treatments of the history and nature of American street gangs are now available to an extent never before achieved,[1] so this chapter provides data and viewpoints on a few selected issues that seem pivotal to understanding the status of street gangs in the 1990s. In particular, I will cover

- definitional approaches to street gangs
- recent changes in street gang structure, activity, and prevalence
- predominant approaches to gang intervention and control[2]

Cycles and Definitions

If accepted definitions of what constitutes street gangs change, this redefinition could lead to the appearance of changes or cycles of gang activity. In the same way, if our understanding of gang structure changes, this altered perception could lead to the appearance of cycles in gang activity. It is important, then, to be as clear as we can on what we include in the concept of the street gang—and what we exclude as well.

Surprisingly, most important gang researchers for several decades have been describing roughly the same phenomenon, while failing to agree on a uniform definition or description. My preference over the years has been not to "define" gangs but rather to describe their modal characteristics. The existing variety of gang forms makes definition problematic but broad characterization useful. Here's where I ended up, after excluding motorcycle gangs; prison gangs; supremacist groups like skinheads; and generally nonviolent cohorts such as stoners, tagger crews, and "normal" adolescent peer groups that do on occasion get themselves into illegal patterns of activity:

> What's left? Groups of young people, who may range in age from ten to thirty or occasionally older, whose cohesion is fostered in large part by their acceptance of or even commitment to delinquent or criminal involvement. They are principally but not exclusively male, principally but not exclusively minority in ethnicity or race, normally but not necessarily territorial, and highly versatile in their criminal offenses. These offenses are not predominantly violent, but they are disproportionately violent when compared to other youth groups or individuals.[3]

Equally important, in my view, is that street gangs are delinquent groups that have passed a "tipping point" in their confrontational stance *as a group*. They have set themselves apart from their neighborhoods *in their own perceptions,* and many members of the local community have come to see them as a group apart. In other words, the street gang comes to see itself as such, and so does the community.

If we accepted prison gangs into this depiction, we could claim an upswing in gangs in the late 1970s and early 1980s. If we accepted stoners, a 1980s upswing would have been followed by a 1990s downturn. Inclusion of skinheads would give us a 1980s upswing continuing into the 1990s.[4] Inclusion of tagger crews would yield an upsurge or new cycle in the 1990s. Further, each of these changes would have shown dramatic differences in geographic locations.

Examples of Asian, Drug, and Entrepreneurial Gangs

Similarly, if we accepted the demonstration of dramatically new forms of street gang structures and included these in our depiction of street gangs, we would see the emergence of new gang cycles. Three examples are particularly relevant: Asian gangs, drug distribution gangs, and quasi-corporate gangs.

Asian gangs come in a variety of forms, most but not all of these being ethnically differentiated. Backgrounds differ—Chinese, Korean, Japanese, Vietnamese, Cambodian, Hmong, Pacific Islander, Filipino—yielding different structures. They tend as a group to be less street-oriented than non-Asian gangs, sometimes less territorial (especially Vietnamese gangs), and sometimes more focused on particular forms of crime (drug sales, extortion, "home invasions," all of which exemplify instrumental rather than expressive violence). Southeast Asian gangs have increased most dramatically in recent years, truly stretching our notions of territoriality and criminal versatility. Yet they still seem "ganglike" and evince standard control practices from law enforcement. Because they are hard to penetrate and typically victimize their own compatriots, who are reluctant to rely on the police, Southeast Asian gangs have proliferated in the absence of effective social controls. Where they operate, they create their own cycles.

Drug gangs have emerged in the public eye as a second new phenomenon because of overstated law enforcement and media attention to crack cocaine distribution in particular. Still, the following seems to be true:

- A number of individual street gang members have engaged at varying rates in the sale and distribution of crack and other drugs. Crack is most common among black distributors.
- Some cliques of street gangs have broken off to concentrate on drug sales, but most street gangs per se have not been transformed into drug gangs.
- In some cities, independent drug gangs have emerged that have drug sales as their primary focus. Washington, D.C., and Detroit have been depicted as such instances in particular.

There have been enough instances of drug gangs, as distinct from street gangs, that we can describe typical differences between them as follows:

Street Gangs	Drug Gangs
Versatile ("cafeteria-style") crime	Crime focused on drug business
Larger structures	Smaller structures
Less cohesiveness	More cohesiveness
Looser leadership	More centralized leadership
Ill-defined roles	Market-defined roles
Code of loyalty	Requirement of loyalty
Residential territories	Sales market territories
Members may sell drugs	Members do sell drugs
Intergang rivalries	Competition controlled
Members younger, on average, but wider age range	Members older on average, narrower age range

With a reported increase in gang involvement in drug sales and thus greater likelihood of drug gang proliferation, inclusion of these groups under the rubric of "street gangs" would obviously have the effect of exacerbating the street gang proliferation nationally. As things now stand, I see drug gangs for the most part as gangs—but not street gangs. The distinction is helpful in understanding each kind of gang, while combining them simply muddies the research waters.

Much of the difference between street gangs and drug gangs stems from their criminal focus. For street gangs, this tends to be diffuse and versatile, with the majority of delinquent and criminal acts being relatively mild in seriousness. Nothing in this pattern *requires* particular structural attributes beyond the requirements of youthful group loyalty and territoriality associated with gang rivalry.

But the newer drug gangs, because of their focus on "business" and the peculiar nature of the drug distribution enterprise, do tend to form in a narrower structural band. Business roles develop to ensure methods of sale, distribution, enforcement, and connections to higher-level suppliers. The safety of the enterprise calls for smaller, more cohesive, and secretive groups, with imposed limits on individual departures from group norms. The differences, on average, justify a different nomenclature and different intervention approaches to street gangs and drug gangs.

For example, from what we know about drug gangs (see the earlier list of differences and Padilla's [1992] informative ethnography of one such group[5]), they seem to be legitimate targets for the normal technologies and practices of police narcotics divisions and the Drug Enforcement Agency (DEA) at the federal level. Police gang units would have little to contribute here. But in contrast, the use of narcotics units and federal agencies to combat local street gangs can be both inappropriate and counterproductive.

The inappropriate aspect is that the narcotics groups work on the assumption of conspiracy of the sort that fits well with drug *cartels*. Street gangs are not cartels; they haven't the cohesion, the organization, the loyalty, or the technology to engage the sophisticated armament of the DEA and federal prosecutors.

The counterproductive aspect of narcotics agency control of street gang stems from the peculiar group dynamics that form and reinforce gang structure. Gang members will use, distort, reverse, and manipulate any incoming "message" to increase the internal cohesion of the gangs. A jail sentence yields reputation; arrest and release yields invincibility; targeting by police builds reputation, as does media attention. In such a context, garnering attention from "narcs" and "feds" merely strengthens the gang bonds. Control attempts thus tend to defeat their own purposes.

A third purported phenomenon which could well yield changes in gang prevalence and new cycles of gang crime is that of the "quasi-corporate" street gang. Described in several varieties by Skolnick et al. (1992) and Taylor (1991) with respect to drug marketing, and by Sanchez-Jankowski more broadly, these groups, if they exist, constitute an unusually rational, economically focused mechanism for gang businesses.[6] They are not unlike the Blackstone Rangers and Vice Lords in Chicago, the "supergangs" that were the recipients of millions of dollars in public and private War on Poverty money in the 1960s.

A number of scholars and police officers have seriously questioned the available ethnographic descriptions of these businesslike gangs, while others have welcomed the description as heralding a new era in the evolution of street gangs. Our own national assessments (carried out by my research team and I) of street gang structures and gang member migration in over 1,100 U.S. towns and cities fails to confirm the pattern described by the several writers noted earlier, except in a few isolated cases. It's hard to equate an aberration with a cycle.

Still, whether exaggerated or not, the reported appearance of corporate-style gangs serves the purpose of underlining the implications of different gang definitions for control purposes. An organized market-oriented criminal enterprise calls forth technologies of legal and social response different from those inspired by a loosely organized, fluctuating amalgam of street youths. The confusion of the two would not bode well for effective community response.

The Problem of Cycles

Gang cycles—purported and real changes in gang behavior—are more common than they often seem to be, yet less common than media attention would suggest. Every reporter newly assigned to the gang beat seems to reinvent what has been stable, yet overlooks significant changes. The same is often true of police and prosecution officials newly assigned to gang duty, and to many academics as well, newly come to the street gang arena. Thus it is no surprise that public policy officials and politicians often initiate plans and programs that suffer egregiously from misinformation. They turn for their knowledge, understandably, to the news reports, enforcement officials, and occasionally to the academics whose turfs are delineated in both time and space.

These cycles in which gang observers are caught up are not "merely academic," to use a most unfortunate phrase. It is important for several reasons to assess the cycles and understand how they relate to gang definitions, patterns, and control. First, failure to appreciate the existence of gang cycles leads us to misunderstand the nature of gang phenomena. Second, failure to connect gang cycles to gang patterns closes a unique window on understanding how we organize our society: the gang is a byproduct of that organization and thus reflects its nature.

Third, gang intervention and control efforts can be both misguided and incorrectly assessed in their effects if the cycles are not appreciated. For example, gang intervention programs initiated soon after cyclical peaks of gang activity *seem* to have produced downturns, when those were occurring anyway. This pattern has led to the perpetuation and spread of such programs as panaceas, whereas they may have had no real effect at all. Philadelphia and Los Angeles have yielded prime examples of such false but replicated results.[7]

Examples can also be found in recent treatises on gangs in Detroit by Carl Taylor; in California by Jerome Skolnick; and in the three cities of Los Angeles, Boston, and New York by Martin Sanchez-Jankowski.[8] In each case, there are descriptions of street gang structures and activities that suggest radically new and different patterns basically unrelated to what has gone before. In each case, a better appreciation of gang cycles and gang history would have placed these descriptions into broader paradigms of street gangs. Failure to appreciate when and where gang cycles occur has yielded three descriptions generalized well beyond likelihood and credibility. Public policy based upon such generalizations, as has happened in the case of Skolnick's work, can be both wrong and damaging.

Varieties of Cycles

These cycles of street gang activity to which I refer are of several sorts. Some of them are merely seasonal. Historically, gang activity normally peaked during the summer months in Eastern cities—Chicago, Boston, New York—and street workers assigned to gangs were not allowed vacation time during those months. Yet in Los Angeles, gang activity was lower during the summer and street workers took their vacations then.

In one of the more interesting gang ethnography reports, Leon Jansyn related gang cohesiveness to delinquent activity levels.[9] His data suggested that when gang cohesiveness dropped to a rather low level, certain gang members responded by initiating cohesion-building activities—criminal events—with the seemingly deliberate intention of increasing gang cohesiveness. This is an interesting suggestion of group dynamics at work, but because Jansyn's observations took place over a one-year period, a plausible alternative explanation would be that he was observing a normal, seasonally based cycle of gang activity. He did not consider this cycle-based hypothesis, and so we cannot be confident of his cohesion hypothesis despite its appealing logic.

Seasonality may be more likely among gangs of predominantly school-aged members. Among the Latins, a large group studied in Los Angeles over an eighteen-month period, two factors related directly to gang cohesiveness.[10] The first was battles with rival gangs. The second was the school calendar. Gang cohesiveness rose just before every change in the school calendar—the beginning and end of each semester, and the beginning of Easter and Christmas holidays. This happened in spite of the fact that most of the active Latin members were not in school. It is the community rhythms occasioned by the school calendar that seem to be causal here. Gang activity reflected community tensions around school events. The rise in cohesiveness always took place just *before* the break in the calendar, an anticipatory function probably related both to youth excitement and to parental and community concern.

A second form of cycle might be called "epochal." Within any given city, and in separate areas of larger cities with widespread gang presence, gang activity seems often to move in cycles of as much as five and ten years. Thus, one sees peaks and valleys in reported gang activity over extended periods of time in patterns that relate directly and yet complexly to public policy initiatives about gangs.

Several points are of interest here. One is that the cycles are more locally than nationally recognizable. When Chicago gang activity is peaking, New York may be in decline. Cycles tend to be city-specific.

Also, cycles can differ between areas of a city. Recent examples in Los Angeles are most instructive. If one looks merely at the overall gang-related homicide rate in Los Angeles County, one sees a steady linear increase from 1982 through 1992—a straight line from a "low"[11] of 205 homicides to a high of 803. There is no cycle evident in this pattern, although an earlier (1980) peak of 351 homicides reminds us that the currently observed linear progression probably is part of a longer cycle whose down phase simply hasn't occurred yet. The progression cannot go on forever—gang homicides in the county currently account for almost 40 percent of *all* homicides.

But *within* Los Angeles county, major gang areas during this same period have seen distinct cycles. Well-documented and different lows and highs have occurred in individual cities such as El Monte, Compton, and Long Beach, and in broad regional areas such as East Los Angeles and South Central Los Angeles. Similar sub-area differences have been demonstrated by Block in Chicago,[12] and by numerous reports from the various boroughs of New York over several decades. Thus, in addition to city-specific cycles, there are sub-area and neighborhood cycles. These may be masked by reports that cover areas whose cycles cancel each other out in the aggregate.

For policy makers, such cycles can be important in determining where and when to intervene with social and enforcement programs; but more subtle is the danger that policy makers will confuse cycles with intimations of program success and failure. Let me start with the example of Philadelphia in the 1970s.

In the late 1960s, a special commission was appointed to deal with an alarming increase in gang killings in Philadelphia. Thirty gang-related deaths were recorded in 1968, while twenty-four more occurred in just the first six months of 1969.[13] To its credit, the commission became alerted to the problem of cycles when it sought information from New York, Baltimore, and Washington, D.C., which revealed gang activity declines in these cities in prior years. But understandably, the commission was concerned with the Philadelphia situation, which was on the upswing.

As the city slowly acknowledged and came to grips with the situation

over the next few years, specific developments occurred that speak directly
to the connection between natural cycles and program success. One of these
in particular has drawn attention because of its local impact and because of
its effect in other cities. I refer to the Crisis Intervention Network (CIN), a
creative program of gang surveillance, mobile street workers in cars dis-
patched by central phone to hot spots in the community, and active encouragement of gang parent groups.

The Philadelphia gang homicide figures peaked at forty-five recorded
cases in 1974, and decreased dramatically thereafter to almost zero within a
few years. CIN was widely credited with success for this enormous improvement. Yet there are problems in giving such credit for the cycle's downturn,
problems that have seldom received the same attention as the credit. For
instance, the downturn started before CIN was beginning its very first small
pilot program. CIN implementation *followed,* rather than preceded, the cycle
peak—not a good pattern for attributing the downturn to CIN.

Still, CIN may well have contributed to the continuation of the downturn.
The problem with assessing this contribution is that other things were going
on as well. The police department was cracking down on gangs, even using
blatantly illegal suppression tactics (as described by police officials in a
personal interview). Sister Falaka Fatah had initiated the widely praised
House of Umoja gang project. Other social agencies turned their attention to
the gang problem (in perhaps less direct fashion), and local neighborhood
and block clubs emerged—mothers' groups, grandmothers' groups—to
reassert local control over street gangs. Imagine a gathering of gang members
on the corner, when suddenly appears a group of grandmothers swinging
brooms and marching toward the corner. Few gangs I know will fail to get the
message and move on.

In sum, CIN alone cannot very well have initiated the cycle change. The
program may have contributed thereafter, but there is no way to assess this.
It also may *not* have contributed, but there is no way to assess this either. It
would have been foolish for CIN not to claim credit, and equally foolish for
policy makers to assume that claim was valid. But Los Angeles policy makers
did.

As Los Angeles approached a cycle peak in 1979, public officials visited
CIN in Philadelphia and became convinced of its "success." They transported
the program to Los Angeles. Little attention was paid to the fact that Philadelphia is a city of communities—block and neighborhood identities are widespread and viable—whereas Los Angeles has few communities recognized
as such by their residents. A program based on neighborhood identities was
adopted nonetheless, and was soon followed by the anticipated claim of
success.

From the 1980 peak of 351 homicides, a rapid decline showed 292 cases
in 1981 and 205 in 1982. The first claim for Community Youth Gang Services
(CYGS) success came from the member of the county board of supervisors

who was most instrumental in bringing the program to Los Angeles. His claim was made in mid-1980, *prior to the implementation* of even the first CYGS team activity in the county areas. More teams were activated later in 1980 and teams in the *city* of Los Angeles, awaiting separate city funding, did not begin to appear until a year later (mid-1981). So the declining gang homicide figures for 1981 and 1982 were for the shakedown and initial years of CYGS. As in Philadelphia, the initial decline can in no way be attributed to the program; the existence of the program can be attributed to the cycle incline, but that's not anyone's point.

At most, as in Philadelphia, the program in Los Angeles may have contributed to a continuation of the decline in 1982. But the program has survived from that day to this, in various forms yet always larger than any other undertaking of its kind in the nation. It has continued throughout the period of the current upward cycle, to the current level of 803 deaths in 1992. This raises the interesting if troublesome question, Why is it that claims of program impact always follow a decline in gang activity, but that never is a claim made about the *incline*? Every decline is like a new gold strike—claims are staked out, but abandoned on the upswing. I grant that my question is a rhetorical one, but it is one that reminds us to maintain a skeptical view of agencies and politicians who only report their efforts in good times.

This brings us to a third form of cycle, which we can call the "illusory cycle." These are likely non-cycles that nonetheless appear to be genuine through misleading reports or through cycles of reporting. It was widely noted in the late 1960s that gang activity had died down because gang-involved communities turned their attention to more political issues—civil rights issues of black power and la raza. This was the era of the Black Panthers and Brown Berets. Little empirical data have been offered to substantiate this decline, just as little research ever appeared a decade and more earlier to support the contention (of the early 1950s) that gang activity had been sapped by an epidemic cycle of drug use among potential gang members. Walter Miller stated the point very succinctly: "Youth gangs aren't 'back.' They never went away, except in the media."[14]

Spergel has noted recently that figures for numbers of gangs and numbers of gang members vary widely in reports from different sources. He also cites such places as Fort Wayne and Louisville as yielding dramatically different figures over periods of just a few years.[15] These could reflect genuine gang changes. They could also reflect different sources, different data collection or recording procedures, even different definitions of a gang. Let me cite just two examples from my book *The American Street Gang*:[16]

A study of gang member migration[17] included interviews with police gang experts in hundreds of U.S. cities. In one of these, the expert listed 1986 as the year that gangs first appeared there. The city is Boston, one of the most thoroughly studied gang cities in America—in the mid-1950s!

In a series of interviews with police departments in 1991, I received denials of any gang presence in a number of them. Within a year of those interviews, questionnaires sent to them as part of the gang migration study revealed cities that had changed their response. It's not that gangs had suddenly appeared; in each case, the reported year of gang onset was prior to the interview response claiming no gangs. The onset dates were from one to five years prior to the interview and, in one case, as early as the 1960s. There were seven such cities—not a large number, but enough to suggest that cycle existence can be confounded by sources of information.

Another example is revealed by our recent research on the proliferation of cities with gangs. Most comments about the 1950s and 1960s suggest that there were perhaps a dozen of these; New York, Chicago, Philadelphia, Boston, Los Angeles, San Francisco, El Paso, and San Antonio were the best known. But now we know there were about sixty such cities before 1960. Smaller cities, cities without research on gangs, and cities in a denial phase simply weren't part of our common knowledge.

The 1960s added over 40 cities for a total of at least 100. The 1970s, following the period of the Vietnam War and massive urban unrest, have generally been noted as a quiescent period, when the gang problem was reduced or, at worst, remained stable. However, we now know that another 80 new gang cities emerged during the 1970s. The period seemed quiescent because media attention had focused elsewhere, as had that of researchers and funding agencies. Thus, by 1979 there were at least 180 gang cities, and the trend had hardly started.

In the decade of the 1980s, the proliferation of gang cities slowly achieved some recognition but not with any clarity. There were reports that gang cities might now number in the low hundreds, whereas in fact there were at least 800 by 1991, and perhaps as many as 1,100.[18] This underreporting is easily understandable; until 1992 no one had undertaken a thorough national assessment.

Even more striking is the marked diffusion and acceptance of the claim, made by some major enforcement officials and a few academics and reified by the media, that the 1980s gang proliferation was caused by the crack cocaine explosion and gang involvement in crack distribution. Careful research has failed to document this cause-and-effect relationship. Simple logic would do so as well:

- Crack has been distributed principally by blacks, yet black gangs constitute only half or so of all those in America.

- Crack first appeared on a national scale in 1985 and increased thereafter, whereas many of the gang cities were established prior to that date and many others prior to the time crack finally got to them in the late 1980s.

• Many gang cities did not—and still do not—have much of a crack prob-lem. Some heavily involved crack cities do not have street gangs.

In other words, the attribution of the cycle upswing in gang-involved cities to the emergence of crack cocaine can be at best only a partially valid attribution. Many of the reports are factually incorrect, serving needs other than accurate public information. The attribution has also led to inadvisable, even some absurd, policy recommendations and programs. Not the least of these is the involvement of the Federal Bureau of Investigation; the Bureau of Alcohol, Tobacco, and Firearms; and the Drug Enforcement Agency in street gang control on the assumption that street gangs are of the same character as the organized drug distribution rings with which these agencies are familiar. They are not, by a long shot, of the same character.

Cycles and Recent Changes

In none of the foregoing do I mean to downplay the importance of significant changes that have featured the world of street gangs. Indeed, I find some of these changes to be astounding in their scope, and very challenging for those who would venture to control or reverse them. Five somewhat intercon-nected changes deserve attention: the increase in drug distribution involve-ment, the expansion of the age range of gang members, the greater variety of gang structures, increased violence (or lethality of violence), and the proliferation of gangs. Generally, the increases in each case are evident in comparing the 1950s and 1960s, when gang research itself showed a cycle peak, and the 1980s and early 1990s, when a new research cycle took place (one that seemingly has not yet peaked).

1. Drug distribution.   Street gang members—many of them, not all of them—have been involved in drug *use* for as long as researchers have been observing their behavior. If alcohol use were included, usage rates would be substantially higher yet. But normally this drug use is casual and episodic, a matter of friends buying small amounts from friends. Drug use has been part of the larger "cafeteria-style" involvement in a wide variety of offense behav-iors among gang members. Drug *selling* among members has been part of this varied pattern, rather than a special focus.

There was nothing in this pattern to provide special openings for gang intervention or control programs. *Members* sold and distributed drugs to some extent, but *gangs* did not. The emergence in the late eighties of *new, drug-selling* gangs has created a new cycle—not a new *street* gang cycle—with implications for control measures. Let's go down the list of drug gang characteristics on page 219 as they compare with those of street gangs:

- As a group focused on drug *business,* the drug gang is more vulnerable to undercover operations and to control by interfering with *demand,* that is, drug customers.

- As smaller and more cohesive structures, they are more readily targeted and delimited by law enforcement intelligence operations.

- Their more centralized leadership invites police and prosecution strategies that concentrate efforts on the few—crime enforcement takes precedence over general gang suppression.

- Market-defined roles and interpersonal loyalties make it more difficult to "turn" drug gang members (establish informants); yet, once turned, individual members can, by virtue of the gang networks, lead investigators to a more thorough dismantling of the gang structure.

- Since territories have more to do with sales markets than with common residence, drug gangs tend to be less ingrained in the local neighborhood. Local communities are less tied to drug sellers than to resident street gang members and are therefore more readily mobilized against the presence and the threat of the drug gang.

- Finally, older average membership makes drug gang members less protected by juvenile statutes and more susceptible to the harsher penalties of adult criminals. It also increases the likelihood that deterrent practices will work better, in that the older, market-oriented drug gang member works on a calculated, rational paradigm more than his young street gang counterpart. This is, at least, a reasonable hypothesis.

Clearly, it would be useful to report the level of drug dealing now prevalent among street gangs, but relevant research has not been undertaken in any systematic fashion. The best guess is that this level remains part and parcel of overall gang crime involvement—part of the pattern, but not generally a prominent part.

By the same token, it would be useful to know how prevalent the new drug distribution gangs are, but relevant research is not yet available. Thus, it is also true that we can't gauge special violence levels associated with drug gangs. While a few neighborhood-specific or city-specific studies have appeared, they were undertaken in order to illustrate drug gang factors; they cannot speak to prevalence or representativeness.

In sum, to the extent that distinctive drug distribution gangs have emerged (and they have; the argument is about their pervasiveness), then this is a *new* cycle whose control might be more in our hands than in theirs. A combination of community mobilization and targeted enforcement activities could very conceivably reduce the pervasiveness and longevity of what is now an upward trajectory of the cycle. My strongest caveat is that we must remain sensitive to the differences between street gangs and drug gangs.

2. Proliferation of street gangs.   As noted earlier, the proliferation of cities experiencing the emergence of street gangs has shown no sign of abating to this date. There will *have* to be a cycle of gang proliferation, but so far we see only an extended upswing. The Gang Cities Onset Chart (Figure 10.1) rather dramatically depicts the upswing of this cycle; more than half of the gang cities emerged after 1985. I posit two sets of factors as principally to blame for this pattern, neither of which is easily within our control. The first is the spread and deepening of the urban underclass throughout many of our cities; the second is the diffusion of "gang culture" nationally via the news and entertainment media.

More specifics on both these factors are presented in *The American Street Gang*. In the space available here, I can only note the obvious. If persistent and pervasive poverty, if increased racial segregation and density, if the decrease in available social services, and if the increase in working class unemployment all continue to deepen in our inner cities and take hold in our working class suburbs, we will sow more seeds of the street gang response. Local youth will depend less on what adult society has to offer, and more upon each other. Reducing street gang cycles and violence can't be accomplished by police suppression, court crackdowns, or legislative hardening alone; nor can it be accomplished by street-level intervention programs, nor by community mobilization, nor even by early prevention efforts, so long as our cities are allowed to become the residue of our civilization. Control without long-term prevention will at best give short-term satisfaction; it cannot dam up the gang spawning stream.

FIGURE 10.1
Gang Cities Onset Chart, Cumulative Numbers

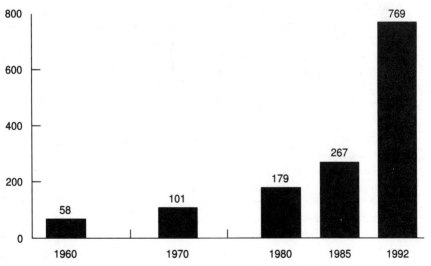

Now add to this a side effect of one of our society's most prideful developments, the communications industry, and we have a paradox indeed. Thanks to movies (*Colors, Boyz 'N the Hood, American Me*), and to TV news and documentaries on gangs and to youth-oriented TV shows on MTV and other channels, gang "style" has been diffused to youth across the country. Millions of youngsters now learn how to dress, talk, act, and even feel like gang members. It doesn't take a big city ghetto to teach about gang life; our media carry it to every vulnerable corner. To attempt to control this diffusion is to confront some of our most sacred democratic traditions—freedom of speech, press, expression. Voluntary controls, unless severe, won't stem the communication of gang styles. Even our police and research experts, funded at times by federal and state agencies, contribute to this cultural diffusion through lectures, demonstrations, seminars, and workshops on gang behavior, given to other officials, schoolteachers, and parent groups. The depiction of gang life is a commodity, volunteered and marketed to every at-risk and gang-involved sector of our society. There is, in effect, no control on this diffusion process.

3. Age distribution.   As might be expected, the proliferation of street gangs increases the likelihood of a wider range of some gang characteristics. The age distribution is one of these. In earlier decades, the terms "delinquent gang" or "juvenile gang" were appropriate because gangs were predominantly young. Age ranges from eleven to twenty and age means around sixteen were commonplace. Now, however, it is not uncommon to find gangs whose memberships include many twenty-year-olds, some thirty-year-olds, and even a few forty-year-olds. This pattern tends to be seen in chronic gang cities, while the newly emergent cities of the past ten years or so often report more gangs with a restricted adolescent membership.

This expansion of the age range has implications for gang control. The higher ages may well reflect urban underclass problems of unemployment and increased minority density. Older members may well be more criminally hardened and sophisticated, and thus less amenable to various forms of social intervention. They may also be more inclined to turn to violence for instrumental purposes. There is little in this gang age expansion that bodes well for gang control.

4. Structural forms.   Also associated with gang proliferation is an increase in the variety of modal gang structures. Drug gangs are one such modal form. In addition, there are perhaps larger proportions of young, age-homogeneous adolescent gangs, especially in the newer gang cities. There are some ethnic patterns as well.

One of these latter are Vietnamese gangs and some other Southeast Asian groups of a similar style: small, mobile, property-crime-oriented, preying on their own ethnic communities, and using violence in instrumental rather than expressive (gang rivalry) fashions.[19]

Another disturbing pattern is the rise of white supremacist or skinhead groups. They don't accord well with the earlier description of street gangs, but in many instances may still merit the general gang terminology. [20] These groups, given their very special hate messages, raise difficult ethical (and constitutional) questions when one considers intervention techniques, and they are not rare, appearing now in perhaps 10 percent of our gang-involved cities.

This much is clear; the change in age distribution and the greater variety of gang forms that have accompanied gang proliferation increase the importance of understanding *differences* in gang structures before considering forms of gang intervention. *The* American gang is not a single structure justifying a single or simplistic approach to control. *The* American gang must now be understood as a generic term begging for careful differentiation— unless, of course, these structural changes are merely the upswing of a massive cycle which will soon go down again. I doubt the likelihood of this, but in the spirit of this chapter, one must be alert not to consider the *present* to be a necessary vector into the future.

5. Street gang violence.   Street gang activity, as noted earlier, goes through various cycles in both time and space. Such cycles seldom occasion a great deal of concern—consider the very moderate public responses of the 1960s and 1970s—unless they contain highly visible components of violence, especially violence against people other than gang members. It is the violent cycles that arouse major response, usually in the form of a suppressive response from legislation and law enforcement officials. I know of no data that demonstrate a reduction of gang violence—a down cycle—as a result of such responses, although anecdotes to that effect are not uncommon.

Yet gang violence does cycle; it ebbs and flows in response to something. One of the questions I am most commonly asked is why gang violence has just increased or just decreased. I have no good answer, no answer based upon properly collected data; but let me offer a hypothesis about the down-cycles, the ebbs in the unfathomable pattern.

My hypothesis is that reductions in street gang violence are not the result of various forms of community or justice system response. Rather, they are responses by gang members to their own relative state of activity. It's as if there were a social biofeedback system. I've seen this process at work during my early days as a street observer of gang life. Gangs can in fact get over their heads in their rivalries, escalating the intergang violence to the point of shared anxiety and fear. I posit this as a response to their "relative state of activity" because in the sixties it took far fewer changes than today to evoke the generalized fear response. One *can* get inured to ambient levels of violence, such that new plateaus must be reached before the next response kicks in. In 1991 alone, well over 2,000 people died in gang-related incidents in the United States. The proliferation of ready-to-hand firearms in the past decade has, if anything, accelerated the problem. Over 90 percent of gang-related homicides are caused by guns—usually handguns. These guns are pervasive in gang areas. Any gang member can avail himself of a good weapon in a matter of minutes. Listening to gang members these days reveals a fatalism and an acceptance of firearm resolutions of conflict that require a far higher *absolute* level of danger to evoke the fear response and subsequent violence subsidence. For each new plateau, it is the *relative* violence increase that yields the subsequent reduction. Our intervention programs, mounted belatedly toward the top of the new plateau, give us false confidence that it is we, the interveners, who have produced the reduction.

If this hypothesis has any merit, it says that increases in gang violence carry their own inevitable seeds of self-response and violence reduction.[21] But it says nothing about when this will happen, or by what manifest mechanism (reduction in gang participation, search for alternative activities, calls for gang truces, and so on). It also suggests, as will the cohesion hypothesis to be discussed later in this chapter, that our best interventions may be those aimed not to *trigger* violence reduction but to reinforce it when it begins to occur. As an example, the suggestion might be not to try to initiate gang truces from outside but to reinforce any that are indigenous, gang-initiated efforts.

This may be the lesson of the truces begun by Los Angeles gang members just before the Rodney King riots in 1992 and reinforced by various community groups (but not the police) thereafter. In this instance, various factions of the Crips and Bloods in the general area that was to contain the flash points of the riots came together pretty much on their own to consider reducing the continually accelerating intergang violence. "Unity" parties were held in several housing projects in the Watts area of South Central Los Angeles.[22]

According to one activist involved in the initiation of the truce, it resulted when gang members in one of the hottest areas "agreed they were tired of the warfare and the violence."[23] This is in line with the hypothesis noted earlier; and for some months following the riot, the truce held. It received public attention from the media and support from local black politicians and community leaders, including Louis Farrakhan of the Nation of Islam.

But the mechanics remained in large part in the hands of gang members. The unity parties were theirs (though under heavy surveillance and some harassment from the police). Police reports, sometimes with pleasure and sometimes with much skepticism, suggested that the period of the truce *in the area directly involved* saw a significant reduction in intergang violence. In the two police districts most involved, gang-related homicides dropped by 31 percent and 43 percent respectively during the year, while they continued to rise in other, non-truce-involved areas.

This down-cycle could be truce-initiated, or it could be yet another example of a spurious finding—the reduction and the truce being merely two facets of a more general phenomenon and not causally related. But the coincidence is worth noting, as is the general context that, over many years, truces arranged by outsiders have generally been ineffective (or have even backfired).

6. Cycles and recent changes summarized.   With respect to changes in gang characteristics, it might be thought that the cyclical nature of gang activity would yield a picture of little linear change over time—that is, that the back-and-forth swings of the pendulum would cancel each other out. But this is not the case. Through all the periodic cycles, gangs and gang problems have grown. The cycles end at higher plateaus, on average, as if the pendulum seldom reverts to its original lower level, while often reaching a higher level when on the upswing.

Thus, over several decades, the upper age limit has increased; the variety of minority ethnic gangs has increased; the variety of gang structures has increased; associated gang violence has increased. On the basis of our own national assessments, the United States by the end of 1992 contained around 9,000 street gangs with total membership at about 400,000. This latter figure is of course a tiny portion of our total gang-age population, but since it is concentrated in certain sections of our towns and cities, it has considerable impact in those sections.

Further, most gang-involved cities have ten or fewer gangs and fewer than 500 gang members; the bulk of the proliferation is proliferation of a relatively small problem. Yet if the current cycle is still on the upswing, then many of these less serious situations could contain the seeds of larger growths. The current cycle of gang proliferation and its associated violence is unlikely to revert to the level of the 1960s, so serious attention must be paid to developing alternative approaches to cycle interruption.

Cycles, Cohesiveness, and Control

In my research notes, in reports from other scholars, and in news reports over the years, I count literally scores of gang cycles: New York, Los Angeles, Louisville, Fort Wayne, Philadelphia, Baltimore, San Francisco, and so on—the list is extensive. It is clear by now that street gangs do cycle, gang areas do cycle, gang cities do cycle. Cycles need not be national, or regional, or city-wide. Gangs come and go; gang activity waxes and wanes, including the violence that so effectively draws our attention.

It seems almost as clear, as one reviews gang intervention efforts subject to respectable evaluations, and as one reviews unevaluated claims of intervention successes, that gang intervention attempts fail more often than not. What *seem* to be successes in reducing gang activity are too easily explained by other factors, while the claimants remain silent on the failures. My tentative conclusion has to be that we have not found ways to intervene effectively in most street gang situations.

What are we to do, then? Left to itself, street gang violence apparently will expand and contract on its own, reaching higher plateaus of severity as gang proliferation continues. The standard liberal and conservative answers have not proved particularly useful to date, partly because they have seldom been effectively implemented on other than short-term bases, but also because they are determined more by political philosophy than by knowledge or understanding of gang dynamics.

Liberally oriented gang interventions have been of several varieties, including broad attempts at community organization, more focused street work programs designed to transform specific gang structures, and the targeting of individual gang members for social and therapeutic help.[24]

Community organization has included interagency collaborations as well as empowerment of local residents. Since street gangs are seen as byproducts of community disorganization, the expected impact of community organization is, by design, indirect. Evidence suggests, however, that it is so indirect as to be negligible.

Street work programs, by contrast, are very direct. Workers assigned to active street gangs use their personal skills to aid gang members and their families via court appearances, employment contacts, educational help, individual and group counseling, and other immediate interventions. Carefully evaluated street work programs in Boston, Chicago, and Los Angeles have revealed the considerable success that can be achieved in reaching gang members in this fashion: members returned to school or tutored; jobs or job training facilitated; parents counseled; court interventions managed; intergang disputes deferred temporarily. All these intermediate goal attainments have been realized. Yet the same street work programs also reveal an absence of impact on gang crime, and in some instances an increase in gang crime. The mechanism for this latter seems to be that active gang programming inadvertently leads to increased gang cohesiveness and size, and this increase in turn yields higher levels of gang-related crime. This is a theme to which I will return shortly.

Finally, it should be clear that no matter how effective individual social and therapeutic help may be, it can have little impact on gang structures, which contain anywhere from a score to several hundred gang members at a time. Nor can it have an effect on the social surroundings in which gangs are spawned. Attempts to change the orientation and behavior of gang leaders specifically, thereby affecting gang structures and their neighborhood contexts, have also proved to be illusory. Gang "leaders" are seldom as influential as believed, and gang structures are too loose-knit to be seriously changed by intervening in the lives of the few youths designated as leaders by outside observers.

In short, typical liberal-based gang interventions have failed to manifest much utility. They appeal to our best instincts, but are too indirect, too narrow, or else produce boomerang effects by producing increased gang cohesiveness.

Failures of such programs, plus the burgeoning gang problem and increased intolerance of gang violence, has in the past fifteen years or so produced a series of conservative-based interventions. These have included legislative crackdowns (tougher sentences for gang members, redefining gang activities to increase vulnerability to law enforcement), use of civil abatement procedures, enhanced prosecution efforts, and various forms of police suppression (interagency task forces, large-scale neighborhood sweeps, selective enforcement or harassment, and so on). Some confusion of antinarcotics and antigang suppression has also developed.

The assumptions underlying these conservative approaches are generally those of deterrence theory. Swifter, more certain, and more severe punishments applied to gang members are thought to incapacitate and deter them, and also discourage other youth from participating in gang behavior. Unfortunately, little credible evidence has been adduced to support this position, and the rapid escalation of gang existence and gang violence from the late 1980s to the mid-1990s clearly supplies no support. In fact, there is good reason to believe that suppression approaches can produce precisely the same effect as the earlier liberal approaches—namely, increased gang cohesion. Street gangs tend to be oppositional:[25] they thrive on enemies, be these their rival gangs or the police. The more they feel pressure, the tighter they are likely to become. If true, it is a bit ironic that liberal and conservative approaches may produce the same adverse results, albeit inadvertently.

What can be offered instead? Certainly community empowerment makes sense, if only because residents have a right to live without abject fear in their own homes and streets. Further, a community mobilized against control by gangs will have more legitimacy in the eyes of gang members than do the police, the occupying force.

Certainly every effort should be made to reduce the persistent and pervasive poverty that defines the urban underclass. This is a valuable goal in itself, no matter what its long-term effect on reducing the proliferation of gang structures.

Gang worker programs, on the other hand, are candidates for elimination. I believe there is no way that targeting gang structures for attention can avoid reinforcing those very structures. *Street* workers, not allocated to gangs but to youth generally, would remain a legitimate way to reduce the gaps in positive youth-adult relationships.

Similarly, I would eliminate police and prosecutorial programs that are specifically *gang*-based, *gang*-targeted. We already have the laws needed to respond to the acts of individual gang members. Adding the gang aura to these defeats the deterrent purpose by adding to gang identity, to the psychological benefit to be derived from one's gang reputation. Gang suppression, in other words, is too likely to lead to gang enhancement.

It's hard to tell gang workers *not* to do what comes naturally to them, or to tell police officers *not* to do what comes naturally to them. But this issue of gang cohesiveness is critical. I believe it has as much to do with individual gang cycles as any single factor. Street gangs are not "normal" groups. As noted earlier, their dynamics have reached beyond a tipping point, to where gang members reinterpret our actions in terms that reinforce their bonds to one another. Services offered are proof of how "bad" they are; suppression efforts reinforce gang identity; publicity feeds gang reputations.

This sense of internal cohesion is not strong, unless it is reinforced from the outside. The internal sources of cohesion are weaker than the external sources. One of the latter, not discussed above, may be the most pervasive of all—racism. It should not escape notice that the vast majority of gang members are of racial and ethnic minority status. Even when gangs were predominantly Caucasian in the decades before the World War II, they tended to be of minority status—first- or second-generation Poles, Germans, Italian, east Europeans, Irish, and so on. Color may have changed—minority status has not. The sense of being part of a larger minority group reinforces the cohesiveness of the street gang that is itself homogeneously minority. Where minority status, urban and even suburban segregation, poverty, and poor social service are all tied together, they feed one another.

Direct gang intervention in such circumstances cannot fairly be expected to produce much long-term effect. Understanding and using gang dynamics is a starting point. Understanding and using our society's dynamics is far more important.

EDWARD DONNERSTEIN
AND DANIEL LINZ

11

THE MEDIA

In this chapter we attempt to answer questions most often posed to us as scholars of mass media and psychology concerning the relationship between exposure to media violence and aggressive behavior. Often those who inquire about media violence frame the question about its effects in an "either/or" proposition. Either television violence causes violence on the street and in the home, or television is a mirror held up to an already violent society. Our goal in this chapter is to correct or confirm beliefs about television violence effects. In addition, we will report on the specific studies that have examined the question of whether media violence is related to violent crime.

In this chapter we will explore the perceptions of the American public and policy makers about the impact of media violence on behavior. We examine the types of mass media images that may be most problematic and the theoretical models attempting to account for a connection between violence exposure and behavior. Finally, we will assess the empirical evidence of such a relationship and policy solutions to the problem of mass media violence. In the end, the answer to the question of whether TV violence is the cause of violence or a mirror held up to a violent society will be yes. By that we mean that both assertions are true. Media violence as a form of entertainment is attractive to many members of our society, many of whom are already predisposed toward aggression. Media violence is also a causal factor in the stimulation of violent behavior including crime.

Violence in American Society

As a nation we rank first among all developed countries in the world in homicides. In 1992 there were over 1.9 million violent crimes in the United States, including 25,000 homicides. Among individuals fifteen to twenty-four years old, homicide is the second leading cause of death, and for African American youth it is the primary cause of death. In the United States, the homicide rate is increasing at six times the population rate, with little or no end in sight (American Psychological Association 1993). What accounts for these alarming trends?

Violent and criminal behavior is the result of a multiplicity of factors. Throughout this book gang membership, drug and alcohol use, gun availability, poverty, racism, and other factors are explored as contributors to violence. In recent years the American Psychological Association (1993), National Academy of Sciences (Reiss and Roth 1993), and Centers for Disease Control (1991) have examined the causes of violent behavior. These groups have concluded that violence is determined by multiple factors. Permeating each of these investigations, however, is the idea that the mass media are not an innocent bystander to the problem of violence but that they contribute to violent behavior. This conclusion is based on careful and critical readings of the social science research collected over the past forty years.

The American Public's View of Mass Media Violence

Public opinion data suggest that Americans are very concerned about the amount and impact of violence in the mass media. In a 1989 poll conducted by the Associated Press for Media General Research, 82 percent of the respondents indicated that they thought movies were too violent, and 72 percent found television too violent. When asked if this violence is harmful to society, 80 percent believed that it is, with 47 percent seeing media violence as "very harmful"—double the percentage of the early 1980s. Likewise, a poll conducted by the *Times Mirror* indicated that, while 53 percent of those polled in the early 1970s believed that media violence "desensitizes" people, by 1993 this figure had grown to 78 percent (*Los Angeles Times* 1993). This poll found that the American public is more troubled by violence than by other aspects of film or program content. Twice as many people reported being "upset" with violence in the mass media than with other content categories such as sex, nudity, profane language, or drug use. Over half of the respondents said they would support governmental intervention to limit television and movie violence.

Media violence is not equally unacceptable to all viewers, however.

Many viewers like it, or are at least unconcerned about it. The *Times Mirror* poll showed a pronounced generation gap in tolerance for violence. Violence tends to be popular among young adults. Those under thirty are far more likely to be heavy consumers of violent programming and movies. Seventy-four percent of those under thirty reported heavy consumption of violence, and 50 percent of the thirty- to forty-nine-year-olds fell into that category. Only 20 percent of the fifty-and-older adults reported heavy violence viewing. Younger adults also report being far less bothered by violence on television and are less likely to feel that violence is harmful to society than are older Americans. They are also less prone to believe that televised violence is itself a cause of real life violence.

Does this mean we are raising a generation of viewers desensitized to violent media? A recent survey of children suggests not, at least among *selected* groups of younger viewers. A recent survey of children who view Nickelodeon found that these children perceived television violence to be a serious problem (Reynolds 1993). Eighty percent of the children believed that there was too much violence on television, and 91 percent found real violence more disturbing than cartoon violence. Most interesting was the finding that 89 percent believed that warning labels should be put on shows that contain violence. In a national poll of children age ten to seventeen (a group who reports that the media is an important influence on their lives) 59 percent indicated they found television too violent, and 67 percent said movies were too violent (*Newsweek* 1993).

Defining Violence in the Mass Media

Much of the debate on media violence has concentrated upon the impact of "televised" violence. For many individuals this has referred strictly to portrayals transmitted through the television sets in people's homes and has involved programming on the major broadcast networks, ABC, CBS, and NBC. Television is much different in the mid-1990s, however, from the way it was a decade or so earlier. Today most viewers have access to cable television and numerous channels. Many of these more specialized channels are devoted nearly exclusively to movies or other forms of entertainment traditionally found outside the broadcast television environment. Children and adults are now exposed to vastly different types of programs since the advent of cable television than that available on commercial television. The introduction of the video cassette recorder (VCR) has also changed the types of media we view in our own homes. Children now have access to depictions they would not have been exposed to via commercial television, movie theaters, or even over cable.

When we consider the question of media violence we must consider the fact that children may not just be viewing what we as adults remember as "television." Recent studies have indicated that children with VCR and/or cable access have seen more R-rated films than their non–cable/VCR counterparts (Donnerstein, Slaby, and Eron 1994). The fact that many of these films would not be shown on commercial television in the first place—or if they were shown would be edited to exclude extreme instances of violence and sex—suggests that children are being exposed to more graphic violence, sexual content, and "mature" themes than ever before. Consequently, when we discuss the effects of "televised" violence we must include all the types of mass media viewers may encounter, including R-rated and X-rated fare that now routinely appears on the screen in many homes.

Precisely defining *violence* for scientific study and safely generalizing research findings beyond particular research domains to be useful to policy debates has also proved to be troublesome. As several legal scholars have pointed out (for example, Krattenmaker and Powe [1978]), to be useful as the basis of criminal justice policy, studies of the causes of violence must rest upon a definition that considers several social/normative concerns. The researcher should ideally take as an objectively observable conception of violence behavior that produces social concern. Critics have asked: Is violence the apparent infliction of pain? Must the infliction of pain be intentional? Is it violent to inflict pain on an inanimate object? Must the pain be intended to produce a net harmful effect on the victim? Must the person inflicting the pain be unauthorized by law to do so? Is emotional aggressiveness between people an element of antisocial violence? These questions pose problems for the interpretation of the results of many studies of media violence. Without agreement on a definition of violence in media portrayals, the meaning of violent acts measured after subjects have been exposed to the media makes the usefulness of empirical research questionable.

The majority of investigations of the effects of media violence have relied on laboratory experiments. In the typical experiment subjects are exposed to media violence and then asked to punish a fellow subject (actually a confederate of the experimenter) for inadequate performance on a task by administering electric shocks or other aversive stimuli. In other studies researchers have examined willingness to intervene or emotional responsiveness to subsequent aggressive behavior after subjects have viewed violence.

Critics such as Krattenmaker and Powe contend that researchers have studied acts of violence under somewhat mutually inconsistent and debatable definitions of the term. In early studies Albert Bandura and his colleagues treated hitting a Bobo doll in a setting where doll hitting is not subject to any sanction as violent behavior (Bandura 1971). If one were to substitute a live clown for the doll the definition of violence being employed would change. The Buss Aggression Machine used in early laboratory studies of aggressive behavior only *apparently* inflicts pain. Many who used it thought they were producing net positive effects for the "victim." A few experimenters have indicated that giving shocks in an experimental setting is not perceived as aggressive by participants unless the individual giving the shocks is viewed as violating some accepted norm. Finally, in the most important of the correlational studies (discussed later) researchers relied either on the interviewee's own subjective, unexplained definitions of violence or on the interviewer's own concepts, including mere verbal aggression (Huessman and Eron 1986).

These criticisms do not mean that the studies are invalid. Instead they mean that any individual study by itself cannot be considered conclusive because many people may disagree with the definition of violence employed in selecting materials for study. The existence of a variety of studies employing slightly different definitions of violence but arriving at the same conclusion strengthens our confidence in the findings.

There is, according to the critics, an objective and determinable definition of violence that includes the following: the purposeful, illegal infliction of pain for personal gain or gratification that is intended to harm the victim and is accomplished in spite of societal sanctions against it.

Contrary to the critics' assumptions, researchers have generally agreed on a definition of violence that embraces many of the critics' concerns. One leading researcher in the field of aggression, Robert Baron, has summarized the definition acceptable to most social scientists and implicit in most research on the effects of televised violence: "any form of behavior directed toward the goal of harm: or injuring another living being who is motivated to avoid such treatment" (Baron 1977).

Both definitions include the notion that to be objectively defined, aggression must be some sort of goal-directed or purposeful behavior. Both definitions assume that people are motivated to avoid it on the individual level or to devise sanctions at the group level to prohibit it.

The question for researchers and critics alike is, To what extent do the activities portrayed in the media and the behavior of subjects measured after exposure to these media depictions conform to the definition of violence agreed upon by both social scientists and members of the legal/policy-making community? The researcher who attempts experimental work in the domain of media violence and aggressive behavior cannot ethically devise an experimental manipulation that will cause a subject actually to inflict harm upon another. Thus, social science research is continually subject to the criticism that it is impossible to investigate adequately the effects of media violence as just defined because it requires that the experimenter create exactly the kind of behavior that (1) no researcher in a laboratory may seek to cause and (2) no real-world observer can hope to witness systematically.

While behavioral scientists cannot inflict actual harm in the laboratory, scientists in this area are not prohibited from leading subjects to *believe* that they are actually inflicting harm on another person, as long as the subject is thoroughly debriefed after participating in an experiment. This is important for two reasons: First, there is good evidence that subjects in laboratory aggression experiments do in fact perceive themselves as inflicting actual harm although they recognize that the harm is of a rather uncommon variety (such as administering shocks or blasts of noxious noise). Second, although the violent act committed by the laboratory subject is rather unusual, it is far from meaningless or inconsequential to the aggressor. Intending to hit someone with an axe handle but resorting instead to a baseball bat because axes are less available does not change the meaning of the aggressive act. It is the meaning—the idea of inflicting harm, the intention behind the aggressive act, whether it be shock, pricking someone with a pin, or shoving someone—that can be generalized from the laboratory to the real world.

The basic point here is that the generalizability of laboratory results to real-world aggressive acts does not depend solely on the physical similarity between the aggressive activity performed in the laboratory and an aggressive act outside the laboratory. The validity of a laboratory study—the degree to which its results can be generalized to the real world—depends upon the meaning that subjects assign to the situation they are in. Available evidence points strongly to the fact that subjects define the act of giving someone an electric shock as aggressive, as a means of inflicting harm. Second, there is a heightened tendency to inflict harm as a result of exposure to violent media depictions. There is good reason, then, to believe that people exposed to violent media depictions outside the laboratory will exhibit a greater tendency toward harmful behavior.

The validity of an experiment does not hinge on whether or not the setting has surface realism (Berkowitz and Donnerstein 1982). It is quite appropriate to generalize from the results of a laboratory experiment on aggression to real-world aggression if we can be sure that persons inside and outside the laboratory assign the same meaning to events around them. In the case of research on television violence it is the meaning the subject imparts to aggression performed in the laboratory that can be generalized outside the laboratory. For example, Malamuth (1986) has shown that males exposed to sexual violence in a laboratory experiment and later asked to administer shocks (1) knows that his victim is female, (2) understands that the shocks are painful, and (3) believes that his female victim is receiving them.

Variables Contributing to the Media Violence and Aggression Relationship

It is often asked, What kinds of media violence cause violent or aggressive behavior? Are cartoons likely to have the same effect as *Rambo?* Does a broadcast of an NFL game result in the same effects as *Die Hard?* Research has not generally proceeded on a genre by genre basis. Instead, researchers have attempted to identify characteristics that vary across many television and movie genres. They have then examined the impact of these variables in experimental laboratory studies.

The best way to describe the effects of exposure to violent media is to say that for some people, some of the time, exposure to violence will result in aggressive behavior (also see Donnerstein, Linz, and Penrod [1987]). There are many environmental and personal factors operating to restrain the individual from actually engaging in aggressive behavior. The main effects of observed violence for the average viewer most of the time probably are aggressive ideas that might come to mind for a brief period. These can result in possible harsh judgments of others, or hostile words that might be uttered to some offending party soon after exposure. The likelihood of actual violence among most viewers is very low. On the other hand, if conditions are right, exposure to media violence may lead to aggressive behavior. Aggressive behavior following a violent media depiction will most often depend on both exposure to the depiction itself and a combination of individual viewer characteristics and features of the environment.

Whether or not a person will choose to expose himself or herself to media violence in the first place might depend on several factors, such as prior histories of personal aggressiveness or apprehension about crime and violence that may be alleviated by exposure to crime shows in which "good guys" win. The approval or disapproval of media violence by fellow observers also appears to play a role in whether or not aggressive reactions are displayed or restrained. The mere availability of a victim after seeing violence, as well as more subtle victim characteristics such as similarity between available targets after exposure and victims portrayed in the media event, may influence subsequent aggressiveness. Even simple attentional factors, such as whether the viewer attends primarily to the violence depicted in the story or focuses instead on a myriad of other scenes and stimuli present in most media depictions, will determine if an individual will behave aggressively after exposure.

Other research has pointed to demographic characteristics such as age and sex that may affect aggressive responding after exposure to media violence (see Huston et al. [1992]). Investigators have noted, for example, that older children are more likely to comprehend violent TV shows in terms of the "aggressor's" intentions or motivations rather than in terms of raw outcomes. In other words, if the character meant well but the result nonetheless was violent, older children will not necessarily become more aggressive following the depiction. Young children, who are less able to make these subtle distinctions, seem to respond in "all or nothing" fashion to violence, becoming increasingly aggressive no matter what the content of the violence depiction. On the other hand, older viewers, such as college-age subjects, may be especially reactive to certain types of portrayals (for example, revenge scenarios) and not particularly aggressive after viewing others. Males are more likely than females to show increased aggression after exposure to a violent film, although these differences may be diminishing because of changes in the pattern of socialization for girls in our society.

In a recent review of the media violence research literature, Comstock and his associates have systematically categorized the conditions that tend to produce aggressive behavior following exposure to media violence (Comstock and Strausburger 1990; Comstock and Paik 1991). Four general factors contribute to aggressive behavior following exposure to violent media. The first is efficacy—whether the aggressive behavior seen on the screen is rewarded or punished. The second is normativeness—the degree to which violence is justified or lacks negative consequences for the perpetrators. The third is pertinence—the similarity or relevance of the media scene or situation to the viewer's social context. Finally, the susceptibility of the viewer to the media depiction is an important contributory factor. Does the viewer become aroused or frustrated easily? Is the viewer predisposed to aggression? From these four dimensions, Comstock has derived fifteen situations where aggressive behavior is likely to follow from exposure to violence in the media. Findings from laboratory experimental studies support the connection between media violence and aggressive behavior in these situations. Aggressive behavior is more likely to follow violent media depictions if

1. Those who act aggressively are rewarded or not punished (see Bandura [1971]).

2. The violent behavior is seen as justified (see Berkowitz and Rawlings [1963]).

3. Cues in the portrayed violence have a similarity to those in real life (see Berkowitz and Geen [1967]; Donnerstein and Berkowitz [1981]).

4. There is a similarity between the aggressor and the viewer (see Rosenkrans [1967]).

5. The viewer strongly identifies with the aggressor or imagines being in the aggressor's place (see Turner and Berkowitz [1972]).

6. Behavior that is motivated to inflict harm or injury is portrayed (see Geen and Stonner [1972]).

7. The consequences of violence are lowered—for example, there is no pain, sorrow, or remorse (see Berkowitz and Rawlings [1963]).

8. Violence is portrayed more realistically or seen as a real event (see Atkin [1983]; Feshbach [1972]).

9. Violence is not subjected to critical commentary (see Lefcourt et al. [1966]).

10. The violent portrayals seem to please the viewer (e.g. Slife & Rychiak, 1982).

11. The violence includes physical abuse in addition to verbal aggression (see Liberman Research [1975]).

12. The viewer is left in a state of arousal following the violence (see Zillmann [1971]).

13. Viewers are predisposed to act aggressively (see Thomas [1982]).

14. Viewers are in a state of frustration after they view violence, either from an external source or from the viewing itself (see Geen [1968]).

15. The violence is unrelieved or is not interrupted (see Liberman Research [1975]).

Exposure to media violence promotes aggressive behavior, but it does so under certain conditions and for certain persons. Each of these variables plays a role in heightening the probability that aggressive behavior will occur after exposure to media violence.

Measuring the Amount of Violence on Television

Research shows that there are about 5–6 violent acts per hour on prime time and 20–25 acts on Saturday morning children's programs (Gerbner and Signorielli 1990). Within the United States this accounts for about 188 hours of violent programs per week, or around 15 percent of program time (Huesmann 1992). In addition to broadcast television, cable TV adds to the level of violence through new, more violent programs, and by recycling older violent broadcasts. A recent survey by the Center for Media and Public Affairs (Lichter and Amundson 1992) identified 1,846 violent scenes on broadcast and cable between 6:00 A.M. and midnight on one day in Washington, D.C. The most violent periods were between 6:00 and 9:00 A.M. with 497 violent scenes, and between 2:00 and 5:00 P.M. with 609 violent scenes. Most of this violence is presented without context or judgment as to its acceptability, and most of the violence in the morning and early afternoon is viewed by children. More interesting was the type of violence portrayed. Serious assaults accounted for 20 percent of the violence and gunplay 18 percent.

Americans watch a lot of television and therefore may be frequently exposed to violence. Recent surveys indicate that about 98 percent of American households have television, with multiple sets in many homes (Huston et al. 1992). Within these homes the television is on about twenty-eight hours a week for children two to eleven years of age and twenty-three hours for teens. These are fairly stable patterns that have been found over many years of research. It is now known that television viewing occupies more time than any other nonschool activity and accounts for more than half of leisure activities, particularly among children. Furthermore, there is more viewing among black and Hispanic children, independent of social or economic status (Tangney and Feshbach 1988), and many of the poorest and potentially most vulnerable groups in our society are the heaviest viewers of television, because of a lack of alternative activities (see Kuby & Csikszentmihalyi [1990]).

If children watch on the average two to four hours a day of television, then by the time a child leaves elementary school he or she may have seen 8,000 murders and more than 100,000 other acts of violence. As the young person nears the end of the teenage years he or she has been witness to over 200,000 violent acts within the media (Huston et al. 1992). This figure would actually increase with more exposure to cable premium channels or viewing of R-rated films on the VCR. Huston et al. report that popular films like *Die Hard 2* (264 violent deaths), *Robocop* (81), and *Total Recall* (74) have far more violence than broadcast television.

Another important concern now that television program content has expanded to include R-rated movies is who the violence is directed against. Content analysis has revealed that in popular R-rated horror films, women are killed at a ratio of almost 3 to 1 compared with prime time television, and 2 to 1 compared with other R-rated films (Linz and Donnerstein 1994). In addition, there is an association in these films of sexual content with the victimization of females. The analyses showed that 33 percent of occurrences of sex were connected to violence (male or female). Fourteen percent of all sex incidents were linked to a death of a female. Further, nearly 22 percent of all innocent female protagonists were killed during or following a sexual display or act. Compare this finding—that 33 percent of all occurrences of sex are paired with violence in horror films—with other film genres. In common X-rated films there is substantially less violence associated with sex and virtually no deaths (Yang and Linz 1990). This is important to note given the changes in technology and program access for children that we discussed earlier.

Perhaps surprisingly, the level of violence on *broadcast* television re-mained relatively constant from the early 1970s through the early 1990s (Gerbner 1992). But no one is sure how much violence is on cable television or whether violence is increasing or decreasing. Recently, the National Asso-ciation of Cable Broadcasters has agreed to monitor violence levels for three years. This monitoring project, unlike its predecessors, will focus on in-creases or decreases in media violence shown to have negative effects. This focus will enable social scientists and media policy makers to more clearly frame the terms of the television violence debate.

The Relationship between Television Violence and Aggressive Behavior

Over the past few decades many professional organizations have conducted exhaustive reviews of studies on the relationship between media violence and aggressive behavior. These investigations have been summarized in major governmental and organizational reports. Consistently, the reports acknowledge that media violence is related to aggressive behavior in children, adolescents, and adults. Most of these studies have not involved assessment of the relationship between television violence viewing and crime. Nevertheless, social scientists are generally agreed that there is a relationship between televised violence and aggressive behavior and that this relationship may include serious criminal behavior.

In 1972 the surgeon general released a report based on a review of existing literature and specifically commissioned research. The research was quite clear in showing that children were exposed to a substantial amount of violence on TV and that they had the capacity to remember and learn from this type of material. The Surgeon General's Report concluded that there was strong evidence to indicate that over several measures of aggressive behavior there was a significant and consistent correlation between television viewing and aggressive behavior. Second, the report concluded, on the basis of upon experimental evidence, that there was a directional, causal link between exposure to televised violence and subsequent aggressive behavior by the viewer. Although controversial at the time because of the belief in the academic community that a stronger statement could be made about a causal relationship (see Liebert and Sprafkin [1988]), the Surgeon General's Report concluded: "At least under some circumstances, exposure to televised aggression can lead children to accept what they have seen as a partial guide for their own actions. As a result, the present entertainment offerings of the television medium may be contributing, in some measure to the aggressive behavior of many normal children. Such an effect has now been shown in a wide variety of situations" (Surgeon General's Scientific Advisory Committee on Television and Social Behavior 1972, 5).

Ten years after the release of the Surgeon General's Report, the National Institute of Mental Health (NIMH), at the request of the surgeon general, issued a report that summarized the state of knowledge on televisions effects since the time of the 1972 report. The report concentrated on many areas in which television could influence the behavior of individuals, with only about 10–15 percent of its content dealing with televised violence. Its conclusions, on violence however, were unequivocal.

> After ten more years of research, the consensus among most of the research community is that violence on television does lead to aggressive behavior by children and teenagers who watch the programs. This conclusion is based on laboratory experiments and on field studies. Not all children become aggressive, of course, but the correlations between violence and aggression are positive. In magnitude, television violence is as strongly correlated with aggressive behavior as any other behavioral variable that has been measured. The research question has moved from asking whether or not there is an effect to seeking explanations for the effect. (National Institute of Mental Health 1982, 6)

Several important new findings had emerged over the ten-year period between the two reports. First, the age range of the effects could now be extended to include preschoolers and older adolescents. Also, the effects were not considered gender-specific. Research showed that both boys and girls were affected by exposure to televised violence. Second, and somewhat disturbing given the findings of a decade before, researchers concluded that the amount of violence on television had not decreased since the surgeon general's 1972 report. Finally, studies revealed that certain viewers learn more than aggressive behavior from violent programming on television. Viewers may learn to identify with victims of crime and violence. Several studies indicated that heavy viewing of violence and crime lead to fear and apprehension about being the victim of violent assault.

In 1985 the American Psychological Association (APA) released a position paper that endorsed the findings that televised violence had a causal effect on aggressive behavior. A year later APA established a task force to review the existing literature on the positive and negative influences of television, particularly on targeted populations such as children, the elderly, women, and minorities. Besides this charge, the task force was instructed to make recommendations about how to mitigate the negative influences and to find ways of working more closely with the media industry in promoting improved mental health aspects of television. The task force made it clear that its concerns were with a large domain of human behavior and that it wanted to move beyond violence and aggression. Nevertheless, its conclusions, released in 1992 (Huston et al. 1992) and based upon an exhaustive review of the literature, were straightforward. As with the NIMH report of ten years earlier, the task force concluded that high levels of television viewing are correlated with aggressive behavior and the acceptance of aggressive attitudes. Furthermore, these correlations are fairly stable over time, place, and demographics. An examination of hundreds of experimental and longitudinal studies supported the position that viewing violence in the mass media is causally related to aggressive behavior. More important, naturalistic field studies and cross-national studies supported the position that the viewing of televised aggression leads to increases in subsequent aggression and that such behavior can become part of a behavioral pattern that lasts well into adulthood (see Huesmann and Eron [1986]).

The APA continued its investigation into the effects of media violence with the establishment in 1991 of a Commission on Youth and Violence. While this commission was interested in the entire array of factors potentially related to aggression and youth, media effects were given consideration. The final report of the commission was released in late 1993, and six conclusions were stated:

1. Nearly four decades of research on television viewing and other media have documented the almost universal exposure of American children to high levels of media violence.

2. There is absolutely no doubt that higher levels of viewing violence in the mass media are correlated with increased acceptance of aggressive attitudes and increased aggressive behavior. In addition, prolonged viewing of media violence can lead to emotional desensitization toward violence.

3. Children's exposure to violence in the mass media, particularly at young ages, can have lifelong consequences. Aggressive habits learned early in life are the foundation for later behavior. Aggressive children who have trouble in school and in relating to peers tend to watch more television; the violence they see there, in turn, reinforces their tendency toward aggression. These effects are both short-term and long-lasting.

4. In addition to increasing violent behaviors toward others, viewing violence on television changes attitudes and behaviors toward violence in significant ways. Even those who do not themselves increase their violent behaviors are significantly affected by their viewing of violence in three ways:

- Viewing violence increases fear of becoming a victim of violence, with a resultant increase in self-protective behaviors and increased mistrust of others.

- Viewing violence increases desensitization to violence, resulting in calloused attitudes toward violence directed at others and a decreased likelihood to take action on behalf of the victim when violence occurs (behavioral apathy).

- Viewing violence increases viewers' appetites for becoming involved with violence or exposing themselves to violence.

5. Films that depict women as willingly being raped have been shown to increase men's beliefs that women desire rape and deserve sexual abuse. Male youth who view sexualized violence or depictions of rape on television or in film are more likely to display callousness toward female victims of violence, especially rape. Laboratory studies also have shown an increase in men's aggression against women after exposure to violent sexual displays, as well as increased sexual arousal. In addition, research indicates that these attitude and arousal patterns may have some relationship to actual real-world aggression toward women.

6. The effects of viewing violence on television can be mitigated. Children can be taught "critical viewing skills" by parents and in schools so that they learn to better interpret what they see on television. (American Psychological Association 1993)

These reports, along with others from the Centers for Disease Control, and the National Academy of Sciences lend substantial support to the premise that exposure to media violence can influence the perceptions, attitudes, and behaviors of many young children and adolescents.

The Effect of Television Violence on Violent Crime

Many findings from the studies reviewed in the preceding paragraphs have come from laboratory experiments. In these studies analogues to actual aggression have been used. Subjects' levels of aggression following violence exposure have been measured in terms of electric shocks supposedly delivered to confederates of the experimenter or through similar outcome measure tasks that may lack real-world validity. Other, nonexperimental studies that have measured the correlation between violence viewing and aggressive behavior have employed more realistic aggression measures but lack the causal certainty of an experiment. Field experiments have been conducted, and their findings generally support those obtained in the laboratory. In the field, however, one cannot ethically do an experiment that involves illegal or criminal behavior as an outcome.

In order to examine adequately the relationship between media violence and crime, investigators must rely on nonexperimental field methods such as longitudinal studies, comparative national studies, or attempts to compare the co-occurrence of media broadcasts with the onset of violence. Three research projects employing these techniques have been undertaken. Taken together, these studies strongly suggest that exposure to media violence is a causal factor in criminal behavior.

The South African, Canadian, U.S. Comparison Study

Centerwall (1989a) notes that South Africans have lived in a fully modern state for decades, with one exception—they had no television until 1975. Tensions between Africaner- and English-speaking communities concerning programming content stalled the introduction of TV for years. In fact, for twenty-five years approximately two million white South Africans were excluded from exposure to television. The medium was introduced in the United States twenty-five years earlier. Television was introduced into Canada a few years after its introduction in the United States.

In order to test whether exposure to television is a cause of violence Centerwall compared homicide rates in South Africa, Canada, and the United States. Since blacks in South Africa live under different conditions than blacks in the United States, he limited his comparisons to white homicide rates in both these countries and the total homicide rate in Canada (which was 97 percent white in 1951). The homicide rate was chosen as a measure of violence because homicide statistics are extremely accurate.

From 1945 to 1974, the white homicide rate in the United States increased 93 percent. In Canada, the homicide rate increased 92 percent. In South Africa, where television was banned, the white homicide rate declined by 7 percent.

Centerwall examined several other factors that could possibly explain the fact that violence increased in the United States and Canada but not in South Africa. Many of the more obvious explanations could be ruled out. He argues that economic growth cannot account for the murder rate growth. All three countries experienced significant economic growth between 1946 and 1974 (Canada 124 percent, the United States 75 percent, South Africa 86 percent). Civil unrest such as antiwar and civil rights activity cannot be an explanation because the homicide rate in Canada also doubled without similar civil unrest. Other possible explanations include changes in age distribution, urbanization, alcohol consumption, capital punishment, and the availability of firearms. None of these provides a viable explanation for the observed homicide trends (Centerwall 1989b). The only appreciable difference among the three countries was the absence of television in South Africa.

Centerwall found a ten- to fifteen-year lag between the introduction of television and the subsequent increase in homicide rate in the United States and Canada. He attributes this time lag to the fact that television exerts its behavior-modifying effects primarily on children. Since homicide is primarily an adult activity, the lag represents the time needed for the "television generation" to come of age.

The relationship between television and the homicide rate holds within the United States as well. Different regions of the United States acquired television at different times. The regions that acquired television first were also first to see higher homicide rates. Urban areas acquired television before rural areas. As expected, urban areas saw increased homicide rates several years before the occurrence of a parallel increase in rural areas. White households in the United States acquired television sets approximately five years before minority households. The white homicide rate began increasing in 1958, four years before a parallel increase in the minority homicide rate.

The epidemiological approach used by Centerwall can be criticized on several grounds. First, it assumes that the United States, Canada, and South Africa are comparable countries on every factor save the introduction of TV. It is, of course always possible that some heretofore unidentified difference aside from the introduction of TV between the countries accounts for the differences in murder rates. Centerwall has done an admirable job of specifying falsifiable hypotheses to evaluate the claim that exposure to television alone accounts for the relationship. However, the possibility of a yet unexamined factor accounting for differences between these societies' murder rates cannot presently be ruled out.

Second, Centerwall can only measure the onset of television as a whole in the societies he studies. He has no measure of exposure to television content, specifically violent content. His research can only suggest that with television comes violent crime. There is no theory of media and behavior that would predict that merely owning a television will lead to violent behavior. Most theories, as we note later, emphasize exposure to violent programming as a causal factor in the development of violent habits. It could be argued that TV programming contains many violent depictions and that those who later engaged in violence must have been exposed to this content over the years. Centerwall has no evidence that this is the case, however. To be more convincing, Centerwall must either develop a theoretical explanation for why television itself, independent of content, causes violence or more reliably establish the link between those who have committed murder and the type of TV content they have been exposed to.

Finally, a critical test of Centerwall's thesis would be increases in white homicide rates in South Africa in the 1990's. If Centerwall's ideas are correct, we should observe a doubling in homicide rates by the end of the decade. Unfortunately for this test, the recent political changes in South African society may preclude us from ever knowing the answer to this question. However, Centerwall (1989a) has found that as of 1983 the white South African homicide rate had reached 3.9 homicide deaths per 100,000 white population—an annual rate greater than any observed in the pretelevision years, 1945 through 1974, the last year before television was introduced. In contrast, Canadian and American homicide rates did not increase between 1974 and 1983.

Publicized Media Events and Real-World Violence.

Another approach to understanding TV violence and crime is to compare the rates of criminal violence with the onset of the TV events. Research by Phillips and his associates provides some initial evidence for a stable empirical relationship between highly publicized media events and the facilitation of real-world violence (Phillips 1974; 1979; 1982a and b; 1983a and b; Bollen and Phillips 1981; 1982; Phillips and Bollen 1985; Phillips and Carstensen 1986; Phillips and Hensley 1984).

Phillips and Hensley (1984) examined the patterns of over 140,000 U.S. homicides from 1973 to 1979 before and after publicity about prizefights, murder acquittals, life sentences, and executions. Regression analyses were used to measure the change in homicides while controlling for fluctuations due to day of week, month, and year and the effects of holidays. The researchers found that the number of homicides showed a significant increase several days after the fight—a finding replicated in other research (Phillips 1983a). They also found evidence of an inhibition effect. The number of homicides taking place after publicized stories about death sentences, life sentences, and executions was lower several days following these events.

One of the more compelling features of the Phillips research is the match between the content of the media events and the patterns of violence observed later. Studies of mass media imitative effects in the laboratory have shown that a violent media portrayal is most likely to be imitated if the violence is real, exciting, rewarded, justified, and intended to injure and if the perpetrator identifies with the character who uses aggression successfully in the media event (Comstock and Paik 1991). Thus, findings by Phillips and Hensley (1984) that the number of homicides taking place after death sentences and life sentences decreased while the rates remained unchanged following acquittals can be predicted from knowledge of the content of the publicized event. Similarly, Phillips (1983b) found that the number of homicide victims increased in the population of the race of the defeated prizefighter. These results were congruent with laboratory research that showed that angered subjects were more aggressive toward targets who showed similar characteristics with the filmed victim (Berkowitz and Geen 1966) and with the finding that subjects are especially aggressive if they identified with the character who used aggression successfully (Turner and Berkowitz 1972).

This set of studies can be criticized on several grounds. Baron and Reiss (1985) present evidence suggesting that imitation effects attributed to mass media events are statistical artifacts of the mortality data, the timing of the media events, and the methods employed in the research. Most troubling, they suggest that a close examination of the data suggests that several media events assumed to have occurred before increases in violence may actually have occurred after these increases. Grogger (1990) points out that in the capital punishment research, data were aggregated over executing and nonexecuting jurisdictions. His analysis using only jurisdictions where capital punishment is permitted suggests that the conclusions of Phillips and his colleagues must be tempered.

The Twenty-two-Year New York State Studies

Both the Centerwall study and the Phillips studies are archival studies. These inquiries have detected relationships between two sets of events, television ownership and crime, or the media depictions and criminal activity. The first longitudinal study to examine the long-term effects of television violence on aggressive and criminal behavior in individuals was the Huesmann, Eron, Lefkowitz, and Walder (1984) twenty-two-year study of youth in Columbia County, New York. This study, when begun in 1960, was intended primarily to assess the prevalence of aggression in the general population. Originally, the researchers were interested in aggression as a form of psychopathology and how it related to other child, family, and environmental variables. The television viewing habits of the children were studied somewhat as an afterthought.

The researchers examined the entire third grade population of Columbia County, New York (public and private schools), in 1960—875 children. Children were first questioned and tested in classrooms. Their mothers and fathers were also interviewed. Ten years later, in 1970, the investigators located 735 of the original subjects and interviewed 427 of them. Twenty-two years later, in 1982, the investigators reinterviewed 409 of the original subjects again and collected criminal justice data on 632 of the original subjects.

In the first wave the investigators found that eight-year-old boys' aggression as determined from peer nominations was very significantly correlated with the violence ratings of their favorite TV shows, those they watched most often as reported by their mothers. However, there was no relationship between girls' aggression and preference for violent television shows. In the second wave of the study, ten years later, the researchers did not find any evidence of a relation between an eighteen-year-olds' television viewing habits and aggressive behavior for either girls or boys. However, the investigators did find that boys' preferences for more violent shows assessed ten years earlier when they had been in third grade were predictive of how aggressively they behaved now that they were eighteen. The investigators conducted an extensive set of longitudinal regression and structural equation modeling analyses that led them to conclude that it was likely that early exposure to television violence was stimulating the later aggression. Their analysis showed that aggressive habits are moderately stable over time while television viewing habits are not.

In the third wave of data collected when the subjects were on average thirty years old, the investigators also found no relation between these males' current television viewing habits and any current aggressive or antisocial behavior. However, the researchers again found evidence of a longitudinal effect, this time one that spanned the twenty-two years from age eight to age thirty. For boys, early television violence viewing correlated with self-reported aggression at age thirty (especially aggression under the influence of alcohol) and added a significant increment to the prediction of seriousness of criminal arrests accumulated by age thirty (as recorded by New York State). These effects occurred independently of social class, intellectual functioning, and parenting variables (Huesmann 1986). Huesmann and Eron have concluded that early exposure to television violence stimulates aggression over several years, and that early aggression is a statistical precursor of later criminal behavior leading to the longitudinal relation from habitual childhood exposure to television violence to adult crime. Their analyses suggest that approximately 10 percent of the variability in later criminal behavior can be attributed to television violence (Huesmann and Eron 1986).

Unfortunately, the sample on which this conclusion was based is very small because of technical difficulties in locating the original television data on subjects who were not interviewed at an intermediate point (television violence was not a focus of major interest when the study was begun). As

Huesmann and Eron note, while the results are significant, they mostly reflect the behavior of a few high violence viewers and must be treated very cautiously. Nevertheless, this study supports the conclusions from laboratory experiments that exposure to media violence stimulates aggression and suggests that, as a result, there might be a relation for males between early violence viewing and adult aggression and criminality. However, the study provides no evidence of a relation for females.

Critics of the Huesmann and Eron work have questioned whether correlational studies, even if they are longitudinal, can ever demonstrate causality. Freedman (1984; 1986; 1992) admits that the Huesmann and Eron studies are the most promising piece of evidence in favor of a causal effect of violent TV, but he is troubled by what he considers to be an odd pattern of results. Specifically, he finds puzzling the fact that the correlation between watching TV violence at grade three and aggression at age thirteen is greater than that between later TV violence and aggressiveness at age thirteen. He is also concerned about the fact that the "aggression time 1" correlation and "aggression time 2" correlation is larger than the correlation between early TV violence and "time 2 aggression." Freedman asserts that under a cumulative theory of TV violence and aggression, synchronous correlations between violence viewing and aggression must increase with age. Freedman also notes that the pattern was found for only one of three measures of aggression and only for boys, not for girls. Finally, those correlations that are found are small.

Huesmann, Eron, Berkowitz, and Chafee (1992) reply that later analysis has turned to a more conservative analysis approach in form of regression or path analysis that have addressed many of these concerns. With this approach one predicts as much of later aggression as possible from early aggression and then examines whether TV violence viewing adds significantly to the prediction. Almost all the path coefficients obtained in this manner from early violence viewing to later aggression are positive in a 1984 study by Huesmann, Lagerspetz, and Eron.

Further, Huesmann et al. (1992) point out that Freedman, like many other skeptics, falls into the trap of discounting correlations that seem small in absolute value, no matter how significant they are. Rosenthal (1986) has argued against this discounting, especially when it comes to socially significant phenomena. Correlations that seem to explain relatively little variance may in fact indicate socially very significant effects.

Finally, while Freedman does recognize that a cumulative developmental process might be a plausible theory, he draws the wrong conclusions from such a theory, according to Huesmann et al. (1992). For example, Freedman asserts that under a cumulative theory synchronous correlations between violence viewing and aggression must increase with age. This might happen, reply Huesmann et al., but it is not a necessary implication of such a theory. As children mature, their viewing patterns change substantially; time spent with TV generally increases throughout childhood, then decreases during adolescence (Comstock and Paik 1991). Viewing patterns are not very stable over time, and their variability may change. It is perfectly plausible for heavy, early violence viewing to have a cumulative effect in promoting later aggression, while later aggression may not always correlate highly with the later violence viewing (Huesmann and Eron 1986).

The developmental theory that Huesmann and Eron have proposed suggests that aggression, as a characteristic way of solving problems, is learned at a young age and becomes more impervious to change as the child grows older. Under this developmental model one would expect exposure to media violence at a young age to be correlated with concurrent and later aggression; whether media violence viewing and aggression were correlated among older teenagers or adults would be irrelevant. Media violence affects aggression in adulthood by teaching young children lasting aggressive habits, not by changing adults' habits (Huesmann 1986). We describe this and other theoretical approaches in the next section.

Theories of Media Violence and Aggression

Two theoretical approaches dominated early investigations of the impact of mass media violence. Both approaches were fashioned around basic principles in classical conditioning and instrumental learning. Since the mid-1980s researchers have taken issue with the idea that either classical conditioning or other learning theories give a full account of the effects of exposure to violent mass media (Berkowitz 1984). Berkowitz and his colleagues (Berkowitz and Rogers 1986) have proposed that, far from being firmly learned patterns of response, many media effects are immediate, transitory, and relatively short-lived. They have offered an explanation influenced by theorizing in cognitive psychology (Neisser 1967). Basically, the explanation is extremely straightforward and is as follows: When people witness an aggressive event through the mass media, ideas are activated which for a short time tend to evoke other related thoughts. These thoughts then come to influence subsequent social evaluations or interactions. Berkowitz suggests that aggressive ideas brought on by viewing violence in the mass media can prime other semantically related thoughts, increasing the probability that they will come to mind. Once these additional thoughts have come to mind they influence aggressive responding in a variety of ways.

Besides the fact that such an explanation does not advance us much beyond common sense notions of why aggression increases after exposure to media, another issue that can be taken with this theorizing is that it is primarily one-sided. Media effects are presumed to arise from the environment. There is no attempt to account for recipient expectations, active audience construal of messages, or the continued interaction of the viewer with the mass media.

This one-sided approach has left two very important questions unaddressed. First, what are the consequences of exposure to mass media violence for future violent media use? Once the individual has been exposed to mass media violence is he or she altered in a way so that future goals and plans incorporate violence viewing? A second and perhaps more narrowly focused question concerns the emotional consequences of repeated viewing of mass media violence. Does repeated exposure to violence cause viewers to become desensitized or less emotionally reactive to the consequences of real life violence? We will attempt to answer the first question by describing a model that emphasizes the reciprocal nature of the viewer and the media event—a developmental theory of mass media violence effects proposed by Huesmann (1986), which we briefly noted earlier. The second question is addressed in work on the effects of repeated exposure to violence and desensitization.

Huesmann (1986) draws upon ideas in social cognitive theory to explain the effects of televised violence, especially the notion that learning the appropriate course of action in a situation involves the retention of behavioral rules or "scripts" through mental rehearsal. In this model, as in social cognitive modeling, social strategies learned through watching violent television are tried in the immediate environment and if reinforced are retained and used again. The most important contribution of the social developmental model proposed by Huesmann, however, is the explication of personal and *interpersonal* factors as intervening variables that link violence viewing and aggression.

Past empirical research has established five variables as particularly important in maintaining the television viewing–aggression relation (see Huesmann [1986]). These are the child's (1) intellectual achievement, (2) social popularity, (3) identification with the television characters, (4) belief in the realism of the violence shown on television, and (5) amount of fantasizing about aggression. According to Huesmann, a heavy diet of television violence sets into motion a sequence of processes, based on these personal and interpersonal factors, that results not only in the viewers' being more aggressive but also in their developing increased interest in seeing more television violence.

This process is illustrated in Figure 11.1. It may be described as follows: Children who are heavy viewers of television violence will see characters solving interpersonal problems by behaving aggressively. To the extent that these children identify with the aggressive characters they observe and believe the aggression is realistic, they will fantasize about and encode in memory the aggressive solutions they observe. If aggressive behaviors are emitted in the appropriate situations, the aggressive behaviors will be

258   EDWARD DONNERSTEIN AND DANIEL LINZ

FIGURE 11.1
Huesmann's Reciprocal Model of Long-Term Effects of Mass Media
Violence

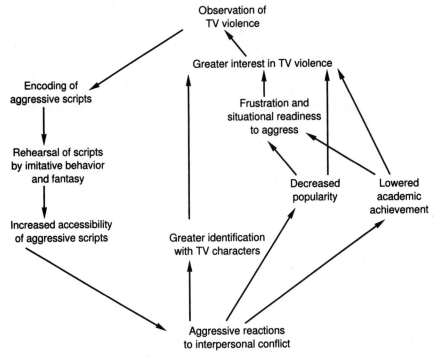

SOURCE: L. R. Huesmann, "Psychological Processes Promoting the Relation between Exposure to Media Violence and Aggressive Behavior by the Viewer," *Journal of Social Issues* 42 (3): 125–40.

reinforced with desirable outcomes. But if aggressive behavior becomes habitual, it will interfere with social and academic success. The more aggressive child will become less popular at school with peers and especially with teachers. These academic and social failures may lead to aggression; but, just as important, they may also lead to more regular television viewing. It is hypothesized that children might obtain from television satisfactions that they are denied in their social lives and might be better able to justify their own aggressive behavior after seeing more aggression in the media. The cycle of aggression, academic and social failure, violence viewing, and fantasizing which mutually facilitate each other then continues.

Desensitization to Media Violence

The model advanced by Huesmann (1986) deals nearly exclusively with *cognitive* processes that may operate with long-term exposure to media violence. In this model heavy emphasis is placed on cognitive scripts and abstract rules for social behavior that may be imparted to the viewer through continued use of violent mass media. Another important factor, however, is the role of emotions. Generally, research on affective reactions to violent messages has been concerned with the possibility that continued exposure to violence in the mass media will undermine feelings of concern, empathy, or sympathy viewers might have toward victims of actual violence. Most of the previous work on desensitization to media violence has involved exposure to rather mild forms of television violence for relatively short periods of time (for example, Cline, Croft, and Courrier [1973]; Thomas [1982]; Thomas et al. [1977]). More recently, Linz, Donnerstein, and Penrod (1984; 1988) measured the reactions of college-age men to films portraying violence against women, often in a sexual context, viewed across a five-day period. Comparisons of first- and last-day reactions to the films showed that, with repeated exposure, initial levels of self-reported anxiety decreased substantially. Furthermore, subjects' perceptions of the films also changed from the first day to the last day. Material that was previously judged to be violent and degrading to women was seen as significantly less so by the end of the exposure period. Subjects also indicated they were less depressed and enjoyed the material more with repeated exposure. Most important, these effects generalized to a victim of sexual assault presented in a videotaped reenactment of a rape trial. Subjects who were exposed to the sexually violent films rated the victim as less severely injured compared with a no-exposure control group. In another study (Linz, Donnerstein, and Penrod 1988) subjects were also less sympathetic to the rape victim portrayed in the trial and less able to empathize with rape victims in general, compared with no-exposure control subjects and subjects exposed to other types of films. Longer film exposure was necessary to affect the violence-viewing subjects' general empathetic response.

Linz, Donnerstein, and Penrod (1984; 1988) suggested that the viewers were becoming comfortable with anxiety-provoking situations much as they would if they were undergoing desensitization therapy. Further, it was suggested that self-awareness of reductions in anxiety and emotional arousal may strongly influence the formation of other perceptions and attitudes about the violence portrayed in the films that are then carried over to other contexts. Once viewers are emotionally "comfortable" with the violent content of the films, they may also evaluate the film more favorably in other domains. Material originally believed to be offensive or degrading to the victims of violence may be evaluated as less so with continued exposure. A reduction in the level of anxiety may also blunt viewers' awareness of the frequency and intensity of violence in the films. Reductions in anxiety may serve to decrease sensitivity to emotional cues associated with each violent episode and thereby reduce viewers' perceptions of the amount of violence in the films. Consequently, by the end of an extensive exposure period, viewers may perceive aggressive films as less violent than they had initially. These altered perceptual and affective reactions may then be carried over into judgments made about victims of violence in other, more realistic settings.

The Television and Film Industry View of the Research

Historically the media industry has been steadfast in denying a relationship between media violence and aggression and also in opposing any governmental intervention. At the time of the release of the 1972 Surgeon General's Report there were intensive lobbying efforts by the industry for more qualified conclusions. After the release of an NIMH ten-year follow up to the Surgeon General's Report, ABC published a major critique of the research on televised violence and aggression. In this report (American Broadcasting Corporation 1982), ABC drew the following conclusions:

1. The research does not support the conclusion of a causal relationship between televised violence and aggressive behavior.
2. There exists a significant debate within the academic community over the relationship.
3. There has been a decrease in the overall amount of violence on TV in recent years.

At the same time as the release of the ABC report, NBC published a large-scale field study on the relationship between exposure to TV violence and aggression in children (Milavasky et al. 1982). The study, with a sample of 3,200 children followed over a three-year period, concluded that no significant relationship exists between exposure to televised violence and a variety of measures of aggression. Independent researchers who examined the data collected by NBC disagreed with this conclusion.

Over the ensuing years the media industry claimed that they were reducing violence on TV. Nevertheless, attacks on the research continued, even up to the present time. For example, prior to a nationally televised meeting with Senator Paul Simon and representatives of the media industry in August of 1993, Jack Valenti, president of the Motion Picture Association of America issued a press release on media violence. In it he said, "I do not believe television is a prime cause of violence in society. They [researchers] failed to make the connection. . . . Congress and the TV industry should authorize someone, a dispassionate researcher, to certify and measure all research that has been done to date—because it doesn't prove anything" (Valenti 1993a). Two months later before a Senate hearing on media violence, Valenti, while indicating the industry will be responsible in dealing with the problem, nevertheless said, "We in the creative community have a minimum regard for research which offers up the Three Stooges and Roadrunner cartoons as violent, dangerous materials to be handled with extreme care. Yet many folks declare the research to be definitive, beyond rebuttal" (Valenti 1993b). At these same hearings Howard Stringer, president of CBS, commented, "We do not concur with the more expansive lockstep causal relationship postulated by many of the social scientists who have studied television violence . . ." (Stringer 1993). Nevertheless, he went on to indicate that CBS is attempting to reduce violent programming. Other well-known individuals in the film industry have also said that there is no relationship between media violence and aggression:

> [Mike Medavoy, chairperson of TriStar Pictures] I do think that to make a claim that films are largely responsible for violence in society is ludicrous. Most of the ideas that come from movies are found in the news. We basically try to reflect society.

> [James Cameron, director of *The Terminator, Terminator 2, and Aliens*] I disagree with the idea that the solution to the problem of violence is to take violence out of movies. If all there was to do was to go see *Driving Miss Daisy,* people would still cut other people's heads off with a chainsaw, because that is the center of our nature.

> [Richard Donner, director of the *Lethal Weapon* films] If people see gratuitous violence in any of the *Lethal Weapon* movies, I wonder if they've seen the same movie. It's entertainment. That's my obligation. (*Mother Jones* 1993)

The Government and the Problem of Television Violence

As of late 1993, there were no fewer than eight bills in various stages in the United States Congress designed to deal with the issue of televised violence. At no time in history has there been so much government activity around the problem of media violence, including congressional hearings, televised conferences, and head-to-head debates about the pros and cons of violence in the media. Leading senators, the attorney general, the surgeon general, and even the president and first lady have spoken out against violence in the media. While we will look at this current concern, we should in no way assume that this political interest is new. For over forty years, Congress, networks, and the public have involved themselves with the issue of mass media violence and its potential impact on violent crime in our society.

In 1952 the House Subcommittee on Interstate and Foreign Commerce held the first hearings on violence in radio and television. Two years later, Senator Estes Kefauver, who at the time chaired the Senate Subcommittee on

Juvenile Delinquency, held a series of hearings on the impact of media violence on children. While both hearings speculated upon the relationship between the mass media and violent behavior, the research at the time was minimal, and network representatives were quick to point out that no causal links had been established.

While continuing examinations occurred over the next decade, it was not until 1969 that the mass media and violence link became a major target for congressional inquiry and action. Following a series of national riots and violence in 1968, the National Commission on the Causes and Prevention of Violence issued a report that noted that the mass media were in fact contributors to the problem of violence in our society. While several bills were offered in Congress to reduce the amount of violence on television, none became law. It was at this time that Senator John Pastore requested that the surgeon general of the United States begin a major investigation into the role television plays in aggressive behavior. The five-volume report, *Television and Growing Up: the Impact of Televised Violence,* was issued by the surgeon general in 1972 and became for years a mainstay of thought on the assumed relationship between the media and violent behavior.

Despite continuing research on the topic, congressional legislation was not forthcoming. There was basically no challenge to the industry's position that self-regulation was the only appropriate solution to the media violence problem (if one existed). It was not until 1990 that the first major congressional action took place. In that year Congress passed legislation authored by Senator Simon and Representative Glickman that granted an antitrust exemption to the members of the broadcast and cable industry for the specific and limited purpose of allowing them to work jointly to address the problem of television violence. It should be noted that even this bill had a great deal of difficulty becoming law. As in previous years, the response of the broadcast and cable industry was minimal. Although the industry eventually issued a statement of guidelines regarding media violence, the statement received an unenthusiastic response from Congress. Additional hearings on TV violence were held; and, although there had been some overtures by the industry, both the public and Congress were skeptical of the industry response.

In response to the increased pressure from policy makers and the public, the four networks and the cable industry adopted a policy of airing parental advisories before programs containing "excessive violence." Critics argued that, while this action represents a step in the right direction, it falls short of meaningful action because parents are often unable or unwilling to monitor and control children's viewing. Critics also are skeptical of a system where the broadcasters have complete control over whether a program is considered to contain "excessive violence." Consequently, members of Congress have introduced several bills addressing the issue in various ways. As of fall 1993, there were no fewer than eight congressional bills in various stages attempting to impose standards on the mass media. Some of these are as follows:

- *S.1383, Children's Protection from Violent Programming Act (Sen. Hollings, Sen. Inouye):* Would require the Federal Communications Commission (FCC) to establish rules prohibiting the distribution of violent programming during hours when children are likely to make up a "substantial portion of the viewing audience." Would allow the FCC to exempt news programs, documentaries, educational programs, and sporting events, along with pay-per-view and premium cable channels. Broadcast licensees who repeatedly violate the law could have their licenses repealed by the FCC.

- *S.943, Children's Television Protection Act (Sen. Durenberger):* Would require both audio and visual warnings on programs that are violent or portray unsafe gun practices. Violators would be subject to civil fines. Cartoons are included; news programs, documentaries, educational programs, and sports events are exempt.

- *S.973/H.R. 2159, Television Violence Report Card Act (Sen. Dorgan, Rep. Durbin):* The FCC would be required to survey the programming of the networks and cable quarterly, evaluate the programming on the basis of the amount of violent programming, and issue quarterly "report cards" for shows and their sponsors.

- *H.R. 2888, Television Violence Reduction through Parental Empowerment Act (Rep. Markey):* Would require that all TV sets sold in the United States be equipped with technology to (1) enable viewers to block certain shows, channels, and time slots and (2) enable viewers to block shows with a common rating (such as "V" for violent). Broadcasters would also be called upon to implement an industry-wide parental advisory system for programs containing excessive violence and electronically transmit a code for such shows.

- *H.R. 2756, Parents Television Empowerment Act (Rep. Kennedy):* Would require the FCC to establish a toll-free hotline to collect comments and complaints from the public concerning TV programs which contain violence. The FCC would issue a quarterly report summarizing the comments and complaints and listing the fifty most troublesome shows, their sponsors, their production company, and other information.

- *H.R. 2837, Television and Radio Program Violence Reduction Act (Rep. Bryant):* Would require the FCC to establish standards on television and radio broadcasts of violence. News programs, documentaries, educational programs, and sporting events would be exempt. Violators would be subject to civil fines and license revocation. The FCC would be required to consider a licensee's compliance before removing a license.

- *S.Res. 122/H. Res. 202, Sense of the Congress Resolution on TV Violence (Sen. Kassebaum, Rep. Slattery):* Calls for broadcasters and cable operators to take violent programs off the air as well as to classify programs based on the amount of violence they contain. Also calls for on-screen program advisories.

It is doubtful that congressional activity will abate soon. Senator Paul Simon, who has been actively involved in the TV violence debate, has taken a strong position on the effects of media violence, including possible solutions to its problem (Simon 1993). Simon observes, "This is no longer theory. The evidence that television violence does harm is now just as overwhelming as the evidence that cigarettes do harm." He made seven suggestions to members of the entertainment industry recently on what he believed needed to be done regarding the media violence issue. First, there should be recognition by the creative community that self-restraint is essential for a democracy to function. According to Simon, "The best way to protect your industry from the dangerous and heavy hand of government is to exercise self-restraint. The gauge of whether we are a civilized society is not to what extremes we can indulge ourselves." Second, the entire industry needs to be involved, including cable, film, and independents. Third, there needs to be a continuity of effort and concern in this area. In this regard Simon called for an ongoing monitoring of TV violence, and a possible Advisory Office on Television Violence, so there will be a continuing effort among the industry to deal effectively with the violence issue. As Simon notes, "if within the industry you do not exercise self-restraint, neither will many of those who are concerned. Extremes in behavior invite extremes in response." Fourth, he suggested that glamorized violence should be avoided, and that the realities of violence need to be presented. Furthermore, Simon believes, it is important for the industry to begin to consider nonviolent solutions to conflict in their dramatic presentations. The concern over violent promotions was Simon's fifth issue. He suggested that such promotions be reduced and that they be eliminated during times when children are in the audience. Sixth was his suggestion that the television medium should be used to educate the public about the harmful effects of violence, particularly media violence. Last, Simon wanted to remind the audience of the international impact of the American media. As he noted when discussing concerns that other countries had with violence in the American media, "The revulsion in many nations to parts of the American culture is not a reaction to the Chicago Symphony Orchestra . . . nor is it in response to our finer movies or television shows. We should ask ourselves what messages we wish to send to other nations." In total, Senator Simon's message was clear—there is too much violence on television, and something needs to be done.

IV

CRIME
CONTROL
STRATEGIES

PHILIP J. COOK AND MARK H. MOORE

GUN CONTROL

In the search for more effective ways to reduce violent crime, establishing more stringent controls on gun commerce and use has the broad support of the American public. Guns are the immediate cause of almost 40,000 deaths a year and are used to threaten or injure victims in hundreds of thousands of robberies and assaults. It makes sense that if we could find a way to make guns less readily available, especially to those inclined toward crime and violence, we could reduce the level and seriousness of crime.

But not everyone accepts this perspective on guns. Some argue that guns are the mere instruments of criminal intent, with no more importance than the type of shoes the criminal wears. If the type of weapon does not matter, then policy interventions focused on guns would have little utility. This argument is taken another step by those who argue that while the type of weapon used by the perpetrator does not matter much, the type of weapon available to the victim for use in self-defense matters a great deal. The conclusion, then, is that measures that deprive the public of their guns would increase the social burden of crime.

This point and counterpoint makes it appear as if the debate over gun control is primarily concerned with facts about the role of guns in crime and self-defense. If this were true, one might hope that empirical research might eventually resolve the matter, and the proper choice of gun control measures would become clear.

In reality, however, there are important values at stake here, and particularly conflicts concerning the proper relationship between the individual, the community, and the state. Even a definitive empirical demonstration that a gun control measure would save lives will not persuade someone who believes that any infringement on the individual right to bear arms is tantamount to opening the door to tyranny. Further, empirical research in this area will never resolve all the important factual issues, so the value conflict will flourish in the face of uncertainty about the consequences of proposed reforms.

The purpose of this essay is to set out a framework for thinking about the next steps that should be taken in the search for an effective gun control policy. We begin with a review of the more-or-less uncontroversial facts about trends in gun ownership and use, and the reasons why Americans are inclined to arm themselves. A discussion follows of the more controversial question, whether guns influence levels or seriousness of crime. We then identify the important values at stake in adopting any gun control policy, and go on to describe the existing policies and the mechanisms by which they and other such measures have their effect. Finally, we make recommendations about promising next steps.

Gun Ownership, Use, and Misuse

Guns are versatile tools, useful in providing meat for the table, eliminating varmints and pests, providing entertainment for those who have learned to enjoy the sporting uses, and protecting life and property against criminal predators, so their broad appeal is not surprising. They are an especially common feature of rural life, where wild animals provide both a threat and an opportunity for sport. As America has become more urban and more violent, however, the demand for guns has become increasingly motivated by the need for protection against other people.

Patterns of Gun Ownership

The December 1993 Gallup Poll estimated 49 percent of households possess a gun, a result that affirms one of the remarkable constants in American life: the fraction of American households owning a gun has remained at about half since polling on the subject began in 1959 (Kleck 1991). The same poll estimated that 31 percent of adults personally own a gun, a result also little changed over recent decades.

While the prevalence of gun ownership has remained steady at this extraordinarily high level, it appears that the number of guns in private hands has been increasing rapidly. Since 1970 total sales of new guns have accounted for over half of all the guns sold during this century, and the total now in circulation is on the order of 200 million (1992 figures from the U.S. Bureau of Alcohol, Tobacco, and Firearms. See also Kleck [1991] and Cook [1991]). How can this volume of sales be reconciled with the flat trend in the prevalence of ownership? Part of the answer is in the growth in population (and the more rapid growth in the number of households) during this period; millions of new guns were required to arm the baby boom cohorts. Beyond that is the likelihood that the average gun owner has increased the size of his collection (Wright 1981). The most recent Gallup Poll estimates suggest that gun-owning households average 4.5 guns, up substantially from the 1970s.[1]

One addition for many gun-owning households has been a handgun. The significance of this trend toward increased handgun ownership lies in the fact that while rifles and shotguns are acquired primarily for sporting purposes, handguns are primarily intended for use against people, either in crime or self-defense. The increase in handgun prevalence corresponds to a large increase in the relative importance of handguns in retail sales: since the early 1970s the handgun fraction of new-gun sales has increased from one-third to near one-half (Cook 1993).

Some of the increased handgun sales have been to urban residents who have no experience with guns but are convinced they need one for self-protection, as suggested by the surges in handgun sales after the Los Angeles riots and other such events. But while the prevalence of handgun ownership has increased substantially over the past three decades, it remains true now as in 1959 that most households that possess a handgun also own one or more rifles and shotguns. The 1993 Gallup Poll found that just 17 percent of gun-owning households have only handguns, while 32 percent have only long guns and 51 percent of gun owners have both.

These statistics suggest that people who have acquired guns for self-protection are for the most part also hunters and target shooters. Indeed, only 13 percent of gun owners say that their guns are *strictly* for self-protection, although twice that many sometimes carry a gun for protection and fully 41 percent keep a gun loaded. Most grew up in a house with a gun and expect that their children will also have guns.

The demographic patterns of gun ownership are no surprise: most owners are men, and the men who are most likely to own a gun reside in rural areas or small towns, and were reared in such small places (Kleck 1991). The regional pattern gives the highest prevalence to the states of the Mountain Census Region, followed by the South and Midwest. Blacks are less likely to own guns than whites, in part because the black population is more urban.[2] The likelihood of gun ownership increases with income and age.

The fact that guns fit much more comfortably into rural life than urban life raises a question. In 1940, 49 percent of teenagers were living in rural areas; by 1960 that percentage had dropped to 34 and by 1990, to 27. What will happen to gun ownership patterns as new generations with less connection to rural life come along? Hunting is already on the decline: the absolute number of hunting licenses issued in 1990 was about the same as in 1970, indicating a decline in the percentage of people who hunt. Confirming evidence comes from the National Survey of Wildlife-Associated Recreation, which found that 7.2 percent of adults age sixteen an over were hunters in

1990, compared with 8.9 percent in 1970.[3] This trend may eventually erode the importance of the rural sporting culture that has dominated the gun "scene." In its place is an ever greater focus on the criminal and self-defense uses of guns.

Uses of Guns against People

A great many Americans die by gunfire. The gun death counts from suicide, homicide, and accident have totaled over 30,000 for every year since 1972. In 1991 there were 38.3 thousand firearms deaths, a rate of 15 per 100,000 U.S. residents. All but 2,000 were either suicides or homicides. While homicides garner the bulk of the public concern, there were actually 800 more gun suicides than homicides. The remainder were classified as accidents or unknown.

There are different points of reference to make sense of these numbers. For example, in terms of Americans killed, a year of gun killing in the United States is the equivalent of the Korean War. Another familiar reference is highway accidents: nearly as many Americans die of gunfire as in motor vehicle crashes, and the former have shown a strong secular increase while the latter have declined.

It is criminal homicide and other criminal uses of guns that cause the greatest public concern. Gun accident rates have been declining steadily over the past two decades,[4] and suicide only seems a threat to those whose loved ones are at risk. Interestingly there has been little variation in the homicide rates over the past two decades: the homicide rate per 100,000 has fluctuated between 8.1 and 10.6. Between 60 and 70 percent of these were committed with guns, mostly (80 percent) handguns. The peak rates, occurring in 1980 and 1991, were about the same magnitude.

Homicide is not a democratic crime. Both victims and perpetrators are vastly disproportionately male, black, and quite young. With respect to the victims, homicide is the leading cause of death for black males age fifteen to thirty-four, whose victimization rate (in 1990) was ten times as high as for white males in this age range, and nearly fifty times as high as for white females.[5] (The evidence suggests that most victims in the high-risk category are killed by people with the same demographic characteristics.) About 75 percent of the homicide victims in this age group were killed with firearms. Thus we see a remarkable disparity between the demography of gun sports and of gun crime: sportsmen are disproportionately older white males from small towns and rural areas, while the criminal misuse of guns is concentrated among young urban males, especially minorities.[6] And it is young black men who have suffered the greatest increase in homicide rates since 1985; by 1991 the homicide victimization rate for fifteen- to twenty-four-year-olds in this group had tripled, reaching an all-time high of 159 per 100,000.[7]

Of course, most gun crimes are not fatal. For every gun homicide victim there are roughly six gun-crime victims who receive a less-than-mortal wound (Cook 1985) and many more who are not wounded at all. Indeed, the most common criminal use of guns is to threaten, with the objective of robbing, raping, or otherwise gaining the victim's compliance; relatively few of these victims are physically injured, but the threat of lethal violence and the potential for escalation necessarily make these crimes serious. According to the 1991 National Crime Victimization Survey (NCVS), there were 286,000 gun robberies, 440,000 aggravated assaults (of which 88,000 caused injury) and 15,000 rapes in that year, for a total estimated volume of gun crimes of about 741,000. For each of these crime types, guns are used in only a fraction of all cases, as shown in Figure 12.1. When a gun is used, it is almost always a handgun, which accounts for upward of 90 percent of these crimes.

While guns do enormous damage in crime they also provide some crime victims with the means of escaping serious injury or property loss. The National Crime Victimization Survey is generally considered the most reliable source of information on predatory crime, since it has been in the field over two decades and incorporates the best thinking of survey methodologists. From this source it would appear that use of guns in self-defense against criminal predation is rather rare, occurring perhaps 65,000–80,000 times per year. This amounts to less than 1 percent of all violent crimes (McDowall, Loftin, and Wiersema 1992b). Of particular interest is the likelihood that a gun

FIGURE 12.1
Personal Crimes of Violence, 1991

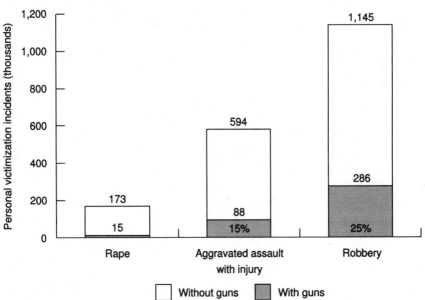

SOURCE: National Crime Victimization Survey data.

will be used in self-defense against an intruder. Cook (1991), using the NCVS data, found that only 3 percent of victims were able to deploy a gun against someone who broke in (or attempted to do so) while they were at home. Remembering that half of all households have a gun, we conclude that it is quite rare for victims to be able to deploy a gun against intruders even when they have one handy.

Using other surveys, Gary Kleck has come up with far higher estimates of one million or even two million or more self-defense uses each year (1991; 1993). Indeed, Kleck concludes that guns are used more commonly in self-defense than in crime. At the moment there is no clear resolution to the puzzle of the vast disparities in the survey-based estimates.[8] Nor is there any clear sense of how many homicides were justifiable in the sense of being committed in self-defense (Kleck 1991; Tennenbaum 1993). Of course, even if we had reliable estimates on the volume of such events, we would want to know more before reaching any conclusion. It is quite possible that most "self-defense" uses occur in circumstances that are normatively ambiguous: chronic violence within a marriage, gang fights, robberies of drug dealers, encounters with groups of young men who simply *appear* threatening. In one survey of convicted felons in prison, the most common reason offered for carrying a gun was self-defense (Wright and Rossi 1986). Self-defense conjures up an image of the innocent victim using a gun to fend off an unprovoked criminal assault, but in fact many "self-defense" cases are not so commendable.

Instrumentality and Availability

Do "guns kill people" or do "people kill people"? In murder trials the killer's motivation and state of mind are explored thoroughly, while the type of weapon—usually some type of gun—is often treated as an incidental detail. Yet there is compelling evidence that the type of weapon matters a lot in determining whether the victim lives or dies. If true, then depriving potentially violent people of guns would save lives, an essential tenet of the argument for restricting gun availability. But then a second question arises. How can we use the law to deprive violent people of guns if such people are not inclined to be law abiding? The saying "If guns are outlawed, only outlaws will have guns" may ring true.[9] There is also some evidence on this matter, suggesting that some "outlaws'" decision of what weapon to use *is* influenced by the difficulty and legal risks of obtaining and using a gun.

In this section we develop the evidence on these two issues, designated "instrumentality" and "availability." The same two issues should also be raised in an assessment of the self-defense uses of guns, and we do so in the third part of this section.

Instrumentality

In some circumstances the claim that the type of weapon matters seems indisputable. There are very few drive-by knifings, or people killed accidentally by stray fists. When well-protected people are murdered it is almost always with a gun; over 90 percent of lethal attacks on law enforcement officers are with firearms, and all our murdered presidents have been shot. When lone assailants set out to kill as many people as they can in a commuter train or schoolyard, the only readily available weapon that will do the job is a gun. But what about the more mundane attacks that make up the vast bulk of violent cases?

The first piece of evidence is that robberies and assaults committed with guns are more likely to result in the victim's death than are similar violent crimes committed with other weapons. In the public health jargon, the "case fatality rates" differ by weapon type. Take the case of robbery, a crime that includes holdups, muggings, and other violent confrontations motivated by theft. The case fatality rate for gun robbery is three times as high as for robberies with knives, and ten times as high as for robberies with other weapons (Cook 1987). For aggravated (serious) assault it is more difficult to come up with meaningful probability estimates, since the crime itself is in part *defined* by the type of weapon used. (A threat delivered at gun point is likely to be classified as an aggravated assault, while the same threat delivered while shaking a fist would be classified as a simple assault.) We do know that for assaults where the victim sustains an injury, the case fatality rate is closely linked to the type of weapon (Zimring 1968 and 1972; Kleck and McElrath 1991), as is also the case for family and intimate assaults known to the police (Saltzman et al. 1992).

Case fatality rates do not by themselves prove that the type of weapon has an independent causal effect on the probability of death. Possibly it is true that the type of weapon is simply an indicator of the assailant's intent and that it is the intent, rather than the weapon, that determines whether the victim lives or dies. In this view—which has been offered as a reasonable possibility by Wolfgang (1958); Wright, Rossi, and Daly (1983); and others— the gun makes the killing easier and is hence the obvious choice if the assailant's intent is indeed to kill. But if no gun were available, then most would-be killers would still find a way. Fatal and nonfatal attacks form two distinct sets of events with little overlap, at least in regards to the assailant's state of mind.

Perhaps the most telling response to this argument is due to Franklin Zimring (1968; 1972), who concluded that there is actually a good deal of overlap between fatal and nonfatal attacks: even in the case of earnest and potentially deadly attacks, assailants commonly lack a clear or sustained intent to kill. Whether the victim lives or dies then depends importantly on the lethality of the weapon with which the assailant strikes the first blow or two. For evidence on this perspective, Zimring notes that in a high percentage of cases the assailant is drunk or enraged, unlikely to be acting in a calculating fashion. Zimring's studies of wounds inflicted in gun and knife assaults demonstrate the difference between life and death is evidently just a matter of chance: whether the bullet or blade found a vital organ. The point is that it is relatively rare for assailants to administer the coup de grâce that would ensure their victim's demise. For every homicide inflicted with a single bullet wound to the chest, there are two survivors of a bullet wound to the chest, and similarly for knife attacks.

Zimring's argument in a nutshell is that robbery murder is closely related to robbery, and assaultive homicide is closely related to aggravated assault; death is in effect a probabilistic byproduct of violent crime. While the law determines the seriousness of the crime by whether the victim lives or dies, the outcome is not a reliable guide to the assailant's intent or state of mind. One logical implication of this perspective is that there should be a close link between the overall volume of violent crimes and the number of murders. One study provided confirmatory evidence, demonstrating by use of data on changes in crime rates in forty-four cities that an additional 1,000 gun robberies "produces" three times as many extra murders as an additional 1,000 robberies with other weapons (Cook 1987). The instrumentality explanation for this result is simpler and more persuasive than an argument based on changes in the prevalence of homicidal intent among robbers.

Another type of intervention provides further evidence on the importance of separating guns from violent crime. A recent study, based on six cities in three states, found that mandatory sentencing enhancements for those convicted of using a gun in a crime are effective in reducing the homicide rate (McDowall, Loftin, and Wiersema 1992a). Apparently these laws persuade some robbers and other violent people to substitute other weapons for guns, with the result that their attacks are less likely to be fatal.

Zimring's reasoning can be extended to a comparison of different types of guns. In the gun control debate the prime target has been the handgun, since handguns are used in most gun crimes. But rifles and shotguns tend to be more lethal than handguns: a rifle is easier to aim and the bullet travels with higher velocity than for a short-barreled weapon, while a shotgun blast spreads and causes a number of wounds when it strikes. To the extent that assailants substitute rifles and shotguns for handguns in response to handgun control measures, the result may be to increase the death rate (Kleck 1984).[10] Unfortunately, there is little evidence on the question of whether effective handgun control would lead robbers and other violent people to substitute long guns (more lethal) or knives (less).

"Instrumentality effects" are not limited to differences in case fatality rates. The type of weapon also appears to matter in other ways. For example, gun robbers are far less likely to attack and injure their victims than robbers using other weapons, and are less likely to incur resistance (Conklin 1972; Cook 1976 and 1980; Skogan 1978). (In cases where the victim is attacked and injured, the likelihood of death in gun robberies is far higher than with knives or blunt objects, which accounts for the relatively high case fatality rate in robbery.) We also have evidence that aggravated assaults follow similar weapon-specific patterns (Kleck and McElrath 1991). The most plausible explanation for this pattern of outcomes is simply that a gun gives the assailant the power to intimidate and gain his victim's compliance without use of force, whereas with less lethal weapons the assailant is more likely to find it necessary to back up the threat with a physical attack.

The intimidating power of a gun also helps explain the effectiveness of using one in self-defense. According to one study of NCVS data, in burglary of occupied dwellings only 5 percent of victims who used guns in self-defense were injured, compared with 25 percent of those who resisted with other weapons.[11] Other studies have confirmed that victims of predatory crime who are able to resist with a gun are generally successful in thwarting the crime and avoiding injury (Kleck 1988; McDowall, Loftin, and Wiersema 1992b). But the interpretation of this result is open to some question. Self-defense with a gun is a rare event in crimes like burglary and robbery, and the cases where the victim does use a gun differ from others in ways that help account for the differential success of gun defense. In particular, other means of defense usually are attempted after the assailant threatens or attacks the victim, whereas those who use guns in self-defense are relatively likely to be the first to threaten or use force (McDowall, Loftin, and Wiersema, 1992b). Given this difference in the sequence of events, and the implied difference in the competence or intentions of the perpetrator, the proper interpretation of the statistical evidence concerning weapon-specific success rates in self-defense is unclear (Cook 1986 and 1991).

In sum, we postulate that the type of weapon deployed in violent confrontations appears to matter in several ways. Because guns provide the power to kill quickly, at a distance, and without much skill or strength, they also provide the power to intimidate other people and gain control of a violent situation. When there is a physical attack, then the lethality of the weapon is an important determinant of whether the victim survives. But when the assailant's purpose is robbery, intimidation, or self-defense rather than inflicting injury, then a gun appears to be more effective than other weapons in achieving that purpose, and without actual use of violence. These hypothesized effects receive support from the empirical work that has been published in this area, but that evidence surely leaves room for doubt.

Availability

If the type of weapon transforms violent encounters in important ways, as suggested in the preceding discussion, then the extent to which guns are available to violence-prone people is a matter of public concern. "Availability" can be thought of in terms of time, expense, and other costs. Violent confrontations often occur unexpectedly, and in such cases the weapons that will be used are among those that are close at hand; the relevant question is whether a gun is *immediately* available. But logically the next question concerns the likelihood that when a violent confrontation occurs, a gun will be there. In particular, do the costs of obtaining a gun and keeping it handy influence the likelihood of gun use in violence?

Arthur L. Kellermann and his associates (1992 and 1993) provide evidence on the importance of the first issue, immediate availability. In case-control studies of violent events occurring in the home, they found that the likelihood of both suicide and homicide are greatly elevated by the presence of a gun in the home. The authors selected each "control" from the same neighborhood as that in which the killing occurred, and through their matching criteria and use of multivariate statistical techniques attempted to control for other differences between the cases and controls. But there is no guarantee that this effort to control for other factors that might be confounded with gun possession was successful, so the proper interpretation of these findings remains controversial.[12] If we accept the authors' interpretation, then two propositions follow:

1. If a member of the household owns a gun, then at-home suicide attempts and armed assaults are more likely to involve a gun than otherwise.
2. A gun is more deadly than other weapons would have been in these circumstances (an instrumentality effect).

From the more aggregate perspective, we can ask whether the extent to which guns are readily available in the community influences the mix of weapons used in violent crime (and suicide). A recent cross-national comparison for eleven countries indicates a strong positive correlation (.72) between the household prevalence of gun ownership and the fraction of homicides committed with a gun (Killias 1992), suggesting that the overall scarcity of guns in a country influences weapon choice in violent events. But within the American context, many commentators have expressed doubt that guns are in any sense scarce, or that anyone (including youth and violent criminals) would find it more difficult to obtain a gun than, say, a kitchen knife. But regional comparisons suggest otherwise.

The prevalence of gun ownership differs rather widely across urban areas, from around 10 percent in the cities of the Northeast to upwards of 50 percent in the Mountain states. (The obvious explanation for these large differences has to do with the differing importance of rural traditions in these areas.)[13] The overall prevalence of gun ownership is highly correlated with the percentage of homicides, suicides, and robberies that involve guns in these cities (Cook 1979 and 1985). Thus, where gun ownership is prevalent in the general population, guns are also prevalent in violence. A natural explanation for this pattern is in terms of intercity differences in scarcity. Predatory criminals obtain most of their guns from acquaintances, family members, drug dealers, and other street sources, rather than from licensed dealers. The ease of making such a "connection" will be greater in a city where guns are prevalent. Further, the black markets for guns, which are the ultimate source for perhaps half or more of the crime guns, will tend to be more active in cities where gun ownership is prevalent (Wright and Rossi 1986; Wright, Sheley, and Smith 1992; Moore 1981).

It helps in thinking about the availability of guns to realize how frequently they change hands. For youthful criminals, acquiring a gun is typically not a one-time decision. One interesting statistic from a survey of inner city male high school students helps make the point: 22 percent said they currently owned a gun, while an additional 8 percent indicated that they had owned one or more guns in the past, but did not at the time of the interview. Further, the number who said they carried a gun on occasion exceeded the number who owned one, suggesting loans and other temporary arrangements are important features of this scene (Wright, Sheley, and Smith 1992). In this environment, a realistic objective for policy may be to reduce the percentage of a delinquent career in which the typical youth is in possession of a gun, rather than to strive to deprive delinquent youth of guns entirely. Where guns are relatively scarce and expensive, a youthful criminal may be slower to acquire a gun and quicker to sell it when he does, simply because keeping the gun will be more costly in terms of what other pleasures the youth has to give up in order to keep one.

Of course, for a gun to be available for use during a violent encounter, it is not enough for the assailant to have a gun—he must also be carrying it at the time. Since most violent crime occurs away from home, one important aspect of gun availability is the propensity to go armed. Most states prohibit carrying concealed, but do not treat violations as serious offenses. A notable exception is the Bartley-Fox Amendment in Massachusetts, which in 1975 legislated a mandatory one-year prison sentence for anyone convicted of carrying a gun without a license. This mandatory sentence provision received tremendous publicity at the time it was implemented. The immediate impact was clear: thousands of gun owners applied for licenses required to carry a handgun legally. Several studies analyzed subsequent trends in violent crime. Pierce and Bowers (1981) concluded that the short-term impact was to reduce the fractions of assaults and robberies involving guns and, presumably as a consequence, to reduce the criminal homicide rate (see also Deutsch [1979]). Apparently some streetwise people were deterred from carrying, and as a result were more likely to commit their robberies and assaults, when the occasion arose, with weapons other than guns. As a result of the instrumentality effect, the result was to reduce the death rate in these attacks.

In sum, we find evidence indicating that while guns are certainly a prevalent feature of the mean streets of American cities, they are not yet at the point of complete saturation. It is a remarkable fact that less than one-third of robberies are committed with a gun, despite the relative profitability of gun robbery (Cook 1976); the legal and other costs of obtaining, possessing, and carrying a gun are sufficient to discourage some violent people from doing so, at least some of the time. Stronger conclusions will necessarily await better evidence.

One important question remains. While the general availability of guns appears to influence the choice of weapons in violent crime, and the likelihood that a violent crime will result in the victim's death, does gun availability influence the overall *volume* of violent crime? The available evidence provides little reason to believe that robbery and assault rates are much affected by the prevalence of gun ownership (Cook 1979; Kleck and Patterson 1993). The fact that the United States is such a violent country [14] does not have much to do with guns; the fact that our violent crimes are so deadly has much to do with guns.

The Values at Stake

Used in the manner of our rural sporting tradition, a gun provides recreation, food, and, arguably, a way of learning a sense of responsibility. When kept behind the counter of a small grocery in a high crime neighborhood, a gun may help stiffen the owner's resolve to stay in business while serving as part of the informal social control system for local youth. When used as an instrument of gang warfare, a gun becomes part of the nation's nightmare of crime that terrorizes urban residents and cuts short far too many lives.

These different uses of guns all have value to those who use them in these ways. Society as a whole, however, values some uses less highly than do the individual owners. The "great American gun war" is an ongoing debate and political struggle to determine which uses will be protected, and which sacrificed to achieve some greater social good. There is widespread consensus that disarming the gangs would be a step in the right direction (a conclusion that the gang members themselves may or may not agree with), but the social value of preserving current opportunities for self-defense and sporting use is far more controversial.

The debate over gun control policy makes broad use of both consequentialist and deontological arguments. A consequentialist framework is concerned with ascertaining and valuing the consequences of proposed reform, while the deontological framework is concerned with how a proposed reform measures up in terms of its assignment of civic rights and responsibilities. Advocates on both sides tend to make use of both consequentialist and deontological claims. Thus, control advocates typically argue their case both by pointing to the reductions in fatalities engendered by the proposed reform and by insisting that gun owners, as a matter of principle, should be willing to relinquish some of their rights to own guns in the interests of achieving these benefits. The anti-control advocates argue that gun ownership serves to reduce crime rather than increase it, and that they have a constitutional right to own guns.

Much of the rhetoric in the debate stems from three broad perspectives. Two of these, the public health and welfare economics perspectives, are predominantly consequentialist, while the third is primarily deontological.

The Public Health Perspective

Public health advocates are primarily concerned with the loss of life and limb caused by the use of guns against people. They are not much concerned with whether any particular shooting is criminal or not; all loss of life is equally serious. Thus lives lost to gun accident, suicide, and criminal homicide are of equal public concern.

Assigning suicide the same importance as homicide is profoundly important in evaluating the gun "problem." There are more gun deaths from suicide than homicide, and the demographic incidence of suicide is in most respects the mirror image of homicide.[15] Looking at homicide statistics we conclude that guns are a far greater problem in cities than elsewhere, especially in minority communities, and would focus gun control efforts there. But including suicide as an equally important prevention target suggests that guns are a major problem in suburban and rural areas as well.

In any event, the bottom line in the public health framework is whether a proposed control measure would reduce the incidence of injury and death. There is little concern with the value of sporting uses of guns. From this perspective, the modest pleasures associated with recreational shooting and the dubious benefits from self-defense should yield to society's overwhelming interest in reducing gun deaths. Preserving life is the paramount value in this scheme.

The Welfare Economics Framework

Like the public health framework, the welfare economics framework is predominantly consequentialist, but with a wider array of consequences and greater attention to individual preferences. It leads us to view the gun "problem" in terms of the harm inflicted on others, with much less attention to suicides and self-inflicted accidents. The socially costly uses are virtually coterminous with those that are prohibited by law. But there is no presumption that punishing criminal uses is an adequate response, and there remains the possibility that the benefits of preemptive controls on guns, such as a ban on carrying concealed, would outweigh the costs. The costs of such controls include the public costs of enforcement and the private costs of compliance (or evasion) of these regulations. In principle we could determine whether they are worthwhile by comparing these costs with the benefits stemming from whatever reductions in gun crime are accomplished.

In this calculus of cost and benefit, where does self-defense fit in? For most gun owners, the possibility that the gun will prove useful in fending off a robber or burglar is one source of its value.[16] Indeed, if guns had no value in self-protection, a ban on possession of guns in the home would quite likely be worthwhile, since other, sporting uses of guns could be preserved by* allowing people to store firearms in shooting clubs and use them under regulated conditions. This arrangement would be akin to the military policy for controlling the use of rifles and ammunition by servicemen on military bases, and is somewhat more liberal than the current policy governing fireworks in most states (and far looser than policies regulating the distribution of high explosives). So we believe that the self-defense uses of guns are more important than sporting uses in assessing the costs of restrictions on home possession and carrying in urban areas.

Some have even argued that the private valuation of guns in this respect understates their public value, because the widespread possession of guns has a general deterrent effect on crime (Snyder 1993; Kleck 1991). Indeed, one survey of imprisoned felons found that a paramount concern in doing their crimes was the prospect of meeting up with an armed victim (Wright and Rossi 1986). What we do not know is whether the predominant effect on criminal behavior is desisting, or displacement to victims who are not likely to be armed, or a change in technique. If the latter two predominate, then the externality is negative rather than positive (Clotfelter 1993).

Thomas Jefferson offered another reason why gun ownership and use may be undervalued in private decisions, as explained in this quotation: "A strong body makes the mind strong. As to the species of exercises, I advise the gun. While this gives a moderate exercise to the body, it gives boldness, enterprize and independence to the mind. Games played with the ball and others of that nature, are too violent for the body and stamp no character on the mind."[17]

If gun sports are especially suited to building character, then perhaps these sports should be viewed as "merit" goods on a par with the opera or art museum, and deserving of subsidy by the public. (But Jefferson would surely have changed his mind about the relative merits of guns and ball games if he could have foreseen the invention of baseball).

The "Rights and Responsibilities" Perspective

The welfare economics framework helps organize the arguments pro and con for gun controls, and suggests a procedure for assigning values. But for those who believe in the "right" to bear arms, it is not a completely satisfactory approach. The debate over gun control can and should be conducted, at least in part, in the context of a framework that defines the appropriate relationship between the individual, the community, and the state.

Very much in the foreground of this debate lies the Second Amendment, which states, "A well regulated Militia, being necessary to the security of a free State, the right of the people to keep and bear Arms, shall not be infringed."

The proper interpretation of this statement has been contested in recent years. Scholars arguing the constitutionality of gun control measures focus on the militia clause, and conclude that this is a right given to state governments. Others assert that the right is given to "the people" rather than to the states, just as are the rights conferred in the First Amendment, and that the Founding Fathers were very much committed to the notion of an armed citizenry as a defense against both tyranny and crime (Kates 1983 and 1992; Halbrook 1986). The Supreme Court has not chosen to clarify the matter, having ruled only once during this century on a Second Amendment issue, and that on a rather narrow technical basis.[18] Indeed, no federal court has ever overturned a gun control law on Second Amendment grounds.

Regardless of the concerns that motivated James Madison and his colleagues in crafting the Bill of Rights, the notion that private possession of pistols and rifles is a protection against tyranny may strike the modern reader as anachronistic—or perhaps all too contemporary when one recalls such groups as the Branch Davidians and the Aryan Nation. Much more compelling for many people is the importance of protecting the capacity for self-defense against apolitical assailants.

Some commentators go so far as to assert that there is a public duty for private individuals to defend against criminal predation, now just as there was in 1789 (when there were no police).[19] The argument is that if all reliable people were to equip themselves with guns both in the home and out, there would be far less predatory crime (Snyder 1993; Polsby 1993). Other commentators, less sanguine about the possibility of creating a more civil society by force of arms, also stress the public duty of gun owners, but with an emphasis on responsible use: storing them safely away from children and burglars, learning how to operate them properly, exercising good judgment in deploying them when feeling threatened, and so forth. In any event, the right to bear arms, like the right of free speech, is not absolute, but is subject to reasonable restrictions and carries with it certain civic responsibilities.

In conclusion, these three perspectives—public health, welfare economics, and civic rights and responsibilities—each provide arguments about the public interest that seem familiar and important. Each is well represented in the ongoing debate over the appropriate regulation of firearms. In practice, the public health perspective helps focus greater attention on suicide, while the perspective that stresses civic rights strengthens the case for protecting self-defense uses of guns. We are not inclined to argue the relative merits of these differing perspectives in the abstract, but will have more to say about policy evaluation in the next sections.

Alternative Gun Control Policies

Commerce in guns and the possession and use of guns are regulated by federal, state, and local governments. To assess the options for reform it is first helpful to understand the current array of controls and why they fail to achieve an acceptably low rate of gun violence.

The Current Array of Policies

The primary objective of federal law in this area is to insulate the states from one another, so that the stringent regulations on firearms commerce adopted in some states are not undercut by the greater availability of guns in other states. The citizens of rural Wyoming understandably favor a more permissive system than those living in the crime-ridden District of Columbia, and both can be accommodated if transfers between them are effectively limited. The Gun Control Act of 1968 established the framework for the current system of controls on gun transfers. All shipments of firearms (including mail order sales) are limited to federally licensed dealers who are required to obey applicable state and local ordinances. There are also restrictions on sales of guns to out-of-state residents. [20]

Federal law also seeks to establish a minimum set of restrictions on acquisition and possession of guns. The Gun Control Act stipulates several categories of people who are denied the right to receive or possess a gun, including illegal aliens, convicted felons and those under indictment, and people who have at some time been involuntarily committed to a mental institution. People with a history of "substance abuse" are also proscribed from possessing a gun. Dealers are not allowed to sell handguns to people younger than twenty-one, or to sell long guns to those younger than eighteen, although there is no federal prohibition of gun possession by youth. These various prohibitions are implemented by a requirement that the buyer sign a form stating that he or she does not fall into any of the proscribed categories.

A number of states have adopted significant restrictions on commerce in firearms, especially handguns. As of 1993, a majority of states require that handgun buyers obtain a permit or license before taking possession of a handgun. All but a few state transfer-control systems are "permissive," in the sense that most people are legally entitled to obtain a gun. In a few jurisdictions, however, it is very difficult to obtain a handgun legally. The most stringent is Washington, D.C., where only law enforcement officers and security guards are entitled to obtain a handgun (Jones 1981). In 1993 Congress adopted the Brady Bill, which requires that dealers in states that lack their own screening system for handgun buyers enforce a five-day waiting period between the purchase and transfer. The dealers are required to notify law enforcement officials shortly after the purchase, in order that they might run a background check on the buyer.

State and local legislation tends to make a sharp distinction between keeping a gun in one's home or business and carrying a gun in public. All but a few states either ban concealed weapons entirely or require a special license for carrying concealed weapons. Local ordinances typically place additional restrictions on carrying and discharging guns inside city limits.

Some types of firearms are regulated more stringently than others in federal and state law. The National Firearms Act of 1934 imposed confiscatory taxes on gangster-style firearms, including sawed-off shotguns and automatic weapons (such as the Tommy gun). The Gun Control Act banned the import of small, cheap handguns,[21] and more recently the federal government has banned the importation of certain "assault" weapons. States typically regulate handguns more closely than long guns, since the former account for most of the firearms used in crime.

Beyond this array of legislated restrictions on gun commerce and use are a variety of other approaches to reducing gun violence. A number of lawsuits have been brought in recent years that attempt to hold manufacturers, dealers, or owners accountable for the damage done by their guns. Many schools have taken steps to keep guns off school property and educate students on violence prevention. Ministers preach against gun violence, while psychologists counsel suicidal patients to remove all guns from their homes.

Some sense of the variety of possibilities here is suggested by this list of recent efforts, proposed or adopted, to extend additional control over firearms commerce and use:

1. imposing a heavy federal tax on ammunition
2. banning the sale and possession of assault rifles at the state level
3. limiting handgun sales to no more than one per month per customer
4. requiring that gun buyers pass a test demonstrating their knowledge of law and good practice in handling a gun
5. raising the fees charged to acquire a federal license for gun dealing
6. trying local drug dealers in the federal courts if they are in possession of a gun at the time of their arrest
7. offering cash, tickets to sporting events, or even toys in exchange for guns
8. establishing minimum mandatory sentences for illegally carrying guns

9. using public education campaigns and the cooperation of the television industry to stigmatize storing unlocked, loaded guns in households

10. giving the police power to revoke licenses and search intensively for guns in residences where court restraining orders have been issued against spouses

11. using magnetometers to reduce weapons carrying by teenagers in city high schools

12. developing a "parents compact" to promote parent's efforts to prevent their children from possessing or carrying guns

In the face of the rather daunting array of possibilities, policy makers need guidance on which approaches hold the most promise of reducing firearms violence, and at what cost to legitimate owners. Reliable information is difficult to obtain; even when particular control measures have been evaluated in some fashion (and such evaluations are rare in practice) the results are not going to be definitive. There will always be some degree of uncertainty in estimating the consequences of any one intervention, since there is no such thing as a controlled experiment in this area. And further uncertainty arises when we attempt to predict the consequences of implementing a similar intervention in another time and place. Still, some evidence is available concerning which general approaches show the most promise.

In searching for worthwhile reforms, we find it useful to classify alternative gun control measures into three categories:

1. those designed to affect the supply and overall availability of guns

2. those designed to influence who has these weapons

3. those designed to affect how the guns are used by the people who have them

On the basis of combined empirical evidence and logic, the generic strengths and weaknesses of each category can be sketched. The result is a rough map of the relevant terrain with some of the details missing, but nonetheless a useful guide.

Reducing Overall Supply and Availability

Many gun control measures focus on the supply and availability of the guns themselves (or, in one imaginative leap, on the ammunition that makes them deadly). The basic idea is that if guns (or ammunition) become less readily available, or more expensive to purchase, then some violence-prone people will decide to rely on other weapons instead, and gun violence will be reduced.

Within this broad strategy are a variety of tactics. We prohibit commerce in automatic weapons and teflon-coated bullets, and impose a modest federal tax on the production of more ordinary firearms and ammunition.[22] A few jurisdictions have adopted restrictive policies with respect to handguns, hoping to prevent growth in the number in circulation. Buy-back programs seek to reduce the existing stock, although these efforts have been very limited in time and space.

Many commentators have suggested that this approach is doomed by the huge arsenal of guns currently in private hands. How can we discourage violence-prone people from obtaining guns when there are already enough in circulation to arm every teenager and adult in the country?

In response, we note that the *number* of guns in circulation is only indirectly relevant to whether supply restrictions can hope to succeed; of direct consequence is the price and difficulty of obtaining a gun. Most violent crimes are not committed with guns, in part because most predatory youth are not in possession of a gun at any given point in their careers. While of course they can obtain one if they are sufficiently determined, the time and money they would have to devote to this effort have other valuable uses. And if they do happen to come into possession of a gun, through theft or other means, there remains a choice to them whether to keep it or exchange it for cash or drugs or clothing. Our discussion of availability in a previous section helps establish the evidence on these matters—availability does seem to matter, even within the current context of widespread private ownership.

Basic economic reasoning suggests that if the price of new guns is increased by amending the federal tax or other means, the effects will ripple through all the markets in which guns are transferred, including the black market for stolen guns. If the average prices of guns go up, some people— including some violence-prone people—will decide that there are better uses for their money. Others will be discouraged if, in addition to raising the money price, the amount of time or risk required for a youth obtain a gun increases. While there are no reliable estimates of the elasticity of demand for guns by youth, we submit that youth are likely to be more responsive to price than to more remote costs (such as the possibility of arrest and punishment). Those who argue that youthful offenders will do whatever is necessary to obtain their guns may have some hard-core group of violent gang members and drug dealers in mind, but surely not the much larger group of kids who get into trouble from time to time.[23]

Few jurisdictions have adopted a policy intended to reduce the general availability and ownership of handguns, and none have done so for rifles and shotguns. This approach is a blunt instrument, with less public support than other gun control measures. But now a substantial increase in the federal tax is under discussion for the first time in memory. Potentially even more important is the growing possibility of successful tort litigation against manufacturers of cheap concealable handguns, which if successful would raise the price of the cheapest guns (Teret 1986).

Another approach to raising prices is to impose safety requirements on gun manufacturers. Proposals in this area include "childproofing" guns so that they are inoperable by children; requiring that domestically manufactured guns meet the same safety requirements as imports, including protections against accidental discharge; and requiring safety devices such as trigger locks and loaded chamber indicators (Teret and Wintemute 1993). As it is now, firearms manufacturers are remarkably free of safety regulation, in part because the Consumer Product Safety Commission has no authority over personal firearms. While such regulations may be welcomed by gun buyers who are seeking some protection against gun accidents, they would have little direct effect on suicide and criminal misuse of firearms. To the extent that complying with such regulations made guns more costly, however, there could be some indirect effect comparable to raising the federal tax.

A more far-reaching proposal is to encourage the manufacture of guns that are "personalized," in the sense that they would be equipped with an electronic sensing device that would "recognize" a ring on the owner's finger, or even the owner's fingerprint. Such devices are currently under development. If they prove reliable, law enforcement agencies may adopt them to protect officers from being assaulted with their own guns. If all new handguns were equipped with such devices, it would gradually reduce the number of gun accidents and reduce the profitability of stealing guns.

Restricting Access

The second broad class of gun control policy instruments are those designed to influence who has access to different kinds of weapons. The intuitive notion here is that if we could find a way to keep guns out of the hands of "bad guys" without denying access to the "good guys," then gun crimes would fall without infringing on the legitimate uses of guns. The challenges for this type of policy are, first, to decide where to draw the line and, second, to develop effective barriers to prevent guns from crossing this line.

Who should be trusted with a gun? Federal law rules out several large groups, including drug users and illegal aliens, but there are no ready means of identifying those who fall into these categories. Public records provide more information on criminal background, and there is an important debate concerning what sort of criminal record should be disqualifying. Any felony conviction strips an individual of the right to own a gun under federal law, although many felons are able to obtain a court order allowing them to possess guns after they have served their sentences.

This approach to drawing the line rests on the premise that owning a gun is a right granted to all adults[24] unless they do something to disqualify themselves, such as committing a serious crime. A quite different approach would be to treat gun ownership as a privilege, as is the case, say, with driving a vehicle on public highways.[25] And as in the case of the driving privilege, one eminently sensible requirement for those who seek to acquire a gun is that they demonstrate knowledge of how to use it safely and legally.[26] It is an intriguing possibility that such a requirement would engender considerable growth in the National Rifle Association's safety training programs, since many of those wishing to qualify for a license would need to enroll in such a course.

Wherever the line is drawn, there is the serious problem of defending it against illegal transfers. That task is currently being done very poorly indeed. The major loopholes stem from the widespread abuse of the federal licensing system, the lack of effective screening of those who seek to buy guns from dealers, a vigorous and largely unregulated "grey" market by which used guns change hands, and an active black market supplied by theft, scofflaw gun dealers, and interstate gun-running operations.

Federal licensing system.   The U.S. Bureau of Alcohol, Tobacco, and Firearms is the agency charged with the regulation of federally licensed gun dealers. It is a small agency whose jurisdiction includes not only regulatory inspections of gun dealers but also criminal investigations of violations of federal gun laws, and both regulatory surveillance and criminal investigation of the explosives, alcohol, and tobacco industries as well. Obtaining a federal dealer's license from BATF is just a matter of paying a small fee and filling out a form, and in 1993 there were 260,000 people who had done so—far more than were genuinely in the business of selling guns to the public. BATF lacks the resources to screen applicants effectively or to inspect their operations after issuing the license (Violence Policy Center 1992). Thus, the federal licensing system, which was intended to act both as the gatekeeper in the federal system for insulating the states from each other and as a system for keeping particular groups of dangerous people from obtaining guns, is not performing as intended by Congress. Recent proposals call for a substantial increase in the licensing fee, which would reduce the number of licensees enough to make effective regulation of dealers a realistic goal.[27]

What would effective regulation accomplish? Some dealers knowingly engage in off-the-book sales to youth, criminals, and others who are not entitled to buy a gun legally or who do not want any public record of their purchase. These people can also buy guns from nondealers (as discussed later), but a licensed dealer can offer them their pick of any new gun offered for sale by a manufacturer or importer. Their unique privilege of obtaining guns by mail order from catalogs is what provides scofflaw dealers with a profitable niche in the illicit market. There is no systematic evidence on how important these illicit dealers are in supplying the guns used in crime; occasionally a police investigation will turn up a dealer who has sold hundreds or thousands of guns illegally (Dabbs 1994).

Screening.   People who seek to buy handguns from a dealer are required to submit to state permit requirements or, if there are none, a five-day waiting period required by federal law. If the dealer and purchaser comply with this requirement, there is some chance that disqualified buyers will be identified and screened out. But felons, youth, and others who are not permitted to purchase a gun may ask a qualified friend or relative to make a "straw man" purchase from a dealer on their behalf, or find a scofflaw dealer who is willing to sell guns off the books. Most common of all is simply to purchase a gun from a nondealer.

Black and grey markets.   There is a remarkably active and open market for used guns which is largely unregulated, a market where buyers and sellers find each other through "gun shows," word of mouth, or the classified ads. These transactions are often entirely legal—someone who sells a gun or two on occasion is not subject to any federal requirements except that they not knowingly sell to a felon, illicit drug user, or other person prohibited from possessing a gun.[28]

One leak that seems particularly important in supplying criminals is theft. Household burglaries and other thefts yield approximately 400,000 firearms each year,[29] and for obvious reasons these guns are more likely than others to be used in robberies and other violent crime. To reduce this source of crime guns, it may be possible to impose some obligation on gun dealers and gun owners to store their weapons securely (as we now do on pharmacists who sell abusable drugs), or to step up enforcement against "fences" who happen to deal in stolen guns. Another intriguing possibility is for the police to focus more attention on disrupting local, street-level gun markets. The analogy to drug enforcement comes to mind. But gun markets appear quite different from heroin and cocaine markets for several reasons.

First, the supply of guns to this market is diffuse, involving myriad potential sellers who enter the market when they happen to have an extra gun or two, rather than the more concentrated illicit supply system that characterizes the cocaine and heroin markets. Every burglar who steals a gun then has the opportunity to become a dealer for the purpose of disposing of the gun, selling to other youth they know. Alternatively, they may sell to middlemen, although there is some evidence that fences who handle other stolen merchandise are reluctant to deal in guns. Drug dealers sometimes take guns in trade, and thus become middlemen. And police investigations occasionally turn up a licensed dealer who has been active in making illicit sales. But our impression is that the bulk of the sales in the black market are by people who have no commitment to this line of business.

Second, because guns are a durable good, and are both purchased and used less frequently than drugs, the total number of transactions in the market is much smaller than in the illicit drug market. There are also fewer repeat buyers. This means that the illicit gun markets are less visible than drug markets in local communities, but relatively easy to penetrate by the police informants and undercover agents.

Third, because in most areas there is a large legal market standing along-side the illicit market, the prices that can be charged in the illicit market are typically lower than in other markets for guns, just as is true for stolen jewelry or televisions. The exception may be in very tight control jurisdictions, such as New York and Boston, where prices are apparently high enough to moti-vate a good deal of gun running from jurisdictions with weaker controls. There is some evidence that these gun-running operations tend to be small (Moore 1981).

Thus, the illicit gun market consists of a relatively large number of rela-tively unspecialized enterprises. It is filled with burglars who happen to find some guns next to the silver, some small entrepreneurs who brought a small stock of guns back from the South, or armed robbers or gangs who have accumulated an arsenal for their own purposes, and are sometimes willing to trade or sell a gun to a colleague. The type of enforcement that would be appropriate in attacking such markets is probably a high volume "buy and bust" operation (Moore 1983). Law enforcement agencies may be reluctant to launch an operation of this sort, given the danger inherent in dealing with guns and the legal difficulties in proving that the guns they are buying are in fact stolen and being sold illegally.

Controlling Uses

The third broad class of gun control policy instruments is concerned with limiting unsafe and criminal uses of guns. Most prominent are sentencing enhancement provisions for the use of a gun in crime. One clear advantage of this approach as compared with other gun policies is that it does not impinge on legitimate uses of guns. A recent analysis of crime trends in jurisdictions that adopted such sentencing provisions provides evidence that they can be effective in reducing the homicide rate (McDowall, Loftin, and Wiersema 1992a).

Another and far more controversial tactic is to focus local law enforce-ment efforts on illegal possession and carrying. The potential effectiveness of this approach is suggested by the success of the Bartley-Fox Amendment in Massachusetts, discussed earlier. This sort of gun enforcement typically re-quires proactive police efforts, and there is considerable variation among police departments in how much effort they direct to halting illegal posses-sion and gun carrying (Moore 1980). The controversy over enforcement stems in part from the concern that police, if sufficiently motivated, may conduct illegal searches in the effort to get guns off the street. More funda-mentally, treating illegal carrying as a serious crime puts in jeopardy millions of otherwise law abiding people who carry guns for self-protection.[30]

Rather than a general effort to get guns off the streets, a more focused effort can be directed at prohibiting guns in particularly dangerous locations such as homes with histories of domestic violence, or bars with histories of drunken brawls, or parks where gang fights tend to break out, or schools where teachers and students have been assaulted.[31] Often, in seeking to reduce the presence of weapons in these particularly dangerous places, groups other than the police may be mobilized to help make the laws effective. Victimized spouses or their advocates might help enforce rules against guns in violence-prone households, liquor-licensing agencies might be enlisted to help keep guns out of bars, the recreation department might be mobilized to reduce gun carrying in public parks, and so on. The point is that there may be some particular "hot spots" for gun offenses that could be targeted as places to concentrate gun enforcement efforts much as we focus a great deal of attention on keeping guns and bombs out of airplanes.

Conclusion: What's to Be Done?

Given the important value conflicts and empirical uncertainties surrounding gun control policies, some caution in recommending public or governmental action is warranted. But recommending caution is far from recommending inaction. Indeed, we think that it is time to get on with the business of actively exploring alternative gun control initiatives to develop more effective interventions than those we now rely upon. Exploration and experimentation are urgent for several reasons.

First, the current toll of gun violence demands action. Interventions to restrict the availability of guns are unlikely to have much effect on the overall rate of violence, but they do have the potential to reduce the number of fatalities. A substantial portion of the 38,000 gun deaths each year can surely be prevented without infringing too heavily on the public fisc or individual rights. A "war on guns" seems a far more promising avenue to saving lives than the costly war on drugs.

Second, it is only through trying alternative approaches that we can hope to develop confident conclusions about what works. Learning from experience is not automatic, but it can happen if reforms are coupled with systematic evaluation. With additional evidence may come a shift in the politics of gun control as well. Currently advocates on both sides mix value statements concerning rights or social welfare with factual claims concerning potential efficacy. For example, those who assert an individual right to bear arms usually also claim that widespread private ownership of guns reduces crime, implying that the value at stake here (freedom from government interference) can be preserved without social cost. If the factual claims were sufficiently robust that advocates had to accept the fact that their position entailed real costs, we would begin to learn something about how strongly these values are actually held.

The goal of gun control policy over the next decade should be to develop and evaluate specific gun control measures that can reduce gun crimes, suicides, and accidents, while preserving as much legitimate use of guns as possible. There is no reason to believe that there is a single best policy. Rather, we are looking for a portfolio of policies that reflects the full array of gun "problems." To some extent this portfolio should differ according to local circumstances and values, with an emphasis on suicide prevention in Iowa and street violence in Washington D.C.

Our suggestions are organized according to level of government.

Action at the Federal Level

The Federal Government is best positioned to make guns more valuable and harder to obtain, while insulating the states from one anothers' supply of guns. Among the next steps that appear most promising are these:

1. Raising the tax on guns and ammunition to make the cost of acquiring and owning particular kinds of guns more accurately reflect the social costs and benefits of having them. Incidentally, we would favor converting the current excise tax, which is proportional to the wholesale price, to a flat tax. Cheap handguns do as much damage as expensive ones. On the one hand, we recognize that this tax is regressive, and will be particularly burdensome on poorer people who want a gun. On the other hand, the benefit of such a tax, reductions in gun crimes and accidents, will also accrue disproportionately to the poor, who are vastly over-represented among the victims of gunshot wounds.

2. Reducing the number of federally licensed gun dealers by raising the license fee to several hundred dollars per year, while increasing BATF's capacity to regulate dealers' activities.

3. Requiring all gun transfers to pass through federally licensed dealers, with the same screening and paperwork provisions as if the gun were being sold by the dealer.

4. Stepping up criminal enforcement efforts against gun-running operations.

5. Providing funding and technical know-how to enhance the quality and completeness of state and federal criminal records files and facilitating access by law enforcement agencies to these files.[32]

6. Enhancing cooperation with the local law enforcement efforts in investigating and prosecuting those who deal in stolen guns.

7. Mandating that new guns meet minimum safety requirements to reduce gun accidents, while encouraging research in devices to personalize guns.

The federal government is also in the best position to accumulate the national experience with gun control policy initiatives. Much as the National

Institutes of Health try to accelerate learning about what is effective in dealing with cancer by monitoring treatments and outcomes in nationally established protocols, so the National Institute of Justice should expedite the search for more effective gun control policies by noting and evaluating the large number of diverse policy interventions that will be launched at different levels of government over the next few years. To facilitate such evaluations, better data are needed. The Fatal Accident Reporting System is a good model. It has provided the raw material for evaluation research in traffic fatalities. A similar system for intentional violent injuries could be implemented without much difficulty.

Beyond this, the surgeon general and attorney general together could use their "bully pulpit" to help create an environment in which local governments, community groups, and private individuals would begin to change their attitudes and behaviors with respect to guns. Such measures have proven effective over the long run in reducing smoking, drunk driving, and drug use; perhaps they could become effective in changing behavior with respect to guns. Specifically, it is important to remind gun owners of the need to keep their weapons secure from theft, to transfer them only to responsible others, to keep them out of the hands of their children, and so on. The message should be: guns are dangerous, particularly in an urban environment, and it behooves owners learn how to store them safely and use them responsibly.

Action at the State Level

The agenda for each state will and should depend on its circumstances. In the past the states have been the laboratory for instituting a variety of licensing and regulatory programs, as well as establishing different sentencing schemes for use of guns in crime and for carrying illegally. Technology transfer can take place only if these innovations are subjected to careful evaluation.

A battle in the state arena looms over the extent of liability for manufacturers, sellers, and owners of guns when a gun is used to injure someone. Lawsuits based on a variety of liability theories are moving through the courts. The implicit threat posed by these lawsuits is that if manufacturers and sellers are held responsible for the damage done by handguns, the monetary liability would be prohibitive. This possibility is appealing to those who are impatient with the more moderate results achievable through the political process.

The most notable victory for the plaintiffs to date was in the Maryland courts (*Kelly v. R. G. Industries*), where the jury found the manufacturer of a small cheap handgun liable for an injury it caused (Teret, 1986). In that case the Maryland legislature enacted a law that exempted the manufacturers against such claims but at the same time established a process for banning commerce in certain types of small, cheap handguns. Thus the plaintiff's lawyers were successful in improving the terms of political trade by changing the status quo, and the result, while still quite moderate, went farther to control guns than otherwise would have been possible.

Action at Metropolitan or Municipal Levels

Perhaps the greatest opportunities to work on reducing gun violence in the immediate future lie in the cities where the toll of gun violence—especially criminal violence, and particularly youth violence—is so high. It is there that the scales balancing the competing values of rights to gun ownership on one hand, and the social interest in reducing gun violence on the other tilts most significantly toward reducing gun violence. It is there that one might expect gun owners to willingly surrender some of their privileges, or to accept a greater public responsibility in the ways that they acquire, possess, use, and transfer their weapons.

What works against this outcome, of course, is fear of crime and the fervent belief by some that a gun will provide protection. Thus, one important goal of gun control policy at the local level should be not simply to reduce the availability of guns but to find other, less socially costly means that people can use to produce security and reduce fear. In many cities, this is one of the important goals of shifting to a strategy of community policing. Community policing is designed to help mobilize citizens into effective self-defense groups that can work in partnership with the police forces. If such groups became common, the need for individual gun ownership might abate. Another goal of community policing is to work directly on the fear of crime as well as on actual criminal victimization. To the extent that these efforts help to dissipate some ill-founded fears, these measures, too, might reduce the felt need for individual gun ownership, and with that, increase the range of feasible and desirable gun control policies.

The particular targets of city efforts against gun violence that seem important to us are three:

1. reducing gun carrying by offenders on city streets
2. reducing youth access to and use of all kinds of weapons
3. keeping guns out of places that have records of violent conflicts such as rowdy bars, homes where domestic violence often occurs, or other community "hot spots"

Exactly how to accomplish these particular objectives remains unclear, but it is not hard to list particular actions one could imagine police departments undertaking. Indeed, bringing gun crime down would be a good exercise in problem solving to turn over to an innovative police agency.

Action at the Community and Household Level

Over the long run, effective gun control may be best achieved by action at the community and household level rather than at the governmental level. Just as the battle against the costly social consequences of smoking and drinking (and to some degree, drug abuse) are now being advanced through volunteer community initiatives, so it may be that the problem of gun violence, and the role of guns in contributing to that violence, may be eased as individuals become more responsible and more attentive to their own and their neighbors' interests in deciding whether to own a gun, how to use it, and to whom to transfer it. If we get together to deal with the threat of violence, the fear that leads many to keep a loaded firearm handy may abate, thus sparing their households from this particular hazard. And in particularly risky circumstances, where there is ongoing domestic violence or a member of the household is suicidal, neighbors, counselors, and social workers must be prepared to insist that any guns be removed from the premises.

The challenge of finding the best portfolio of gun control measures is daunting in the face of our considerable uncertainty about what works and the profound disagreements about which values should be paramount. But with continuing attention to the evidence generated by the state and local innovations, and a vigorous public dialogue on the importance of both rights and responsibilities in this arena, there is every hope of doing better.

DAVID BOYUM AND
MARK A. R. KLEIMAN

13

ALCOHOL
AND OTHER DRUGS

Discussions about crime control—at cocktail parties, in classrooms, and on Capitol Hill—inevitably turn to the subject of drugs. For one thing, violence among drug dealers, who in inner city neighborhoods appear to shoot each other (and occasional passersby) with frightening regularity, is at the heart of public anxiety over crime. Moreover, one of the few universally accepted propositions about crime in the United States is that active criminals are disproportionately substance abusers. In Manhattan, urine tests indicate that over three-quarters of those arrested have recently taken illicit drugs; in few major cities is the proportion less than half (National Institute of Justice 1993). A majority of jail and state prison inmates report that they were under the influence of drugs or alcohol (or both) at the time of their current offense (United States Department of Justice 1988 and 1991).

For most Americans, such statistics, bolstered by images of urban drug killings, underscore the need for vigorous drug enforcement. They see drug trafficking as inherently violent, and drug use as a catalyst for criminal (and other delinquent) behavior, both through the inhibition-reducing and aggression-stimulating effects of intoxication and through the impacts on character and lifestyle of long-term substance abuse. Since, it is widely believed, drug dealing and use lead to crime, enforcement efforts to suppress these activities will tend to reduce crime (Office of National Drug Control Policy 1994).

Others have reached a very different conclusion. In their view, it is drug policy, and not drug abuse, that is principally responsible for the observed drugs-crime connection (Nadelman 1988). Noting that many heavy users of illicit drugs commit crimes to finance their habits, they argue that prohibition and enforcement, which by raising the prices of illicit drugs make those habits more expensive, increase rather than decrease crime. As to violent crime among dealers, that is even more obviously attributable to prohibition; when alcohol was an illicit drug, alcohol dealers settled their differences with firearms, just as cocaine dealers do today. But two contemporary liquor store owners are no more likely to shoot one another than are two taxi drivers. This reasoning has led a small but vocal minority of scholars and politicians to the conclusion that in order to reduce predatory crime, the drug laws, being criminogenic, should be repealed or, at least, that drug law enforcement should be radically cut back.

But "legalizers" and "drug warriors" alike ground their policy recommendations in partial and one-sided analyses of the relationship between drugs and crime. By creating black markets, prohibition can cause crime. But so too can intoxication and addiction, even when the underlying drug is legal. Thus, the answer to the question, Do drugs, or drug laws, cause crime? is, Yes. The right question, from a crime control perspective, is, What set of drug laws, enforcement practices, and other policies would cause the least crime? Of course, the crime-minimizing set of drug policies might not be the best set of policies, all things considered; other components of the public health and welfare are also involved. The present chapter will, however, largely restrict itself to the crime control aspects of the drug policy problem.

Even that problem is complicated enough, with causal chains that look like loops, evidence that remains stubbornly ambiguous, and policies whose effects, even as to their direction, may depend on difficult-to-predict details of implementation. It might turn out, for a given drug, that an intelligently implemented prohibition would outperform any practicable system of legal availability, but that the less-than-ideal legal system that might actually emerge would outperform prohibition as it currently operates (or vice versa). More obviously, the crime control costs and benefits of various drug policies are likely to vary sharply from drug to drug, even among those currently illicit, in somewhat complicated ways.

Nevertheless, we will attempt a systematic exploration of the myriad ways in which drugs and drug policy might, as a conceptual matter, cause or prevent predatory criminal behavior, and a review of what evidence there is about the existence and sizes of the logically possible effects. From there, we will turn to a review of drug abuse control policies, asking how legal status, the enforcement of drug and other criminal laws, and prevention and treatment programs, as applied to a variety of drugs, are likely to influence the levels of predatory crime. Last, we will summarize what all of this suggests for the design of a crime-control-oriented drug policy.

The Drugs-Crime Connections

There seem to be three links between drugs and crime. First, there are the crime-facilitating effects of drug use itself: the intoxication and addiction that, in certain circumstances, appear to encourage careless and combative behavior. The second and third drugs-crime connections stem from policies of drug prohibition and enforcement: the crimes that attend the workings of the black market—violence among dealers and the corruption of law enforcement—and the crimes committed by users to obtain money with which to buy drugs.

Abuse-related Crime

More crimes—and especially violent crimes—are committed under the influence of alcohol than under the influence of all illegal drugs combined (U.S. Department of Justice 1988 and 1991). That alcohol, a legal and inexpensive drug, is implicated in so much crime suggests that substance abuse itself, and not just economic motivation or the perverse effects of illicit markets, can play a significant role in crime. This hardly comes as a surprise. Anything that weakens self-control and reduces foresight is likely to increase lawbreaking along with other risky activities that promise immediate benefits and only the possibility of future costs (Wilson and Herrnstein 1985). And most of us have witnessed firsthand individuals who, when drunk or high, became reckless and aggressive, if not violent. Moreover, although aggressiveness is often an unwanted or at least unintended side effect of intoxication, those who intend to act aggressively sometimes become intoxicated to unleash their rage or to steel themselves for a violent encounter.[1]

Yet the claim that drugs cause aggressive behavior is hard to prove. Of all psychoactive substances, alcohol is the only one that has been shown in behavioral experiments to commonly (but not always) increase aggression (Roth 1994; Reiss and Roth 1993). Heroin and marijuana, for example, seem to generate pacific rather than aggressive pharmacological effects (although short tempers are common during withdrawal from opiate addiction) (Martin 1983; Dewey 1986). In general, sweeping assertions about intoxication and aggression do not withstand scrutiny; the relationship holds only for people with certain types of personalities, using certain substances, in certain settings (Fagan 1990).

But the immediate effects of intoxication are not the only, or necessarily the most significant, effects of drug taking on offending. Both the pharmacology of various drugs and the sociology of their acquisition and use may alter the behavior of heavy users in ways that increase their propensities toward offending, even when not under the influence. Chronic intoxication routinely hurts school and job performance, makes its victims more present-oriented and less likely to delay gratification, and damages relationships with friends and family. All of this, one would assume, makes violent and other criminal behavior more likely.

At least where cocaine is concerned, there is a chemical aspect to the matter as well. Stereotypes are rarely devoid of truth, and it is hard to dismiss the widespread belief among inner city residents and drug treatment personnel that chronic cocaine and crack abuse produce paranoid, irascible behavior (Weiss and Mirin 1987; Post 1975). From a pharmacological perspective, cocaine and amphetamines are quite similar; and amphetamine abuse is clearly related to aggressive behavior (Bejerot 1970; Grinspoon and Bakalar 1985). Indeed, the difference in the levels of violence between the active street heroin markets of fifteen years ago and the active street cocaine markets of today seems to reflect in part the irritability that tends to characterize chronic, heavy cocaine users. That in experiments cocaine has failed to consistently stimulate violent behavior is not conclusive here; if the connection between cocaine and violence is conditionally causal—meaning that cocaine use encourages violence, but only in particular contexts, and perhaps only after long-term abuse—then experiments will necessarily have a hard time identifying a cocaine-violence link.

Crime Attributable to Drug Markets

In many cities, there is rampant violence among drug dealers. Because selling drugs is illegal, business arrangements among dealers cannot be enforced by law. Territorial disputes among dealers; employee discipline; punishment for stealing, informing, or not paying debts; and disagreements over the price, quantity, and quality of drugs are all likely to be settled by force. Since dealers have an incentive to be at least as well armed as their competitors, violent encounters among dealers, or between dealers and customers, will often prove deadly. Moreover, perpetrators of inter-dealer or dealer-customer violence are unlikely to be apprehended: enforcement drives transactions into locations that are hidden from the police, and victims, themselves involved in illegal behavior, are unlikely to file a report.

Drug dealers are more often and more heavily armed than they would be in other lines of work; dealing provides both the motivation and the wherewithal for weapons acquisition. In homicides that were considered drug-related in New York City in 1984, 80 percent of the victims were killed with a handgun, compared with only 47 percent in homicides that were not considered drug-related (Goldstein and Brownstein 1987). While guns can be a deterrent, perhaps reducing the number of violent encounters, their presence tends to raise the lethality of incidents that do take place. The net effect is probably a decrease in black eyes, an increase in fatalities (see Chapter 12 in this volume).

The arms race among drug dealers may spill over to other residents of drug-involved neighborhoods; survey reports of significant proportions of inner city high school students carrying guns for self-protection may represent evidence of such an effect (Sheley and Wright 1993). The process, once started, may be largely self-sustaining, and it is possible that a decline in cocaine dealing (or its elimination by legalization) would not greatly change the patterns of weapons acquisition and use that the cocaine trade certainly helped to establish. The vicious cycle of violence, fear, gun acquisition, more violence, and more fear may have taken on a life of its own (Kennedy 1994). It is not clear how much of the violence among drug dealers is attributable to the drug trade itself, as opposed to the propensities of the individuals employed in it or the economic, political, social, or cultural conditions of drug-impacted communities. Violent drug dealers tend to live and work in poor, inner city neighborhoods, where violence is common, independent of the drug business. On an individual level, a willingness to engage in violence is part of the implicit job description of a drug dealer in many markets. And the logic of natural selection suggests that active dealers (as opposed to those who are dead, incarcerated, or scared out of the business) are those who were best able to use violence, intimidation, and corruption to protect their position.

Recent research suggests that urban violence is less directly related to the drug trade than it has been in the past, and that many violent incidents commonly thought to be drug-related—because they occur between dealers, between members of drug-dealing gangs, or at a known dealing location (Goldstein et al. 1990)—are in fact not. Instead, the occasion of the dispute may be an insult, a woman, a sidelong glance, or seemingly nothing at all. Or it may involve gang territory; in studying street gang crime in Chicago from 1987 to 1990, Carolyn and Richard Block concluded that gang-motivated homicides were most often turf-related (gang turf, not drug turf), while only 8 of 288 homicides were related to drugs (Block and Block 1993). Observers note that the combatants are easily provoked—"live wires" is a common description—especially when they themselves are chronic crack smokers. (Spending one's working life in a violent business, or living in a violent community, also contributes to having a short fuse.)

Other researchers stress the role of an inner city culture in which respect is earned through violence, and where backing down from a confrontation not only is the ultimate loss of face but may actually increase future vulnerability (Ferguson 1993). "In fact, among the hard-core street-oriented," writes sociologist Elijah Anderson, "the clear risk of death may be preferable to being 'dissed' by another" (Anderson 1994, 92). Still others note that those involved in violent incidents typically have a history of delinquency (including violence) dating back to early childhood (Wasserman 1993). While data on these kinds of factors are difficult to assemble, Jeffrey Fagan came up with some revealing evidence in a survey of over 500 active drug dealers in the Central Harlem and Washington Heights neighborhoods of New York City. Fagan reports an association, among these dealers, between violent activity within the drug trade and violence and criminal activity outside of the drug business. "It appears," he concludes, "that processes of self- and social selection result in the participation of generally violent and criminally active people in drug selling" (Fagan 1992, 117).

The drug trade also contributes to crime by diverting inner city youths away from legitimate pursuits of school and employment (Inciardi and

Pottieger 1991). Not only does the drug business introduce them to criminal enterprise, it also increases their risk of substance abuse, and weakens their prospects for legitimate work (prison time makes for a bad résumé entry),[2] all of which make it more likely that they will engage in criminal activity even outside of the drug business.

If the drug trade diverts individuals away from the above-ground economy, it also diverts the resources of the criminal justice system. This too may encourage crime. There are more than a million drug arrests a year in the United States; without question, this imposes a tremendous burden on police, courts, and prisons. More than half of the residents of federal prisons are committed for drug offenses; in state prisons, the figure is roughly 30 percent (U.S. Department of Justice 1992). In a world of finite criminal justice resources, diverting some of those resources to drug law enforcement reduces the risks of committing nondrug crimes and the number of nondrug offenders incapacitated (Blumstein 1993).

While shifting criminal justice resources toward drug offenses certainly reduces the deterrent to nondrug crime, however, not all of it reduces isolation benefits, because most of those who are prosecuted for drug crimes have very high rates of nondrug offending as well. Indeed, there is some evidence that, on average, those incarcerated for drug offenses and those incarcerated for other crimes have committed nondrug offenses with the same frequency (Cohen and Nagin 1993). So using a prison cell to house an arrested drug offender may buy, in incapacitation, as much reduction in nondrug crimes as would using that prison cell to house someone caught for a nondrug offense. In fact, if making drug arrests involves less police work than making nondrug arrests, it is possible that arresting and prosecuting individuals for drug offenses is an efficient approach to reducing nondrug crime.

Such a policy would still reduce the deterrence against predatory crime among all offenders and both the deterrence and isolation effects among nondrug-dealing offenders, and for the significant minority of drug offenders with little or no other criminal activity (couriers, many low-level marijuana and hallucinogen dealers), the costs of arrest, prosecution, and imprisonment are deadweight losses from a crime control perspective. In any case, very long sentences as provided by federal drug laws and many state drug laws for a wide range of offenses are likely to be crime-increasing for two independent reasons. First, the deterrent value of any given amount of punishment can be increased by spreading it more evenly across the class of those eligible to be punished, increasing certainty at the expense of severity (Cook 1981). Long sentences do the opposite. Second, the incapacitating effect of isolation depends on the "personal crime rates" of those incarcerated, and offending tends to diminish with age. The longer the sentence, the older the offender during its later years, and the fewer the offenses that are prevented by his (rarely her) incarceration. ("Three strikes and you're out" laws, which provide for life imprisonment without parole for repeat serious offenders, are especially subject to this objection.)

Economically Motivated Crime among Users

The proposition that drug abusers commit crimes to get money to buy drugs is straightforward enough. The desire for drugs among habitual users can be an extraordinarily powerful one, and for many heavy users of expensive drugs, crime is the only feasible source of the requisite funds. Once again, there is plenty of circumstantial evidence. Fred Goldman found that among heroin addicts, ninety cents of each criminally earned dollar was spent on heroin (Goldman 1976; 1977; 1981). In studying New York City heroin addicts, Bruce Johnson and his colleagues found a close match between criminal income and drug expenditures (Johnson et al. 1985; Johnson, Anderson, and Wish 1988). Similar correlations have been found for criminally active cocaine users (Collins, Hubbard, and Rachal 1985).

Yet, like many conjectures about drugs-crime connections, the idea that users commit crime for drug money is hard to prove. What we know is that there is a clear association between heavy use of expensive drugs and income-generating crime, and that this relationship holds for individual users, who commit more crime during periods of heavy use and less crime during periods of lower use or abstinence (Chaiken and Chaiken 1990).

But there are other possible explanations for the observed relationship between drug use and crime. Drug use itself may induce antisocial behavior (including crime), and there may be other factors, such as indifference to risk and willingness to deviate from established norms, that cause both drug abuse and crime. (This is sometimes called the "criminal subculture" theory of drugs and crime). Lastly, there could be the paycheck effect: just as some heavy drinkers splurge at their local bar on payday, drug-involved offenders may buy drugs because crime gives them the money to do so. In other words, income-generating crime may cause drug use.

Despite this methodological difficulty, common sense leads us to believe that a nontrivial amount of crime among addicts is economically motivated. And many drug-involved offenders acknowledge this: according to a 1989 survey of convicted jail inmates, 39 percent of cocaine and crack users claimed to have committed their current offense to get money to buy drugs (U.S. Department of Justice 1991).

What can also be said, with more certainty, is that economic motivation is an incomplete theory of crime among heavy drug abusers. First, the survey of jail inmates just cited also implies that 61 percent of cocaine and crack users committed their current offense for reasons *other* than drug money. Second, there is a substantial body of research indicating that, while drug use does appear to intensify and perpetuate criminal behavior, it usually does not initiate it (Ball, et al. 1981; Weisman, Marr, and Katsampes 1976). Most street drug users appear to have been involved in crime before drug use.[3] So, while the need for drug money may be a motivating factor for some crime among criminally active users, it did not, in most cases, cause them to become criminals. Third, most crime, even among drug addicts, appears to be opportunistic rather than planned, a complicating fact for a theory that assumes some level of economic rationality (Cook 1986). Fourth, as noted earlier, more crimes are committed under the influence of alcohol than under the influence of all illegal drugs combined. (U.S. Department of Justice 1988 and 1991). Presumably, few of them are committed to get money to buy booze.

Making Sense of the Drugs-Crime Connections

It has become common for researchers to characterize drug-related crime according to a highly influential typology of drug-related violence advanced several years ago by P. J. Goldstein (1985). Goldstein offered three models: the psychopharmacologic, the economically compulsive, and the systemic. The psychopharmacologic model suggests that drug abuse will cause some individuals, either in the short run or long run, to be more prone to violent behavior. The economically compulsive model accounts for behavior that is economically motivated. The systemic model captures the violence intrinsic to the drug trade.

The framework, which is broadly similar to the categories we outlined above, is a good starting point for thinking about the drugs-crime connection, in part for what it clarifies, but also for what it obscures. The framework clarifies in this sense: if there is a drug-crime connection, that is if the observed patterns of association are not merely spurious, then any causal relationships will be described, almost by definition, by one or more of the three models.

However, what seem to be mutually exclusive logical categories are less neat and clean when one attempts to identify them with empirical observations. The killing of one crack dealer by another in a business dispute appears "systemic," but may in fact stem from the effects on both of them of their chronic cocaine abuse and their consequent irritability. In contrast, a killing with no obvious nexus to the illicit business—over jewelry or a pair of sneakers—may employ the weapons, and reflect the personal operating styles, acquired in the drug trade. Moreover, there are apt to be important contributory nondrug causes that are not captured at all by Goldstein's framework. Perhaps the key factor is an inner city culture that does not allow either party to a dispute to walk away peacefully while maintaining reputation and self-respect.

Another danger posed by such a framework is the tendency to overgeneralize. Some scholars, for example, have pointed out the great variability in drug trade violence, noting that it is difficult to generalize across time and drug, and emphasizing the role of context-specific factors (Watters, Reinarman, and Fagan 1985). Ansley Hamid, for one, has argued that "the rate, type and volume of violence attaching to the use or distribution of any particular drug result from its unique impacts upon particular neighborhoods" (Hamid

1990, 32). Hamid stresses that much violence we are now witnessing in inner city neighborhoods is peculiar to the particular circumstances surrounding the growth of crack. In addition to the economic and social deterioration of inner city communities, he points to aspects of the crack trade that are not typical for other illegal drug businesses—very young dealers, centralized retail distribution operations, curbside sales.

A final danger of any such framework is that it can highlight differences where, from a policy perspective, it may not matter. Consider the evidence that drug users commit more crime during periods of heavy addiction, less during periods of abstinence or reduced use. Is this because heavy drug use increases the economic motivation to commit crimes, or is the heightened criminal activity the product of the intoxicating and dehumanizing effects of some patterns of drug use? For certain policy decisions, the answer may be irrelevant. Either explanation implicitly endorses policies that reduce drug use, for a reduction in drug use will, other things being equal, reduce crime. For policy purposes, it is often sufficient to know whether depressing the brake or accelerator makes the car go slower or faster. Arguing about why can sometimes distract us from learning how to drive.

Differences across Drugs

It is common to talk about illicit drugs as if they were a single substance. While this is convenient, it often obscures important differences. Illicit drugs vary in pharmacologic effects, patterns of use, prices, and availability.

Surely, the nature of the connection between drugs and crime must vary across drugs. Of the three major illicit drugs of abuse (marijuana, cocaine, and heroin), one would expect marijuana to be the least implicated in crime. Marijuana habits are cheap compared with cocaine and heroin habits, and so there is probably much less economically motivated crime committed by its users. Marijuana dealing is comparatively discreet and therefore relatively peaceful, in part because marijuana users make fewer purchases than heroin or cocaine users. (Because they do not typically engage in the sort of binge use that stops only when their drug supply is exhausted, marijuana smokers are able to buy in bulk and hold an inventory.) Finally, marijuana does not appear to generate much abuse-related crime. Those high on marijuana are not typically violent, and marijuana is less likely to bring its users into a criminal subculture. This reasoning is supported by the observation that although marijuana is the most widely used illicit drug, it shows up less often than cocaine in arrestee urine samples, and in many cities less frequently than opiates (National Institute of Justice 1993).

The differences between cocaine and heroin are less clear. Although there are some indications that heroin use is on the rise, active criminals are still much more often using cocaine or crack. Violence is more common in the cocaine business, but this may be change if, as some recent evidence suggests, cocaine organizations enter the heroin trade and retail dealers sell both drugs. Pharmacologically, cocaine addicts are more prone to aggression and thus, presumably, to violent crime. Criminally active heavy cocaine and heroin users probably commit income-generating crime at roughly similar rates; in dollar terms, their drug habits appear comparable.[4] However, chronic heroin users appear to be more persistent in their habits than chronic cocaine users, and if this translates into longer criminal careers, lifetime offending rates could be higher among heroin abusers.

Drug Abuse Control Policies

In what follows, we survey a variety of drug abuse control policies, discussing their likely impacts on both drug abuse and crime. For purposes of taxonomy, policies are grouped into three categories: legal status, law enforcement, and prevention and treatment.

These classifications parallel the custom of distinguishing drug policy strategies as either supply reduction or demand reduction, but that distinction probably obscures more than it reveals. The distinction is straightforward on the surface: drug consumption is a function of demand and supply, of individuals' desire to use drugs and the expense, difficulty, and risk of obtaining them. But the line between demand reduction and supply reduction policies is hard to draw. Typically, drug enforcement is considered supply reduction, while prevention and treatment are placed on the demand side. But suppose high drug prices, stemming from drug enforcement, convince an addict he can no longer support his habit, prompting him to enter a treatment program that reduces his appetite for drugs. And what if, relieved of the financial pressures of his addiction, the addict gives up dealing as well, thereby reducing the supply of drugs? Has enforcement become a demand-side policy and treatment a supply-side one?

Legal Status

The sale and possession of heroin and cocaine is a criminal offense everywhere in the United States. Other substances—such as alcohol, tobacco, and pharmaceuticals—are not completely prohibited, but their purchase and sale is more-or-less regulated. In practice, the legal status of marijuana use often falls somewhere in between: although use is prohibited by federal law, genuine possession arrests (simple possession rather than possession with intent to distribute) are rare, and in some states, possession of small amounts is a noncriminal offense.

There is no sharp line distinguishing prohibition from decriminalization or regulation; all three limit the legal access to drugs. Morphine, PCP, codeine, and cocaine are all listed under Schedule II of the Controlled

Substances Act, yet we generally think of cocaine and PCP as prohibited, and codeine and morphine as regulated. Prohibition is nothing more than extremely tight regulation, and regulation is simply targeted prohibition.

Drug policy can use regulation to control a variety of behaviors connected to drug sales and use. Laws can regulate intoxicated behavior, such as driving while intoxicated (DWI) or public drunkenness. Laws can regulate commerce, placing restrictions on potency and form, defining commercial behavior, and limiting the times and places of sale. Beer and whiskey are allowed to have only a certain alcohol content; cigarettes cannot be advertised on television. There can be limits on the purpose of use, as we now have for prescription drugs. There can be restrictions on who uses, such as the prohibition for minors, although enforcing those restrictions is a different matter.

Prohibition is less discriminating in its approach. It threatens all sellers, buyers, and users, rather than some, with criminal penalties. It also expresses a collective sentiment that drug use is dangerous, if not wrong in itself (Moore 1991). Decriminalization tries to find a middle ground between regulation and prohibition. It threatens sellers as in a prohibitory regime, but by and large lets users alone. (This was the regime called Prohibition when applied to alcohol.)

In comparison with a legal, unregulated regime, the prohibition, decriminalization, or regulation of drugs will reduce consumption, and thereby the crime that is attributable to the pharmacology of drug consumption. Legal status may also have an impact on user crime, apart from the effect on consumption. For instance, the fact that decriminalization does not brand apprehended users criminals may make them less prone to break other laws.

Regulation will usually result in a smaller black market than will prohibition or decriminalization, although a well-enforced prohibition could easily have a smaller illicit market than poorly enforced regulation. (Partly this is a matter of definition; more adolescents obtain alcohol than buy any illicit drug, but the alcohol supply system for juveniles does not involve professional illicit dealers.) Decriminalization will tend to result in the largest black market; there is no legal market, and buyers are not as strongly deterred as they would be by a prohibitory regime. Size matters: other things equal, a large black market for a given drug will tend to entail more black-market-related crime than a tiny market for the same drug. But the marijuana market, with more customers than the heroin market (and comparable total expenditures), is much less violent.

Despite the vast territory of potential policy that lies between complete prohibition and virtually free legal commerce, drug policy is commonly framed as a matter of prohibition versus legalization (Kleiman 1992b). This dichotomy has a censoring effect on drug policy discourse; discussants are labeled and divided into warring camps, and middle ground policies that do not jibe with the extremes of either prohibition or legalization go unnoticed for that reason, or are summarily dismissed as being steps down the slippery slope to the enemy's position. Nonetheless, the legalization question is too prominent for us to ignore, and so we will comply with convention before turning to what seem to us more immediately pressing questions. To explore the crime control issues at stake, and the range of possible effects, we consider in turn the legalization of three currently illicit drugs: marijuana, PCP, and cocaine.

Legalizing marijuana.   Making marijuana legally available to adults on more-or-less the same terms as alcohol would tend to reduce crime both by greatly shrinking the illicit market and by reducing alcohol consumption via substitution (since drinking seems to have a greater tendency to unleash aggression than does smoking pot). Insofar as some marijuana users are now committing income-producing crimes to pay for their habits, the price reduction which would follow legalization would also tend to decrease crime. In addition, if, as many studies suggest, marijuana is a "gateway" to other illicit drugs primarily because it is illicit (Clayton and Voss 1981), the legalization of marijuana, by breaking the link between marijuana users and illicit drug dealers, would be expected to somewhat reduce the number of cocaine and heroin users (substitution effects might work in the same direction). It is rather difficult to see any effects of marijuana legalization that would be crime-increasing, unless legalization for adults increased use by teenagers in ways that decreased either their prudence or their legitimate opportunities.

This does not strictly imply that marijuana legalization on the alcohol model would be, on balance, desirable. The almost inevitable increase in overall intoxication, and in the number of persons who become heavy, chronic marijuana users, would create offsetting noncrime costs. Either the current prohibition or some legalization, under much stricter controls on quantity and on intoxicated behavior than now apply to alcohol, might be the better course (Kleiman 1992b). But if crime control were the only social objective, marijuana prohibition, at least as it is currently implemented, could not stand. [5]

Legalizing PCP.   By contrast, the legalization of phencyclidine (PCP) would almost certainly increase crime. The illicit markets in PCP remain small, both in the number of users and in the revenues involved. (Revenues are small in part because the easily synthesized PCP remains cheap even as a forbidden commodity.) Thus, legalizing PCP would not eliminate much crime related to the illicit market, avoid much economic crime by users, or free much in the way of law enforcement resources. Even a small increase in crime related to intoxication and addiction would make PCP legalization a net crime increaser.

It is quite possible that PCP does not fully deserve its evil reputation as the generator of bizarrely aggressive behavior; some of that effect surely relates to the sociology of its users rather than the pharmacology of the drug.

Evidence for this possibility is that ketamine, a closely related product used by a much more sophisticated and less impoverished group of users, has no such reputation. It is also possible that other chemicals produced in the course of careless illicit synthesis and mixed with what is sold on the street as PCP are responsible for a considerable share of PCP-related crime.

Still, given that PCP today represents a tiny contributor to crime, legalizing it as a measure of crime control would be a far-fetched notion. Thus, marijuana and PCP form the two ends of spectrum of drugs in terms of the effects of legalization on crime rates.

Legalizing cocaine.   But of course the main event on the legalization fight-card is not marijuana or PCP, but cocaine. It is cocaine whose trafficking and consumption in the face of prohibition causes enormous amounts of crime and causes a massive hemorrhage of enforcement resources. Would legalizing cocaine reduce crime?

No one knows. Even were the details of the "legalization" better specified than they usually are by proponents or opponents, the effects of cocaine legalization would be so numerous, so profound, and so unpredictable that any strongly expressed opinion on the subject must reflect some mix of insufficient intellectual humility and simple bluff. No one knows, and there is no plausible way of finding out, short of actually legalizing cocaine over a wide region for a long time. (Even then one couldn't be sure, as other factors would be changing.) A survey of the likely effects of cocaine legalization will serve to justify this sweeping negative claim.

If cocaine were sufficiently legal so that the heavy users, who account for the vast bulk of illicit purchases, could instead obtain legal supplies—which would mean, in effect, selling unlimited quantities, as is now the case with alcohol—illicit cocaine dealers would be put out of business. In the short run, this might increase predatory crime, as some turned to theft as the next-best alternative to honest work in the absence of an illicit cocaine market, and others tried to muscle in on the remaining illicit drug markets (if any). Also in the short run, the supply of guns purchased for use in the cocaine trade and with its proceeds would remain in the hands of young men with short fuses.

In the long run, however, smaller illicit market revenues would translate into less illicit market crime, and the shrinking of the illicit business with the greatest attractiveness to young men with few marketable skills would tend to increase their job market participation and decrease the proportion of them with prison records and expensive weapons. At the same time, about 20 percent of the nation's law enforcement, prosecution, and corrections resources would be freed up to deter and punish predatory crime instead of cocaine dealing. (It is possible, though not certain, that the resulting reduction in the incarceration rate would tend to increase the stigma on incarceration and thus its deterrent value.) Thus the legalization of cocaine would have two large crime-decreasing effects, one via the crime associated with illicit markets and the other through relieving the strains on criminal justice institutions.

Whether cocaine legalization had a similar effect on the income-producing crime of cocaine users would depend on its details, and especially on the price set by taxation. Legalization near current black market prices (about $100 per gram) would presumably increase user crime, since there would be more users because of reduced stigma and enforcement risk and increased availability but no less need of money among those who did become heavy users. Moreover, some of the income needs of heavy users now satisfied by dealing would have to be satisfied by theft instead.

At prices closer to the free market price (five dollars per gram, or about twenty-five cents per rock of crack), income-motivated crime by users would probably decrease; since habits would be much cheaper to finance, a smaller proportion of chronic users would resort to crime as a source of income, and it is doubtful that total spending on cocaine would go up (this would require a greater than twentyfold increase in cocaine use). But how about intoxicated crime, and the crime resulting from the long-term effects of addiction? Here legalization, even at high prices, is almost certainly worse than prohibition, and legalization at low prices substantially worse than that. Since cocaine (as opposed to coca leaf) has never been legal anywhere since the invention of crack cocaine smoking, there is no compelling way to estimate the number of people who would try it if it were legal and cheap, or the proportion of them who would go on to, and persist in, habits of very heavy use, or the proportion of heavy users who would become aggressive either under the immediate influence of the drug or because of its chronic effects. (Probably a smaller proportion than now do so, given the reduction of economic pressures, the elimination of the need to deal with criminals in the black market, and the dilution of the cocaine addict pool by persons with less initial commitment to criminal lifestyles; but how much smaller is anyone's guess.)

Let anyone who doubts that the horrible cocaine/crime situation of today could get worse contemplate the alcohol/crime problem, and recall that alcohol plus cocaine is a frequent drug combination. Even without the nightmare fantasy of developing as many cocaine addicts as there now are alcoholics, cocaine legalization could greatly increase the level of cocaine abuse and the level of alcohol abuse, thus creating a double pharmacologic source of crime increase to set off against the likely decreases in economic and systemic crime.

Given what a miserable experience heavy, chronic cocaine use can be for the user and his or her intimates and neighbors, and given the near certainty that any thoroughgoing legalization would increase substantially the number of persons going through that experience, we would think legalization justified only if there were a very strong balance of probabilities in favor of a noticeable crime decrease. In this case, our agnosticism in terms of its crime control effects leaves us opposed to cocaine legalization as an overall proposition.

Law Enforcement

Traditionally, legal scholars drew a distinction between acts that were considered *mala in se*, or inherently evil, and those that were *mala prohibita*, not immoral in themselves, but merely proscribed by the laws of society (Blackstone 1890). The thinking is out of favor today; too many sociologists and philosophers have pointed out that even definitions of murder differ greatly across societies (MacIntyre 1981). But the spirit of the idea lives on, and the common differentiation between "predatory" and "consensual" crimes— murder, theft, or robbery as opposed to prostitution, bookmaking, or drug trafficking—reflects in part a feeling that some behaviors are just plain wrong, while others simply have bad effects.

Moreover, the distinction is useful in thinking about drug enforcement. It reminds us that the purpose of such policy is not simply to catch and punish "bad guys." Although retribution is an objective in enforcing any criminal law, drug enforcement is, or at least ought to be, principally an effort to influence the conditions of potential drug taking, such as the price and availability of drugs.

Raising prices.   One of the primary aims of current drug policy is to raise the prices of illicit drugs. The logic is that of elementary economics: purchases of heroin, cocaine, or marijuana, as of any commodity, are influenced by price. Other things being equal, one expects lower prices to be accompanied by greater use, and higher prices to go with less consumption.

A prohibitionist drug policy attempts to raise drug prices through the vigorous enforcement of laws prohibiting the sale and possession of drugs. Imprisoning traffickers and dealers, seizing their drugs, money, and physical assets—all of these actions impose costs on the drug trade, costs which are presumably passed on to consumers in the form of higher prices (Reuter and Kleiman 1986). A regulatory drug policy can raise price through taxation.

But any reduction in drug use that is obtained in this manner is purchased at a high cost. Where drugs are prohibited, higher drug prices brought about through enforcement can amplify black market violence. Enforcement shrinks the size of the drug trade (in terms of quantity sold, not necessarily revenues) but in the process makes the business more lucrative for those who survive. The higher gross margins increase the incentive for dealers to engage in violence and corruption to protect themselves and their livelihood. Where drugs are taxed, higher taxes may foster the creation or growth of a black market. Under either legal status, high prices can have another unwanted effect: users whose habits become very expensive to support, but who cannot or will not quit, may turn to theft, drug dealing, or prostitution as a source of income.

The key to the connection between drug prices and crime is the strength of the relationship between drug prices and consumption: what economists call the price-elasticity of demand. If consumption falls only slightly as prices rise (i.e., if demand is highly inelastic), then enforcement efforts that successfully drive up the price of drugs will have only a moderate impact on consumption, bringing only a slight reduction in those crimes attributable to drug abuse. Worse, if the percentage change in consumption is smaller than the percentage change in price (i.e., less than unit elasticity), total expenditures go up along with prices, and we would expect to see users committing more crimes for drug money. Higher prices and greater revenues would also be expected to increase drug-related violence. Even in this case, it is in principle possible that the fall in abuse-related crime would be greater than the combined increases in crime committed by dealers seeking competitive advantage and crime perpetrated by users looking for drug money, but the arithmetic of relatively inelastic demand is discouraging.

If, on the other hand, the demand for drugs is more than unit elastic, effective drug enforcement will have more positive consequences. Higher prices will cause a more-than-proportional drop in consumption, lowering total expenditures on drugs. This should cause a decline in crime connected to abuse and in crime motivated by economic need, and leave dealers with fewer illicit dollars to fight over (and potential dealers with fewer illicit opportunities to divert them from licit employment).

The price-elasticity of demand for a given drug is not an unchanging constant, like its molecular weight. It varies from user to user, and thus may rise and fall as the mix of users changes. It also varies with the price itself; other things being equal, one would expect the price-elasticity of demand to rise with price, since the impact of, say, a 10 percent price increase on a user's budget will tend to be greater if the drug is already expensive. It varies as well with the availability and price of substitutes (in the economic sense of that term): other drugs, other recreations, and help in shedding unwanted drug habits.

Moreover, the short-run price-elasticity—the effect of today's price change on today's consumption—is different from the long-run elasticity, which takes into account the effect of price change on consumers' habits and personal routines. In the case of gasoline during the two oil shocks of the 1970s, for example, the stock of automobiles and the distribution of commuting distances were both fixed. Over time, though, higher fuel prices led people to buy more efficient cars and to move closer to work (or led work to move closer to them). The long-run elasticity was near unity, though the short-run elasticity was only about 0.1 (Pindyck 1979).

Accurately estimating the elasticity of demand for a legal commodity is very difficult. There are countless factors other than price that influence demand, and distinguishing these—in effect, holding nonprice factors constant—is a methodological challenge. Estimating the elasticity of demand for illicit drugs is considerably harder. The usual problems are magnified by the lack of reliable data. If one were estimating the elasticity of demand for gasoline, for instance, one could easily find accurate figures on gasoline prices and consumption. But with illicit drugs, prices are not reliably or consistently measured, and quantity, since it is not an observable variable, must be indirectly estimated.

As a result, most of the research and discussion on the demand for illicit drugs has been speculative rather than empirical. Much of this work implicitly assumes that the demand for illicit drugs is almost perfectly inelastic. For instance, advocates of drug legalization commonly argue that higher prices do little to curtail use, and that the drastically lower prices that would prevail in a legal regime would not significantly increase consumption (Trebach, in Trebach and Inciardi 1993).

This assumption is based partly on the model of "addiction" as involving a fixed daily "habit" not subject to the user's choice, a model only vaguely applicable to heroin and almost completely irrelevant to cocaine, which tends much more to binge use. Even for those who are in fact heavy daily users and who struggle to maintain their habits to avoid withdrawal—the group whose elasticity of demand would seem at first blush to be lowest—demand will still be somewhat elastic if drug purchases now make up a very large proportion of the user's income. To assume that demand for addictive drugs is highly inelastic is also to ignore the effects of price on initiation, intensification, quitting, and relapse, the four processes by which the addict pool grows or shrinks.

Moreover, available evidence provides little support for the low elasticity theory. Historically, sharp increases in heroin prices seem to bring about similarly sharp decreases in heroin-related overdoses (DuPont and Greene 1973; Boyum 1992). And higher cocaine prices are correlated with fewer cocaine-related emergency room episodes, fewer cocaine-related deaths, and a lower percentage of arrestees testing positive for recent cocaine use, while lower cocaine prices are correlated with the opposite effects (Hyatt and Rhodes 1992).

A number of studies have estimated, or reviewed estimates, of the elasticity of demand for alcohol and tobacco, which, of course, are also addictive drugs for some users (tobacco for most). Given the variety of methodological approaches employed, it is not surprising that the estimates vary widely. But most of the research suggests that the demand for alcoholic beverages and cigarettes is only moderately inelastic (elasticity of demand smaller in absolute value than, but close to, -1). The findings make it hard to credit the idea that illicit drug demand is very inelastic, particularly when one considers that illicit drugs are much more expensive than alcohol or cigarettes.

As far as empirical estimates of the elasticity of demand for illicit drugs go, only two studies have been widely regarded as methodologically respectable. Both examined the link between heroin prices and crime in the early 1970s, and only indirectly looked at elasticity of demand (Brown and Silverman 1974; Silverman and Spruill 1977).

Brown and Silverman found, for New York City, a positive correlation between the price of heroin and rates of different types of crime. Significantly, the association was generally stronger for the revenue-raising crimes (such as robbery, burglary, and auto theft) that addicts would commit to finance drug purchases than it was for violent crimes.

Data for the other eight cities examined did not provide much support for the New York City findings. Some cities (for example, Houston) revealed a positive relationship between drug prices and crime, while other cities (Boston is one) showed a significant negative relationship. In other cities (Chicago, Detroit, Miami), results were mixed.

Silverman and Spruill performed a similar, but more detailed, analysis for Detroit alone. The data showed a strong association between heroin prices and crime, especially for property crimes. Overall, Silverman and Spruill estimated that a 50 percent increase in the price of heroin would result in a 14 percent increase in total property crime.

Several important points are raised by these two widely cited studies. First, that the association between drug prices and crime was positive in some cities, negative in others, and unclear in most underscores that a variety of factors other than drug prices affect crime levels, and that some of these factors may affect the relationship between drug prices and crime.

Particularly important in this regard may be the availability of treatment. In a careful study of heroin use in Washington, D.C. in the early 1970s, Robert DuPont and Mark Greene found that heroin use declined in conjunction with a rise in heroin prices and a fall in reported crimes (DuPont and Greene 1973). Their analysis suggests that the crime rate fell because of a decline in heroin addiction, just as the crime rate had increased over the previous decade because of a growth in addiction. A sharp increase in heroin prices, the result of vigorous law enforcement efforts, was instrumental in reducing heroin use, but only, in their view, because treatment was made available. In effect, DuPont and Greene argue that the association between heroin prices and crime is negative when treatment is available, positive when it is not.

Moreover, studies like Brown and Silverman's or Silverman and Spruill's can only measure the elasticity of demand in the short run. Thus, their estimates are likely to understate the effect of price changes once users have the opportunity to discover and habituate themselves to substitute drugs, enter and complete treatment programs, and so on.

For the purposes of drug policy, we are primarily interested in the long-run elasticity of demand, because the size of the user population over time is a function of long-run initiation and quit rates. It is quite possible that the demand for illicit drugs is inelastic in the short run and elastic in the long run. In the short run, demand is above all a function of consumption among current addicts. Their demand is unlikely to respond quickly to a price increase; not only is it difficult for them to immediately adjust their habits, but they know that most jumps in illicit drug prices reflect temporary interruptions in supply rather than lasting trends. If the higher price persists, thereby maintaining and giving credibility to the economic pressure, it becomes more worthwhile for them to invest in changing their habits.

At the same time, the higher price reduces both initiations and progressions from initiation or moderate use to heavy use (Moore 1990). In principle, the addictive nature of drugs may contribute to these effects. A rational person considering whether or not to take an addictive drug should be more strongly influenced by a change in its price than he would be if the drug were not addictive, because the effect of the drug's price on his lifetime budget is greater (Becker, Grossman, and Murphy 1991). The evidence from cigarettes, however, suggests that most new users of even highly addictive substances do not expect to become hooked (Cleary et al. 1988).

Over time, these changes in initiation and quit rates, even if small, can significantly alter the size of the user population. And if the demand for drugs is more elastic in the long run than in the short run, we should expect time horizon to affect the connection between drug prices and crime. Specifically, it is conceivable that higher drug prices increase crime in the short run, as current users commit more offenses to finance their now-costlier habits and dealers fight over a market with larger revenues, but decrease crime in the long run, as the user population shrinks and the illicit market shrinks with it.

The price of one drug may also influence the consumption of another, either positively or negatively, and this relationship may hold either at a moment or over time. Insofar as two drugs compete for users' time and money, as rival brands of beer do, a price rise for one will increase consumption of the other (substitution). If they are used together, as various depressants such as alcohol, heroin, and minor tranquilizers are with cocaine, then raising the price of one will tend to decrease the consumption of the other (complementarity). A special kind of complementarity, acting over time and only in one direction, involves situations where consumption of one drug increases the probability of trying another (which might be true, for example, of tobacco and other smoked drugs, or alcohol and other intoxicants, or marijuana and other illicit drugs). This unidirectional complementarity over time is known in the drug literature as the "gateway effect"; its existence remains highly contested (Clayton and Voss 1981).

The frequency of polydrug consumption among many heavy users suggests that both substitution and complementarity are likely to be important effects, but estimating them presents great methodological challenges. There is, however, some empirical evidence of interdrug substitution. John DiNardo found that raising the legal drinking age appears to increase marijuana use (DiNardo 1991). Comparing states that decriminalized marijuana in the 1970s with those that did not, Karyn Model has found that marijuana decriminalization tends to increase the frequency of marijuana-related visits to hospital emergency rooms, but to decrease the frequency of emergency room incidents involving other drugs, and decrease the homicide rate (which may reflect substitution of marijuana for alcohol) (Model 1991 and 1994).

To the extent that drugs are substitutes, drug policy should concern itself with the relative, and not just the absolute, prices of illicit drugs. In particular, we would want to make sure that the prices of the most harmful and addictive drugs (heroin and cocaine) are very high vis-à-vis the prices of the less-dangerous ones (marijuana) (Moore 1979). Failure on this score could be quite damaging. According to one researcher who has conducted focus groups with heroin users, many current heroin addicts claim to have turned to heroin in the late 1970s when marijuana supplies dried up (Rocheleau 1994).

That drugs can be substitutes and complements further complicates the analysis of drug prices and crime. It implies that one cannot consider the impact of a change in the price of one drug without considering the effects on consumption of other drugs. Without substitutability or complementarity, an increase in the price of marijuana would have a negligible impact on crime. As noted above, a marijuana habit is not terribly expensive to support, marijuana dealers rarely shoot each other in turf battles, and marijuana users are not typically violent or criminal. However, with cross-price effects, an increase in the price of marijuana could materially influence crime. Users might switch to, or increase their consumption of, cocaine, heroin, or alcohol, which would tend to increase crime. At the same time, reduced marijuana use might mean fewer initiations to cocaine and heroin.[6]

Overall, we simply do not know whether, on balance, higher drug prices increase or decrease crime. By driving up prices, drug enforcement curtails drug consumption and the crime that is attributable to drug abuse. But higher prices may also increase crime committed by users to obtain drug money as well as violence among dealers. The net effect is uncertain. Furthermore, there is no reason to assume that there is a consistent relationship between drug prices and crime. More likely, the connection is context-specific, different for different drugs, cities, time periods, and price levels.

Mark Moore has pointed out that ideally we would like to have two completely separate drug markets (see Wilson [1985, 220]). In one market, which would be open only to confirmed addicts, drugs would be sold at low prices, thereby reducing the need for addicts to commit crimes. In the second market, drugs would be expensive, thus deterring the initiation of new users. In practice, maintaining such an arrangement is difficult, as the history of British efforts to allow addicts legal access to drugs attests (Turner 1991); nonaddicts have an incentive to achieve addict status, and arbitrage frustrates efforts to prop up prices in the high price market.

There is one drug for which higher prices would clearly be crime-decreasing: alcohol. According to surveys of jail and state prison inmates, more crimes, and especially violent crimes, are committed under the influence of alcohol than under the influence of all illicit drugs combined (U.S. Department of Justice 1988 and 1991). Arguably, alcohol-related crime represents the single largest external cost of substance abuse.

A number of policy actions could reduce alcohol-related crime. Increasing taxes on alcohol is the most obvious. Alcohol consumption is responsive to price, and at present, the federal and state tax burden on the average drink is only about ten cents, roughly one-tenth its total price. Both economic efficiency and fairness dictate that alcohol taxes should be high enough to cover the costs that drinkers impose on others. As it is, they do not even come close; even studies that exclude the costs of alcohol-related crime suggest that drinkers pay for only a third of their external costs (Manning et al. 1989). A good case can thus be made for alcohol taxes at the level of a dollar per drink (Kleiman 1992a). The effect on alcohol-related crime (including domestic violence and child abuse) would likely be substantial.

Of course, such a tax would have disadvantages. Trafficking and consumption of "moonshine" and other illegal alcohol products would increase, bringing with it damage from black market crime and adulterated drinks. But evidence from those foreign countries where alcohol is taxed more highly than in the United States—and from the early 1950s, when U.S. alcohol taxes were, in terms of purchasing power, several times higher than they are now—suggests that these effects would present only minor problems. It appears that the safety and convenience of legal alcohol, and loyalty to legal brands, are tough to compete with.

Restricting availability.   A number of years ago, Mark Moore pointed out that the demand for an illicit drug is a function not simply of its cash price but rather of its "effective price," a measure that includes, in addition to its dollar price, toxicity of adulterants, access time, and risks of victimization and arrest (Moore 1973). These nonmonetary elements of the effective price can be thought of as the drug's "availability" to its users (Rocheleau and Kleiman 1993).

Three observations make the distinction between price and availability important. First, there is not a perfect correlation between price and availability; some kinds of enforcement actions affect price more than availability, while others affect availability more than price. Second, reductions in availability (that is, increases in the nonmoney price) will not have the same unwanted side effects as an increase in price. Third, the nonmoney price is likely to be much higher for new drug users than for experienced ones. (Note that where drugs are not prohibited, regulation can be used to reduce availability. With alcohol, for example, states determine not only who is allowed to sell—by requiring licenses—but also what, where, and when.)

In principle, if enforcement could decrease the availability of a drug without increasing the dollar price, we would get the benefits of a price rise in the form of reduced consumption without its costs in increased expenditures and illicit revenues. In practice, enforcement cannot choose its effects so neatly and cleanly, but some types of enforcement do a better job of decreasing availability than others. The important distinction is between high-level and street-level enforcement. High-level enforcement (including interdiction and source country eradication efforts) boosts the dollar price of drugs, but has little impact on availability, other than by shrinking the overall size of the market. In contrast, street-level enforcement can directly affect availability. By threatening retail sellers, street-level enforcement can shrink their numbers, restrict their locations, and generally make them more cautious. Street-level enforcement also scares buyers. All of this should increase the nonmoney price of drugs, and there is some evidence that concentrated street-level enforcement, especially against relatively small markets, can increase treatment admissions among users and decrease crime rates (Kleiman et al. 1988).

By making it more difficult and risky for retail buyers and sellers to complete transactions, street-level enforcement reduces drug consumption with fewer side effects than would accompany a policy that simply raised drug prices. A more crucial advantage of street-level enforcement is that retail drug markets are responsible for much of the violence and declining quality of life in inner city communities. Insofar as it can scale back the volume and flagrancy of the retail drug trade, and in turn the violence that goes with it, effective street-level enforcement might help reclaim for law-abiding citizens large areas of their neighborhoods.

In practice, the results of intensive retail drug enforcement efforts are mixed, and evidence of a general relationship between the overall level of retail enforcement and the overall crime rate is lacking. Lynn, Massachusetts, and Tampa, Florida, are success stories, but failures are far greater in number (Kleiman et al. 1988; Kennedy 1993). Still, the victories have provided not only hope but some important lessons about the components of a successful strategy.

What appears to be key is a shift away from the traditional approach of simply seizing drugs and arresting dealers toward a comprehensive and integrated strategy of market disruption (Kennedy 1993). The basic game plan of such a disruption scheme is to coordinate active community involvement with the resources of multiple government agencies in order to assault the drug market with a barrage of measures, which together make it so difficult for the market to operate that it virtually collapses.

Tampa's much heralded Quick Uniformed Action against Drugs (QUAD) program was something of a model operation in this regard. With targeted enforcement, the police pressured sellers to continually change their venues, and scared away buyers by seizing their cars in "reverse stings" where the police posed as dealers. Citizen information was used to identify and seize drug stashes. With the cooperation of other city authorities, abandoned houses were razed, bars and small stores implicated in drug dealing were closed down, and local ordinances were employed to clear crowds from known trafficking sites. Where six months of conventional enforcement had failed to curtail street trafficking, six months of the QUAD program virtually eliminated public drug dealing, bringing considerable reductions in violence, disorder, and fear (Kennedy 1993).

The usefulness of retail-level drug law enforcement as a crime control measure is likely to depend strongly on how large and widespread the retail market is for the drug under consideration and whether there is a risk that the number of users of the drug is about to rise substantially. A crackdown on a small market is both more likely to succeed and less expensive in enforcement resources. If sales are widespread, cracking down in one area may only have limited benefits. Retail enforcement is likely to be especially valuable for a drug for which initiations are rising, or seem poised to rise, because an increase in the nonmoney costs of drug acquisition weighs particularly heavily on new users.

Thus, enforcement against retail-level cocaine dealing was a much more attractive program in 1985 than it is today; the market was smaller, but the number of actual and potential new users was larger. With heroin prices very low, but retail availability still quite spotty, retail heroin enforcement, especially in cities where heroin dealing is not yet widespread, may be a good investment of police resources today.

Sanctions for intoxication.   Much of the social damage caused by drug users occurs while they are intoxicated. As noted earlier, a majority of jail and state prison inmates report that they were intoxicated when they committed their current offense. Even allowing for the possibility that intoxication contributes to the likelihood of arrest, it seems that something like half of all crimes are committed under the influence of drugs or alcohol.

Presumably, some of these crimes would not have been perpetrated in the absence of intoxication, in large part because being drunk or high clouds judgment and diminishes self-control. In other words, for some individuals, in certain circumstances, the threat of punishment is a sufficient deterrent to crime when they are sober, but inadequate when they are intoxicated.

One approach to combating intoxication-generated crime is to discourage intoxication in the first place, or at least intoxication in settings where damaging behavior is particularly likely. Such a policy can take one of three forms: the law can proscribe intoxication per se, as do laws against drunkenness; or it can cast its net more narrowly, either with respect to persons—forbidding intoxication only to those who have committed crimes under the influence—or conduct—forbidding only dangerous or harmful intoxicated behavior. In practice, the last approach could involve two steps: first,

318 DAVID BOYUM AND MARK A. R. KLEIMAN

punishing intoxicated individuals who are engaged in activities (such as driving) where their intoxication significantly increases risks to others; second, treating intoxication as an aggravating, rather than a mitigating, factor in punishing crimes (either in sentencing or crime definition). However, such policies raise difficult philosophical questions, and retributive considerations probably argue against some of them.

It is not difficult to justify laws against intoxication, at least intoxication in public. Becoming drunk or otherwise high is (for most people) voluntary behavior, and insofar as the risks it imposes on others are substantial, it amounts to reckless endangerment. But in only a small percentage of cases does intoxication lead to criminal or other antisocial acts, and it is hard to imagine severe punishments for intoxication, especially drunkenness. And if the penalties are light (on the order of a speeding ticket), they would provide little additional deterrent to the punishment for crimes.

Making intoxication an aggravating circumstance in crime commission is more problematic. Deterrence theory supports the idea: if intoxication weakens self-command, then logically it requires the threat of a greater punishment to deter someone who is drunk or high than to deter someone who is sober. However, is it really more blameworthy to commit a crime in a semiconscious drunken stupor than when stone-cold sober? If anything, notions of culpability are more consistent with intoxication being a mitigation, rather than an aggravation of responsibility; the criminal law recognizes diminished capacity, and intoxication can contribute to behavior we would consider unrepresentative of a person's character.[7]

There are probably variations on these policies that are more palatable to our sense of justice. For instance, the law could proscribe, and punish with some severity, reckless intoxication, rather than intoxication per se. Implicit in such an approach is the notion that intoxication increases the likelihood of socially irresponsible or criminal behavior, and so those who get intoxicated have a duty to do so in a setting that minimizes these risks. Being armed while intoxicated, for example, could reasonably be forbidden.

Another avenue is to target only those previously convicted of offenses committed while intoxicated. In this way, the law would acknowledge both that not all individuals are crime-prone while intoxicated and that intoxication or intoxicated behavior is not always characteristic of an individual. With multiple offenses, the "I wasn't myself" defense is no longer convincing. Interestingly, John Stuart Mill advocated such a policy:

> Drunkenness, for example, in ordinary cases, is not a fit subject for legislative interference; but I should deem it perfectly legitimate that a person, who had once been convicted of any act of violence to others under the influence of drink, should be placed under a special legal restriction, personal to himself; that if he were afterwards found

drunk, he should be liable to a penalty, and that if when in that state he committed another offense, the punishment to which he would be liable for that other offense should be increased in severity. (Mill 1989, 98)

However, while Mill's proposal to forbid intoxication to those convicted of intoxicated offenses is unexceptionable, the suggestion for enhanced penalties seems dubious on retributive grounds. Given that intoxication weakens judgment and self-control, it is hard to argue that committing a crime when drunk is worse than committing the same crime when sober, even when the perpetrator has a checkered past. Ultimately, any policy that treats intoxication as an aggravation has to be justified on the grounds that the policy's deterrent value outweighs the violation of retributive principles. Given that a majority of violent crimes, including perhaps two-thirds of homicides, are committed under the influence of drugs and alcohol, such a claim deserves consideration.

There is also a practical problem with Mill's proposal. In effect, it tells problem drinkers that they can drink, but not get drunk, a bad strategy according to most substance abuse counselors. Perhaps it is better to require those with a history of drinking problems (such as committing a crime while drunk) to follow a course of abstinence. Since enforcing such individual prohibitions would be difficult without the assistance of retail alcohol sellers, such an approach would seem to require some form of personal drinking licenses that could be revoked for intoxicated misbehavior (Kleiman 1992a).

Sentencing policy.   Not all drug offenders inflict the same level of damage on society. Indeed, research suggests that a small number of them represent society's most active and vicious criminals, and that they account for the lion's share of the violent and property crime perpetrated by drug offenders. These individuals ought to be a particular focus of criminal justice efforts.

An especially important step would be to use prison space more efficiently. Given limited prison capacity, it makes sense to give priority to housing the most active and violent offenders. Current federal policy is perhaps the most prominent example of the wrong approach. Under the law, relatively minor participants in drug trafficking, some with no prior arrests, frequently face long mandatory prison terms. According to a recent Department of Justice analysis, 21 percent of all federal prisoners are "low-level drug law violators" with no record of violence or incarceration. Of these, 42 percent are drug couriers (or "mules"), rather than dealers or principals in trafficking organizations (Heymann 1994). Since those prisoners' cells could instead be holding more dangerous offenders, the result of long mandatory sentences for minor drug offenders is to increase crime. Even if long sentences were given to offenders worth locking up, deterrence theory suggests that this would not be the best way to employ limited cell capacity to deter drug dealing: certainty (maximized by handing out many shorter sentences) is more important than severity (Cook 1981).

Prevention and Treatment

The demand for drugs can be reduced in two ways: by altering the subjective states (attitudes, opinions, and preferences) of users and potential users or by changing the objective conditions of drug use to make it less pleasant or more hazardous. Even if attitudes were systematically harder to influence than objective conditions, there are at least two reasons why attitudes might nonetheless be the object of policy intervention, through either prevention or treatment programs. First, given the constraints of the justice system, supply reduction strategies have only limited capacity to raise the prices or reduce the availability of mass market drugs. Second, in a liberal society, it is generally preferable that citizens behave responsibly, and obey the laws, for reasons of internal, rather than external, motivation. It is better, for instance, if our fellow citizens refrain from mugging us because they believe mugging is wrong, and not because they are afraid of getting caught. (It does, of course, matter how attitudes or values are internalized. Big Brother–like tactics might be useful in preventing drug abuse, but at substantial cost to civic and republican values. In the view of many, even some of the current antidrug messages tread rather close to the line, both as to their freedom with the facts and their approach to prejudice and fear (Gersh 1988; Trebach, in Trebach and Inciardi 1993)).

There are several ways in which changes in attitudes can influence drug abuse and its consequences. First, attitudes can reduce initiation, either because potential users believe drug use to be wrong or dangerous, or because drug use is stigmatized. (A worry here is that the same attitudinal changes that reduce initiation may increase the rates of progression to heavy use, and of misbehavior, among those who do initiate.)

Second, attitudes can affect the progression to habitual use, or influence the time, place, and character of intoxicated behavior. An obvious helpful example is the practice of choosing a "designated driver." A less obvious illustration is the Japanese perspective that intoxication is something to be flaunted rather than concealed, as is typical in Western societies. By being public about their drunkenness, the Japanese make it easier for those who are intoxicated to acknowledge their incapacities and for those who are sober to identify them.

Third, attitudes can influence the frequency and duration of cessation. Attitudes about addiction, attitudes towards ex-addicts, and beliefs about the probability and difficulty of successful cessation all matter.

Lastly, attitudes can influence involvement in drug dealing, which in turn impacts drug use and its consequences. When potential dealers enter the drug trade, they increase the availability and lower the price of drugs. They also tend to increase drug use and crime, since most of them eventually become users themselves.

Prevention.   Prevention programs are an effort to change attitudes about drug use. From a policy perspective, successful prevention programs are a clear winner; they offer the benefit of reduced drug use without the baggage of black market side effects. That's the good news. The bad news is that few prevention programs have demonstrated that they can consistently reduce the number of their subjects who use drugs. And the positive results that have accompanied some programs have often proved difficult to replicate in other settings. Added to this are concerns about some of the methods employed; many prevention instructors and some antidrug advertising disseminate or broadcast demonstrably false information about the physical and psychological effects of drug use (Horgan 1990). The programs would have to be marvelously effective to justify this kind of misinformation.

Despite these difficulties, prevention programs deserve continued research and evaluation. Their focus should also be broadened to include prevention of drug dealing, especially given the growing evidence that dealing is less disapproved of than drug drug taking among inner city adolescents. On average, it is much more valuable to convince a youth not to sell drugs than to convince him not to try them. Many young persons lead successful lives despite having experimented with, or occasionally used, drugs. Fewer, especially in inner city neighborhoods, prosper when they have sold drugs.

How to best prevent dealing is unclear, but since kids are clearly attracted by the promise of money, efforts would probably include an anti-conspicuous-consumption campaign. This could involve, among other steps, uniforms and dress codes in schools to curtail the visible competition in expensive clothing, footwear, and jewelry. An anti-dealing strategy might also develop community alternatives to "hanging out," such as after-school or late night recreational programs. Somewhat surprisingly, "midnight basketball" leagues have been shown to noticeably reduce the rates of some crimes where they have been tried.

While a discussion of education, social welfare, and economic policy is beyond the scope of this chapter, it is also important to note that the appeal of drug dealing or use depends partly on the alternatives. To the extent that there are better employment or educational or recreational opportunities, we should expect less involvement in drug use and dealing. Drug prohibition may have important effects here, since a criminal record depreciates one's value in the job market. While this risk may keep some from using or selling drugs, it makes things more difficult for those who are not deterred. This cost needs to be weighed against the limited benefits of routine retail-level drug enforcement in cities with large-scale (as opposed to nascent) drug markets.

Drug abuse treatment.   From a crime control perspective, successful treatment of drug-involved offenders is another unequivocal winner. The criminal activity of addict-offenders seems to rise and fall in step with their drug consumption; and, importantly, the relationship holds whether reductions in drug use are unassisted or the product of formalized treatment (Anglin and Speckart 1986; Nurco et al. 1988). Moreover, a treatment-induced reduction in demand does not bring with it the side effects of an enforcement-induced reduction (higher drug prices, depletion of criminal justice resources). Lastly, many drug-involved offenders sell drugs in addition to using them, and some may exit the drug trade if they gain control over their own habits.

Discussion of drug treatment seems to be dominated by two issues: whether or not treatment "works," and what can be done to increase the availability of treatment. Treatment advocates insist that drug treatment is effective and often call for "treatment on demand." Skeptics counter that abstinence is short-lived for the vast majority of treatment clients, and argue that a significant expansion in treatment services would, in effect, throw good money after bad. In fact, treating drug-involved offenders clearly has benefits in excess of its costs, but merely offering more treatment may not be the best approach to getting more offenders treated.

Evaluation studies indicate that all the major drug treatment modalities—therapeutic communities, methadone maintenance, outpatient drug-free programs—are modestly successful, at least according to most outcome criteria (Anglin and Hser 1990; Gerstein and Harwood 1990). The usual yardsticks are *post-treatment* levels of drug and alcohol use (rates of abstinence and relapse), and employment activity. While these measures may be sufficient for evaluating treatment for a stockbroker, they overlook what is perhaps the most important benefit of treating drug-involved offenders.

Findings from the Treatment Outcome Prospective Study (TOPS), to date the most comprehensive evaluation study of treatment effectiveness, indicate that the largest reductions in criminal activity, by a wide margin, occur *during* treatment. Among TOPS subjects treated three months or longer, about 60 percent of residential clients, and about one-third of outpatient methadone and outpatient drug-free clients, reported criminal activity in the year prior to entering treatment. Yet fewer than 10 percent of the clients in outpatient methadone and outpatient drug-free programs, and only 3.1 percent of residential clients, reported committing predatory crimes during treatment. In fact, this reduction in criminal activity is so large that on cost-benefit grounds it would probably justify the treatment costs, even if treatment had no effect on post-treatment behavior (Hubbard et al. 1989).

Two points are often missed in discussions of treatment availability. First, many drug-involved offenders will enter treatment only if coerced; simple availability is often not a sufficient enticement. Second, drug enforcement and the criminal justice system are the most powerful mechanisms for getting drug-involved offenders into treatment; high effective prices can convince users that maintaining their habits is too costly, and courts can offer or compel treatment as a condition of parole or probation.

For maximum crime control, treatment resources should be aimed at drug-involved offenders. Arguing against this approach is the fact that criminally active drug users are often poor candidates for treatment, at least as evaluated by treatment providers, who often have their eyes fixed on long-term abstinence as the target outcome. And indeed, despite having a captive clientele, most prison-based drug treatment programs have not been shown to reduce recidivism rates (Gerstein and Harwood 1990).

However, a small number of prison therapeutic communities (TCs), with strong linkages to community-based treatment programs—such as the Stay'n Out program in New York—appear to work. An equally important research finding is that those who are coerced into nonprison treatment by the criminal justice system fare as well as, if not better than, those who enter such programs voluntarily (Anglin and Hser 1990). Together, these findings argue for more prison-based TCs (of course modeled on the better programs), and an expansion in the legally coerced treatment for nonincarcerated users identified by the criminal justice system. (The former is actually relatively inexpensive, since housing, which is a major cost of TCs, is already paid for. Typically, an in-prison TC adds only a few thousand dollars to the annual cost of prison alone.)

Evaluations of treatment programs indicate that monitoring of drug use by urine testing enhances outcomes (Hser, Longshore, and Anglin 1994). This raises the interesting question of whether carefully implemented programs of coerced abstinence—regular urinalyses combined with swift and sure sanctions for dirty or missed tests—could achieve some of the benefits of treatment at a much lower cost (BOTEC Analysis Corporation 1990).

Coerced abstinence.   Casual users account for no more than one-quarter of the total volume of cocaine consumed in the United States, and for an even smaller fraction of the volume of heroin consumed. This is not because heavy users are very numerous. On the contrary, the total number of active heavy cocaine users and heavy heroin users in the United States probably comes to no more than three million persons, of whom about three-quarters derive a substantial share of their income from criminal activity (Rhodes, Scheiman, and Carlson 1993). These criminally active heavy users are the main contributors to crime related to illicit drugs, both through their own criminal activity and through their contribution to illicit market demand.

Since the sorts of crimes committed to support heroin and cocaine habits are likely to result in fairly frequent arrest and conviction, a significant number of cocaine- and heroin-involved offenders are under the jurisdiction of the criminal justice system at any given moment, most of them on probation or parole. Their identification as offenders already being made, their identification as heavy drug users requires nothing more than a chemical test of urine or hair, and whether they continue to use is similarly straightforward to determine.

Given the very high personal crime rates characteristic of drug-involved offenders who remain heavily drug-involved, the substantial cost of imprisonment might not be too high a price to pay to avoid the crimes they commit while free, even putting aside the crimes committed by the drug traffickers they support (Cavanagh and Kleiman 1990). From the crime control perspective, this would certainly be a better use of the cells than long sentences for minor drug dealers, who are certain to be replaced within the illicit labor market.

But it may not be necessary to imprison drug-involved offenders to reduce their drug consumption. The threat of incarceration for continued drug use might be adequate to deter many of them. The question is simply whether someone whose continued liberty is in principle conditional on obeying certain rules can in practice be effectively deterred from continuing to take illicit drugs and committing crimes to buy them.

The two keys to deterrence, especially for persons with short planning horizons and poor judgment concerning risk—two characteristics likely to produce, and likely to be produced by, addiction to expensive illicit drugs— are certainty and swiftness. Severity is of less importance. The observation that quitting any drug habit involves repeated attempts and repeated failures only increases the importance of creating predictable but not catastrophic penalties for the failures that are almost certain to occur (and, ideally, rewards for periods of success).

Unfortunately, the current drug-testing practices of probation and parole departments do not pay attention either to what is known about deterrence or to what is known about recovery from addiction. Infrequent testing, and even more infrequent sanctioning for missed or dirty tests, are combined with unnecessary severity. Several months in prison is not an uncommon sanction for a "technical violation" involving drugs—in California, the single most common reason for a prison admission is a failed drug test—and sanctions of years are not unknown. Few better ways could be devised of absorbing large amounts of scarce punishment capacity with the minimum benefit in terms of deterrence or relapse management.

The alternative would be frequent (say, twice-weekly) tests and automatic, but mild, sanctions: perhaps two days' confinement for the first failure, escalating with repeated failures over a short period. Such a system has been proposed (DuPont and Wish 1992) and employed with some apparent success in various pilot programs (BOTEC Analysis Corporation 1990; Kushner 1993), but has never been made routine in a large jurisdiction, or even carefully tested with experimental controls.

One reason for the failure of coerced abstinence to gain even a serious test is that it does not engage the professional interests of drug treatment providers, drug enforcement agents and prosecutors, or corrections officials. Another reason is that the proposal does not fit comfortably within the categories (supply versus demand, tough versus soft) that dominate the drug policy debate.

But if such a program could be made to work on a large scale, the results might be dramatic: a reduction in total cocaine volume of 40 percent, far exceeding the impact of any other plausible program, would not be out of range. This would shrink not only the crime rates of those tested but the illicit markets they prop up, and thus both dealing-related violence and the pull illicit markets exercise over poor adolescents. The cost, which has been estimated at about $2,500 per participant per year or about $5 billion for a complete national program, would be at least partly offset by reduced imprisonment rates for the participants and for the cocaine and heroin dealers driven from the shrunken illicit markets. The availability of formal treatment would almost certainly decrease the violation rate among participants, but might not be essential to the program's functioning.

Summary of Policy Implications

Because so much crime appears connected to the sale and chronic use of drugs, and because crime is widely thought the most serious of the harms associated with drug abuse, many Americans consider drug policy to be a massive crime prevention program. This view, which does not see any trade-offs between reducing drug abuse and reducing crime, is analytically unsound. Any drug policy that includes efforts to limit or hinder access to drugs will generate, along with its benefits, unwanted side effects. Specifically, such policy will decrease some types of crime, while increasing other sorts; in principle, the net effect can go either way.

Moreover, there is no reason to assume a consistent relationship between particular drug policy strategies and crime. More likely, policy effects are highly sensitive to the specific circumstances of implementation, and vary across drugs, cities, and time periods. To take one example: enforcement that results in increased heroin prices might lead to lower crime in cities where methadone maintenance is readily available, and higher crime where methadone programs are scarce.

Given such uncertainties, we are agnostic on some of the most hotly debated issues of drug policy, such as whether legalizing cocaine in some form would reduce crime. At the end of the day, what can be said with any colorable show of confidence can be briefly said:

- Reducing the incidence of drunkenness will reduce crime, unless the control measures create a substantial illicit market. Increased taxation (up to some multiple of current rates) and a campaign of persuasion to make drunkenness less fashionable both seem like good candidates. Denying access to alcohol to those who have committed crimes under the influence would be harder to achieve, but the potential rewards would be large.

- Reducing the volume of cocaine consumed without raising its price will also reduce crime. Making treatment more available to nonincarcerated offenders is one way to do so.

- Very long sentences for minor, nonviolent drug offenders increase predatory crime by wasting prison cells without much influencing the price or availability of drugs.

- Police tactics to disrupt certain kinds of flagrant drug dealing can reduce crime even if they do little to reduce drug consumption.

- Using the probation and parole systems to coerce abstinence among persons under their supervision could greatly reduce crime committed to buy drugs and the violence and disorder incident to drug dealing.

- Although heroin is much cheaper now than it was ten or twenty years ago, it remains hard to find for most consumers in most areas of the country. Keeping it that way by moving aggressively against emerging retail heroin markets will tend to reduce crime.

- If, as seems to be so, marijuana acts as a substitute (in the economic sense) for alcohol and cocaine, then anything that reduces the effective price of marijuana relative to that of alcohol or cocaine will tend to reduce crime.

While this list of relatively firm conclusions is short, each item on it is of potentially great significance. If drug abuse control policy were made primarily for practical reasons, and primarily with an eye to the control of predatory crime, such policies might be close to its center, and the result would probably be a substantial reduction in crime.

However, those who rely for their careers on the support of the public have found that, like Calvin Coolidge's preacher in his attitude toward sin, they can get along on drugs and crime by being "against it." Only a change in public attitudes is likely to remedy that situation, and it will take more than essays on policy analysis to bring about such a change.

LAWRENCE W. SHERMAN 14

THE POLICE

"More cops mean less crime." This claim is an article of faith in American politics, a bipartisan dogma from City Hall to the White House. Consider the following dialogue at a neighborhood civic meeting between Philadelphia Mayor Ed Rendell and civic leader Glenn Devitt in 1994:

> Rendell told the crowd how his administration had reorganized police patrols to put almost 300 more officers on the street. "We're not seeing them!" Devitt said to loud applause. Rendell said the police department's response time is "better than every single American city." To which a chorus yelled back: "It's not good enough!" More applause. [1]

High visibility and low response time are the twin pillars of modern police strategy, implying the more police the better. Yet there is growing evidence that the *number* of police on the street is far less important than the *tasks* police perform. Spreading more police out across a big city and lowering response time, the research shows, will have little effect on crime—no matter what neighborhood groups may think. But more police attacking the risk factors for crime—like guns on the street and "hot spot" street corners—could make a substantial difference in crime.

American police once paid more attention to risk factors than to "visible" patrol and rapid response. Several decades ago, for example, police routinely checked businesses at night for unlocked doors. They checked taverns for people carrying guns. They monitored repeat offenders and paroled felons. But these crime prevention tasks fell by the wayside as the number of 911 calls to big city police skyrocketed in the 1980s, more than doubling in some agencies[2] and rising far faster than the number of crimes. The nature and causes of this increase are poorly understood, but its consequences are all too apparent: police tasks are now primarily responsive to past crimes, rather than preventive of future crimes.

Like investors balancing income and growth, taxpayers must decide how to balance their investment in police resources between past and future crimes. We attack past crimes to achieve justice, with the hope that justice will deter future crimes. But the odds are against us, with few crimes solved and even fewer punished. To prevent future crimes, police are increasingly turning back to old-fashioned strategies and inventing new ones. While less glamorous than cops-and-robbers chases, these dogged efforts to reduce the opportunities for crime may have far more payoff. The problem is to get the balance right between punishment and prevention, between making arrests and achieving civil obedience. While we would like to think the two goals are compatible, substantial research shows that often they are not.

This chapter begins with the most visible question about police and crime prevention: How many police do we need? President Clinton's 1992 campaign pledge to put 100,000 more police on the streets (about a 20 percent increase in uniformed patrol) would constitute the biggest national increase in police presence in this century. Recent research shows how the additional officers could best be used.

The chapter then describes two developing police strategies for crime prevention and the evidence to date on their effectiveness: "community policing" (or police as security guards) and "problem solving" (or police as public health agents). The chapter concludes with an assessment of the tough choices we must make in order to achieve more effective policing.

How Many Police Do We Need?

The United States has some 504,000 state and local police officers providing general-purpose law enforcement, with an additional 61,000 officers policing transit systems, public housing, state university systems, and other special areas.[3] This works out to about 1 general purpose officer for every 500 Americans, or 20 per 10,000. The number of uniformed officers patroling the streets is about half the total, after we subtract supervisors, detectives, and support services jobs like training, radio communications, and computer operation. The number of patrol officers must be further adjusted for the number of hours spent on the streets after off-duty time, vacations, training, and court time are subtracted. A reasonable estimate is about 200 patrol shifts per year per officer, with a maximum of seven hours on patrol each shift, or about 16 percent of the hours in a year. Thus, at any given time, there is an average of 40,000 patrol officers on the streets out of the 500,000 sworn officers employed.

Applying this ratio of 8 in 100 to President Clinton's proposal, the nation would go from having one officer on patrol at any given time for every 6,250 Americans (1.6 per 10,000) to one officer for every 5,208 Americans (1.9 per 10,000). This 20 percent increase does not seem likely to make much difference in crime, at least under the conventional theories of high visibility and rapid response time. Nor is it likely to produce the substantially higher arrest rates that some advocates argue will reduce crime. Even if the increase did improve visibility, response time, and arrest rates, the evidence from two centuries of police history and a quarter century of careful research suggests that all three issues are more complicated than they seem.

Does Visibility Matter?

Many serious scholars are convinced that police visibility is irrelevant to the crime rate. University of Arizona professors Michael Gottfredson and Travis Hirschi, for example, conclude that "The idea that a substantial effect on the crime rate can be achieved simply by increasing the numbers of police—and thereby restricting opportunities [for crime]—is . . . contrary to . . . empirical research."[4] University of Delaware professor Carl Klockars goes even further, saying that "it makes about as much sense to have police patrol routinely in cars to fight crime as it does to have firemen patrol routinely in firetrucks to fight fire."[5]

A cursory look at the ratio of police to serious crime across American cities supports this view, with some of the safest cities having very few police per capita, and some of the most heavily policed cities having very high crime rates.[6] In San Diego, for example, the 1992 homicide rate was 13 per 100,000, and the total serious violent crime (homicide, rape, robbery, and aggravated assault) rate was 1,284 per 100,000. Washington D.C.'s homicide rate was almost six times higher, at 75 per 100,000, and its total serious violent crime rate was over twice as high at 2,832 per 100,000. Yet Washington has almost five times as many police per capita, at 7.5 local police per 1,000 people, compared with San Diego's 1.6. (That does not begin to count all the other uniformed police patrol agencies in Washington, such as park police and Secret Service embassy police). Even when Washington increased its police force by a congressionally mandated 19 percent, from 3,974 in 1989 to 4,740 in 1990, total serious violent crime did not fall; it rose by 15 percent, and homicide rose by 9 percent.

The conclusion that police strength does not affect the crime rate is consistent with a highly influential experiment conducted by the Kansas City, Missouri, police in the early 1970s. That experiment systematically compared crime rates in three groups of patrol beats. One group was given two to three times as much patrol coverage as usual. Another group had patrol entirely withdrawn, except to answer calls for service. A third group was left unchanged at normal patrol coverage. The results showed no difference in crime across the three groups.[7] Despite methodological criticisms of the experiment,[8] many mayors and police chiefs concluded from this evidence that increasing police patrols would not be cost-effective.

A large body of evidence, however, supports a contrary view: *police presence can reduce or even increase the crime rate substantially in specific places at specific times, depending upon what the police do.* This evidence comes from police history, police strikes, the "hot spots" phenomenon, police crackdowns, and more advanced police experiments.[9]

Police history. The past 150 years of police history provides an important natural experiment in the effects of police visibility. For most of the past thousand years, neither Europe nor North America had visible police patrol. An often-incompetent night watch system was limited to larger cities, and posed little deterrent threat to criminals. Policing was essentially a voluntary communal effort, relying on groups of citizens' responding to shouted summonses to "stop the thief." English communities could even be fined by the Crown for failing to catch an escaping criminal suspect.[10]

By the mid-eighteenth century, English thinkers found this system totally inadequate for the huge and often anonymous city of London, even with the rise of bounty-hunting private detectives. No less creative a person than the author of *Tom Jones,* Mr. Henry Fielding, published a treatise calling for professional police, then persuaded the government to secretly pay for a small group of them after a bloody crime wave in the summer of 1753.[11] By 1830, a lengthy policy debate over public safety versus individual liberty was resolved, and a large, uniformed patrol force was established as the Metropolitan Police of London. New York and many other cities followed London's example, creating a major experiment in the effects of foot patrol in highly dense urban environments. Instead of shouting for their neighbors, city residents could now shout "police" with a good chance that an officer would hear them and respond. Officers on foot patrol were highly visible in these closely packed communities, where up to a hundred people could see the police officer at a time.

The result of these developments is hard to measure with precision. There is substantial evidence that serious violent crime and public disorder declined in response to the "invention" of visible police patrol. Other social changes, however, were also associated with the drop in crime. Increasing democratization and wider voting rights, for example, could have produced less alienation and less crime. Or the growth of the urban middle class and of public education might have strengthened informal social controls. Nonetheless, the sharp drop in violent crime in London after 1830 is an impressive fact associated with police visibility.[12]

Equally impressive, though no more definitive, is the fact that serious crime in the United States began to rise in the 1950s and 1960s as police visibility dropped substantially. While many other social changes were also occurring at that time, it is important to note the massive out-migration from highly dense environments where police were very visible to low density, suburban environments where police were rarely seen. Even within city limits, the rising prevalence of automobile ownership shifted the population toward single family, large lot housing and away from multiple family, small lot housing. Given the same ratio of police to population, the falling ratio of population to square mile drastically lowered the odds that police would encounter a crime in progress or a criminal about to commit a crime. Police responded to this change by shifting from foot to automobile patrol. But the intensity of police watching from patrol cars, and the frequency of stopping to question suspicious persons, may have declined substantially relative to these activities during foot patrol.

The predominant police theory during that era shifted from high visibility to rapid response. While police thinker O. W. Wilson still advocated the use of patrol to create an aura of "omnipresence" to prevent crime,[13] police purchases of radio-equipped patrol cars were often justified as helping to catch more crooks during or after the occurrence of crime. The long-term effect on police strategy was a transition from "wall-to-wall cops" visible patrol to a "dial-a-cop" rapid response.[14] That transition was impressively, if not conclusively, linked to a rise in serious crime. While many other social factors have been cited to explain the crime increase, the *causal* evidence for them is no more compelling than it is for the police strategy correlation.

Police strikes.   Police strikes are the ultimate experiment: what would happen if we had no police? In Boston and Liverpool in 1919, in Montreal in 1969, in Helsinki in 1973, and even in Nazi-occupied Copenhagen, the evidence is consistent: all Hell breaks loose.[15] Robberies in particular show sudden increases, as well as fights and property crime. Hospital admissions for violent injuries in Helsinki rose substantially. In Montreal, the hourly burglary rate rose by 13,000 percent, and the hourly bank robbery rate rose by 50,000 percent. This evidence should leave no doubt that even homogeneous, well-educated, low crime societies need police to control crime. The argument is not over whether the medicine of policing is required but over what the dosage should be.

Hot spots of crime.   Police strikes remove police from all parts of the city simultaneously. But crime does not occur in every place in the city. Over half of all crime comes from less than 3 percent of the addresses in a city, and crime at those "hot spot" addresses is bunched by "hot" days of the week and times of day. Thus, most addresses, and even most blocks, in any city go for years without any crime—even in high crime neighborhoods.[16]

Spreading patrol visibility out evenly in space and time means applying it *un*evenly to crime. While every citizen gets a "fair share" of policing, this strategy may be as useful as giving everyone his or her fair share of penicillin—regardless of whether the person is sick. And by reducing penicillin dosage for those who are sick, the net effect may be that the treatment helps no one. The Kansas City Patrol Experiment tested this strategy, spreading police out fairly evenly across these peaks and valleys of spatial and temporal variations in crime. Like standard American policing, the experiment invested most police time on the low-crime valleys and offered little extra presence on the high-crime peaks. Regardless of the scientific issues with the experiment, it is this illogical (but politically attractive) "fair share" strategy that may be at fault.

A more sensible question, then, is whether police visibility can make a difference if concentrated at high crime places and times. So far, at least, the answer is yes. When police have taken that approach, evaluation findings have generally shown police can reduce, or at least displace, the targeted crime problems.[17] Police visibility may matter immensely, but not with the "fair share" approach the Philadelphia civic group wants. Concentrating police visibility where the crime is may protect those civic group members much better than the spread-out strategy they demand, for all citizens are more likely to be attacked by stranger crime in public hot spots than in their own homes. One hundred percent of the robberies in one year in Minneapolis, for example, occur at just 2 percent of that city's addresses.[18]

The need for hot spot police visibility has increased as the population has become less dense over the past half century. The decline in density limits opportunities for many crimes to the few places at which people or property are highly concentrated, like commercial centers. Modern zoning has segregated high density commercial activity from low density residential land use far more markedly than ever before, giving police a choice. One alternative is to dilute police presence to virtual invisibility by patrolling low crime residential areas. The other is to make police omnipresent in crime hot spots. Two kinds of evidence suggest that this second strategy might work: evaluations of police crackdowns and a controlled experiment in hot spot patrol.

Crackdowns and displacement.   Police crackdowns are defined as sudden, massive increases in police presence or enforcement activity. They have produced substantial short-term reductions in crimes as diverse as drunk driving, robbery, drug dealing, prostitution, and youthful disorder, usually in small geographical areas. Whether these crimes have all been pushed to other locations is impossible to say for sure, but the evidence is against it.[19] A review of eighteen police crackdowns around the United States and in five other countries shows that fifteen were successful, with little clear evidence of displacement.[20] The London prostitution crackdown, for example, found no indication that the prostitutes pushed from one area had been arrested in any other area of London.

Further evidence against displacement comes from two sources. One is the observation in many evaluations of just the opposite effect. Rather than displacing crime to surrounding areas, crime prevention measures reduce crime in nearby areas where they have not been implemented. The "phantom" or carryover effect may reflect the second source of evidence against displacement: the concentration of crime in hot spots. That is, if criminal opportunities are limited to hot spots, the prevention of crime in one hot spot seems unlikely to displace crime out of a hot spot. If any displacement occurs, it should be to another hot spot providing a similar opportunity structure. But if police visibility is high in all hot spots in a community, the potential for displacement is theoretically much lower.

The key to making crackdowns work is to keep them short and unpredictable. Long-term police crackdowns all show a "decay" in their deterrent effects over time. Short-term crackdowns, in contrast, show a free bonus of "residual deterrence" after the crackdown stops, while potential offenders slowly figure out that the cops are gone. Random rotation of high police visibility across different short-term targets can accumulate free crime prevention bonuses and get the most value out of police visibility. Even if displacement to other hot spots occurs, the unpredictable increases in police presence at any hot spot may create generally higher deterrent effects from the same number of police officers.

The hot spots patrol experiment.   This theory of increased but unpredictable police presence was put to the test in the Minneapolis Hot Spots Patrol Experiment in 1988–1989. Three hours a day of intermittent, unpredictable police presence was applied to a randomly selected 55 out of the worst 110 hot spot intersections in the city. The other 55 received normal patrol coverage, primarily in response to citizen calls for service. The net difference was about 250 percent more police presence, confirmed by over 6,000 hours of observations by an independent research team. The impact on all reported crime was modest but statistically significant at 13 percent, and even greater for some serious crimes like robbery (over 20 percent). The level of disorder, including fights and disturbances, noted by independent observers was 50 percent lower at the hot spots with higher police visibility than at hot spots in the control group. [21]

Further analysis of the experiment showed the value of frequent rotation of police across different hot spots, rather than long spells of patrol at any one hot spot. The independent observations made it possible to measure how long it took from the time a police car left the hot spot until the first act of crime or disorder was observed there. The analysis showed that the longer the police stayed, the longer the hot spot was crime-free after the police departed—but only up to a point. Five minutes of police presence was more effective than one minute, and ten minutes better than five. But much more than ten minutes of police presence produced diminishing returns. Merely driving through the hot spot had almost no measurable benefit. Thus, the optimal way to use police visibility may be to have police travel from hot spot to hot spot, staying about ten minutes at each one. [22]

The validity of this conclusion, however, may still depend heavily upon what police *do* in the hot spots. The Minneapolis patrols were fairly passive, with officers rarely stepping out of their cars to talk to people or interrogate suspects. More aggressive efforts may have reduced crime even further—or made it worse.

The English police have a name for the phenomenon of more police presence actually increasing crime: "provocative policing." One high Scotland Yard official explained it by describing his early career alone on a foot beat with no radio as a time when he had to use verbal persuasion to keep young male drunks under control. He often broke up fights with minimal problems. "Nowadays," he says, "if a constable runs into any resistance, he calls for backup, and several police cars arrive, but that can just attract even more young men into the fray—so twenty people go to jail for assault."[23] Police visibility is clearly not as simple or consistent as aspirin. Its effect on crime may depend very heavily on how it is administered and how it is absorbed.

Does Response Time Matter?

Even when we don't see the police, we are comforted to know that they will come quickly if we call them. And if a burglar is breaking into our house, we want police to come as quickly as possible. This scenario makes response time a strongly emotional subject, even though it is highly misleading.

In theory, rapid police response should prevent injury, increase arrests, and deter crime. In practice, it seems to do none of these things. Criminals often cause injury in the first seconds of a crime, giving no time for anyone to summon police. Many storekeepers have been killed, for example, while reaching for robbery alarms as the masked gunman walked in the door; in early 1994, several Dallas residents were followed home and shot just as they stepped out of their cars in their own driveways. If police do arrive while the robber is still present, there can be a shootout in which innocent bystanders die in the crossfire, or the victims may be taken hostage. Many banks have abandoned both armed guards and robbery alarms for that reason. As for the burglar breaking into an occupied home, most police advise residents to get out of the home as quickly as possible, and only then call the police. Few people would wait for a fire truck before leaving a burning house, by the same logic.

The more basic problem with reducing injury through lowered response time is that only a minuscule fraction of all calls to police report immediate potential for injury. Most calls report verbal disputes, false commercial burglary alarms, and past property crimes. Reducing response time across the board, to all kinds of calls, is both wasteful and dangerous (as police officers drive fast to reach the crime scene). Thus, when Philadelphia's mayor accepted the premise that quicker response was better, he failed to make this critical distinction. *Just as the value of police visibility appears limited to a*

small fraction of all locations, the value of rapid response time is limited to a small fraction of all calls.
This claim must be qualified by the evidence from police strikes, which shows basically the effect of no response at all. But marginal reductions in average response time, from reasonably soon to even faster, seem pointless. There is little practical difference between three and five minutes for police response, even though the difference in cost is substantial. What is important is that a burglary in progress–occupied dwelling call (or similar events) be answered within minutes or seconds, regardless of the overall average response time.

For the same reasons, reduced response time has little effect upon arrest rates. Even among serious crimes—a minority of all calls to the police—only 25 percent of all crimes involve any contact between a victim and an offender. Three out of four serious crimes are discovered after the fact, and over 90 percent of crimes are either not serious, discovered later, or both. Immediate response to serious crimes in progress now results in an arrest in only 2.9 percent of serious crime calls. The prospects for increasing that rate are small, since much of the "response" time is actually victim response—or delay. In almost half of all cases where victims confront the offender, citizens wait over five minutes before calling police. And the chances of catching an offender after a five-minute delay are no greater than after a sixty-minute delay.[24] The capacity of police to make on-scene arrests is thus limited by citizen delay in calling police, something that is not very easy to change.

Do Arrest Rates Matter?

Even if we could increase arrest rates, it would probably not cause crime to decrease. In theory, more arrests should increase the certainty of punishment and prevent crime through deterrence. But in practice, raising the arrest rate can have several unintended side effects, wiping out any benefits and sometimes even backfiring to cause more crime.

The first problem is that every arrest takes police off the street to do paperwork, sometimes for many hours. The more arrests police make, therefore, the less visibility they provide. The deterrent effects of an arrest and of patrol presence in the streets have never been systematically compared. But the longer arrests take to process, the less advantage they should have over patrol. The amount of time it takes to process arrests varies enormously from one city to the next, from an hour in some small towns up to an entire shift of duty in New York City. Even where it can be done in one hour or less, taking one or two officers off the street for that time means a substantial reduction in patrol visibility. If visibility deters more crime than arrest, then increasing the arrest rate could raise the crime rate—with different trade-offs for each specific type of offense.

This problem would be different if most arrests were for serious felonies.

They are not. Most arrests are for misdemeanors, such as taking inexpensive property or hitting someone (without injury) in an argument, and not for a felony like a burglary or armed robbery. Very few arrests result in prosecution, and most arrests are followed by release within twelve hours. Arrest without prosecution is the most commonly used form of punishment, with fifty-six times more people arrested than committed to prison each year.[25] This reflects, in part, the low seriousness of the offenses leading to most arrests.

Police help preserve their visibility by under-using their arrest powers. Legally trained observers of police encounters with crime victims and accused offenders consistently find that police make arrests in less than half of all cases where they have adequate legal cause, and in only slightly more than half of all felony cases.[26] When police do make arrests, the reasons may vary from the seriousness of the offense to the rudeness of the offender. When they do not make arrests, it is often because they can find other "solutions" to the situation, such as restitution or separation. For example, police could persuade a suspect to return the property or leave the scene for the night. Police scholars call this "peacekeeping," in contrast to "law enforcement."[27]

Even if arrests caused no loss of police visibility, arrests may often be less effective than peacekeeping in preventing future crime. Many offenses are acts of revenge, the legal punishment of which may simply provoke more revenge.[28] Some police argue that arrests can escalate a dispute, causing more violence in the future. Given the speedy release of most arrestees in revolving-door justice, there is little police can do after the arrest is made to protect potential victims. Nowhere is this dilemma more clearly documented than in the problem of domestic violence.

Controlled experiments and domestic violence.   Documentation of the dilemma police face in deciding whether or not to arrest comes from the most powerful research design available in human sciences: the randomized controlled trial.[29] This design was first developed in medical science, but has been used with increasing frequency over the past decade of police research.[30] The design increases our certainty about cause and effect by eliminating most other possible theories besides the one being tested. It does that by making two groups as nearly equal as possible in virtually every respect except the police action (or medicine) being tested. If the two groups then differ in their subsequent behavior, that difference is usually viewed as the direct result of the difference in police treatment. The method for making the two groups as similar as possible is to declare a single group legally eligible for either treatment, and then use a mathematical formula giving every member of the large group an equal probability of being assigned to each of the two subgroups—what is usually called "random assignment," which is anything but random in the colloquial sense of "haphazard." The significance of randomized controlled experiments is that they give us far greater knowledge about the effects of police action on crime than we have ever gained from less powerful research designs. This knowledge is often surprising, sometimes influential, and occasionally perplexing.

In 1984, the first controlled experiment in the use of arrest reported that misdemeanor domestic violence in Minneapolis was substantially reduced when police made arrests rather than using alternative, peacekeeping strategies.[31] This result received widespread publicity, and helped to prompt a nationwide effort to increase the arrest rate for misdemeanor domestic assault.[32] Fortunately, the National Institute of Justice decided not to stop at one experiment, but to further test the hypothesis in other cities. The results of the replications were even more important, although far less publicized and influential than those of the original Minneapolis experiment. Taken together with the Minneapolis results, three experiments now show evidence of a deterrent effect of arrest, while three others show evidence of a criminogenic effect.[33]

Further analyses shed some light on the different results. While there were no consistent differences *between* the two groups of experiments, there were consistent differences *within* at least four of them. In Milwaukee, Omaha, Dade County (Florida) and Colorado Springs, albeit to varying degrees, arrest consistently deterred employed batterers but increased repeat violence among unemployed men.[34] A further reanalysis of the Milwaukee experiment suggests that this pattern may have more to do with the neighborhoods where arrests are made than with individual employment status. That is, even employed people in neighborhoods of high unemployment become more violent when arrested than when warned, and even unemployed people in neighborhoods of low unemployment tend to be deterred by arrest.[35] Whatever the reasons for these results, they show that more arrests are no simple guarantee of less crime, as arrest advocates suggest.[36] The effect of the arrest rate "pill" may depend heavily on the condition of the "patients."

Despite these findings about *domestic* crime, increasing the arrest rate may still be an effective strategy for preventing crimes against *strangers*. Arrest for minor public infractions by pedestrians and motorists, for example, shows a clear connection to robbery: the more police enforce traffic and disorderly conduct laws, the less robbery there is.[37] High rates of enforcement in public places may convey a sense of control that generally deters street crime, especially among strangers.[38]

This benefit may not depend on arrests as much as it does on intensive police patrol. A field experiment in San Diego found that when police cut back on field interrogations in one area, street crimes went up substantially.[39] To be sure, field interrogations can easily become "provocative policing," and several blue-ribbon commissions have blamed the practice for starting riots.[40] A polite and formal police manner, however, may reduce the side effects of this robbery prevention strategy.

So how many police do we need? We need at least as many police as it takes to provide high visibility in crime hot spots. We do not need a large number of police waiting in reserve like firefighters to keep the average response time low. We do need to create high levels of traffic enforcement and field interrogations. Beyond these requirements, how many police we need depends on how much we want them to act like security guards, public health agents, or both.

Community Policing: Police as Security Guards

Many police are insulted by the idea of their acting like security guards. They should not be. In the past two decades, people have voted with their wallets, increasing spending far more rapidly on security guards than on public police. Revenues in the security guard industry rose a projected 11 percent in 1994, from $12.7 billion to $14 billion.[41] In contrast, local public police personnel numbers grew by only 5 percent over the six years from 1986 to 1992.[42] Thus, private security may be growing more than eleven times faster than city police, perhaps out of public preference for crime prevention. When a terrible crime happens, the public expects the public police to bring the offenders to justice. But when citizens want to prevent crime at a specific place of business or in a residential area, they hire a security guard.

What security guards do is to *control risk factors.* They do not roam far and wide looking for action, as many young police officers do. Guards stay within their assigned area, such as a shopping mall or office building. Most of all, guards are on constant lookout for things causing elevated risks of harm to that community. These risks range from a water spill on the floor, to suspicious odors, to a suspicious-looking person. The security guard immediately attacks these risk factors, either directly or by summoning people with appropriate expertise. When the elevated risk is returned to normal, the guard goes back to looking for other risk factors.

Police can do this as well, but they rarely do. It was therefore surprising when a uniformed police officer patrolling our Washington, D.C., alley recently knocked on our door to ask if someone had tried to break into our car. We came outside to find our rear car door wide open, probably left that way by one of the kids. We locked up the car and thanked the officer, but we were no longer surprised. We discovered that the police officer was employed not by our local police department but by the federal agency which patrols—like security guards—the foreign embassies in our neighborhood. As most big city police will tell you, the "real" police don't have time to check doors any more.

For all the diverse definitions of community policing,[43] it may boil down to this: police treating a neighborhood the way a security guard treats a client property. Part of that treatment is the personal "service" orientation that so many suburban and small town police have long adopted, cultivating and listening to clients to understand their needs.[44] But more important may be the focus on risk control through careful scrutiny of everything happening in the neighborhood. This is the core of the nostalgia for the "cop on the beat," and the reason many people understand community policing as mere foot patrol. It is not the walking, but the exclusive attention to a small territory foot patrol implies, that the public prefers. And that is what makes community policing so expensive, especially as population density declines.

The key difference between police and security guards is that police protect public places, not private property, which makes their job much harder. Security guards have the law of trespass on their side, the power to expel unwanted people they define as risks. Police once exercised such powers illegally, especially in small communities where criminals could be run out of town. Police no longer have that luxury. Guards can even set up metal detectors and screen people for guns as a condition of entry to private property. Police must try to control risks in a wide-open environment, where everyone has a right to be. Even so, the law gives police some powerful tools to control risk factors in public places. Three of the most important risk factors are intimately connected: guns, convicts, and juveniles.

Controlling Guns

The leading risk factor for criminal harm in the United States is handguns. A great deal of evidence shows a strong connection between the gun density of a community and its rates of gun injury.[45] More important, but still unmeasured, may be the rate at which people carry guns illegally on the streets—especially people likely to use them. The growth of this practice among teenagers may be the leading cause of the doubling of the juvenile arrest rate for homicide between 1985 and 1989.[46] Carrying the gun, even for "self-defense," makes it more likely to be used. Disputes once settled by fists now get settled by fusillades from semiautomatics, with innocent bystanders killed at a rising rate.[47]

Police have often felt helpless to deal with the record homicide rates hitting many cities in the 1990s. But there is a clear and effective strategy they can pursue to get guns off the streets: security-guard-style traffic enforcement. More precisely, intensive traffic enforcement in gun crime hot spots has been found to increase gun seizures, reduce gun crime, and reduce shootings in a high homicide patrol beat in Kansas City, Missouri. The yield from this strategy is about one gun in every twenty-eight traffic stops, compared with about one gun for every sixty-six pedestrian stops. These rates may vary across cities. But in Kansas City, the only better way to take guns away from high-risk users is to raid drug houses. Drug raids seize one gun for every 145 officer hours worked, compared with 165 officer hours per gun seized in traffic enforcement and 658 officer hours across all police activities. [48]

More important is the effect of gun seizures on violent crime. When the Kansas City police added 2,200 officer hours of "security guard" patrol—slightly more than one officer year—in gun crime hot spots in one target neighborhood for three months, the number of guns seized rose to eleven per 1,000 residents, compared with only four per 1,000 residents in a high homicide rate control group area in another precinct. Gun-related crimes in the target area dropped by 58 percent from the prior year, compared with only a 29 percent drop in the control group area. Shots fired in the target area dropped by 81 percent, compared with to only a 32 percent drop in the control group area. By both measures, doubling the gun recovery rate in the Kansas City Gun Experiment was associated with more than doubling the reduction in gun violence.

It is also interesting to note what did *not* work in Kansas City. A more traditional "community involvement" strategy of door-to-door visits seeking anonymous gun tips was implemented very thoroughly by officers in the target beat—an area with one drive-by shooting every two weeks and a homicide rate twenty times the national average. Making contact in 80 percent of the 1,000 dwellings through more than 1,400 visits in thirty-five days of regular patrol time, the officers handed out flyers with the telephone number of a gun tips hotline. The middle-aged, predominantly African American homeowners told the all white officers (and an independent evaluator) they were delighted with the program. But the program failed to produce gun tips, and had no impact on crime. The result is a sobering comment on the widespread enthusiasm for "police-community partnerships." These may have many benefits, but reduced gun violence does not appear to be among them—at least not when attempted this way.

There are many legal and constitutional questions to be addressed if police mount a serious effort to seize guns carried illegally. The Supreme Court decision of *Terry v. Ohio* gives police the tool of frisking the outside of a person's clothes for weapons, if they can articulate the reasons they suspect the person of carrying a gun. [49] The full extent of possible reasons has not yet been tested in the courts, and court challenges seem inevitable if police attempt to make wider use of this decision. Some officers may also be shot or killed in such efforts. But this strategy is one of the few clear responses to the homicide problem terrifying the nation. It may also be one of the few ways to get beyond legislative gridlock on gun control to a public policy that can have some measurable impact.

Getting guns off the street has the advantage of appealing to a wide range of ideologies, from those who want to ban further handgun sales to those who conclude there is no need for further legislation. The latter position [50] may make little sense in the long run; police efforts to seize illegal guns may be overwhelmed if the number of high-powered handguns in circulation doubles or triples in the next several decades. But for the present, seizing illegal guns might begin with the support of a broad, if not universal, political consensus. So might undercover "buy-and-bust" policing of illegal gun markets, a largely untried but promising idea.

Controlling Convicts

One clear risk factor in any community is the release of parolees convicted of violent felonies. While some parolees do stop offending, their average recidivism rates are high enough to merit close attention. Most police agencies currently do little to monitor them, even though the agencies often have ready access to data on the parolee's home and work addresses. Retail security guards study pictures of people who have shoplifted in the past; community policing could do the same for people who have raped and robbed in the past. Persons on probation can also be monitored by police, and have been in several smaller Los Angeles area police departments focusing on high-risk probationers.[51] Large-scale computerization of pictures and current address information has yet to be reported. But mobile data terminals (MDTs) to be installed in many patrol cars in the late 1990s will increase police time devoted to checking on suspicious persons and cars.

Another method of tracking high-risk convicts is the use of specialized repeat offender units. Usually working undercover, these units combine surveillance and "sting" strategies to catch the offenders in the act of crime. The resulting evidence is stronger than in most arrests made after the fact, thus increasing the odds of the offender being imprisoned. A controlled experiment evaluating the Washington, D.C., repeat offender program (ROP) found a substantial increase in offenders sentenced to prison when targeted by ROP.[52] And while the Washington program was later abolished by a new police chief, other police departments around the country have adopted similar programs.[53]

Despite these exceptions, patrol beat officers are rarely briefed about convicts or high-risk offenders living on their beats. It is not clear what effect patrol surveillance of parolees would have. Frequent field stops could let parolees know they were being watched, which might deter them from further crime. This approach may also become "provocative policing," however, angering criminals into more offending.

What is clear is that police have enormous legal powers to investigate parolees. In some states, for example, police can stop and frisk them at any time, without probable cause. Using that power may be an excellent way to keep guns off the streets, if nothing else. It may also be a way to return dangerous parolees to prison very quickly. That in turn creates powerful reasons for police to use these powers, if their police agencies can organize the information systems needed to supply the patrol officers with current lists of resident parolees.

Controlling Juveniles

On average, juveniles are far less dangerous than parolees. But there are far more juveniles, and collectively they appear to generate more crime than any other demographic group. Some shopping malls have reacted to juvenile crime by banning teenagers altogether during certain hours.[54] Some police agencies have adopted a similar "security guard" approach, attempting to ban juveniles from public streets at certain times and places. This effort is supported by two legal tools: truancy laws and curfews.

Truancy enforcement is a prime example of an historical crime prevention strategy that has disappeared in the last half of this century. Children unsupervised during the day may just go fishing. They may also shoplift, burgle, sell guns, and rob. Getting the kids off the streets from 8:30 to 3:30 could substantially reduce the number of crimes, even allowing for the many crimes committed at school.

Whether this theory works out in practice awaits careful evaluation, but the programs are being implemented. The Newark, New Jersey police worked in collaboration with the school board to develop a truancy enforcement program in the 1980s, driving a school bus around town during school hours and picking up school-age children spotted on the streets. The children were taken to a study center where they were detained until their parents came or they could be transferred back to their schools. Similar programs have been tried in the 1990s in Philadelphia, Atlanta, St. Louis, San Jose, Oklahoma City, Washington, and New York City.[55] While no careful evaluations are available, there are some indications of crime prevention success. There is also opposition from civil libertarians, and some concern about provocative policing.

Similar concerns have been voiced about curfew enforcement, which may have even more theoretical potential to reduce violent crime. Much more violence overall occurs at night than by day, although it is not clear that juvenile violence follows that pattern. Many juvenile homicides are committed in broad daylight, especially those involving disputes with other teenagers as opposed to robberies of adults. But very young teenagers committing late night murders of a British tourist in Florida, or an ATM customer in San Antonio, help to fuel the call for juvenile curfew enforcement.

Curfews have expanded rapidly in the 1990s, with 100 New Jersey communities adopting them in 1993 alone.[56] Enforcement appears to vary widely, especially since few legislatures appropriate additional funds for police time to take children off the streets. Just as arrests reduce patrol time, so does processing curfew violators. The net effect of full curfew enforcement on crime is thus open to question. No rigorous evaluations are available. But there is reason to believe that curfews work better with a program to "pull" children off the streets to complement police efforts to "push" them off—that is, providing attractive legitimate activities while ordering juveniles not to gather on the streets.

The San Antonio curfew enacted in 1991 was accompanied by early evening youth programs costing $2 million. By 1993, crimes against juveniles had dropped by 77 percent, and arrests of juveniles had declined 5 percent, during the curfew hours of midnight to 6:00 A.M. Whether these changes were due to the program is unclear.[57] But the idea of opening school buildings for supervised recreation until late at night has been debated in the U.S. Congress, and a carefully evaluated demonstration project could reveal both costs and benefits. In many areas, late night recreation would have to be heavily secured. Shootouts can happen just as easily on the basketball court as on the streets.

However juveniles are monitored, they are clearly a risk factor the public wants police to control. Residents want protection from their own neighbors, and some parents want protection from their own children. Much research suggests that this task is easier if teenage males do not make up too large a percentage of the total population in a neighborhood, as they do in some public housing projects.[58] This *Lord of the Flies* effect of unsupervised young males makes the police job that much harder. It also reveals the alternative— or complementary—strategy for police to control risk factors. Rather than dealing with male teenagers individually, police might do better by reducing their residential concentrations through public housing policies. The difference is like that between swatting mosquitoes and filling in the swamps—the basic premise of "public health" policing.

Problem Solving: Police as Public Health Agents

What security guards and public health agents have in common is that they both control risk factors. What makes them different is the time frame of those risks: guards address immediate risk situations, while public health addresses long-term patterns of risk. In the late 1970s, police theorist Herman Goldstein introduced public health strategies to police work with the concept of problem-oriented policing, or P.O.P. to its supporters.[59] He recommended breaking big crime problems (like robbery) down into specific patterns (like night robberies of convenience stores) and developing specific responses to each identifiable pattern. Requiring two clerks to work in convenience stores at night, as the Gainesville, Florida, police recommended in the mid-1980s, is a prime example of P.O.P. (even though the strategy had no measurable impact).[60] In contrast, a "security guard" community policing approach would require that police pay frequent visits to repeat robbery locations, looking for suspicious persons.

Given the extraordinary successes of public health in the last century, there is great promise in applying the same methods to policing. From eliminating tuberculosis to preventing polio, the science of epidemiology has a strong track record in risk analysis and risk control. The methods of risk *analysis* are easily applied to policing, where it has identified hot spot crime locations, repeat offenders, and repeat victims. The methods of risk *control*, however, are much harder to apply. Absent vaccines for crime problems, about the best we can do is what seat belts, air bags, motorcycle helmets, bulletproof vests, and condoms for AIDS prevention do: target high-risk situations and attempt to construct barriers to harm.

That is exactly the approach taken by the academic field of situational crime prevention developed in England in the 1980s.[61] Its successes, broadly defined, are impressive. Skyjacking was virtually eliminated by establishing a barrier to weapons on planes (metal detectors).[62] Robberies of bus drivers fell dramatically with exact change fares and a barrier to cash availability.[63] Public housing burglaries fell with the elimination of coin-operated gas heating systems.[64] Book theft from libraries fell with electronic access control inserts.[65]

All of these examples, however, are ad hoc solutions. There is no underlying theory, like the biochemistry of vaccines, that can guide police from one crime problem to the next. Each specific crime problem tests anew the ingenuity of anyone attempting to solve—or more modestly, to manage—that problem. History predicts that such trial-and-error efforts will fail more often than they succeed, at least on the first several attempts.

That is just what has happened in many of the police agencies adopting P.O.P. since the early 1980s, although few of them are eager to admit it. Policing is an occupational culture driven by rapid responses to short-term problems, unaccustomed to judgments about success or failure. The new assignment of long-term problem solving has often caused occupational culture shock. Admirably, police have not given up, although some have lowered their expectations for speedy success. The hard lesson to learn is that failure in problem solving is not personal but technological. No doctor blames herself for a failure to cure AIDS, and no police officer should blame herself for a failure to cure repeat robberies. There is no shame in failing at what no one has invented a technology to accomplish.

The ability of police to change the underlying causes of specific problems is limited by two key constraints. One is their diagnostic experience. Both seasoned physicians and auto mechanics often fail to diagnose the underlying cause of a symptom. Police have even less experience at problem solving to draw upon. Although some officers have been doing problem solving for years, they have not shared their experience the way doctors and auto mechanics have. The complexity of many crime patterns, such as hundreds of crimes a year at a low income apartment complex, requires all the diagnostic experience and insight the profession can offer. Officers confronting such problems have few places to turn for a second opinion or a consulting expert.

The second constraint is the need for what some have called third-party policing: other organizations and actors monopolize the power to make the decisions affecting underlying causes of crime patterns. Only landlords can screen tenants and move to evict them, not police officers. Only parking facility owners can build fences around the first three floors of a structure. Only bartenders can decide whether to serve people who are already intoxicated. These third parties can make problem solving succeed or fail, and there is often little police can do to influence them. One study of problem solving in Minneapolis was thus suitably entitled "Convincing the Recalcitrant."[66]

Many of these recalcitrant third parties are other agencies of government. Public housing administrations, liquor-licensing authorities, traffic departments, youth recreation services, and even libraries (which continually call police about homeless people) have all refused to cooperate with police attempts to change underlying causes of situational crime patterns. This is a paradox of police "professionalism": historically, police exercised many powers of licensing and building inspection, but they got rid of those duties in order to focus on criminal law enforcement. Now empowered with a broader view of crime prevention, some police would like to have those regulatory powers back.

Three areas of regulation may provide fertile ground for crime prevention through problem solving, if supported by careful research and evaluation: liquor sales, automatic teller machines (ATMs), and nighttime business operations.

Liquor Licenses

Liquor sales are highly correlated with crime, in several ways. High crime neighborhoods often have a high density of liquor stores per capita, which may or may not increase the per capita level of alcohol consumption. The connection between alcohol and crime is not entirely clear, but it qualifies as a risk factor. The connection of taverns to crime is much clearer. Research in several cities shows greatly elevated risks of violent crimes on blocks where taverns are located. In Milwaukee, for example, 12 percent of all homicides in the 1980s were connected to taverns.[67]

The striking thing about taverns is how few of them have any violent crime at all. Most tavern violence in Milwaukee and Kansas City occurs at less than 10 percent of the taverns. By focusing on the small number of hot spots, police might be able to remove the underlying situational causes of the violence. Lax tavern management, gang conflicts among patrons, drug dealing, or other causes might be more amenable to change if police had greater leverage over liquor-licensing decisions. Fears of police corruption, however, have kept police largely powerless to have violent taverns shut down. If police are to work like public health agents, they need the power to close down polluted wells.

ATM Locations

In some cities, police have obtained the power to regulate the location of ATMs. That power is based on the assumption that locations vary in their safety for all-night cash transactions. That assumption may be correct, but it has never been proved. Police have no sound basis to rely on in approving or disapproving ATM locations. They do have substantial in-house records about ATM crime, but no published analysis of those records is available. Had such an analysis been done, it might have stopped the New York City Council from regulating all ATMs equally in 1992—with the requirement that banks either post security guards or offer computerized controlled access enclosures at every one.[68] Even that idea remains untested, and may be as ineffective as it is costly.

The ATM question is a good example of the need for much greater reliance on public health methods, particularly epidemiology. It is very crude risk analysis to declare all ATMs dangerous. Careful study of ATM sites for traffic patterns, lighting, shrubbery or sightlines could reveal the risk factors associated with higher or lower crime rates. Absent such analysis, police regulation of ATMs is based on mere speculation.

Nighttime Business Operation

Much the same can be said about nighttime businesses. In 1993, the police chief of Washington, D.C., suggested closing robbery-plagued businesses after dark.[69] The community response was a storm of criticism over the police failure to protect honest merchants. Had the chief conducted an epidemiological analysis of the factors associated with high and low robbery rates at different nighttime retail locations, he might have been able to suggest a less Draconian solution. Given the huge number of jobs at stake, nighttime closings will remain a last resort. The Florida legislature has singled out convenience stores for nighttime regulation, based on claims of crime prevention success by the Gainesville police. But the public interest will be far better served by more selective strategies for keeping night businesses safe.

Learning from Experience: Evaluating Crime Prevention

The long-term success of police problem solving will depend heavily on its methods of evaluation. It is tempting to declare every project a success, especially without controlled measurement. Only problem solving explicitly judges policing by its results (such as crime trends), rather than its activities (arrests made, calls answered). It is thus unfortunate that the problem-solving movement has so far paid little attention to the complexities of evaluation.[70]

A recent program in Indianapolis attempts to fill that gap. The Indianapolis Model of Police Accountability for Community [problem-solving] Targets (IMPACT) is a computerized record of all registered attempts to solve problems. Officers beginning such efforts obtain approval from supervisors for their target selection and plan of action, then set evaluation criteria and a time frame for judging success. Success is measured for both implementing the action plan (for example, getting a liquor license revoked) and achieving the impact of that plan (for example, reduced crime at a tavern). All evaluations include a control (comparison) group, such as another patrol beat or the entire city. A civilian criminologist serves as an IMPACT analyst in each patrol district to draw final conclusions and write up the history of each problem-solving effort.

IMPACT creates an institutional memory for the lessons of problem solving. If attempting to bar trespassers from a high crime apartment complex fails to reduce crime, that experience goes into the IMPACT file. Three years later, an officer in another district working on a similar problem can read about the earlier experience with trespassers. As years go by and thousands of problem-solving efforts are documented in the IMPACT file, key word searches of the computerized textbase will provide more and more guidance to aid future problem solving.

At the same time, IMPACT helps to quantify a police agency's problem-solving performance. Departments trying to do more problem solving have been hampered by the traditional emphasis on arrests made and calls for service answered. IMPACT enables police to publish annual reports on problems attacked and solved, balancing if not surpassing the traditional measures. It can also show progress on key priorities, such as number of guns seized and number of gun crimes prevented at target locations.

Tough Choices for Crime Prevention

If police efforts are focused on crime prevention, we can use as many officers as we can get. Police visibility in hot spots, security-guard-style community policing, and public-health-style problem solving can all contribute to crime prevention. The greatest potential is for increased efforts at gun detection to reduce inner city homicide. If national policy were focused on that goal, all 100,000 of the federally funded officers would be assigned to neighborhoods with homicide rates ten times higher than the national average. That decision would reduce the homicide rate substantially. It would also be a tough choice.

We are unlikely to abandon the "fair share" approach to policing, even though it limits our ability to prevent crime. The argument that all taxpayers deserve equal police services fits the security guard–client model. But it ignores the public health model of contagion. The spread of gun violence throughout our society is growing rapidly, even while total violent crime changes little. In Indianapolis, for example, gun crimes more than doubled from 1988 to 1993, while total violent crime declined slightly.[71] Concentrating police crime prevention in the places with highest gun crime may be the most effective way to protect everyone, not just residents of the high crime locations.

The choice between fair share and crime-focused policing is not the only tough decision we face. We must also choose between rapid responses and solutions to persistent crime patterns. We must choose visible patrol or more arrests, security guards or public health agents, guns off the street or every burglary investigated. And we must make these choices consciously, rather than letting them just slide along. Whether we admit it or not, we cannot have it all.

The challenge of these choices is to find the right balance. No one proposes that police give up answering 911 calls or arresting felons. But if we compromise on all these tough choices, we may do everything poorly and nothing well. Police and elected officials must explain the tough choices and mobilize consensus behind a few achievable goals, rather than promising to do everything. Reduction of gun violence could be the primary achievable goal. Doing that one thing well could justify many tough choices indeed.

CHARLES MURRAY

THE
PHYSICAL
ENVIRONMENT

Common sense and everyday experience tell us that the physical environment is related to the risk of crime. That's why most people avoid poorly lighted streets and run-down neighborhoods, thinking that they are more vulnerable targets in such places. This calculation about the specific chance of becoming a victim goes hand in hand with another common sense understanding about crime: one of our best protections against crime is to live in a community where neighbors watch out for each other and stand ready to call the police or to intervene directly when they spot a malefactor.

But how do cause and effect work in such situations? Is the risk of crime high because the neighborhood is run-down, or is the neighborhood run-down because too many of its residents are criminals? Is crime low because criminals know that the neighbors will call the police, or will neighbors call the police only in neighborhoods where they already feel safe?

In 1961, Jane Jacobs published her seminal book, *The Death and Life of Great American Cities,* which, among its many other themes, proposed a new way of looking at the relationship between the physical environment and crime.[1] Jacobs proposed that crime in urban residential areas could be reduced if those areas became less anonymous and less isolated. Orient buildings so that it is easy for neighbors to see what is going on, she argued. Make sure that public and private spaces are clearly separated, and that public spaces are situated near high-use private spaces.

Despite the great overall impact of *The Death and Life of Great American Cities,* its crime prevention implications were not much discussed until 1972, when an urban planner named Oscar Newman expanded upon Jacobs's ideas and gave his theory a memorable label, "Defensible Space" in a book of that title.[2] His book came at a time when crime had become a major issue, Newman himself was an adept promoter of his ideas, and he made a bold claim: defensible space would work not only in ordinary urban neighborhoods, but in the most crime-ridden of urban environments, the public housing project. Within two years after *Defensible Space* appeared, major demonstration projects were already under way. Within another year, the Law Enforcement Assistance Administration had funded a multi-million dollar project to extend defensible space theory to other environments as well—a commercial strip, a residential area, a school, and a transportation system. By 1975, Hartford, Connecticut, was applying the concepts of defensible space to an entire neighborhood. Around the world, new public housing projects were designed with Newman's precepts in mind.[3] "Defensible space" was in vogue.

The widespread media attention that Newman's work attracted was undoubtedly encouraged by Newman's bold presentation of his thesis, but the ideas behind defensible space were also immediately plausible. In the broadest sense, Newman had to be right that some physical environments are less conducive to crime than others. In terms of specific research findings, what have we learned? The summary answers are:

- The most provocative hypothesis of defensible space has been that residents would change their behavior, defending their space against criminals given the right environmental design. This has not been demonstrated. The wrong physical environment may deter people from acting against crime, but providing a better physical environment has not been proved to produce new anticrime behaviors.

- Defensible space as a method for reducing crime has some utility, in combination with other measures and in the context of certain neighborhood characteristics. These effects are modest and inconsistent, however.

- "Situational crime prevention," a broader conception of the relationship between the physical environment and crime, has demonstrated promise in reducing certain types of crime.

Defensible Space Theory

In Newman's original formulation, "defensible space theory" embraced three propositions about the relationship between people's physical environment and crime: territoriality, natural surveillance, and "image and milieu."[4]

Territoriality

The instinct to demarcate and defend territory has long been observed among animals. In the mid-1960s, Robert Ardrey popularized the theory that territoriality characterizes human behavior as well.[5] Newman applied Ardrey's thesis to crime, arguing that people perceive certain areas as their own space, which can and should be defended: A family that has a sense of territoriality about the entryway to its apartment will be more likely to defend it against intruders than a family that does not. A community that has a shared sense of territoriality will be more likely to act in concert against intruders than a community that has none. Proper design can establish real and symbolic barriers and demarcation lines that foster this sense of territoriality.

Natural Surveillance

The "observability" of crime can likewise be improved, defensible space theory holds, by designing the use of space to increase the number of friendly "eyes on the street." The greater the number of observers, the greater the probability that an offender will be seen in the act, thereby aiding law enforcement and deterring criminals.

Image and Milieu

Proper design, it is thought, can alter the visual impact of a neighborhood or housing project. Offenders are alert to visual cues, and can be deterred from or encouraged to invade a given space (housing project, neighborhood residence) on the basis of them. A vandalized, run-down housing project, for example, looks disorganized and vulnerable.

At the heart of these propositions about the relationship of the manmade environment to crime is the concept of "informal social control"—the means whereby a community exerts pressure to prevent violations of its norms. The rationale is that defensible space increases the effectiveness of informal social control, which in turn reduces crime. This two-step process distinguishes defensible space theory from traditional physical means of deterring crime by such things as better locks, higher fences, and stouter doors.

Can the Creation of Defensible Space Reduce Crime? Fear of Crime?

The initial attraction of defensible space theory lay in its potential for policy. The lament of the 1960s had been that crime was so embedded in basic social and economic conditions that little could be done until those conditions were changed. Newman said this was too pessimistic—that physical design changes could in and of themselves "release latent attitudes in tenants which allow them to assume behavior necessary to the protection of their rights and property."[6] A housing project or neighborhood that scored "low" on defensible space could reduce its crime by the right physical changes in that space. The residents' "latent attitudes" would be released. A series of demonstration projects in the 1970s attempted to test this expectation.

Reducing Crime

Newman's most evocative arguments had to do with public housing projects, and the first major test appropriately came at two public housing projects in New York City, Clason Point and Markham Gardens. The design changes included establishment of play areas, improvements in the appearance of the projects, better lighting, fencing to divide areas into semiprivate spaces, and barriers and channels for pedestrian traffic.

The evaluation found a few ambiguous signs of more "neighboring" and a greater sense of territoriality, but no consistent reduction in crime. In one of the sites, burglary and robbery decreased, but vandalism doubled. After installation of street lights at Clason Point, crime decreased between 5:00 and 9:00 at night, but increased even more between midnight and 5:00 A.M., for a net increase.[7] At best, these early demonstrations of defensible space in public housing could point only to highly selective, tenuous examples of success in reducing crime—examples that had to be ignored when crime went up. The most persuasive explanation is that the evaluators were observing fluctuations that had little to do with the design changes.

Defensible space theory also suggested ways in which neighborhoods could reduce crime. These got their most direct test through the Asylum Hill project in Hartford, Connecticut, implemented in 1976 and evaluated (in two stages) through 1979. Asylum Hill was a working class, racially mixed residential neighborhood surrounded by commercial areas. The physical changes introduced by the project consisted of alterations in the streets and intersections—closing some off to create cul-de-sacs, narrowing the openings at intersections to create the effect of a "gateway" into the residential area, and using one-way streets to discourage commercial traffic. The purpose of the changes was to reduce "outsider" vehicular traffic, increase pedestrian traffic among residents, and demarcate the boundaries of the neighborhood—all translated straight from the precepts of defensible space theory.

The physical changes were implemented in half of Asylum Hill. The principal remaining components of the project, implemented throughout Asylum Hill, consisted of a specially assigned neighborhood police team and a police advisory committee of local residents.

The evaluation vindicated some of the expectations of defensible space theory. Three years after the changes were put in place, residents showed significantly improved use of the neighborhood, ability to recognize strangers, willingness to intervene in suspicious situations, and positive perceptions of their neighbors. There was ambiguous evidence that the project had reduced fear of crime, based on the fact that fear of crime held steady in Asylum Hill while it was rising elsewhere in Hartford. However, the project did not reduce crime. Burglary and robbery decreased significantly in the first year after implementation but rose thereafter to the levels experienced by the city as a whole.[8]

In addition to these ambitious efforts to implement defensible space theory, a large number of street-lighting projects were undertaken around the country. This wave of projects told the same story. First came the enthusiastic anecdotal accounts of huge reductions in crime after better street lights were installed, followed by the evaluators and debunking. In a review of all the recorded street-lighting demonstrations up to 1977 (forty-one, of which fifteen were deemed important enough to warrant a full-scale assessment), researchers concluded that the occasional short-term improvements were ephemeral. No project had produced a statistically significant reduction in crime.[9] More positive results were produced by one of the major demonstration projects funded by the federal government, where a combination of security surveys and better street lighting of a commercial strip in Portland, Oregon, was followed by a statistically significant reduction in commercial burglaries. It was impossible to tell how much of this effect was owed to better lighting and how much was owed to improved security procedures.[10]

Reducing Fear of Crime

The advocates of defensible space hypothesized that the built environment could reduce the fear of crime independently of effects on crime itself. The rationale for wanting to reduce fear (independently of reducing real crime) had two elements: fear can affect everyone, whether or not victimization occurs, and fear is often exaggerated, bearing little relationship to the real level of risk.[11] When people have an unreasonably high fear of crime, it is good (according to this line of argument) to reduce it, even if crime stays the same.

The one measure that clearly seems to reduce fear of crime, at least in the short term, is better street lighting. In a Baltimore project, 66 percent of the residents interviewed said they felt safer after street lighting was improved. The comparable figure in Milwaukee was 82 percent. Smaller decreases in fear were found in Tucson, Denver, and Norfolk.[12]

What about reducing fear of crime through the more subtle design changes? The Clason Point project found no effects. Residents reported a markedly increased sense of safety, but they attributed it entirely to the improved lighting and not to any other of the defensible space innovations.[13] In Asylum Hill, fear of robbery and burglary held steady through the three years of observation, during a period when fear of crime was rising in the rest of Hartford. The authors concluded that the fear of crime in North Asylum Hill was significantly lower than it would have been without the project, writing that this was "a critical finding" in support of defensible space theory,[14] but drawing confident "would have been" conclusions in the context of imprecise experimental conditions is always problematic.

Taken as a whole, the early returns on environmental changes were not wholly negative, but neither did they give much hope that design changes could produce dramatic changes. The early high hopes for defensible space were modified accordingly. By the mid 1980s, a rough consensus had formed about defensible space as Newman had conceived it. "Territoriality" remained an interesting concept, but not much was known, pro or con, about whether it could be applied to practical problems of crime prevention. Increasing "natural surveillance" might have effects on residential burglary, vandalism in large housing projects, and school break-ins, though the evidence is ambiguous.[15] Design changes to promote "image and milieu" might have some positive effects on the perceptions that people had about their living spaces, but did not seem to have much effect on crime. In any case, changes in the built environment would have to be part of a broader crime control package. The physical changes may facilitate social cohesion and thereby increase informal social control, but only when supplemented by community organizing efforts, better policing, and improved police-community relations.

Since the mid-1980s, most of the continued interest in defensible space has shifted from public housing projects (where not much can be done to redesign existing spaces without prohibitive expense) to innovations of the Asylum Hill type, in which planners make design changes that are supposed to make a neighborhood of single family houses more defensible. The chief design feature has been street closure. Sometimes streets are made into cul-de-sacs. In other cases, a long barrier may be placed diagonally across a four-way intersection, creating residential loops.

Results have been mixed. In Los Angeles, Operation Cul-de-Sac began in 1990 and within a few months was claiming an 85 percent reduction in drive-by shootings and reduced drug trafficking in the target neighborhoods. But when the special foot patrols that accompanied the street closures were discontinued, crime went back up, and the street barriers themselves have fallen into disrepair, covered with graffiti. In contrast, projects in threatened neighborhoods of Dayton, Bridgeport, and Fort Lauderdale report a variety of positive results in the atmosphere and cohesiveness of the neighborhood.[16]

As in the pioneering defensible space projects of the 1970s, marked reductions in crime have not occurred anywhere, however. This leads to a larger issue: what, after all, should be expected of successful changes in the built environment? Proponents of design changes argue plausibly that an immediate reduction in crime is not necessary in order to call a project a success. A change in neighborhood characteristics that may eventually lead to a more stable neighborhood and lower crime may in itself be considered a major step forward.

With success defined in these less ambitious terms, what explains the difference between the successful and unsuccessful projects? One consistent lesson seems to be that street closings work only if the neighborhood takes the lead, "forcing" the municipality to implement a plan that the neighborhood has designed and sponsored—the process that occurred in the successful projects in Bridgeport and Dayton. In contrast, many of the failed street closings in South Central Los Angeles occurred with only pro forma involvement of the community. Similarly, Chicago Mayor Richard Daley announced that "we're going to cul-de-sac the city," only to find an outpouring of protest from low income black neighborhoods that feared being shut off from the rest of the city and shut in with the gangs.[17]

But neighborhood initiative is no guarantee of success. The Los Angeles neighborhood of North Hills lobbied for cul-de-sacs for years before finally getting them (with neighborhood residents paying the bill for the barriers themselves). But the barriers brought unintended consequences. They could be used by gang members to escape from police. They did indeed reduce traffic (one of the intended outcomes), but sometimes that was an advantage for criminals. Anne Jordan, in her review of this and other street-closing projects, reported that some residents "blame the barriers for high apartment vacancy rates, the reluctance of some lenders to make loans in the area, and a sharp decline in property values."[18]

In short: There are no strategies for altering the built environment that can confidently be expected to produce even the intermediate outcome of improved neighborhood functioning, let alone reducing crime. The prevailing lesson has been that "it all depends."

The Community, the Physical Environment, and Crime

Depends on what? I began by stating that in some broad sense Oscar Newman had to be right: we all recognize from personal experience that the physical environment affects our behavior in relation to crime. We all know from experience that informal social control is a real phenomenon. Yet attempts to reduce crime, or even to improve community functioning, through environmental design have fallen far short of expectations. Was the relationship between crime and the physical environment overstated? Misstated? Illusory? Or have we failed to try the right modifications, the right "treatment," or the right environment?

Only the demonstration projects provide a direct answer to the question of whether *changes* in defensible space design can produce *reductions* in crime. But demonstration projects are expensive. The bulk of the research since defensible space came into vogue has dealt not with attempts to manipulate the environment but with "natural variation" in design settings. The task has been to understand, first, whether the differences in design settings are associated with differences in crime and, second, if so, why.

In a now-classic article entitled "Broken Windows," James Q. Wilson and George Kelling described how crime and the physical condition of a neighborhood can be intertwined. Their core image is the broken window left unrepaired—which, as sociologist and police officer alike have observed, invariably leads to more broken windows. "A piece of property is abandoned, weeds grow up, a window is smashed," they wrote. "Adults stop scolding rowdy children; the children, emboldened, become more rowdy. Families move out. . . . Many residents will think that crime, especially violent crime, is on the rise, and they will modify their behavior accordingly. They will use the streets less often, and when on the streets will stay apart from their fellows. . . . It is more likely that here, rather than in places where people are confident they can regulate public behavior by informal controls, drugs will change hands, prostitutes will solicit, and cars will be stripped."[19]

Subsequently, Wesley Skogan has elaborated on the role of disorder as a progenitor of crime.[20] But whereas Wilson/Kelling and Skogan argue persuasively that physical deterioration facilitated certain behaviors which in turn facilitate crime, they have not been optimistic that repairing all the broken windows will repair the behaviors. Once the social processes, community bonds, and norms of behavior have broken down, the solution must involve more than just physical change.

This seems to be the consistent lesson of the technical literature that has grown up around the issue. In many ways, researchers have found that people think and behave as defensible space theory predicts. Oscar Newman himself, with Karen Franck, conducted research showing that large buildings were associated with decreased interaction among the residents, with less use of adjoining spaces, and that these reactions in turn made crime more likely.[21] Similarly, in a study of sixty-six neighborhoods in Baltimore, the correlation between an "incivilities" factor and crime rate was .63, very large by the standards of social science, and the relationship between the physical environment and crime rates was .38, also substantial and significant. But when the socio-demographic characteristics of the neighborhood were held constant, the link between the physical environment and crime became insignificant.[22]

The underlying dynamics were most clearly revealed by an ethnographic study of a housing project in a northeastern city. The researcher, Sally Merry, found that the residents of the housing project feared the places that defensible space theory says they should fear: space that was not "owned" by anyone, for example, and places where they were shielded from view. But most of the project was well designed in terms of defensible space. The occurrence of robberies was split about evenly between places which were and were not architecturally "defensible."[23] Merry took advantage of this natural variation to explore how the residents' responses to robberies had varied.

Merry found that almost all of the interventions by neighbors occurred in the defensible areas—which is consistent with defensible space theory—but that the people who did the intervening were a special subgroup of unusual people, consisting of people who had lived in the neighborhood for a long time and who were highly committed to it. Furthermore, their commitments were delineated by ethnic group, with the Chinese, the African American, and the Syrian-Lebanese group each drawn in on itself. "Even if buildings are low," Merry wrote, with "entrances and public spaces clearly linked to partic-ular apartments, residents will not respond to crime if they feel that the space belongs to another ethnic group, if they believe that the police will come too late or they will incur retribution for calling them, or if they are unable to distinguish a potential criminal from the neighbor's dinner guest."[24]

Meanwhile, many of the offenders have as much local knowledge as the residents, and act accordingly. Merry was able to gain the confidence of seven young men from the project who committed many of the robberies. They were extremely pragmatic. Perhaps symbolic barriers and demarcation lines were operating on their psyches at some unconscious level, but it sounded very much as if the *real* risk of being observed, *real* risk of someone calling the police, and *real* risk of being cut off without an escape route governed their thinking. "One street is considered good robbing space be-cause the people who live there are thought never to look out," Merry wrote:

> A plaza outside the elderly housing is poor because the old people are always looking out their windows. Some people are thought to look out their windows only after they hear a noise while others watch all the time. Only the latter concern the robbers. Some are known to do nothing and are ignored; others are reputed to intervene actively. Of this latter group, some shout and tell the criminal to stop but do not call the police: these succeed in moving the crime around the corner. Others are be-lieved likely to call the police, and robbers are very cautious about committing crimes within sight of these apartments.[25]

These observations get to the nub of the limits on defensible space as a strategy for preventing crime. A well-designed physical environment can help a civil, law-abiding community in its efforts to protect itself from intrud-ers. Deterioration in the physical environment can set forces in motion that undermine a community. But once disorder has set in, changes in the physi-cal environment are unlikely to have much effect unless they are reinforced by other changes for the better in the socio-demographic setting. Indeed, once disorder has set in, the same design features that can be helpful to a functioning community can become helpful to the outlaws—"offensible space," as one architect has called it, in which the principles of territoriality, natural surveillance, and milieu become tools that enable criminals to carry on their activities with less risk of being interrupted by the police. [26] Thus, as I reported earlier, some of the street barricades in Los Angeles have been used by drug dealers as a means of eluding police pursuit. [27]

Situational Crime Prevention

If the promises of defensible space have gone largely unfulfilled, a less dramatic theoretical approach based on environmental design shows promise. Itself part of a broader scholarly field known as environmental criminology that has developed largely outside the United States, "situational crime prevention" has demonstrated reductions of a wide variety of crimes. [28]

The underlying theme of environmental criminology is that crimes require convergence in time and space of a motivated offender, a suitable target, in the absence of a capable guardian. [29] Situational crime prevention, as the applications of environmental criminology are called, does not try to do anything about the motivation of the offender. It does not try to attack the root social or psychological causes of crime. The issues of community life which are at the heart of defensible space theory play only a minor role. Situational crime prevention simply tries to reduce the opportunities for crime by increasing the effort that the offender must invest, increasing the risks he must take, and reducing the rewards.

The theoretical underpinnings of environmental criminology are drawn broadly from a view of crime as a quasi-rational activity in which criminals "go to work" and try as best they can to get the most from the least effort while incurring the least risk. This view of the offender has been buttressed by a number of studies which use offenders as informants. [30] Like the offenders interviewed by Merry, most of the people who commit large numbers of robberies and burglaries select their targets. Whether they do so well or poorly, they are at least trying to minimize their risks and effort. When a burglar sees a German Shepherd sitting on the front porch, he seldom tries to figure out how to bypass the dog; he chooses another house. [31] When a robber of convenience stores sees that the store has two clerks, he is likely to look around for a store with just one. [32]

A key finding in studies of situational crime prevention is that the calculus of risks and rewards does not have to be decisively altered to be effective. An instructive example is prevention of library and bookstore thefts by electronic detection systems. To a determined shoplifter (or library lifter), the system hardly poses an insuperable obstacle. And yet such systems are effective even when only a small portion (or even none) of a library's books have actually been coded with the magnetic strip. [33] The point is not that people are caught, but that most people who steal books are not highly motivated thieves, and are easily deterred.

In other cases, the crime prevention effect can take advantage of peculiarities inherent in the crime. The dramatic reductions in obscene phone calls that have been documented after introduction of Caller ID service even when only about 1 percent of telephone subscribers use Caller ID offers an example. In a technical sense, the obscene phone caller does not face a large increase in risk if he is willing to choose victims at random, and hardly any increase in risk at all if the offender is willing to use a pay telephone.[34] But drinking and masturbation are commonly involved in obscene phone calls, which makes public telephones unsuitable, and obscene phone callers typically like to call particular women—who, if they are subjected to an obscene phone call once, are much more likely than the random citizen to get Caller ID.

Ronald Clarke has created a typology for the many discrete forms of situational crime prevention, shown in Table 15.1.

Many of the examples represent measures that prudent readers would naturally take in their homes or businesses. Others, such as "hotel registration" under the category of "rule setting," are not ordinarily seen as crime prevention techniques at all, but do in fact play such a role. Together, as Clarke argues through his compilations of many case studies from around the world, they can play an important role in reducing crime.

Is the crime thus prevented in one location displaced to another? The answers are still incomplete, but the best current estimate is that some displacement occurs, but seldom anywhere near 100 percent. One of the most sophisticated studies of displacement, conducted by the Rand Corporation, examined what happened to robberies of subway change booths before and after New York City introduced an "exact fare" system for buses in 1969.[35] At first glance, the precipitous drop in bus robberies seemed matched by an increase in subway change-booth robberies. After closer examination, a much more interesting phenomenon seems to have been at work. In 1968, bus robbery became "popular." Rand's researchers argued that a multiplier effect operates in a local crime scene. When a few incidents demonstrate that a certain type of crime is safe and lucrative, it attracts imitators very rapidly. Then when an effective anticrime technique is developed, that crime becomes "unpopular" just as rapidly, sometimes dropping much more than the real effectiveness of the new technique would seem to warrant. Some of this reduction is displaced to other targets, but incompletely. These conclusions, echoed in the larger literature, point to gaps in knowledge of the circumstances in which criminals persist in a given level of criminal activity and ones in which they are deflected.[36] The conservative conclusion at this point is that situational crime prevention has a proven track record for reducing many types of specific crimes at specific types of location, and probably has more diffuse positive effects as well, of less certain magnitude.

TABLE 15.1
The Twelve Techniques of Situational Prevention

Increasing the effort	Increasing the risks	Reducing the rewards
Target hardening	*Entry/exit screening*	*Target removal*
Steering locks	Border searches	Removable car radios
Bandit screens	Baggage screening	Exact change fares
Slug rejector devices	Automatic ticket gates	Cash reduction
Vandal-proofing	Merchandise tags	Removing coin meters
Toughened glass	Library tags	Phone cards
Tamper-proof seals	Electronic point of sale systems	Paying by check
Access control	*Formal surveillance*	*Identifying property*
Locked gates	Police patrols	Cattle branding
Fenced yards	Security guards	Property marking
Parking lot barriers	Informant hotlines	Vehicle licensing
Entry phones	Burglar alarms	Vehicle parts marking
ID badges	Red light cameras	PIN for car radios
PIN numbers	Curfew decals	LOJACK[a]
Deflecting offenders	*Surveillance by employees*	*Removing inducements*
Bus stop placement	Bus conductors	"Weapons effect"
Tavern location	Park attendants	Graffiti cleaning
Street closures	Concierges	Rapid repair
Graffiti boards	Pay phone location	Plywood road signs
Litter bins	Incentive schemes	Gender-neutral phone lists
Spittoons	Closed-circuit TV systems	Parking Camarro off street
Controlling facilitators	*Natural surveillance*	*Rule setting*
Spray-can sales restrictions	Pruning hedges	Drug-free school zones
Gun control	"Eyes on the street"	Public park regulations
Credit card photos	Lighting bank interiors	Customs declaration
Ignition interlocks	Street lighting	Income tax returns
Server intervention	Defensible space	Hotel registration
Caller ID	Neighborhood Watch	Library check-out

a. Trade name for a transmitter concealed in the body of a vehicle.
SOURCE: Ronald V. Clarke, ed., *Situational Crime Prevention: Successful Case Studies* (New York: Harrow and Heston, 1992).

Conclusion

The growing knowledge about the relationship of the physical environment to crime generally confirms that if the environment is changed so as to raise the immediate, tangible risks and costs of crime, then, *ceteris paribus,* crime will go down. The finding itself is unsurprising, but it nonetheless has broad policy implications, as may be seen by running through the list of situational crime prevention techniques shown in Table 15.1. Much can be done through existing technology and procedures to make crime tougher for criminals to commit and easier for law-abiding citizens to prevent.

But such improvements fall far short of the exciting hopes that greeted defensible space. What does one make of another common sense finding, now substantiated by social science, that cohesive communities are less attractive to criminals than disorganized ones? True, many of the innovations arising from defensible space theory are sensible and inexpensive to incorporate in new housing. If nothing else, the innovations tend to make the housing more livable and attractive. They may also have some value in forestalling deterioration in a low crime area that is threatened with encroachment by outsiders. But defensible space improvements are likely to have the least effect in places with the worst crime problems. In such places, informal social controls are likely to be the weakest, meaning that few residents are likely to take advantage of natural surveillance and territoriality. Meanwhile, the criminals in such places are likely to have intimate local knowledge that will lead them to ignore symbolic changes in the built environment and enable them to turn concrete changes to their own advantage. Defensible space has two faces. When neighbors are allies, measures that make it easier for them to see who comes and goes from one another's houses may help prevent a burglary. In neighborhoods where the neighbor may very well *be* the burglar, the same measures can be a menace.

BRIAN FORST

PROSECUTION AND SENTENCING

One of the most vexing of all public policy questions is this: What should be done with those who violate the law? Many believe that our crime problem is largely the product of a system that is too soft on criminals. How lenient are prosecutors and judges *really?* Or is the problem that offenders too often slip through the system on legal technicalities? Others see the problem as one of a racially biased system. Is there merit in those concerns as well?

These "hot button" issues can be addressed by starting with basics. Most agree that case processing should be just, effective, and speedy; but authorities disagree broadly and often bitterly over the specifics. For prosecutors, the central questions are how to allocate scarce resources and how best to proceed for each of a bewildering variety of cases involving street crime, domestic violence, drug violations, child abuse, white collar offenses, and repeat offenders. For judges and legislators, the problem is how to sentence any particular category of offender so that a proper balance is found among the often conflicting goals of crime prevention, fairness, reform of the offender, and economy.

Typical Case Dispositions

To provide a background for considering how the system ought to work, let us see what actually happens to the approximately three million arrests for index crimes (homicide, forcible rape, robbery, burglary, aggravated assault, larceny, and arson) each year.[1] It is well known that most offenses do not end in arrest and that most arrests do not end in incarceration; incarcerations have been increasing sharply, however, over the past twenty years, and not just because of increases in the number of offenses. In 1970, imprisonments were fewer than 1 percent of all reported index crimes. By 1989 the rate had more than doubled, rising to 2.2 percent.[2]

Thanks to improvements in the record-keeping technology of prosecution over the past twenty years, we have learned a great deal about what happens between arrest and final case disposition. Figure 16.1 depicts the outcomes of 100 typical arrests for felony offenses in a cross section of jurisdictions throughout the United States.[3]

To begin with, about one-third of all felony arrests involve juvenile offenders. Statistics about the outcomes of those cases are not readily available, largely because of a widespread reluctance to maintain and use juvenile records for analytic purposes. To the extent that we do know about the dispositions of the million-plus felony cases involving juveniles annually, we can say that they tend to involve more variation in handling than adult felony

FIGURE 16.1
Typical Dispositions of 100 Felony Arrests in the United States, 1988

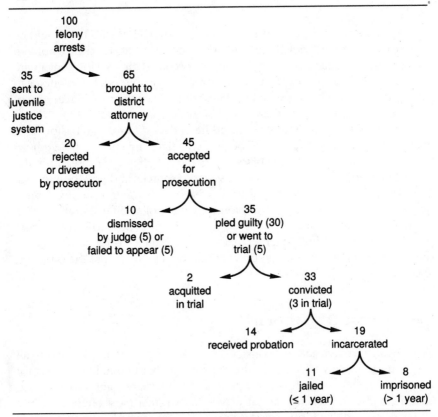

cases from jurisdiction to jurisdiction and, generally, fewer long-term commitments.[4]

We know considerably more about what happens to adults arrested for felony crimes. About one-third of these cases are either rejected outright at the initial screening stage or dropped by the prosecutor soon afterward; some 70 percent are accepted for prosecution (about 45 of the original 100 felony arrests displayed in Figure 16.1). In about 10 of those 45, the judge dismisses the case because of evidence insufficiency, procedural difficulty (for example, the prosecutor is not prepared), or the triviality of the offense; 5 more are eventually dropped because the defendant fails to appear in court after having been released on money bond, personal recognizance, or third-party custody. (About 30 of the 45 defendants whose cases are accepted for prosecution are released prior to trial, and about 5 of those are rearrested before the first case is resolved.[5]) Some 30 (almost 90 percent) of the 35 remaining defendants plead guilty, often to obtain a lighter sentence than they would receive if found guilty in trial; the other 5 go to trial and are most often found guilty.[6] Most of the 33 thus convicted are incarcerated, and the majority of those are given jail terms of less than a year.

Variation in Screening and Plea-Bargaining Practices

These numbers are not uniform across jurisdictions. The Constitution says precious little about prosecutorial rules and standards; prosecutors are free to go about their business in quite different ways from one jurisdiction to another, and even among offices within the same jurisdiction.[7] Prosecutors in some offices are much more inclined to obtain convictions by plea rather than take cases to trial. Conventional wisdom holds that these differences are due to variations in the workloads per prosecutor from office to office, but that is not the whole story—jurisdictions with huge caseloads often have low ratios of pleas to trials, while those with much smaller caseloads often have high ratios.[8]

Prosecution *policy*—whether to be more selective at the screening stage and then put more effort into bringing cases to trial, or to take on more risky cases and put more effort into negotiating guilty pleas in return for charge reductions in all cases—appears to be as important a determinant of the ratio of pleas to trials as does the press of large caseloads. In screening arrests for prosecution, some offices apply the arrest standard of "probable cause," while in others a much higher standard of "trial-worthiness" is used. The former tend to have higher plea-to-trial ratios and higher conviction rates, but lower rates of imprisonment, than the latter.[9] Less clear is how each approach serves the interests of justice and effectiveness, respectively.

Many have argued that plea bargaining is simply wrong and should be abolished, since it deprives defendants of their day in court and deprives victims of the security of long terms of incarceration for offenders. But the abolition of or constraints on plea bargaining practices by legislation or voter referendum has proven to be at best ineffective and often counterproductive.[10] It is clear that little good would be served by attempting to force all cases through the court; many, perhaps most, pleas involve cases in which an offender has no defense and simply wishes to expedite the process, often in exchange for minor concessions by the prosecutor.

Factors Associated with Conviction and Incarceration

The numbers presented in the preceding section tell us little about the factors that determine *which* cases are selected for prosecution and harsher sanctions in any jurisdiction. Note in Figure 16.1 that about five-eighths of the adult felony cases that fail to end in conviction are weeded out by the prosecutor and are never seen by a judge. To learn about the factors that influence felony case dispositions, we would do well to begin by focusing on these dropped cases and on the reasons given by prosecutors for rejecting them.

It turns out that the vast majority of all felony cases dropped by the prosecutor are rejected because of insufficiency of evidence—the police fail to produce adequate physical evidence (such as stolen property or implements of the crime) or testimonial evidence from victims or eyewitnesses.[11] The next major reason given by prosecutors, although far less common than evidentiary insufficiency, is triviality of the offense (often reported as declined "in the interest of justice"). The defendants in these cases are generally not viewed as serious threats to the community. Most are dropped outright, while others are "diverted," often with the stipulation that the defendant must complete a program of counseling or instruction aimed at rehabilitation.

Many of the cases dropped or diverted are not trivial, however. Cases of assault and rape, in particular—often cases involving serious injury—are frequently dropped by prosecutors because they arise between people who knew each other prior to the offense, typically in domestic settings. Studies of felony arrest processing in several jurisdictions have shown that in the majority of violent offense cases, the assailant is known to the victim, and many involve members of the same family.[12] Prosecutors usually regard such cases as unattractive; the victims, after having called the police to arrest the offender, are frequently uncooperative.[13] Because of uncooperative witnesses, prosecutors reject arrests for crimes of assault within families at a rate of over 40 percent—nearly three times the rate for assault cases involving strangers.[14] Males who make a habit of assaulting their female partners may commit serious crimes in the home as frequently as other offenders with more serious criminal records do on the street.[15] Although some progress has been apparent during the past few years, prosecutors still are somewhat loath to give such cases the attention that may be warranted by conventional standards of justice.

It is widely believed that many, if not most, felony cases presented to prosecutors are dropped for another reason—legal "technicalities" related to Fourth Amendment exclusionary rule violations. In fact, fewer than 1 percent of all felony arrests are dropped on such grounds; most of those are drug cases involving questionable procedures for searching for drugs.[16] While the exclusionary rule may retard the ability of the police to arrest a large number of offenders and bring apprehended offenders to the prosecutor, it does not appear to play a major role in the prosecutor's decision to reject or dismiss cases.[17]

Of course, the reasons for case rejections officially recorded by public agents are not necessarily to be believed. On this question, however, independent empirical evidence exists to validate the official reasons. Convictions are systematically more likely to follow arrest when police produce and document physical evidence in the case than when such evidence is not produced. Likewise, when police produce information about two or more witnesses (including victims), convictions are more likely to follow. Finally, when police are able to make the arrest soon after an offense occurs, physical evidence is more likely to be found, and conviction is more likely to follow, than when more time elapses between the offense and the arrest.[18]

There should be nothing surprising in the finding that arrests with the strongest tangible and testimonial evidence are most likely to produce convictions. Older generations brought up on *Perry Mason* and younger generations brought up on *L.A. Law* alike know that the evidence needed to convict in a courtroom must be sufficient to prove guilt beyond a reasonable doubt. More important is the fact that the *police* are responsible for obtaining physical evidence and information about witnesses, as well as for providing information to witnesses that induces them to support the prosecutor in convicting offenders. It turns out that some police officers consistently produce arrests that end in convictions at a rate that substantially surpasses random chance.[19] Interviews have revealed that those officers tend to be more persistent about finding witnesses and more conscientious about follow-up investigation than officers with low rates of conviction.

In short, whether an arrest ends in conviction depends in the first place on factors over which the prosecutor has no direct control: the strength of the evidence as presented to the police officer, the effectiveness of the officer in bringing the best available evidence (both tangible and testimonial) to the prosecutor, and the seriousness of the offense. Nonetheless, prosecution resources and practices—and the exercise of discretion—do play a significant role in determining whether arrests lead to conviction.

Unbridled Prosecutorial Discretion?

District attorneys normally exercise considerable latitude in choosing the approximately 60 percent of felony arrests brought by the police that will be prosecuted—so much so that the district attorney has been said to exercise "the greatest discretion in the formally organized criminal justice network." [20] The typical urban prosecutor's office, presented with about 100 felony cases per attorney each year, obviously cannot give celebrity status attention to each and every case.

In fact, for many if not most cases the decision whether to prosecute is virtually automatic—for cases in which the evidence is either extremely weak or strong and cases involving either trivial or very serious offenses. Numerous studies agree that prosecutors' case-screening and -handling decisions have been influenced primarily by the strength of the evidence and the seriousness of the offense. [21] In the late 1970s and early 1980s many prosecutors, stimulated largely by federal support, instituted programs to focus resources as well on cases involving repeat offenders. [22] Prosecutors' decisions are assuredly not random.

Within those boundaries, however, there is substantial discretion. In deciding whether to accept cases, in selecting charges to file with the court, in negotiating pleas with defense counsel, in preparing cases more or less extensively for trial, and in recommending sentences to judges, prosecutors have considerable room to maneuver. Written policies used in even the most rule-conscious offices do not provide unambiguous instructions about how to handle every type of case. Because of this discretion, even the best statistical models of prosecutors' decision making are incapable of accurately predicting screening, charging, or plea-bargaining decisions in particular cases.

When asked to explain the rationale behind the decisions, most prosecutors are inclined to say that case-handling decisions, like medical decisions, involve both science and craft, and that experienced prosecutors know how to blend the technical requirements of the law with the good judgment that comes from years of practice. Unfortunately, this tells us nothing about the underlying goals that influence their decision-making process. Nor do we know whether prosecutors consciously make case selection and handling decisions with such goals in mind. Most prosecutors argue that while justice, crime control, and speedy case processing are all worthy goals, each case is unique. Whether to accept a case, what charges to file, how much time to spend preparing it for a court proceeding, what charge or charges to allow the defendant to plead to in return for dropping other charges (or what sentence to recommend to the judge if the defendant pleads guilty to a particular charge) in any given case cannot be determined by pondering over abstract goals or resorting to a formula derived from such goals. Until a strong argument can be made for instituting a more explicit set of rules or guidelines for making case-processing decisions based on well-established empirical links between the rules and such tangible goals as reduced case-processing time and crime control, decisions about individual cases are likely to continue to be made in a subjective and largely unpredictable manner.

Prosecutors may, however, be pushing the political, if not the lawful, limits of their discretion. Authorities from both ends of the political spectrum have voiced strong objection to the clear appearance of increasing politicization of prosecution policies and practices. The accusation of abusive prosecution has been made by the defense counsel for former Washington, D.C., mayor Marion Barry and taken up by much of the nation's African American community in response to Barry's 1990 cocaine bust, as well as by civil libertarians opposed to the unpredictable prosecution of drug conspiracy cases. It has been made just as fervently by the *Wall Street Journal* and other conservative sources in criticizing the zeal of U.S. attorneys in going after arbitrarily selected high status individuals under the amorphous Racketeer Influenced and Corrupt Organization (RICO) statute and that of independent prosecutors in a variety of sensational affairs.[23] Much less has been written about cases involving low-level street offenders, but the lack of any systematic review of prosecutors' decisions about which cases to file in court and how much attention to give to each should lead one to wonder about evenhandedness in those cases as well. An issue that liberals and conservatives alike can agree upon and regard as critical in the high profile cases alone is one that deserves to be taken seriously.

Prosecutors may disagree on the proper goals of prosecution, or on the best method of achieving a goal, but it is difficult to object to a more coherent and consistent basis for making case-processing decisions in a prosecutor's office. Prosecutors themselves can take the initiative in identifying those areas in which guidelines for more uniform practices are most needed and putting them in place, so that their work can be made both more explicit and more evenhanded. If they do not, others may do it for them.

The Exercise of Discretion in Sentencing

Until the 1980s, sentencing decisions were not substantially more predictable than prosecution decisions. The seriousness of the offense, an important factor in prosecution, has also been critical in sentencing. The offender's prior record as well has been found to have an independent effect on the severity of the sentence.[24] A third factor associated with sentence severity is whether the defendant pleads guilty; those who do tend to receive lighter sentences than those similarly charged who take their chances and are found guilty in trial. [25]

The sentencing decision appears to have been shaped most decisively, however, by the sentencing judge. Research on sentencing variation prior to the era of the structuring of sentencing discretion found the sentence to be affected more by the sentencing judge than by all other factors combined. This finding has been confirmed both in studies in which identical cases were shown to several judges for an opinion about the appropriate sentence and in studies of sentences given in real cases, using detailed case descriptions from presentence investigation reports to control statistically for other factors influencing sentence severity. [26]

Judges have been responsible for several kinds of unwarranted sentence disparity. Some judges are inclined simply to give more severe (or lenient) sentences than others. Those who support rehabilitation as the primary goal of sentencing, for example, have been found to give more lenient sentences, while those who support the more strictly utilitarian goals of deterrence and incapacitation tend to give harsher sentences. [27] There are also more selective kinds of variation; a judge who is neither especially tough nor lenient on the whole may be more lenient than most judges, for example, with defendants found guilty in trial or with persons convicted of drug trafficking. And finally, there is a natural element of inconsistency among the sentencing decisions of an individual judge, and some tend to be more inconsistent than others. Sentence disparity has been much more than just a matter of overall toughness or leniency.

Under the rules of sentencing that have prevailed throughout the United States for most of the twentieth century, judges exercised discretion in determining not only who would be incarcerated and who would be given terms of probation but also the minimum term before eligibility for parole for persons selected for prison. Judges also had the extraordinary option of selecting concurrent or consecutive terms of imprisonment for separate conviction charges in individual cases.

What about the effect of racial or sexual discrimination? Blacks, who make up 12 percent of the U.S. population, constitute nearly half of U.S. prison populations. [28] After reviewing the then-available research evidence on the effect of the defendant's race on the sentence he receives, a 1983 National Academy of Sciences panel concluded that "factors other than racial discrimination in sentencing account for most of the disproportionate representation of blacks in U.S. prisons. . . . Blacks are overrepresented in prison populations primarily because of their overrepresentation in arrests for the more serious crime types." [29] The panel did acknowledge the likelihood of racial discrimination in the decisions of some individual judges in some jurisdictions, stating that any such discrimination, however small is unacceptable. [30]

Black representation in prisons increased significantly because of the mid-1980s war on drugs, with its emphasis on trafficking in crack cocaine. Tougher sanctions in crack cocaine cases, designed primarily to deal with a problem that had reached epidemic proportions in many inner cities during the 1980s, thus produced the unintended effect of much higher minority prison populations. While these tougher sanctions may have actually made a serious drug abuse problem somewhat less serious, it is certainly in order to ask whether that benefit justifies the harsh medicine of long prison terms and the corresponding large increase in minority prison populations. (This matter is addressed in further detail later, in the discussion of problems associated with sentencing guidelines.)

Similarly, the disproportionate number of males in prison is primarily the result of disproportionate numbers of males being arrested for serious crime. When studies do find gender differentials in sentencing, they have usually been to the advantage of women offenders.[31] There are other sources of variation in sentencing—suburban and rural courts, for example, tend to be more severe than urban courts[32]—but such discrepancies are not generally regarded as "unwarranted" in the same sense as the variations discussed above.

Incentives of Prosecutors and Judges

By and large, case selection and sentencing practices have been consistent with the broadest notion of justice. Prosecutors and judges have tended to act in such a way as to ensure that those offenders who pose the greatest threat to the community are convicted and incarcerated—a tendency consistent with the utilitarian principle of crime control through incapacitation and deterrence. The practice of reserving the most severe sanctions for the most serious offenders is consistent both with the notion of "just deserts" and with the principle of deterrence. Likewise, the inclination of prosecutors and judges to conserve scarce court resources by giving more lenient sentences to offenders who plead guilty serves the interests of speedy justice and economy. Other notions of justice, such as those emphasizing restitution and rehabilitation, could of course be given more emphasis; the practices just described are not necessarily incompatible with those notions.[33] Given the substantial obstacles confronting prosecutors and judges—large caseloads, limited resources, and broadly conflicting views about what the system ought to be accomplishing—it would be inappropriate to conclude that either group has not been acting generally in the interests of justice.

It would be equally inappropriate to assert that prosecutors and judges do not respond to incentives. Like other professionals, they care about their professional reputations; they tend to operate in ways that induce both their peers and the public they serve to respect their judgment and take note of their effectiveness.

As typically publicly elected officials, district attorneys in particular are usually inclined to conduct themselves so as to appeal to the general public. Unfortunately, public assessments of the effectiveness of district attorneys may have little to do with the actual achievement of justice. One district attorney may be especially conscientious, for example, about taking on cases involving highly active offenders, even when these cases require the commitment of additional resources (for example, to give extra attention to the needs of reluctant witnesses). If as a result the crime rate were reduced by 10 percent, our inability to prove cause and effect would prevent even the district attorney from knowing for certain whether his or her conscientiousness paid off. Another district attorney may routinely drop cases involving repeat offenders unless they happen to be easy cases, taking on only those that do not require much attention; the D.A. may then boast of a 90 percent conviction rate for the narrow subset of cases that went to trial or resulted in guilty pleas. Since information about cases dropped by the prosecutor is not generally made available to the public, a prosecutors' legitimate crime control efforts, or lack thereof, typically go unnoticed.

What does give public visibility to the district attorney? Most conspicuous are the outcomes of the handful of exceptional cases that appear in the newspapers and on news broadcasts.[34] Also important is the image that the D.A. projects in press conferences and public appearances on a variety of issues; for example, the prosecutor can gain visibility by announcing crackdowns on organized crime or drug dealing. U.S. Attorney Rudolph Giuliani adopted such an approach in his high profile targeting of white collar offenders in the Southern District of New York in the late 1980s. If a prosecutor says he is tough on criminals and appears to put up a good fight in the exceptional cases that make the news, any failures in managing his office efficiently or in dealing effectively with the larger pool of cases involving predictably dangerous offenders—cases that rarely make the news—will not jeopardize his prospects for reelection or advancement to higher political office.

The "career criminal" prosecution programs, created in 1975, illustrate the tension that can arise between the goals of justice and crime prevention, on the one hand, and the incentives facing prosecutors on the other. These programs were initiated by the Law Enforcement Assistance Administration (LEAA) to deal with the problem posed by those relatively few offenders who, as researchers found repeatedly, account for a disproportionate share of cases involving serious crimes.[35] It had been perceived generally that prosecutors did not give extra attention to cases involving those more criminally active offenders—cases that were often otherwise unattractive. This perception was later validated empirically.[36] To provide an incentive for prosecutors to target more attorney time on such cases, LEAA offered additional resources to local prosecutors for the creation of career criminal programs. Many prosecutors, interested in the additional resources, applied for and obtained them, creating sections of the office in which attorneys worked on fewer cases and processed them through all the stages of prosecution ("vertically") rather than in the production line process ("horizontally") that characterizes conventional prosecution.

Subsequent evaluations of those programs, however, produced mixed results. On the one hand, career criminal units were found to allocate a much greater concentration of resources to cases involving potential career criminals—perhaps four or five times more than would have been conventionally applied.[37] On the other hand, the criteria used by the prosecutors to identify career offenders tended to be less than optimal. Rather than pinpointing the most criminally active suspects, most jurisdictions developed criteria designed to be easy to administer and produce interesting cases. Career criminal units typically targeted offenders with at least one prior felony conviction and current charges involving a serious crime—often homicide, rape, or assault. Such criteria are better than none, but prosecutors can do even better by basing case selection on criteria that correspond more closely to the actual characteristics of dangerous, high-crime-rate offenders: prior arrests for serious crimes, a juvenile record, youthfulness, drug use, and known involvement in robbery or burglary. Those characteristics had been shown to be the strongest predictors of predatory crime in research at the University of Pennsylvania, the Rand Corporation, and elsewhere;[38] yet for the most part they failed to appear in career criminal targeting criteria. The public has been deeply concerned about crime and generally supportive of career criminal programs, but in practice career criminal units tended to employ criteria that focused largely on criminals in the twilight of their careers, bypassing the offenders likely to inflict the most harm on society.

The programs appear, nonetheless, to have improved prosecution, on balance. Career criminal prosecution units atrophied when federal funding disappeared, but an awareness of the need to consider not only the strength of the evidence and the seriousness of the offense but also the dangerousness of the offender has been a legacy of the units that lives on in conventional prosecution systems.

A few prosecutors have attempted more recently to improve their operations and simultaneously improve their relations with the public by developing "community-oriented" prosecution programs. Patterned after community-oriented policing programs that aim to improve police performance by building bridges to the community, these programs assign individual attorneys to cases involving crimes in specific neighborhoods. The basic idea is that prosecutors can be more effective when they descend from their professional perches and get to know the neighborhood better. Additional economies are likely to derive from working with the same few police officers who are responsible for the same neighborhoods.[39] These programs have not yet received rigorous assessment, but they make good sense and reflect a healthy spirit that characterized successful service delivery in the 1980s—serving customers more effectively by getting to know them better.[40]

Ironically, public scrutiny tends to be directed more at "soft" judges than at prosecutors and their case selection criteria and case management systems. One measure of the relative importance of prosecutorial and judicial discretion is revealed in Figure 16.1: for every felony case that a judge presides over in trial, thirteen felony cases are brought to the prosecutor by the police. Since judges are less often elected officials and often have judicial tenure, they may place a smaller premium on public sentiment than do district attorneys. Judges do typically wish to establish reputations of fairness in their exercise of discretion and efficiency in clearing the court docket, but these reputations are established primarily among peers (despite frequent disagreement among peers about the goals of sentencing) rather than with the public. At the same time, however, judges are not oblivious to public sentiment. No judge cares to read in the newspaper that a defendant he or she released on personal recognizance was rearrested for murder.

The incentives of prosecutors and judges, in short, are consistent with broad standards of justice, but leave substantial opportunity for disparity and inefficiency in the exercise of discretion. The goals of prosecution and sentencing have not been made sufficiently clear, and detailed information about the decisions made by prosecutors and judges has not been made sufficiently accessible to induce prosecutors and judges to make decisions about individual cases that correspond closely or consistently to any particular standard of justice or efficiency.

Structuring the Exercise of Prosecutorial Discretion

Aware of ample room for improvement, prosecutors and judges, as well as state and federal legislators and criminal justice system reformers, have set out to introduce procedures designed to produce greater accountability, uniformity, and efficiency in the decisions and practices that follow arrest. In the 1970s prosecutors began to rely on computers for tracking individual cases and caseloads of individual attorneys, printing subpoenas, producing periodic reports showing various aggregate dimensions of office performance, and providing data so that office policy could be analyzed in depth. Lack of information about prosecutor operations prior to the use of computers limits opportunities to measure the benefits of improved information technology; the proliferation of management information systems in a setting that traditionally has been ambivalent about such technology, however, suggests that prosecutors gain benefits from these systems that exceed the costs. And despite the limitations of career criminal programs noted earlier, the adoption and retention of essential principles of those programs in many offices after the withdrawal of federal support further attests to a growing sense of accountability among prosecutors for aggregate and somewhat elusive concepts such as crime control. Prosecutors, like other lawyers, have tended to focus traditionally on individual cases and litigation related to them rather than on jurisdiction-wide, or even office-wide constructs of performance.[41]

These changes have been initiated with the full involvement of prosecutors. Other attempts to reform prosecution practices, imposed from outside, have been less successful. For example, legislative attempts to abolish plea bargaining that have not enlisted the full support of the prosecutor have proved subject to circumvention through the replacement of charge bargaining with sentence bargaining and through an increase in the rate at which cases are dropped by the prosecutor.[42]

Structuring More Consistent Sentencing Policies

Reforms in prosecution practices over the past generation have been fairly modest when compared with the sweep of change in sentencing policy. Indeed, no quarter of the criminal justice system has seen more extensive change during the 1980s and 1990s than has our system of sentencing. This was largely the product of legislators taking on a much larger role in the toughening of sanctions than during any earlier period.[43] It was the product also of research findings—first on the ineffectiveness of rehabilitation programs,[44] second on disparity in judicial sentencing practices.[45]

For most of the twentieth century, the notion that prisons should correct the behavior of inmates—not just warehouse them or subject them to punishments of the sort that characterized less civilized eras—seemed like a humane culmination of Montesquieu's eighteenth-century notion of enlightenment and Zebulon Brockway's nineteenth-century progressive spirit. It also seemed to satisfy a more pragmatic notion that advancements in medical and behavioral-scientific therapies could be tailored to fit the individual needs of the inmate. From 1935 to 1975, indeterminate sentencing was the American way of sentencing, used in all of the states, in the District of Columbia, and by the federal government.[46] Under that system, judges determined who would go to prison, and parole boards determined both when prison inmates were ready for release to the community and whether certain behaviors of persons thus released warranted return back to prison.

Support for indeterminate sentencing began to erode when reformers and public entertainments (the movie *A Clockwork Orange* is the classic example) raised questions about the ethics of the rehabilitation model. The erosion accelerated following a well-publicized search and failure by Robert Martinson and his associates to find any systematic evidence that our system of indeterminate sentencing actually worked—that prison programs rehabilitated offenders and that parole boards could really determine with any degree of precision when inmates eligible for release had been cured of their criminal propensities. This substantial lack of evidence made a mockery of the term "correctional institution." More significantly, it raised fundamental questions about the wisdom of maintaining a sentencing policy that was not only failing to achieve its primary objective but doing so in a manner that lacked coherence and evenhandedness. Even members of the judiciary began to step forward to register complaints about indeterminate sentencing.[47] The state of Maine led the movement away from the rehabilitative model with a return to the determinate sentence in 1975.

In turning away from the goal of rehabilitation, sentencing authorities are left with several alternative rationales for determining an appropriate sentence for any particular class of offender: general deterrence, special deterrence, incapacitation, and retribution or "just deserts." The basic idea of *general deterrence* is that by punishing one person, we dissuade others from committing future such acts; it assumes that prospective offenders engage in a rational process of determining whether the expected costs associated with the punishment that may follow a given crime are sufficient to offset the expected rewards associated with the crime and thus prevent the crime. While the theory of general deterrence has received empirical support for many categories of offenses, such support in crimes of passion and in violent crimes committed by juveniles has been notably absent.

The notion of *special deterrence* holds that individual offenders will be dissuaded from repeating an offense after having experienced the unpleasantness of a prison term; if rehabilitation is the "carrot" approach to incarceration, special deterrence is the "stick." Evidence in support of special deterrence, like that for rehabilitation, has been the exception rather than the rule.[48] The idea of *incapacitation* is simply that offenders separated from society will not be able to inflict harms on innocent people during their period of incarceration. *Retribution* reflects the ancient eye-for-an-eye rationale for sentencing: the appropriate sentence is one that corresponds in severity to the heinousness of the crime.[49]

With such an array of alternative rationales for determining an appropriate sentence—even leaving aside the liberal-conservative dimension of the debate—it should not be surprising that there is little consensus on sentencing policy. In moving away from the indeterminate sentence, states have gone in several different directions. Some (California, Colorado, Connecticut, Illinois, Indiana, Maine, New Mexico, and North Carolina) have adopted *statutory determinate sentencing laws,* in various degrees of specificity and severity. Still other states (Delaware, Kansas, Louisiana, Maryland, Michigan, Minnesota, Oregon, Pennsylvania, and Washington) have adopted *sentencing guideline* systems: some *voluntary* and mostly ineffective as disparity reduction agents[50] and some more clearly structured as *presumptive guide-*

line systems, based on explicit "typical" sentences or sentence ranges for particular categories of offense and offender—often presented in the form of a matrix that displays the offense and offender seriousness levels along the columns and rows, with the presumptive guidelines shown in the cells— subject to reduction for mitigating circumstances, enhancements for aggravating circumstances, and appellate review. Sentencing guideline systems vary in other ways too: Some are determined by sentencing commissions and others by statute. Some are *descriptive,* based on past norms; and others, *prescriptive,* based on either just deserts or utilitarian notions.[51] Many states have retained indeterminate sentencing and parole boards, some essentially unchanged from the systems put in place fifty years or more earlier.

Surely the most visible and controversial of the sentencing reforms is the guideline system created under the federal Sentencing Reform Act (SRA) of 1984. The SRA created a seven-member Sentencing Commission to direct a program of research in support of sentencing guidelines that went into effect in late 1987; it also ended the federal parole system and established a system of appellate sentence review. The federal sentencing guidelines have been roundly criticized, especially by federal judges and liberals, but by pragmatists of other stripes as well. They are despised by the judges for excessively limiting the exercise of discretion and for their complexity and difficulty of use. They are deplored by defense counselors for their harshness, for shifting sentencing authority from judges to prosecutors,[52] and for being based on offense elements and prior record rather than conviction charges. They are disliked by many federal officials for their dissimilarity to the prior system of sentencing and for the disruption they brought to a system perceived by many as one that had been working well enough before the change.[53]

Perhaps the most compelling of all criticisms of the federal guidelines is that they were developed with too little attention paid to either ethical considerations of basic justice or pragmatic concerns about their effects on prison populations. From 1982 to 1992, the number of convictions in federal courts increased by 52 percent while the number sentenced to prison increased by 92 percent.[54] The federal prison population increased by 60 percent from the end of 1987 to mid-1992.[55] The average time served until first release for those imprisoned increased from 14.9 months in 1986 to 23.6 months in 1992, with the largest increases in prison time for drug trafficking—from 22.7 months to 34.7 months over the six-year period.[56] The number of prison years given to convicted drug traffickers nearly tripled, from 10,663 in 1986 to 30,242 in 1992, in large part because of congressionally imposed mandatory minimum sentences for drug offenses.[57] With the drug arrest rate for blacks over three times that for whites, these increases have fallen disproportionately on African American males.[58] It is surely reasonable to ask whether the benefit of drug market disruption is justified by the considerable costs— financial, administrative, and ethical.[59] The federal sentencing guidelines appear to have reduced certain types of unwarranted disparity[60] but, especially in combination with mandatory minimum sentences, have produced other types of unwarranted disparity along the way; and by some reckonings they have produced unwarranted *severity* to boot.

This does not mean that sentencing guidelines determined by commissions are doomed to fail. Indeed, the experiences of several of the commission-based sentencing guideline systems at the state level have in fact been quite positive. Michael Tonry has observed that Delaware, Minnesota, Oregon, Pennsylvania, and Washington have produced guidelines that appear to have reduced unwarranted disparity, including racial and gender discrimination, without deeply upsetting judges and other interested parties.[61] Two keys to the success of these systems are that they tend to be thoughtfully crafted with a view to their effects on prison populations, and they are insulated from uncontested political pressures to get forever tougher on criminals. Tonry notes that the commission-based sentencing guideline approach is "the only reform strategy that commands widespread support and continues to be the subject of new legislation."[62] Voluntary guideline systems have produced no systematic evidence of disparity reduction, and statutory determinate sentencing laws have been too diverse to lend themselves to generalization.[63]

A critical aspect of both the federal guidelines and other presumptive guideline systems that discourages sentence disparity is appellate review. Sentences that fall outside the guidelines may be appealed by either the defendant or the state. In such cases, two factors are available to the appellate judge that facilitate the sentence appeal process: an explicit sentence guideline sanctioned by law and an explicit rationale given by the sentencing judge for diverging from the guideline. Appellate review of sentencing otherwise has not been an important factor in the United States, since most states do not have presumptive guidelines; appellate review plays an important role in virtually every other common law nation.[64]

Most states have expanded *mandatory sentences* for selected categories of offenses such as drugs and felonies involving firearms, and for multiple felony convictions. Among the more significant of the mandatory minimum sentencing statutes are New York's 1973 Rockefeller Drug Law, aimed at narcotics traffickers and users; Massachusetts's 1974 Bartley-Fox Amendment, requiring that anyone caught possessing an unregistered handgun will receive a one-year prison term; the 1977 Michigan Felony Firearm Statute, which adds two years to any felony term involving firearm possession; New York's 1980 gun law; the federal drug control acts of 1986, 1988, 1990, and 1992, assigning long mandatory prison terms to drug traffickers and doubling them for offenders with prior convictions; and three-strikes-and-you're-out-for-life provisions enacted in several states in the mid-1990s for persons convicted of three violent felony offenses.[65]

Mandatory sentencing is perhaps the most controversial of all legislative changes in sentencing. Often the product of get-tough political posturing rather than thoughtful analysis, mandatory minimums are typically directed at offenders who tend already to receive tough sanctions under preexisting sentencing provisions. The combination of tough guidelines in many states with increases in mandatory minimum sentences in virtually all states and the federal system has produced what one authority has called "probably . . . the most disastrous decade in the history of American penology."[66]

Severe mandatory minimums for offenders with long records can be especially counterproductive; they often work at cross-purposes with the goal of "selective incapacitation"—reserving prison space for the most dangerous and criminally active offenders. To the extent that offenders tend to accumulate longer records as they grow older, tough mandatory minimums for persons with long records without regard to age can have the effect of reserving prison space primarily for offenders nearing the ends of their criminal careers. Further reductions in incapacitation benefits are produced when parole boards accelerate the release of dangerous offenders to accommodate the incarceration of less dangerous drug offenders sentenced under mandatory minimum statutes.

Mandatory minimum statutes can be counterproductive in other ways as well, reducing defendants' incentives to plead guilty[67] and lengthening case-processing times, inducing prosecutors to dismiss cases and reduce charges excessively (thus depriving the community of potentially important deterrent effects), overturning thoughtfully crafted sentence guidelines, and creating dreadful overcrowding conditions in prisons. Moreover, in lengthening the sentences of some offenders while reducing others to zero, mandatory minimums actually *increase* the disparity in sanctions. The legislator's compulsion always to take a tough stand where the public's concern about crime is an issue, in spite of strong evidence against the effectiveness of mandatory minimum laws, makes other allegations of "political correctness" look trivial; it may accomplish little other than to give the public a false sense of security, while inflicting substantial costs and other harms on society.[68]

How Punitive *Should* Sentences Be?

Mandatory minimums, and tougher sentencing laws generally, are neither inherently unjust nor ineffective. A just and effective sentencing system would ensure that a particular category of offense and offender receive a particular sanction, one that would indeed be mandatory in the sense that it would eliminate unwarranted disparity. "Proper" sentence lengths could be determined under any of several different frameworks:

1. historical or cross-cultural norms
2. a just-deserts perspective
3. the utilitarian framework

From a *historical* perspective, sentences in the United States became generally tougher during the 1980s. Imprisonments for index crimes and for drug
crimes have increased sharply—the ratio of imprisonments to index crimes
more than doubled during the 1970s and 1980s, as I have noted. Imprisonments have increased for violent crimes as well: the average prison time
served per violent crime roughly *tripled* from 1975 to 1989.[69] *Cross-cultur-
ally*, sentences in the United States have been similar to those in most other
countries for violent offenses in terms of certainty and severity, and are a
good deal tougher than those in most other countries for property offenses.[70]

From a *desert-based* perspective, more serious offenses warrant more
severe sanctions; the difficulty is in determining precisely how severe a
punishment to assign to any particular crime in the first place. Legislative
deliberation is certainly a legitimate way of ascertaining, in a democracy,
what criminal sanction is deserved for a particular type of offense. When the
public becomes more outraged about crime (ironically, often in times of
stable crime rates), they are more inclined to press their legislators for
tougher sanctions on retributive grounds. Sentences increased during the
1980s and 1990s in a climate in which politicians worried a good deal more
about being characterized as "soft" on crime than about being characterized
as insensitive to prison populations or costs. One can imagine that at some
point, perhaps when public concern about prison costs relative to crime itself
increases, sentences may return to earlier levels. The logic of just deserts, in
any case, allows us only to assess whether one punishment is too tough
relative to that for another offense; it provides no basis for determining an
inherently proper level of punitiveness for a particular category of offense
and no guidance as to the overall correspondence of sentence severity to
offense seriousness.

Under a *utilitarian* system, the problem is to determine for each category of offense and offender the sentence that minimizes the total social cost
of crime and punishment, taking into account both the costs of punishment
and the value of the crimes prevented by those punishments by way of
deterrence and incapacitation.[71] It is surely easier to estimate the additional
prison cost of a one-year increase in sentence than it is to estimate the value
to the public of the crime prevention gained by that additional year. We
simply do not yet know enough about the deterrent and incapacitative effects
of sentences to permit useful estimates on the benefits side of the calculus.
We do know that increases in the certainty of punishment have a greater
crime reduction impact than do proportionate increases in severity of punishment,[72] but this does not tell us whether the current levels of either certainty
or severity are in a socially optimal range. Even if we knew the number of
crimes prevented by the one-year incarceration of a particular category of
offender, we would have difficulty determining the number and value of lives
saved and injuries not inflicted. The utilitarian system offers an elegant framework within which researchers can organize their estimates, but not yet one

for determining whether sentences are too harsh or too lenient. For some time to come, we will have to live with other ways of assessing the overall toughness of sentencing policy—primarily, historical norms and cross-cultural comparisons.

Alternatives to Incarceration

Thoughtful sentencing reform considers more than just the term and nature of imprisonment. It must consider also whether prison is the most effective alternative for certain classes of offenders. Other criminal sanctions may be equally or even more productive in reducing crime and may do so at a considerable saving to the public. An affluent nation with a high crime rate may be both able and willing to put a larger proportion of its population behind bars than any other in the world—more than 1 percent of the U.S. adult male population, well over a million in absolute number[73]—but we will do well to consider alternatives to prison and jail for offenders who can be safely and effectively punished in other ways.

A long-standing alternative to incarceration is the *fine,* an amount that the court orders the offender to pay the state. Fines are justified in part to repay both the criminal justice system for case-processing costs and society for other disruptions imposed by the crime, and in part as a form of punishment for the offender. Related alternatives to incarceration are *restitution,* based on the notion that convicted offenders should pay back their victims for the losses imposed,[74] and *forfeiture,* the seizure of goods and implements associated with the crime. These sanctions are less expensive to administer, and they tend to produce less stigma than prison; moreover, they can provide compensation to the victim and, especially in the case of crimes without identifiable victims, to society. On the other hand, the collection of fines and enforcement of restitution are not automatic; they require resources and record keeping and, if not carried out, breed further cynicism toward the criminal justice system.

Tough questions for sentencing decision makers involve the matter of equity for offenders at the margin of incarceration: How large a fine or term of community service is equivalent to, say, thirty days in jail? Should the offender be given the choice in these marginal cases? What role should the status of the offender play in the shaping of such alternatives? Different jurisdictions will inevitably arrive at different answers to these questions. Regardless of those answers, it is important that they be uniformly applied to offenders within that jurisdiction.

Another problem with both fines and restitution is that some offenders are in a much better position than others to satisfy the financial requirements imposed by the court. An irony of fines and restitution is that these sanctions may induce the poor offender to commit further crimes to satisfy the conditions imposed by the court. Indeed, fines often go unpaid—in the neighbor-hood of $2 billion annually.[75] But there is further irony: A term of incarceration for those unable to pay, even when the offender is given the choice, amounts to discrimination against the poor; and a larger fine for a person better able to pay may be viewed as lacking evenhandedness.[76]

Other important alternatives to conventional incarceration include *community service, shock probation* (resentencing the prisoner to probation after a short prison term), *intensive probation supervision*—often involving *house arrest* and *electronic monitoring*—and *community-based corrections.* These alternatives, which are considered more fully in Todd Clear and Anthony Braga's chapter in this volume (Chapter 18), have become increasingly important as our prison populations have continued to soar during the 1980s and 1990s. A potentially important risk associated with the harsher of these alternatives is that they may not be used as alternatives to incarceration at all, that they may be imposed instead on offenders who would ordinarily have received lesser sanctions (a phenomenon that has been referred to as "net widening"[77]), thus making it more difficult for the offenders to reintegrate back to society, or that they may be inappropriately used in *addition* to incarceration.

An equally important risk, of course, is that justice officials may divert dangerous offenders from incarceration to alternative sanctions that offer insufficient protection to the public. Much more research is needed to determine the relative effectiveness of these various alternative sanctions for various classes of offenders, so that policy makers can make these critical decisions in a more fully informed way.

Directions for Further Reform: The Effective Use of Information

Until fairly recently, prosecutors and judges operated in a statistical void, uncharacteristic of other major components of the criminal justice system and inconsistent with contemporary standards of management and public accountability. But information on prosecution and sentencing has been accumulating now for nearly a generation, inducing district attorneys and those responsible for the fashioning of sentencing policy to shift their thinking from the single-case litigation perspective instilled by conventional legal training to an orientation that considers the aggregate information in the context of goals of prosecution and sentencing. Thus a fundamental and revolutionary aspect of reform in prosecution and sentencing is under way.

The technical work that remains has to do largely with the development of more coherent guidelines for decision making by prosecutors and judges and the further production, dissemination, and use of sound statistical information to support those decisions. The process of developing guidelines for prosecution and sentencing is itself important for its tendency to induce more systematic consideration of the means of achieving the goals of justice. Once developed, the guidelines serve as explicit statements of policy—primarily to render decision making by prosecutors and judges more uniform, but also to provide essential information to other decision makers. Defendants and their counselors, for example, should be less likely to accept inferior offers from prosecutors when the sanctions associated with a particular combination of conviction charges and prior record are explicit.[78]

Sound guidelines also provide standards against which data can be used to assess criminal justice performance. If the data indicate that the standards are inappropriate—for example, stringent screening standards and harsh sentencing guidelines may produce high arrest rejection and case dismissal rates—a conscious choice can then be made either to make the guidelines less stringent or to improve performance (for example, to improve evidence by using investigative resources available to the prosecutor more efficiently and increase witness support by maintaining better contact with witnesses, perhaps using paralegal assistants).

The data can also be used to assess and improve existing criteria for case selection, targeting, and bail release decisions, and sentencing policy. Evidence suggests clearly that criteria derived from empirical analysis of computerized data maintained by prosecutors and courts can yield results that substantially surpass those associated with conventionally derived criteria at each important stage of criminal justice decision making. I have noted the need for such criteria in selecting cases with a view toward crime reduction through incapacitation; if only eight out of a hundred felony arrestees are to be imprisoned, it would seem worth devoting extra attention to those revealed in the data as the most dangerous of the arrestees with convictable cases. Desert-based sentencing systems, for example, may tend to inflate prison populations over time with older, less dangerous people. A similar example is provided by bail decisions. Many of the persons who are detained in jail pending trial have been found to have characteristics that make them predictably less prone to pretrial misconduct—few prior arrests, current employment, no drug use, current offense not robbery or burglary—than others arrested for felony offenses and released. It is clear that if criteria are fashioned from recent data to provide an empirically sound basis for selecting persons for pretrial release, jail populations can be reduced without increases in either pretrial crime or failure to appear in court.[79]

Critical to the effective use of data to support criminal justice decisions is that the data be *reliable*. Prosecutors are usually quick to express concern, as they should, about the need for prompt, accurate information about evidence from investigators, forensic laboratories, and lineups. A crime-control-oriented prosecutor should show as much concern about the quality of data indicative of defendant dangerousness, including arrest history ("rap sheet") information, juvenile record, and a urinalysis test result to indicate whether the defendant was on drugs at the time of arrest. Prosecutors and judges have not been conditioned to seek out such information to support prosecution and sentencing decisions, despite widespread concern about "false positives"—people selected for incarceration who in fact would not commit another crime if released. The availability and use of reliable rap sheets, juvenile records, and urinalysis test results, when combined with existing information, would provide demonstrably more accurate assessments of defendant dangerousness than current information alone is capable of providing; more accurate assessment means *fewer* false positives. [80]

Data used by prosecutors and courts, properly processed, can also help improve performance in other areas of the criminal justice system. For example, district attorneys can induce the police to bring better arrests by periodically providing information to police supervisors about the outcomes of the arrests brought to prosecution, itemized by department, precinct, and officer. This information could include data about the frequencies of each major type of outcome (such as those displayed in Figure 16.1) and the reasons for case rejections and dismissals. Information about case outcomes could also be given routinely to the victims and witnesses in those cases. The systematic dissemination of information can also nurture cooperation between prosecutors on the one hand and police, victims, and witnesses on the other. Public support of the criminal justice system is not enhanced by the routine failure of prosecutors to provide feedback to victims and witnesses; similarly, police incentives to produce better evidence are weakened when prosecutors routinely fail to provide information about arrest outcomes to police officers and their supervisors. [81]

Where from Here?

Public and police support of prosecutors and judges is important, but more support is not absolutely essential. The criminal justice system has demonstrated that it can function without strong public support, without tight cohesion among its components, and with minimal levels of accountability and efficiency. Despite a host of reforms, prosecutors and judges can still find ways of conducting business more-or-less in the traditional manner, with a disproportionate focus on cases that go to trial and a low level of attention to performance in the aggregate. Improvements such as those that have been suggested in this chapter—further development of sound prosecution and sentencing guidelines and the use of reliable data to support the decisions made by prosecutors, judges, and others—can be largely ignored.

Yet they are not being ignored. Guidelines have gained increasing acceptability, even under the cloud of a flawed system of federal sentencing guidelines; and statistical information about prosecution and sentencing is becoming almost abundant. Why? A mundane reason is that information technology has advanced to a stage that makes it irresistible even to many who have long been reluctant to modify their familiar ways of doing business. This technology in turn produces the data that, when analyzed, often make the need for guidelines more apparent. A second inducement to reform in prosecution and sentencing is pressure—from peers in other jurisdictions; legislators; the media; and, especially in the case of prosecutors, political opponents. While much of this pressure is uninformed, contemporary systems of accountability make it increasingly difficult for a prosecutor to reject inducements to employ sound principles of management or for a judge to reject reasonable attempts to structure the exercise of sentencing discretion. The incentives of prosecutors and judges appear, in short, to be coming into closer alignment with the broader goals of prosecution and sentencing; and this is a hopeful development.

Much of what remains to be done lies in three areas. One is the depoliticization of the criminal process. Prosecutors must be held accountable for more than just the glitzy cases that make the news, and sentencing policy must be insulated from the folly of legislators seeking only more severe punishment to deal with a problem that is deeply rooted in family dysfunction and community breakdown. This does not mean that sentences necessarily should be more lenient; if we cannot figure out how to rehabilitate dangerous offenders, we will of course have to continue to incapacitate them. It does mean that it may be prudent to look more diligently than we have for ways of rehabilitating families and communities and reforming media rather than relying *exclusively* on incarceration to deal with crime. Ever tougher prison terms may strike some as smart politics, but the long-term prospects of that approach alone are grim. Prosecution and sentencing have proved to be reformable without political pandering and without violation of democratic processes. Guidelines developed by state sentencing commissions and community-oriented prosecution systems serve as prime examples.

A related area of reform has to do with public education. While the detailed process of developing prosecution policy and sentencing guidelines may be much like the making of sausage—most people don't really want to know all the particulars—it is critical that the public be informed, if not included, in the shaping of fundamental goals of prosecution and sentencing and the principles behind guidelines.

Finally, prosecutors, sentencing commissions, and individual judges—most states do still rely on judges to determine the sentence—must be induced to take a larger, more systemic view of their various roles and responsibilities. The one-case-in-a-vacuum perspective of case screening, plea bargaining, and sentencing—and the disparity that that approach engenders—has produced throughout society deep cynicism about the administration of justice and doubt about the objectives of the system. Failure to shape sentencing guidelines and mandatory minimums with a view to their effects on prison populations is an equally compelling example of nonsystemic decision making with potentially immense, dire consequences. Prosecutors and sentencing authorities stand to improve matters substantially by giving greater consideration to alternatives to conventional prosecution and adjudication—such as arbitration for minor crimes and disputes within households and between neighbors—and effective alternatives to incarceration for offenders who are not dangerous. For serious and minor offenses alike, guidelines for prosecutors and judges should be fashioned in a way that achieves a balance that the public can support among the goals of crime prevention, fairness, reintegration of offenders back to society, and economy.

How we deal with offenders—and victims—will be assessed inevitably on grounds of justice, and on grounds of efficiency. But assessments of our system of criminal sanctions transcend the domains of crime, justice, and efficiency. In the end, how we deal with the people involved in crime is a fundamental statement of what kind of people we are.

ALFRED BLUMSTEIN

PRISONS

In the precursor to this volume, I began my essay on prisons with the observation that "the most critical administrative problem facing the United States criminal justice system through the 1980s will be that of crowded prisons. Pressure will continue to mount for more and harsher prison sentences, seriously straining the already limited capacity of penal institutions."[1]

Escalating Prison Populations

The essay from which I quote was written in 1981, and the period of the 1980s certainly bore out that forecast. That impact is displayed most vividly in Figure 17.1, which depicts the U.S. incarceration rate (prisoners per capita) from 1924 to 1993. The fifty-year period from the early 1920s to the early 1970s was characterized by an impressively stable incarceration rate averaging 110 per 100,000 of general population (or 0.11 percent of the population) in prison at any time, with a coefficient of variation (the standard deviation of the series of annual observations divided by the mean of the series) of only 8 percent.

Indeed, that stability through a period that included such disruptive events as the Great Depression (when incarceration rates increased somewhat) as well as World War II (when the nation had greater needs for men of imprisonment age, and perhaps even better means for controlling them) was so striking (and was consistent with similar stability in a number of other countries) that it suggested a homeostatic process leading to this stability.[2]

Especially in light of what has happened more recently, the homeostatic process proposed seems to have been a reasonable characterization of that period, when incarceration policy was largely within the control of functionaries within the criminal justice system: When prisons got too crowded (presumably because crime rates were climbing), then those functionaries could simply raise the threshold of the kind of offending behavior that warranted imprisonment, or lower the threshold of the assurance of "rehabilitation" before a prisoner was released on parole. Similarly, when more slack capacity became available (perhaps because crime rates were declining), then those shifts in threshold could be reversed.

However valid that explanation might have been for those first fifty years, it certainly did not explain what happened between the mid-1970s and the mid-1990s. Clearly, some fundamental societal and political changes gave rise to the steady climb seen in the right-hand portion of Figure 17.1. The 1993 incarceration rate of 351 per 100,000 (involving 948,881 prisoners in state and federal institutions)[3] was over three times the rate that had prevailed for the earlier fifty years. The nation had entered a new regime in which prison populations kept climbing as a replacement for the previous stable punishment policy.

In this chapter, I would like to identify some of the factors contributing to this changed environment, to assess the appropriateness of this growth in response to those factors, and then to consider whether some policy changes

FIGURE 17.1
Incarceration Rate by Year

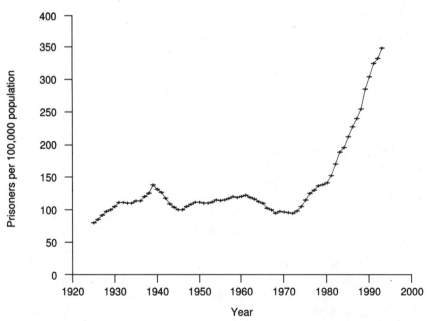

might be appropriate. Some of the factors that are natural candidates for having contributed to that growth include crime rate changes (all else equal, more crime should lead to more prisoners), demographic changes (more people in the crime-prone demographic groups, even with no change in demographic-specific criminal tendencies, should lead to more prisoners), and policy changes (more punitive sanction policies should lead to more prisoners). A central policy shift that we have to consider is the "war on drugs" that became intense in the late 1980s. That was a major new policy initiative, stimulated, of course, by the growth of the crack cocaine usage that began in the mid-1980s.

Once I identify the contribution of the various factors to the growth, I then go on to examine some of the approaches that are being used or that might be considered to try to address the seemingly uncontrolled growth.

Trends in Crime Rates

In order to examine the first of these alternative explanations—the growth in crime rates—we can examine the *Uniform Crime Reports* (UCR) crime rates that are tabulated by the FBI each year based on reports by police departments, which in turn receive reports of crimes, usually from individual victims.[4] The two crimes for which the reports are probably most reliable and well defined are those for murder and robbery, and these are also two of the most prevalent violent crimes in prison, accounting respectively for 10.6 and 14.8 percent of prison inmates.[5]

Figure 17.2 presents a graph of the annual reported rates of robbery and of murder (whose rate is scaled up by a factor of 25 to bring it into the same numeric range as robbery for ease of comparison). As is evident from the figure, the reported crime rates for these two crimes over this period of dramatic growth in prison population have fluctuated somewhat but have generally remained within a fairly confined range of 200 to 250 per 100,000 population for robbery and 8 to 10 per 100,000 for murder. Both the murder and the robbery rates peaked in about 1980, declined through the early 1980s, and then climbed again during the late 1980s with the spawning of the crack epidemic and the war on drugs. Both rates dropped from 1991 to 1992, but then murder increased while robbery decreased from 1992 to 1993. Further observations will be required before we can conclude that we are at a turning point.

The fluctuations have been around fairly flat trend lines. For murder, the trend line is not statistically significantly different from zero, while the robbery rate has fluctuated with almost the same pattern around a trend line that is increasing somewhat,[6] but only 1.36 percent per year.

Figure 17.3 compares the time series of the reported crime rate for robbery with that for burglary (with the burglary rate scaled down by a factor of 6 for comparability). Both followed a similar pattern until the start of the drug

FIGURE 17.2
UCR Murder and Robbery Rates

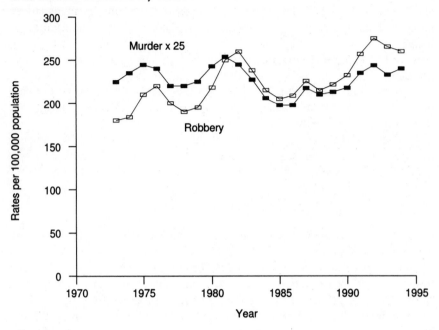

FIGURE 17.3
UCR Robbery and Burglary Rates

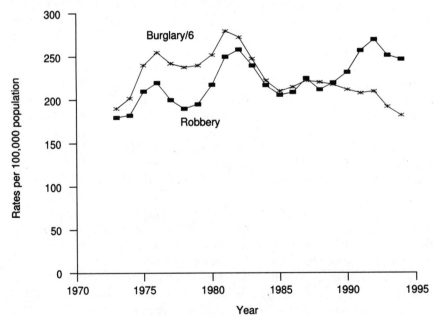

problems of the mid-1980s, and then diverged, with robbery increasing and burglary declining somewhat. One might speculate that, if the growth in drug abuse was responsible for the growth in the crime rates of the late 1980s, then it may well be that the drug users who stole in order to buy drugs would have had a preference for robbery—which is likely to yield money that can be converted to drugs easily and quickly—over burglary, which is more likely to lead to property that still has to be sold to get the money to buy the drugs.

Aside from drug offenses, murder, robbery, and burglary are the three most prevalent offenses represented in prison, together accounting for over one-third of the prisoners. It is clear that the rates of these three crimes did not increase dramatically between the mid-1970s and mid-1990s, thereby making it very unlikely that the growth in prison population was a consequence of growing crime rates.

As a further, related observation, crime rates have also not *decreased* dramatically, either, perhaps suggesting that the considerable growth in prison population (quadrupling from the mid-1970s to the mid-1990s) has not succeeded in significantly *reducing* the crime rate. But the reasons for that seeming lack of response to the increase in sanctions is a complex question. Much of the increase in prison population is attributable to the dramatic increase in incarceration for drug offenses. According to Beck et al., "inmates sentenced for a drug offense accounted for 44% of the increase in the prison population from 1986 to 1991."[7] While that incarceration is unlikely to have had much impact on the rate of drug offending (largely because of replacement of incarcerated or deterred drug sellers by others), it should have had an effect of incapacitating the other offenses that at least some of the incarcerated drug offenders may have committed if they were free.

It is clear, however, that there has been a real increase in sanctions imposed per crime committed. This is reflected in an increase in the probability of incarceration following a crime as well as an increase in time served.[8] The increase in incarceration probability has been documented by Langan, and the increase in both probability of incarceration and time served by crime type by Cohen and Canela-Cacho.[9] These shifts should have had some deterrent effect on crime rates, and they almost certainly had an incapacitation effect on these crimes.

The difficult question then is why crime rates did not decline in the face of these presumed crime reduction effects associated with increased incarceration. One possible explanation is that the growth in imprisonment kept crime rates from increasing significantly because of exogenous factors (externally caused factors). That is certainly possible, but there has been no clear indication of what those exogenous factors might be and what the associated rate of growth might have been.

Another explanation is the possibility, suggested by Golub, for example, that the incapacitative effect is counteracted by a delay in the termination of criminal careers of those incarcerated.[10] Then, when they leave prison, they resume their criminal careers at the point they left them when they went into prison, with no evidence of termination in prison.

Furthermore, since the massive incarceration of drug offenders is likely to include many who were not involved in other forms of criminality, these would be likely to be transformed into more conventional offenders as a result of their prison experiences and socialization. These effects could be augmented by the results of their frustration at finding legitimate job opportunities available to them as a result of their prison record. These effects could also contribute to the compensation for the major crime reduction consequences that should have accompanied the growth in prison populations, but did not. This is an extremely important issue that needs far more development than can be given in this essay.

Demographic Effects on Prison Populations

Oddly, the growth of the prison population through the 1980s came at a time when the prospects appeared reasonably bright with respect to crime, at least initially. Crime rates, which are extremely age-sensitive, were expected to decline during the 1980s as the large birth cohorts of the postwar baby boom (those cohorts born in the period 1947 to 1962) passed out of their late teens (the years of most active criminal activity) into their early twenties and beyond.

The age sensitivity of criminal activity is illustrated in Figure 17.4, which displays the age-specific arrest rates [11] in 1985 for murder and aggravated assault, and Figure 17.5, which displays these rates for burglary and robbery. It is clear that these age-specific rates peak in the sixteen-to-eighteen age range for each of the relevant crimes. Following that peak, the rates then drop quickly, especially for property crimes. They fall to about half the peak rate in the early twenties for property crimes and for robbery (which is certainly a property crime from the viewpoint of the offender, even though its violent nature has it classed as a "violent crime" in UCR tabulations), and in the mid-thirties for the assaultive person crimes.

Since age is so salient a factor in crime commission, we also need information on the changing age composition of the American population. [12] This is reflected in Figure 17.6, which depicts the number of people at each age in the U.S. population. [13] If we think of eighteen as being a peak crime age, then the people who were eighteen in 1980 are thirty-two in 1994. From Figure 17.6, it is apparent that those people (and those slightly older) were among the largest cohorts in U.S. demographic history. Thus, if the age-specific rates were unaffected by cohort size, then larger cohorts should give rise to a larger number of crimes. In fact, there is some evidence [14] that larger cohort sizes lead to an increase in the age-specific crime rates, amplifying the composition effect of the larger cohort size alone.

These demographic effects on crime and on prison populations were

Prisons   393

FIGURE 17.4
Aggravated Assault and Murder in 1985

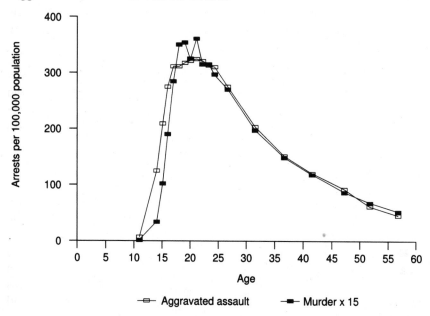

FIGURE 17.5
Robbery and Burglary in 1985

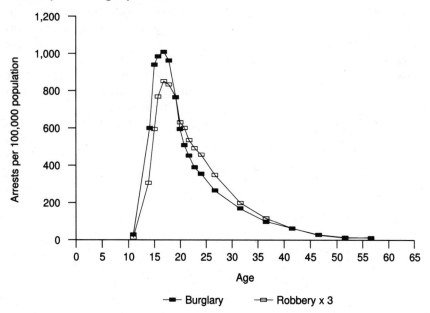

FIGURE 17.6
Age of U.S. Population in 1994

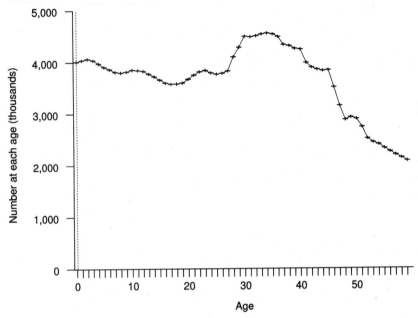

SOURCE: Jennifer Cheeseman Day, *Population Projections of the United States by Age, Sex, Race, and Hispanic Origin: 1993 to 2050*, United States Bureau of the Census Series P25-1104 (Washington, D.C.: U.S. Government Printing Office, 1993).

examined in a study that used data reflecting demographic changes and policy choices of the 1970s.[15] Data from Pennsylvania were used to make projections about crime and prison populations based on trends displayed during the 1970s. During that time, policy was fairly stationary, so that the results were driven strongly by demographic shifts,[16] which were changing rather rapidly as the baby boom generation passed through their teens and twenties. The study estimated that crime rates would reach a peak in 1980 and then decline subsequently. The predicted peak actually occurred in Pennsylvania and in the United States generally, as shown in Figures 17.2 and 17.3.

Based on those demographic considerations, the downturn of the early 1980s was expected to continue until the early 1990s, when the "echo boomers"—the children of the baby boomers—were expected to enter the peak crime age. As can be seen from Figure 17.6, the smallest age cohort relevant to the crime problem in the United States is the cohort born in 1976; this group was just eighteen in 1994, and so its criminal activity should diminish subsequently. But subsequent cohorts will be larger, and so demographic factors should reemerge as contributing to crime growth later in the 1990s and beyond.

Of course, demographic shifts are only one of the many factors influencing crime rates. Even though crime rates in the early 1980s followed demographic influences, other factors assumed much greater importance in the late 1980s, particularly the crack cocaine epidemic that began in the mid-1980s and continued to be a focus of intense law enforcement activity.

The age shift that contributed to an easing of crime rates in the early 1980s also contributed to *growth* in the prison populations. This seeming paradox results from the difference between the peak crime ages and the peak imprisonment ages. As shown in Figures 17.4 and 17.5, arrest rates peak between the ages of sixteen and eighteen. In contrast, the peak imprisonment ages are the late twenties, with a median age of prisoners close to thirty. The difference results mainly from the fact that very few people under eighteen are sent to prisons, which are intended primarily for adults. [17] Also, those in the adult age ranges who are convicted of crimes are generally put on probation for their first—or first few—convictions for all but the most serious crimes. By the time they have accumulated a sufficient number of convictions to become serious candidates for prison, they are well into their twenties.

As a result, even though crimes were expected to decline, prison populations were expected to increase over the 1980s as the bulge of the baby boom (with a peak at about the 1960 cohort) continued to flow through the high imprisonment ages. But it was also expected that, by the early 1990s, those cohorts would also be past the peak imprisonment ages, and so prison populations were expected to begin to decline—at least based on these considerations of the age composition of the population.

Of course, all projections are based on a number of assumptions, and do not countenance new developments that cannot be foreseen at the time the projections are made. The emergence of the crack epidemic of the late 1980s was an important factor in the reversal of the anticipated decline in crime rates. Also, the changing policy environment surrounding crime and punishment during the 1980s could override any influence of demographics alone.

Shifts in Policies

The period of the 1980s and beyond saw a major shift in the political environment, and hence the policies related to imprisonment. For most of the first two-thirds of the twentieth century, the dominant perspective on imprisonment viewed it as a vehicle for "correction" or "rehabilitation." The notion was that upon release, a prisoner should be less likely to commit crimes. Prison professionals would recommend an offender's release when he was judged to be "rehabilitated."

But faith in rehabilitation was severely challenged in the early and mid-1970s by a succession of experimental studies that evaluated a variety of alternative rehabilitative strategies. The dominant finding of these studies of adults was a "null effect," i.e., that no particular approach consistently works any better than any other in changing postrelease criminal behavior.[18] The implication was that individual traits of offenders and of the environment to which they are returned after release may have far more influence on subsequent recidivism than exposure to any particular rehabilitative program.

There remains a controversy between those who contend that prison makes criminals better and those who believe it makes them worse. The former group argue that prison improves some criminals by virtue of either its rehabilitative effects (that is, the prisoner is taught skills that enable him to function more effectively in the community) or by its "specific deterrent" effect (its unpleasantness discourages future criminality by the individual who is imprisoned). Others argue to the contrary that prison is harmful because it socializes prisoners, especially younger ones, into a hardened criminal culture. The frequent null effect finding does not necessarily invalidate either of these positions, but it does suggest that there is probably merit on both sides, and that the opposing effects roughly balance each other in the aggregate. Some individuals emerge from prison with sufficient distaste for the experience—and sufficient control over their own subsequent behavior—to avoid the risk of subsequent imprisonment by desisting from crime. Other, weaker individuals very likely are socialized into a criminal culture—or at least are frustrated by the limitations they find in the legitimate labor market—and may then commit more and more serious crimes than they might otherwise have committed.

If one had a sure means of distinguishing those who would benefit from prison from those who would be harmed by it, and if judges were willing to employ such means (and especially accepting the inequitable treatment that would result), then there might be a more significant rehabilitative effect from imprisonment. So far, however, criminal justice authorities have been saved from having to face the legal and ethical dilemmas involved in making such decisions by the inability of anyone to offer a valid method of identifying the appropriate candidates for rehabilitation through imprisonment.

The loss of confidence in rehabilitation has contributed significantly to the growth in prison populations. It is ironic that the initial assault on the rehabilitation approach came from a de-incarceration perspective which argued that since there was so little the criminal justice system could do to change behavior, then there should be less intervention with offenders. They also claimed that those exercising the release authority—parole boards and their associated professionals—were engaged in an arbitrary exercise of power over individuals' liberty, and so declaimed the disparity of treatment that resulted.

To some degree, these arguments about disparity were accepted, and there were a variety of attempts to limit discretion over the time served by prisoners. Some of these emerged from the parole boards themselves, and included structured parole guidelines, with formulations on the additional time to be served based on attributes of the offender as well as on the court's sentence. Legislatures passed determinate-sentencing laws, initially intended to prescribe by statute the time to be served for each offense category, with "enhancements" for certain aggravating factors like gun use or inflicting serious bodily injury.

Rather than diminish or even limit the use of imprisonment, as the initial advocates wished, this political shift did transfer the emphasis away from rehabilitation to the more explicitly punitive deterrent and incapacitative effects of prison as the only means left to the criminal justice system to address the objective of reducing crime. This reflected a pressure for greater retribution and an intensified desire by the public for crime control. Judges have also felt the influence of the growing public hostility toward criminals and of increasing demands for severe punishment, and have undoubtedly responded to those pressures.

The standards for what level of punishment constitutes "just deserts" have thus been increasing. Even parole boards, the subject of criticism for releasing prisoners before they served their "full sentences," responded to the political environment and became more cautious about who they released and when they did so, and also became more aggressive about returning parole violators to prison. All these changes brought control over sanction policy out of the criminal justice system into the open political arena, and opened the door for changes in legislation and in practice that have contributed to the uncontrolled growth of prison populations that characterized the late 1970s and the 1980s.

Once the policy moved into that political arena, there was little that could be done to recapture concern for limiting prison populations. The public, concerned as it always is about crime, has little sympathy for the offenders, and responded with enthusiasm to political calls for increasing sentence severity. Wherever judges are elected, the campaign commercial involving a prison cell door being slammed shut has become a widespread cliché. In a modern age of rapid media response, many political figures find it attractive to follow the report of any heinous crime with a call for increasing the sentence for that kind of crime. If some judge was found to have sentenced an offender to probation, then that was taken as evidence of the irresponsible leniency of the entire judiciary, and so a bill calling for mandatory minimum sentences would be introduced. In an evolving political environment where every campaign manager is looking for ways to label an opponent as "soft on crime," once such bills got to the floor of a legislature, they would be passed with overwhelming majorities. It was left largely to the legislative skill and political courage of the chairs of the judiciary committees to bottle up bills that were irresponsible.

The result of this process has been a major transfer of discretion within the criminal justice system to the prosecutor, mostly from the judge. It is the prosecutor who decides what charges to file in a particular case, what charge revisions to accept in exchange for a guilty plea, and how those changes relate to various laws limiting sentencing discretion in particular cases. Since prosecutors tend to deal with each case as a discrete entity, they have no particular concern.for aggregate effects like impacts on prison populations. Also, since prosecutors are almost always elected to office, and usually have ambitions for higher office, it is consistent with their professional responsibilities as well as their political ambition to be seen demanding higher sanctions. Even if they agree that such sanctions may not apply in a particular case, it strengthens their negotiating position in a plea bargain to be able to threaten a charge that will result in a severe sanction if the defendant does not accept the plea bargain.

There have been some attempts to restrain this process. The most notable is the creation of sentencing commissions, either by action of the judiciary or by statute. Such commissions are given the assignment of creating a coherent schedule of sentences that reflect both the gravity of the offense committed and the prior record of the convicted offender. In some cases, most notably in Minnesota, the commissions are expected to assure that their sentencing schedule is compatible with the available capacity of the state prison system. Most, whether required to do so or not, take some account of the impact of their sentencing schedules on prison populations. While the intent here has been to take the establishment of sentencing out of the hands of the legislative process, that has not prevented legislatures, including the Congress, even after creating a sentencing commission, from acting on bills to establish mandatory minimum sentences, even when that would distort the coherence of the established sentencing schedule. Obviously, any legislation so enacted has to take precedence over the rules of a sentencing commission.

The structural arrangements for decision making in legislatures or within the criminal justice system regarding sentencing policy are such that the costs associated with increased punitiveness (prison crowding, larger corrections budgets) are almost never faced by those who act punitively (such as legislators, prosecutors, judges). Thus, it is easy for these decision makers to respond to the public's demands for harsher measures. In most states, this has led to an increase in the severity of sentences and a growth in prison populations.

The Crack Cocaine Epidemic and the Drug War

The other major new element that has entered the issue of prison populations is the emergence of the crack cocaine epidemic beginning in the mid-1980s and the massive criminal justice response to that problem.

It is easy to recognize that the drug problem is an issue of serious concern to American society. Many people are debilitated by taking drugs, and there is particular concern by parents that their children, whom they see as vulnerable, will become captured by drugs.

Further, there is a profound nexus between drugs and crime more generally. In 1986, 52 percent of prisoners reported that they had at some time used major drugs [19] and 35 percent reported that they had been under the influence of a major drug at the time they committed the crime that led to their current imprisonment. [20]

Given the seriousness of the problem, the American public in the mid-1980s vigorously demanded that something be done about the drug problem. Democratic political systems require a strong response to such vigorously articulated demand—even when there is no clear means of effective response. Unfortunately, our political system learned an overly simplistic trick: when it responds to such pressures by sternly demanding increased punishment, that approach has been found to be strikingly effective—not in solving the problem, but in alleviating the political pressure to "do something." The public generally seems to accept that approach to almost any behavior it finds objectionable, and without much questioning as to whether that approach will be effective in the particular context of concern.

As a result, there has been a succession of punitive efforts to attack the drug trade. Many states have adopted mandatory minimum sentences for drug dealing that are comparable to the sentences for homicide; in Pennsylvania, for example, the sentencing guideline for sale of more than 100 grams of cocaine is the same as for voluntary manslaughter. The consequence of these efforts has been a dramatic growth in the number of arrests for drug offenses and the filling of prisons with drug offenders.

Figures 17.7 and 17.8 show the growth from 1965 to 1992 in arrest rates for adults and juveniles for drug offenses, by race. [21] Since the early 1970s, the rate for white adults has been fairly steady, about 300–400 per 100,000. On the other hand, the rate for nonwhites (primarily African Americans) climbed steadily from 1980 to 1985, then began to grow exponentially at a rate of about 15–20 percent per year until it reached a peak in 1989, and then continued at a high rate.

The growth in drug arrests for juveniles, depicted in Figure 17.8, is rather different from that for adults. From 1965 until about 1980, arrest rates for white and nonwhite juveniles were very similar; indeed, from 1970 until 1980, the arrest rate for whites was higher than for nonwhites. But arrest rates for both groups were growing from a rate of about 10 per 100,000 juveniles in 1965 to a peak about thirty times higher in 1974 (329 for whites and 257 for nonwhites).

The intensity of the crackdown shows itself in prison populations. In 1994, over 60 percent of the prisoners in federal prisons and about 25 percent of those in state prisons were there on a drug charge. This contrasts sharply with the rates in 1986, only eight years earlier, when drug offenders accounted for only 8.6 percent of state prisoners. [22] The growth has been extremely rapid, and has been even more extreme in the rate of new commitments. In New York State, for example, in 1991, drug offenders were 45

FIGURE 17.7
Drug Arrest Rate, Adults

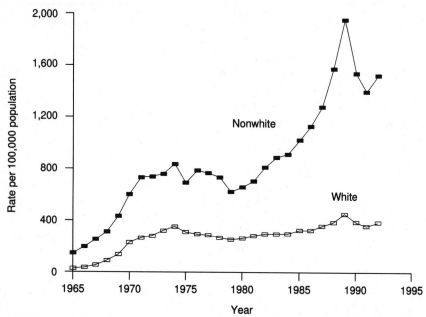

SOURCES: Federal Bureau of Investigation, *Age-Specific Arrest Rates and Race-Specific Arrest Rates for Selected Offenses, 1965–1988* (Washington, D.C.: Uniform Crime Reporting Program, 1990). More recent data were provided by the FBI's Uniform Crime Reporting Program.

percent of new commitments to prison and 34 percent of prison populations. Despite the enormous magnitude of the efforts and the impacts on the criminal justice system, accepting those costs would not necessarily be unreasonable if the approach were truly effective in reducing drug abuse. There is, however, no indication that the efforts have been at all successful. Of course, that result is not at all surprising. Anyone who is removed from the street is likely to be replaced by someone drawn from the inevitable queue of replacement dealers ready to join the industry. It may take some time for recruitment and training, but experience shows that replacement is easy and rapid.

A similar situation applies to general deterrence. One of the rationales most frequently cited for increasing the level of drug sanctions is that sellers will be deterred from engaging in drug transactions. There is little question that some actual or potential sellers, learning of the severe sanctions, are indeed deterred. But as long as there remain willing replacements, that deterrent effect is of little import. As long as the market demand persists and there is a continued supply of sellers, there should be little effect on drug transactions.

It is difficult to discern whether the continued escalation of sanctions has been carried out in ignorance of these basic insights, or whether the polices

FIGURE 17.8
Drug Arrest Rate, Juveniles

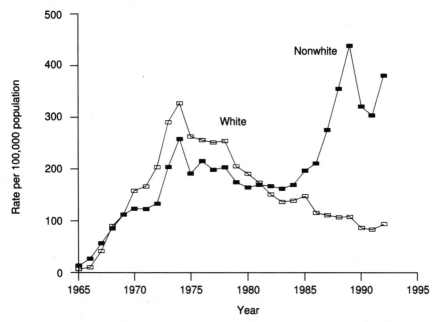

SOURCES: Federal Bureau of Investigation, *Age-Specific Arrest Rates and Race-Specific Arrest Rates for Selected Offenses, 1965–1988* (Washington, D.C.: Uniform Crime Reporting Program, 1990). More recent data were provided by the FBI's Uniform Crime Reporting Program.

have been adopted more cynically. It is not unreasonable to believe that the people who establish the high sanction policies fully understand the limitations of the policies but need some means to respond to the public pressure to "do something." Lacking any better alternative to propose, they merely increase the sanctions, not so much because they think that response will work, but because they have come to realize that it is an effective way to relieve the political pressure.

The basic observation about drug markets is that they are inherently demand driven. As long as the demand is there, a supply network will emerge to satisfy that demand. While efforts to assault the supply side may have some disruptive effects in the short term, the ultimate need is to reduce the demand in order to have an effect on drug abuse in the society. That requires efforts in treatment of current users and prevention among potential users.

Responses to the Population Growth

The major growth in prison populations can thus be attributed roughly equally to the consequences of the punitiveness involved in pursuing the drug wars and to an increase in punitiveness generally. This growth comes at a time when many state budgets are under severe fiscal stress: taxpayer revolts have been manifested in various tax limitation referenda and voters' rejection of initiatives to increase prison capacity, whether through bond issues or through tax increases. In the face of these severe pressures, governments would very much like to find ways to respond to the growth in prison population.

The responses are basically of three forms:

1. *Null strategy:* Do nothing and let the prisoners pile up.
2. *Construction:* Persist in current strategies and build whatever additional capacity is needed.
3. *Alternatives:* Find a way to divert some of the flow from prisons through a mixture of "front door" approaches (that is, moving offenders to sanctions and treatments other than incarceration) and "back door" approaches (that is, releasing prisoners under some form of control in the community).

Each of these approaches has its costs, including political costs for the legislature or the administration that must implement them. The costs associated with the different strategies, however, would be borne by different individuals or groups in each case.

The various strategies also differ in the time required to implement them. Some could be put into place immediately, whereas others might require several years to develop institutional arrangements (for example, the creation of a sentencing commission to develop sentencing guidelines) before they could contribute to the reduction of prison overcrowding. The longest time is associated with new construction (a minimum of two and, more likely, as many as seven or eight years).

Null Strategy

The easiest strategy in the short run is to make no systematic changes. Prosecutors can continue to demand severe sentences; judges can avoid public criticism by responding to those demands; and wardens can demonstrate their managerial skill by accepting the prisoners and, absent court intervention, putting two or more in a cell, using hallways and recreational areas for residential purposes as necessary, and keeping the increasingly crowded prisons under control.

Crowding inevitably involves diminished control of the prisons by authorities; control tends to be transferred to the inmates, and often to the most brutal group of inmates. This inevitably results in greater suffering by those inmates who are not members of the controlling group; but since prisoners' political influence is generally weak, their suffering is likely to be invisible to the general public. Unless it is forcibly brought to public attention by the press or through the legal process, it is likely to be overlooked and ignored in the general political environment. Overcrowding and its consequences have become so commonplace that they hardly make news anymore.

A further consequence of the shift in control is the deterioration in staff morale and the attendant increase in staff turnover, which in turn accelerates the transfer of control to the prison inmates. Yet these problems rarely come to public attention. Overcrowding prevails as long as the disruption stays short of riot and does not prompt court intervention.

Court intervention, when it occurs, usually follows suits brought under the Eighth Amendment's prohibition against cruel and unusual punishment. Many such actions have been initiated by the American Civil Liberties Union Prison Project, with some success. Prisons in a majority of states have come under court intervention because overcrowding produced conditions that the courts viewed as unacceptably severe. In its decision in *Rhodes v. Chapman,* however, the Supreme Court ruled that double celling per se was not unconstitutional, particularly if it was a temporary expedient to respond to overcrowding in a prison that was not otherwise cruel. Even though that decision was carefully drawn to apply to one particular institution, it did represent an important reversal of momentum in federal court interventions, and has significantly inhibited court intervention in overcrowding cases.

The one consequence of prison overcrowding that actually rattles the public is the prison riot. But such events are rare, and the techniques of riot control in prisons appear to have reached a level of effectiveness such that explosive prison riots are relatively unlikely, even in very difficult circumstances.

For all of the reasons described, it is relatively easy for a state to follow a null strategy, to close its eyes to the potential impacts of overcrowding and to hold its breath hoping that no disasters follow and that the courts keep their hands off. Yet, to the extent that a state government wants to avert these consequences and reduce these risks, either legislative or executive leadership is needed to pursue one of the more active strategies for accommodating the imbalance between the growing populations and the limited capacity.

Construction of New Capacity

The traditional response to prison crowding has been the construction of additional prison capacity, but that is expensive. It costs approximately $75,000 to construct a prison cell and about $20,000 per year to maintain a prisoner in a state prison. It is rare, however, for these costs to receive any attention in the debate over punishment policies. It is not clear to what extent attitudes toward punishment would change if all sentencing policy proposals had to be accompanied by a "prison impact statement" reflecting the expected change in the number of prisoners that would result and the expected costs to house and supervise them.

Moreover, new construction does not answer the immediate crisis of prison overcrowding. There is a long delay from the time the decision is made to construct additional capacity until it becomes available to house prisoners. The legislature must authorize it, a site must be chosen that the neighbors will accept (although the traditional NIMBY—"not in my backyard"—concern is increasingly being replaced by a view that sees a prison as an economic development opportunity), and the institution must be designed, the money appropriated, and the facility finally built. The process normally takes at least two years and can take up to seven years.

In many states, new capacity would be helpful simply as a replacement for obsolete and archaic prisons, provided the governments wanted to replace them. In such cases, new construction is not totally wasteful. But state governments faced with severe fiscal stress are generally reluctant to put replacement of old prisons very high on their list of priorities. Taxpayers are resistant to any growth in taxes, and more often reject bond issues to pay for new prisons, even when those new facilities are required to carry out the taxpayers' vigorous calls for increased sanction policies. Consistency in that regard has never been required of the electorate, or even of their elected officials. The public seems fully prepared to demand increased punishment severity, but is not necessarily willing to pay for it.

The construction strategy was an important part of a set of recommendations prepared by former attorney general William Barr, in which he called for restricting parole practices and increasing time actually served by violent offenders, mandatory minimum penalties for gun offenders, armed career criminals, and habitual violent offenders. To achieve these tougher sanction policies in order to enhance incapacitation, he called for "providing sufficient prison and detention capacity to support the criminal justice system."[23]

One approach that has received attention as a means of increasing capacity is the idea of privatizing the operation of prisons. This has the same appeal to the presumed efficiencies and innovativeness that is often associated with suggestions to privatize other governmental functions. The attractiveness is complicated here because punishment is so distinctively a function that government reserves to itself and prohibits private individuals from doing. But it is still possible for government to make all the decisions about who should go to what institution, how long he should stay there, and to oversee any private institution in order to assure that the conditions of confinement are within the prescribed limits. While there have been a number of privately constructed and operated prisons established, there is still no clear indication that they can be operated with any more than a few percent greater efficiency, and so there has been no significant growth in the number of such institutions.[24] Private prisons could well have some advantages, but none have been shown to be sufficiently dominant that they significantly shift the choice of whether to engage in new construction.

One of the arguments most frequently voiced against new prison construction rests on the presumption that the prison population would fill up added capacity because of "Parkinson's Law,"[25] which suggests that the population will simply expand to fill the available capacity. There is a reasonable intuitive basis for this presumption, and many judges knowingly avoid sending convicted criminals to prison because of concern about prison crowding. On the other hand, during the 1960s when there was spare prison capacity in the United States, there was also a definite reduction in prison population.

One study attempted to test this hypothesized Parkinsonian link between prison population and capacity by examining the time series relationship between state prison populations and corresponding changes in prison capacity.[26] The analysis claimed that each new prison cell would be filled in two years' time. The widespread attention and acceptance accorded that finding are indicative of both its intuitive appeal and the desire by many to use the concept to limit the construction of additional prison capacity in any but the most extreme circumstances. The study, however, was found to be severely flawed technically—the result primarily of a computational error.[27] While the possibility of a Parkinsonian relation between population and capacity still exists (the failure to confirm a hypothesis does not prove the contrary), it is clear that a much more elaborate model must be formulated that will take account, at a minimum, of such considerations as the number of persons convicted of the most serious crimes, budget constraints on creating additional capacity, the level of seriousness of offenders not being sent to prison, and court orders limiting prison populations.

While there is undoubtedly a strong desire in many quarters to increase sanction severity, especially for violent offenders, for whom incapacitation seems most appropriate, there is also a widespread reluctance to continue to achieve these goals by continuing to increase prison capacity. In most states, the corrections budget, even ignoring new construction, is the only one being increased, and there is widespread concern about the other governmental functions that are being sacrificed to meet this increasing demand. Thus, in the face of fiscal pressures, there is a widespread desire among state governments to find means of accommodating the focus on the violent offenders without the large capital and operating expenditures associated with construction of additional capacity. To do that, the general theme is to find means of dealing with the nonviolent offenders through means other than imprisonment. This has spawned a variety of approaches that used to be known as "alternatives to incarceration," but, in the face of pressure for "punishment," have come to be designated as "intermediate punishments."

Intermediate Punishments

There are important reasons—principally those of cost and of the time lag from a decision to build until the additional capacity is operational—why states are reluctant to address their prison crowding problems primarily through increasing their prison capacity. Yet the continuing demand for more incarceration in the face of the limited current capacity suggests a need for using the available capacity more effectively. This requires a view of prison capacity as a scarce resource, and the issue becomes one of allocating that scarce resource more effectively and efficiently. There does seem to be a growing consensus that the focus of the incarceration should be on the violent offender—the individual who is not likely to be deterred by any threat of a criminal sanction and who, at least during his period of violent activity, can be removed as a threat to the community only through incarceration.

Intermediate punishment (IP) involves a variety of approaches for controlling, in a community setting, those who represent a relatively smaller threat, but who require some kind of punishment involving restraint, partly for retributive reasons and partly to make it clear to them that they cannot continue their criminal activity with impunity.

The approaches involve some combination of finding who is most appropriate for the IP, and then selecting from an array of IP alternatives by assigning an appropriate IP to that individual. The array of alternatives has been enumerated by Morris and Tonry, [28] and are discussed more extensively in Chapter 18 of this volume, "Community Corrections." They include community service requirements; intensive probation supervision with much closer surveillance than is possible under normal probation workloads with excessive numbers of cases; work release; house arrest enforced through electronic monitoring with a bracelet placed on the offender that links him electronically to his telephone in order to monitor whether he is at home; or "boot camps," which invoke the rigorous discipline of Marine recruit training, but for a much shorter time than would normally be served in prison.

Unfortunately, there has been very little careful evaluation of these approaches. One striking exception has been the randomized field experiments conducted by Petersilia and Turner in sixteen jurisdictions to evaluate intensive supervision programs (ISPs). [29] As with so many other experimental evaluations, they find no major impact on the recidivism of the persons placed in ISP. They do find a greater risk of technical violation as a result of the more intensive surveillance of the individuals in the programs. They also find that, even though the programs might have been introduced with the intention of diverting prisoners to a lesser level of control, the people assigned tend to be offenders who would otherwise have been more likely to be assigned to probation. As a result, even the anticipated cost saving is frustrated because the ISP results in an escalation of an average routine supervision cost of $4,700 to an ISP cost of $7,200, rather than the anticipated savings from a typical $20,000 prison cost. They do find, however, that ISP is attractive for drug offenders at an early stage of their criminal careers.

Thus, for first-time offenders, and especially for drug offenders, or for others who represent no direct threat or danger to the community, such approaches seem to offer important possibilities. They would be consistent with a general strategy of continual monitoring of individuals under the control of the criminal justice system. As offenders conform, they will be put under conditions of looser control; as they are found to be failing, through reports of criminal activity, or even with urinalysis when drug abuse is an important part of their behavioral problem, then they can be moved to a tighter form of control. Ultimately, of course, prison will be necessary for many of these.

Increasingly, these intermediate punishments are being incorporated into sentencing guidelines. The problem in implementing them, however, is that an infrastructure of capability to manage the intermediate punishment programs is needed, and most jurisdictions do not have that capability. Thus, it is likely that judges will continue to be confronted with a choice between meaningless probation or perhaps excessive control in prison for many of the convicted people they deal with.

Prison Population Reduction

States that are facing severe prison congestion and that feel compelled to avoid overcrowding—usually because they are required to do so by court order—need to find some means of allocating their limited number of cells. Obviously, it would be desirable if that allocation could be in terms of maximizing the protection of public safety, by keeping in prison those who represent the greatest current threat to public safety, and releasing those for whom the risk is least. Indeed, to some degree, that was the approach taken by the parole boards in the period before the politicization of crime policy.

Such risk assessments are certainly not easy. But even if one could make an assessment of each individual's potential harm in the community, there would be limits to the degree to which that could be acted on. Some prisoners may no longer be a risk, but are required to serve a particular sentence for reasons that are strictly retributive; those constraints are fully consistent with the mixed purposes of sentencing.

It is also true, however, that, while the corrections departments that operate prisons have considerable discretion in whom they may release to accommodate new prisoners, statutes usually prohibit them from releasing prisoners under mandatory minimum sentences. Thus, the growing prevalence of such prisoners—usually intended to serve a political need rather than one addressing crime control—severely inhibits the ability of the releasing authorities from addressing matters of public safety optimally.

The approaches to population control are typically characterized as "front-door" and "back-door" strategies. The front-door strategies involve diverting from prison to alternative sentences or programs the most marginal of the offenders who might otherwise be sent to prison. Probation, established in the middle of the nineteenth century, is the most common such assignment, and it is now the sanction assigned to the great majority of convicted first-time offenders, mostly for the less serious offenses.

In most jurisdictions, judges are faced with a choice between probation and prison; these alternatives span a great range of severity. A judge confronted with a repeat burglary offender who has already been on probation may seek an intermediate response that represents an escalation in severity; for many such offenders, imprisonment is too severe a sanction. It is here that the development of intermediate sanctions represents an important opportunity for responding in ways that go beyond simple probation, but stop short of imprisonment.

These programs handle a mixture of offenders—some who would otherwise have gone to prison if the programs were not available, and others for whom prison would not have been likely and who would have been put on probation. Most evaluations have found that the people assigned to these programs tend to be individuals who would have been on probation rather than those who would have gone to prison,[30] but rules could be established that make it more likely that such programs would be used for people for whom some degree of escalation in their punishment is called for, but to a level short of imprisonment.

While front-door strategies operate to divert offenders from entering prison, back-door strategies are concerned with increasing the release rate by shortening the time served by those who do go to prison. In the presence of constraints on total prison capacity, one can choose between sending more people to prison for a shorter time or fewer people for a longer time. Considerations of both deterrence and incapacitation argue for the former. Indeed, many jurisdictions that have been under court order to restrict prison populations have been forced to use back-door policies that have involved releasing prisoners at fractions as small as one-quarter of their specified prison sentence. This has stimulated strong pressure for "truth in sentencing" to assure that the full sentence is served, although there continues to be ambiguity about what the "true" sentence is. This is especially problematic in states with "indeterminate" sentencing structure, where the presumption is that release is permitted upon expiration of the minimum sentence, but much of the rhetorical debate focuses on time served that falls short of the maximum sentence.

Research on deterrence has consistently supported the position that sentence "severity" (that is, the time served) has less of a deterrent effect than sentence "certainty" (the probability of going to prison).[31] Thus, from the deterrence consideration, there is a clear preference for increasing certainty, even if becomes necessary to do so at the expense of severity. This suggests a preference for the use of back-door approaches (that diminish severity) in order to strengthen certainty when capacity constraints force a choice.

This view is supported from the standpoint of incapacitation also. The longer the time served, the more likely it is that the individual would have terminated his criminal activity. In this sense, additional prison time is "wasted" after his career is terminated. Studies of the duration of criminal careers suggest that property offenders "retire" from crime at a rate of 10 percent to 20 percent per year, and at a lower rate for violent offenders,[32] and this termination rate increases appreciably after they pass their early forties. In any given year, then, one might expect about 10 percent of the individuals in prison to have terminated their criminal activity if they were on the outside. It is, however, difficult to identify just which of those prisoners have terminated at any time. Because of this process of termination of criminal careers, incapacitation is best accomplished by incarcerating individuals during the period when they are most likely to be criminally active, which is the period closest to the time of conviction.

Thus, from the perspective of incapacitation as well as that of deterrence, allocation of limited capacity to more, shorter sentences is more effective than allocating to fewer, longer ones. These considerations do not negate the value of long sentences for retributive reasons, but it should be recognized that use of long sentences for punishment in the face of a capacity constraint may well require diminished efficiency in the use of limited prison resources for crime reduction.

All the strategies considered so far can be implemented without taking direct account of the current population or the current degree of crowding in a state's prisons. But one can also link sentencing policies more directly to prison population. It is possible to devise strategies that explicitly tie a measure of crowding (for example, the relationship between population and capacity) to sentencing practices. This is most often done through sentencing guidelines that are linked to prison capacity.

The best example of a planned policy sensitive to prison capacity is the sentencing guidelines matrix developed by the Minnesota Sentencing Guidelines Commission or the recent one developed in North Carolina.[33] The Minnesota commission's initial work followed from an explicit legislative mandate to "take account of prison capacity" in developing its guidelines, and used prison capacity as a specific constraint on the sentencing schedule that emerged. Thus, if some commission member wanted to increase the prescribed sentence for robbery, he had to identify the offenses for which he would like to reduce the sentences in exchange. Such a procedure requires a technology (such as some kind of simulation or impact-estimation model) that enables the policy group to calculate for each possible sentencing schedule the prison capacity it would consume. This in turn requires information on the expected number of convicted offenders in each category within the sentencing schedule (typically based on an offense gravity score and on the seriousness of the offender's prior conviction record) in order to estimate the prison capacity that the schedule would consume.

The existence of this prison capacity constraint imposes a rare discipline on the policy debate. In most settings where sanction policies are debated, advocates of tougher sentences gain political benefits without having to consider the costs of their actions. But the availability of this discipline has undoubtedly contributed to making Minnesota the state with the second lowest incarceration rate in the nation—78 prisoners per 100,000 population in 1991 when the national rate was 310 per 100,000 population. Also, the growth in incarceration rate from 1971 to 1991 was only 94 percent in Minnesota, less than half the growth of 221 percent for the nation as a whole.[34]

It is also possible to introduce a policy that employs a population-responsive "safety valve" that releases prisoners when overcrowding becomes excessive. Under that approach, established in Michigan, a corrections commission is charged with monitoring the population of the state's prisons in relation to their capacity, and with reporting to the governor when the population of the prisons exceeds their capacity for longer than thirty days. Upon receipt of such a report, the governor is then mandated to reduce the minimum sentences of every prisoner by up to ninety days, thereby increasing the population eligible for parole. This does not represent an automatic release of all these prisoners, because they still have to appear before the parole board, which can still retain the dangerous convicts until their maximum sentences expire. This strategy was explicitly designed to diffuse the political cost of accommodating prison population to capacity. The legislature enacts the law; the independent corrections commission declares the condition of overcrowding; the governor orders the reduction of minimum sentences; and the parole board orders the actual release. This approach was intended to provide all participants with a politically palatable means of acting responsibly to avoid the consequences of prison overcrowding. Nevertheless, even this carefully designed scheme failed to survive the Michigan political environment when the governor refused to exercise his mandated obligation to reduce the minimum sentences. That failure undoubtedly contributed to Michigan's having the highest incarceration rate (388 per 100,000 population) of the eleven states of the Midwest (which had an aggregate incarceration rate of 255 per 100,000).

There might be more radical approaches to rationing the limited number of prison spaces. One is suggested by a former corrections commissioner in Connecticut, John Manson: A "ration" of prison cells is allocated to each court and its judges or prosecutors, who must then take their limited allocation into account in making their own sentencing decisions or recommendations.[35] Then, if a court has used up its allocation and wants to send an additional convicted offender to prison, the court is required to identify which cell from among its allocation should be vacated. The judge must then release a current occupant in order to obtain the needed space for the new one. This approach forces the judge (or the prosecutor before him) to assume concern for the political costs of facing up to the problem of prison crowding, and to take those costs into account in making sentencing decisions. So far, no jurisdictions have adopted this approach, for reasons that are fully understandable. But it does force a focus on the allocation issues of concern, and directs attention to the other, more conventional approaches.

All of these approaches to controlling the prison population require an explicit formulation of the excessively flexible concept of "prison capacity." As long as double or triple celling is a possibility, capacity remains a very poorly defined notion, and represents no constraint whatsoever on any of the policy makers or decision makers within the criminal justice system. When considerations such as reasonable limits on prisoner capacity become more explicit and are taken into account, then capacity does become a more meaningful limit, and explicit policy statements can be formulated to define it. This can be done by a commission, including representatives of the legislature, the judiciary, the correctional administration, and prosecutors.

Some Projections for the Future

The Developing Violence Problem

Even though aggregate homicide rates have been relatively stable from the mid-1970s to the mid-1990s (see Figure 17.2), there are some distressing aspects in the disaggregated information that suggest that violence is a more serious problem than is reflected in the aggregate rate. This is of special concern because of some dramatic growth in the violence being committed by young people, both because that may reflect a cohort effect which might continue into the future with the current young cohorts, and also because incoming cohorts will be of larger size.

The structure of the age-specific rates for homicide have changed appreciably since 1985. This is reflected in Figure 17.9, which shows how the involvement of young people from fourteen through twenty-two in murder changed dramatically over the short period from 1985 (where the pattern was very similar to that which prevailed for the previous fifteen years) to 1992. The previous pattern, which was relatively flat from age eighteen through twenty-four, has been shifted to one with a very high peak at age eighteen at more than double the rate only seven years earlier. Furthermore, while stranger-to-stranger homicides are relatively rare among adults (only 20 percent), they are much more common among juveniles (34 percent). It is the stranger-to-stranger homicides that are particularly distressing to most people, because they see it as much more random, and so increasing the possibility that they will become victims, even though they consider themselves at no risk from their own intimates.

The growing propensity for young people to be involved in homicide is

FIGURE 17.9
Age-Specific Murder Rate, 1985–1992

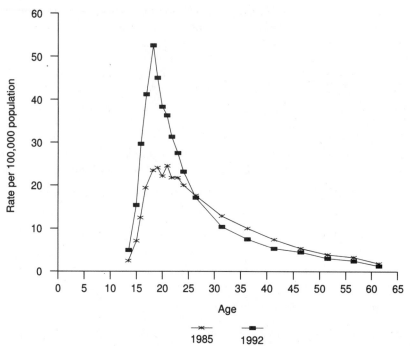

also reflected in Figure 17.10, which depicts the rate of homicide since 1976 by males aged fourteen through seventeen. White rates have increased by about 50 percent, but the rates for the young black males tripled in the seven years after 1985. The graph showing victimization rates for this group would appear very similar—the principal victims are also young black males.

The third important feature of the developments since the mid-1980s is the growing involvement of guns in the murders by and of these young men. In Figure 17.11, it is apparent that the use of guns against victims aged thirty or more declined somewhat from 1976 to 1992. But the use of guns by and against young people increased appreciably from the mid-1980s, from 62 percent to 83 percent.

It seems reasonable to consider the possibility that these major changes in homicide by young people, especially with guns, can be attributed to some mixture of the drug industry and our nation's efforts to control it. The nature of the industry has made guns a necessary tool of the trade for those who participate in it, and use of violence a standard means of dispute resolution as well as self-defense. Since that industry is often quite pervasive in many communities, it is inevitable that others in those communities will also arm themselves, at least as a self-defensive measure, and possibly also as a means of enhancing their status among their peers. The presence of violence in that

FIGURE 17.10

Male Homicide Rate/100,000 for Ages Fourteen through Seventeen

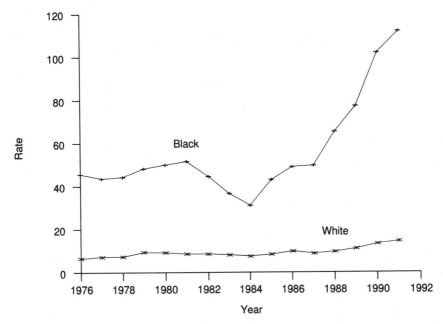

SOURCE: Based on data developed by Glenn Pierce and James Fox of Northeastern University from the Supplementary Homicide Reports provided by police departments to the FBI's Uniform Crime Reporting Section.

industry, whether it occurs as part of training and selection of new recruits or as dispute resolution between competing sellers or between sellers and buyers, undoubtedly sets a tone in the community, undoubtedly generates a greater inurement to violence generally, and so stimulates violence by others. This leads to an escalation of violence as more weapons diffuse through the community; and it does not look as if it is likely to reverse itself until we somehow find ways to diminish the presence of the drug markets, or at least to capture the guns from the young people involved in them. Experience since the mid-1980s does not encourage the belief that the intense efforts by the criminal justice system in attacking the supply side of the market is likely to be effective in reaching that goal. We have to explore other approaches.

Growing Politicization of Crime Policy: The "Three Strikes" Laws

While the serious problem of violence continues to grow, especially in urban areas, the political response to the problem continues to be of increasingly simplistic form. The concept of the mandatory minimum sentence dominated the actions of the 1980s, regardless of any judgment of whether long

FIGURE 17.11

Percentage Homicide Victims Killed by Guns, by Victim Age, United States

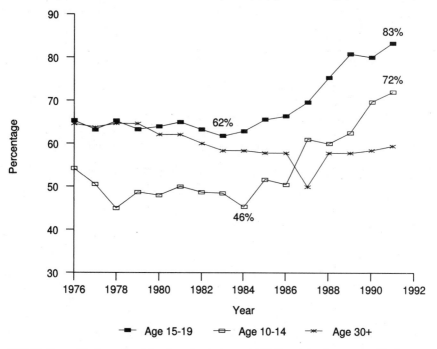

SOURCE: Prepared by Jacqueline Cohen from data in the annual *Uniform Crime Reports* issued by the FBI.

sentences were effective or not. The idea that has emerged as the pat solution of the 1990s is the variety of "three strikes and you're out" laws—an even more appealing sound-bite than the multisyllabic "mandatory minimum sentence." Washington was the first state to enact such a law through the referendum process, and it was followed in rapid succession by the U.S. Congress, California, and a number of other states.

At first glance, the idea behind the three-strikes principle certainly seems reasonable: Let's find the truly incorrigible criminal who represents a serious threat to the rest of us, and lock him away for a long time. Indeed, that is what the criminal justice system tries to do today. Anyone who has three separate convictions for serious violent felonies like murder or forcible rape is likely to go to prison for at least twenty years, more likely more, and very often for life. In fact, most states already have "three-time loser" laws that permit sentences beyond statutory maximums for people with serious prior criminal records. Such laws usually permit parole, however, at some point as the prisoner ages. Preventing any form of release until the person dies is the dominant feature of most of the new three-strikes laws, and that is likely to contribute to a reduced effectiveness of any prison capacity in reducing crime.

The basic issue that has to be considered in addressing a three-strikes rule from the viewpoint of incapacitation is the anticipated future duration of the criminal career of the offender after he commits his third "strike." If all his prior crimes were violent, there is a reasonable expectation that he will indeed continue to be a serious threat, and a life sentence is quite reasonable; that reasonableness is enhanced if there will be an opportunity at a later time to assess whether continuing his imprisonment is an effective use of prison space. Indeed, that is what parole boards were traditionally charged with doing before sentencing policy became so saliently involved in the political process.

It is evident from the age-crime curves (Figures 17.4 and 17.5) that a three-strike offender in his twenties is very unlikely to continue as a threat beyond age fifty, when the prisoner still has a future life expectancy—and future prison occupancy—of more than 25 years. That represents a cost to the taxpayers of about half a million dollars for each such offender, who is almost certainly no longer a threat to anyone.

However unlikely such long careers may be for young, violent offenders, they are even more unlikely for property offenders (including robbers), whose careers tend to be appreciably shorter. Thus, it is important to resist the temptation, following a particularly heinous version of some property offense, to add additional offenses to the three-strikes legislation, even if the property incident undoubtedly represents an attractive platform for doing so. It is even more inappropriate to include drug offenses as "strikes," as the U.S. Congress has done.

Much better information is needed on the anticipated future duration of the criminal careers of different categories of offenders, so that the truly persistent ones can be retained in prison and the less risky ones released to make space available for others—especially the growing number of violent ones—for whom incapacitation is more appropriate.

The previous discussion has emphasized incapacitation, but it may be that the purpose of the three-strikes laws is general deterrence. However hard it is for rational folks to conceive of it, there are some people who simply do not respond to whatever threat is presented to them. The problem is that any serious three-strikes candidate probably falls into that category. For people who see no attractive options in the legitimate economy, and who are doubtful that they will live another ten years in any event, the threat of an extended prison stay is likely to be far less threatening than it would be to a well-employed person with a family. Most candidates for three-strikes punishment would face a sentence of at least ten or twenty years or more for that third offense anyway. If even that threat fails to inhibit that third crime, how much greater an increment of deterrent threat will these individuals—who are not well known for their propensity to engage in careful long-range planning—see when the threat is extended to life in prison? Obviously, we have no strong empirical evidence on the elasticity of this incremental deterrent threat, so it would be desirable to conduct measurements in states that have passed such laws to gauge the magnitude of the response in terms of crime reduction by offenders vulnerable to three-strikes legislation.

We can certainly anticipate that the legislative process will not wait for the results of such research and that there will be a growth in the enactment of three-strike laws as the public's fear of violence and frustration with real crime problems increases. But these are complex and important issues, and it is unfortunate that the political response to them takes such simplistic forms.

When such laws are passed, it is critical that the set of offenses defined as "strikes" be strictly limited to the most seriously violent. And it is important to retain the possibility of release when the offender passes age fifty or has served a full but finite sentence, whichever is later. Otherwise, we will be filling our prisons with minor offenders well past their period of active criminality, and will not have room for others who are currently active and pose a much more serious threat.

One of the problems with such laws is that, however carefully the initial legislation is drawn, we can certainly expect the list of offenses included as "strikes" to expand over time. Even when a punishment policy is formulated narrowly, there are many precedents for expanding its scope. The law becomes a platform onto which other offenses can easily be added. This happens when a particularly striking or serious version of that offense (for example, a "carjacking" version of a robbery) hits the news. Then, we can anticipate a rush by legislators to be the first to introduce a bill adding that offense to the law. Once that proposal gets to the floor, then no one can oppose it for fear of being labeled "soft on crime" by his or her opponent in the next election.

Developing a Rational Strategy for the Use of Prisons

Any development of a rational strategy regarding prisons must recognize several key facts:

- There has been a massive growth in prison populations between the mid-1970s and the mid-1990s, with no demonstrated strong effect on crime rates.
- There has been a major growth in the use of imprisonment for drug offenders, and prison is demonstrably ineffective for diminishing drug selling or drug abuse, except for being able to coerce drug treatment.
- Prisons are expensive, costing about $20,000 per year per prisoner to operate, and these funds are diverted from other needs (such as education

or economic development, or even juvenile institutions, where rehabilitation is most likely with the right programs and resources applied) which might have some possibility of diminishing the future calls for prison.

- Prisons are generally ineffective for rehabilitation of adults.

- While the threat of a lengthy prison sentence is undoubtedly very effective at deterring white collar crimes that tend to be committed by middle class individuals, they are probably far less effective in deterring the crimes committed by underclass individuals, who are the primary occupants of prisons, and for whom the increment of pain associated with prison time may be far less severe than it would be for those ensconced in a comfortable job.

- Incapacitation through imprisonment is probably the only effective means of restraining the violent crimes that are committed by some individuals otherwise out of social control, and so incarceration of these people should be a high priority for the use of limited prison capacity.

- It is important to find ways to remove prison policy from a primarily political agenda that reacts to the crime of the moment, and to develop a coherent schedule and process of imposing punishment and controlling offenders.

With these basic observations, and in recognition of the growing public concern over violence resulting from the explosive mixture of young people who see no hope for their future in the legitimate society, the spreading violence associated with the drug industry, and the growing presence of guns stimulated by that industry, we can begin to develop a mixture of short- and long-term strategies for dealing with the prison problem.

For the short term, there is little we can do but respond to the growing violence with arrest, conviction, and incarceration, at least for the period when the individual can be expected to continue to act violently. In order to do this, we have got to make room in our prisons for those for whom prison is most appropriate for reasons of incapacitation, those who are likely to engage in violence on the outside.

In order to provide that capacity, we should seek to make much greater use of intermediate punishments for those accused of nonviolent offenses, and especially of drug dealing. In order to do this, we have to provide the resources and expertise to our communities to enable them to carry out their responsibilities in these intermediate punishments. In particular, there could be much better use of police and their presence, along with greater access to modern information systems and telecommunications, for control of people on intermediate punishment (including those on probation and parole release) within the community.

We should repeal mandatory minimum sentencing laws, which were passed in the passion of some issue at one point in time, and may no longer be appropriate. In general, one finds those sentenced under mandatory minimum sentencing laws to have appreciably less serious prior records than those sentenced otherwise, and so, at the margin, prison might be better used for offenders that are more like the latter group. If political conditions preclude outright repeal, then we should pass a generic "sunset" law causing all mandatory minimum laws to expire automatically two years after enactment unless explicitly reenacted. This is especially necessary for the mandatory minimum laws that apply to drug offenses, which are of doubtful effectiveness and account for the majority of prisoners serving time on mandatory sentences.

More generally, we have to reconsider the inappropriate use of prison for the problem of drug abuse. Certainly drug abuse is a serious problem to be addressed, but there is no indication that the attacks by the criminal justice system on the supply side of the market have been successful in dealing with it. Indeed, it could well be that the crime and violence problems created by the drug markets are more severe than those created by the abusive drugs they sell. There should be a gradual transformation of those efforts to a public health model with prevention and treatment focused on the demand side, and tight regulation of the supply side. This is not a problem that will be solved in the short term, but the strategies for dealing with the problem must be addressed in the short term.

For the intermediate term, it would be most desirable to find ways to take the issue of punishment policy out of the rabid political arena, where the conditions under which the debate occurs can lead to the enactment of much irresponsible policy. One means for achieving that is through the creation of sentencing commissions, even though they are also affected by political pressures. But, since they are explicitly charged with the development of a coherent sentencing structure, they are more likely to maintain a reasonable degree of coherence in the sentences they develop. The major distortion to most sentencing commissions' schedules have been associated with the mandatory minimum laws passed by legislatures, often even after establishing the sentencing commission.

For the longer term, it seems essential that we get at some of the major factors that are contributing to important and large segments of our nation's population having no stake in legitimate conformity, and so having greatly diminished sensitivity to the sanctions available to the criminal justice system. That problem is a direct consequence of the erosion of family structure and the associated abandonment in far too many cases of the obligation of socialization of growing children. The society will have to consider how the inadequate efforts in these families may be augmented, whether that is done merely by the widespread introduction of day-care centers in the schools (to enable the teenage mothers to finish school, to begin socializing their children, and to teach those mothers basic parenting skills) or by a massive array of boarding schools to which mothers might send their children. Any such efforts, of course, are likely to be expensive, perhaps enormously so, and the benefits are still very uncertain; but, even if successful, they are not likely to be realized for at least ten years, when another political administration is in office.

In light of the short political planning horizons and the very limited availability of funds for such efforts, we are not likely to see significant efforts of this sort pursued in the near future. In that event, it is likely that we will be needing appreciably more prison capacity in the decades to come.

TODD R. CLEAR AND ANTHONY A. BRAGA

COMMUNITY CORRECTIONS

For the first half of this century, discussions about the offender in the community encountered a straightforward policy context. Nearly every offender under community correctional authority was either on probation or on parole. Probationers were, for the most part, first-time offenders or minor offenders, and they received probation terms as acts of judicial leniency allowing them to remain in the community despite their crime. Parolees, by contrast, were more serious felons, often recidivists, who reentered the community after periods of confinement.

Following World War II, penal authorities began to doubt the wisdom of keeping the prison as the primary correctional strategy. Interest in community-based correctional approaches grew, and it became common for second- and even third-time felons to receive sentences of probation, with special conditions established by the court. Even some violent felons were retained in the community, as it was argued the effects of prison were primarily negative (Clear and Cole 1994).

The postwar optimism about community correctional methods quickly waned. Since the mid-1970s, a backlash about offenders in the community has dominated correctional thinking. Ironically, while public confidence in community-based methods seems at an all-time low, the number of offenders under community controls has increased dramatically, from fewer than one million in 1975 to over three million, today. Since 1980, in fact, rates of growth in probation caseloads have been similar to rates of prison population growth (compare Austin [1990] with Langan [1994]). Today, three out of every four offenders under correctional control are currently supervised in the community (Dillingham 1990).

Since the mid-1980s, disquiet about offenders under community supervision has maintained a collision course with an equivalent dismay over burgeoning prison populations. On the one hand, it has bothered policy makers that so many offenders, some of whom stand convicted of serious crimes, receive so little in the way of official control under traditional probation and parole methods. Yet the alternative, ever-expanding prison capacity, seems equally unpalatable in times of strained tax revenues.

The prison-probation dilemma has led to the development of the concept of intermediate sanctions, sometimes called intermediate punishments. The first well-articulated case for intermediate sanctions was made by Morris and Tonry (1990). They argued that for a large group of middle range offenders, prison is too punitive and costly, yet traditional probation is inadequate as a punishment or a control. Forced to choose between these extremes, judges often opt for prison, wishing for a less onerous, credible alternative. What is needed, therefore, is a range of correctional strategies falling between prison and probation.

As Morris and Tonry were making their argument, correctional leaders were beginning to fill in the programmatic vacuum between prison and probation. Today, nearly every correctional system has an array of intermediate programs, most of them community-based. These programs range from residential and semicustodial (such as day reporting centers and home detention) to fully community-based approaches such as intensive supervision. Critics argue that these new programs are frequently poorly integrated into an overall philosophy or correctional strategy (O'Leary and Clear 1994), but it can no longer be argued that corrections in the community is merely probation and parole. The context for community corrections has shifted forever.

The Changing Context of Community Corrections

In the face of unprecedented growth accompanied by a deepening credibility crisis, community corrections officials have not only diversified their programs but have shifted their methods to emphasize surveillance and control practices more resonant with the get-tough atmosphere in which corrections now operates. Compared with the first half of this century, three differences are apparent in contemporary community corrections: resources, sentencing, and intermediate sanctions/programs.

Resources

Even though community corrections absorbed a greater increase in offenders than did the prison during the 1980s, it was the prison budget that grew.

Langan (1994) estimates that state and local prison funding has doubled in the period from 1977 to 1990, but during the same period, probation funding remained constant. Now, although nearly three-fourths of correctional clients are in the community, about one-tenth of the correctional budget goes to supervise them.

Apparently, community supervision has been seen as a kind of elastic resource that could handle whatever numbers of offenders the system required it to. Neglect in funding resulted in caseloads routinely in excess of 150 probationers, often as high as 300 or more (Cunniff and Shilton 1991). There is no uniformly accepted standard for the optimal caseload size, and studies suggest that even experience with smaller caseloads does not promise that such a number will ever be documented by scientific method (Banks et al. 1977). But since some studies indicate that the average probation or parole officer carrying a large caseload can make between 90 and 120 face-to-face contacts in a month (Bemus and Baird 1988), we can conclude that current caseloads do not afford much supervision. Under these conditions, it is unusually good if an offender is seen monthly in brief office visits, lasting fifteen minutes or less.

Relative decreases in resources seem to be associated with changes in supervision outcomes. It is more likely today that community supervision will end in failure: the proportion of parolees and conditional release violators representing new prison admissions increased from 15.8 percent in 1979 to 26.8 percent in 1988 (Byrne, Lurigio, and Baird 1989), and current estimates are that between 30 percent and 50 percent of all new prison admissions are likely to be community supervision failures (Austin and Tillman 1988). Indeed, the fastest-growing component of the prison population are those offenders who fail under community supervision (Taxman and Byrne 1994).

Resources alone almost certainly do not explain this change in effectiveness. A greater emphasis on surveillance and control converge with a severe shift in resources to weaken the incentives for working with offenders who are struggling to make it in the community. Swift revocation removes part of the workload from the community supervision agent and places it back on the prison. It also means the community corrections agency avoids the possibility of a more serious, credibility-damaging crime being committed by an "uncooperative" client.

Sentencing

The types of sentences offenders receive have changed the meaning of community-based corrections. In particular, there has been an increased use of split sentences, mandatory minimums, and mandatory supervision (Clear, Byrne, and Dvoskin 1993).

An offender receiving a split sentence (also called "shock probation") is sentenced to a period of incarceration and is then released to probation.

Typically the institutional portion of the split sentence is served in jail; however, a recent review by Dawson (1990) found that one out of four of these cases involved a prison sentence. The median jail time was six months followed by three years of probation; prison cases had a median time of four years followed by three years of probation (Dawson 1990). Dawson also found that 40 percent of all probation cases and 21 percent of all convictions were split sentence cases, while both straight prison sentences and straight probation sentences are now less popular among judges (33 percent and 16 percent for all convicted felons, respectively).

A related change is mandatory sentencing, which shifts the control of sentencing and release decisions from judges to the legislature. Mandatory sentences specifying punishments for certain crimes (for example, drunk driving, drug offenses, sex crimes) are now a widespread practice, and presumptive sentencing statutes have been passed in more than twenty states (Byrne 1990).

The move toward fixed sentences has been accompanied by the growing use of supervised mandatory releases. Between 1977 and 1990, the proportion of discretionary parole releases dropped from 71.9 percent to 40.5 percent, while unconditional releases stayed fairly constant and supervised mandatory releases increased from 5.9 percent to nearly 30 percent of all prison releases (Bureau of Justice Statistics 1991).

These sentencing changes have meant that probationers and parolees look increasingly alike. A study by Petersilia and her colleagues (1985) found that 25 percent of felony probationers were "indistinguishable" in terms of prior criminal records or current offenses from those sentenced to prison. Many probationers have experienced incarceration as a condition of their community supervision; many offenders who would ordinarily have been considered good candidates for probation now receive mandatory prison terms. This may be especially true for those offenders now receiving mandatory minimum sentences for drug offenses, who represent as many as one-third of the prisoners in some state prison systems.

Intermediate Sanctions

Community programs have become more stringent in the conditions they impose on offenders and more varied in the programs they operate.

The increased use of probation conditions is an attempt to both punish the offender via restitution and fines and to better control the behavior of offenders via urine testing, curfews, and so forth (Taxman and Byrne 1994). Dawson (1990) found that in 48 percent of all felony probation cases judges imposed special conditions including restitution (36 percent), fines (18 percent), and various types of mandatory treatment (17 percent). Similarly, Cuniff and Shilton (1991) found that 55 percent of felony probations had special conditions imposed on them, frequently more than one.

The expanded conditions are applied and enforced by a growing variety of community-based programs. Instead of merely using traditional probation and parole, most community supervision agencies now operate a range of programs. Some of these new intermediate sanctions are designed primarily as short-term solutions to prison crowding and are presented as cost-effective alternatives to prison. Other programs seek to respond to specific offender problems such as drug abuse or aggressive behavior, and these programs are promoted on their ability to reduce recidivism. Some of the new intermediate sanctions programs are residential, as well, showing how the differences between institutional corrections and community corrections are no longer as distinct as once they were.

The combined effects of diminished resources, changes in sentencing practices, and programmatic elaboration has changed the community-based penal system in two fundamental ways. It has changed the kinds of offenders under supervision in the community, and it has changed the way these offenders are supervised.

Changes in Offenders under Supervision

It is not an anomaly for an offender to be living in the community. Since three-fourths of correctional clients are under community supervision, and since most prison sentences result in time served of about two years or less, it seems safe to say not only that having offenders in the community is normal but that any other circumstance would be almost unthinkable. To make it unusual for offenders to be retained on the streets would require more fundamental changes in resources and in policy than even the most strident critics of community-based penology have imagined. What are these offenders like, and how do they behave (or misbehave)?

According to a recent review by the Bureau of Justice Statistics (1992), 48 percent of probationers are felons (current offense) and 31 percent are misdemeanants. The typical felony probationer is an unmarried, minority male, twenty-eight years old, sentenced to a forty-two-month term for a nonviolent offense conviction (Cuniff and Shilton 1991). Only 12 percent of felony probationers were convicted of a violent offense (homicide, rape, robbery, and aggravated assault), while the vast majority of conviction offenses involve property or public order offenses (Cuniff and Shilton 1991). A study of one stratified sample of probationers found that over half had no prior felony conviction (Langan 1994).

The increased number of felons on probation can be partially attributed to the changes in sentencing strategies highlighted earlier. In 1986, rates for split sentences were as follows: murder 5 percent, rape 17 percent, robbery 13 percent, aggravated assault 21 percent, burglary 25 percent, larceny 21 percent, drug trafficking 28 percent, and other felonies 20 percent (Dawson

1990). Cuniff and Shilton (1991) further reported that persons convicted of drug offenses (trafficking, possession) make up 35 percent of the total felony probation workload. The effects of drug use and the corresponding "war on drugs" have been particularly apparent for community corrections. Nurco, Hanlan, and Kinlock (1990) have estimated that more than half of the three million persons on probation or parole are drug-involved, either as sellers or as users, or both. Research has shown that probationers who continue their drug use during their supervision tend to have further involvement in criminal activity (Turner, Petersilia, and Deschenes 1994).

Probation misbehavior varies considerably; it ranges from very minor rule violations to major, significant felony offenses. A Wisconsin study (Baird, Clear, and Harris 1986) found that only 13 percent of probation cases were accused of a major or moderately serious crime and only 5 percent were accused of the most serious person offenses; 11 percent were accused of rule violations or minor crimes. Approximately two-thirds of these violators committed only a single violation while on probation, and barely 10 percent committed three or more violations (Baird, Clear, and Harris 1986). A stratified, national sample showed a much higher concentration of probationer noncompliance: 49 percent of probationers ended their probation terms without full compliance with the rules of probation (Langan 1994). Studies of probationer misbehavior while on ISP show that a majority of technical violations are incurred as a result of failure to pass a mandatory urine test (see Petersilia and Turner [1993]). Indeed, the proliferation of cheap urine testing, more than any other condition, has led to an increase in the number of technical violations identified by corrections staff.

Changes in Supervision Programming

The programs used to supervise offenders in the community have changed substantially, especially as regards the development and expansion of intermediate sanctions. In the following sections we list and describe the main programs in community-based corrections, arranged by type and degree of supervision provided to the offender.

Traditional Probation Programs

Traditional probation is currently the most extensively used sanction in the correctional system. Approximately two-thirds of offenders under correctional supervision are on probation, and this number has been increasing by 5 percent to 8 percent a year since 1980 (Byrne and Pattavina 1992), or at a rate of 9,000 new cases a month (Byrne 1989).

Innovations in traditional probation.   For years, experts believed that the effectiveness of traditional probation supervision could be increased by reducing the size of probation caseloads. However, dozens of studies failed to show that caseload reduction alone is enough to reduce recidivism (Banks et al. 1977). According to Carter and Wilkins, caseload size "is not significant in contrast to the nature of the supervision experience, the classification of offenders, officers and types of treatment, and social systems of the correctional agency" (1976, 394). Without structure to the supervision process, most observers have felt that probation supervision results too often in inappropriate activities with inappropriate offenders (Clear and O'Leary 1983).

In 1981, the National Institute of Corrections (NIC), a division of the Federal Bureau of Prisons, set about to develop a way to structure probation and parole supervision through a classification-workload system (Baird 1981). Restricted and/or reduced correctional budgets led to a surge of interest in the development of a more effective method of structuring community supervision. Consequently, a more structured classification-based case management system evolved based on time studies of supervision under Wisconsin-type risk/need classifications (see Baird, Heinz, and Bemus [1979]). Called a "model" system of caseload management, the approach consisted of three fundamental components:

- supervision classification using standardized risk and needs assessment criteria

- written and systematic strategies for supervision planning

- workload accounting based upon studies of the amount of time it takes to supervise a case (National Institute of Corrections 1981)

Classification involves the use of a standardized scale to assess individual clients in terms of risk to the community and need for assistance. Probationers are differentiated into levels (minimum, medium, maximum) based on scores. Clients who have the highest scores for risk or need receive the maximum available supervision.

Within risk and need categories, cases are assigned "work units" in accordance with the necessary amount of time required to supervise them, based on time studies. Each probation officer is responsible for a certain number of work units, and cases are assigned so that no time requirements exceed the officer's time available for supervision. The model system is designed to be responsive to an influx of cases, so the highest risk cases get maximum supervision while less serious cases receive less supervision, even when caseloads are increasing. By 1991, the model system or a derivative had been adopted in almost all adult probation or parole systems, and in most juvenile supervision systems (Burke and Adams 1991).

Administrators who have adopted the system report success in using the workload formula approach to provide probation agencies with a supervision strategy that responds to an influx of cases while accounting for risk to the community and assistance to the client. The NIC model system approach has been so well received that agencies without classification-workload systems are said to be "probation dinosaurs" (Clear and Gallagher 1985).

Community service and financial penalties.   Community service is labor performed by the offender, generally for a public agency or nonprofit organization, to remedy some of the harm caused by the crime or compensate society for it. As an alternative to jail sentences, this sanction has attractive features: the person "pays back" to the offended community, all offenders are charged equally (in hours) regardless of their circumstances, and the cost is considerably less than that of incarceration (McDonald 1989). One advantage of community service approaches has been that they provide a relatively efficient way to sanction repetitive minor offenders, such as misdemeanants, without tying up scarce jail space in response to these often minor illegal activities.

Fines, penalties, and forfeitures have also been advanced as an alternative approach to punishment. Advocates of financial penalties argue that they are well suited to a capitalist society that places importance on wealth. Not only can the profits of criminal behavior be eliminated, but also substantial punishment can be inflicted on offenders by the imposition of a financial penalty, without the severe costs of incarceration (Hillsman and Greene 1992). These penalties are thought to be punitive, since their severity can be adjusted for the seriousness of the offense and for the offender's financial circumstances (called the "day fine") (see von Hirsch, Wasik, and Greene [1989]). Day fines are based on a system of "units"; these fine units are derived from the proportion of the offender's daily income that is considered equitable for purposes of fining (Hillsman and Greene 1992). Some observers have argued that fines are potentially very different from and much fairer than forfeitures, which can be arbitrary and very disproportionate in their impact on offenders.

Restitution is a financial penalty that seeks to recompense the victim for the losses suffered as a result of the crime. Restitution is often combined with community service; the offender reimburses the specific victim for the losses, but also "repays" the symbolic victim—the community—with labor.

Intermediate Programs

In order to fill in the penal vacuum between probation and prison, a range of new, intermediate programs has emerged. Below we describe the main versions now in existence.

Intensive supervision.   Intensive supervision programs (ISPs) have been presented as part of the new "tough" image of community supervision that is responsive to the prison crowding problem (Byrne 1990). ISPs normally require multiple weekly face-to-face contacts, including evening visits to the home. They also typically employ urine testing and electronic monitoring to augment the level of surveillance. There are two general types of intensive supervision programs: probation diversion (called probation enhancements) and institutional diversion programs. Probation enhancement programs divert offenders from traditional probation sentences. They select probationers who have committed offenses deemed too serious for routine supervision (Petersilia and Turner 1993). Prison diversion programs select lower-risk offenders sentenced to prison and provide supervision for them in the community (Pearson and Harper 1990; Erwin 1986).

ISPs appeal to both liberal and conservative policy makers. For liberals, ISPs claim to divert prisoners from incarceration without appearing soft on crime; for conservatives, they claim to allow an increase in control over offenders without additional cost to corrections (Byrne 1990).

Home confinement and electronic monitoring programs.   House arrest programs (with and without electronic monitoring) have been promoted for reasons similar to those used in support of ISP: they promise to alleviate the prison and jail crowding problem in a politically palatable manner (Baumer and Mendelsohn 1992). Offenders receive prison sentences but serve their sentences in their homes; home detention is enforced using an electronic sensor that indicates whether the offender is complying with the home restriction. These programs are thought to be cost-effective in that it costs the state nothing to house or feed the offender, and often the electronic monitor is paid for by the offender's own resources. The number of offenders participating in electronically monitored home confinement programs has increased dramatically from 95 in 1986 to nearly 12,000 in 1990 (Renzema 1992).

Day reporting centers.   Day reporting centers (DRCs) are facilities where probationers go for day-long intervention and treatment. As recently as 1990, only six states used day reporting centers (Parent 1990), though that number is rising with the program's popularity. DRCs use a plethora of correctional treatment methods similar to those used in halfway houses, but without the difficulties and costs associated with a residential facility. McDevitt and Miliano (1992) report that despite similarities in program elements (such as frequent client contact, drug testing, and formalized scheduling), the various DRCs they examined operated quite differently. Therefore, they state, "it is difficult to define specifically what a day reporting center is; each center is unique" (1992, 154).

Like most intermediate sanctions, DRCs were originated to alleviate prison crowding by providing an early release mechanism for inmates who were close to their parole dates or completion of their sentences (McDevitt and Miliano 1992). However, DRCs are currently being used as alternative sanctions for prison-bound offenders, especially those who are failing in traditional or enhanced probation programs.

Boot camp/shock incarceration. This alternative involves a sentence to a short (thirty to ninety days) but harsh confinement experience that is modeled after military boot camps, followed by a period of probation supervision (Parent 1989). In some respects, these programs are a throwback to early forms of imprisonment that extolled the virtues of hard work and daily discipline. The idea of these programs is to "shock" offenders in two ways: first, by removing them from the community and, second, by subjecting them to harsh, unrelenting conditions of physical exertion.

The Effectiveness of Corrections in the Community

In this section we will examine the effectiveness of specific community-based correctional strategies.

Evaluating Probation

Probation as a crime control strategy has been regarded by some observers as a farce, leaving offenders virtually unsupervised and free to commit new crimes and violate release conditions with impunity (Byrne and Pattavina 1992). But the popular criticisms of probation are not completely justified by the facts. Studies show that up to 80 percent of all probationers complete their terms without a new arrest (BJS 1991). Despite the fact that the seriousness of probationers' offenses has been increasing, it is still true that many of the individuals currently on probation are low-risk offenders, with no prior criminal convictions. Thus, high success rates for probationers should not be surprising. In fact, some scholars argue that many low-risk probationers could be handled successfully through the use of nonsupervision alternatives such as day fines (von Hirsch, Wasik, and Greene 1989).

Although the majority of offenders on probation do not get rearrested, studies also confirm that a subgroup of probationers have high rates of criminal activity (Petersilia et al. 1985). Byrne and Kelly (1989) have estimated that approximately 10 percent of probationers are high risks and that 60 percent of these high-risk offenders will be rearraigned within one year of probation. A 1985 Rand study in two California counties found that 65 percent of felons on probation were rearrested for crimes such as robbery, burglary, or assault (Petersilia et al. 1985). The release of the Rand study led to a chorus of criticism of probation nationwide.

Yet misbehavior by offenders on probation appears to vary greatly from place to place, and depends upon the length of follow-up. Vito (1986) applied the Rand methodology to a Kentucky sample and found that felony rearrest rates were a much lower 22 percent. Geerken and Hayes (1993) summarized follow-up studies of probationers and found that felony rearrest rates varied from a low of 12 percent to a high of 65 percent—the Rand study cited above (see Table 18.1). Finally, a long-term follow-up of California parolees released from prison in 1962 found that two-thirds were subsequently reincarcerated in prison or jail at least once (Gottfredson and Gottfredson 1992). However, most of the cohort's arrests were for "nuisance" offenses; only 9 percent of the arrests were for personal felony offenses.

Because of the wide differences in probationer behaviors under supervision, increasing attention has been paid to the need for classification systems which allow conventional probation to focus resources on the most risky and needy clients (for example, those with extensive priors or a history of unemployment or drug dependency) within a caseload (Clear and Gallagher, 1983). This is the essence of the NIC "model" system described earlier, and research suggests that this approach is promising (Andrews and Bonta 1994; Markley and Eisenberg 1987; Baird, Heinz, and Bemus 1979).

Classification may hold promise for more effective probation supervision. A recent survey of felony probationers in the United States revealed that 10 percent of these offenders should have been classified as high-risk, intensive supervision cases (Langan and Cunniff 1992). Nearly half of these felons were rearrested on felony charges within three years. These high-risk offenders were much more likely to have drug abuse problems and other felony convictions, and required special supervision programs. However, many large probation agencies operating under severe budget constraints have had to eliminate special programs and reduce staff, and classification systems for these agencies may be of limited usefulness (Matthews 1991).

It must be admitted that we know relatively little about the impact of traditional probation on offenders. Evaluators have tended to ignore traditional probation practices in favor of focusing on newer alternatives such as ISP and house arrest. Lipton, Martinson, and Wilks's (1975) review of 231 institutional and community treatment program evaluations (published between 1945 and 1967) yielded only seven acceptable assessments of either a probation or a parole program. Only one of these evaluations randomly assigned offenders to different types of probation (see Lipton, Martinson, and Wilks 1975).

Evaluating Intensive Supervision

In the early 1980s, Georgia's Intensive Probation Supervision was widely hailed as an innovative approach to combating that state's prison overcrowding problem. Many policy makers emulated Georgia's acclaimed program

TABLE 18.1.

Seventeen Studies Reporting Recidivism Rates for Probationers

Study	Instant offense	Follow-up period	Failure criterion	Failure rate (%)
1	Internal Revenue laws (72%)	Postprobation: 5½–11½ years	Conviction	16.4
2	Burglary; forgery and checks	To termination: 4–7 years	2 or more violations/revocations (technical and new offenses)	30.2
3	Bootlegging (48%) and forgery	Postprobation: 6–12 years	Conviction	17.7
		On probation: 18–30 months	Inactive letter, bench warrant, revocation	20.2
4	Auto theft; forgery and checks	To termination	Revocation (technical and new offenses)	52.5
5	Larceny and burglary	Postprobation: minimum of 4 years	Arrest or conviction	41.5
		Postprobation: 20-month average	Revocation and postrelease conviction	55.0
6	Property	To termination: 1–2 years	Revocation	18.3
7	Burglary, larceny, and vehicle theft	Postprobation: 6 months–7 years	Arrest and conviction	30.0
8	Property	Postprobation: 3–4 years	Arrest	29.6
9	Felonies	40 months from term initiation	Rearrest	65.0
10	Felonies	36 months from term initiation	Rearrest	22.0
11	Felonies	40 months from term initiation	Rearrest	22.0
12	Felonies	3 years from term initiation	Rearrest	33.0
13	Felonies	5 years from term initiation	Rearrest	12.0
			Violations	6.0
			Rearrests and violations	26.0
14	Felonies and misdemeanors	From term initiation to 5-1-87 (median 3.4 years at risk)	Rearrest	39.0
15	Felonies	3 and 4 years from term initiation	Rearrest	36.40
			Reconvicted	31.35
			Incarcerated	15.17
			Imprisoned	9.11
16	Felonies	3 years from term initiation	Rearrest	43.00
17	Index offenses	To term expiration	Rearrest	50.00

SOURCE: M. Geerken and H. Hayes, "Probation and Parole: Public Risks and the Future of Incarceration Alternatives," *Criminology* 31 (1993): 549–64.

because it promised an approach to the prison crowding problem that left the community safe. Administrators liked the program because it was a visible way of reasserting the value of community supervision.

According to a review by the United States General Accounting Office (GAO) (1990), jurisdictions in every state had instituted an ISP for adult offenders, though only eighteen states had formally evaluated their programs. Most of these evaluations had serious flaws in their research designs; yet, taken together, these evaluation studies presented a generally negative view of the effectiveness of ISP programs in terms of cost-effectiveness, diversionary impact, and recidivism reduction (see Clear and Braga [1994]). More recently, Petersilia and Turner (1993) of the Rand Corporation completed the largest random assignment field experiment ever conducted in corrections, looking primarily at probation enhancement ISPs. The demonstration project ran from 1986 to 1991 and involved fourteen separate ISP programs in nine states. The results are worth a detailed review.

Recidivism.   The study concluded that ISP offenders "did not have lower recidivism rates—in terms of arrests, technical violations, or convictions—than offenders on routine supervision at any of the sites" (Petersilia, Peterson, and Turner 1992, 30). No difference was found between ISP clients and regular probation clients in terms of arrests or convictions. Approximately one-third of the offenders in both experimental and control groups had been rearrested at the end of the one-year follow-up period; 21 percent of both groups were reconvicted within one year. However, 65 percent of ISP offenders had a technical violation, as compared with 38 percent of offenders on routine supervision. This large number of technical violations was viewed as a program effect of ISPs arising from systematic monitoring of probationer behavior. Some observers were encouraged by the high rate of technical violations and saw it as an indicator that ISPs took active offenders off the streets earlier, but Petersilia and Turner (1993) report that there was no correlation between an arrest for new crimes and technical violations.

Cost.   For the twelve probation enhancement programs in the Rand study, intensive supervision was considerably more costly than conventional probation and parole ($7,200 versus $4,700 per year). In Oregon's jail diversion program, ISP costs were 75 percent those of prison costs to begin with (Petersilia and Turner 1993). Half of the ISP clients recidivated and were incarcerated, while almost half of the prisoners later served short prison terms. As a result, the overall costs of the two sanctions are comparable. The conclusion was that ISPs were not less costly, overall, than the previous program arrangements.

Crowding reduction.   In the Rand studies, intensive supervision "was associated with more technical violations and more commitments to prison than routine supervision" (Petersilia, Peterson, and Turner 1992, 26). Thus, the potential of ISP as a means to reduce overcrowding is seriously eroded by high rates of program failure. In Georgia, only half of the ISP offenders successfully complete the program (Petersilia 1987); in New Jersey, close to 50 percent return to prison, usually for a technical violation (Pearson and Harper 1990). When high revocation rates are combined with the use of ISP for offenders who are not prison-bound, the net effect of ISP programs may be to increase prison populations (Tonry 1990).

Evaluating Home Confinement and Electronic Monitoring

As recently as 1990, the GAO (1990) concluded that we simply "do not know" about the effectiveness of the various home confinement models because they have not been systematically evaluated. Since then Baumer and Mendelsohn (1992) have released the results of their experimental research on Indiana's home confinement programs, while Austin and Hardyman (1991) have completed their evaluation of Oklahoma's house arrest program.

Almost all home confinement programs with an electronic monitoring component have reported technical problems with the equipment, resulting in both false positives (erroneous reports that the offender is home) and false negatives (erroneous reports that the offenders is not home). Although the equipment is potentially fallible, it provides "considerably more intensive and consistent levels of attempted contacts" than does manual monitoring (Baumer and Mendelsohn 1990, 37).

Offenders report "time on electronic monitoring to be moderately difficult, but . . . better than jail" (Baumer and Mendelsohn 1992, 60). Further, when these offenders were asked whether staying at home was hard or easy, fewer than half regarded the experience as easy or very easy. However, Baumer and Mendelsohn did find that the electronic monitoring was more demanding and stressful for the offender's family than manual monitoring methods.

Decision makers want to know whether offenders violate their curfews or get rearrested. In Indiana, slightly over 40 percent of the home confinement population had at least one program violation and between one-third and one-half of all "programmed contacts" were not successful, suggesting a violation (Baumer and Mendelsohn 1992). Offender self-reports paint a similar portrait of noncompliance for both manual and electronic monitoring (40 percent unauthorized absences versus 47 percent unauthorized absences, respectively).

Since the first wave of house arrest programs targeted low-risk offenders, it is not surprising that new arrests are relatively uncommon. Many programs accept only nonviolent property offenders and individuals who have not been charged with or convicted of crimes such as domestic violence, child abuse, and incest. Renzema and Skelton (1990) report a rearrest rate of 3.7 percent for electronic monitoring programs, while Baumer and Mendelsohn (1990) report a rate of 3.3 percent. With the exception of one program reporting a 16 percent rearrest rate, Petersilia (1987) found most house arrest programs to have about a 5 percent arrest rate. Baumer and Mendelsohn (1992) also suggest that home confinement results in improvements in employment; offenders on house arrest seem to obtain jobs and maintain better job attendance.

Some offenders appear to do better on home confinement than others. For example, offenders charged with felony DWIs had better compliance rates and lower rearrest rates than other offenders. Baumer and Mendelsohn (1992) believe that these individuals were low rate offenders and less committed to a criminal lifestyle; thus, the home confinement sanction in combination with a prohibition on alcohol helped control their behavior. House arrest programs have been used more successfully with offenders at the postconviction stage than at the preconviction stage. Preconviction clients were significantly more likely to abscond (Baumer and Mendelsohn 1990).

The results of a randomized field experiment (focusing on a preparole supervised release program in Oklahoma) conducted by the National Council on Crime and Delinquency confirm that increased surveillance translates directly into increased risk of program failure. Offenders supervised with electronic monitoring "had higher rates of both technical violations and new arrests" than the offenders placed on supervised release without electronic monitoring (Austin and Hardyman 1991, 21). Offenders monitored using continuous electronic monitoring devices had higher failure rates (33.3 percent) than offenders monitored using intermittent monitoring systems. Yet overall, all monitored offenders tended to be successfully terminated, with an average time from release to termination of 126.6 days for the electronically monitored group and 105.4 days for the controls.

Austin and Hardyman concluded that the program was cost effective because the preparole community supervision (PPCS) program ". . . averted $9,295 per PPCS offender per year" (1991, 30). In findings similar to those of Baumer and Mendelsohn (1990), the evaluators suggested that the electronic monitoring device itself was not a critical element of a community supervision program in Oklahoma. They also argued that Oklahoma should expand the group of offender types that are eligible for this program, because "electronic monitoring can be as effective with violent and drug offenders as with property and alcohol offenders" (Austin and Hardyman 1991, 33).

Evaluating Boot Camp/Shock Incarceration

MacKenzie and Parent (1992) provide the most recent summary of what we currently know about the implementation and impact of boot camps for young adult offenders. Evaluation research on the different program models has been quite limited, with no randomized field experiments to date. A variety of nonexperimental and quasi-experimental research studies have been completed on programs operating in Georgia (Georgia Department of Corrections 1989), Florida (Florida Department of Corrections 1989), New York (New York State Division of Parole 1989), and Louisiana (MacKenzie 1991).

Although this is an admittedly limited group of evaluations, MacKenzie and Parent offer some tentative conclusions about shock incarceration.

- No research suggests that offenders who complete shock incarceration programs will have lower recidivism rates in comparison with other offenders.

- As currently designed, shock incarceration programs neither deter nor rehabilitate offenders.

- There is no support for the idea that prison crowding will be reduced by shock programs by decreasing the recidivism of offenders.

- Punishment may be one of the most desirable features of these programs from the perspective of the public and policy makers.

- Policy makers need to recognize that these programs may be difficult to implement in their jurisdiction, because of the types of staffing problems that are likely to emerge (such as turnover, training, recruitment, and burn out). (1992, 114–15)

Evaluating Day Reporting Centers

Although there are more than 100 day reporting centers (DRCs) in the United States (see Parent [1990]), the available evaluation research on DRCs has been descriptive, with no available research that employed either an experimental or a quasi-experimental design. McDevitt and Miliano (1992) have provided a description of six Massachusetts day reporting centers (see also Parent [1990]). In Massachusetts, offenders from county houses of corrections and jails are eligible, and DRCs are operated as early release mechanisms for those offenders without "recent disciplinary reports on file" (McDevitt and Miliano 1992, 154). Some of the DRC programs did have electronic monitoring as a component.

The majority (nearly 80 percent) of offenders placed in DRC programs completed the programs successfully; 16 percent were terminated because of technical violations, while "5 percent were returned to higher custody because they committed new crimes or had escaped" (McDevitt and Miliano 1992, 160). As have many programs, the DRC movement has proceeded without the benefit of sound evaluation research on program implementation and impact.

Residential Community Corrections Programs

Latessa and Travis (1992) have reviewed evaluation research on residential community corrections (RCC) programs. They found that often these programs are quite small, are quite varied in the programs they run, and serve a mixed clientele. Moreover, most of these programs operate in the private sector and do not like to be externally evaluated. For these reasons, good evaluations of RCCs are rare. Allen and his colleagues (1976) reviewed thirty-five studies of correctional halfway houses and found that an equal number of the quasi-experimental and experimental studies reported either no differences between groups or lower recidivism among halfway house residents. Latessa and Allen (1982) identified forty-four separate evaluations of halfway house programs and again found inconsistent results.

There is some general evidence to suggest that RCCs may work better than direct release to parole because they assist in reintegrating the offender into the community. Latessa and Travis (1992) review a number of more recent evaluations and find a possible "treatment effect" associated with placement in an RCC program. However, they also emphasize that next to nothing is known about the implementation and impact of the latest wave of surveillance-oriented RCC programs, which often place relatively little emphasis on offender needs or treatment and instead use drug testing to monitor program compliance.

Community Service Programs

Douglas McDonald (1992) recently completed a review of the evaluation research on the use of unpaid community service as a criminal sentence. No randomized field experiments could be identified. The focus of his review was on the results of the Vera Institute of Justice's community service sentencing project, which used a quasi-experimental design (see McDonald [1986]). The results of this study "give no support to the idea that community service either rehabilitates offenders better or deters further crime more effectively than a short jail term" (McDonald 1992, 189). In terms of cost, McDonald reported that because the sanction was used as a probation enhancement as often as it was used as an alternative to jail, "the project did not result in direct savings to the city's budget for jail operations" (1992, 190).

Day Fines

Although much has been written about the use of fines as an intermediate sanction (see Hillsman and Greene [1992] for an overview), we know remarkably little about the implementation of day fines programs or about the impact of this sanction on offenders. However, the Bureau of Justice Assistance has recently funded day fine demonstration projects at several sites across the country, while the National Institute of Justice is supporting a large-scale evaluation (using a quasi-experimental design) of the implementation and impact of day fines.

Intervention Programs

The most recent wave of changes in offender management in the community is an emerging interest in programs of intervention. These are behavioral change programs that target specific offender problems and seek to reduce recidivism by reducing the impact of these "criminogenic" problems. Andrews et al. (1990) report that intervention programs for high-risk offenders can reduce rearrest rates by 25 percent or more (see also Andrews and Bonta [1994]). These estimates are based upon meta-analytic studies, which combine the results of numerous small evaluation studies into one large study. Meta-analysis, because it "adds up" the results from unrelated studies, has been criticized as leading to suspect conclusions (Lab and Whitehead 1990; Logan and Gaes 1993). Lipsey (1992) has concluded that convincing overall positive results of intervention programs were difficult to discern from the studies in his meta-analytic review. Nevertheless, recent positive findings in broad evaluations of intervention approaches have been associated with a renewed interest in prospects for practices that may change offenders in community settings.

A particularly popular version of these new intervention programs is "cognitive skills training," a strategy developed by Robert Ross and Elizabeth Fabiano (1985). This intervention system improves offenders' general life skills, especially those involving thinking and reasoning. It is argued that these life skills generalize to all areas of personal functioning, and that they can provide ways to solve problems without resort to criminal behavior.

A version of the skills development approach is the "relapse prevention" model, which is commonly used for sex offenders but has applicability to other types of offenses as well. Relapse prevention is built around helping the offender understand "precursors" of criminal relapse, and teaching the offender how to avoid the circumstances that lead to those precursors.

Removing Offenders from Community Supervision

Offenders in the community who violate the conditions of their sentences face the possibility of revocation and prison. But there is evidence that, although violation of programmatic conditions is common, revocation and return to prison are not: while as many as half of all offenders fail to abide fully by the terms of their sentences, only one-fifth of the violators go to prison or jail (Langan 1994). This gap between behavior and consequences seems further to erode confidence in the effectiveness of community-based programs for offenders. Critics portray an image of wanton disregard for program rules followed by little or no sanction from program managers. The result, it is sometimes argued, is a continuing breach of community safety.

This argument is appealing, but is not completely accurate. The question of what should be done when an offender violates the rules of supervision is not a simple one, for several reasons.

First, there is some evidence that the rules being applied to offenders under community supervision are increasing in number and in scope. This has been accompanied by a systematic increase in surveillance capacity to enforce the rules—predominately through urine testing. If more rules and more surveillance are being applied to an increasingly serious population of offenders, then it should not surprise us that noncompliance is observed at higher rates.

Noncompliance may indicate an undisciplined life—which is entirely consistent with the type of person who enters the penal system—but it need not mean a breach of community safety. Indeed, two studies (Baird, Clear, and Harris 1986; Petersilia and Turner 1993) have shown that the violation of technical rules by an offender is not associated with an increased likelihood of arrest for a crime, suggesting that rule violations should not always raise public safety concerns. In fact, some studies have shown that rule violations may be more a matter of bureaucratic manifests than of crime control (Robison and Takagi 1976).

Recognizing this—and recognizing, too, that prisons are already crowded with community corrections failures—many of those who administer community sanctions stress creative responses with rule violators. Instead of an immediate return to prison upon the first violation, a graduated system of sanctions is employed. Depending on the type of rule being violated, the sanctions may begin with increased reporting or more frequent urine tests; continued problems in the program may lead to community service work, restrictions on freedom, or even a few days in jail. In this type of enforcement system, prison is a final resort, reserved only for persistent violators or for those whose violations presage a return to crime.

Thus, while it is fair to recognize the high rates of noncompliance among offenders in the community, it is inaccurate to portray these failures as indications that the programs are not effective. Of the 80 percent of rule violators who are not returned to prison, it may be that most receive a limited sanction of some sort. It may also be that most of these violators are eventually in compliance with program requirements and that few of them are rearrested.

Challenges for Corrections in the Community

There can be no question that, for the foreseeable future, most offenders will be managed in community supervision programs. Given this review of the evidence about these programs, what are the prospects for community-based programs? What challenges do they face? We suggest that there are five challenges, as described in the balance of this chapter.

Prison Crowding and Its Costs

It seems safe to say that unless the existing programs are revamped in extraordinary ways, community corrections agencies will remain of only marginal importance as solutions to problems of institutional crowding. This may seem at least ironic or even preposterous, but our review shows that for the most part community-based programs are designed and run in ways that make them virtually predestined to exacerbate rather than ameliorate prison crowding.

For one thing, most programs' articulation of a target group leads to *enhanced* levels of control and costs, not reduced levels. Most ISPs are probation enhancement programs rather than confinement diversion programs. They seek a "tougher" probation to replace traditional methods, and they target the "toughest" probation cases. This approach can reduce crowding and related costs only by substantial reductions in failure rates compared with traditional probation. As we have seen, the stringent conditions and strict enforcement associated with these programs means they actually produce a *higher* failure rate by promoting revocations that may have little to do with crime (Petersilia and Turner 1993).

Similarly, most shock incarceration programs target first-time offenders, and most exclude violent or previously incarcerated offenders. Often, boot camp programs are limited to persons under a certain age, no higher than early twenties. In most correctional systems in the United States, first-time property offenders do not go to prison anyway. The only first-time offenders who receive terms of confinement are drug offenders—in accord with today's negative attitude toward drugs, these offenders are often excluded from program eligibility as well. By designating such a limited target group, boot camps often guarantee their own irrelevance to the problems confronting institutional corrections systems.

Not only does the choice of target group cast doubt on these programs, but the programs' methods do as well. What has been called "catch 'em and snatch 'em" probation is oriented toward maximum surveillance and minimum tolerance. It is not surprising that these programs lead to high rates of return to prison. The net effect of these programs, then, can be extremely damaging. For example, probation enhancement programs take offenders that would otherwise *not* be prison-bound and place them in programs that actually *increase* their exposure to confinement.

If community corrections are to be able to confront with any durability the problem of prison crowding, three changes will be needed in the design of these programs.

First, the target groups for these programs should be narrowly defined so as to maximize the probability that the program is getting only prison- or jail-bound offenders. Because most jurisdictions experience considerable sentencing disparity, this is not an easy task: many offenders have a moderate chance of serving either prison or nonprison sentences. The two "safe" target groups, in terms of diversion, are offenders whose crimes are serious (particularly violent offenders or drug distributors), and persons who are seriously failing under regular community supervision (see Gendreau, Cullen, and Bonta [1994]). Because of the obvious political considerations attaching to the first choice, most programs opt for community failures. (Although we would point out that in terms of prison cell savings, a person facing a lengthy term for a serious crime represents a far better investment than a person about to serve a few months for a technical violation).

Second, the methods used to supervise these offenders must change. Adjectives like "tough," and "no-nonsense" sound good and inspire public confidence. But these methods often do not conform well to the lives of the people under community supervision. For many of those under community supervision, increased structure and controls may ultimately be helpful, but expecting an easy adjustment to those changes is unrealistic. When these programs adopt a stance which seeks any opportunity to remove a person from the streets, they can be assured of finding plenty of people to remove. What is needed instead is a philosophy that offenders will be kept on the streets by whatever means are available. According to this idea, occasional rules violations are to be expected and worked through with the client.

Third, the consequences of program failure will need to be mediated. Often, the reverse is true: program failures are "taught a lesson," by receiving expanded prison terms. Not only are these terms often undeserved, because they are disproportionate to the conduct for which they are imposed, but they are counterproductive. For example, if a person who would have received a six-month penalty is diverted to one of these programs, we know chances of failure increase. But even if this were not true, when the costs of failure increase as well—say, to a one-year term—the chances that the program will achieve prison savings is made even more remote, for even a 50 percent reduction in failure would amount to a wash in resources, overall.

Surveillance and Its Effectiveness

Of what good is close contact, if its only rationale is to identify the malfeasant and take firm action? Surveillance and control are not values in themselves; they are useful only if they lead to positive results. We have seen that closer surveillance increases program failure rates in ways that do not seem to be associated with crime reduction. Indeed, the use of electronic monitors seems unrelated to actual program compliance—the tighter the monitor, the more frequent the failure—and also, in some ways, unrelated to crime (Austin and Hardyman 1991). Thus, the logical reason for watching people so closely—that doing so will prevent crime or increase compliance—is not supported by the data.

If close supervision is not necessarily effective, is it perhaps benign? There is no direct way to answer this question, but most of us might admit to an uneasiness with the expanded use of surveillance and control by a government agency when the payoff seems so unclear. Putting government agents in peoples' homes in order to find reasons to remove them from those homes should strike all of us as a bit troubling, and a wholesale advancement of this technical capacity might be more than troubling.

The emphasis on surveillance and control also detracts from the time and attention devoted to service delivery. Since both the Rand evaluation and an earlier evaluation of Massachusetts's ISP (Byrne and Kelly 1989) reported significantly lower recidivism rates when offenders received treatment (for substance abuse, employment difficulties, and family problems), an emphasis on treatment seems to be a promising avenue for crime control in the community (see Gendreau, Cullen, and Bonta [1994]).

Ultimately, the question comes down to, Why? That is, what is the reason for the control, and what value is obtained by more nearly perfect knowledge of the person's behavior? In the case of offenders whose crimes become more frequent (or more likely) when drugs are in their system, a program of urine testing makes intuitive sense as a preventive measure. This can be especially well argued, when the resulting offense is likely to be serious, such as a sex offense against a child. However, without an attitude change about how requirements are enforced, a general program of urine testing is likely to expose the ordinary offender to sanctions that decrease our chances of achieving goals of cost containment and community adjustment.

A case can be made, then, that program requirements need to be tailored to individual cases and their circumstances, not applied across the board. Moreover, sanctions need to be designed in ways that promote compliance by trial and error, not by simple threat.

Program Design and Offender Risk

One of the ironies of the changes in community corrections is that the most powerful programs are being front-loaded on the least risky offenders. Boot camps are reserved for youthful first-time offenders; ISPs are restricted to property offenders; electronic monitors are given only to the employed. It is understandable that new programs seek "safe" clients with whom to demonstrate their impact, but a growing body of evidence suggests this is not a wise use of these resources (Byrne and Brewster 1993).

Put in another way, New Jersey's ISP, which provides daily contact with offenders and eligibility for treatment programs that otherwise have waiting lists, is reserved for the *very best risks* in the New Jersey prison system. The worst risks eventually come out on regular parole, in caseloads of a hundred or more. We might wonder if this is not an upside-down use of resources.

Meta-analyses find that intervention programs work best with high-risk clients (Palmer 1992). The reasons are simple: it is not easy to affect a base expectancy failure rate of 5 percent—low-risk—but even a moderately well designed program of structure stands a chance to reduce a 50 percent base rate of failure—high-risk. Yet again, these new programs routinely select from the lesser risk clients in the system. Is it any surprise that the evaluation results seem always to suggest little impact and to be based on small sample sizes?

If these programs are to provide maximum bang for the buck, we must recognize that they need to target cases that have high probability of failure, and bring the failure rates down (not the current strategy, which is too often to target low probability cases and which sends failure rates up).

Overall Community Safety

Studies of offenders in the community find that they account for a minor portion of overall crime in the community. This is counterintuitive, but true. An estimate by Geerken and Hayes (1993) finds that Louisiana probationers and parolees account for only 7 percent of felony arrests in a given year. A federal study estimated that young parolees represented 6 percent of all arrests during their release period. Perhaps this is why Spelman (1994) has estimated that the potential benefits of large increases in incapacitation are quite small, on the order of 4–8 percent. Likewise, the National Research Panel of the National Academy of Sciences has estimated that the tripling of time served by violent felons since 1975 has produced only a 10–15 percent reduction in violent crime (Reiss and Roth 1993).

Clearly, the number of felons under supervision in the community has only marginal implications for the safety of the communities in which they reside. A full review of the evidence on this question is not possible here, but it appears that the way the question has been posed in the past has been wrong. We should not ask *whether* the offender should be on the streets, but *how* the offender should be managed on the streets. In this regard, it appears that

- Intervention programs are promising when applied to higher risk offenders.
- Expanded use of nonprison alternatives does not need to result in expanded criminal behavior, if low-risk offenders are diverted from prison.
- The relaxation of stringent program requirements for low-risk cases need not be associated with increased criminality.

- The levels of criminality, as indicated by arrests, in traditional community programs are low in most jurisdictions.

These are all good indicators that an increased investment in and policy emphasis on community-based methods will not lead to decreases in community safety, and may well increase community safety.

The Problem of Justice

In the 1970s, debate about the meaning justice, and how best to achieve it through the sanctioning process, occupied the penological community. It is testimony to the distance we have come from that debate that only in this last section do we finally raise the question of justice. It is a sad demonstration of the state of public policy that a lengthy discussion of the offender in the community could proceed with so little intrusion of the question of what is just.

In the 1980s, the calibration of penalties in this country has changed. The advent of three-strikes legislation, the example of the federal sentencing guidelines, the ubiquity of mandatory penalties has meant that what is seen as "right" or "fair" is different, as a matter of scale, from what was held to be true twenty years ago. The irony is that while the popular public idea has it that this is a lenient nation, we have become markedly less so over the course of two decades.

It is hard for community penalties to compete with confinement for public favor when the question is punishment and the standard is measured in years and even decades. Certainly, some research suggests that some prisoners would rather stay in prison than be released on the most stringent supervision programs—the dubious distinction of being more onerous than prison is an odd badge for a community program to wear (see Clear and Braga [1994]; Petersilia [1994]; Petersilia and Deschenes [1994]).

Perhaps in the future the justice question will no longer be dominated by images of harshness, discipline, loss, and suffering. In their place might be appeals to the capacity to make amends to victims and the community, to the maintenance of family ties and parenting possibilities, to the opportunity to contribute to society rather than merely be a net drain on its resources.

When—if ever—the popular idea of justice loses its current mean-spirited distortion and becomes broad enough to embrace these ideas of basic social justice, community-based methods will have the potential for sustained importance and a central place in the scheme of policy making.

JOHN J. DIIULIO, JR.,
STEVEN K. SMITH, AND
AARON J. SAIGER

THE FEDERAL ROLE IN CRIME CONTROL

Congress finds further that crime is essentially a local problem that
must be dealt with by State and local governments if it is to be
controlled effectively.

— *Title I, 1968 Omnibus Crime Control and Safe Streets Act*

The Congress finds that legalization of illegal drugs, on the Federal or
State level, is an unconscionable surrender in a war in which, for the
future of our country, and the lives of our children, there can be no
substitute for total victory.

— *Section 5011, 1988 Anti–Drug Abuse Act*

In the last three decades, violent crimes have increased by 300
percent. Over the last three years, almost a third of Americans have
either had themselves or someone in their families victimized by
crime. . . . What are we going to do about this? . . . We have to
recognize, as all of you know, that most laws—criminal laws—are
state laws and most criminal law enforcement is done by local police
officials.

—President Bill Clinton, *remarks before Ohio Peace Officers Training
Academy, London, Ohio, February 15, 1994*

As the other chapters in this volume make clear, there is no shortage of
general ideas about how government can combat crime. But general ideas
are not public policies, public policies are not self-executing, and even well-
executed public policies do not always produce predictable and desirable
results.

The American political system is designed in ways that make it difficult to translate national policy choices into effective subnational administrative action. Administratively, the single most important feature of the system is federalism, the constitutional and political division of authority between the national government and the state and local governments. Many countries (Germany, Canada) have some type of federal system, but in none do subnational political units retain as much power over so many domains (education, law enforcement) or regularly exercise as much influence in national policy making as state and local governments do in the United States. In a recent study of "government capabilities in the United States and abroad," federalism was identified as one of the most distinctive, and probably the most consequential, feature of America's national policy-making process.[1]

And so it is. Since the end of World War II, virtually every major domestic policy initiative in the United States has involved state and local governments. This pattern is illustrated in the shared Social Security financing and payment arrangements under the Social Security Act (administered by the states subject to federal review for compliance with minimum standards set by the secretary of health and human services), the management for active state and local participation in land use under the Federal Land Policy and Management Act (regionally administered subject to federal review for compliance with planning criteria set by the secretary of the interior), and the state implementation of the Clean Air Act, under which state officials develop specific plans for environmental cleanup (subject to standards set by the Environmental Protection Agency).[2]

From welfare to economic development, health reform to environmental policy, transportation to housing, the national government in the United States has almost no direct hand in administering the domestic policies it establishes. Instead, the national government employs various tools to get state and local governments to govern in accordance with nationally stated (though often vaguely defined) goals. Some tools are formal: grants, tax expenditures, regulations, contracts, and loans. Others are informal: arguments, threats, and cajolery. But whatever tools it uses, rare are the circumstances in which policies formulated in Washington are implemented with ease and efficiency beyond the beltway.

Administratively and politically, all national domestic policies are to one degree or another prisoners of federalism. In America's federal system, different levels of government routinely "impose conflicting programs, raising implementation costs and making problems of coordinating objectives" virtually unresolvable.[3]

As a rule, when Washington attempts to act in policy areas where state and local governments have traditionally been dominant, and when it tries to alter how citizens or bureaucrats behave (getting people on public assistance to choose work over welfare, getting local cops to do more foot patrol) rather than, or in addition to, altering individuals' incomes or institutions' budgets (sending unemployed single mothers their monthly welfare checks, sending local governments federal dollars to do with what they please), the problems of intergovernmental relations and policy implementation amount.

These problems can be diminished, but they cannot be entirely dissolved, by keeping national programs focused on straightforward economic or other clear-cut objectives; some of the most famous studies of implementation failures are tales of limited (and, at the time they were tried, quite popular) national programs that nonetheless bit the dust of administrative federalism.[4]

Nor can the problems be met simply by developing abstract principles governing what functions belong to which levels of government. As generations of policy makers have learned, the "question of what level of government should act to solve a particular problem is seldom decided by rational criteria."[5] The realities of governance in America's federal system permit no firm attachments to any "sorting out" principles, while contemporary political pressures often trigger national action in areas where the federal government has little, if any, knowledge or capacity to act effectively, and state governments are hardly better prepared.[6]

For good or ill, considerations of what it actually takes to implement national policies via state and local governments have rarely conditioned national policy responses to complex social and economic maladies. So it is today with crime policy.

Between 1968 and 1994, the national government of the United States assumed ever greater responsibility for making, administering, and funding the country's criminal justice policies. But crime has been, and continues to be, a state and local responsibility. In a typical year, subnational governments spend over six times as much on all justice activities (police, courts, corrections), convict almost seventy times as many violent criminals, and hold nine times as many prison inmates as the federal government does.[7] Likewise, the federal government investigated approximately 114,000 suspects for federal offenses in 1991.[8] By comparison, in 1991 state and local law enforcement agencies reported an estimated fourteen million arrests, including slightly more than one million for drug violations alone.[9] In few areas of domestic governance does Washington remain so much the junior partner.

Today, however, many policy makers, judges, journalists, analysts, activists, and average citizens insist the federal role in crime control can and should be expanded greatly. For example, some believe that the national government should supply the human and financial resources for programs intended to prevent at-risk juveniles from getting into trouble with the law, help adults convicted of crimes to resist illegal drugs, and ameliorate the social and economic conditions (poverty, joblessness, chronic welfare dependency) that are widely supposed to be among the root causes of crime.

Others believe that the national government can and should provide state and local justice agencies with whatever technical, legal, or financial assistance they need to put more police officers on the streets, crack down on violent and repeat criminals, and build and operate additional jails and prisons. Still others believe that the federal government should adopt a broad mix of prevention and punishment policies.

The federal government will in all likelihood expand its role in making, administering, and funding crime policy. But it is by no means clear that it can do so with predictable and desirable consequences. Nor is it clear whether anything it does will ultimately meet the goals of those who called upon it to act in the first place. Whatever is desired—prevention and programs, punishment and prisons, or both—those who look to Washington ought not to look past the political, intellectual, and most of all, administrative obstacles to a broader and more effective federal role in crime control.

Political and Intellectual Barriers

Historically, Americans have demanded a justice system that apprehends and visits harm upon the guilty (delivers punishment); makes offenders either more virtuous or more law abiding, or both (provides rehabilitation); dissuades actual and would-be offenders from criminal pursuits (achieves specific and general deterrence); protects innocent citizens from being victimized by convicted criminals in state custody (effects incapacitation); and invites most convicted criminals, following a court-sanctioned period of state custody, to return to society with most or all of the rights of free citizenship restored to them (accomplishes reintegration).

Not only have Americans wanted a justice system that could somehow achieve these multiple, vague, and contradictory goals; they have wanted one that could do so without violating the public conscience (flouting humane treatment), jeopardizing the public law (infringing civil rights and liberties), draining the public purse (disregarding cost containment), and abandoning the tradition of state and local public administration (contravening federalism).

Any justice system would be hard-pressed to achieve some or all of these goals (punishment, rehabilitation, deterrence, incapacitation, reintegration) while honoring many or most of these constraints (humane treatment, civil rights and liberties, cost containment, federalism). Compared with the United States, in most contemporary democracies the goals of the justice system are more rationalized (either punishment, deterrence, and incapacitation or rehabilitation and reintegration), and the constraints on how the justice system operates are relatively few (limited rights for the accused and convicted, direct national administration and finance of all or most justice agencies).[10]

But some key features of the American justice system are changing. Mounting evidence suggests that the tradition of state and local justice administration, and the concomitant proscription against a large national government role in crime control, may be weaker today than at any point in American history. In a February 1994 poll of 1,531 adult Americans, 83 percent of respondents believed that the federal government could do much more to make the crime problem better.[11] In a May 1987 poll of 1,500 adult Americans, 52 percent of respondents claimed that the federal government was not spending enough to control crime, while 33 percent said that spending levels were "about right" and 9 percent said that they were "too big."[12] There is growing public sentiment that Washington can and should become an equal or senior partner with subnational governments in crime policy.

This shift in public sentiment has been in the works for about six decades. In the 1930s a number of studies challenged the decentralized character of the American justice system and called for centralizing reforms at the state and local level.[13] The 1967 report of the President's Commission on Law Enforcement and the Administration of Justice did not call for a vastly expanded federal role in all aspects of crime control (policy making, administration, funding). But it did call on the federal government to expand dramatically its technical and financial support of ongoing anticrime efforts and centralizing administrative reforms at the subnational level (state and local planning, scientific research, grants for operational innovations).[14]

Over the last quarter century, federal policy makers have reinforced the idea that the national government can and should be centrally involved in crime control. In his successful 1968 presidential campaign, Richard M. Nixon made "law and order" a national political issue, and it has since been a permanent fixture of the federal policy agenda.[15]

Indeed, the question is no longer whether the national government should be involved in crime control, but how. For example, in the 1930s many people denounced the new U.S. Bureau of Prisons (BOP) as an affront to federalism; as late as the mid-1970s, some were still waging a federalism argument against the agency's existence or expansion.[16] By the 1990s, however, the BOP held about 10 percent of the nation's prison population. A proposal to place tens of thousands of state prisoners in "regional" federal facilities met with some opposition, but virtually none of it was based on a principled defense of federalism. Similarly, as late as the 1960s and 1970s, the idea of using U.S. military forces in any aspect of civilian law enforcement, including the "war on drugs," met with instant and widespread opposition. But in the 1990s national military personnel were enlisted in many antidrug efforts. Such debate as occurred over this radical break with tradition was mainly concerned with the nature and extent of the military's involvement, not whether it should be involved in civilian law enforcement in the first place.[17]

As public thinking about crime has become more Washington-centered, it has also become more conservative. In his comprehensive review of post-1965 survey research and polling data on crime, William G. Mayer concludes:

> The conventional wisdom on this issue is that . . . public opinion became increasingly outraged by horror stories about brutal criminals set free on legal technicalities or through the ministrations of misguided social workers. And, in this case, the conventional wisdom turns out to be quite accurate. From the mid-1960s to the late 1980s, there is clear, strong evidence that American public opinion became substantially more conservative in its assessment of how to deal with crime.[18]

But this confluence of trends on crime—rising support for national action and tough anticrime measures—has not led to a thoroughgoing rationalization of justice system goals and constraints. To anyone familiar with the basic history and political dynamics of crime in America, that should not be too surprising.

The history of crime policy in America is replete with examples of shifts in public sentiment about how to handle criminals. From the colonial era to the present, the proverbial pendulum of public opinion on crime and punishment has swung back and forth.[19] But even in "get tough" or "do justice" periods there has been substantial public support for efforts to prevent at-risk juveniles from turning to crime and to keep ex-offenders from returning to it. And even in "go easy" or "show mercy" periods there has been no lack of public support for catching and punishing criminals.[20]

Arguably, the history of these swings in opinion reflects the profound conflict of values within the American penal credo, a credo that demands both justice and mercy, both punishment and forgiveness, both stern custody and humane treatment.[21]

But even if the public were to resolve this tension in favor of one set of values or the other, it is by no means certain that crime policy and justice operations would reflect the settled view of the majority. On many domestic issues, there is a gap between persistent majority preferences and actual public policies.[22] Political science research on criminal justice is scarce, but it is clear that crime is an issue on which there is often a high degree of opinion-policy incongruence.[23] As Mayer has shown, since 1965 public opinion on crime has been moving to the right.[24] But it is not clear that public policy on crime has followed public opinion on it. For example, in the 1980s the public demanded more police, but most big-city police forces contracted. Likewise, the public demanded long, fixed mandatory prison terms. Many states passed such laws, but about three of every four persons under correctional supervision at any given time were placed on probation or parole, and most violent criminals and recidivists spent well under half their sentences in confinement.[25] And in the early 1990s, such highly popular anticrime measures as mandatory sentences of life without parole for thrice-convicted violent criminals (three-strikes-and-you're-out initiatives) were mainly the fruit of grassroots campaigns by victims' rights organizations in the state of Washington and in other jurisdictions where legislators had previously failed to consider the policy or voted it down.[26]

Of course, it is conceivable that, on the march to an enlarged federal role, Americans and their elected representatives could lay aside their historic ambivalence about the goals of the justice system and relax one or more of the constraints that they have traditionally placed upon its operations. For example, as some fear and others hope, the public and its leaders could opt to bring the full weight of the national government to bear on urban street crime, focus more or less exclusively on the goal of public protection, and rely primarily on incarceration as the means to that end.

But neither the history nor the political science of the subject suggests that any such decisive policy shift is likely. If experience is any guide, the national government will continue do something to satisfy each of a diverse set of views on crime policy, without adopting any one, single, overarching vision of how best to combat crime.

Even if the political barriers to a broader and more effective federal role in crime control could be lowered—an end to public ambivalence about the goals and constraints of the justice system, the dawn of perfect opinion-policy congruence on crime—the intellectual hurdles to it would nonetheless remain quite high. To the extent that criminology offers a scientific understanding of the causes of crime, it is mainly with respect to variables (age, gender) over which policy makers can exercise little, if any, direct control. Despite the many advances in research and thinking reported on in the other chapters in this volume, criminology has yet to produce an empirically meaningful body of policy-oriented knowledge.

Still, it is important to remember that the scientific study of crime in America has benefited greatly from the national government's quarter-century-old effort to produce, preserve, and disseminate data and analyses relevant to understanding and controlling crime. As is true in such areas as health policy, the national government's biggest comparative advantage in crime policy may well be as a spur to scientific research. This point is further addressed at the close of this chapter.

Administrative Barriers

According to one estimate, by 1994 the number of federal crimes had grown to 3,000.[27] Until the 1980s, the federal government was primarily concerned with crimes committed on federal property; against federal officials, by federal officials; or in other narrowly defined, statutorily mandated areas of jurisdiction. The scope of these federal statutory crimes was quite limited. But the "war on drugs" of the 1980s, culminating in the Anti–Drug Abuse Act of

1988, changed all that. Today, the federal government employs a wide range of crime control measures that state and local governments have neither the authority nor, in many cases, the resources to employ.

Basically, the federal government can employ three anticrime strategies:

1. Policy making: The federal government can regulate a virtually unlimited range of activities believed to contribute to street crime (assault, rape, robbery, burglary, drug dealing, murder) and white collar crime (fraud, deceptive business practices, illegal financial transactions). For example, all levels of government can regulate such things as the availability of handguns; indeed, many states have gun-control and antidrug laws that are stricter than the federal government's. But only the federal government can regulate such things as immigration flows, interstate commerce, and global corporate activities.

2. Policy administration: The federal government can declare an undesirable activity a federal crime, thereby bringing the full force of federal law enforcement (the Federal Bureau of Investigation, the Drug Enforcement Agency, even the U.S. military in overseas drug interdiction efforts), prosecution (U.S. attorneys), and adjudication (literally "making a federal case" before a federal court) to bear on the activity.

3. Policy funding: The federal government can provide human, financial, and informational resources (technical experts or advisers, money, studies and statistics that compare crime trends across many jurisdictions) and is in a unique position to coordinate (or legally mandate) interjurisdictional anticrime plans.

To date, the federal government has made two substantial forays into crime policy. The first effort, discussed in the next section as Case 1, centered on the Law Enforcement Assistance Administration (LEAA). The second effort, discussed as Case 2, was the war against drugs and the development of the block grant Edward Byrne Memorial State and Local Law Enforcement Assistance Program (hereafter the Byrne Program) administered by the main administrative successor to the LEAA, the Bureau of Justice Assistance (BJA). The record in each case provides a wealth of information about the administrative nature of American federalism, the irreducible complexities of intergovernmental relations, and the impediments to effective national government action against crime and other complex social problems.

Case 1: The Rise and Demise of the LEAA, 1968–1982

The LEAA was established by Title I of the 1968 Omnibus Crime Control and Safe Streets Act. A brainchild of President Lyndon B. Johnson's Commission on Law Enforcement and the Administration of Justice, the LEAA was launched during the first Nixon administration. The LEAA sponsored law enforcement training institutes for state and local officials, began to develop national criminal justice data-gathering and information-sharing networks, spurred ambitious criminal rehabilitation programs, and encouraged local community-based crime control initiatives. [28]

Essentially, however, the LEAA was a grant-making agency. The initial trickle of federal dollars into state and local coffers began with the Law Enforcement Assistance Act of 1965. This act, administered by the U.S. Department of Justice, Office of Law Enforcement Assistance, provided slightly more than $20 million over fiscal years 1966–1968 to state and local agencies and other criminal justice organizations. [29] This program was repealed and superseded by the 1968 act that created the LEAA.

Title I of the 1968 act stated that

> the declared policy of the Congress is to assist State and local governments in strengthening and improving law enforcement at every level by national assistance. It is the purpose of this title to (1) encourage States and units of general local government to prepare and adopt comprehensive plans based upon their evaluation of State and local problems of law enforcement; (2) authorize grants to States and units of local government in order to improve and strengthen law enforcement; and (3) encourage research and development directed toward the improvement of law enforcement and the development of new methods for the prevention and reduction of crime and the detection and apprehension of criminals. [30]

The LEAA's primary mission was to curb organized crime and control urban civil disorders. [31] Other efforts at crime fighting in the 1968 legislation authorized expanded wiretapping and electronic surveillance to fight organized crime, and outlawed firearms possession by felons and other specifically defined individuals.

But in no sense did the LEAA represent a full-scale federal effort to combat crime. The LEAA was never a vehicle for the statutory expansion of federal crimes and sanctions (making crime policy) or for the direct implementation of federal crime laws (administering crime policy). Congress had specifically prevented the LEAA and the executive branch from expanding their operational involvement in local crime-fighting activities. This was mainly a result of pressures within Congress and of concerns that the LEAA represented a possible first step toward the nationalization of state and local police agencies. Section 518(a) of the 1968 act specifically warned against federal operational encroachment on state and local law enforcement: "Nothing contained in this title or any other Act shall be construed to authorize any department, agency, officer, or employee of the United States to exercise any direction, supervision, or control over any police force or any other law enforcement agency of any state or any political subdivision thereof."

Thus, the LEAA was designed and functioned basically as a check-writing machine for channeling federal dollars to state and local governments (funding crime policy). As has often happened when federal money has been made available to state and local governments, recipients of the LEAA's funds demanded and got more. In this case, they exerted pressure to expand the scope of allowable expenditures from strictly law enforcement (mainly policing) to other areas of criminal justice. For example, changes to the LEAA as a result of the 1970 Omnibus Crime Control Act required that LEAA grant 20 percent of all funds allocated to it for correctional programs and facilities.[32]

Thus, as Table 19.1 shows, during fiscal years 1969 through 1977, the LEAA's budget increased in every year except one. In real (inflation-adjusted) terms, the LEAA's fiscal 1972 budget was greater than the total budget for the Justice Department in fiscal 1968. By 1980 the LEAA had spent about $8 billion on state and local crime control.[33]

But the LEAA's demise was as rapid as its rise. During his successful 1976 bid for the presidency, Jimmy Carter charged that the LEAA had wasted billions of dollars "while making almost no contribution to reducing crime."[34] Whether or not this charge was accurate, the fact remained that crime rates were much higher in 1976 than they were in 1968. For example, between 1968 and 1976 the total annual crime rate (number of crimes per 100,000 resident population) rose from 3,370 to 5,287; over the same period, the violent crime rate rose from 298 to 468.[35]

Meanwhile, the LEAA's statewide criminal justice planning activities were

TABLE 19.1
Distribution of LEAA Funds, Fiscal
1969–1979

Fiscal year	Funds distributed (constant dollars, 1979)
1969	$118,692
1970	$501,346
1971	$948,199
1972	$1,213,571
1973	$1,398,639
1974	$1,281,951
1975	$1,207,751
1976	$1,033,035
1977[a]	$1,147,655
1978	$720,710
1979	$646,488

a. Includes $204,960 from 1976-TQ during fiscal year conversion.
SOURCE: Law Enforcement Assistance Administration, *LEAA Eleventh Annual Report: Fiscal Year 1979* (Washington, D.C.: United States Department of Justice 1980), 97. Recalculated in constant 1979 dollars.

widely perceived as a failure.[36] The federal government was awash in new data on crime, but nobody, least of all in Washington, seemed to know what to do with it.

The LEAA's budget dropped like a rock between fiscal years 1978 and 1980, and it lost most of its research and related functions to other agencies of the Justice Department. The Reagan administration phased out the LEAA in 1982, but by that time the agency had already been in fiscal limbo for about three years.

There were many different schools of thought about whether the LEAA had actually failed to help state and local governments control crime, and, if so, why. Some argued that the LEAA simply had not spent enough. In contrast, others argued that the LEAA had spent plenty but had spent it badly, overspending on police and underspending on prevention and treatment programs (or vice versa). Still others argued that the crime problem was simply beyond the reach of government action, whatever the federal role.

Regardless of what explanation they favored, most observers agreed that in funding state and local criminal justice agencies the LEAA was funding a loose confederation of literally thousands of different agencies operating under a mind-boggling array of political and legal constraints. But what if, some asked, the LEAA had not been restricted to funding state and local efforts? What if, in effect, the federal government made crime policy as well and allowed states the administrative flexibility they required to meet national goals? Would that have resulted in either a workable national crime control strategy or a reduction in crime, or both?

Case 2: The War on Drugs, 1982–1993

As the 1980s ushered in the war on drugs, the federal government began taking a different approach from that of the LEAA. President Ronald Reagan's 1983 budget message to Congress stated plainly: "Public safety is primarily a state and local responsibility. This administration does not believe that providing criminal justice assistance in the form of grants or contracts is an appropriate use of federal funds."[37] Except for drips of LEAA money that were already in the pipeline to states and localities, the LEAA's funding faucets remained shut.

But in the 1980s, while Washington reconsidered its role as a crime policy funder, it vastly increased its role as a crime policy maker and administrator. Table 19.2 characterizes the differences between these two eras in federal-state relations in crime control. The federal crime-fighting programs of the 1980s and early 1990s were characterized by a statutorily based emphasis on incarcerating drug traffickers and possessors, gang members, and firearms violators. Under the color of the 1986 and 1988 Anti–Drug Abuse Acts, federal law enforcement agencies, and U.S. attorneys around the country, began to play a major role in what had previously been a state and

TABLE 19.2
Federal-State Relations in Crime Control

Type of activity	LEAA 1968–80	War on drugs, 1980–92
Making policy		
Statutory expansion of federal crimes		
and sanctions	Low	High
Administering policy		
Involvement of Federal agencies at state		
level	Low	High
Funding policy		
Direct Federal funds to state and local		Low (1982–88)
agencies	High	Moderate (1989–93)

local effort as local officials increasingly worked with federal prosecutors and investigators.

The Bush administration (1989–1993) brought Washington near to its first full-court press in making, administering, and funding crime policy. As Table 19.3 shows, in these years the war on drugs activated federal agencies across the bureaucratic spectrum in a call to budgetary arms. Moreover, as Table 19.4 indicates, between fiscal years 1989 and 1992, federal antidrug

TABLE 19.3
Federal Drug Control Budget Authority, 1991

	Millions of dollars
Total	10,841.4
Department of	
Justice	3,842.4
Health and Human Services	1,924.9
Defense	1,042.5
Treasury	977.6
Transportation	749.6
Education	683.1
Veterans Affairs	473.1
State	257.6
Housing and Urban Development	150.0
Labor	67.6
Interior	35.7
Agriculture	16.1
Judiciary	294.1
Agency for International Development	202.9
Office of National Drug Control Policy	104.3
ACTION	12.5
U.S. Information Agency	7.3
Small Business Administration	0.1

SOURCE: Office of National Drug Control Policy, *National Drug Control Strategy: A Nation Responds to Drug Use* (Washington, D.C., January 1992), 144–45.

TABLE 19.4
Byrne Antidrug Law Enforcement
Formula Grant Appropriations, Fiscal
1988–1992

Fiscal year	Thousands of dollars
1989	118,800
1990	395,101
1991	423,000
1992	423,000

SOURCE: United States General Accounting Office, *War on Drugs: Federal Assistance to State and Local Drug Enforcement*, GAO/GGD-93-86 (Washington, D.C., April 1993), 5.

formula grants more than tripled, to some $423 million. The National Drug Control Budget increased from approximately $1.5 billion in 1981 to $12.7 billion in 1993; 28 percent of the 1993 drug budget ($3.5 billion) was targeted as direct assistance to state and local governments.[38] Between 1980 and 1992 the number of federal convictions for drug trafficking increased about 300 percent, and the number of convicted drug traffickers sentenced to prison increased about 400 percent.[39] Furthermore, the number of drug offenders behind federal prison bars increased from fewer than 5,000 to more than 27,000 between 1980 and 1990.[40]

The states mirrored the federal government in arresting, prosecuting, and incarcerating drug offenders. Between 1982 and 1991, the number of arrests for drug abuse violations increased by more than 50 percent to over one million.[41] Between 1979 and 1991 the fraction of state prisoners who were drug offenders rose from about 6 percent to 21 percent.[42]

But it is difficult to find anyone who thinks that the federal war on drugs has been any more successful than the LEAA was in meeting expectations. The criticism of the federal drug war comes not merely from drug legalization advocates but from mainstream analysts and law enforcement officials themselves.[43] And although they cannot be taken simply as a referendum on the efficacy of the federal drug war, the 1994 public opinion surveys that identified crime as the nation's number one problem and demanded more action from Washington could hardly be read as a vote of public confidence.[44]

But those who would argue that the problem with the federal drug war has been mainly a problem of strategy (too much enforcement, not enough treatment) need to be reminded that, even if we actually knew what worked in the way of crime prevention or criminal rehabilitation (and precious little is known), no federal policy in criminal justice or other areas is self-executing. Indeed, the record of federal policy making is replete with examples of major domestic policy initiatives that stalled or sank after striking the administrative icebergs of intergovernmental implementation.[45]

Even what look like relatively simple federal funding programs can pose simply enormous implementation problems. Consider, for example, what happened after the LEAA was fiscally neutered in 1980 and laid officially to rest in 1982. The Anti–Drug Abuse Acts of 1986 and 1988 created a new block grant program to fund state and local justice agencies. Administratively, a new office within the Department of Justice—the Bureau of Justice Assistance (BJA)—picked up where the LEAA had left off, albeit with a much smaller budget (roughly $425 million in formula grants and $50 million in discretionary grants annually since fiscal year 1990).

The BJA is strictly a grant-making agency.[46] It makes no arrests, tries no cases, and incarcerates no one. Instead, it is a federal agency that disburses funds to states, monitors its grantees' expenditures, and reviews crime control strategies. Each state must designate an agency (usually a "state planning agency") to prepare "a statewide strategy for drug and violent crime control programs which improve the functioning of the criminal justice system, with an emphasis on drug trafficking, violent crime and serious offenders." The state submits this strategy to BJA, and within sixty days the BJA approves the strategy and awards the grant money, which is calculated on a straightforward population-based allocation formula.

But what is a "drug and violent crime control strategy"? The answer, in practice, is pretty much whatever the state agencies say it is.[47] The state agencies that receive block grant funding have wide discretion to determine which types of programs to emphasize. As the Byrne Program is defined, high-level drug investigations are as good (or bad) as street-level sweeps; traditional policing is no more prized (or devalued) than community policing; drug treatment programs are neither more nor less acceptable than "user accountability" or "zero tolerance" efforts. Fundamentally, grant recipients need only to stay within the boundaries set by the twenty-one statutorily specified "purpose areas." Purpose areas for allowable expenditures range from "prison industry projects" to "multijurisdictional task forces" to "anti-terrorism plans for deep draft ports, international airports, and other important facilities."[48] These "purpose areas" encompass virtually any conceivable crime- or drug-related initiative. The BJA has little administrative authority to steer the states in any specific strategic direction.

The state agencies distribute their Byrne Program funds to state and local operational agencies. In fiscal year 1993, about 65 percent of the funds went to local projects. During fiscal years 1991 to 1993, the single largest funded priority, representing one-third of the funds, was multi-jurisdictional task force activities.[49]

The Byrne Program requires that a certain fraction of funds (consistent with the fraction of total statewide criminal justice spending contributed by the local governments) go to local, rather than state, projects. Also, according to the Crime Control Act of 1990, states must allocate at least 5 percent of their formula grant funds to improve criminal justice records. In fiscal year 1993, this resulted in more than $26 million being devoted to criminal justice record improvement.[50] Beyond that, the states are free to administer the monies largely as they wish, but the interstate and intrastate differences in how the federal dollars get spent, by whom, and under what conditions are tremendous. Projects funded under the formula grant must receive at least 25 percent nonfederal support in cash. Also, except for multi-jurisdictional task forces, projects can be funded for no more than forty-eight months.[51]

Thus, the Byrne Program implementation chain runs from Congress to BJA to the states to the state-selected grantees, often multi-jurisdictional conglomerates that involve several interlocking relationships among localities and agencies. Some large states require counties to prepare local criminal justice strategies, and then to stand as sub-subgrantors to the operational areas in their local areas; others have no such structures. Likewise, some states require that the BJA program planners coordinate their work with their state counterparts in drug treatment and prevention; others have no such requirements.

The BJA gives money to fifty-six state and territorial planning entities. Each of these agencies has multiple subgrantees. Many states make over fifty subgrants a year. This is not what some public administration experts have called "double discretion" but more like "triple," "quadruple," or "quintuple discretion."[52] The administrative complexity of the Byrne Program makes it difficult, and perhaps impossible, to assess the program's impact on violent crime, drug trafficking or other specific crime prevention goals on a national scale.

One answer, of course, might be to restrict the states' discretion and strictly limit state spending latitude. But that very "solution" to the inherent problems posed by intergovernmental implementation is what hastened the demise of the LEAA, which earmarked formula funds and tied the hands of state and local officials. Indeed, it was to avoid repeating this mistake that Congress designed the Byrne Program to rely mainly on procedural regulation. In practice, however, this approach has limitations, and the BJA finds itself flooded with required "program and planning data" from subnational jurisdictions that it can neither process nor interpret in a nonarbitrary way.

The BJA has a well-deserved reputation for dedicated employees and first-rate administrators. But the administrative problems of federalism are often bigger than the best bureaucrats can master.

Contemporary Proposals

In mid-1994, the Congress was considering another major crime bill containing at least three key provisions that would require a greater federal role in crime control: life without parole for thrice-convicted violent offenders; making a certain portion of federal funds contingent upon the state action to ensure that prisoners spent at least 85 percent of their sentenced time in confinement; and the addition of 100,000 new, community-oriented police officers.

The impact of the first provision, known popularly as "three strikes and you're out," is likely to be small because a relatively small number of violent recidivists are processed by federal courts. For example, in 1991, there were 34,655 new court commitments to federal prisons. Only 5.4 percent, or 1,871, of them were persons whose sole or "most serious offense" of conviction was a violent offense (homicide, kidnapping, rape, other sexual assault, robbery, assault.)[53] If as many as one-tenth of these convictions were for a third violent felony—a high estimate given the recidivism profile of federal prisoners—then a federal three-strikes law, were it in effect in 1991, would have affected only 187 persons, or about one-half of 1 percent of all persons sent to federal prisons in that year. By comparison, of the 317,000 new court commitments to state prisons in 1991, about 30 percent, or almost 95,000, were for violent offenses.[54] If just one-tenth of them were on their "third strike"—a low estimate given the recidivism profile of state prisoners—then the same law in the states would have affected 9,500 persons, a figure equal to 3 percent of all persons committed to state prisons in 1991, and fifty times the number that would have been put away for life under the federal three-strikes law.

The second provision, known popularly as "truth in sentencing," would have a major impact if the federal government could induce most states to adopt the policy as their own. As of this writing, however, that seems unlikely. Under federal sentencing laws, persons sent to federal prison now serve 85 percent of their sentences in confinement. By contrast, most states place prisoners in the community well before they have served as much as half their sentenced time in confinement. For example, in 1991 thirty-four states released 325,757 prisoners, 90 percent of them to community-based supervision. About half of those offenders had served a year or less in prison before their releases. On average, they served 35 percent of their maximum sentences before release. This average held for all types of offenders. Thus, murderers received a maximum sentence of twenty years but served less than eight years (under 40 percent of their maximum sentences) in prison before their release. Drug traffickers received a maximum sentence of about four years but served only about fourteen months (35 percent of their maximum sentences) in prison before their release.[55] No systematic studies have yet been done which estimate carefully the impact that truth-in-sentencing laws would have on rates of criminal victimization, on prison populations, or on other relevant variables. But it is reasonable to suppose that, over time, such laws would double the prison population in most states. Because of the financial burdens of keeping more offenders behind bars for more years, few states have adopted such laws, and some state leaders have indicated that they would sooner forgo federal funds—which, they believe, would cover only a fraction of the total costs of implementing the laws—rather than comply with any federal truth-in-sentencing policy.

The last provision would increase police manpower and foster community-style policing. This approach has generally won widespread support although several program concerns have been voiced. For example, once all factors are taken into account (three shifts, fractions of officers on desk duty, sick leave, disability leave, vacations), it takes about ten police officers to put one police officer on the beat around the clock.[56] Thus, while 100,000 new officers represents a substantial addition to the approximately 600,000 officers now employed by state and local agencies,[57] in reality it translates into about 10,000 around-the-clock cops. Moreover, the history of federal funding in this area suggests that the funds for new police officers are likely to be distributed widely among scores, even hundreds, of jurisdictions, thereby further diluting the measure's direct impact on particularly high crime areas. Also, as each of the federal crime bills that were under consideration in mid-1994 were written, the federal funds would basically serve as seed money. Within six years or sooner, all jurisdictions receiving the manpower and community-policing funds would assume the full financial burden of maintaining the additional officers on active duty. Finally, with a grant program of this magnitude, the agency that would be responsible for administering the provision, BJA, would have to expand quickly in order to manage the traffic in grant proposals, conduct oversight, and measure impacts.[58]

Conclusion

The other chapters in this volume provide plenty of data and analyses that should help one to decide whether federal policies aimed at stiffening penalties for violent crime, lengthening the amount of time served behind bars by violent and repeat offenders, or increasing the number of police on the streets would have much, some, or virtually no impact on the probability that law-abiding citizens will be murdered, assaulted, raped, robbed, burglarized, or harmed by drug trafficking. They also provide evidence and arguments about the efficacy of juvenile justice programs, drug treatment efforts, and much more.

In closing, our purpose is not to pronounce on the wisdom of any subset of these policy proposals. Rather, it is to remind all of those involved in the crime debate that, whatever their beliefs and proposals, the national government now has little ability to implement policies that depend almost entirely on state and local governments for their actual, day-to-day administration, and which aim at changing the behavior of countless people in government and in the community. The federal government can give money to the states for "prison construction" or "crime prevention." But even in the former case, it will have no shortage of difficulty in tracking just how the money was spent and with what, if any, impact on the "crime problem."

Likewise, the federal government can give billions of dollars to state and local governments to hire more police officers and develop "community policing" strategies. But, even in the abstract, it is very difficult to specify what changes in police behavior would constitute community policing; how to identify, document, and measure the performance of departments that do some form of community policing; and whether, ceteris paribus, departments that institutionalize community policing to some degree achieve desirable public goals either more fully or more efficiently than otherwise comparable departments that remain organized along more traditional lines.[59]

The record in such areas as youth and family policy, environmental policy, welfare policy, transportation policy, and health policy shows how human and financial resources can be drained from the leaky bucket of administrative federalism.[60] To date, the implementation, management, and federalism issues posed by a broader national role in crime control have received very little attention. Criminal justice experts need to interact more closely with public management specialists if they are to gain an adequate appreciation of the realities of intergovernmental administration. And national policy makers need to think more in terms of "management impact statements," that is, assessments of the likely administrative barriers to national policy action in crime and other areas.

Whether the administrative barriers to an expanded national role in crime control can be overcome remains an open question. But to continue to debate and analyze crime policy without due consideration of these administrative challenges is to exaggerate the ease with which crime can be affected by public policy in general, and by national policy in particular.

V

REFLECTIONS

ALFRED BLUMSTEIN AND JOAN PETERSILIA

20

INVESTING IN CRIMINAL JUSTICE RESEARCH

The previous chapters in this book have all reported on various aspects of the crime and criminal justice issues they were addressing. In reviewing those chapters, and in contrasting them with corresponding chapters in *Crime and Public Policy* (Wilson 1983), the precursor to this volume, one sees a significant accumulation of research findings and insights that were not available ten years earlier. Those research findings, however, reflect only a tiny portion of what is required to make effective policy and operational decisions in each of those identified areas. There is still a need for major growth in research on crime and criminal justice. For example:

- We have some information on the variation in offending frequency in different prisoner populations, but we know much less well than we would like to how that applies to offenders generally. Similarly, we have some information on the duration of criminal careers; but current estimates are all for specific offender populations (for example, drug offenders), and we would like to be able to generalize the estimates to a wide variety of populations. Also, some information exists on the distribution of offending rates, but we have little basis for making predictions that apply to specific individuals with particular characteristics.

- We have some evaluations of community-based programs like boot camps, electronic monitoring, and intensive probation; and while the overall results are not encouraging, they do suggest that certain offender populations may be amenable to these prison alternatives. We need further evaluations to identify which subset of offenders, under what program conditions, could be safely placed in such programs.

- We know that community characteristics, such as social cohesion, residential mobility, and informal social control of public space all relate directly to levels of violence and fear of victimization. Further, we also know that the willingness of community members to become involved in crime-fighting programs is critical to the programs' success and long-term survival. Yet, knowledge about how best to involve citizens or what particular activities to engage them in remains obscure. And our knowledge on these matters is particularly weak for low income neighborhoods, where the need is the greatest.

- We have also begun to understand the links between community factors, such as those mentioned above, and other risk factors related to criminality. Sampson (Chapter 9 in this volume) reports on research showing that concentrated urban poverty and social disorganization combine to increase child abuse and neglect, low birth weigh, cognitive impairment, and other adjustment problems, which in turn constitute risk factors for later crime and violence. But we are unsure how best to break the link, and how to design effective programs of prenatal and infant health care, and prosocial family management (to teach child-rearing skills or conflict resolution, for example). Some model programs now exist, but we need to assess the costs and effects of such programs in different settings, with different delivery mechanisms, with different populations.

- We have learned much from policing research, confirming that high visibility and fast response times do not necessarily reduce crime or contribute to its solution. But, as Sherman explains in this volume (Chapter 14) there is some level of police presence that is necessary to make citizens feel safe and to deter potential offenders. Key remaining questions now are, What is the right number of police per population, and how does that differ by type of community, and what police activities are most useful for reducing fear and crime? And, as police are instituting community-based policing experiments nationwide, evaluations need to be conducted to identify those strategies that work best in enlisting the communities' help in the co-production of community safety.

- We have documented the costs and benefits of various strategies in the recent war on drugs, and have amply documented the inability of enforcement strategies alone to reduce drug abuse and drug trafficking. Prisons are now full of drug users and drug sellers, and yet the drug problem continues. Most now agree that the nation should invest in a public treatment system to treat hard-core addicts. But how to design such a system or identify the types of programs or users who would most benefit remains unknown.

So, while it is clear that much important research has been conducted since the early 1980s, it is also clear that we are at an extremely primitive stage of knowledge regarding crime, especially for focused action, and that much more needs to be done.

There is little question but that the locus of research on crime and criminal justice should be the responsibility of the federal government. In marked contrast to efforts at crime control by the operational agencies of police, prosecution, courts, and corrections, which are predominantly a local responsibility, research findings represent a public good to be shared broadly. The provision for such public goods (of which national defense is the most common example) is the natural role for the federal government. Research is not something the individual states are inclined to pursue, because of the perception that the benefits will accrue broadly. Independent state programs are not likely. Also, if research gets done at all by the states, each state's focus is likely to be very narrow, and they are not likely to undertake the broader issues, which have the bigger payoffs but take longer and cost more. Moreover, coordinating the research program at the federal level generates important economies of scale and of scope.

The Federal Research Program on Crime and Criminal Justice

There are already in place a number of federal research programs concerned with crime and criminal justice. Any reasonable observer, however, would find that collection of programs to be far smaller and more fragmented than is appropriate for developing necessary knowledge for the issue that is now rated as the principal concern of the American public (*New York Times* 1994).

There has been a long-standing program of research at the National Institute of Mental Health (NIMH) in its Violence and Traumatic Stress Research Branch. That branch has an annual budget of about $8 million for its violence component. It supports a variety of projects, most of which have a strong mental health orientation.

There is a fledgling program at the Centers for Disease Control (CDC) in their Center for Intentional Injury Research. Until recently, that program had a budget of about $8 million, recently augmented by $7.3 million for study of violence against women. There is also a program at the National Science Foundation under its Law and Social Science Program, with a budget of $2.4 million that covers a broad range of issues on law compliance and judicial process. Aside from these efforts, which are identifiable as research, one can certainly find fragments of policy analysis within various operational agencies such as the FBI, DEA (Drug Enforcement Agency), and the Office of National Drug Control Policy (ONDCP). At most, these would add another few million dollars to the total.

By far the broadest program of research on crime and criminal justice is located at the National Institute of Justice (NIJ) in the U.S. Department of Justice. This program represents one of the smallest research budgets of any federal department, only $22.5 million in fiscal year 1994. This budget is intended to cover its entire range of activities, which comprises a wide variety of dissemination activities, including operating a reference service, and activities such as strategic planning for security at the 1996 Olympics, which are questionable for a research institute. This leaves only about $10 million per year for the research program itself, which has to cover the entire criminal justice system and all aspects of crime and crime control.

It is striking to contrast criminal justice research budgets, which aggregate to well under $50 million dollars, with the resources used for various other research and operational activities. The total NIH budget of $13 billion is almost 1,000 times as large as the NIJ budget. Federal resources directed at law enforcement for drugs alone represent $13 billion. It is clear that the research expenditures in this area are profoundly inconsistent with the magnitude of the problem, with the resources being expended to address the problem, and with the resources committed to other comparably important national issues. The reasons for that are complex and ill-defined. They do warrant some attention, however, in order to identify strategies for improving and enhancing the support for research.

Explaining Limited Support

There are several possible explanations for the limited financial support of justice research.

Policy driven by ideology.   It may be that the policies intended to address crime and criminal justice are so strongly driven by fundamental ideological convictions that neither side wants to confront empirical reality because that might undermine their deeply held beliefs. Of course, this is the same kind of opposition that faced Galileo over 400 years ago when he tried to convince the religious leaders that their notion of a geocentric universe was mistaken. But we believe this is a major reason why policy has so largely ignored research findings that make it quite clear, for example, that punishment for reasons of incapacitation and deterrence is not very helpful in disrupting drug markets, and that increasing the certainty of punishment is more effective than increasing its severity.

These findings are well established and widely accepted throughout the research community, and even among the functionaries within the criminal justice system, and yet the nation persists in imposing ever longer sentences for drug offenders. Also, the very popular three-strikes-and-you're-out bills (requiring lifelong sentences for three convictions of certain types of crimes) keep gaining widespread public acceptance without a critical assessment of which kinds of crimes or offenders they are inappropriate for. Even though the research in both these areas is incomplete, there is enough currently known to provide much better guidance than the legislative and political processes seems willing to absorb or to deal with.

Distortion by the investigator.   It could be that the results of social science research, especially on issues in which the researchers themselves have strong ideological views, are simply too unreliable to trust. There are two sources of unreliability: one the bias imposed by the investigator and the other the contradictory nature of findings in different settings. This challenge to criminal justice research is unfortunately too often true to simply ignore or reject.

One does often see conclusions from research projects that merely confirm the ideological predilections of the investigator, and the more committed that investigator is to a particular policy line the more likely it is that he or she will find results that are in accord with that policy position. Even if there is no distortion of the data (and we have found data distortion to be extremely rare), the researcher can choose a setting or select particular measures which are likely to confirm a prior predilection. It is often true that results may permit various interpretations, measuring "half a glass" and permitting the investigator to decide which to emphasize, the "half full" or "half empty" assessment.

It is also possible for an investigator to shape the interpretation of some data by the form of aggregation chosen. For example, one may get one interpretation if one focuses on homicides, a different one if one focuses on "violent crimes," which are dominated by the much larger number of aggravated assaults and in which homicides are a small part of the total, and a very different interpretation if one measures "serious" crimes, which would also include burglary.

These kinds of biasing of research results are a serious problem because they cast doubt on the entire research enterprise as a result of the distortions introduced by a minority of researchers within the field. The way to address these problems, however, is to provide a forum where such results can be challenged by those who do not share—or who oppose—the ideological perspective of the original investigator.

Since the late 1970s, panels of the National Academy of Sciences (NAS) have been convened to review controversial or conflicting findings in the criminal justice field. The NAS has convened such review panels in the areas of measuring deterrence and incapacitation effects of sanctions, the development of sentencing policy and their articulation in sentencing guidelines, research on criminal careers, and violence research. These panels have almost always found a basis for resolving the conflict directly. If that is not possible, they can identify a critical experiment or formulate the next steps of research that would resolve the conflict. This is an extremely important part of any scientific activity, but it is especially necessary in this area. A credible forum like the NAS has developed strong and effective procedures to assure balance and to remove ideological bias from its reports.

Those efforts could be expanded significantly to address other areas of conflict (for example, the costs of prison versus alternative punishments). Such efforts also have a valuable monitoring effect in informing investigators that their research would come under such scrutiny, and thereby provide a strong incentive to the individual investigators to monitor their own research and avoid the censure that can come from introducing inappropriate distortion.

Skepticism that research will prove useful in combating crime.   In the 1960s and 1970s, there was great faith in the practical value of all social sciences. Those concerned with education, poverty, crime, and other social problems assumed that if we just studied it more deeply, we could contribute to its solution. Such optimism has faded, particularly with respect to crime. Not only is crime believed to be rather intractable given current social conditions, but many believe that practitioners, not researchers, have the best answers for solving the crime problem. In short, craft knowledge is believed to hold more value than that which is empirically derived through research studies.

The skepticism among practitioners toward research is caused by their intellectual traditions as well as the issues they choose to focus on. Researchers often spend the majority of their careers in universities and, as a result, appear to practitioners as divorced from real-world problems and constraints. The issues they choose to look at are often too broad to lend themselves easily to policy manipulation (for example, identifying poverty as a cause of crime) or too narrow to have much policy interest (such as a focus on obscure crimes committed by a small number of offenders). And, when researchers have become involved, say in an evaluation of a national demonstration program, they are more likely to identify what *doesn't* work than what does.

The upshot is that over time, policy makers and practitioners have become skeptical that new discoveries or effective programs will be identified by the scientific community in the same way that they are in the fields of medicine and engineering. Practicing physicians, for example, rely heavily on research and development efforts to keep the field advancing; whereas in criminal justice, practitioners rely more often on their own experience for innovation and progressive thinking. Physicians also regularly read the major research journals in their field (*The New England Journal of Medicine,* for example), whereas justice practitioners seldom read crime research journals (such as *Criminology*). This lack of a strong constituency for research results also creates little incentive to increase justice research funding, and contributes to fewer instances of use once the research is completed.

Researchers and practitioners need to work more aggressively to create a collaborative framework for the conduct and dissemination of policy-relevant research. Practitioners could help focus the research agenda, improve dissemination, and increase the utility of research by making their priorities and needs known to researchers. They could also help create new channels for dialogue between researchers and practitioners. In addition to publishing readable research reports, researchers must identify other forums, potential "consumers," and uses of the research; set priorities for addressing them; and tailor research products accordingly. Researchers and practitioners need to begin to engage in serious dialogue over research results and their implications. Forums for such discussions could, for example, be built into the annual meetings of professional associations (such as the American Correctional Association, or the International Association of Chiefs of Police).

Perspectives of the legal profession on empirical research.   Another important factor inhibiting more significant efforts by the NIJ derives from the inherent perspective on empirical research held by the majority of the legal profession, which, of course, is the dominant professional group within the Department of Justice. This is in marked contrast to the medical profession, whose perspectives dominate the health side of the Department of Health and Human Services (DHHS). In the medical world, from the first year of medical school, through residency, and through general practice, physicians are taught consistently to advert to research findings in order to learn how to do their job better. They are constantly surveying the research literature; those efforts are supported by Medline and other elements of their professional infrastructure intended to keep them up to date with current research. They take it as a matter of pride and a professional obligation to contribute to that research literature.

In the legal profession generally, there is no comparable tradition for empirical research. The counterpart legal research involves searching for cases or statutes that address the issues in their case. Every case is addressed on its own terms, and the relevant precedents are sought. Thus, the search for generalizable knowledge that is the essence of empirical research—and that should provide a basis for public policy—is not a central aspect of legal professional work. Within legal practice, no decisions or actions typically hinge on such generalized knowledge. It is not surprising, then, that no great enthusiasm—as reflected in budgetary commitments—has developed in the Justice Department for an empirical research program at NIJ.

As a result of the differences in these professional perspectives, some of the operating agencies (most notably the Federal Bureau of Prisons, which is not dominated by legal practice and traditions) within the Justice Department have established their own research staffs. But even these agencies must focus on issues associated with operating parts of the Federal criminal justice system. Thus, there is no strong support within the Justice Department for the research program at NIJ, where the primary function is to develop information that will be of use to state and local criminal justice systems.

This lack of commitment to such a mission is reflected in NIJ's budgetary history, shown in Figure 20.1 (both in current dollars and in 1992 dollars).

FIGURE 20.1
National Institute of Justice Appropriations History, Current and 1992
Dollars

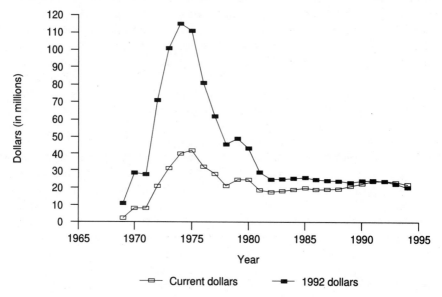

There was a spurt of growth from 1972 through 1974; indeed, the rate of
growth was probably too great to deliver on the expectations imposed.
Perhaps as a result, the budget has declined in real terms almost every year
since then. It has been essentially flat (with slight declines in real terms) since
1981 and has stayed in the range of about $20 million to $30 million since
then—well short of a high priority.

Structure for a Criminal Justice Research Program

The earlier chapters in this volume have addressed many of the issues relevant to criminal justice policy, and many of them have identified critical
research issues that need attention. Drawing on those, we can identify at least
some important program areas which clearly warrant major research endeav-
ors, well beyond the level that could be supported by current funding commitments.

Describe the Nature of Criminal Careers and Their Development and Evolution

It is impressive how little we still know about how the criminal justice system
controls crime. The NIJ did pursue a small program of research on crime

control theory, with a focus on deterrence and incapacitation. That program has resulted in some initial steps toward describing criminal careers in terms of offending frequency (a construct that was not even within the criminological lexicon as recently as the early 1970s) in a limited number of settings and population groups. Unfortunately, the estimates are almost always based on prison populations, whose offending frequency will inevitably be much higher than among the whole range of offenders committing crimes within the community, and so corrections have to be made for the different populations. So far, very little effort has been directed at distinguishing the high frequency offenders who should be of primary interest to the criminal justice system from those who have had only marginal involvement.

Even less well studied has been the question of the duration of criminal careers. That aspect is particularly difficult to observe because one cannot directly see or detect the termination of a criminal career except in long retrospect. Recidivism rates have been used as a proxy, but they are always measured over a fairly short observation period (rarely more than three years and most often for one year), and it is entirely possible for an individual to continue active involvement in a criminal career but not recidivate during the observation period. Alternatively, it is possible for an individual to be rearrested early in the observation period but terminate a career either in prison or well before the observation period is completed. The duration of a career is a particularly important attribute because it provides information on how long one can anticipate continued criminal activity from a group of offenders. If one can reasonably anticipate that duration to be short, then long sentences are highly inefficient, at least from the viewpoint of incapacitation. If the career can be anticipated to be long, then long sentences become more appropriate. Of course, all these aspects of sentence duration must be weighed with other considerations of appropriate retribution or desert as well as resource allocation within the criminal justice system.

Also, it is particularly important to establish the determinants of these two critical characteristics of criminal careers: offending frequency (commonly denoted by the Greek letter lambda, λ) and duration. We know only that intensive drug use increases λ and early involvement in arrest is a precursor of high λ. For career termination, it is widely viewed that effective gainful employment or stable marital relationship are important factors contributing to the termination of a criminal career, but even this presumption has not been well established. Also, how one anticipates or stimulates such career-ending conditions is still somewhat problematic.

In addition to describing criminal careers, it is extremely important to develop an extensive research program that characterizes the evolution of criminal careers, including factors that contribute to career initiation and termination. We need to understand better the contribution of various biological mechanisms, and the instruments of society such as parenting, schools, peers, the criminal justice system, and the interaction among all of these. To think that a few regression equations will provide adequate knowledge for addressing these issues is extremely simplistic. It is critical that an intensive program which includes a variety of community settings, governmental jurisdictions, family structures, and socioeconomic groups be pursued to study this.

Any such effort will require a longitudinal design to study cohorts of individuals, probably starting at birth, or perhaps even prenatally. One important initial step in this direction is the youth development project being funded by the NIJ and the MacArthur Foundation. This effort is estimated to cost about $8 million per year for a period of about ten years in order to track accelerated cohorts from birth through to age twenty-four. The study design establishes overlapping cohorts and tests the influence of family, school, peers, and communities on the emergence of criminal activity. This is an extremely ambitious and exciting project; nevertheless, it is being conducted in only one city (Chicago), which limits the degree to which one can test the generality of its findings to other cities. It would be very desirable to be able to bring a comparable effort to other cities over the next several years.

It is clear that the paths leading to criminal activity are highly dependent on effective socialization into societal norms. That socialization process begins at birth, where the parents are the exclusive socializing instruments, and expands to include influences from preschool experiences, family, school, and peers into the teenage period. Other important factors include churches, which have increasingly become removed from that function; mass media; and all the other social influences that an individual encounters as he or she moves from childhood through to adulthood.

Some facets of that socialization process have received observation and experimentation—for example, parental behavior in a limited number of experiments, media violence in social laboratories. But, in view of the importance of the family in socialization, and the general transition of family structures in the United States away from the traditional nuclear family, we have to learn much more about the socializing effects of diverse kinds of "family environments," including, single parents, day care, foster parents, institutional care, grandparents, and the many other forms of familial environments that are becoming more common. We know very little about what works well, with what kinds of kids, and in what kinds of environments. It would be very desirable to find effective means to train parents or other parent surrogates in different settings. There are at least fragments of knowledge to enable that. But the level of knowledge necessary to do so in ways that would be truly effective that accommodate the different personalities on the part of the parents and the children are far from available. Research must be pursued to first study different kinds of socializing settings and their consequences.

Eventually, different kinds of training experiments should be pursued and their outcomes measured. While there is much to be gained by observation, there is much more that can be done by organized experiments with various kinds of socializing interventions. These might include proactive court intervention in a dysfunctional family, foster placement, or creation of group basketball leagues and teams. The success of any of these would obviously depend on the initial characteristics of the child, since it should be expected that different children with different needs will would be amenable to different kinds of interventions.

Increase Understanding of the Nature and Development of Juvenile Violence

In recent years the nation has become increasingly concerned with violence, and especially homicide, committed by juveniles. It is probable that such violence has contributed significantly to the recent ranking of "crime" as the nation's number one problem in public opinion polls. This contrasts with the traditional form of homicide, which is most common between spouses or intimates, and so need not generate fear among the public more generally. On the other hand, homicide by juveniles tends more often to be against strangers, has increasingly involved the use of guns, and conveys a sense of randomness that can generate a much more widespread sense of vulnerability. The rate of juvenile homicide with guns has grown dramatically since 1985 (see Blumstein, Chapter 17, and Cook and Moore, Chapter 12, in this volume). Much of this growth in juvenile violence has been coincident with the growth in drug markets since 1985, and might well be associated with those drug markets which use guns as their normal methods of both self-defense and establishing a "tough" reputation.

It is extremely important that major effort be directed at understanding the nature of the growth and development of juvenile violence, and how that is related to individual development (the major theme of the large project being carried out in Chicago with the support of the NIJ and the MacArthur Foundation), family structure and environment and its contribution to socialization, community conditions (many poor communities have had no growth in juvenile violence while others have seen major increase in juvenile homicides), the organization of gangs in the neighborhood and the nature of those gangs, and proximity to drug markets and their recruitment of juveniles and to gun markets which sell guns illegally to juveniles.

These are key factors likely not only to affect juvenile violence but to be major aspects of the socialization and development of the future workforce and citizenry of the nation. The fact that there has been a major growth in juvenile violence (between 1985 and 1992, more than a doubling of homicide rates by juveniles aged eighteen and below while there has been no growth in homicides by adults aged twenty-four and above) is not only of concern in itself; it is symptomatic of many key aspects of juvenile development that need major attention. Some attention is now being directed to these problems by foundations and by various government agencies (mostly within the DHHS), but with a knowledge base that is distressingly thin in terms of knowing how best to intervene in these developmental processes.

Assess the Effects of the Justice System on Crime and Offender Behavior, and on Costs

Criminal justice agencies—police, courts, corrections—are the principal means by which we attempt explicitly to control crime and criminals. Research to date has, for the most part, focused on evaluating these individual agencies and assessing their performance. This research has been critical in shaping policies of these agencies. For example, research findings have altered the way police are deployed, how they handle calls for service from the public, and which offenders and offense types receive special handling (for example, career criminals, domestic assault). Research has amply demonstrated the patterns of case attrition, and highlighted the importance of citizens in reporting crime and providing evidence needed to arrest and convict offenders. And corrections research has identified the characteristics most associated with offender recidivism, and has shown the risks associated with placing felons in the community unsupervised. Research has undoubtedly helped these agencies become more efficient in areas ranging from patrol management to probationer classification.

Future research must now grapple with the more complex and difficult question, that of assessing the extent to which formal justice agencies, individually and collectively, contribute to crime reduction in the community through incapacitation and deterrence. We need to move away from the fragmentary studies of individual agencies and toward more comprehensive assessments of how justice agencies influence one another and, together, influence crime. Decisions made in one justice agency have dramatic workload and cost implications for other justice agencies, and later decisions (such as not prosecuting certain arrests) can negate the effects of other's efforts. To date, these systemic effects have not been well studied, and much benefit is likely to come from examining how various policy initiatives affect criminal justice agencies, individually and collectively.

Of particular importance at this time are studies of the impact that more police and alternative policing strategies will have on crime, criminals, and other justice agencies. Communities around the nation are expanding the number of police in the hopes of reducing violence. But as Sherman notes in this volume (Chapter 14), more police do not necessarily mean less crime. The critical factor seems not to be the number of police in a community, but rather to be what the police choose to do with their time and in what locations they are deployed.

Communities expanding the size of their police force will provide numerous natural experiments to study how variations in police size, strategies, and deployment affect fear of crime and victimization. By studying these efforts systematically, we should help answer the important questions: How many police do we need? What types of activities are most useful, in what types of settings? And, if researchers and police officials can work together to vary some of the policing tactics employed, we will be able to study the effects of evolving programs such as monitoring drug hot spots, undercover "buy and bust" operations, policing of illegal gun markets, searching parolees and probationers for weapons, and truancy enforcement. These innovative programs, along with evaluating broader community-based policing initiatives, will help us better understand how the police can best contribute to crime prevention and control. It is also important to study some of the interactions between the policing strategy employed and type of officer it works best with.

It is also critical to monitor the impacts that more police will have on police processing and other agencies' workloads. Simply hiring more police and putting them on the streets will not necessarily increase police presence (and hence, presumably, deterrence). Similarly, generating more arrests will not necessarily result in more convictions and incarcerations, if prosecutors and corrections (either by policy or budget constraints) do not follow through with convictions and incarcerations.

We also believe more solid data are needed to assess the crime and cost implications of alternative criminal sanctions. There is great interest in identifying punishment strategies that are both effective at preventing crime and less expensive than prison. Since the mid-1980s, states have experimented with a variety of intermediate sanctions, such as house arrest and intensive probation, hoping to accomplish these dual goals; and the results have been disappointing. For the most part, the programs have been unable to significantly reduce the recidivism rates of participants. And since most of the program failures are subsequently revoked to prison, intermediate sanctions sometimes end up costing as much or more than prison, because agencies incur the cost of both the intermediate sanction and the prison or jail term imposed as a result of revocation.

While these early evaluations are instructive, their results are by no means definitive. The programs have mostly been surveillance-oriented, and have focused primarily on increasing drug testing and face-to-face contacts with offenders. They have incorporated little treatment or employment training. Most intermediate sanction programs targeted serious career criminals, with lengthy histories of crime and substance abuse. It is possible (and there is some supporting evidence) that intermediate sanctions incorporating treatment, in addition to surveillance activities, do produce lower recidivism rates (Petersilia and Turner 1993). It is also possible that had these programs been targeted toward less serious offenders, or earlier in their criminal careers, the results might have been more encouraging. There is reason to continue experimenting with community-based sanctions, varying target population, program elements, setting, and point in the criminal career for intervention.

These evaluations have also highlighted the importance of technical violations in community supervision. Probation and parole officers spend most of their time monitoring the technical conditions imposed by the courts (such as, no alcohol or drug use). When violations are discovered, additional time is spent in processing the paperwork necessary to revoke offenders. Nationally, about a third of all incoming prisoners are committed to prison for violating their technical probation or parole conditions, rather than for a new crime conviction. And most of those revoked to prison had violated the "no drug use" condition, as detected through urine testing. Such revocations will undoubtedly increase as urinalysis testing for drugs becomes less expensive and more widespread.

This begs an important question: what purpose is served by monitoring and revoking persons for technical violations, and is the benefit worth the cost? If technical violations identify offenders who are "going bad" and likely to commit crime, then we may well wish to spend the time uncovering such conditions and incarcerating those persons. On the other hand, if technical violators are simply troubled, but not criminally dangerous, then devoting our scarce prison resources to this population might not be warranted. Despite the policy significance of technical violations, no serious research has focused on this issue. As the costs of monitoring and incarcerating technical violators increases, research must examine its crime control significance.

There is also the ongoing debate about who is in prison, and whether there exists a group of prisoners who, based on crimes and prior criminal records, could safely be supervised in the community. Proponents of alternatives argue that over the past decade we have vastly expanded the use of imprisonment, and as a result many low-level offenders have gotten caught up in the broader net of social control, and are now in prison. They contend that many (if not most) prisoners are minor property offenders, low-level drug dealers, or technical violators—ideal candidates for community-based alternatives. Those who are against expanding prison alternatives disagree, citing data showing that most prisoners are violent recidivists with few prospects for reform.

It is likely that the truth lies somewhere in between, and that the differences in the numbers cited depend on how one aggregates the data, and what data set one chooses to analyze. It is likely that historical sentencing patterns have resulted in vastly different populations being incarcerated in different states. Research examining the characteristics of inmates in different states (by age, criminal record, and substance abuse history), is necessary to clarify this important debate. It is also critical that we conduct better follow-up studies (ideally, using experimental designs) of offenders who have been sentenced to prison as opposed to various forms of community supervision. By tracking similarly situated offenders, sentenced differently, we will be able to refine our recidivism prediction models, and begin to estimate more accurately the crime and cost implications of different sentencing choices.

Study the Relationship between Drug Markets and Control of Illicit Drugs

Illicit drugs represent a major national problem in many ways. There is a strong nexus between those who commit crimes and those who abuse drugs. There is a very high percentage drug-positive on urinalysis of booked arrestees as measured by the DUF program. The rate is above 50 percent in most of the cities sampled, and is often above 70 percent in cities like New York (Manhattan), Chicago, San Diego, and Philadelphia.

A large fraction of prisoners acknowledge having used drugs in the period before the crime that led to their incarceration. Even legal substances like alcohol, when abused, have a significant pharmacological connection to violence.

Largely because of the concern over the potential for harm these substances represent, the nation has waged a massive effort since the early 1980s, primarily using law enforcement approaches to try to control traffic.in and abuse of substances like marijuana, cocaine, and heroin. That effort has resulted in over 60 percent of federal prisoners and about 25 percent of state prisoners being incarcerated for drug offenses. The cost of the effort draws about $13 billion per year from the federal budget alone, and many billions more from state budgets.

It is clear that this massive effort has contributed to a high volume of seizures of drugs and has led to over a million arrests per year and several hundred thousand prisoners. It is not clear, however, how much impact this effort has yet had on drug markets or on drug abuse. The National Institute on Drug Abuse is charged with the responsibility for research on drug abuse, but those efforts have focused primarily on issues of pharmacological effects and treatment possibilities and have not been directed at overall strategic issues or at the basic operations of drug markets.

So much more remains to be done, particularly from the viewpoint of assessing the effectiveness of alternative approaches (primarily law enforcement, treatment, and prevention) to reducing drug abuse. Any such assessment should be in the context of different kinds of users, different market mechanisms, different price regimes, and different kinds of illicit drugs. Much better information is needed on price behavior with changing supply or demand, and the dynamics of demand in the face of different levels of enforcement. Since a major part of the enforcement strategy involves disrupting street markets, it is important to come to understand how markets recover in another location when the initial market is disrupted, and to learn how long it takes to build up in another location. It is also important to know, when drug abuse levels increase, how much of that is attributable to increased use by already involved drug users and how much is attributable to newly recruited users.

There have been increasing calls for "legalization" or "decriminalization" of currently illegal drugs, but there has yet been very little in the way of specific consideration of detailed alternative modes of providing for the distribution of the currently illegal drugs that might be made more selectively available. Those possibilities cover a broad range from making marijuana available for medical uses to providing cocaine and heroin on supermarket shelves. There has been no systematic exploration of the various possibilities in between these extremes, in terms of estimating how much the anticipated demand would increase, how new black markets would arise, and how the legalized supply would be controlled and kept from children and others who all agree should not have access to such drugs.

Research involving exploration of the effects of various kinds of decriminalization of various kinds of drugs in both the United States (particularly considering the various states that have partially decriminalized marijuana) and in foreign countries (a number have decriminalized various other kinds of drugs at various times). Such exploration is necessary in order to assess the magnitude of the anticipated increase in drug abuse and in which populations; the anticipated diversion from the legalized market to illicit markets; the effects on children, who are of particular concern; the impact on welfare burdens; changes in corruption patterns; changes in other crimes associated with a need to steal money for drugs; and changes in violence that flows from drug markets, both internally for dispute resolution as well as into the more general community as a result of the diffusion of guns from the drug markets. In general, there is now no basis for making a general assessment of the costs and benefits as well as the changing market dynamics associated with such revisions in enforcement policies.

Study the Impacts of the Changing Social Environment on Crime

The United States is changing in profound ways that are likely to increase the nature and extent of crime we experience. The next generation of children is more likely to be born to a single mother, to be raised in a single parent household, to experience poverty, and to be unemployed than previous generations—all factors known to relate to later criminality.

Communities are also changing, experiencing greater geographical mobility and social isolation, which often results in social disorganization and, ultimately, more crime, drugs, and guns. Understanding how these contextual factors relate to the production of crime, and whether they can be countered by justice interventions, is of highest priority. Within this large galaxy of problems, we would like to comment on two issues that seem particularly in need of research at this time: gun acquisition, ownership and use, and community-based prevention programs for youth.

Two-thirds of all homicides reported in 1991 in the United States were committed with firearms, and in over half of them a handgun was the weapon used. Federal laws prohibit criminals and other high-risk individuals from owning guns; however, most offenders acquire them through illegal means or from informal sources, even though the firearms may originally have been sold through legitimate channels. These facts highlight the importance of learning more about the channels facilitating illegal access to guns and examining the effectiveness of licensing and regulation strategies that govern acquisition and firearm use. Creating better and more accessible records of gun sales would also permit research into the operations of illegal gun markets.

A number of strategies are currently being employed by police—for example, gun buy-back programs—but the effects of such programs is unclear. Sherman and Wilson recommend, for example, that police more closely monitor probationers and parolees to identify individuals carrying weapons (see Chapter 14 and Chapter 21 in this volume). This strategy holds some promise because of the relatively high probability that such persons will engage in future crime, and because of the legal authority to search such persons without a warrant. But whether such procedures would prove viable, and at what cost, is only poorly known. It would also be useful to develop means of using modern information systems to help police in this task.

We also need to learn much more about delinquency prevention. It is widely recognized that communities and the families within them, much more than the justice system, provide the greatest hope for intervening successfully in the lives of at-risk youth. Research has consistently demonstrated that one of the best predictors of sustained and serious adult criminality is an early age of initiation and the seriousness of the delinquent career. Most experts urge more aggressive intervention in the lives of youth who are showing early signs of potential delinquency. There is a widespread desire to do this, but the practical difficulty is that we have yet to learn how to design and implement effective prevention programs.

While there are many promising programs, most have not been tried in multiple settings, nor have most shown consistently positive or lasting effects. In addition to program design issues, there are target selection problems. We wish to target programs at the most vulnerable kids who might benefit the most, but we still know very little about how to identify the high-risk child before serious problems occur. While research has discovered multiple antecedents of problem behavior, our ability to predict which kids will get in trouble is still quite primitive. Furthermore, as Ellickson notes (1992), we know that programs designed for kids who are already in trouble can actually make them worse by such means as lumping them together with other misfits or labeling them as problems. Thus, targeting interventions at kids who might get in trouble some time in the future runs the added risk of labeling them before the fact and thereby fostering the behavior we want to avoid.

The challenge is to continue evaluating the new programs being implemented in communities across the nation (like Head Start), with an eye towards identifying the particular characteristics—of kids, settings, and providers—that seem to make the most difference, followed up over longer periods of time. Such studies should focus on identifying at what point in youths' lives to intervene (to foster deterrence and not labeling) with what type of program (family, individual) in what type of setting (criminal justice, foster home, own home). These tasks are particularly difficult because of the long interval between the intervention and the opportunity to observe its effects, but that problem makes it particularly important to initiate such programs early.

Exploit Opportunities to Capitalize on Defense Technological Resources Becoming Available

One of the major challenges for new research is exploiting some of the technological capability becoming available through the reduction of defense expenditures. The technological capabilities are perhaps best represented by the federal laboratories (among them Los Alamos, Sandia Corporation, and the Aerospace Corporation). Some of these are affiliated with the Department of Energy (which has responsibility for nuclear weapons work), and others are affiliated with the Department of Defense or the individual services. They represent an enormous reservoir of technological talent, along with the corporations involved in the defense industry. These corporations would include the nonprofit corporations such as Rand, the Institute for Defense Analyses, and the Mitre Corporation as well as the defense industry (General Dynamics, Raytheon, and others).

All of these organizations will be seeking challenging work to keep their highly sophisticated technical staffs supported and productive. There is some obligation by the Department of Defense to continue support of these organizations, even if not at their prior levels, and so the technical capability could become available for addressing technical questions associated with upgrading the quality of technology involved in the criminal justice area. Some of the issues that would be worth pursuing include issues of nonlethal weapons such as sticky foam (which has been widely publicized recently) and criminalistics (especially pinning down the reliability of DNA analysis). It could also include the possibility of maintaining a fingerprint-like directory of gun barrels and ballistic markings on bullets fired from them. It could also include detection of guns at a distance (an issue highlighted by Wilson in his concluding chapter to this volume).

The major advances, however, are most likely to come from improving the quality of command, control, and communication for maintaining ready access to information about suspects, offenders, and others processed by the criminal justice system, and control over the effective utilization of a police force. There are major opportunities for significant improvement in information management throughout all aspects of the criminal justice system. One can readily view the entire criminal justice function as an information-processing function to collect information about cases and suspects and to reach decisions about those. Compact, high capacity information systems could be used to search through interrogation reports, to assure the availability of accurate and timely criminal justice records at all appropriate stages of the trial and sentencing process, to make predictions of future risk assessment at various stages of the corrections process, and to aid in rehabilitative treatment by matching treatments and treaters to the characteristics of the offenders to be treated.

Information systems that contain identification information about parolees and probationers in a community could be of considerable value to the police of that community. The more capable police become in protecting the community from those potential suspects of crimes, the more likely it is that the community will be willing to accept community-based intermediate punishments for such individuals.

Commitment to a New and Significant Research Program

The issues presented in the previous section are only a few of the salient themes that should be pursued. They represent only a small fraction of the new knowledge that is needed to develop effective policy with respect to crime—including crime prevention—and crime control, including efficient and effective operation of the criminal justice system. These must be pursued, however, if we are to gain a better understanding of crime and its origins, and of how to mobilize our societal resources, including those of the criminal justice system, to control it.

The nation is investing many billions of dollars—over thirty billions in the 1994 Crime Bill alone—in programs intended to address the problem of crime. It is hard to think of another policy area where the concern is so high, the expenditures are so high, and the knowledge base is so thin. In view of that situation, it is particularly troublesome that so little effort is being directed at improving the situation. One might attribute that to a sense of the difficulty of understanding the vagaries of human behavior, but certainly the NIMH budget of over $500 million is no less complex. And the vagaries of behavior in warfare are no less complex, but billions are invested in studying how to be effective in managing military personnel and in using them to the greatest effectiveness in warfare.

In view of the considerable expenditure made for programs to deal with crime—law enforcement, prisons, prevention programs—it is critical to learn how those expenditures can be made to be more effective. The thirty billions committed in the crime bill have been committed to programs for which their advocates would have great difficulty in providing any empirically based estimate of their aggregate impact on crime, let alone an assessment of how specifics of the individual programs can be modified to be more effective. Any service industry would be in deep trouble if it invested less than 3 percent of its total costs in research designed to make it more effective. No one seems to be concerned that the Justice Department, especially as an agent for state and local criminal justice systems, falls impressively short of that mark. .

So significant an agenda cannot be pursued with the necessary intensity, nor can it draw on the best research competence, when the federal budget for it is under $50 million, and especially when the NIJ, the primary agency charged with this broad mission, has an annual budget under $25 million. In order to build a research base and to attract the quality of individuals that are necessary to assure an effective, creative, and responsible research program, there must be a commitment to build a research program that goes well beyond that level of support. It is entirely appropriate to consider doubling the annual budget each year until it reaches a stable level of perhaps $1 billion per year within six or seven years. Certainly, the nation's most important problem warrants at least that kind of commitment. It should be clear that many aspects of the future of the nation will depend on effectively addressing the problems identified here. The crime problem is one of increasing and immediate concern. Many of the issues identified go well beyond crime, however. They also affect the basic social stability of the society as well as the economic vitality of the nation.

The $1 billion should be contrasted with the $11 billion the nation spends on health research through the NIH, the $13 billion a year that are expended in federal funds alone to pursue the drug war, and the more than $30 billion or so likely to be committed from the Crime Bill of 1994.

As one examines the details of the crime bill (crime prevention programs, 100,000 new police officers, prison subsidies, and a three-strikes mandate), it is clear that so many of the features of the bill are incorporated based on pure presumption of usefulness. There is no base of knowledge that will significantly help in the assessment of which features should be adopted and which are wasteful. Furthermore, there is only a weak foundation of knowledge to enable the best functional choice of how best to incorporate these features: which crime types should be included in the three-strikes provisions, how the new police officers can be used best in various cities, and what is the relative cost-effectiveness of various kinds of crime prevention activities. The knowledge for pursuing these issues is simply not yet available; when the knowledge does become available, the potential for improvement in the effectiveness of spending in the anticrime efforts could become considerable.

Experience with the National Institute of Justice over its twenty-five

years makes it clear that such a major effort cannot be organized or executed as a minor part of a department which seems to have an inherently
minimal and peripheral interest in empirical research. Rather, this seems to
call for a separate federal agency that would necessarily have links to the
Department of Justice as well as the nation's entire criminal justice system,
but it must also be linked to the National Science Foundation and its research traditions, to the Department of Health and Human Services (particularly the National Institute of Mental Health and the Centers for Disease
Control) and its recognition of the importance of research as a route to
improved practice.

The program must be protected with strong links to traditions of scientific integrity. Those could come from the president's science adviser, from
the National Science Foundation, and from the National Academy of
Sciences. Some mixture of all of these could have oversight of the scientific
integrity of its program and of its published research.

The Congress, and especially its two judiciary committees, would be in
a good position to provide oversight of the programs of this new agency in
order to assure that the agency is addressing problems that Congress believes
are important.

The director of the agency should be separated from the political process
and should be appointed by the president for a fixed term (of, say, five years).
It is also critical that such an individual have a very strong research background in order to make the technical judgments that are necessary to any
credible research program. A large fraction of previous NIJ directors have
been lawyers; some have done extremely well, others less so, but it is extremely difficult to bring critical questioning of the feasibility of a research
project or program without having a strong background in research.

Because implementation is an important need in this area, the new
agency would have two main branches, one concerned with research and the
creation of research products, and the other concerned with improvement of
policy and practice through dissemination of research results that emerge
from the agency's programs or from elsewhere.

The research branch would establish major centers of excellence in critical areas. These centers would be responsible for carrying out research on a
particular theme as well as for the training of new generations of researchers.
It is extremely important that the population of individuals who carry out
research related to crime and criminal justice be expanded by bringing in
individuals expert in disciplines that have not yet adequately been exploited.
The research branch would fund major research projects in various program
areas. It should also be in a position to carry out intramural research as a
means of strengthening its staff capability. It would inevitably seek to develop field sites where it would manage laboratory opportunities as they
became available within police departments, prosecutor's offices, courts, or
corrections agencies.

The dissemination branch would maintain close connection to other federal departments and especially to the practitioners in the field. Members of this branch would use modern information dissemination capabilities, including electronic mail and electronic bulletin boards. They would organize frequent conferences of users and researchers so that each group understood the other's needs and contributions. They would recognize that they must aggressively pursue the task of diffusing important research results, and find ways to encourage practitioners to seek out research results.

It should certainly be recognized that not all research results will be directly transferable to users. In many cases, the research results will provide the stimulus for new research which will contribute to the research process, and will later contribute to the improvement of practice. The dissemination branch would be responsible for undertaking reviews of research findings to assure that the results are stable and valid. It would have frequent occasion to call on the National Academy of Sciences for review of conflicting findings in important areas. For less salient issues, it would convene balanced review panels to assess research results, and it would be responsible for sorting out well-established from weaker research findings.

In fiscal year 1993, the National Institute of Justice, with a very small amount of funds available for research, received 400 proposals and was able to fund only 40. Staff at the NIJ have made it clear that they could well have funded at least twice that number. It is also the case that they were largely confined to funding projects under $150,000 per year, far below what would be necessary for an effective research program. A major infusion of additional funds would certainly contribute to bringing new talent into the research activity. This is a critical need at a time when some excellent talent is becoming available as other research activity is reducing its funding.

One issue that should be considered is the desirability of adding the Bureau of Justice Statistics to this new agency. In substantive terms, it would be very desirable to link the research activity with the statistics collection activities in order to assure mutual support between these two strongly technical activities.

As an implementation of these proposals, we urge the development of a legislative initiative that would establish this new research agency located outside the Department of Justice, perhaps as an independent agency like the National Science Foundation or perhaps incorporated within the National Science Foundation. It is important that those within the new agency view the Department of Justice as an important client and make it clear that they do have information and insights that would be particularly valuable to that department. It must have strong technical oversight by the president's science adviser (who should have a strong say in the appointment of the director, for example) and the National Academy of Sciences. It should begin with the budget of the NIJ (or NIJ and BJS combined if the BJS is included in the new organization) and there should be a commitment to double that budget each year until it reaches a level of $1 billion per year,

Investing in Criminal Justice Research

at which point it could be leveled out, and further developments considered subsequently.

We view this as a necessary step if the nation is to benefit from the level and quality of research it needs in order to become much more effective in dealing with the developing crime problem.

JAMES Q. WILSON

CRIME AND PUBLIC POLICY

When the United States experienced the great increase in crime that began in the early 1960s and continued through the 1970s, most Americans were inclined to attribute it to conditions unique to this country. Many conservatives blamed it on judicial restraints on the police, the abandonment of capital punishment, and the mollycoddling of offenders; many liberals blamed it on poverty, racism, and the rise of violent television programs. Europeans, to the extent they noticed it at all, referred to it, sadly or patronizingly, as the "American" problem, a product of our disorderly society, weak state, corrupt police, or imperfect welfare system.

Now, thirty years later, any serious discussion of crime must begin with the fact that, except for homicide, most industrialized nations have crime rates that resemble those in the United States. All the world is coming to look like America. In 1981, the burglary rate in Great Britain was much less than that in the United States; within six years the two rates were the same; today, British homes are more likely to be burgled than American ones. In 1980, the rate at which automobiles were stolen was lower in France than in the United states; today, the reverse is true. By 1984 the burglary rate in the Netherlands was nearly twice that in the United States. In Australia and Sweden certain forms of theft are more common than they are here. While property crime rates were declining during most of the 1980s in the United States, they were rising elsewhere (Lynch, Chapter 2 in this volume; Kalish 1988). [1]

America continues to lead the industrialized world in murders. There can be little doubt that part of that lead is to be explained by the greater availability of handguns in this country. Arguments that once might have been settled with insults or punches are more likely to be settled by shootings. But guns are not the whole story. Big American cities have had more homicides than comparable European ones for almost as long as anyone can find records. New York and Philadelphia have been more murderous than London since the early part of the nineteenth century. This country has had a violent history; with respect to murder that seems likely to remain the case. But for most property crimes, much of the rest of the world has caught up and even passed us by.

Indeed, except for homicide, and in particular youthful homicide, things have been getting better in the United States for over a decade. Since 1980, robbery rates (as reported in victim surveys) have declined by 15 percent. The rate at which adults kill each other was no higher in 1990 than it was in 1980, and in many cities it was considerably lower.

This was as it was supposed to be. Starting in around 1980, two things happened that ought to have reduced most forms of crime. The first was the passing into middle age of the postwar baby boom. By 1990 there were 1.5 million fewer boys between the ages of fifteen and nineteen than there had been in 1980, a drop that meant that this youthful fraction of the population fell from 9.3 percent to 7.2 percent of the total. In addition, the great increase in the size of the prison population, caused in part by the growing willingness of judges to send offenders to jail, meant that the dramatic reductions in the costs of crime that occurred in the 1960s and 1970s were slowly (and very partially) being reversed. Until around 1985, this reversal involved almost exclusively real criminals and parole violators; it was not until after 1985 that more than a small part of the growth in prison populations was made up of drug offenders.

Because of the combined effect of fewer young people on the street and more offenders in prison, many scholars, myself included, predicted a continuing drop in crime rates throughout the 1980s and into the early 1990s. We were almost right. Crime rates did decline, but suddenly, starting in around 1985, youthful homicide rates shot up.

Alfred Blumstein (Chapter 17) has estimated that the rate at which young males, ages fourteen to seventeen, kill people has gone up significantly for whites and incredibly for blacks. Between 1985 and 1992, the homicide rate for young white males went up by about 50 percent but for young black males it *tripled*. Meanwhile the homicide rate for older males scarcely changed at all. The public perception that today's crime problem is different from and more serious than that of earlier decades is quite correct. Youngsters are shooting at people at a far higher rate than at any time in recent history. Since young people are more likely than adults to kill strangers (as opposed to lovers or spouses), the risk to innocent bystanders has gone up. There may be some comfort to be had in the fact that youthful homicides are only a small fraction of all killings, but given their randomness it is not much solace.

Our Two Crime Problems

The United States does not have "a" crime problem, it has at least two. Our high (though now slightly declining) rates of property crime are very much like those to be found in most of the industrialized West. They reflect a profound, worldwide cultural change: prosperity, freedom, and mobility have emancipated people almost everywhere from those ancient bonds of custom, family, and village that once held in check both some of our better and many of our worst impulses. The power of the state has been weakened, the status of children elevated, and the opportunity for adventure expanded; as a consequence, we have experienced an explosion of artistic creativity, entrepreneurial zeal, political experimentation—and criminal activity. A global economy has integrated the markets for clothes, music, automobiles—and drugs.

There are only two restraints on behavior—morality, enforced by individual conscience or social rebuke, and law, enforced by the police and the courts. If society is to maintain a behavioral equilibrium, any decline in the former must be matched by a rise in the latter (or vice versa). If familial and traditional restraints on wrongful behavior are eroded, it becomes necessary to increase the legal restraints. But the enlarged spirit of freedom and the heightened suspicion of the state have made it difficult or impossible to use the criminal justice system to achieve what custom and morality once produced.

This is the modern dilemma; and it may be an insoluble one, at least for the West. The Islamic cultures of the Middle East and the Confucian cultures of the Far East believe that they have a solution. It involves allowing enough liberty for economic progress (albeit under general state direction) while reserving to the state, and its allied religion, nearly unfettered power over personal conduct. It is too soon to tell whether this formula—best exemplified by the prosperous but puritanical city-state of Singapore—will, in the long run, be able to achieve both reproducible affluence and intense social control.

The other crime problem has to do with the kind of felonies we have: high levels of violence, especially youthful violence, often occurring as part of urban gang life and produced disproportionately by a large, alienated, and self-destructive underclass. This part of the crime problem, though not uniquely American, is more important here than in any other industrialized nation. Britons, Germans, and Swedes are upset about the insecurity of their property and uncertain about what response to make to its theft, but if Americans only had to worry about their homes being burgled and their autos stolen, I doubt that crime would be the national obsession we are now experiencing. Crime, we should recall, was not a major issue in the 1984 election and had only begun to be one in the 1988 contest; by 1992 it was challenging the economy as a popular concern and in 1994 it dominates all other matters. The reason, I think, is that Americans believe something fundamental has changed in our patterns of crime. They are right. We were unhappy about having our property put at risk, but we adapted with the aid of locks, alarms, and security guards. But we are terrified by the prospect of innocent people being gunned down at random, without warning and almost without motive, by youngsters who afterwards show us the blank, unremorseful face of a seemingly feral, presocial being.

The Characteristics of Repeat Offenders

Criminology has learned a great deal about who these people are. In studies both here and abroad it has been established that about 6 percent of the boys of a given age will commit half or more of all the serious crime produced by all boys of that age. Allowing for measurement errors, it is remarkable how consistent this formula is—6 percent causes 50 percent. It is roughly true in places as different as Philadelphia; London; Racine; and Orange County, California (Farrington, Ohlin, and Wilson 1986, 50–52; Kurz and Moore 1994).

We also have learned a lot about the characteristics of the 6 percent. They tend to have criminal parents; to live in cold or discordant families (or pseudo-families); to have a low verbal intelligence quotient and to do poorly in school; to be emotionally cold and temperamentally impulsive; to abuse alcohol and drugs at the earliest opportunity; and to reside in poor, disorderly communities. They begin their misconduct at an early age, often by the time they are in the third grade. These characteristics tend to be found not only among the criminals who get caught (and who might, owing to bad luck, be an unrepresentative sample of all high rate offenders), but among those who don't get caught but reveal their behavior on questionnaires (Herrnstein, this volume, Chapter 3; Wilson and Herrnstein 1985, chaps. 3, 6, 7, 8, 9, 10; Farrington 1991). And these traits can be identified in advance among groups of randomly selected youngsters, long before they commit any serious crimes—not with enough precision to predict which individuals will commit crimes, but with enough accuracy to be a fair depiction of the group as a whole. Not everyone in the 6 percent looks like this, and some high rate offenders begin their criminal careers much later in life; but in general few criminologists are any longer surprised to find that the typical chronic offender looks pretty much as I have described him.[2]

But a puzzle arises: If 6 percent of the males cause so large a fraction of our collective misery, and if young males are less numerous than once was the case, why are crime rates high and rising? The answer, I conjecture, is that the traits of the 6 percent put them at risk for whatever criminogenic forces operate in society. Magnify those forces and the at-risk boys will respond in exaggerated fashion, though all of us will respond to some degree. As the costs of crime decline or the benefits increase, as drugs and guns become more available, as the glorification of violence becomes more commonplace, as families and neighborhoods lose some of their restraining power—as all of these things happen, almost all of us will change our ways to some degree. For the most law-abiding among us, the change will be quite modest: a few more tools stolen from our employer, a few more traffic lights run when no police officer is watching, a few more experiments with fashionable drugs, and a few more business deals on which we cheat. For the least law-abiding among us, the change will be dramatic: we will get drunk daily instead of just on Saturday night, try PCP or crack instead of illegal cigarettes, join gangs instead of marauding in pairs, and buy automatic weapons instead of making zip guns.

A metaphor: When children play the school yard game of crack the whip, the child at the head of the line scarcely moves but the child at the far end, racing to keep his footing, often stumbles and falls, hurled to the ground by the cumulative force of many smaller movements back down the line. When a changing culture escalates criminality, the at-risk boys are at the end of the line, and the conditions of American urban life—guns, drugs, automobiles, disorganized neighborhoods—make the line very long and the ground underfoot rough and treacherous.

Prevention, Deterrence, and Western Values

Much is said these days about preventing or deterring crime, but it is important to understand exactly what we are up against when we try. Prevention, if it can be made to work at all, must start very early in life, perhaps as early as the first two or three years, and given the odds it faces—childhood impulsivity, low verbal facility, incompetent parenting, disorderly neighborhoods—be massive in scope. Deterrence, if it can be made to work harder (and surely it already works to some degree), must be applied close to the moment of the wrongful act or else the present-orientedness of the would-be offender will discount the threat so much that the promise of even a small gain will outweigh its large but deferred costs.

But in this country, and in most Western nations, we have profound misgivings about doing anything that would give prevention or deterrence a chance to make a large difference. The family is sacrosanct; the family preservation movement is strong; the state is a clumsy alternative. "Crime prevention" programs, therefore, usually take the form of creating summer jobs for adolescents, worrying about the unemployment rate, or (as in a version of the

1994 crime bill) funding midnight basketball leagues. There may be something to be said for all of these efforts, but crime prevention is not one of
them. The high rate offender is well launched on his career before he becomes a teenager or has ever encountered the labor market; he may like
basketball, but who pays for the lights and the ball is a matter of supreme
indifference to him.

Prompt deterrence has much to recommend it; the folk wisdom that swift
and certain punishment is more effective than severe penalties is almost
surely correct.[3] But the greater the swiftness and certainty, the less attention
paid to matters of guilt or innocence and the procedural safeguards essential
to establishing culpability. The courts exist in part to restrain our desire for
swiftness and certainty, and most of us want some such restraints to exist.
Despite their good instincts for the right answers, the people, frustrated by
the restraints (many wise, some foolish) on swiftness and certainty, vote for
proposals to increase severity: if the penalty is ten years, let us make it twenty
or thirty; if the penalty is life imprisonment, let us make it death; if the penalty
is jail, let us make it caning.

The more draconian the sentence, the less (on the average) the chance
of its being imposed; plea bargains see to that. And the most draconian
sentences will, of necessity, tend to fall on adult offenders nearing the end of
their criminal careers and not on the young ones who are in their criminally
most productive years. (The peak ages of criminality are between sixteen and
eighteen; the average age of prison inmates is ten years older.) I say "of
necessity" because almost every judge will give first-, second-, or even third-
time offenders a break, reserving the heaviest sentences for those men who
have finally exhausted judicial patience or optimism. Laws that say, "Three
strikes and you're out," are an effort to change this, but they suffer from an
inherent contradiction: If they are carefully drawn so as to target only the
most serious offenders they will probably have a minimal impact on the
crime rate, but if they are broadly drawn so as to make a big impact on the
crime rate they will catch many petty repeat offenders who few of us think
really deserve life imprisonment.

Prevention and deterrence, albeit hard to augment, at least are plausible
strategies. Not so with many of the other favorite nostrums. Televised violence may have some impact on criminality (Donnerstein and Linz, this
volume, Chapter 11) but I know of few scholars who think the effect is very
large. And to achieve even a small effect we might have to turn the clock back
to the kind of programming we had around 1945, because the few studies
that correlate programming with the rise in violent crime find the biggest
changes occurred between that year and 1974. Boot camps made good copy,
but so far no one has shown that they reduce the rate at which the former
inmates commit crimes (Greenwood, this volume, Chapter 5; Clear and
Braga, this volume, Chapter 18). Guns are almost certainly contributors to the
lethality of American violence, but there is no politically or legally feasible

way to reduce the stock of guns now in private possession to the point that their availability to criminals would be much affected (compare with Cook and Moore, this volume, Chapter 12). And even if there were, law-abiding people would lose a means of protecting themselves long before criminals lost a means of attacking them. Rehabilitating juvenile offenders has some merit, but there are few big success stories. Individually, the best (and best-evaluated) programs have minimal, if any, effects; collectively, the best estimate of the crime reduction value of these programs is quite modest, something on the order of 5 or 10 percent.[4]

Controlling the Streets

What, then, is to be done? Let us begin with policing, since law enforcement officers are that part of the criminal justice system that is closest to the situations in which criminal activity is likely to occur. It is now widely accepted that, however important it is for officers to drive around waiting for 911 calls summoning their help, doing that is not enough. As a supplement to a reactive strategy, comprising random preventive patrol and the investigation of crimes that have already occurred, many leaders and students of law enforcement now urge the police to be "proactive"—to identify, with the aid of citizen groups, problems that can be solved so as to prevent as well as respond to criminality. This is often called community-based policing. But what, exactly, does this entail? Something more than feel-good meetings with honest citizens, but something less than allowing neighborhoods to assume control of the police function.

Let me suggest that, to the extent their resources permit, the police ought to engage in *directed,* not random, patrol, and should make the following the goal of that direction: to reduce, consistent with fundamental liberties, the opportunity for high-risk persons to do those things that increase the likelihood of their victimizing others. Here are some examples:

Stop and pat down persons who the police reasonably suspect may be carrying illegal guns. The Supreme Court has upheld such frisks when an officer observes "unusual conduct" leading him to conclude that "criminal activity may be afoot" on the part of a person who may be "armed and dangerous." This is all rather vague, but it can be clarified in two ways (see Wilson [1994]). Statutes can be enacted that make certain persons, on the basis of their past conduct and present legal status, subject to pat downs for weapons. And technology can be developed that provides the officer with a reasonable suspicion that a suspect is carrying a concealed weapon. The statutes can, as is now the case in several states, make all probationers and parolees subject to nonconsensual searches for weapons as a condition of their remaining on probation or parole. Since three-fourths of all offenders (and a large fraction of all convicted felons) are in the community rather than in prison, there are on any given day over three million convicted criminals on the streets under correctional supervision. Many are likely to become recidivists. Keeping them from carrying weapons will materially reduce the chances that they will rob or kill. It is also possible that courts might declare, under statutory authority, certain dangerous street gangs to be continuing criminal enterprises, membership in which constitutes grounds for police frisks. Since I first proposed such a strategy, I have learned that there are efforts under way in public and private research laboratories to develop technologies that will permit the police to detect from a distance persons who are carrying concealed weapons on the streets; should these efforts bear fruit, they will provide the police with the grounds for stopping, questioning, and patting down even persons not on probation or parole or obviously in gangs. Whether or not the technology works, the police can also offer immediate cash rewards to people who provide information of individuals illegally carrying weapons. Spending $100 on each good tip will have a bigger effect on dangerous gun use than will the same amount spent buying back guns from law-abiding people.[5] Getting illegal firearms off the streets will require that the police be motivated to do all of these things. But if the legal, techno-logical, and motivational issues can be resolved, our streets can be made safer even without sending many more people to prison.

The same directed patrol strategy might help keep known offenders drug free. Most persons jailed in big cities were using illegal drugs within the day or two preceding their arrest. When convicted, some are given probation on condition that they enter drug treatment programs; others are sent to prisons where (if they are lucky) drug treatment programs operate. But in many cities the enforcement of such probation conditions is casual or nonexistent; in many states parolees are released back into drug-infested communities with little effort to insure that they participate in whatever treatment programs are to be found there (see Boyum and Kleiman, this volume, Chapter 13). Almost everyone agrees that more treatment programs should exist, but what many advocates overlook is that steadfast participation is the key to success and many, probably most, offenders have no incentive to be steadfast. Patrol officers could enforce random drug tests on probationers and parolees on their beats; failing to take a test when ordered, or failing the test when taken, should be grounds for immediate revocation of probation or parole, at least for a brief period of confinement. The goal of this tactic is not simply to keep offenders drug free (and thereby lessen their incentive to steal the money needed to buy drugs and reduce their likelihood of committing crimes be-cause they are on a drug high); it is also to diminish the demand for drugs generally and thus the size of the drug market.

Lest the reader embrace this idea too quickly, let me add that as yet we have no good reason to think that it will reduce the crime rate by very much. Something akin to this strategy (albeit one using probation instead of police officers) has been tried under the name of "intensive supervision programs," or ISPs. By means of a set of randomized experiments carried out in fourteen cities, Joan Petersilia and Susan Turner (1993), both then at the Rand Corporation, compared the rearrest rates of offenders assigned to ISPs (with their panoply of drug tests, house arrests, frequent surveillance, and careful records) with those of offenders in ordinary probation. There was no difference. But this study does not settle the matter. For one thing, since the ISP participants were under much closer surveillance than the regular probationers, the former were bound to be caught breaking the law more frequently than the latter. It is possible that a higher fraction of the crimes committed by the ISP group than of those committed by the control group were detected and resulted in a return to prison, which would mean, if true, a net gain in public safety. For another thing, "intensive" supervision was in many cities not all that intensive—in five cities, contacts with the probationers occurred only about once a week, and for all cities drug tests occurred on average only once a month. Finally, there is some indication that participation in treatment programs was associated with lower recidivism rates.

Both antigun and antidrug police patrols will, if done systematically, require big changes in police and court procedures and a significant increase in the resources devoted to both, at least in the short run. (The ISP approach is not cheap, and it will become even more expensive if it is done in a truly intensive fashion.) Most officers have at present no incentive to search for guns or enforce drug tests; many jurisdictions, owing to crowded dockets or overcrowded jails, are lax about enforcing the conditions of probation or parole (Langan 1994). The result is that the one group of high-risk people over which society already has the legal right to exercise substantial control is often out of control, "supervised," if at all, by means of brief monthly interviews with overworked probation or parole officers.

Much crime is opportunistic: idle boys, usually in small groups, sometimes find the opportunity to steal or the challenge to fight irresistible. It is possible to deter such crimes by a credible threat of prompt sanctions, but deterring present-oriented youngsters who want to appear fearless in the eyes of their comrades while indulging their thrill-seeking natures is a tall order. It is easier to reduce their chances for risky group idleness in the first place. Realizing this, many cities are beginning to enforce truancy and curfew laws.

In Charleston, South Carolina, for example, Chief Reuben Greenberg instructed his officers to return all school-age children to the schools from which they were truant and to return all youngsters violating an evening curfew agreement to their parents. As a result, groups of school-age children were no longer to be found hanging out in the shopping malls or wandering the streets late at night. Burglaries and larcenies declined. There has been no careful evaluation of these efforts in Charleston (or, so far as I am aware, in any other big city), but the rough figures are impressive—the Charleston crime rate in 1991 was about 25 percent lower than the rate in South

Carolina's other principal cities and, for most offenses, lower than what that city reported twenty years earlier.

All of these tactics have in common putting the police, as Lawrence Sherman phrases it, where the "hot spots" are (Sherman, this volume, Chapter 14). Most people need no police attention except for a response to their calls for help. A small fraction of people (and places) need constant attention. In Minneapolis, for example, *all* of the robberies during one year occurred at just 2 percent of the city's addresses. To capitalize on this fact, the Minneapolis police began devoting extra patrol attention, in brief but frequent bursts of activity, to those locations known to be trouble spots. A careful evaluation suggested that robbery rates fell by as much as 20 percent and public disturbances by even more.

Some of the worst hot spots are outdoor drug markets. Because of limited resources, a fear of police corruption, or a desire to catch only the drug kingpins, the police in some cities (including, from time to time, New York) neglect street-corner dealing. By doing so, they get the worst of all worlds. The public, seeing the police ignore drug dealing that is in plain view, assumes that they are corrupt whether or not they are. The drug kingpins, who are hard to catch and are easily replaced by rival smugglers, find that their essential retail distribution system remains intact. Casual or first-time drug users, who might not use at all if access to supplies were difficult, find access to be effortless and so increase their consumption. People who might remain in treatment programs if drugs were hard to get drop out when they learn that they are easy to get. Interdicting without merely displacing drug markets is difficult but not impossible, but it requires motivation which some departments lack and resources which many don't have.

The sheer number of police on the streets of a city probably has only a weak, if any, relationship with the crime rate; what the police do is more important than how many there are, at least above some minimum level. But patrol directed at hot spots, loitering truants, late night wanderers, probationers, parolees, and possible gun carriers, all in addition to routine investigative activities, will require more officers in many cities. Between 1977 and 1987, the number of police officers declined in a third of the fifty largest cities and fell relative to population in many more. Just how far behind police resources have lagged can be gauged from this fact: In 1950 there was one violent crime reported for every police officer; in 1980 there were three violent crimes reported for every officer.

Prison

I have said little so far about penal policy, in part because I wish to focus attention on those things that are likely to have the largest and most immediate impact on the quality of urban life. But given the vast gulf between what the public believes and what many experts argue should be our penal policy, a few comments are essential. The public wants more people sent away for longer sentences; many (probably most) criminologists think we use prison too much and at too great a cost and that this excessive use has had little beneficial effect on the crime rate.

My views are much closer to those of the public, though I think the average person exaggerates the faults of the present system and the gains of some alternative (such as "three strikes and you're out"). The expert view as it is expressed in countless op-ed essays often goes like this: "We have been arresting more and more people and giving them longer and longer sentences, producing no decrease in crime but huge increases in prison populations. As a result we have become the most punitive nation on earth."

Scarcely a phrase in those sentences is accurate. The probability of being arrested for a given crime is lower in 1994 than it was in 1974. The amount of time served in state prison has been declining more or less steadily since the 1940s: the median time served for burglary, for example, was thirty months in 1945 and thirteen months in 1984. Only for rape are prisoners serving as much time today as they did in the 1940s. Taking all crimes together, time served fell from twenty-five months in 1945 to thirteen months in 1984. The net effect of lower arrest rates and shorter effective sentences was that the cost of the average adult burglary fell from fifty days in 1960 to fifteen days in 1980. That is to say, the chances of being caught and convicted, multiplied by the median time served if imprisoned, was in 1980 less than a third of what it had been in 1960. [6]

Beginning in around 1980 the costs of crime began to inch up, the result, chiefly, of an increase in the proportion of convicted persons who were given prison terms. By 1986 the "price" of a given burglary had risen to twenty-one days. Also beginning in around 1980, the crime rate (as measured by household surveys) began to decline. It would be foolhardy to explain the drop in crime by the rise in imprisonment rates; many other factors, such as the aging of the population and the self-protective measures of potential victims, were also at work. Only a controlled experiment (for example, randomly allocating prison terms for a given crime among the states) could hope to untangle the causal patterns, and happily the Constitution makes such experiments unlikely. But it is worth noting that changes in the age structure of the population cannot explain even half of either the increase or the decrease in crime rates and that nations with different penal policies have experienced different crime rates. According to David Farrington of Cambridge University, property crime rates rose in England and Sweden at a time when both the imprisonment rate and time served fell substantially, while property crime rates declined in the United States at a time when the imprisonment rate (but not time served) was increasing (Farrington and Langan 1992; Farrington and Wikstrom 1993).

Though one cannot measure the effect of prison on crime with any accuracy, it would be astonishing if it had no effect. For example: By 1986 there were 55,000 more robbers in prison than there had been in 1974. Assume that each imprisoned robber would commit five such offenses per year if free on the street. That means in 1986 there were 275,000 fewer robberies in America than there would have been had these 55,000 men been left on the street.

Nor does America use prison to a degree that vastly exceeds what is found in any other civilized nation. Compare the chance of going to prison in England and the United States if one is convicted of a given crime. According to Farrington and Langan (1992), your chances were higher in England if you were found guilty of a rape, higher in America if you were convicted of an assault or a burglary, and about the same if you were convicted of a homicide or a robbery. Once in prison, you would serve a longer time in this country than in England for almost all offenses save murder. James Lynch has reached similar conclusions from his comparative study of criminal justice policies (this volume, Chapter 2). His data show that the chances of going to prison and the time served for homicide and robbery are roughly the same in the United States, Canada, and England.

Starting in the mid-1980s, drug sentences began to change American penal practice radically. In 1982, only about 8 percent of state prison inmates were serving time on drug convictions. In 1987 that started to increase sharply; by 1994 over 60 percent of all federal and about 25 percent of all state prisoners were there on drug charges. In some states, such as New York, the percentage was even higher. This change can be attributed largely to the advent of crack cocaine. Whereas snorted cocaine powder was expensive, crack was cheap; whereas the former was distributed through networks catering to elite tastes, the latter was mass marketed on street corners. The public was rightly fearful of what crack was doing to their children and demanded action; as a result, crack dealers started going to prison in record numbers. These penalties may or may not deter dealing, but they do not have the same incapacitative effect as sentences for robbery. A robber taken off the street is not replaced by a new robber who has suddenly found a market niche, but a drug dealer sent away is replaced by a new one because an opportunity has opened up.

Reducing drug use requires reducing the demand for drugs, and that in turn requires either prevention programs on a scale heretofore unimagined or treatment programs with a level of effectiveness heretofore unachieved. Any big gains in prevention and treatment will probably have to await further basic research into the biochemistry of addiction and the development of effective and attractive drug antagonists that reduce the appeal of cocaine and similar substances.[7]

In the meantime, it is necessary to build much more prison space, find some other way of disciplining drug offenders, or both. There is very little to be gained, I think, from shortening the terms of existing nondrug inmates in order to free up more prison space. Except for a few elderly, nonviolent offenders serving very long terms, there are real risks associated with shortening the terms of the typical inmate. Scholars disagree about the magnitude of those risks, but the best studies, such as the one of Wisconsin inmates done by Professor John DiIulio of Princeton, suggest that the annual costs in crime committed by an offender on the street are probably twice the costs of putting him in a cell (DiIulio and Piehl 1991; see also Cavanaugh and Kleiman [1990]). That ratio will vary from state to state because states differ in what proportion of convicted persons are imprisoned—some states dip deeper down into the pool of convictees, thereby imprisoning some with minor criminal habits.

But I caution the reader to understand that there are no easy prison solutions to crime, even if we build the additional space. The state prison population more than doubled between 1980 and 1990, yet the victimization rate for robbery fell by only 23 percent. Even if we assign all of that gain to the increased deterrent and incapacitative effect of prison, which is implausible, it is not a vast improvement. Of course it is possible that the victimization rate would have risen, perhaps by a large amount, instead of falling if we had not increased the number of inmates, but we shall never know.

Two things need to be said about imprisonment as a way of reducing crime. The first applies to its incapacitative effect. Very large increases in the prison population can produce only modest reductions in crime rates. That seems counterintuitive. If we double the number of prison inmates or double the sentences they serve, should not the crime rate fall by a like amount? The reader should understand why this doesn't happen; why, that is, that doubling the prison population probably produced only a 10 to 20 percent reduction in the crime rate.

One reason is that judges already send the most serious offenders with the longest records to prison. Very few judges, contrary to what some people think, give slaps on the wrist to robbers and assaulters who are three-time losers. This fact means that as you increase the proportion of convicted offenders who go to prison instead of being put on probation, you dip deeper into the bucket of persons eligible for prison, dredging up offenders with shorter and shorter criminal records. The marginal utility (where utility is the prevention of a crime) of sending each additional offender to prison will, on the average, decline.

Moreover, the most serious offenders typically get the longest sentences. All offenders have a criminal career of a finite length. (Some thugs may mug and murder until the day they die, but they are the exception. Age slows us all down, mugger and victim alike.) Alfred Blumstein and his colleagues have estimated that the criminal career of the average adult who has committed a violent crime is about ten years (Blumstein, Cohen, and Hsieh 1982). This means that if you lengthen the sentence of the persons already going to prison, you shorten the length of their criminal career. At some point you will be keeping them in prison during the years of their life when, if they were on the streets, they would have stopped offending. This does not mean inmates should be set free as soon as some social scientist predicts their careers are over; social scientists cannot make such predictions accurately for given individuals, and in any case many of these inmates (Charles Manson comes to mind) have committed such heinous acts that justice requires very long sentences, or even execution. But lengthening time served beyond some point will, like increasing the proportion of convicted criminals sent to prison, encounter diminishing marginal returns.

The second problem has to do with deterrence. The threat of punishment deters almost all of us to some degree. Even if sending a higher fraction of all criminals to prison for longer periods has only modest (but still quite worthwhile) crime reduction effects, wouldn't the increased chances of going to prison deter would-be offenders? Maybe. A lot depends on what drives the chances of going to prison and how feasible it is to increase those chances in a meaningful way.

Recall my discususion of the decline in the costs of crime, measured by the number of days in prison that result, on average, from the commission of a given crime. It is vastly lower today than in the 1950s. But much of that decline (and since 1974, nearly all of it) is the result of a drop in the probability of being arrested for a crime, not in the probability of being imprisoned once arrested (see Langan [1991]). By my rough calculations, the odds that a robbery reported to the police would result in an arrest for robbery fell, between 1960 and 1989, by about 16 percent. Langan (1991) found that during the period (the late 1970s and early 1980s) when the chances of an accused person going to prison were rising, the chances of a crime resulting in an arrest were still declining. By his account, the arrest rate for robbery fell by 20 percent between 1974 and 1986. Between arrest and conviction lies the prosecutor's decision whether or not to charge, what plea bargain to accept, and what penalty to request. We have few data on how prosecutorial behavior has changed (compare Forst, this volume, Chapter 16).

All of this means that increasing the deterrent effect of prison is not as easy as it may first appear. You will have to first increase the arrest rate; more cops would help, but that is not enough. You will have to find more prosecutors (and public defenders) and make them work harder, because if the chances of prison for a given offense go up, the chances of a defendant taking a plea bargain go down. Then you would to have to shrink judicial discretion, something that judges will fight to the bitter end. They don't like mandatory sentencing laws, and some are willing to find ways of evading those that exist.

Thinking clearly about prison in a democratic society is hard for two reasons. Some people believe (wrongly) that prison is fundamentally incompatible with a free society and so wish to use it as little as possible, while others feel (rightly) that prison is essential to the protection of our freedoms but exaggerate how much can be achieved by its extensive use.

Possibly we can make larger gains by turning our attention to the unexplored area of juvenile justice. Juvenile (or family) courts deal with young people just starting their criminal careers and with chronic offenders when they are often in their peak years of offending. We know rather little about how these courts work or with what effect. There are few, if any, careful studies of what happens, a result in part of scholarly neglect and in part of the practice in some states of shrouding juvenile records and proceedings in secrecy. Some studies, such as one by the *Los Angeles Times* of juvenile justice in California, suggest that young people found guilty of a serious crime are given sentences tougher than those meted out to adults (reported in Greenwood, this volume, Chapter 5). This finding is so counter to popular beliefs and the testimony of many big city juvenile court judges that some caution is required in interpreting it.

There are two problems. The first lies in defining the universe of people to whom sanctions are applied. In some states, such as California, it may well be the case that a juvenile *found guilty of a serious offense* is punished with greater rigor than an adult; but many juveniles whose behavior ought to be taken seriously (because they show signs of being part of the 6 percent) are released by the police or probation officers before ever seeing a judge. And in some states, such as New York, juveniles charged with having committed certain crimes, including such serious ones as illegally carrying a loaded gun or committing an assault, may not be fingerprinted. Since persons with a prior record are usually given longer sentences than those without one, the failure to fingerprint can mean that the court has no way of knowing whether the John Smith standing before it is the same John Smith that was arrested four times for assault and so ought to be sent away or a different John Smith whose clean record entitles him to probation.

The second problem arises from the definition of a "severe" penalty. In California, a juvenile found guilt of murder does, indeed, serve a longer sentence than an adult convicted of the same offense—sixty months for the former, forty-one months for the latter. Many people will be puzzled by a newspaper account that defines five years in prison for murder as a "severe" sentence, and angered to learn that an adult serves less than four years for such a crime.

The key, unanswered question is whether prompt and more effective early intervention would stop high rate delinquents from becoming high rate criminals at a time when their offenses were not yet too serious. Perhaps early and swift though not necessarily severe sanctions could deter some budding hoodlums, but we have no evidence of that as yet.

Attacking the Causes

For as long as I can remember, the debate over crime has been between those who wished to rely on the criminal justice system and those who wished to attack the root causes of crime. I have always been in the former group because what its opponents depicted as "root causes"—unemployment, racism, poor housing, too little schooling, a lack of self-esteem—turned out, on close examination, not to be major causes at all.

Of late, however, there has been a shift in the debate. Increasingly those who want to attack causes have begun to point to real causes—temperament, early family experiences, and neighborhood effects. The sketch I gave earlier of the typical high rate young offender suggests that these factors are, indeed, causal. The problem now is to decide whether any can be changed by plan and at an acceptable cost in money and personal freedom.

If we are to do this, we must confront the fact that the critical years of a child's life are ages one to ten, with perhaps the most important being the earliest years. During those years, some children are put gravely at risk by some combination of heritable traits, prenatal insults (maternal drug and alcohol abuse or poor diet), weak parent-child attachment, poor supervision, and disorderly family environment. If we knew with reasonable confidence which children were most seriously at risk, we might intervene with some precision to supply either medical therapy or parent training or (in extreme cases) to remove the child to a better home. But given our present knowledge, precision is impossible, and so we must proceed carefully relying, except in the most extreme cases, on persuasion and incentives.

But we do know enough about the early causes of conduct disorder and later delinquency to know that the more risk factors (such as parental criminality and poor parental supervision of children) that exist, the greater the peril to the child. It follows that programs aimed at just one or a few factors are not likely to be successful; the children most at risk are the ones that require the most wide-ranging and fundamental changes in their life circumstances. The goal of these changes is, as Travis Hirschi has put it, to teach self-control (this volume, Chapter 6).

Hirokazu Yoshikawa (1994) has recently summarized what we know about programs that attempt to make large and lasting changes in a child's prospects for improved conduct, better school behavior, and lessened delinquency. Four in particular seemed valuable—the Perry Preschool Project in Ypsilanti, Michigan; the Parent-Child Development Center in Houston, Texas; the Family Development Research Project in Syracuse, New York; and the Yale Child Welfare Project in New Haven, Connecticut. All had certain features in common. They dealt with low-income, often minority, families; they intervened during the first five years of a child's life and continued for between two and five years; they combined parent training with preschool education for the child; and they involved extensive home visits. All were evaluated fairly carefully, with the follow-ups lasting for at least five years, in two cases for at least ten, and in one case for fourteen. The programs produced (depending on the project) less fighting, impulsivity, disobedience, restlessness, cheating, and delinquency. In short, they improved self-control.

They were experimental programs, which means that it is hard to be confident that trying the same thing on a bigger scale in many places will produce the same effects. A large number of well-trained and highly motivated case workers dealt with a relatively small number of families, with the workers knowing that their efforts were being evaluated. Moreover the programs operated in the late 1970s or early 1980s before the advent of crack cocaine or the rise of the more lethal neighborhood gangs. A national program mounted under current conditions may or may not have the same result as the experimental efforts.

Try telling that to lawmakers. What happens when politicians encounter experimental successes is amply revealed by the history of Head Start: they expanded the program quickly without assuring quality, and stripped it down to the part that is the most popular, least expensive, and easiest to run, namely, preschool education. Absent from much of Head Start are the high teacher-to-child caseloads, the extensive home visits, and the elaborate parent training—the very things that probably account for much of the success of the four experimental programs.

In this country we tend to separate programs designed to help children from those that benefit their parents. The former are called "child development," the latter "welfare reform." This is a great mistake. Everything we know about long-term welfare recipients indicates that their children are at risk for the very problems that child-helping programs later try to correct. The evidence from a variety of studies is quite clear: even holding income and ethnicity constant, children (and especially boys) raised by a single mother are more likely than those raised by two parents to have difficulty in school, get in trouble with the law, and experience emotional and physical problems (Wilson 1993; Dawson 1988; McLanahan and Sandefur 1994; Furstenberg et al. 1989). Producing illegitimate children is not an "alternative lifestyle" or simply an imprudent action; it is a curse. Making mothers work will not end the curse; under current proposals, it won't even save money. The absurdity of divorcing the welfare problem from the child development problem becomes evident as soon as we think seriously about what we want to achieve. Smaller welfare expenditures? Well, yes, but not if it hurts children. More young mothers working? Probably not; young mothers ought to raise their young children, and work interferes with that unless *two* parents can solve some difficult and expensive issues. What we really want is *fewer illegitimate children,* because such children, except in unusual cases, by being born out of wedlock are being given early admission to the underclass. And failing that, we want the children born to single (and typically young and poor) mothers to have a chance at a decent life.

Letting teenage girls set up their own households at public expense neither discourages illegitimacy nor serves the child's best interests. If they do set up their own homes, then to reach those with the fewest parenting skills and the most difficult children will require the kind of expensive and

506   JAMES Q. WILSON

intensive home visits and family support programs characteristic of the four successful experiments mentioned earlier. One alternative is to tell a girl who applies for welfare that she can receive it only on condition that she live either in the home of *two* competent parents (her own if she comes from an intact family) or in a group home where competent supervision and parent training will be provided by adults unrelated to her. Such homes would be privately managed but publicly funded by pooling welfare checks, food stamps, and housing allowances. One model for such a group home (albeit one run without public funds) is the St. Martin de Porres House of Hope on the south side of Chicago, founded by two nuns for homeless young women, especially those with drug abuse problems. The goals of the home are clear: accept personal responsibility for your lives and learn to care for your children. And these goals, in turn, require the girls to follow rules, stay in school, obey a curfew, and avoid alcohol and drugs (Driscoll 1993). Those are the rules that ought to govern a group home for young welfare mothers.

Group homes funded by pooled welfare benefits would make the task of parent training much easier and provide the kind of structured, consistent, and nurturant environment that children need. A few cases might be too difficult for these homes, and for such children boarding schools—once common in American cities for disadvantaged children, but now almost extinct—might be revived.

Such homes also make it easier to supply quality medical care to young mothers and their children. Such care has taken on added importance in recent years with discovery of the lasting damage that can be done to a child's prospects from being born prematurely and with a very low birth weight, having a mother who has abused drugs or alcohol, or being exposed to certain dangerous metals. Lead poisoning is now widely acknowledged to be a source of cognitive and behavioral impairment; of late, elevated levels of manganese have been linked to high levels of violence (Gottschalk et al. 1991; see also Fishbein and Pease [1988]).[8] These are all treatable conditions; in the case of a manganese imbalance, easily treatable.

My focus on changing behavior will annoy some readers. For them the problem is poverty and the worst feature of single parent families is that they are inordinately poor. To even refer to a behavioral or cultural problem is to "stigmatize" people. Indeed it is. Wrong behavior—neglectful, immature, or incompetent parenting; the production of out-of-wedlock babies—*ought* to be stigmatized. There are many poor men of all races who do not abandon the women they have impregnated and many poor women of all races who avoid drugs and do a good job of raising their children. If we fail to stigmatize those who give way to temptations we withdraw the rewards from those who resist them. This becomes all the more important when entire communities, and not just isolated households, are dominated by a culture of fatherless boys preying on innocent persons and exploiting immature girls.

We need not merely stigmatize, however. We can try harder to move children out of those communities, either by drawing them into safe group homes or facilitating (through rent supplements and housing vouchers) the relocation of them and their parents to neighborhoods with intact social structures and an ethos of family values. Much of our uniquely American crime problem (as opposed to the worldwide problem of general thievery) arises, not from the failings of individuals, but from the concentration of people at risk for failing in disorderly neighborhoods (compare Sampson, this volume, Chapter 9). That concentration is partly the result of prosperity and freedom (functioning families long ago seized the opportunity to move out to the periphery), partly the result of racism (it is harder for some groups to move than for others), and partly the result of politics (elected officials do not wish to see settled constituencies broken up).

Conclusions

I seriously doubt that this country has the will to address either of its two crime problems, save by acts of individual self-protection. We could in theory make justice swifter and more certain, but we will not. We could vastly improve the way in which our streets are policed, but some of us won't pay for it and the rest of us won't tolerate it. We could alter the way in which at-risk children experience the first few years of life, but the opponents of this—welfare rights activists, family preservationists, budget cutters, and assorted ideologues—are numerous and the bureaucratic problems enormous. Instead we debate the death penalty, wring our hands about television, lobby to keep prisons from being built in our neighborhoods, and fall briefly in love with trendy nostrums that seem to cost little and promise much.

Meanwhile, just beyond the horizon, there lurks a cloud that the winds will soon bring over us. The population will start getting younger again. By the end of this decade there will be a million more people between the ages of fourteen and seventeen than there are now; this increase will follow the decade of the 1980s when people in that age group declined, not only as a proportion of the total but in absolute numbers. This extra million will be half male. Six percent of them will become high rate, repeat offenders—thirty thousand more young muggers, killers, and thieves than we have now.

Get ready.

NOTES AND REFERENCES

CONTRIBUTORS

INDEX

NOTES AND REFERENCES

Chapter 1 has no references.

2. James Lynch, "Crime in International Perspective"

Notes

1. See Miller (1977) for a discussion of how urbanization and industrialization in England led to the disruption of traditional institutions, a rise in crime, and the development of the modern police.

2. For illustrations of the case study methodology see Koppel (1992); Dobash and Dobash (1992); Miller (1977). For an illustration of a case study that uses less qualitative information but takes great care getting the statistics right, see Farrington and Langan (1992).

3. For illustration of studies that test quantitative models see Bennett and Lynch (1990); Stack (1984); Gartner and Parker (1990a and 1990b); Messner (1989).

4. For a good discussion of the different types of distortions that various types of statistical systems can introduce see Biderman (1966) and Biderman and Lynch (1991).

5. With somewhat more effort, annual police statistics from individual nations can be used for comparison purposes. Much more information is available in these reports, but they often require translation and extensive work to ensure comparability of crime classes and procedures.

6. Violent crime includes rape, robbery, and various forms of assault, including attempts.

7. The National Crime Victimization Survey (BJS 1992) indicates that only 41.5 percent of simple assaults are reported to the police, 58.4 percent of aggravated

assaults, 54.7 percent of purse snatchings, 28.1 percent of personal larcenies without contact, and 14.6 percent of larcenies involving household property worth under $50.

8. The differences in the proportion of crimes reported to the police are much reduced when the range of countries is restricted to those most similar to the United States. Canadians report 49.8 percent, Americans 52 percent, Australians 46.4 percent, and victims in England and Wales report 58.7 percent. This is probably due to the similarity of the crime mix in these countries, as we will see later in this chapter.

9. Unfortunately police statistics do not always clearly differentiate commercial from noncommercial crime. For a discussion of this in the United States see Biderman and Lynch (1991).

10. Teske and Arnold (1982) have made a detailed comparison of legal codes and crime classification schemes for Germany and the United States.

11. Some police data systems can fall substantially short of total coverage for the nation (Biderman and Lynch 1991). This is in some ways the worst of both worlds, since the result is neither a census nor a systematic sample. Moreover, there is good reason to believe that differences in the coverage of these systems is not constant across nations. Coverage in federated nations may be less adequate than in those more politically or administratively centralized.

12. The data used to compute these rates were taken from FBI (1989, 12) and Home Office (1989, 75).

13. This is due primarily to the fact that property crime is much more prevalent than violent crime. One interpretation is that wealthier people simply have more to steal than the less wealthy. There is also some evidence that the victim survey method may underestimate the victimization experience of the less educated relative to the more educated (Hubble 1990; Lynch 1993b). Since income is highly correlated with education, this type of measurement error may affect the observed differences between income groups.

14. These standardizations were done with the public use file from the 1988 ICS.

15. The ICS has much more potential to illuminate differences in cross-national rates of property crime. Much more complex standardization can be done. The data are particularly well suited for multi-level models wherein nation-level variables can be included with the characteristics of victims to provide a much more nearly complete picture of why nations differ with respect to the level of crime. The small sample sizes in the survey will limit what can be done, but pooling the 1988 and 1992 surveys will help in this regard. There are also some questions about sources of measurement error in the survey that may affect cross-national comparisons (Lynch 1993b). These can and must be dealt with if the ICS is to fulfill its potential.

16. In 1978, for example, I noted that only 9 of the 87 persons convicted of murder in Sweden were imprisoned. I wrote to the director of the agency responsible for Swedish prison statistics questioning the accuracy of the data. He responded that the data were indeed accurate. He noted, however, that in the same year 67 of the persons convicted of murder were sentenced to secure mental institutions for indefinite periods. The decision to include or exclude mental hospitals in the definition of incarceration is the difference between a conviction-based incarceration rate of 87.4 or 10.3.

17. Although flow designs have a number of advantages over stock designs, some of which were mentioned earlier, they also have a number of potential disadvantages. Rather than confounding length of sentence with the propensity to incarcer-

ate as stock studies do, flow designs can confuse delay in court processing with the incarceration rate. The bias introduced by delay can be ignored if we can make one of two assumptions—that the bias is offsetting from year to year, or that delay in processing felony offenses is fairly constant across countries. A second source of possible error in flow designs restricted to a specific type of crime results from changes in charge during court processing. Offenders who are arrested for aggravated assault but plead guilty to and are sentenced for simple assault drop out of a flow study which is restricted to aggravated assaults. Since the offender is arrested for aggravated assault, his arrest will be included in the denominator of the incarceration rate. Because he is admitted to prison for simple assault, his admission will be excluded from the numerator, thereby artificially reducing the incarceration rate. If charge reduction practices are reasonably similar across countries, then they should not affect the accuracy of the comparison.

18. Time served in custody is used rather than imposed sentence because the determinacy of the sentencing process varies across nations. Sentences imposed by the court, for example, can later be modified by correctional administrators via "good time" or by parole boards through decisions to grant early release. It is essential that countries be compared as much as possible on the basis of the final decision made on an offender for a particular crime.

19. As incoming cohorts receive longer sentences, fewer of these inmates will appear immediately in the release cohorts. Hence exiting cohorts have fewer of the more harshly sentenced prisoners in them and more persons with relatively short sentences. Albert Biderman has pointed out that in the case of rapid and substantial increases in sentence length, the time served based on release cohorts would be shorter when the actual time served is increasing.

20. Using crime specific rates does not remove all of the problems inherent in differences in the nature of crime.

21. One of the major difficulties in obtaining crime-specific incarceration rates is selecting the appropriate method for controlling for the volume of crime.

The number of persons convicted for a specific type of crime would be the most desirable base for an incarceration rate, since it includes only those persons who have been found guilty. This would provide the most interpretable measure of the relative punitiveness of sentencing practices cross-nationally. Defining the particular point at which conviction occurs in each country, however, is not simple due to the differences in the structure of the criminal justice process. In the United States, for example, prosecutors can decide not to proceed with a case for reasons other than evidentiary strength. Indeed, there is strong evidence to suggest that the less serious crimes are less likely to be prosecuted (Jacoby et al. 1982) regardless of the evidentiary strength of the case. By deciding not to proceed, the prosecutor makes the decision not to incarcerate.

In systems like that of Germany where prosecutors do not have the same discretion to decline to prosecute (Langbien 1979), the judge may be confronted with many more less serious cases in his sentencing decision, and fewer convicted persons will be incarcerated. If the two systems were compared using an incarceration rate based on convicted persons, then Germany would appear less punitive than the United States when the two systems may be quite similar if some decisions not to prosecute are included as decisions not to incarcerate. Since different actors make the same decisions in different countries, there is no unambiguous choice of decision point for assessing the punitiveness of sentencing practices cross-nationally. Convicted persons may be the most appropriate base for an incarceration rate, but determining when conviction occurs in each system is problematic. Moreover, comprehensive and offense-specific data on sentencing are not widely available.

22. Farrington and Langan (1992, 14) note that about one-half of the persons receiving a noncustodial sentence for homicide were sentenced to secure mental hospitals. In the United States the proportion sentenced to mental hospitals for homicide is negligible. Consequently, it may be better to use the figure .93 as the probability of custody given conviction in England and Wales rather than .86.

23. The arrest data for drugs were taken from BJS (1992, 158). Admissions data for State and Federal prisons were taken from BJS (1993). Jail admissions were estimated by multiplying the admissions to state prison by the proportion of felons sentenced to incarceration who will serve their sentences in jails (as opposed to prison).

24. In this calculation arrest in England and Wales was approximated by adding together all those proceeded against in magistrates court and all of those cautioned by the police for drug offenses. Some may object to the inclusion of cautioning as equivalent to arrest in the United States because it is less severe. If cautions are excluded the incarceration rate for drug offenses is .092. The truth may lie somewhere in between. Under the first assumption the probability of incarceration given arrest in the United States is 2.69 times that in England and Wales. Under the second assumption, the probability of incarceration in the United States is 1.6 times that in England and Wales. Either way the difference is considerable.

25. Some may argue with using other nations as a standard for the appropriate level of incarceration. Utilitarian standards—e.g., crime levels or reductions—or just desserts standards may be more suitable or rational. There is no contesting, however, the fact that cross-national comparisons are widely used to assess criminal justice policy, and, as a result, they merit attention.

26. We must be cautious in drawing conclusions from some of the data presented above because they pertain to the mid-1980s. There is good evidence that sentencing policy may have changed substantially in the later 1980s, at least in the United States (see Chapter 16 in this volume). The probability is that these changes have only accentuated the relationships observed here. The differences between the United States and other nations in the prevalence of incarceration and the time served for lesser violence and property offenses has probably increased, while the differences for more serious violence have remained less pronounced. These are conjectures. Cross-national comparisons based on more recent data are required.

References

Archer, Dane, and Rosemary Gartner. 1984. *Violence and Crime in a Cross-national Perspective.* New Haven: Yale University Press.

Bennett, Richard R., and James P. Lynch. 1990. "Does a Difference Make a Difference? Comparing Cross-national Crime Indicators." *Criminology* 28 (1).

Biderman, Albert. 1966. "Social Indicators and Goals." In *Social Indicators,* ed. Raymond Bauer. Cambridge, Mass.: MIT Press.

Biderman, Albert, and James P. Lynch. 1991. *Understanding Crime Incidence Statistics: Why the UCR Diverges from the NCS.* New York: Springer Verlag.

Bittner, Egon. 1968. "The Police on Skid Row." *American Journal of Sociology.*

———. 1973. *The Functions of the Police in Modern Society.* Cambridge, Mass.: Oelgeschlager, Gunn and Hain.

Block, Richard. 1992. "Comparing National Surveys of Victims of Crime." *International Journal of Victimology*, 1–20.

Bureau of Justice Statistics (BJS). 1992. *Drugs, Crime and the Justice System: A National Report*. Washington, D.C.

———. 1993. *National Corrections Reporting Program, 1990*. Washington, D.C.

Clarke, Ronald, and Derek Cornish. 1986. *The Reasoning Criminal: Rational Choice Perspective on Offending*. New York: Springer Verlag.

Clarke, Ronald, and Pat Mayhew. 1988. "The British Gas Suicide Story and Its Criminological Implications." *Crime and Justice: A Review of Research*, ed. Michael H. Tonry and Norval Morris, 10:107.

Cohen, Lawrence, and Marcus Felson. 1979. "Social Change and Crime Rate Trends: A Routine Activity Approach." *American Sociology Review* 44:588–608.

del Frate, Anna Alvazzi, Ugljesa Zvekic, and Jan J.M. van Dijk. 1993. *Understanding Crime: Experiences of Crime and Crime Control*. Rome: United Nations Interregional Crime and Justice Institute (UNICRI).

Dobash, R. Emmerson, and Russell P. Dobash. 1992. *Women, Violence and Social Change*. London: Routledge.

Dodd, Tricia, and Paul Hunter. 1992. *The National Prison Survey: Report to the Home Office of a Study of Prisoners in England and Wales*. London Office of Population Censuses and Surveys, Social Survey Division.

Doleschal, E. 1977. "Rate and Length of Imprisonment: How Does the U.S. Compare with the Netherlands, Sweden, and Denmark?" *Crime and Delinquency* 23:51.

Farrington, David, and Patrick Langan. 1992. "Changes in Crime and Punishment in England and Wales and America in the 1980s." *Justice Quarterly* 9 (1): 6–46.

Federal Bureau of Investigation (FBI). 1989. *Crime in the United States*. Washington, D.C.: United State's Department of Justice.

Fingerhut, Lois, and Joel C. Kleinman. 1990. "International and Interstate Comparisons of Homicide among Young Males." *Journal of the American Medical Association* 263, no. 24 (June).

Gartner, Rosemary, and Robert Nash Parker. 1990a. "Cross-national Evidence on Homicide and the Age Structure of the Population." *Social Forces* 69 (2): 351.

———. 1990b. Victims of Homicide: A Temporal and Cross-national Comparison." *American Sociological Review* 55:92–106.

Gurr, Ted. 1977. "Crime Trends in Modern Democracies Since 1947." *The International Annals of Criminology* 16:41–85.

Home Office. 1989. *Police Statistics: England and Wales 1988*. London: Her Majesty's Stationery Office.

———. 1992. *Police Statistics: England and Wales 1990*. London: Her Majesty's Stationery Office.

Hubble, David. 1990. "National Crime Survey New Questionnaire Phase-in Research: Preliminary Results." Paper presented at the International Conference on Measurement Errors in Surveys, Tucson, Ariz., November 11–14.

Interpol. 1988. *International Crime Statistics*. Paris: Interpol General Secretariat.

Jacoby, Joan, L. Mellon, E. Ratledge, and S. Turner. 1982. *Prosecutorial Decisionmaking: A National Study*. Washington, D.C.: National Institute of Justice.

Kaiser, G., H. Kury, and H. J. Albrecht, with the assistance of H. Arnold. 1991. *Victims and Criminal Justice*. Freiburg: Max Planck Institute.

Kalish, Carol. 1988. *International Crime Rates*. Washington, D.C.: Bureau of Justice Statistics.

Killias, Martin. 1993. "Gun Ownership, Suicide and Homicide: An International Perspective." In *Understanding Crime: Experiences of Crime and Crime Control*, ed. Anne Alvazzi del Frate, Ugljesa Zvekic, and Jan van Dijk. Rome: United Nations Inter-regional Crime and Justice Institute.

Koppel, David B. 1992. *The Samurai, the Mountie and the Cowboy: Should American Adopt the Gun Controls of Other Democracies*. Buffalo, N.Y.: Prometheus Books.

Langbien, J. 1979. "Land without Plea Bargaining: How the Germans Do It." *Michigan Law Review* 78: 204–10.

Lynch, James P. 1988. "A Comparison of Prison Use in England and Wales, Canada, the United States and West Germany: A Limited Test of the Punitiveness Hypothesis." *Journal of Criminal Law and Criminology* 79 (1): 180–217.

———. 1993a. "A Cross-national Comparison of the Length of Custodial Sentences for Serious Crimes." *Justice Quarterly* 10 (4).

———. 1993b. "The Effects of Survey Design on Reporting in Victim Surveys." In *Fear of Crime and Criminal Victimization*, ed. Wolfgang Bilsky, Christian Pfeiffer, and Peter Wetzels. Stuttgart: Enke Verlag.

Lynch, James P., Steven Smith, Helen Graziadei, and Tanutda Pittayathikhun. Forthcoming. *Profile of Inmates in the U.S. and in England and Wales, 1991*. Washington, D.C.: Bureau of Justice Statistics.

Maurer, Michael. 1991. *Americans behind Bars: A Comparison of International Rates of Incarceration*. Washington, D.C.: The Sentencing Project.

MacCoun, Robert J., Aaron Saiger, James P. Kahan, and Peter Reuter. 1993. "Drug Policies and Problems: The Promises and Pitfalls of Cross-national Comparisons." In *Psychoactive Drugs and Harm Reduction: From Faith to Science*, ed. N. Heather, E. Nadelman, and P. O'Hare. London: Whurr Publications.

Messner, Steven. 1989. "Economic Discrimination and Societal Homicide Rates: Further evidence on the Cost of Inequality." *American Sociological Review* 54:597–611.

Miller, Wilbur. 1977. *Cops and Bobbies: Police Authority in New York and London*. Chicago: University of Chicago Press.

Moitra, S. D. 1986. "Crime and Imprisonment Trends: An Analysis by Individual Crime-Types." *International Journal of Comparative and Applied Criminal Justice* 10 (1): 95–106.

Nettler, Gwynn. 1978. *Explaining Crime*. New York: McGraw-Hill.

Riedel, Marc. 1990. "Nationwide Homicide Data Sets: An Evaluation of the Uniform Crime Reports and National Center for Health Statistics Data." In *Measuring Crime: Large-scale, Long-range Efforts*, ed. D. L. MacKenzie, P. J. Baunach, and R. R. Roberg. Albany, N.Y.: SUNY Albany Press.

Shryock, J., and L. Siegel. 1973. *Methods of Demography*. Washington, D.C.: United States Census Bureau.

Sloan, J. H., A. L. Kellerman, D. I. Reay, J. A. Fenis, T. Koepsell, F. P. Rivara, C. Rice, L. Gary, and J. Logerfo. 1988. "Handgun Regulations, Crime, Assaults and

Homicide: A Tale of Two Cities." *New England Journal of Medicine* 319:1256–62.

Sproule, C., and D. J. Kennett. 1989. "The Use of Firearms in Canadian Homicides, 1972–1982." *Canadian Journal of Criminology* 30:31–37.

———. 1990. "Killing with Guns in the USA and Canada 1977–1983: Further Evidence for the Effectiveness of Gun Control." *Canadian Journal of Criminology* 31: 245–51.

Stack, Steven. 1984. "Income Inequality and Property Crime." *Criminology* 22:229–57.

Teske, R., and H. Arnold. 1982. "Comparison of the Criminal Statistics of the United States and Federal Republic of Germany." *Journal of Criminal Justice* 10:359.

Trebach, Arnold S., and James A. Inciardi. 1993. *Legalize It? Debating American Drug Policy.* Washington, D.C.: American University Press.

van Dijk, Jan, and P. Mayhew. 1993. "Criminal Victimization in the Industrialized World: Key Findings of the 1989 and 1992 International Crime Surveys." In *Understanding Crime: Experiences of Crime and Crime Control,* ed. Anne Alvazzi del Frate, Ugljesa Zvekic, and Jan van Dijk. Rome: United Nations Interregional Crime and Justice Institute.

van Dijk, Jan, P. Mayhew, and M. Killias. 1990. *Experiences of Crime Across the World.* Boston: Klewer.

Waller, I., and Chan, Janet. 1975. "Prison Use: A Canadian and International Comparison." *Criminal Law Quarterly* 3:47.

Young, Warren, and Michael Brown. 1993. "Cross-national Comparisons of Imprisonment." In *Crime and Justice: A Review of Research,* ed. Michael H. Tonry and Albert J. Reiss. Chicago: University of Chicago Press.

3. R. J. Herrnstein, "Criminogenic Traits"

Notes

1. Courtwright 1982.

2. Blumstein and Cohen 1979; Farrington, Ohlin, and Wilson 1986; Gottfredson and Hirschi 1990; Wilson and Herrnstein 1985.

3. Asked to raise their hands if they have committed various minor offenses, virtually all the men and roughly half to two-thirds of the women in Harvard classes raise them.

4. Wolfgang 1980.

5. See summary in Farrington, Ohlin, and Wilson (1986).

6. Farrington 1983.

7. Wolfgang, Figlio, and Sellin 1972.

8. For both rising risk and increased seriousness, see Farrington, Ohlin, and Wilson (1986).

9. From a British Home Office Statistical Bulletin, July 1985, cited in Farrington, Ohlin, and Wilson (1986, 51).

10. See Reichel and Magnusson (1988) and Wikström (1989) for the Swedish statistics; for a summary of Danish findings, see Wilson and Herrnstein (1985).

11. Blumstein, Farrington, and Moitra 1985.

12. Greenwood and Abrahamse 1982.

13. For recent reports, see Farrington (1991a; 1991b; 1992) and Farrington and West (1990).

14. That is to say, they were almost five times as large a proportion of the boys rated aggressive as of the boys rated nonaggressive.

15. A category of adult behavior is included here if and only if it was significantly (i.e., p<.01) associated with childhood aggression for at least two of the three age brackets.

16. Convictions for burglary were significantly associated with other criminal activities, including shoplifting, auto theft, assault, use of illegal drugs, and fraud (Farrington 1992).

17. Farrington observes that behaviors, such as sexual activity, that are signs of antisociality in childhood cease being so in adulthood.

18. All ratios are statistically significantly above 1.0 (p<.01).

19. Loeber, Stouthamer-Loeber, and Green 1991.

20. Besides being resident in or near a small city, nearly all of the boys were white. This is not a nationally representative sample.

21. See reviews in Loeber and Dishion (1983) and Wilson and Herrnstein (1985).

22. Farrington 1985. For a comprehensive meta-analysis of the influence of poor parenting on juvenile conduct disorders and delinquency, the conclusions of which largely support the Cambridge study findings, see Loeber and Stouthamer-Loeber (1986). There is a chicken versus egg problem in any attempt to unravel the impact of the parent on the child from the impact of the child on the parent. A parent might, in other words, be harsh, inconsistent, and indifferent because his or her child is troublesome, in addition to vice versa (Sampson and Laub 1993). For other attempts to construct indexes of later criminal behavior from measures available in childhood, see the review in Loeber and Stouthamer-Loeber (1987).

23. White et al. 1990.

24. Hyperactivity and inattentiveness are among the signs of a more general psychodiagnostic category of "externalizing behaviors." For a review of the correlates in adolescent behavior of this early marker of adjustment disorders, which corroborates the findings of the New Zealand study, see Hinshaw (1992).

25. Nagin and Paternoster 1991. The thesis that past crime disinhibits future crime is consistent with the folklore of criminals, who are frequently quoted as saying that the first time is the hardest. On the other hand, it has been shown that siblings resemble each other in criminal behavior more because they share certain traits than because the crimes of one of them triggers the crime in the others (Rowe and Britt 1991).

26. Hirschi and Hindelang 1977; Quay 1987; Wilson and Herrnstein 1985. Parts of this section overlap with material in Chapter 11 of Herrnstein and Murray (1994).

27. Blumstein, Farrington, and Moitra 1985; Denno 1990. National studies of convicts who get rearrested after release likewise show that low levels of education

(which are presumably correlated with low test scores) are at higher risk for recidivism (Beck and Shipley 1989).

28. Lipsitt, Buka, and Lipsitt 1990.

29. Hirschi 1969; Wilson and Herrnstein 1985.

30. Nicholson and Kugler 1991.

31. Wilson and Herrnstein 1985.

32. Stattin and Klackenberg-Larsson 1993.

33. Gordon 1987; Jensen and Faulstich 1988.

34. Wilson and Herrnstein 1985.

35. Hirschi 1969; Hirschi and Hindelang 1977.

36. Reichel and Magnusson 1988.

37. Colaizzi 1989.

38. Goring 1913.

39. Goddard 1914.

40. A highly critical review of the crime-IQ literature by one of the leaders of the American school of criminologists may have been decisive in the eclipse of IQ (Sutherland 1931).

41. Hirschi and Hindelang 1977.

42. Reichel and Magnusson 1988.

43. In the words of one such textbook, "Hirschi and Hindelang's inferences [on the substantial correlation between crime and IQ] have been supported by research conducted by both American and international scholars (Siegel 1989, 146).

44. A balanced, recent summary says, "At this juncture it seems reasonable to conclude that the difference [between offenders and nonoffenders in intelligence] is real and not due to any of the possible methodological or confounding factors that have been noted in the literature" (Quay 1987, 107f).

45. See reviews in Gordon (1987), Hirschi and Hindelang (1977), Wilson and Herrnstein (1985). A representative study, based on Danish data, is Moffitt et al. (1981).

46. Gordon 1987. Zero order correlations between crime and IQ (within age, race, and sex categories) usually fall between $-.15$ and $-.3$; they are not much attenuated by partialing out SES.

47. Jensen 1980; Linn 1982.

48. The evidence in fact suggests that smart offenders pick crimes with lesser likelihoods of arrest and larger payoffs (Wilson and Herrnstein 1985).

49. The probability of arrest *per crime* may be lower for smart offenders than for dull ones, but chronic offenders commit so many crimes that, whether they are smart or dull, they will probably show up sooner or later in the pool of data about offenders.

50. Moffitt and Silva 1988.

51. Hindelang, Hirschi, and Weis 1981; Hirschi and Hindelang 1977; Wilson and Herrnstein 1985.

52. Reichel and Magnusson 1988.

53. Kandel et al. 1988.

54. In this sample, there was no significant correlation between IQ and SES, and IQ remained a significant predictor of offending even after the effects of parental SES and the sons' own level of education were entered as covariates in an analysis of covariance.

55. White, Moffitt, and Silva 1989.

56. Werner and Smith 1982.

57. Werner 1989; Werner and Smith 1982.

58. Werner 1989.

59. Farrington et al. 1988. For the significance of childhood shyness, see also Ensminger, Kellam, and Rubin (1983).

60. Caspi 1987.

61. For an attempt to explain why these traits evolve into criminal behavior in some people but not in others, see Loeber and Blanc (1990).

62. Sampson and Laub 1993; Wilson and Herrnstein 1985.

63. Examples of some of the inconsistencies that can be traced to varying measurements of personality traits are given in Arbuthnot, Gordon, and Jurkovic (1987). The issue is also discussed in Eysenck and Gudjonsson (1989).

64. A sampling of this technical literature, including individual studies and reviews: Arbuthnot, Gordon, and Jurkovic 1987; Ellis 1987; Farrington 1991a; Hinshaw 1992; Hirschi 1969; Loeber and Blanc 1990; Moffitt 1990; Wilson and Herrnstein 1985.

65. Loeber and Blanc 1990; Robins 1978; Robins 1986.

66. As on the Minnesota Multiphasic Personality Inventory (MMPI) and California Psychological Inventory (CPI), for example. See review of the relevant literature in Wilson and Herrnstein (1985). A different set of inventories, developed by Hans Eysenck, yields comparable outcomes (Eysenck and Gudjonsson 1989).

67. Arbuthnot, Gordon, and Jurkovic 1987; White et al. forthcoming. The lack of consistency for measures of impulsivity relates to the fact that the measures themselves do not intercorrelate very highly. There may be various sorts of impulsivity, with varying correlations with offending (Stanford and Barratt 1992; White et al. forthcoming).

68. Gottfredson and Hirschi 1990; Hinshaw 1992.

69. Gottfredson and Hirschi 1990; Rowe, Osgood, and Nicewander 1990.

70. The distinction between the disposition of criminality and the behavior of committing crime is drawn in Gottfredson and Hirschi (1990) and Hirschi and Gottfredson (1986). An attempt to pin down and to evaluate the "latent trait" of criminality is presented in Rowe, Osgood, and Nicewander (1990).

71. Herrnstein and Murray 1994; Rowe 1994.

72. For reviews of this literature, see Loehlin (1982; 1985), Plomin (1986), Plomin, Chipauer, and Loehlin (1990), and Willerman (1979). So many ways to subdivide personality make it impossible to summarize the literature succinctly. In an article reporting, among other things, evidence for the heritability of the tendency toward optimism or pessimism, the authors reveal both the diversity of personality traits and the strength of the evidence for heritability: "The ubiquitous evidence for genetic influence on personality questionnaires makes it no longer interesting to document heritability for yet another personality trait" (Plomin et al. 1992, 922). Many of the personality traits implicated in criminal behavior have genetic factors involved in them.

73. Chapter 6, by Mednick and Moffitt, is a detailed discussion of the biological correlates of criminal behavior.

74. For a review as of 1985, see Wilson and Herrnstein (1985). For more recent work, see Baker (1986); Cloninger and Gottesman (1987); Mednick, Gabrielli, and Hutchings (1987); and Moffitt (1987). For the small fraction of offenders who specialize in violent crimes alone, the heritable influence on offending is evidently smaller than it is for the more typical serious offender, who does not much specialize.

75. This is a recurrent finding, reviewed in Cloninger and Gottesman (1987) and Wilson and Herrnstein (1985). Most of the better studies are of Scandinavian twin populations; for a recent, American study coming to essentially the same conclusion, see Rowe and Osgood (1984).

76. Only "about" one-half because assortative mating for a trait increases the correlation between fraternal twins. The effects of this complication would need to be weighed for a specific estimate of the heritability of criminality.

77. Plomin and Daniels 1987; Rowe 1994.

78. For evidence that the greater similarity in anti-civil behavior between identical, compared with fraternal, twins is due to shared genes rather than shared family environment, see Rowe (1986).

79. Rowe and Gulley 1992.

80. Carey 1992; Rowe and Gulley 1992.

81. And it is self-evidently refuted by evidence from other species. For example, poodles behave differently from terriers. Raising a poodle to act like a pit bull terrier is not a promising project.

82. See reviews in Eysenck and Gudjonsson (1989) and Wilson and Herrnstein (1985). Many studies (e.g., Goring 1913) have observed that offenders are shorter than nonoffenders. Among the reasons for this difference, one may be the lack of ectomorphy, since ectomorphy is positively correlated with height.

83. The childhood sample is described in Sheldon, Harte, and McDermott (1949). A summary of their behavior over more than thirty years is in Hartl, Monnelly, and Elderkin (1982).

84. For recent reviews see Denno (1988), Eysenck and Gudjonsson (1989), and the various relevant chapters in Mednick, Moffit, and Stack (1987).

85. Lewis et al. (1979) and Lewis et al. (1989), with a review in Pallone and Hennessy (1992).

86. For an attempt to tie the various physical correlates together, and to reconcile the mixed findings with hormones, within a theory that relates criminal behavior to the influence of male hormones on the development of the brain, see Ellis (1987).

87. And, to the degree that female offending has been overtaking male, it probably has more to do with the feminization of poverty and the rise in drug offenses than to the rise of feminism per se (Dillingham 1991; Wilson and Herrnstein 1985).

88. Wilson and Herrnstein 1985.

89. Greenfield and Minor-Harper 1991; Stephan and Jankowski 1991.

90. Three times in one article, the *New York Times* assured its readers that any link between crime and the XYY pattern has been discredited (Goleman 1992).

91. Witkin et al. 1976.

92. Maxson 1981; Maxson and others 1982.

93. Kraus 1991 and n.d.

94. For injuries at work as an individual trait, see Herrnstein and Murray (1994).

95. Kraus 1991, 14, 11.

96. Kraus 1991, 16.

97. Shown by excess urinary kryptopyrroles, sometimes called the "mauve factor" because of its tendency to produce discolored urine.

98. Pallone and Hennessy 1992.

99. I.e., by parole boards.

100. Monahan 1981.

101. After a serial murder or an otherwise notorious criminal case, journalists routinely call and ask why it happened. This must be a familiar experience to anyone who has a reputation for expertise in criminal behavior. If I answer by saying that their question is ill-posed, they usually call someone else.

References

Arbuthnot, Jack, Donald A. Gordon, and Gregory J. Jurkovic. 1987. "Personality." In *Handbook of Juvenile Delinquency,* ed. Herbert C. Quay, 139–83. New York: Wiley, 1987.

Baker, Laura A. 1986. "Estimating Genetic Correlations among Discontinuous Phenotypes: An Analysis of Criminal Convictions and Psychiatric Diagnoses in Danish Adoptees." *Behavior Genetics* 16:127–42.

Beck, Allen J., and Bernard E. Shipley. 1989. *Recidivism of Prisoners Released in 1983.* United States Department of Justice, Bureau of Justice Statistics Special Report NCJ-116261.

Blumstein, Alfred, and J. Cohen. 1979. "Estimation of Individual Crime Rates from Arrest Records." *Journal of Criminal Law and Criminology* 70:561–85.

Blumstein, Alfred, David P. Farrington, and Soumyo Moitra. 1985. "Delinquency Careers: Innocents, Desisters, and Persisters." In *Crime and Justice: A Review of Research,* ed. Michael H. Tonry and Norval Morris, 6:187–219. Chicago: University of Chicago Press.

Carey, Gregory. 1992. "Twin Imitation for Antisocial Behavior: Implications for Genetic and Family Environment Research." *Journal of Abnormal Psychology* 101:18–25.

Caspi, Avshalom. 1987. "Personality in the Life Course." *Journal of Personality and Social Psychology* 53:1203–13.

Cloninger, C. Robert, and Irving I. Gottesman. 1987. "Genetic and Environmental Factors in Antisocial Behavior Disorders." In *The Causes of Crime: New Biological Approaches,* ed. Sarnoff A. Mednick, Terrie E. Moffitt, and Susan A. Stack, 92–109. New York: Cambridge University Press, 1987.

Colaizzi, Janet. 1989. *Homicidal Insanity, 1800–1985.* Tuscaloosa, Ala.: University of Alabama Press.

Courtwright, David T. 1982. *Dark Paradise: Opiate Addiction in America before 1940.* Cambridge, Mass.: Harvard University Press.

Denno, Deborah W. 1988. "Human Biology and Criminal Responsibility: Free Will or Free Ride?" *University of Pennsylvania Law Review* 137:615–71.

————. 1990. *Biology and Violence: From Birth to Adulthood.* New York: Cambridge University Press.

Dillingham, Steven D. 1991. *National Update.* United States Department of Justice, Bureau of Justice Statistics Special Report NCJ-129863.

Ellis, Lee. 1987. "Neurohormonal Bases of Varying Tendencies to Learn Delinquent and Criminal Behavior." In *Behavioral Approaches to Crime and Delinquency: A Handbook of Application, Research, and Concepts,* ed. Edward K. Morris and Curtis J. Braukmann, 499–518. New York: Plenum.

Ensminger, Margaret E., Sheppard G. Kellam, and Barnett R. Rubin. 1983. "School and Family Origins of Delinquency: Comparisons by Sex." In *Prospective Studies of Crime and Delinquency,* ed. Katherine T. Van Dusen and Sarnoff A. Mednick, 73–97. Boston: Kluwer-Nijhoff.

Eysenck, Hans J., and Gisli H. Gudjonsson. 1989. *The Causes and Cures of Criminality.* New York: Plenum.

Farrington, David P. 1983. *Further Analyses of a Longitudinal Survey of Crime and Delinquency.* Washington, D.C.: National Institute of Justice.

————. 1985. "Predicting Self-reported and Official Delinquency." In *Prediction in Criminology,* ed. David P. Farrington and R. Tarling, 150–73. Albany, N.Y.: State University of New York Press.

————. 1991a. "Antisocial Personality from Childhood to Adulthood." *The Psychologist* 4:389–94.

————. 1991b. "Childhood Aggression and Adult Violence: Early Precursors and Later Life Outcomes." In *The Development and Treatment of Childhood Aggression,* ed. D. J. Pepler and K. H. Rubin, 5–29. Hillsdale, N.J.: Erlbaum.

————. 1992. "Explaining the Beginning, Progress, and Ending of Antisocial Behavior from Birth to Adulthood." In *Facts, Frameworks, and Forecasts,* ed. Joan McCord, 253–86. New Brunswick, N.J.: Transaction.

Farrington, David P., Bernard Gallagher, Lynda Morley, Raymond J. St Ledger, and Donald J. West. 1988. "Are There Any Successful Men from Criminogenic Backgrounds?" *Psychiatry* 51:116–30.

Farrington, David P., Lloyd E. Ohlin, and James Q. Wilson. 1986. *Understanding and Controlling Crime: Toward a New Research Strategy.* New York: Springer-Verlag. .

Farrington, David P., and Donald J. West. 1990. "The Cambridge Study in Delinquent Development: A Long-Term Follow-up of 411 London Males." In *Criminality: Personality, Behavior, Life History,* ed. H. J. Kerner and G. Kaiser, 115–38. New York: Springer-Verlag.

Goddard, Henry H. 1914. *Feeble-Mindedness: Its Causes and Consequences.* New York: Macmillan.

Goleman, Daniel. 1992. "New Storm Brews on Whether Crime Has Roots in Genes." *New York Times,* 15 September, C1.

Gordon, Robert A. 1987. "SES versus IQ in the Race-IQ-Delinquency Model." *International Journal of Sociology and Social Policy* 1913. 7:30–96.

Goring, Charles. 1913. *The English Convict: A Statistical Study.* London: Darling and Son.

Gottfredson, Michael R., and Travis Hirschi. 1990. *A General Theory of Crime.* Stanford, Calif.: Stanford University Press.

Greenfield, Lawrence A., and Stephanie Minor-Harper. 1991. *Women in Prison.* United States Department of Justice, Bureau of Justice Statistics Special Report NCJ-127991.

Greenwood, Peter W., and A. Abrahamse. 1982. *Selective Incapacitation.* Santa Monica, Calif.: Rand.

Hartl, Emil M., Edward P. Monnelly, and Roland D. Elderkin. 1982. *Physique and Delinquent Behavior: A Thirty-Year Follow-Up of William H. Sheldon's Varieties of Delinquent Youth.* New York: Academic Press.

Herrnstein, Richard J., and Charles Murray. 1994. *The Bell Curve: Intelligence and Class Structure in American Life.* New York: Free Press.

Hindelang, Michael J., Travis Hirschi, and J. G. Weis. 1981. *Measuring Delinquency.* Beverly Hills: Sage.

Hinshaw, Stephen P. 1992. "Externalizing Behavior Problems and Academic Underachievement in Childhood and Adolescence: Causal Relationships and Underlying Mechanisms." *Psychological Bulletin* 111:127–55.

Hirschi, Travis. 1969. *Causes of Delinquency.* Berkeley: University of California Press.

Hirschi, Travis, and Michael Gottfredson. 1986. "The Distinction between Crime and Criminality." In *Critique and Explanation: Essays in Honor of Gwynne Nettler,* ed. Timothy F. Hartnagel and Robert A. Silverman, 55–69. New Brunswick, N.J.: Transaction.

Hirschi, Travis, and Michael J. Hindelang. 1977. "Intelligence and Delinquency: A Revisionist Review." *American Sociological Review,* 42:571–87.

Jensen, Arthur R. 1980. *Bias in Mental Testing.* New York: Free Press.

Jensen, Arthur R., and Michael E. Faulstich. 1988. "Difference between Prisoners and the General Population in Psychometric *g.*" *Personality and Individual Differences* 9:925–28.

Kandel, Elizabeth, Sarnoff A. Mednick, Lis Kirkegaard-Sorensen, Barry Hutchings, Joachim Knop, Raben Rosenberg, and Fini Schulsinger. 1988. "IQ as a Protective Factor for Subjects at High Risk for Antisocial Behavior." *Journal of Consulting and Clinical Psychology* 56:224–26.

Kraus, Richard T. 1991. Forensic report. Honeoye Falls, N.Y.

———. N.d. "An Enigmatic Personality: Case Report of a Serial Killer." Unpublished.

Lewis, Dorothy O., Richard Lovely, Catherine Yeager, and Donna Della Femina. 1989. "Toward a Theory of the Genesis of Violence: A Follow-up Study of Delinquents." *Journal of the American Academy of Child and Adolescent Psychiatry* 28:431–36.

Lewis, Dorothy O., Shelley S. Shanok, Jonathan H. Pincus, and Gilbert H. Glaser. 1979. "Violent Juvenile Delinquents: Psychiatric, Neurological, Psychological, and Abuse Factors." *Journal of the American Academy of Child Psychiatry* 18:307–19.

Linn, Robert. 1982. "Ability Testing: Individual Differences, Prediction, and Differential Prediction." In *Ability Testing: Uses, Consequences, and Controversies,* ed. Alexandra K. Wigdor and Wendell R. Garner, 335–88. Washington, D.C.: National Academy Press.

Lipsitt, Paul D., Stephen L. Buka, and Lewis P. Lipsitt. 1990. "Early Intelligence Scores and Subsequent Delinquency: A Prospective Study." *American Journal of Family Therapy* 18:197–208.

Loeber, Rolf, and Marc Le Blanc. 1990. "Toward a Developmental Criminology." In *Crime and Justice: A Review of Research*, ed. Michael H. Tonry and Norval Morris, 12:375–473. Chicago: University of Chicago Press.

Loeber, Rolf and R. Dishion. 1983. "Early Predictors of Male Delinquency? A Review." *Psychology Bulletin* 94:68–99.

Loeber, Rolf, and Magda Stouthamer-Loeber. 1986. "Family Factors as Correlates and Predictors of Juvenile Conduct Problems and Delinquency." In *Crime and Justice: A Review of Research*, ed. Michael H. Tonry and Norval Morris, 7:29–149. Chicago: University of Chicago Press.

———. 1987. "Prediction." In *Handbook of Juvenile Delinquency*, ed. Herbert C. Quay, 325–82. New York: Wiley.

Loeber, Rolf, Magda Stouthamer-Loeber, and Stephanie M. Green. 1991. "Age at Onset of Problem Behaviour in Boys, and Later Disruptive and Delinquent Behaviours." *Criminal Behavior and Mental Health* 1:229–46.

Loehlin, John C. 1982. "Are Personality Traits Differentially Heritable?" *Behavior Genetics* 12:412–28.

———. 1985. "Fitting Heredity-Environment Models Jointly to Twin and Adoption Data from the California Psychological Inventory." *Behavior Genetics* 15:199–221.

Maxson, Stephen C. 1981. "The Genetics of Aggression in Vertebrates." In *The Biology of Aggression*, ed. Paul F. Brain and David Benton, 69–104. Rockville, Md.: Sythoff and Noordhoff.

Maxson, Stephen C., Timothy Platt, Paul Shrenker, and Alice Trattner. 1982. "The Influence of the Y-Chromosome of Rb/1Bg Mice on Agonistic Behaviors." *Aggressive Behavior* 8:285–91.

Mednick, Sarnoff A., William F. Gabrielli Jr., and Barry Hutchings. 1987. "Genetic Factors in the Etiology of Criminal Behavior." In *The Causes of Crime: New Biological Approaches*, ed. Sarnoff A. Mednick, Terrie E. Moffitt, and Susan A. Stack, 74–91. New York: Cambridge University Press.

Mednick, Sarnoff A., Terrie E. Moffitt, and Susan A. Stack, eds. 1987. *The Causes of Crime: New Biological Approaches*. New York: Cambridge University Press.

Moffitt, Terrie E. 1987. "Parental Mental Disorder and Offspring Criminal Behavior: An Adoption Study." *Psychiatry* 50:346–60.

———. 1990. "The Neuropsychology of Juvenile Delinquency: A Critical Review." In *Crime and Justice: A Review of Research*, ed. Michael H. Tonry and Norval Morris, 12:99–169. Chicago: University of Chicago Press.

Moffitt, Terrie E., William F. Gabrielli, Sarnoff A. Mednick, and Fini Schulsinger. 1981. "Socioeconomic Status, IQ, and Delinquency." *Journal of Abnormal Psychology* 90:152–56.

Moffitt, Terrie E., and Phil A. Silva. 1988. "IQ and Delinquency: A Direct Test of the Differential Detection Hypothesis." *Journal of Abnormal Psychology* 97:330–33.

Monahan, John. 1981. *The Clinical Prediction of Violent Behavior*. DHHS Publication No. (ADM)81–82 ed., Crime and Delinquency Issues: A Monograph Series. Rockville, Md.: United States Department of Health and Human Services.

Nagin, Daniel S., and Raymond Paternoster. 1991. "On the Relationship of Past to Future Participation in Delinquency." *Criminology* 29:163–89.

Nicholson, Robert A., and Karen E. Kugler. 1991. "Competent and Incompetent Criminal Defendants: A Quantitative Review of Comparative Research." *Psychological Bulletin* 109:355–70.

Pallone, Nathaniel J., and James J. Hennessy. 1992. *Criminal Behavior: A Process Psychology Analysis.* New Brunswick, N.J.: Transaction.

Plomin, Robert. 1986. *Development, Genetics, and Psychology.* Hillsdale, N.J.: Erlbaum.

Plomin, Robert, H. M. Chipauer, and John C. Loehlin. 1990. "Behavioral Genetics and Personality." In *Handbook of Personality Theory and Research,* ed. L. A. Pervin, 225–43. New York: Guilford.

Plomin, Robert, and Denise Daniels. 1987. "Why Are Children in the Same Family so Different from One Another?" *Behavioral and Brain Sciences* 10:1–60.

Plomin, Robert, Michael F. Scheier, C. S. Bergman, N. L. Pedersen, J. R. Nesselroade, and Gerald E. McClearn. 1992. "Optimism, Pessimism and Mental Health." *Personality and Individual Differences* 13:921–30.

Quay, Herbert C. 1987. "Intelligence." In *Handbook of Juvenile Delinquency,* ed. Herbert C. Quay, 106–17. New York: Wiley.

Reichel, Howard, and David Magnusson. 1988. *The Relationship of Intelligence to Registered Criminality.* University of Stockholm Reports from the Department of Psychology 676.

Robins, Lee N. 1978. "Sturdy Childhood Predictors of Adult Antisocial Behavior." *Psychiatric Medicine* 8:611–22.

———. 1986. "Changes in Conduct Disorder over Time." In *Risk in Intellectual and Social Development,* ed. Dale C. Farran and James D. McKinney, 227–59. New York: Academic Press.

Rowe, David C. 1986. "Genetic and Environmental Components of Antisocial Behavior: A Study of 265 Twin Pairs." *Criminology* 24:513–32.

———. 1994. *The Limits of Family Influence: Genes, Experience, and Behavior.* New York: Guilford Press.

Rowe, David C., and Chester L. Britt III. 1991. "Developmental Explanations of Delinquent Behavior among Siblings: Common Factors vs. Transmission Mechanisms." *Journal of Quantitative Criminology* 7:315–32.

Rowe, David C., and Bill L. Gulley. 1992. "Sibling Effects on Substance Use and Delinquency." *Criminology* 30:217–33.

Rowe, David C., and D. Wayne Osgood. 1984. "Heredity and Sociological Theories of Delinquency: A Reconsideration." *American Sociological Review* 49:526–40.

Rowe, David C., D. Wayne Osgood, and Alan Nicewander. 1990. "A Latent Trait Approach to Unifying Criminal Careers." *Criminology* 28:237–70.

Sampson, Robert J., and John H. Laub. 1993. *Crime in the Making: Pathways and Turning Points through Life.* Cambridge, Mass.: Harvard University Press.

Sheldon, William H., Emil M. Hartl, and Eugene McDermott. 1949. *Varieties of Delinquent Youth: An Introduction to Constitutional Psychiatry.* New York: Harper.

Siegel, Larry J. 1989. *Criminology.* 3d ed. St. Paul, Minn.: West Publishing.

Stanford, Matthew S., and Ernest S. Barratt. 1992. "Impulsivity and the Multi-impulsive Personality Disorder." *Personality and Individual Differences* 13:831–34.

Stattin, Hakan, and Ingrid Klackenberg-Larsson. 1993. "Early Language and Intelligence Development and Their Relationship to Future Criminal Behavior." *Journal of Abnormal Psychology* 102:369–78.

Stephan, James J., and Louis W. Jankowski. 1991. *Jail Inmates, 1990.* United States Department of Justice, Bureau of Justice Statistics Bulletin NCJ-129756.

Sutherland, Edwin H. 1931. "Mental Deficiency and Crime." In *Social Attitudes,* ed. Kimball Young. New York: Holt.

Werner, Emmy E. 1989. "High Risk Children in Young Adulthood: A Longitudinal Study from Birth to 32 Years." *American Journal of Orthopsy* 59:72–81.

Werner, Emmy E., and Ruth S. Smith. 1982. *Vulnerable but Invincible: A Longitudinal Study of Resilient Children and Youth.* New York: McGraw-Hill.

White, Jennifer, Terrie E. Moffitt, Avshalom Caspi, Dawn J. Bartusch, Douglas J. Needles, and Magda Stouthamer-Loeber. 1994. "Measuring Impulsivity and Examining Its Relationship to Delinquency." *Journal of Abnormal Psychology* 103, no. 2 (July).

White, Jennifer L., Terrie E. Moffitt, Felton Earls, Lee Robins, and Phil A. Silva. 1990. "How Early Can We Tell?: Predictors of Childhood Conduct Disorder and Adolescent Delinquency." *Criminology* 28:507–33.

White, Jennifer L., Terrie E. Moffitt, and Phil A. Silva. 1989. "A Prospective Replication of the Protective Effects of IQ in Subjects at High Risk for Juvenile Delinquency." *Journal of Consulting and Clinical Psychology* 57:719–24.

Wikström, Per-Olof H. 1989. *Project Metropolitan: Age and Crime in a Stockholm Cohort.* University of Stockholm, 26.

Willerman, Lee. 1979. *The Psychology of Individual and Group Differences.* San Francisco: W. H. Freeman.

Wilson, James Q., and Richard J. Herrnstein. 1985. *Crime and Human Nature.* New York: Simon and Schuster.

Witkin, Herman A., Sarnoff A. Mednick, Fini Schulsinger, Eskild Bakkestrøm, Karl O. Christiansen, Donald R. Goodenough, Kurt Hirschhorn, Claes Lundsteen, David R. Owen, John Philip, Donald B. Rubin, and Martha Stocking. 1976. "Criminality in XYY and XXY men." *Science* 193:547–54.

Wolfgang, Marvin E. 1980. "Some New Findings from the Longitudinal Study of Crime." *Australian Journal of Forensic Science* 13:12–29.

Wolfgang, Marvin E., R. M. Figlio, and T. Sellin. 1972. *Delinquency in a Birth Cohort.* Chicago: University of Chicago Press.

4. Patricia A. Brennan, Sarnoff A. Mednick, and Jan Volavka, "Biomedical Factors in Crime"

Notes

Preparation of this chapter was supported by a grant from the Harry Frank Guggenheim Foundation and a Research Scientist Award from the National Institute of Mental Health.

1. Cloninger and Guze 1970; Glueck and Glueck 1974; McCord and McCord 1958; Roberts 1978; West and Farrington 1977.

2. Robins 1966.

3. Lange 1929.

4. Christiansen 1977b.
5. Smith 1974.
6. Christiansen 1977a.
7. Dalgaard and Kringlen 1976.
8. Carey 1992.
9. Rowe 1983.
10. Christiansen 1977a.
11. Grove et al. 1990.
12. Crowe 1974.
13. Cadoret et al. 1985.
14. Cadoret et al. 1987.
15. Bohman 1978.
16. Bohman et al. 1982.
17. Cloninger et al. 1982; Sigvardsson et al. 1982.
18. Sigvardsson et al. 1982.
19. Kety et al. 1968.
20. Schulsinger 1972.
21. Mednick et al. 1984.
22. Mednick et al. 1984.
23. Bohman et al. 1982; Cloninger et al. 1982.
24. Mednick et al. 1984.
25. Baker et al. 1989.
26. Mednick et al. 1984.
27. Moffitt 1987.
28. Little 1861; Rosanoff, Handy, and Plesett 1934b; Pasamanick, Rodgers, and Lilienfield 1956; Mungas 1983; Litt 1971.
29. Kendall et al. 1992.
30. Rantakallio 1992.
31. Kandel 1989.
32. Lewis and Shanok 1977.
33. Lewis et al. 1979.
34. Kandel and Mednick 1991.
35. Werner 1987.
36. Kandel et al. 1989.
37. Kolb and Wishaw 1990.
38. Mesulam 1986.
39. Moffitt and Henry 1991.
40. Bryant et al. 1984.
41. Yoshimasu 1961.
42. Moffitt 1988; Yeudall, Fromm-Aach, and Davies 1982.
43. Hare 1984; Hoffman, Hall, and Bartsch 1987; Sutker and Allain 1983.

44. Flor-Henry 1973; Nachshon 1988; Yeudall 1978.
45. Yeudall et al. 1981; Hart 1987; Mungas 1988; Yeudall and Flor-Henry 1975.
46. Moffitt 1990; Nachshon 1983; Wilson and Herrnstein 1985.
47. Moffitt 1988.
48. Weiger and Bear 1988.
49. Luria 1980.
50. Kolb and Wishaw 1990.
51. Volavka 1995.
52. Scerbo and Raine forthcoming.
53. Gottschalk et al. 1991.
54. Kimura et al. 1978.
55. Volavka 1995.
56. Lidberg, Asberg, and Sundqvist-Stensman 1984; Linnoila et al. 1983.
57. Brown et al. 1989.
58. Scerbo and Raine forthcoming.
59. Volavka 1995.
60. Mirkin and Coppen 1980.
61. Hawley et al. 1985.
62. Venables 1987.
63. Cacioppo, Tassinary, and Fridlund 1991.
64. Hare 1978.
65. Tharp et al. 1980.
66. Hemming 1981.
67. Hare 1982; Raine and Venables 1988.
68. Schmidt, Solant, and Bridger 1985.
69. Venables 1989; Raine et al. 1990b.
70. Buikhuisen et al. 1985.
71. Dawson et al. 1989.
72. Hare 1978.
73. Raine et al. 1990a.
74. Blackburn 1979; Raine and Venables 1984; Raine 1987.
75. Hare 1978.
76. Tharp et al. 1980; Hare 1982; Raine and Venables 1981; Buikhuisen et al. 1985; Raine and Venables 1988; Raine et al. 1990a.
77. Mednick 1977.
78. Hinton, O'Neill, and Dishman 1979; Levander et al. 1980; Hemming 1981; Buikhuisen et al. 1985.
79. Trasler 1987.
80. Hare 1978; Raine and Dunkin 1990.
81. Venables 1987.
82. Volavka 1987; Venables 1988.

83. Mednick and Volavka 1980.
84. Mednick et al. 1982.
85. Petersen et al. 1982.
86. Mednick et al. 1982; Petersen et al. 1982.
87. Volavka 1987; Venables 1988.
88. Raine and Mednick 1989.
89. Schoenthaler, Moody, and Pankow 1991.
90. Kessler and Moos 1970.
91. Sarbin and Miller 1970.
92. Witkin et al. 1977.
93. Schiavi et al. 1984.

References

Baker, L., W. Mack, T. Moffit, S. A. Mednick. 1989. "Etiology of Sex Differences in Criminal Convictions in a Danish Adoption Cohort." *Behavior Genetics* 19:355–70.

Blackburn, R. 1979. "Cortical and Autonomic Response Arousal in Primary and Secondary Psychopaths." *Psychophysiology* 16:143–50.

Bohman, M. 1978. "Some Genetic Aspects of Alcoholism and Criminality." *Archives of General Psychiatry* 35:269–76.

Bohman, M., R. Cloninger, S. Sigvardsson, and A. L. von Knorring. 1982. "Predisposition to Petty Criminality in Swedish Adoptees: I, Genetic and Environmental Heterogeneity." *Archives of General Psychiatry* 39:1233–41.

Borgstrom, C. A. 1939. *Eine Serie von Kriminellen Zwillingen.* Archiv für Rassenbiologie.

Brown, C. S., T. A. Kent, S. G. Bryant, R. M. Gevedon, J. L. Campbell, A. R. Felthaus, and E. S. Barratt. 1989. "Blood Platelet Uptake of Serotonin in Episodic Aggression." *Psychiatry Research* 27:5–12.

Bryant, E. T., M. L. Scott, C. J. Golden, and C. D. Tori. 1984. "Neurophysiological Deficits, Learning Disability, and Violent Behavior." *Journal of Consulting and Clinical Psychology* 52:323–24.

Buikhuisen, W., E. Bontekoe, C. D. Plas-Korenhoff, and S. Buuren. 1985. "Characteristics of Criminals: The Privileged Offender." *International Journal of Law and Psychiatry* 7:301–13.

Cacioppo, J., L. Tassinary, and A. Fridlund. 1991. *Principles of Psychophysiology: Physical, Social and Inferential Elements.* Cambridge: Cambridge University Press.

Cadoret, R. J., T. W. O'Gorman, E. Troughton, and E. Heywood. 1985. "Alcoholism and Antisocial Personality." *Archives of General Psychiatry* 42:161–67.

Cadoret, R. J., E.. Troughton, and T. W. O'Gorman. 1987. *"Journal of Studies of Alcohol."* 48:1–8.

Carey, G. 1992. "Twin Imitation for Antisocial Behavior: Implications for Genetic and Family Environment Research. *Journal of Abnormal Psychology* 101:18–25.

Christiansen, K. O. 1977a. "A Preliminary Study of Criminality among Twins." In *Biosocial Bases of Criminal Behavior*, ed. S. A. Mednick and K. O. Christiansen. New York: Gardner.

Christiansen, K. O. 1977b. "A Review of Studies of Criminality among Twins." In *Biosocial Bases of Criminal Behavior*, ed. S. A. Mednick and K. O. Christiansen. New York: Gardner.

Cloninger, C. R., S. Sigvardsson, M. Bohman, and A. L. von Knorring. 1982. "Predisposition to Petty Criminality in Swedish Adoptees: II, Cross-fostering Analysis of Gene-Environment Interaction." *Archives of General Psychiatry* 39:1242–47.

Cloninger, C. R., and S. B. Guze. 1970. "Female Criminals: Their Personal, Familial, and Social Backgrounds." *Archives of General Psychiatry* 23:554–58.

Crowe, R. R. 1974. "An Adoption Study of Antisocial Personality." *Archives of General Psychiatry* 31:785–91.

Dalgaard, O. S., and E. Kringlen. 1976. "A Norwegian Twin Study of Criminality." *British Journal of Criminology* 16:213–32.

Dawson, M. E., D. L. Filion, and A. M. Schell. 1989. "Is Elicitation of the Autonomic Orienting Response Associated with Allocation of Processing Resources?" *Psychophysiology* 26:560–72.

Flor-Henry, P., 1973. "Psychiatric Syndromes Considered as Manifestations of Lateralized Temporallimbic Dysfunction." In *Surgical Approaches in Psychiatry*, ed. L. Laitiner and K. Livingston. Lancaster, England: Medical and Technical Publishing.

Glueck, S., and E. Glueck. 1974. *On Delinquency and Crime*. Springfield, Ill.: Thomas.

Gottschalk, L. A., T. Rebello, M. S. Buchsbaum, H. G. Tucker, and E. L. Hodges. 1991. "Abnormalities in Hair Trace Elements as Indicators of Aberrant Behavior." *Comprehensive Psychiatry* 28:212–23.

Graber, B., K. Hartmann, J. A. Coffman, C. J. Huey, and C. J. Golden. 1982. "Brain Damage among Mentally Disordered Offenders." *Journal of Forensic Science* 27:125–34.

Grove, W. M., E. D. Eckert, L. Heston, T. J. Bouchard, N. Segal, and D. T. Lykken. 1990. "Heritability of Substance Abuse and Antisocial Behavior: A Study of Monozygotic Twins Reared Apart." *Biological Psychiatry* 27:1293–1304.

Hare, R. D. 1978. "Electrodermal and Cardiovascular Correlates of Psychopathy." In *Psychopathic Behavior: Approaches to Research*, ed. R. D. Hare and D. Schalling. New York: Wiley.

———. 1982. "Psychopathy and Physiological Activity During Anticipation of an Aversive Stimulus in a Distraction Paradigm." *Psychophysiology* 19:226–7

———. 1984. "Performance of Psychopaths on Cognitive Tasks Related to Frontal Lobe Function." *Journal of Abnormal Psychology* 93:133–40.

Hart, C. 1987. "The Relevance of a Test of Speech Comprehension Deficit to Persistent Aggressiveness." *Personality and Individual Differences* 8:371–84.

Hawley, R. J., L. F. Major, E. A. Shulman, and M. Linnoila. 1985. "Cerebrospinal Fluid 3-Methoxy-4-Hydroxyphenylglycol and Norepinephrine Levels in Alcohol Withdrawal: Correlations with Clinical Signs." *Archives of General Psychiatry* 42:1056–62.

Hemming, J. H. 1981. "Electrodermal Indices in a Selected Prison Sample and Students." *Personality and Individual Differences* 2:37–46.

Hendricks, S. E., D. F. Fitzpatrick, K. Hartmann, M. A. Quaife, R. A. Stratbucker, and B. Graber. 1988. "Brain Structure and Function in Sexual Molesters of Children and Adolescents." *Journal of Clinical Psychiatry* 49:108–12.

Hinton, J., M. O'Neill, and J. Dishman. 1979. "Electrodermal Indices of Public Offending and Recidivism." *Biological Psychology* 9:297–309.

Hoffman, J. J., R. W. Hall, and T. W. Bartsch. 1987. "On the Relative Importance of 'Psychopathic' Personality and Alcoholism on Neuropsychological Measures of Frontal Lobe Dysfunction." *Journal of Abnormal Psychology* 96:158–60.

Hucker, S., R. Langevin, G. Wortzman, J. Bain, L. Handy, J. Chambers, and S. Wright. 1986. "Neurophysiological Impairment in Pedophiles." *Canadian Journal of Behavioral Science* 18:440–48.

Hucker, S., R. Langevin, G. Wortzman, R. Dickey, J. Bain, L. Handy, J. Chambers, and S. Wright. 1988. "Cerebral Damage and Dysfunction in Sexually Aggressive Men." *Annals of Sex Research* 1:33–47.

Kandel, E. 1989. "Perinatal Complications and Modeling of Aggressive Behavior: A Test of an Interactive Theory of Violent Offending." Doctoral dissertation, University of Southern California.

Kandel, E., P. A. Brennan, S. A. Mednick, and N. M. Michelson. 1989. "Minor Physical Anomalies and Recidivistic Adult Violent Criminal Behavior." *Acta Psychiatrica Scandinavica* 79:103–7.

Kandel, E., and S. A. Mednick. 1991. "Perinatal Complications Predict Violent Offending." *Criminology* 29:519–29.

Kendall, K., G. Andre, K. Pease, and A. Boulton. 1992. "Health Histories of Juvenile Offenders and a Matched Control Group in Saskatchewan, Canada." *Criminal Behaviour and Mental Health* 2:269–86.

Kety, S. S., D. Rosenthal, P. H. Wender, and F. Schulsinger. 1968. "The Types and Prevalence of Mental Illness in the Biological and Adoptive Families of Adopted Schizophrenics." In *The Transmission of Schizophrenia*, ed. D. Rosenthal and S. S. Kety. Oxford: Pergamon.

Kimura, M., N. Yagi, and V. Itokawa. 1978. "Effect of Subacute Manganese Feeding on Serotonin Metabolism in the Rat." *Journal of Toxicology and Environmental Health* 4:701–7.

Kolb, B., and I. Q. Wishaw. 1990. *Fundamentals of Human Neuropsychology*. New York: Freeman.

Kranz, H. 1936. *Lebensschicksale Kriminellen Zwillingen*. Berlin: Julius Springer.

Lange, J. 1929. *Verbrechen als Schicksal*. Leipzig: George Thieme. English ed., London: Unwin, 1929.

Langevin, R., M. Ben-Aron, G. Wortzman, R. Dickey, and L. Handy. 1987. "Brain Damage, Diagnosis, and Substance Abuse among Offenders." *Behavioral Sciences and the Law* 5:77–94.

Langevin, R., G. Wortzman, R. Dickey, P. Wright, and L. Handy. 1988. "Neuropsychological Impairment in Incest Offenders." *Annals of Sex Research* 1:401–15

Langevin, R., G. Wortzman, P. Wright, and L. Handy. 1989. "Studies of Brain Damage and Dysfunction in Sex Offenders." *Annals of Sex Research* 2:163–79

Legras, A. M. 1932. *Psychese en Criminalitet bij Twellingen*. Utrecht: Kemink en Zonn.

Levander, S. E., D. S. Schalling, L. Lidberg, A. Bartfai, and Y. Lidberg. 1980. "Skin Conductance Recovery Time and Personality in a Group of Criminals." *Psychophysiology* 17:105–11.

Lewis, D. O., and S. S. Shanok. 1977. "Medical Histories of Delinquent and Nondelinquent Children: An Epidemiological Study." *American Journal of Psychiatry* 134:1020–25.

Lewis, D. O., S. S. Shanok, and D. A. Balla. 1979. "Perinatal Difficulties, Head and Face Trauma, and Child Abuse in the Medical Histories of Seriously Delinquent Children." *American Journal of Psychiatry* 136:419–23.

Lidberg, L., M. Asberg, and U. B. Sundqvist-Stensman. 1984. "5-Hydroxyindoleacetic Acid Levels in Attempted Suicides Who Have Killed Their Children." *Lancet* 2:928.

Linnoila, A. M., M. Vikkunen, M. Scheinin, A. Nuutila, R. Rimon, and F. K. Goodwin. 1983. "Low Cerebrospinal Fluid 5-Hydroxyindoleacetic Acid Concentration Differentiates Impulsive from Nonimpulsive Violent Behavior." *Life Science* 33:-2609–14.

Litt, S. M. 1971. "Perinatal Complications and Criminality." Doctoral dissertation, University of Michigan.

Little, W. J. 1861. "On the Influence of Abnormal Parturition, Difficult Labours, Premature Birth and Asphyxia Nonatorum on the Mental and Physical Condition of the Child, Especially in Relation to Deformities." *Transactions of the Obstetrical Society of London* 3:293–344.

Luria, A. R. 1980. *Higher Cortical Functions in Man*. New York: Basic Books.

McCord, J., and W. McCord. 1958. "The Effects of Parental Role Model on Criminality." *Journal of Social Issues* 14:66–75.

Mednick, S. A. 1977. "A Biosocial Theory of the Learning of Law-abiding Behavior." In *Biosocial Bases of Criminal Behavior*, ed. S. A. Mednick and K. O. Christiansen. New York: Gardner.

Mednick, S. A., and J. Volavka. 1980. "Biology and Crime." In *Crime and Justice: A Review of Research*, ed. N. Morris and M. H. Tonry. Chicago: University of Chicago Press.

Mednick, S. A., J. Volavka, W. F. Gabrielli, and T. Itil. 1982. "EEG as a Predictor of Antisocial Behavior." *Criminology* 19:219–31.

Mednick, S. A., W. F. Gabrielli, and B. Hutchings. 1984. "Genetic Influences in Crininal Convictions: Evidence from an Adoption Cohort." *Science* 224:891–94.

Mesulam, M. M. 1986. "Frontal Cortex and Behaviors." *Annals of Neurology* 19:319–23.

Mirkin, A. M., and A. Coppen 1980. "Electrodermal Activity in Depression: Clinical and Biochemical Correlates." *British Journal of Psychiatry* 137:93–97.

Moffitt, T. E. 1987. "Parental Mental Disorder and Offspring Criminal Behavior: An Adoption Study." *Psychiatry* 50:346–60.

———. 1988. "Neuropsychology and Self-reported Early Delinquency in an Unselected Birth Cohort." In *Biological Contributions to Crime Causations*, ed. T. E. Moffitt and S. A. Mednick. Dordrecht, Holland: Martinus Nijhoff.

————. 1990. "The Neuropsychology of Juvenile Delinquency: A Critical Review." In *Crime and Justice: A Review of Research*, ed. M. H. Tonry and N. Morris. Chicago: University of Chicago Press.

Moffitt, T. E., and B. Henry. 1991. "Neuropsychological Studies of Juvenile Delinquency and Juvenile Violence." In *Neuropsychology of Aggression*, ed. J. S. Milner. Boston: Kluwer.

Mungas, D. 1983. "An Empirical Analysis of Specific Syndromes of Violent Behavior." *Journal of Nervous and Mental Disease* 171:354–61

————. "Psychometric Correlates of Episodic Violent Behavior: A Multi-disciplinary Neuropsychological Approach." *British Journal of Psychiatry* 152:180–87.

Nachshon, I. 1983. "Hemisphere Dysfunction in Psychopathy and Behavior Disorders." In *Hemisyndromes: Psychobiology, Neurology, Psychiatry*, ed. M. Myslobodsky. New York: Academic Press.

————. "Hemisphere Function in Violent Offenders." In *Biological Contribution to Crime Causation*, ed. T. E. Moffitt and S. A Mednick. Dordrecht, Holland: Martinus Nijhoff.

Pasamanick, B., M. E. Rodgers, and A. M. Lilienfield. 1956. "Pregnancy Experience and the Development of Behavior Disorders in Children." *American Journal of Psychiatry* 112:613–18.

Petersen, I., M. Matousek, S. A. Mednick, J. Volavka, and V. Pollock. 1982. "EEG Antecedents of Thievery." *Acta Psychiatrica Scandinavica* 62:331–38.

Raine, A. 1987. "Effect of Early Environment on Electrodermal and Cognitive Correlates of Schizotypy and Psychopathy in Criminals." *International Journal of Psychophysiology* 4:277–87.

Raine, A., and J. J. Dunkin. 1990. "The Genetic and Psychophysiological Basis of Antisocial Behavior: Implications for Counseling and Therapy." *Journal of Counseling and Development* 68:637–44.

Raine, A., and T. Lencz. 1993. "The Neuroanatomy of Electrodermal Activity." In *Electrodermal Activity: From Physiology to Psychology*, ed. J. C. Roy. New York: Plenum.

Raine, A., and S. A. Mednick. 1989. "Biosocial Longitudinal Research into Antosocial Behavior." *Revue d'Epidemiologie et de Sante Publique* 37:515–24.

Raine, A., and P. H. Venables. 1981. "Classical Conditioning and Socialization:; A Biosocial Interaction? *Personality and Individual Differences* 2:273–83.

————. 1984. "Electrodermal Non-responding, Schizoid Tendencies, and Antisocial Behavior in Adolescents." *Psychophysiology* 21:424–33.

————. 1988. "Skin Conductance Responsivity in Psychopaths to Orienting, Defensive, and Consonant-Vowel Stimuli." *Journal of Psychophysiology* 2:221–25.

Raine, A., P. H. Venables, and M. Williams. 1990a. "Orienting and Criminality: A Prospective Study." *American Journal of Psychiatry* 147:933–37.

————. 1990b. "Relationships between Central and Autonomic Measures of Arousal at Age 15 Years and Criminality at Age 24 Years." *Archives of General Psychiatry* 47:1003–7.

Rantakallio, P., M. Koiranen, and, J. Mottanen. 1992. "Association of Perinatal Events, Epilepsy, and Central Nervous System Trauma with Juvenile Delinquency." *Archives of Disease in Childhood* 67:1459–61.

Roberts, L. N. 1978. "Aetiological Implications in Studies of Childhood Histories Relating to Antisocial Personality." In *Psychopathic Behavior: Approaches to Research,* ed. R. D. Hare and D. Schalling. New York: Wiley.

Robins, L. N. 1966. *Deviant Children Grown Up.* Baltimore: Williams and Wilkins.

Rosanoff, A. J., L. M. Handy, and I. R. Plessett. 1934. "The Etiology of Manic-Depressive Syndrome with Special Reference to Their Occurrence in Twins." *American Journal of Psychiatry* 91:247–86.

Rosanoff, A. J., L. M. Handy, and F. A. Rosanoff. 1934. "Criminality and Delinquency in Twins." *Journal of Criminal Law and Criminology* 24:923–34.

Rowe, D. C. 1983. "Biometrical Genetic Models of Self-reported Delinquent Behavior: A Twin Study." *Behavior Genetics* 13:473–89.

Kessler, S., and R. H. Moos. 1970. "The XYY Karotype and Criminality: A Review." *Journal of Psychiatric Research* 7:153–70.

Sarbin, T. R., and J. E. Miller. 1970. "Demonism Revisited: The XYY Chromosomal Anomaly." *Issues in Criminology* 5:195–207.

Scerbo, A., and A. Raine. Forthcoming. "Neurotransmitters and Antisocial Behavior: A Meta-analysis."

Schiavi, R. C., A. Theilgaard, D. R. Owen, and D. White. 1984. "Sex Chromosome Anomalies, Hormones and Aggressivity." *Archives of General Psychiatry* 41:93–99.

Schmidt, K., M. V. Solant, and W. H. Bridger. 1985. "Electrodermal Activity of Undersocialized Aggressive Children: A Pilot Study." *Journal of Child Psychology and Psychiatry and Allied Disciplines* 26:653–60.

Schoenthaler, S. J. Moody, and L. Pankow. 1991. "Applied Nutrition and Behavior." *Journal of Applied Nutrition* 43:31–39.

Schulsinger, F. 1972. "Psychopathology: Heredity and Environment." *International Journal of Mental Health* 1:190–206.

Sigvardsson, S., R. Cloninger, M. Bohman, and A. L. von Knorring. 1982. "Predisposition to Petty Criminality in Swedish Adoptees: III, Sex Differences and Validation of the Male Typology." *Archives of General Psychiatry* 39:1248–53.

Slater, E. 1953. "The Incidence of Mental Disorder." *Annals of Eugenics* 6:172.

Smith, C. 1974. "Concordance in Twins: Methods and Interpretation." *American Journal of Human Genetics* 26:454–66.

Stumpfl, F. 1936. *Die Ursprunge des Verberchens: Dargestellt am Lebenslauf von Zwillingen.* Leipzig: Goerg Thieme.

Sutker, P. B., and A. N. Allain. 1983. "Behavior and Personality Assessment in Men Labeled Adaptive Sociopaths." *Journal of Behavioral Assessment* 5:65–79.

Tharp. V. K., I. Maltzman, K. Syndulko, and E. Ziskind. 1980. "Autonomic Activity During Anticipation of an Aversive Tone in Non-institutionalized Sociopaths." *Psychophysiology* 17:123–28.

Trasler, G. 1987. "Biogenetic Factors." In *Handbook of Juvenile Delinquency,* ed. H. C. Quay. New York: Wiley.

Venables, P. H. 1987. "Autonomic and Central Nervous System Factors in Criminal Behavior." In *The Causes of Crime: New Biological Approaches,* ed. S. A. Mednick, T. Moffitt, and S. Stack. New York: Cambridge University Press.

————. 1988. "Psychophysiology and Crime: Theory and Data." In *Biological Contributions to Crime Causation,* ed. T. E. Moffitt and S. A. Mednick. Dordrecht, Holland: Martinus Nijhoff.

————. 1989. "The Emanuel Miller Memorial Lecture 1987: Childhood Markers for Adult Disorders." *Journal of Child Psychology and Psychiatry and Allied Disciplines* 30:347–64.

Volavka, J. 1987. "Electroencephalogram among Criminals." In *The Causes of Crime: New Biological Approaches,* ed. S. A. Mednick, T. E. Moffitt, and S. Stack. Cambridge: Cambridge University Press.

————. 1995. "Neurochemistry of Violence." In *Neurobiology of Violence.* Washington, D.C.: American Psychiatric Press, forthcoming.

Volkow, N. D., and L. Tancredi. 1987. "Neural Substrates of Violent Behavior: A Preliminary Study with Positron Emission Tomography." *British Journal of Psychiatry* 151:668–73.

Weiger, W. A., and D. M. Bear. 1988. "An Approach to the Neurology of Aggression." *Journal of Psychiatric Research* 22:85–98.

Werner, E. E. 1987. "Vulnerability and Resiliency in Children at Risk for Delinquency: A Longitudinal Study from Birth to Adulthood." In *Primary Prevention of Psychopathology,* ed. J. D. Burchard and S. N. Burchard. Newbury Park, Calif.: Sage.

West, D. J., and D. P. Farrington. 1977. *The Delinquent Way of Life.* New York: Crane Russak.

Wilson, J. Q., and R. Herrnstein. 1985. *Crime and Human Nature.* New York: Simon and Schuster.

Witkin, H. A., S. A. Mednick, F. Schulsinger, E. Bakkestrom, K. O. Christiansen, and D. R. Goodenough. 1977. "Criminality, Aggression, and Intelligence among XYY and XXY Men." In *Biosocial Bases of Behavior,* ed. S. A. Mednick and K. O. Christiansen. New York: Gardner.

Wright, P., J. Nobrega, R. Langevin, and G. Wortzman. 1990. "Brain Density and Symmetry in Pedophilic and Sexually Aggressive Offenders." *Annals of Sex Research* 3:319–28.

Yeudall, L. T. 1978. "The Neuropsychology of Aggression." Clarence Hinks Memorial Lecture, University of Western Ontario, Canada.

Yeudall, L. T., O. Fedora, S. Fedora, and D. Wardell. 1981. "Neuropsychology and Aggression." *Australian Journal of Forensic Science* 13:4.

Yeudall, L. T., D. Fromm-Auch, and P. Davies. 1982. "Neuropsychological Impairment of Persistent Delinquency." *Journal of Nervous and Mental Disease* 170:257–65.

Yeudall, L. T., and P. Flor-Henry. 1975. "Lateralized Neuropsychology of Aggression." Clarence Hinks Memorial Lecture, University of Western Ontario, Canada.

Yeudall, L. T., and D. Fromm-Aach. 1979. "Neuropsychological Impairments in Various Psychopathological Populations." In *Hemisphere Asymmetries of Function and Psychopathology,* ed. J. Gruzelier and P. Flor-Henry. New York: Elsevier.

Yoshimasu, S. 1961. "The Criminological Significance of the Family in Light of the Studies of Criminal Twins." *Acta Criminologiae et Medicinae Legalis Japanica* 27.

5. Peter W. Greenwood, "Juvenile Crime and Juvenile Justice"

Notes

1. Wolfgang, Figlio, and Sellin 1981.

2. DaVanzo 1992.

3. Menard and Elliott 1993.

4. Burglary, larceny-theft, auto theft, and arson.

5. Murder, rape, aggravated assault, and robbery.

6. Although juvenile arrest rates in California for all types of violent felonies have been increasing somewhat faster than those for adults between 1988 and 1994, they appear to have leveled off and stabilized since 1990 (California Department of Justice 1992; Fellmeth 1994).

7. Greenwood 1992.

8. Reiss and Roth 1993.

9. United States Department of Health and Human Services 1990.

10. Reiss and Roth 1993.

11. Johnston, O'Malley, and Bachman 1991.

12. Elliott, Huizinga, and Ageton 1985.

13. Blumstein et al. 1986.

14. Empey 1979.

15. Schwartz and Van Vleet 1992.

16. Feld 1989.

17. The U.S. Justice Department's Office of Juvenile Justice and Delinquency Prevention is responsible for delinquency research and demonstration projects while the National Institute of Justice funds research concerning adult offenders.

18. Greenwood et al. 1983.

19. Greenwood et al. 1983.

20. Greenwood 1986.

21. United States Department of Justice 1993.

22. California Department of Justice 1990.

23. *Los Angeles Times* 1993.

24. *Wall Street Journal* 1993.

25. Feld 1989.

26. Feld 1984.

27. Greenwood 1994.

28. Greenwood et al. 1983, 149–50.

29. See Schwartz (1989).

30. See Krisberg and Austin (1993).

31. Coates, Miller, and Ohlin 1982.

32. Krisberg, Austin, and Steele 1991.

33. Coates, Miller, and Ohlin 1982.

34. Bartollas, Miller, and Dinitz 1976; Feld 1977.

35. Coates, Miller, and Ohlin 1982; Empey and Lubeck 1971; Greenwood and Turner 1993.

36. Lipsey 1991.

37. Thornberry et al. 1989.

38. Thornberry et al. 1989.

39. Deschenes, Greenwood, and Adams 1993; MacKenzie 1990.

40. Altschuler and Armstrong 1991.

41. See Greenwood, Deschenes, and Adams (1993).

42. Lipton, Martinson, and Wilks 1975; Sechrest, White, and Brown 1979.

43. Andrews et al. 1990.

44. Lipsey 1991.

45. Greenwood and Turner 1993.

46. Skogan 1990.

47. Elliott, Huizinga, and Menard 1989.

48. Panel on High-Risk Youth 1993.

49. Panel on High-Risk Youth 1993.

50. Hawkins et al. 1992.

51. Yoshikawa 1994.

52. Lally, Mangione, and Honig 1988.

53. Berrueta-Clement et al. 1984, 37.

54. Loeber, Dishion, and Patterson 1984.

55. Patterson, Chamberlain, and Reid 1982.

56. Gottfredson 1986; Gottfredson, Gottfredson, and Hybl 1990.

57. Bell, Ellickson, and Harrison 1993.

58. Jones and Offord 1989.

59. Reiss and Roth 1993.

References

Altschuler, David M., and Troy L. Armstrong. 1991. "Intensive Aftercare for the High-Risk Juvenile Parolee: Issues and Approaches in Reintegration and Community Supervision." In *Intensive Interventions with High-Risk Youths: Promising Approaches in Juvenile Probation and Parole,* ed. Troy L. Armstrong. Monsey, N.Y.: Willow Tree Press.

Andrews, D. A., Ivan Zinger, R. D. Hoge, James Bonta, Paul Gendreau, and Francis T. Cullen. 1990. "Does Correctional Treatment Work? A Clinically Relevant and Psychologically Informed Meta-Analysis." *Criminology* 28 (3): 369–404.

Bartollas, C., S. J. Miller, and S. Dinitz. 1976. *Juvenile Victimization: The Institutional Paradox.* New York: Wiley.

Bell, Robert M., Phyllis L. Ellickson, and Ellen R. Harrison. 1993. *Do Drug Prevention Effects Persist into High School? How Project ALERT Did with Ninth Graders.* RP-237. Santa Monica, Calif.: Rand.

Berrueta-Clement, J., J. Schweinhart, L. Barnett, A. W. Epstein, and D. Weikart. 1984. *Changed Lives: The Effects of the Perry Preschool Program on Youths through Age 19.* Ypsilanti, Mich.: High Scope Press.

Blumstein, Alfred, Jacqueline Cohen, Jeffrey Roth, and Christy Visher, eds. 1986. *Criminal Careers and "Career Criminals."* Washington, D.C.: National Academy Press.

California Department of Justice. 1990. *Crime and Delinquency in California, 1980–1989.* Sacramento: Bureau of Criminal Statistics and Special Services, July.

———. 1992. *Crime and Delinquency.* Sacramento.

Coates, R., A. Miller, and L. Ohlin. 1982. *Diversity in a Youth Correctional System.* Cambridge, Mass.: Ballinger.

DaVanzo, Julie. 1992. "Families, Children, Poverty, Policy." In *Urban America: Policy Choices for Los Angeles and the Nation,* ed. James B. Steinberg, David W. Lyon, and Mary E. Vaiana. Santa Monica, Calif.: Rand.

Deschenes, Elizabeth P., Peter W. Greenwood, and John Adams. 1993. "An Evaluation of the Nokomis Challenge Program in Michigan." *Journal of Contemporary Criminal Justice* 9, no. 2 (May): 146-67.

Elliott, Delbert S., David Huizinga, and Susanne S. Ageton. 1985. *Explaining Delinquency and Drug Use.* Beverly Hills: Sage.

Elliott, Delbert S., David Huizinga, and Scott Menard. 1989. *Multiple Problem Youth: Delinquency, Substance Use, and Mental Health Problems.* New York: Springer-Verlag.

Empey, La Mar T. 1979. *American Delinquency: The Future of Childhood and Juvenile Justice.* Charlottesville: University Press of Virginia.

Empey, La Mar T., and Steven G. Lubeck. 1971. *The Silverlake Experiment: Testing Delinquency Theory and Community Intervention.* Chicago: Aldine.

Feld, Barry. 1977. *Neutralizing Inmate Violence: Juvenile Offenders in Institutions.* Cambridge, Mass.: Ballinger.

———. 1984. "Criminalizing Juvenile Justice: Rules of Procedure for Juvenile Court." *Minnesota Law Review* 69:141–276.

———. 1989. "The Right to Counsel in Juvenile Court: An Empirical Study of When Lawyers Appear and the Difference They Make." *Journal of Criminal Law and Criminology* 79:1185–1346.

Fellmeth, Robert C. 1994. *California Children's Budget, 1994–1995.* San Diego: University of San Diego, Children's Advocacy Institute.

Gottfredson, Denise, 1986. "An Empirical Test of School-Based Environmental and Individual Interventions to Reduce the Risk of Delinquent Behavior." *Criminology* 24 (4): 705–32.

Gottfredson, Denise C., Gary D. Gottfredson, and Lois G. Hybl. 1990. *Managing Adolescent Behavior: A Multi-Year, Multi-School Experiment.* Center for Research on Elementary and Middle Schools, Report no. 50. Baltimore: Johns Hopkins University Press, November.

Greenwood, Peter W. 1986. "Differences in Criminal Behavior and Court Response among Juvenile and Young Adult Defendants." In *Crime and Justice: A Review of Research,* ed. Michael H. Tonry and Norval Morris, 7:151–87. Chicago: University of Chicago Press.

———. 1992. "Substance Abuse Problems among High-Risk Youth and Potential Interventions." *Crime and Delinquency* 38, no. 4 (October): 444–58.

———. 1994. "Strategies for Improving Coordination between Enforcement and Treatment Efforts in Controlling Illegal Drug Use." *Journal of Drug Issues* (forthcoming).

Greenwood, Peter W., Elizabeth Piper Deschenes, and John Adams. 1993. *Chronic Juvenile Offenders: Final Results from the Skillman Aftercare Experiment.* MR-220-SKF. Santa Monica, Calif.: Rand.

Greenwood, Peter W., Albert Lipson, Allan Abrahamse, and Franklin Zimring. 1983. *Youth Crime and Juvenile Justice in California: A Report to the Legislature.* R-3016-CSA. Santa Monica, Calif.: Rand.

Greenwood, Peter W., and Susan Turner. 1993. "Evaluation of the Paint Creek Youth Center: A Residential Program for Serious Delinquents." *Criminology* 31, no. 2 (May): 263–79.

Hawkins, J. David, Richard F. Catalano, Jr., and associates. 1992. *Communities That Care: Action for Drug Abuse Prevention.* San Francisco: Jossey-Bass.

Johnston, Lloyd D., Patrick M. O'Malley, and Gerald M. Bachman. 1991. *Drug Use among American High School Seniors, College Students, and Young Adults, 1975–1990.* Washington, D.C.: National Institute of Drug Abuse.

Jones, Marshall B., and David R. Offord. 1989. "Reduction of Antisocial Behavior in Poor Children by Nonschool Skill-Development." *Journal of Child Psychology* 30 (5): 737–50.

Krisberg, Barry, and James F. Austin. 1993. *Reinventing Juvenile Justice.* Newbury Park, Calif.: Sage.

Krisberg, Barry, James Austin, and P. Steele. 1991. *Unlocking Juvenile Corrections.* San Francisco: National Council on Crime and Delinquency.

Lally, J. R., R. Mangione, and A. Honig. 1988. "The Syracuse University Family Development Research Project: Long-Range Impact of an Early Intervention with Low-Income Children and Their Families." In *Parent Education as Early Childhood Intervention: Emerging Directions in Theory, Research, and Practice,* ed. D. R. Powell. Vol. 3 in *Annual Advances in Applied Developmental Psychology.* Norwood, N. J.: Ablex.

Lipsey, Mark W. 1991. "Juvenile Delinquency Treatment: A Meta-Analytic Inquiry into the Variability of Effects." In *Meta-Analysis for Explanation: A Casebook.* Beverly Hills: Sage.

Lipton, Douglas, Robert Martinson, and Judith Wilks. 1975. *The Effectiveness of Correctional Treatment: A Survey of Treatment Evaluation Studies.* New York: Praeger.

Loeber, Rolf, Thomas J. Dishion, and Gerald R. Patterson. 1984. "Multiple Gating: A Multistage Assessment Procedure for Identifying Youths at Risk for Delinquency." *Journal of Research for Crime and Delinquency* 21, no. 1 (February): 7–21.

Los Angeles Times. 1993. "A Nation's Children in Lockup," 22 August.

MacKenzie, D. L. 1990. "Boot Camp Prisons: Components, Evaluations, and Empirical Issues." *Federal Probation* 54 (3).

Menard, Scott, and Delbert S. Elliott. 1993. "Data Set Comparability and Short-Term Trends in Crime and Delinquency." *Journal of Criminal Justice* 21:433–45.

Panel on High-Risk Youth. 1993. *Losing Generations.* Washington, D.C.: National Academy Press.

Patterson, Gerald R., P. Chamberlain, and J. B. Reid. 1982. "A Comparative Evaluation of a Parent-training Program." *Behavior Therapy* 13:638–50.

Reiss, A. J., and J. A. Roth, eds. 1993. *Understanding and Preventing Violence.* Washington, D.C.: National Academy Press.

Schwartz, Ira M., 1989. *(In)Justice for Juveniles: Rethinking the Best Interests of the Child.* Lexington, Mass.: Lexington Books.

Schwartz, Ira M., and Russell Van Vleet. 1992. "Public Policy and the Incarceration of Juveniles: Directions for the 1990s." In *Juvenile Justice and Public Policy,* ed. Ira M. Schwartz, 151–64. New York: Lexington Books.

Sechrest, L., S. O. White, and E. D. Brown, eds. 1979. *The Rehabilitation of Criminal Offenders: Problems and Prospects.* Washington, D.C.: National Academy of Sciences.

Skogan, Wesley G. 1990. *Disorder and Decline: Crime and the Spiral of Decay in American Neighborhoods.* New York: Free Press.

Thornberry, Terence P., Stewart E. Tolnay, Timothy J. Flanagan, and Patty Glynn. 1989. *Children in Custody, 1987: A Comparison of Public and Private Juvenile Custody Facilities.* New York: University at Albany, March 7.

United States Department of Health and Human Services. 1990. *Health: United States, 1989.* Hyattsville, Md.: Public Health Service.

United States Department of Justice. 1993. *The Juvenile Court's Response to Violent Offenders: 1985–1989.* Washington, D.C.: Office of Juvenile Justice and Delinquency Prevention.

Wall Street Journal. 1993. "Bad Boys," 28 September.

Wolfgang, M., R. M. Figlio, and T. Sellin. 1981. *Delinquency in a Birth Cohort.* Cambridge, Mass. First published Chicago: University of Chicago Press, 1972.

Yoshikawa, Hirokauze. 1994. "Prevention as Cumulative Protection: Effects of Early Family Support and Education on Chronic Delinquency and Its Risks." *Psychological Bulletin* 115 (1): 1–27.

6. Travis Hirschi, "The Family"

Notes

1. See Rowe (1994).

2. For development of this point of view, and its general policy implications, see Gottfredson and Hirschi (1990). The classification of theories as stressing inheritance, invention, or learning is from Roshier (1989).

3. Shalala 1994.

4. A persistent problem for learning theories of crime is their inability to explain how crime got started in the first place. If crime is learned from others, how

and where did others learn it? In the present case, Secretary Shalala suggests that the factors placing families at risk of violence include "joblessness, poor housing, substance abuse and lack of day care." If her analysis is correct, parents and children would appear to acquire violence from fundamentally different sources. In fact, however, this tradition rarely distinguishes between physical abuse and poverty. Both represent an (institutional) assault on the individual that demands and justifies crime.

5. See, for example, Becker (1981, chap. 11).

6. There are several reasons for this decision: Whatever the validity of the argument that apparent family socialization effects are really effects of genetic inheritance in disguise, this argument threatens in equal manner the learning and invention perspectives. Also, the immediately relevant policy position of the biological argument (that family process and structure may be ignored) is represented in a comparison of the other two perspectives. Finally, as a theory of crime, the biological perspective is the least developed of the three. As a result, it is difficult for someone untrained in this perspective to represent it in the manner it deserves.

7. Apparently, the condition of the family was in fact relatively stable until 1960 or later. According to Steven Ruggles, the proportion of black and white children ages 0–14 living with both parents remained essentially constant between 1880 and 1960. Between 1960 and 1980, however, the percentage of children living without both parents went from 32 to 53 among blacks, and from 9 to 16 among whites (Ruggles 1994, 140).

8. See, for example, the discussion in Sutherland and Cressey (1978, chap. 10).

9. Mannheim 1965, 618. Mannheim was among those inclined to see the family as a criminogenic influence: "It is often striking to observe how, especially in the case of delinquents . . . their whole being is, for good or ill, centred around the family" (p. 609).

10. Glueck and Glueck 1950. Family cohesion has often been overlooked in subsequent discussion and analysis of the Gluecks' data.

11. My discussion is based on Patterson (1980) and on the original version of this chapter (Hirschi 1983). In that version I reduced the number of elements in Patterson's child-rearing model from seven to three, and made much of the fact that social learning theory had only recently rediscovered punishment. For present purposes, I am less concerned with the specific elements of a child-rearing model and more concerned about the willingness of the parents to attend to their children, whatever the techniques they employ.

12. Loeber and Stouthamer-Loeber 1986.

13. Widom 1989.

14. For an extended exposition of this point, see Hirschi and Gottfredson (1994).

15. The lack of specialization among offenders is a fact of primary significance for crime research, theory, and policy. It says that a general tendency of offenders is common to a wide variety of offenses. Ironically, it also says that we should look outside the offender for the causes and cures of specific criminal acts.

16. I used these intervening processes to explain family structure effects in the original version of this chapter (Hirschi 1983). In a subsequent article on the same topic (Hirschi 1991), I used an expanded list of family activities for the same purpose. That list is reproduced in slightly modified form in this chapter, as part of the section

"Other Family Activities Relevant to Delinquency," through "A stable family . . . makes a very good excuse, indeed," on page 129.

17. Sampson and Laub 1993, 82.

18. Cohen and Felson 1979.

19. The quotation is from Judith Blake (1961, 89), as quoted by Shirley Foster Hartley (1975, 67).

20. Currie 1985, 193–94.

21. Loeber and Stouthamer-Loeber 1986, 72.

22. Currie 1985, 197.

23. Bennett 1994.

24. Mannheim 1965, 609.

25. Davis 1948, 395.

26. At the moment, feminists attack the family as the bastion of patriarchy and suppression of women (see Wilson [1993]). In the past, the left attacked the family as the bastion of capitalism and bourgeois morality. Of the two critiques, the feminist is the more fundamental. Political views, left and right, run in families, and parents can, if they wish, spend their children's inheritance. However, reproduction requires more from women than from men. Women bear and nurse children, and are therefore more likely to become attached to them. The family was presumably invented for precisely this reason. It alone guarantees that men will assist women in the child-rearing task. Women thus have more to gain by escaping family entanglements altogether; and more to lose from partial involvement in an incomplete family.

27. It was not always so. Not long ago the state convicted men of "bastardy," and exerted some effort to tracking down those guilty of nonsupport. The decriminalization movement of the modern era typically recommended that the police be freed of such duties so that they could concentrate on real crime. For policy recommendations in this area based on the assumption that criminologists derive from their technical studies moral insight superior to that of ordinary citizens, see Morris and Hawkins (1969). For a contrary view, see Roshier (1989).

28. Bronislaw Malinowski (1930), quoted by Kingsley Davis (1948, 400).

29. Glueck and Glueck 1950, 100.

30. Christensen 1960. The 30 percent figure applies to children born within nine months of marriage. Most of the marriages in question were not forced in any meaningful sense of the term.

31. *Arizona Daily Star* 1989.

32. *Arizona Daily Star* 1989.

33. As is evident from the situation in Jamaica described by Judith Blake Davis. See note 19.

34. McLanahan 1991. See also Coleman (1990, 596).

35. Junger 1994.

36. According to Beverly and Otis Dudley Duncan, multivariate analysis "lends some support to the notion that the son raised in a family headed by a female is handicapped with respect to occupational success, even when allowance has been made for . . . his education and point of entry into the occupation structure" (1969, 273–85), quoted by Kriesberg (1970, 181).

37. Buck 1938, 240.

38. McClanahan 1991, 12.
39. This argument is fully developed in Gottfredson and Hirschi (1990).
40. See Travis Hirschi (1969, chap. 3).
41. Sampson 1992.
42. Farrington 1994, xxiii.
43. Rosenquist and Megargee 1969, 457.
44. Compare the data in Hirschi (1991) with the 1931 Shaw and McKay data summarized by Gwynne Nettler (1984, 309–11).
45. See McClanahan (1991); Hirschi (1991); Coleman (1990).
46. Sampson and Laub 1993, chap. 4.
47. Hirschi 1991, 62.
48. The teenage mother is presumably handicapped by her relative inability to recognize deviant behavior. In fact, however, this element of the monitor-recognize-punish child-rearing model remains problematic. Descriptions of actual failure to recognize deviance suggest its transparent motivation. If the child's version of events is accepted by the parent ("That's a lie! I didn't touch that teacher!"), no further action is required.
49. Skocpol and Wilson 1994. In Arizona, an unmarried mother wishing to add a natural father's name to the birth certificate must obtain his notarized consent or a court order. At the same time, the state does not recognize common law marriage. Whatever the legal considerations behind such practices, they strike me as contrary to sound family policy, which would require positive effort to identify the father of the child.
50. Tremblay et al. 1992.
51. See, for example, Morris and Hawkins (1969).
52. See, for example, Kissman and Allen (1993).
53. Glueck and Glueck 1968, 88.
54. Glueck and Glueck 1968, 87.

References

Arizona Daily Star. 1989. "Rise in Premarital Pregnancies Cited," 22 June, 1.
Becker, Gary S. 1981. *A Treatise on the Family.* Cambridge, Mass.: Harvard University Press.
Bennett, William J. 1994. "Raising Cain on Values." *Newsweek,* 18 April, 23.
Blake, Judith. 1961. *Family Structure in Jamaica.* Glencoe, Ill.: Free Press.
Buck, Pearl. 1938. *The Good Earth.* New York: Pocket Books.
Christensen, Harold T. 1960. "Cultural Relativism and Premarital Sex Norms." *American Sociological Review* 25:1–39.
Cohen, Lawrence E., and Marcus Felson. 1979. "Social Change and Crime Rate Trends: A Routine Activity Approach." *American Sociological Review* 44:588–608.
Coleman, James S. 1990. *Foundations of Social Theory.* Cambridge, Mass.: Belknap Press of Harvard University Press.
Currie, Elliott. 1985. *Confronting Crime.* New York: Pantheon Books.

Davis, Kingsley. 1948. *Human Society*. New York: Macmillan.

Duncan, Beverly, and Otis Dudley Duncan. 1969. "Family Stability and Occupational Success." *Social Problems* 16:273–85.

Farrington, David. 1994. *Psychological Explanations of Crime*. Aldershot, England: Dartmouth.

Glueck, Sheldon, and Eleanor Glueck. 1950. *Unraveling Juvenile Delinquency*. Cambridge, Mass.: Harvard University Press.

———. 1968. *Delinquents and Nondelinquents in Perspective*. Cambridge, Mass.: Harvard University Press.

Gottfredson, Michael, and Travis Hirschi. 1990. *A General Theory of Crime*. Stanford, Calif.: Stanford University Press.

Hartley, Shirley Foster. 1975. *Illegitimacy*. Berkeley: University of California Press.

Hirschi, Travis. 1969. *Causes of Delinquency*. Berkeley: University of California Press.

———. 1983. "Crime and the Family." In *Crime and Public Policy*, ed. James Q. Wilson, 53–68. San Francisco: ICS Press.

———. 1991. "Family Structure and Crime." In *When Families Fail . . . The Social Costs*, ed. Bryce J. Christensen, 43–65. Lanham, Md.: University Press of America.

Hirschi, Travis, and Michael R. Gottfredson, eds. 1994. *The Generality of Deviance*. New Brunswick, N.J.: Transaction.

Junger, Marianne. 1994. "Accidents." In *The Generality of Deviance*, ed. Travis Hirschi and Michael R. Gottfredson, 81–112. New Brunswick, N.J.: Transaction.

Kissman, Kris, and Jo Ann Allen. 1993. *Single-Parent Families*. Newbury Park, Calif.: Sage.

Kriesberg, Louis. 1970. *Mothers in Poverty*. Chicago: Aldine.

Loeber, Rolf, and Magda Stouthamer-Loeber. 1986. "Family Factors as Correlates and Predictors of Juvenile Conduct Problems and Delinquency." In *Crime and Justice: A Review of Research*, ed. Michael H. Tonry and Norval Morris, 29–149. Chicago: University of Chicago Press.

Malinowski, Bronislaw. 1930. "Parenthood—the Basis of Social Structure." In *The New Generation*, ed. V. F. Calverton and S. D. Schmalhausen. New York: Macauley.

Mannheim, Herman. 1965. *Comparative Criminology*. Boston: Houghton-Mifflin.

McLanahan, Sara S. 1991. "The Long-Term Economic Effects of Family Dissolution." In *When Families Fail . . . The Social Costs*, ed. Bryce J. Christensen, 5–25. Lanham, Md.: University Press of America.

Morris, Norval, and Gordon Hawkins. 1969. *The Honest Politician's Guide to Crime Control*. Chicago: University of Chicago Press.

Nettler, Gwynne. 1984. *Explaining Crime*. New York: McGraw-Hill.

Patterson, G. R. 1980. "Children Who Steal." In *Understanding Crime*, ed. Travis Hirschi and Michael Gottfredson, 73–90. Bevery Hills: Sage.

Rosenquist, Carl M., and Edwin I. Megargee. 1969. *Delinquency in Three Cultures*. Austin: Texas University Press.

Roshier, Bob. 1989. *Controlling Crime*. Chicago: Lyceum Books.

Rowe, David. 1994. *The Limits of Family Influence*. New York: Guilford Press.

Ruggles, Steven. 1994. "The Origins of African-American Family Structure." *American Sociological Review* 59:136–51.

Sampson, Robert. 1992. "Family Management and Child Development: Insights from Social Disorganization Theory." In *Facts, Frameworks, and Forecasts,* 63–93. Vol. 3 of *Advances in Criminological Theory,* ed. Joan McCord. New Brunswick, N.J.: Transaction.

Sampson, Robert, and John Laub. 1993. *Crime in the Making.* Cambridge, Mass.: Harvard University Press.

Shalala, Donna E. 1994. "Fight 'Terrorism in the Home.' " *Arizona Daily Star,* 5 May.

Skocpol, Theda, and William Julius Wilson. 1994. *Arizona Daily Star,* 14 February, A15.

Sutherland, Edwin H., and Donald R. Cressey. 1978. *Criminology.* Philadelphia: Lippincott.

Tremblay, Richard E., Frank Vitaro, Lucie Bertrand, Marc LeBlanc, Helene Beauchesne, Helene Boileau, and Lucille David. 1992. "Parent and Child Training to Prevent Early Onset of Delinquency." Chap. 6 in *Preventing Antisocial Behavior,* ed. J. McCord and R. Tremblay. New York: Guilford Press.

Widom, Cathy Spatz. 1989. "The Cycle of Violence." *Science* 244:160–66.

Wilson, James Q. 1993. "The Family-Values Debate." *Commentary,* April, 24–31.

7. Jackson Toby, "The Schools"

Notes

1. Reinhold 1989.
2. Toby 1992.
3. Rimer 1993.
4. *New York Times* 1993.
5. Butterfield 1980.
6. United States Department of Health, Education, and Welfare 1978; Gottfredson and Gottfredson 1985.
7. U.S. Department of Health, Education, and Welfare 1978.
8. U.S. Department of Health, Education, and Welfare 1978, 33–37.
9. Parker et al. 1991.
10. The first is McDermott (1979); the second, Bastian and Taylor (1991).
11. Louis Harris and Associates 1993.
12. Martin 1988.
13. Bastian and Taylor 1991, 2.
14. From unpublished special tabulations made available to me by the directors of the survey, Robert Leitman and Katherine Binns of Louis Harris and Associates.
15. Garofalo, Siegel, and Laub 1987.
16. Wilson 1985.

17. Toby 1957. See also his concluding remarks in Glazer (1992) on the deterioration of the value consensus supporting education.

18. Coleman 1961.

19. Salisbury 1958.

20. Toby 1983; Moles 1990.

21. Herndon 1968; Holt 1964; Kohl 1967; Kozol 1967.

22. Coleman, Hoffer, and Kilgore 1982.

23. Dworkin 1987.

24. Rubel 1977 and 1980.

25. U.S. Department of Health, Education, and Welfare 1978, 70–71.

26. U.S. Department of Health, Education, and Welfare, 147.

27. U.S. Department of Health, Education, and Welfare, 232.

28. Harris 1984.

29. U.S. Department of Health, Education, and Welfare 182.

30. U.S. Department of Health, Education, and Welfare, 190.

31. See Chapter 6 in this volume.

32. DeWitt 1993.

33. U.S. Department of Health, Education, and Welfare 78, 129. The same equivocal conclusion was reached about security measures in Gottfredson and Gottfredson (1985, 118–21).

34. Daniels 1985, 100–17.

35. Norimitsu Onishi 1994.

36. United States Department of Education 1987; Rohlen 1983.

37. In a rejoinder to Chester E. Finn, Jr., who argued that education was too important to allow children to choose to drop out merely because they wished to do so, I responded that coercion can only succeed in disrupting the educational process for willing students. See Toby (1989a).

38. Toby 1989b; Toby and Armor 1992.

39. Rapson 1980; Hawaii Crime Commission 1980.

40. Toby 1980.

41. Coleman, Hoffer, and Kilgore 1982.

42. United States Supreme Court 1975.

43. Toby 1983.

44. U.S. Department of Health, Education, and Welfare 1978, B-6.

45. Toby 1950; Schafer and Polk 1967.

46. Bachman, Green, and Wirtanen, 1971; Elliott and Voss 1974.

47. The theory explicated by Gottfredson and Hirschi, namely, that the failure to learn self-control as a child accounts for a wide range of deviant and criminal behaviors throughout the life cycle, would predict this result. See Gottfredson and Hirschi (1990).

48. Dornbusch 1974.

49. Sowell 1974. When Dunbar stopped being selective in 1955, it developed all of the academic and behavior problems of neighborhood schools in the inner city.

50. Wilkerson 1993.
51. Rosenbaum and Kariya 1989.
52. Rosenbaum 1989.
53. Farrington 1993.
54. Moles 1990.
55. Toby 1958.

References

Bachman, Jerald G., Swayzer Green, and Ilona D. Wirtanen. 1971. *Dropping Out: Problem or Symptom?* Vol. 3 of *Youth in Transition.* Ann Arbor, Mich.: Survey Research Center.

Bastian, Lisa D., and Bruce M. Taylor. 1991. *School Crime: A National Crime Victimization Survey Report.* Washington, D.C.: Bureau of Justice Statistics.

Butterfield, Fox. 1980. "Peking Is Troubled about Youth Crime." *New York Times,* 11 March.

Coleman, James S. 1961. *The Adolescent Society.* New York: Free Press.

Coleman, James S., Thomas Hoffer, and Sally Kilgore. 1982. *High School Achievement: Public, Catholic, and Private Schools Compared.* New York: Basic Books.

Daniels, Lee A. 1985. "The Halls of Boston Latin School." *New York Times Magazine,* 21 April, 100–17.

DeWitt, Karen. 1993. "Teachers Ask for Help with School Violence." *New York Times,* 15 January, 18.

Dornbusch, Sanford M. 1974. "To Try or Not to Try." *Stanford Magazine* 2 (Fall/ Winter): 51–54.

Dworkin, Anthony G. 1987. *Teacher Burnout in the Public Schools: Structural Causes and Consequences for Children.* Albany: State University of New York Press.

Elliott, Delbert S., and Harwin L. Voss. 1974. *Delinquency and Dropout.* Lexington, Mass.: Lexington.

Farrington, David P. 1993. "Understanding and Preventing Bullying." In *Crime and Justice: A Review of Research,* ed. Michael H. Tonry, 17:381–458. Chicago: University of Chicago Press.

Garofalo, James, Leslie Siegel, and John Laub. 1987. "School-related Victimizations among Adolescents: An Analysis of National Crime Survey (NCS) Narratives." *Journal of Quantitative Criminology* 3:321–38.

Glazer, Nathan. 1992. "The Real World of Urban Education." *The Public Interest,* no. 106 (Winter), 57–75.

Gottfredson, Gary D., and Denise C. Gottfredson. 1985. *Victimization in Schools.* New York: Plenum.

Gottfredson, Michael R., and Travis Hirschi. 1990. *A General Theory of Crime.* Stanford, Calif.: Stanford University Press.

Hawaii Crime Commission. 1980. *Violence and Vandalism in the Public Schools of Hawaii.* Honolulu.

Herndon, James. 1968. *The Way It Spozed to Be.* New York: Simon and Schuster.

Holt, John. 1964. *How Children Fail.* New York: Pittman.

Kohl, Herbert. 1967. *Thirty-six Children*. New York: New American Library.

Kozol, Jonathan. 1967. *Death at an Early Age: The Destruction of the Minds and Hearts of Negro Children in the Boston Public Schools*. Boston: Houghton Mifflin.

Louis Harris and Associates. 1984. *The Metropolitan Life Survey of the American Teacher 1984*. New York: Metropolitan Life Insurance Company.

————. 1993. *The Metropolitan Life Survey of the American Teacher 1993: Violence in America's Public Schools*. New York: Metropolitan Life Insurance Company.

Martin, Douglas. 1988. "For Teachers Battered by Students, Psychological Wounds Linger." *New York Times*. 26 June.

McDermott, M. Joan. 1979. *Criminal Victimization in Urban Schools*. Washington, D.C.: United States Government Printing Office.

Moles, Oliver C. 1990. *Student Discipline Strategies: Research and Practice*. Albany: State University of New York Press.

New York Times. 1993. "Math Teacher Hurt in Classroom Attack." 25 November.

Onishi, Norimitsu. 1994. "Teaching the Mechanics of Success: Airlines Are Weak and Jobs Few, but Aviation High Thrives." *New York Times*, 16 January.

Parker, Robert Nash, William R. Smith, D. Randall Smith, and Jackson Toby. 1991. "Trends in Victimization in School and Elsewhere, 1974–1981." *Journal of Quantitative Criminology* 7 (March): 3–17.

Rapson, Richard L. 1980. *Fairly Lucky You Live in Hawaii! Cultural Pluralism in the Fiftieth State*. Lanham, Md.: University Press of America.

Reinhold, Robert. 1989. "Killer Depicted as Loner Full of Hate." *New York Times*, 20 January.

Rimer, Sarah. 1993. "Model School Tries to Cope with Killing in a Classroom." *New York Times*, 14 April.

Rohlen, Thomas P. 1983. *Japan's High Schools*. Berkeley, Calif.: University of California Press.

Rosenbaum, James E. 1989. "What If Good Jobs Depended on Good Grades?" *American Educator* 13 (Winter).

Rosenbaum, James E., and Takehiko Kariya. 1989. "From High School to Work: Market and Institutional Mechanisms in Japan." *American Journal of Sociology* 94 (May): 1334–1365.

Rubel, Robert J. 1977. *The Unruly School: Disorders, Disruptions, and Crime*. Lexington, Mass.: D. C. Heath.

————, ed. 1980. *School Crime and Violence*. Lexington, Mass.: D. C. Heath.

Salisbury, Harrison. 1958. *The Shook-Up Generation*. New York: Harper.

Schafer, Walter E., and Kenneth Polk. 1967. "Delinquency and the Schools." In *Juvenile Delinquency and Youth Crime*. The President's Commission on Law Enforcement and Administration of Justice. Washington, D.C.: United States Government Printing Office.

Sowell, Thomas. 1974. "Black Excellence: The Case of Dunbar High School." *The Public Interest* 35 (Spring): 1–21.

Toby, Jackson. 1950. "Educational Maladjustment as a Predisposing Factor in Criminal Careers: A Comparative Study of Ethnic Groups." Ph.D. dissertation, Harvard University.

———. 1957. "Orientation to Education as a Factor in the School Maladjustment of Lower-Class Children." *Social Forces* 35 (March): 259–66.

———. 1958. "Hoodlum or Businessman: An American Dilemma." In *The Jews: Social Patterns of an American Group*, ed. Marshall Sklare. Glencoe, Ill.: Free Press.

———. 1980. "Crime in American Public Schools." *The Public Interest*, no. 58 (Winter): 29–32.

———. 1983. "Violence in School." In *Crime and Justice: A Review of Research*, ed. Michael H. Tonry and Norval Morris, 4:1–47.

———. 1989a. "Coercion or Choice?" *The Public Interest*, no. 96 (Summer): 134–36.

———. 1989b. "Of Dropouts and Stay-ins: The Gershwin Approach." *The Public Interest*, no. 95 (Spring): 3–13.

———. 1992. "To Get Rid of Guns in Schools, Get Rid of Some Students." *Wall Street Journal*, 3 March.

Toby, Jackson, and David Armor. 1992. "Carrots or Sticks for High School Dropouts?" *The Public Interest*, no. 106 (Winter): 76–90.

United States Department of Health, Education, and Welfare. 1978. *Violent Schools— Safe Schools: The Safe School Study Report to the Congress*. Washington, D.C.: United States Government Printing Office.

United States Supreme Court. 1975. *Goss v. Lopez*. 491 U.S. 565.

United States Department of Education. 1987. *Japanese Education Today*. Washington, D.C.: United States Government Printing Office.

Wilkerson, Isabel. 1993. "In School with Their Children, Parents Try Again." *New York Times*. 28 November.

Wilson, James Q. 1985. *Thinking about Crime*. New York: Vintage.

8. Richard B. Freeman, "The Labor Market"

Notes

I have benefitted from the research assistance of Ronald Chen.

1. See Freeman (1983) and Chiricos (1987).

2. Economics does not support the traditional focus on unemployment as *the* key labor market variable affecting crime. Rather, it posits that the decision to commit crime depends on the present value of economic returns to criminal activity compared to the present value of economic returns to legal activity. The returns to crime depend on: the chance of success, the money (utility) obtained from crime, less the value of the time spent at crime, the chance of being caught and convicted, the length of sentence and resultant earnings lost due to imprisonment. The crime decision should also depend on the effects of crime on future earnings opportunities and, because crime is risky, on attitudes toward the risks involved in crime, which range from risk of injury and death to risk of arrest, conviction, and incarceration.

3. These figures are approximate because we do not have data for parole and probation for 1993, but must extrapolate 1990 figures.

4. These figures are larger than figures giving percentages of the various *populations* incarcerated or under supervision since not all adult men are in the workforce. I report figures relative to the workforce because my focus is on the links between crime and the labor market.

5. The Uniform Crime Reporting Index is based on statistics that local law enforcement agencies report to the FBI as part of the Uniform Crime Reporting Program. The crime index is based on seven crime categories: murder and nonnegligent manslaughter, forcible rape, robbery, aggravated assault, burglary, larceny-theft and motor vehicle theft, and arson.

6. Much of the information discussed here is taken from Boggess and Bound (1993).

7. I relate crimes to the male population, because the vast bulk of arrestees, prisoners, and persons who self-report crime are men.

8. The numbers I use are much smaller than those in Zimring and Hawkins (1991, 95–96) or in Wilson and Abrahamse (1992, table 3).

9. In 1970 the proportion of the population that consisted of fifteen- to thirty-four-year-old men was 14.7 percent. In 1980, the proportion had risen to 17.6 percent. But in 1990, it had fallen to 16.3 percent.

10. The one contrary analysis that I have found is Trumbull's (1989) study of unemployment and crime across North Carolina counties, where he obtained a negative coefficient on the unemployment rate. But this does not mean that county data are inconsistent with more aggregate state or SMSA data: in an analysis of 120 counties in Kentucky, Howsen and Jarrell (1987) obtain positive coefficients on percentage unemployed or not in the workforce.

11. Calculated from United States Department of Commerce, (1991, table B-2.)

12. While most ethnographies conclude that monetary incentives underlie gang activity, there is a general consensus that Chicano gangs are more turf-motivated (Moore 1992; Jankowski 1991; Vigil 1990), and Jankowski also reports that Irish gangs in Boston are also more turf- than crime-business-oriented, in part because of connections with adults in the world of work that are missing in other communities.

13. The crime question is on the 1980 survey and refers to past crimes. We do not know the exact timing of the crime. I compare it with the employment status in 1979, but results are similar if I assume the crime was committed in 1980.

References

Beck, Allen J., and Bernard E. Shipley. 1989. *Recidivism of Prisoners Released in 1983*. Bureau of Justice Statistics Special Report, NCJ-116261. Washington, D.C.: United States Department of Justice, April.

Blau, Judith R., and Peter Blau. 1982. "The Cost of Inequality: Metropolitan Structure and Violent Crime." *American Sociological Review* 47:114–129.

Boggess, Scott, and John Bound. 1993. "Did Criminal Activity Increase during the 1980s? Comparisons across Data Sources." National Bureau of Economic Research Working Paper 4431. Cambridge, Mass., August.

Bondeson, Ulla V. 1989. *Prisoners in Prison Societies*. New Brunswick, N.J.: Transaction.

Bureau of Justice Statistics (BJS). 1992. *Sourcebook of Criminal Justice Statistics 1991.* Washington, D.C.: United States Department of Justice.

———. 1993. *Criminal Victimization 1992.* NCJ-144776. Washington, D.C.: United States Department of Justice, October.

Cappel, Charles L., and Gresham Sykes. 1991. "Prison Commitments, Crime, and Unemployment: A Theoretical and Empirical Specification for the United States, 1933–1985." *Journal of Quantitative Criminology* 7 (2): 155–99.

Carroll, Leo, and Pamela Jackson. 1983. "Inequality, Opportunity, and Crime Rates in Central Cities." *Criminology* 21:178–95.

Chin, Ko-Lin. 1990. "Chinese Gangs and Extortion." In *Gangs in America,* ed. C. Ronald Huff. New York: Sage.

Chiricos, Theodore G. 1987. "Rates of Crime and Unemployment: An Analysis of Aggregate Research Evidence." *Social Problems* 34, no. 2 (April): 187–211.

Cohen, Lawrence E., Marcus Felson, and Kenneth C. Land. 1980. "Property Crime Rates in the United States: A Macrodynamic Analysis, 1947–1977, with Ex Ante Forecasts for the Mid-1980s." *American Journal of Sociology* 86 (1): 90–118.

Conley, D., and J. Debro. 1992. "The Ecology of Crime and Drugs in a Southern City: The Ethnographic Study of the English Avenue Community in Atlanta." Presented at the Social Science Research Council Conference on the Urban Underclass, Ann Arbor, Mich., June 8–10.

Cook, Philip J. 1975. "The Correctional Carrot: Better Jobs for Parolees." *Policy Analysis* 1:11–54.

Crowley, Joan E. 1984. "Delinquency and Employment: Substitutions or Spurious Associations," Chap. 8 in *Youth and the Labor Market: Analyses of the National Longitudinal Survey,* ed. Michael E. Borus. Kalamazoo: W. E. Upjohn Institute for Employment Research.

Curtis, R. 1992. "Highly Structured Crack Markets in the South Side of Williamsburg, Brooklyn." Presented at the Social Science Research Council Conference on the Urban Underclass, Ann Arbor, Mich., June 8–10.

Dale, Mitchell W. 1976. "Barriers to the Rehabilitation of Ex-Offenders." *Crime and Delinquency* 22 (July): 322–37.

Economic Report of the President. 1993. Washington, D.C.: United States Government Printing Office, February.

Ehrlich, Isaac. 1974. "Participation in Illegitimate Activities: An Economic Approach." In *Essays in the Economics of Crime and Punishment,* ed. Gary Becker and William Landes. New York: National Bureau of Economic Research.

Elder, Glen H., Jr. 1985. "Perspectives on the Life Course." In *Life Course Dynamics,* ed. Glen H. Elder, Jr., 23–49. Ithaca, N.Y.: Cornell University Press.

Elder, Glen H., Jr., Cynthia Gimbel, and Rachel Ivie. 1991. "Turning Points in Life: The Case of Military Service and War." *Military Psychology* 3: 215–31.

Fagan, J. 1992. "The Dynamics of Crime and Neighborhood Change." Presented at the Social Science Research Council Conference on the Urban Underclass, Ann Arbor, Mich., June 8–10.

———. 1992. "Introduction: Crime, Drugs, and Neighborhood Change." Presented at the Social Science Research Council Conference on the Urban Underclass, Ann Arbor, Mich., June 8–10.

Farrington, David P., Bernard Gallagher, Lynda Morley, Raymond J. St. Ledger and Donald J. West. 1986. "Unemployment, School Leaving, and Crime." *British Journal of Criminology* 26 (4): 335–56.

Federal Bureau of Investigation (FBI). Various years. *Crime in the United States.* Washington, D.C.: United States Department of Justice.

Ferguson, Ronald F. 1994. "Tables for Discussion of Young Black Males and Work at U.S. Department of Labor." July 20.

Finn, R. H., and Patricia A. Fontaine. 1985. "The Association between Selected Characteristics and Perceived Employability of Offenders." *Criminal Justice and Behavior* 12, no. 3 (September): 353–65.

Freeman, Richard B. 1983. "Crime and Unemployment," Chap. 6 in *Crime and Public Policy,* ed. James Q. Wilson. San Francisco: ICS Press.

———. 1987. "The Relation of Criminal Activity to Black Youth Employment." *Review of Black Political Economy* 16, no. 1–2 (Summer/Fall): 99–107.

———. 1992. "Crime and the Employment of Disadvantaged Youth." In *Urban Labor Markets and Job Opportunity,* ed. George Peterson and Wayne Vroman. Washington, D.C.: Urban Institute Press.

Freeman, Richard B., and Harry J. Holzer, eds. 1986. *The Black Youth Employment Crisis.* Chicago: University of Chicago Press for National Bureau of Economic Research.

Glaser, Daniel. 1969. *The Effectiveness of a Prison and Parole System,* abridged ed. Indianapolis: Bobbs-Merrill.

Gilliard, Darrell K., and Allen J. Beck. 1994. *Prisoners in 1993.* Bureau of Justice Statistics Bulletin, NCJ-147036. Washington, D.C.: United States Department of Justice, June.

Good, David H., Maureen A. Pirog-Good, and Robin C. Sickles. 1986. "An Analysis of Youth Crime and Unemployment Patterns." *Journal of Quantitative Criminology* 2 (3): 219–36.

Gottfredson, D. 1985. "Youth Employment, Crime and Schooling." *Developmental Psychology* 21:419–32.

Grogger, Jeffrey. 1994a. "Criminal Opportunities, Youth Crime, and Young Men's Labor Supply." Department of Economics, University of California, Santa Barbara, February.

Grogger, Jeffrey. 1994b. "The Effect of Arrests on the Employment and Earnings of Young Men." *Quarterly Journal of Economics,* forthcoming.

Greenberg, David F. 1975. "The Incapacitative Effect of Imprisonment: Some Estimates." *Law and Society* Summer, 541–80.

Hagan, John. 1993. "The Social Embeddedness of Crime and Unemployment." *Criminology* 31 (4): 465–91.

Hagan, John, and Alberto Palloni. 1988. "Crimes as Social Events in the Life Course: Reconceiving a Criminological Controversy." *Criminology* 26 (1): 87–100.

Hale, Chris, and Dima Sabbagh. 1991. "Testing the Relationship between Unemployment and Crime: A Methodological Comment and Empirical Analysis Using Time Series Data from England and Wales." *Journal of Research in Crime and Delinquency* 28, no. 4 (November): 400–29.

Hamid, A. 1992. "Flatbush: A Freelance Nickels Market." Presented at the Social Science Research Council Conference on the Urban Underclass, Ann Arbor, Mich., June 8–10.

Hindelang, Michael, Travis Hirschi, and Joseph G. Weiss. 1981. *Measuring Delinquency.* Beverly Hills: Sage.

Holzer, Harry. 1986. "Black Youth Nonemployment: Duration and Job Search." Chap. 2 in *The Black Youth Employment Crisis,* ed. Richard B. Freeman and Harry J. Holzer. Chicago: University of Chicago Press for National Bureau of Economic Research.

Howsen, Roy M., and Stephen B. Jarrell. 1987. "Some Determinants of Property Crime: Economic Factors Influence Criminal Behavior but Cannot Completely Explain the Syndrome." *American Journal of Economics and Sociology* 46 (4): 445–57.

Jankowski, M. 1991. *Islands in the Street: Gangs and the American Urban Society.* Berkeley: University of California Press.

Land, Kenneth C., David Cantor, and Stephen T. Russell. 1994. "Unemployment and Crime Rate Fluctuations in the Post–World War II United States: Statistical Time Series Properties and Alternative Models." In *Crime and Inequality,* ed. John Hagan and Ruth D. Peterson. Stanford, Calif.: Stanford University Press, forthcoming.

Land, Kenneth C., Patricia L. McCall, and Lawrence E. Cohen. 1990. "Structural Covariates of Homicide Rates: Are There Any Invariances across Time and Social Space?" *American Journal of Sociology* 95, no. 4 (January): 922–63.

Langan, Patrick. 1991. "America's Soaring Prison Population." *Science* 251 (March 29):1568–73.

Lee, David Sang-Yoon. 1993. "An Empirical Investigation of the Economic Incentives for Criminal Behavior." B.A. thesis in economics, Harvard University, March.

Long, S. K., and Witte, A. 1981. "Current Economic Trends: Implications for Crime and Criminal Justice." In *Crime and Criminal Justice in a Declining Economy,* ed. K. N. Wright, 69–143. Cambridge, Mass.: Oelgeschlager, Gun, and Hain.

Messner, Steven F. 1982. "Poverty, Inequality, and the Urban Homicide Rate." *Criminology* 20:103–14.

———. 1983. "Regional and Racial Effects on the Urban Homicide Rate: the Subculture of Violence Revisited." *American Journal of Sociology* 88 (5): 997–1007.

Moore, J. 1992. "Institutionalized Youth Gangs: Why White Fence and El Hoyo Maravilla Change So Slowly." Presented at the Social Science Research Council Conference on the Urban Underclass, Ann Arbor, Mich., June 8–10.

Nagin, Daniel, and Raymond Paternoster. 1993. "Enduring Individual Differences and Rational Choice Theories of Crime." *Law and Society Review* 27:201–30.

Needels, Karen. 1993. "Go Directly to Jail and Do Not Collect?: A Long-Term Study of Recidivism and Employment Patterns Among Prison Releasees." Department of Economics, Princeton University, November.

Padilla, F. 1992. "Getting into the Business." Presented at the Social Science Research Council Conference on the Urban Underclass, Ann Arbor, Mich., June 8–10.

Paternoster, Raymond, and Leeann Iovanni. 1989. "The Labelling Perspective and Delinquency: An Elaboration of the Theory and an Assessment of the Evidence." *Justice Quarterly* 6:359–94.

Quicker, J., Y. Galesi, and A. Batani-Khalfani. 1992. "Bootstrap or Noose: Drugs in South Central Los Angeles." Presented at the Social Science Research Council Conference on the Urban Underclass, Ann Arbor, Mich., June 8–10.

Reuter, Peter, Robert MacCoun, and Patrick Murphy. 1990. *Money from Crime.* Santa Monica, Calif.: Rand Drug Policy Research Center.

Sampson, Robert J., and John H. Laub. 1994. "A Life-course Theory of Cumulative Disadvantage and the Stability of Delinquency." In *Developmental Theories of Crime and Delinquency: Advances in Criminological Theory,* ed. Terence P. Thornberry, vol. 6. New Brunswick, N. J.: Transaction, forthcoming.

Sherman, Lawrence. 1993. "Defiance, Deterrence, and Irrelevance: A Theory of Criminal Sanction." *Journal of Research in Crime and Delinquency* 30:445–73.

Sjoquist, David L. 1973. "Property Crime and Economic Behavior: Some Empirical Results." *American Economic Review* 63:439–46.

Tauchen, Helen, Ann Dryden Witte, and Harriet Griesinger. 1993. "Criminal Deterrence: Revisiting the Issue with a Birth Cohort." National Bureau of Economic Research Working Paper 4277, February.

Taylor, C. 1990. "Gang Imperialism." In *Gangs in America,* ed. C. Ronald Huff. New York: Sage.

Thornberry, Terence P., and R. L. Christenson. 1984. "Unemployment and Criminal Involvement: An Investigation of Reciprocal Causal Structures." *American Sociological Review* 49:398–411.

Tittle, Charles. 1988. "Two Empirical Regularities (Maybe) in Search of an Explanation: Commentary on the Age-Crime Debate." *Criminology* 26:75–86.

Trumbull, William N. 1989. "Estimations of the Economic Model of Crime Using Aggregate and Individual Level Data." *Southern Economic Journal* 94:423–39.

United States Department of Commerce. 1991. *Money Income of Households, Families, and Persons in the United States: 1990.* Current Population Reports, Series P-60, no. 174.

———. 1994. Current statistics cited by telephone.

United States General Accounting Office. 1993. *The Job Training Partnership Act: Potential for Program Improvements But National Job Training Strategy Needed.* Testimony, GAO/T-HRD-93-18, April 29.

Vigil, J. 1990. "Cholos and Gangs: Culture Change and Street Youth in Los Angeles." In *Gangs in America,* ed. C. Ronald Huff. New York: Sage.

Vigil, J., and S. Yun. 1990. "Vietnamese Youth Gangs in Southern California." In *Gangs in America,* ed. C. Ronald Huff. New York: Sage.

Vigil, J. D., S. Yun, and J. S. Long. 1992. "Youth Crime, Gangs, and the Vietnamese in Orange County." Presented at the Social Science Research Council Conference on the Urban Underclass, Ann Arbor, Mich., June 8–10.

Viscusi, W. Kip. 1986. "Market Incentives for Criminal Behavior." In *The Black Youth Employment Crisis,* ed. R. B. Freeman and Harry Holzer. Chicago: University of Chicago Press for National Bureau of Economic Research.

Williams, Kirk R. 1984. "Economic Sources of Homicide: Reestimating the Effects of Poverty and Inequality." *American Sociological Review* 49:283–89.

Williams, T. 1989. *The Cocaine Kids.* Reading, Mass.: Addison Wesley.

Wilson, James Q., and Allan Abrahamse. 1992. "Does Crime Pay?" *Justice Quarterly* 9, no. 3 (September): 359–77.

Wilson, James Q., and Richard Herrnstein. 1985. *Crime and Human Nature.* New York: Simon and Schuster.

Witte, Ann D. 1980. "Estimating the Economic Model of Crime with Individual Data." *Quarterly Journal of Economics* 94:57–84.

Wolfgang, Marvin E., Robert M. Figlio, and Thorsten Sellin. 1972. *Delinquency in a Birth Cohort.* Chicago: University of Chicago Press.

Zimring, Franklin E., and Gordon Hawkins. 1991. *The Scale of Imprisonment.* Chicago: University of Chicago Press.

9. Robert J. Sampson, "The Community"

Notes

1. This chapter draws extensively from the more detailed review found in Sampson and Lauritsen (1994). I focus primarily on studies that make inferences about "neighborhoods" or "local communities" within urban areas. Cities and metropolitan areas are large, highly aggregated, and heterogeneous units with politically defined and hence artificial ecological boundaries. Although intra-urban units of empirical analysis (e.g., census tracts, wards, block groups) are imperfect substitutes for the concept of neighborhood or local community, they possess more ecological integrity (they have natural boundaries and social homogeneity, for example) than cities or metropolitan areas and are more closely linked to the causal processes underlying crime.

2. Unfortunately, most ecological research has been forced to rely on official statistics (e.g., police and court records) that may be biased because of nonreporting or discrimination by the criminal justice system. To address these problems, many studies limit the domain of inquiry to serious crimes such as homicide and robbery, where police biases appear to be minimal. A wide-ranging body of research shows that, for serious crimes, police bias and underreporting are very small and/or unrelated to individual-level and community variables of interest. Moreover, self-reported offense behavior and victimization experiences have been brought to bear on the validity of official statistics. As shown in Sampson and Lauritsen (1994), a general convergence of community-level findings between official police statistics and "unofficial" rates of violence has been achieved. Because of this convergence, coupled with the fact that they generate the most fear and calls for public action, this chapter focuses primarily on violent crimes.

3. The systemic conceptualization of community addresses the early criticism that Chicago-school social ecologists overemphasized disorganization and dysfunction. In *Street Corner Society,* W. F. Whyte (1943) argued that what looks like social disorganization from the outside is actually an intricate internal organization. That is, he maintained that the real problem of slums was simply that their social organization failed to mesh with the structure of the society around it. However, public and parochial dimensions of informal social control (e.g., collective supervision of youth, density and strength of local organizations) may be weak even when certain forms of internal social organization (e.g., dense primary group relations, kinship networks, organized crime) are present.

4. Note, too, that the research limitations just described are no worse than those typically found in individual-level research. The difference is that the assump-

tions embodied in individual-level research are usually accepted at face value. Consider, as noted earlier, that many individual or group-level correlates of crime (e.g., race, family supervision) may in fact stem from community-related processes.

References

Block, R. 1979. "Community, Environment, and Violent Crime." *Criminology* 17:46–57.

Block, C. 1991. *Early Warning System for Street Gang Violence Crisis Areas: Automated Hot Spot Identification in Law Enforcement.* Chicago: Illinois Criminal Justice Information Authority.

Bursik, R. 1986. "Delinquency Rates as Sources of Ecological Change." In *The Social Ecology of Crime,* ed. J. Byrne and R. Sampson, 63–72. New York: Springer-Verlag.

———. 1988. "Social Disorganization and Theories of Crime and Delinquency: Problems and Prospects." *Criminology* 26:519–52.

———. 1989. Political Decision-making and Ecological Models of Delinquency: Conflict and Consensus. In *Theoretical Integration in the Study of Deviance and Crime,* ed. S. Messner, M. Krohn, and A. Liska, 105–17. Albany: State University of New York Press.

Bursik, R. J., Jr., and H. Grasmick. 1993. *Neighborhoods and Crime: The Dimensions of Effective Community Control.* New York: Lexington.

———. 1994. "Neighborhood-based Networks and the Control of Crime and Delinquency." University of Oklahoma. Unpublished manuscript.

Coleman, J. 1988. Social Capital in the Creation of Human Capital. *American Journal of Sociology* 94 (Suppl.): 95–120.

———. 1990. *Foundations of Social Theory.* Cambridge, Mass.: Harvard University Press.

Coulton, C., J. Korbin, M. Su, and J. Chow. 1994. Community Level Factors and Child Maltreatment Rates. *Child Development,* forthcoming.

Curry, G. D., and I. Spergel. 1988. "Gang Homicide, Delinquency, and Community." *Criminology* 26:381–406.

Daley, S., and R. Meislin. 1988. "New York City, the Landlord: A Decade of Housing Decay." *New York Times,* 8 February 1988.

Felson, M., and L. Cohen. 1980. "Human Ecology and Crime: A Routine Activity Approach." *Human Ecology* 8:389–406.

Frey, W. 1979. "Central City White Flight: Racial and Nonracial Causes." *American Sociological Review* 44:425–48.

Garbarino, J., and A. Crouter. 1978. "Defining the Community Context for Parent-Child Relations: The Correlates of Child Maltreatment." *Child Development* 49: 604–16.

Glueck, S., and E. Glueck. 1950. *Unraveling Juvenile Delinquency.* New York: Commonwealth Fund.

Greenberg, S., W. Rohe, and J. Williams. 1985. *Informal Citizen Action and Crime Prevention at the Neighborhood Level.* Washington, D.C.: National Institute of Justice.

Hirsch, A. 1983. *Making the Second Ghetto: Race and Housing in Chicago 1940–1960*. Chicago: University of Chicago Press.

Interface. 1985. "Crossing the Hudson: A Survey of New York Manufacturers Who Have Moved to New Jersey." New York. Unpublished report.

Katzman, M. 1980. "The Contribution of Crime to Urban Decline." *Urban Studies* 17:277–86.

Kornhauser, R. 1978. *Social Sources of Delinquency*. Chicago: University of Chicago Press.

Logan, J., and H. Molotch. 1987. *Urban Fortunes: The Political Economy of Place*. Berkeley: University of California Press.

Maccoby, E., J. Johnson, and R. Church. 1958. "Community Integration and the Social Control of Juvenile Delinquency." *Journal of Social Issues* 14:38–51.

Massey, D., and N. Denton. 1993. *American Apartheid: Segregation and the Making of the Underclass*. Cambridge, Mass.: Harvard University Press.

Messner, S., and K. Tardiff. 1986. "Economic Inequality and Levels of Homicide: An Analysis of Urban Neighborhoods." *Criminology* 24:297–318.

Prothrow-Stith, D. 1991. *Deadly Consequences*. New York: HarperCollins.

Putnam, R. 1993. "The Prosperous Community: Social Capital and Public Life." *American Prospect,* Spring, 35–42.

Reiss, A. J. 1986. "Co-offender Influences on Criminal Careers." In *Criminal Careers and Career Criminals,* ed. A. Blumstein, J. Cohen, J. Roth, and C. Visher, 121–60. Washington, D.C.: National Academy Press.

Reiss, A. J., and J. Roth, eds. 1993. *Understanding and Preventing Violence*. Washington, D.C.: National Academy Press.

Robins, L. 1966. *Deviant Children Grown Up*. Baltimore: Williams and Wilkins.

Roncek, D. 1981. "Dangerous Places: Crime and Residential Environment." *Social Forces* 60:74–96.

Rosenbaum, D. 1991. Crime Prevention, Fear Reduction, and the Community. In *Local Government Police Management,* ed. D. Rosenbaum, E. Hernandez, and S. Daughtry, 96–130. Washington, D.C.: International City Management Association.

Rosenbaum, J., and S. Popkin. 1991. "Employment and Earnings of Low-Income Blacks Who Move to the Suburbs." In *The Urban Underclass,* ed. C. Jencks and P. Peterson. Washington, D.C.: The Brookings Institution.

Sampson, R. J. 1985. "Neighborhood and Crime: the Structural Determinants of Personal Victimization." *Journal of Research in Crime and Delinquency* 22:7–40.

———. 1986. Neighborhood Family Structure and the Risk of Criminal Victimization. In *The Social Ecology of Crime,* ed. J. Byrne and R. Sampson, 25–46. New York: Springer-Verlag.

———. 1992. "Family Management and Child Development: Insights from Social Disorganization Theory." In *Facts, Frameworks, and Forecasts,* ed. J. McCord, 63–93. Vol. 3 of *Advances in Criminological Theory*. New Brunswick, N.J.: Transaction.

Sampson, R. J., and J. Wooldredge. 1986. "Evidence that High Crime Rates Encourage Migration Away from Central Cities." *Sociology and Social Research* 90:310–14.

Sampson, R. J., and W. B. Groves. 1989. "Community Structure and Crime: Testing Social-Disorganization Theory." *American Journal of Sociology* 94:774–802.

Sampson, R. J., and J. Lauritsen. 1994. "Violent Victimization and Offending: Individual, Situational, and Community-Level Risk Factors." In *Understanding and Preventing Violence,* ed. A. J. Reiss and J. Roth, vol. 3. Washington, D.C.: National Academy Press.

Sampson, R. J., and W. J. Wilson. 1994. "Toward a Theory of Race, Crime, and Urban Inequality." In *Crime and Inequality,* ed. John Hagan and Ruth Peterson. Stanford, Calif.: Stanford University Press, forthcoming.

Schuerman, L., and S. Kobrin. 1986. "Community Careers in Crime." In *Communities and Crime,* ed. A. J. Reiss, Jr., and M. Tonry, 67–100. Chicago: University of Chicago Press.

Shaw, C., and H. McKay. 1942. *Juvenile Delinquency and Urban Areas,* rev. ed. Chicago: University of Chicago Press, 1969.

Sherman, L., P. Gartin, and M. Buerger. 1989. "Hot Spots of Predatory Crime: Routine Activities and the Criminology of Place." *Criminology* 27:27–56.

Simcha-Fagan, O., and J. Schwartz. 1986. Neighborhood and Delinquency: An Assessment of Contextual Effects. *Criminology* 24:667–704.

Skogan, W. 1986. "Fear of Crime and Neighborhood Change." In *Communities and Crime,* ed. A. J. Reiss, Jr., and M. Tonry, 203–29. Chicago: University of Chicago Press.

———. 1991. *Disorder and Decline.* New York: Free Press.

Smith, D. R., and G. R. Jarjoura. 1988. "Social Structure and Criminal Victimization." *Journal of Research in Crime and Delinquency* 25:27–52.

Sullivan, M. 1989. *Getting Paid: Youth Crime and Work in the Inner City.* Ithaca, N.Y.: Cornell University Press.

———. 1993. *More Than Housing: How Community Development Corporations Go about Changing Lives and Neighborhoods.* New York: Community Development Research Center, New School for Social Research.

Taylor, R., S. Gottfredson, and S. Brower. 1984. "Block Crime and Fear: Defensible Space, Local Social Ties, and Territorial Functioning." *Journal of Research in Crime and Delinquency* 21:303–31.

Taylor, R., and J. Covington. 1988. "Neighborhood Changes in Ecology and Violence." *Criminology* 26:553–90.

Thrasher, F. 1963. *The Gang: A Study of 1,313 Gangs in Chicago,* rev. ed. Chicago: University of Chicago Press.

Tienda, M. 1991. "Poor People and Poor Places: Deciphering Neighborhood Effects on Poverty Outcomes." In *Macro-Micro Linkages in Sociology,* ed. J. Huber, 244–62. Newbury Park, Calif.: Sage.

Wallace, R., and D. Wallace. 1990. "Origins of Public Health Collapse in New York City: The Dynamics of Planned Shrinkage, Contagious Urban Decay and Social Disintegration." *Bulletin of the New York Academy of Medicine* 66:391–434.

Whyte, W. F. 1943. *Street Corner Society: The Social Structure of an Italian Slum.* Chicago: University of Chicago Press.

Widom, C. 1989. "The Cycle of Violence." *Science* 244:160–66.

Wilson, W. J. 1987. *The Truly Disadvantaged: The Inner City, the Underclass, and Public Policy.* Chicago: University of Chicago Press.

Wilson, J. Q., and G. Kelling. 1982. "Broken Windows." *Atlantic Monthly,* March, 29–38.

10. Malcolm W. Klein, "Street Gang Cycles"

Notes

1. See Covey, Menard, and Franzese (1992); Cummings and Monti (1993); Goldstein (1991); Knox (1991); Spergel (forthcoming); Spergel (1990).

2. Much of the basic material is condensed from Klein (forthcoming).

3. Klein forthcoming.

4. Our most recent data reveal seventy-two U.S. towns and cities in which white gangs predominate (60 percent or more) over others. Many of these are su-premacist or skinhead gangs. All but two of these cities attained this white gang predominance since 1980.

5. Padilla 1992.

6. See note 4.

7. For this claim, and others contained in this chapter, I refer the reader to *The American Street Gang* (Klein forthcoming), where I have provided extensive documentation and arguments for the positions taken.

8. Sanchez-Jankowski 1991; Taylor 1991; Skolnick, Correl, Navarro, and Rabb 1992.

9. Jansyn 1967, 600–14.

10. See Part 3 in Klein (1971).

11. No figure such as this should be considered low at an absolute level, even if it is low on a comparative level.

12. Block 1985.

13. Pennsylvania Crime Commission 1969.

14. Miller 1977.

15. Spergel 1990.

16. Klein forthcoming.

17. This is an ongoing study. See Maxson (1993, 1–8).

18. Documentation can be found in Chapter 4 of *The American Street Gang.*

19. See Klein (forthcoming, chap. 4).

20. An informative recent treatise is Hamm (1993).

21. Joan Moore (1990) has made the same point, in much the same words, about East Los Angeles gangs.

22. My information on the South Central truce movements comes from a variety of sources—news reports, conversations with police, "insider" reports second- and third-hand removed, and statements by public and private officials. No independent research has come to light.

23. Quoted in Family and Youth Services Bureau (1992, 5).
24. Full coverage is provided in Klein (forthcoming, chap. 5).
25. Moore and Vigil 1987, 27–44.

References

Block, Carolyn R. 1985. *Lethal Violence in Chicago over Seventeen Years: Homicides Known to the Police.* Chicago: Criminal Justice Information Authority, July.

Covey, Herbert C., Scott Menard, and Robert J. Franzese. 1992. *Juvenile Gangs.* Springfield, Ill.: Charles C. Thomas.

Cummings, Scott, and Daniel J. Monti. 1993. *Gangs.* Albany: State University of New York Press.

Family and Youth Services Bureau. 1992. *Connections* 3:5. A newsletter of the Bureau. Washington, D.C.: Cosmos Corporation.

Goldstein, Arnold P. 1991. *Delinquent Gangs: A Psychological Perspective.* Champaign, Ill.: Research Press.

Hamm, Mark. 1993. *American Skinheads: The Criminology and Control of Hate Crime.* Westport, Conn.: Praeger.

Jansyn, Leon R. 1967. "Solidarity and Delinquency in a Street Corner Group." *American Sociological Review* 31:600–14.

Klein, Malcolm W. 1971. *Street Gangs and Street Workers.* Englewood Cliffs, N.J.: Prentice-Hall.

————. Forthcoming. *The American Street Gang: Its Nature, Prevalence, and Control.* New York: Oxford University Press.

Knox, George. 1991. *An Introduction to Gangs.* Berrien Springs, Mich.: Van de Vere Publishing.

Maxson, Cheryl L. 1993. "Investigating Gang Migration: Contextual Issues for Intervention." *The Gang Journal* 1:1–8.

Miller, Walter B. 1977. "The Rumble This Time." *Psychology Today,* May.

Moore, Joan. 1990. "Gangs, Drugs, and Violence." In *Drugs and Violence: Causes, Correlates, and Consequences,* ed. Mario De La Rosa, Elizabeth Y. Lambert, and Bernard Gropper, 160–76. Washington, D.C.: National Initiative on Drug Abuse.

Moore, Joan, and Richard D. Vigil. 1987. "Group Norms and Individual Factors Related to Adult Criminality." *Aztlan: A Journal of Chicano Studies* 18 (Fall): 27–44.

Padilla, Felix M. 1992. *The Gang as an American Enterprise.* New Brunswick, N.J.: Rutgers University Press.

Pennsylvania Crime Commission. 1969. *Gang Violence in Philadelphia.*

Sanchez-Jankowski, Martin. 1991. *Islands in the Street.* Berkeley: University of California Press.

Skolnick, Jerome H., Theodore Correl, Elizabeth Navarro, and R. Rabb. 1992. "Social Structure of Street Drug Dealing." *American Journal of Police* 9 (1): 1–41.

Spergel, Irving A. Forthcoming. *Youth Gangs: Problems and Response.* New York: Oxford University Press.

Spergel, Irving A. 1990. "Youth Gangs: Continuity and Change." In *Crime and Justice: A Review of Research,* ed. Michael H. Tonry and Norval Morris, 12. Chicago: University of Chicago Press.

Taylor, Carl S. 1991. *Dangerous Society.* East Lansing: Michigan State University Press.

11. Edward Donnerstein and Daniel Linz, "The Media"

Chapter 11 is not annotated.

References

American Broadcasting Corporation (ABC). 1982. *A Research Perspective on Television and Violence.* New York: ABC Television.

American Psychological Association (APA). 1993. *Violence and Youth: Psychology's Response.* Washington, D.C.

Atkin, C. K. 1983. "Effects of Realistic TV Violence vs. Fictional Violence on Aggression." *Journalism Quarterly* 60:615–21.

Bandura, A. 1971. *Social Learning Theory.* New York: General Learning Press.

Baron, R. A. 1977. *Human Aggression.* New York: Plenum.

Baron, J. N., and P. C. Reiss. 1985. "Same Time, Next Year: Aggregate Analysis of the Mass Media and Violent Behavior." *American Sociological Review* 50:347–63.

Berkowitz, L. 1984. "Some Effects of Thoughts on Anti and Prosocial Influences of Media Events: A Cognitive-Neoassociation Analysis." *Psychological Bulletin* 95:410–27.

Berkowitz, L., and E. Donnerstein. 1982. "External Validity Is More Than Skin Deep: Some Answers to Criticisms of Laboratory Experiments." *American Psychologist* 37:245–57.

Berkowitz, L., and R. G. Geen 1966. "Film Violence and the Cue Properties of Available Targets." *Journal of Personality and Social Psychology* 3:525–30.

———. 1967. "Stimulus Qualities of the Target of Aggression: A Further Study." *Journal of Personality and Social Psychology* 5:364–68.

Berkowitz, L., and E. Rawlings. 1963. "Effects of Film Violence on Inhibitions against Subsequent Aggression." *Journal of Abnormal and Social Psychology* 66:405–12.

Berkowitz, L., and K. H. Rogers. 1986. "A Priming Effect Analysis of Media Influences." In *Perspectives on Media Effects,* ed. J. Bryant and D. Zillmann. Hillsdale, N.J.: Erlbaum.

Bollen, K. A., and D. P. Phillips. 1981. "Suicidal Motor Vehicle Fatalities in Detroit: A Replication." *American Journal of Sociology* 87 (2): 404–12.

———. 1982. "Imitative Suicides: A National Study of the Effects of Television News Stories." *American Sociological Review* 47:802–09.

Centers for Disease Control. 1991. *Position Papers from the Third National Injury Conference: Setting the National Agenda for Injury Control in the 1990s.* Washington, D.C.: Department of Health and Human Services.

Centerwall, B. S. 1989a. "Exposure to Television as a Cause of Violence." In *Public Communication and Behavior,* ed. G. Comstock, 2:1–58. New York: Academic Press.

———. 1989b. "Exposure to Television as a Risk Factor for Violence." *American Journal of Epidemiology* 129 (4): 643–52.

Cline, V. B., R. G. Croft, and S. Courrier. 1973. "Desensitization of Children to Television Violence." *Journal of Personality and Social Psychology* 27:360–65.

Comstock, G., and H. Paik. 1991. *Television and the American Child.* San Diego: Academic Press.

Comstock, G., and V. C. Strausburger. 1990. "Deceptive Appearances: Television Violence and Aggressive Behavior." *Journal of Adolescent Health Care* 11:31–44.

Donnerstein, E., and L. Berkowitz. 1981. "Victim Reactions in Aggressive-Erotic Films as a Factor in Violence against Women. *Journal of Personality and Social Psychology* 41:710–24.

Donnerstein, E., D. Linz, and S. Penrod. 1987. *The Question of Pornography: Research Findings and Policy Implications.* New York: Free Press.

Donnerstein, E., R. Slaby, and L. Eron. 1994. "The Mass Media and Youth Violence. In *Violence and Youth: Psychology's Response,* ed. L. Eron and J. Gentry, vol 2. Washington, D.C.: American Psychological Association.

Feshbach, S. 1972. "Reality and Fantasy in Filmed Violence." In *Television and Social Behavior,* ed. J. Murray, E. Rubinstein, and G. Comstock, vol. 2. Washington, D.C.: Department of Health, Education, and Welfare.

Freedman, J. L. 1984. "Effect of Television Violence on Aggressiveness." *Psychological Bulletin* 96:227–46.

———. 1986. "Television Violence and Aggression: A Rejoinder." *Psychological Bulletin* 100:372–78.

———. 1992. "Television Violence and Aggression: What Psychologists Should Tell the Public." In *Psychology and Public Policy,* ed. P. Suedfeld and P. E. Tetlock, 179–90. New York: Hemisphere.

Geen, R. G. 1968. "Effects of Frustration, Attack, and Prior Training in Aggressiveness upon Aggressive Behavior." *Journal of Personality and Social Psychology* 9:316–21.

Geen, R. G., and D. Stonner. 1972. Context Effects in Observed Violence." *Journal of Personality and Social Psychology* 25:145–50.

Gerbner, G. 1992. Testimony before the House Judiciary Committee, Subcommittee on Crime and Criminal Justice, 15 December.

Gerbner, G., and N. Signorielli. 1990. "Violence Profile, 1967 through 1988–89: Enduring Patterns." Unpublished manuscript, Annenberg School of Communication, University of Pennsylvania.

Grogger, J. 1990. "The Deterrent Effect of Capital Punishment: An Analysis of Daily Homicide Counts." *Journal of the American Statistical Association* 85:295–303.

Huston, A. C., E. Donnerstein, H. Fairchild, N. D. Feshbach, P. A. Katz, J. P. Murray, E. A. Rubinstein, B. L. Wilcox, and D. Zuckerman. 1992. *Big World, Small Screen: The Role of Television in American Society.* Lincoln: University of Nebraska Press.

Huesmann, L. R. 1986. "Psychological Processes Promoting the Relation between Exposure to Media Violence and Aggressive Behavior by the Viewer." *Journal of Social Issues* 42 (3): 125–40.

————. 1992. "Violence in the Mass Media." Paper presented at the Third International Conference on Film Regulation, London.

Huesmann, L. R., and L. D. Eron, 1986. *Television and the Aggressive Child: A Cross-National Comparison.* Hillsdale, N.J.: Erlbaum.

Huesmann, L. R., L. D. Eron, L. Berkowitz, and S. Chafee. 1992: "The Effects of Television Violence on Aggression: A Reply to a Skeptic." In *Psychology and Social Policy,* ed. P. Suedfeld and P. Tetlock, 191–200. New York: Hemisphere.

Huesmann, L. R., L. D. Eron, M. M. Lefkowitz, and L. O. Walder. 1984. "The Stability of Aggression over Time and Generations." *Developmental Psychology* 20 (6):1120–34.

Krattenmaker, T. G., and L. A. Powe. 1978. "Televised Violence: Amendment Principles and Social Science." *Virginia Law Review* 64:1123–1297.

Kuby, R. W., and M. Csikszentmihalyi. 1990. *Television and the Quality of Life: How Viewing Shapes Everyday Experiences.* Hillsdale, N.J.: Erlbaum.

Lefcourt, H. M., K. Barnes, R. Parke, and F. Schwartz. 1966. "Anticipated Social Censure and Aggression-Conflict as Mediators of Response to Aggression Induction." *Journal of Social Psychology* 70:251–63.

Liberman Research. 1975. *Children's Reactions to Violent Material on Television.* Report to the American Broadcasting Corporation. New York.

Lichter, R. S., and D. Amundson. 1992. *A Day of Television Violence.* Washington, D.C.: Center for Media and Public Affairs.

Liebert, R. M., and J. N. Sprafkin. 1988. *The Early Window: Effects of Television on Children and Youth.* New York: Pergamon Press.

Linz, D., and E. Donnerstein. 1994. "Sex and Violence in Slasher Films: A Reinterpretation." *Journal of Broadcasting and Electronic Media* 38:243–46.

Linz, D., E. Donnerstein, and S. Penrod. 1984. "The Effects of Multiple Exposures to Filmed Violence against Women." *Journal of Communication* 34(3):130–47.

————. 1988. "The Effects of Long-Term Exposure to Violent and Sexually Degrading Depictions of Women." *Journal of Personality and Social Psychology* 55: 758–68.

Los Angeles Times. 1993a. 2 August, D1.

Los Angeles Times. 1993b. 18 December, A1, A23.

Malamuth, N. M. 1986. "Predictors of Naturalistic Sexual Aggression." *Journal of Personality and Social Psychology* 50:953–62.

Milavasky, J., R. Kessler, H. Stipp, and W. Rubens. 1982. *Television and Aggression: A Panel Study.* New York: Academic Press.

Mother Jones. 1993. "Violence and the Mass Media." November.

National Institute of Mental Health (NIMH). 1982. *Television and Behavior: Ten Years of Scientific Progress and Implications for the Eighties.* Vol. 1, *Summary Report.* Washington, D.C.: United States Government Printing Office.

Newsweek. 1993. 22 November, 52–53.

Neisser, U. 1967. *Cognitive Psychology.* New York: Appleton-Century-Crofts.

Phillips, D. P. 1974. "The Influence of Suggestion on Suicide: Substantive and Theoretical Implications of the Werther Effect." *American Sociological Review* 39:-340–354.

———. 1979. "Suicide, Motor Vehicle Fatalities, and the Mass Media: Evidence toward a Theory of Suggestion." *American Journal of Sociology* 84: 1150–74.

———. 1982a. "The Impact of Fictional Television Stories on U.S. Adult Fatalities: New Evidence on the Effect of the Mass Media on Violence." *American Journal of Sociology* 87:1340–59.

———. 1982b. The Impact of Fictional Television Stories on U.S. Adult Fatalities: New Evidence on the Effect of the Mass Media on Violence." *American Journal of Sociology* 87 (6): 1340–59.

———. 1983a. "The Impact of Mass Media Violence on U.S. Homicides." *American Sociological Review* 48:560–68.

———. 1983b. "The Impact of Mass Media Violence on U.S. Homicides." *American Sociological Review,* 48, 560–568.

Phillips, D. P., and D. A. Bollen. 1985. "Same Time, Last Year: Selective Data Dredging for Negative Findings." *American Sociological Review* 50:364–71.

Phillips, D. P., and L. L. Carstensen. 1986. Clustering of Teenage Suicides after Television News Stories about Suicide." *New England Journal of Medicine,* 11 September, 685–89.

Phillips, D. P., and J. E. Hensley. 1984. When Violence Is Rewarded or Punished: The Impact of Mass Media Stories on Homicide." *Journal of Communication* 34 (3): 101–11.

Reiss, A. J., and J. A. Roth, eds. 1993. *Understanding and Preventing Violence.* Washington, D.C.: National Academy Press.

Reynolds, S. F. 1993. "TV Violence: An American Public Health Epidemic." *California Physician,* October, 41–45.

Rosenkrans, M. A. 1967. "Imitation in Children as a Function of Perceived Similarities to a Social Model of Vicarious Reinforcement." *Journal of Personality and Social Psychology* 7:305–17.

Rosenthal, R. 1986. "Media Violence, Antisocial Behavior, and the Social Consequences of Small Effects." *Journal of Social Issues* 42:141–54.

Simon, P. (United States senator). 1993. Remarks to Television/Film Meeting on TV Violence, Los Angeles, 2 August.

Slife, B. D., and J. F. Rychiak. 1982. "Role of Affective Assessment in Modeling Behavior." *Journal of Personality and Social Psychology* 43:861–68.

Stringer, H. 1993. Testimony before the United States Senate Committee on Commerce, Science, and Transportation, 20 October.

Surgeon General's Scientific Advisory Committee on Television and Social Behavior. 1972. *Television and Growing Up: The Impact of Televised Violence.* Washington, D.C.: United States Government Printing Office.

Tangney, J. P., and S. Feshbach. 1988. Children's Television-Viewing Frequency: Individual Differences and Demographic Correlates." *Personality and Social Psychology Bulletin* 14:145–58.

Thomas, M. H. 1982. "Physiological Arousal, Exposure to a Relatively Lengthy Aggressive Film, and Aggressive Behavior." *Journal of Research in Personality* 16:72–81.

Thomas, M. H., R. W. Horton, E. C. Lippencott, and R. S. Drabman. 1977. "Desensitization to Portrayals of Real-Life Aggression as a Function of Exposure to Television Violence." *Journal of Personality and Social Psychology* 35:450–58.

Turner, C. W., and L. Berkowitz. 1972. "Identification with Film Aggressor (Covert Role Taking) and Reactions to Film Violence." *Journal of Personality and Social Psychology* 21:256–64.

Valenti, J. 1993a. Quoted in *Los Angeles Times*, 2 August 1993.

Valenti, J. 1993b. Testimony before the United States Senate Committee on Commerce, Science, and Transportation, 20 October.

Yang, N., and D. Linz. 1990. "Movie Ratings and the Content of Adult Videos: The Sex-Violence Ratio." *Journal of Communication* 40:28–42.

Zillmann, D. 1971. "Excitation Transfer in Communication-mediated Aggressive Behavior." *Journal of Experimental Social Psychology* 7:419–33.

12. Philip J. Cook and Mark H. Moore, "Gun Control"

Notes

1. Kleck (1991, app. 2) offers another explanation, that the true prevalence trended upward during the past couple of decades, but that survey respondents have become increasingly reluctant to admit to gun ownership during this period. We favor the explanation offered in the text because it is supported by the survey evidence on the number of guns per household, and it makes sense given the growth in household disposable income during this period.

2. It should be kept in mind that these patterns are based on surveys and are subject to potential biases induced by the sensitivity of the topic and the difficulty of contacting a representative sample of young urban males.

3. This survey is conducted annually by the Fish and Wildlife Service of the U.S. Department of the Interior.

4. Much has been made of the unintentional firearm deaths of children; but, tragic as such cases are, it should be noted that they are quite rare. Between 1985 and 1990 the annual average number of deaths for children less than ten years old was ninety-four (Fingerhut 1993).

5. The homicide victimization rate for black females age fifteen to thirty-four was similar to that for white males.

6. On the other hand, the demography of gun suicide looks much more like that of gun sports, with victims coming disproportionately from the ranks of older white males.

7. Pierce and Fox (1992) demonstrate that between 1985 and 1991, the homicide arrest rate for males more than doubled for those under age twenty-one, while actually declining for those age thirty and over.

8. On the one issue of whether guns are used more often to victimize or defend, we note that the 1993 Gallup Poll found that 18 percent of gun owners recalled being threatened with a gun, while just 15 percent had ever used a gun to

defend themselves or their family. The survey did not ask these questions of respondents who did not own a gun, but presumably they would be far less likely to have ever used a gun in self-defense.

9. It is, after all, a tautology.

10. Kleck, like Wright, Rossi, and Daly (1983), claims that Zimring and others have not succeeded in demonstrating that guns are more lethal than knives, but accept with confidence the claim that long guns are more lethal than handguns. See Cook (1991) for a discussion of this paradox.

11. The source is unpublished data provided by the Bureau of Justice Statistics. See Cook (1991) for details.

12. The authors of the case-control study of homicide discuss the possibility that their results are due in part to reverse causation, noting that in a limited number of cases, people may have acquired a gun in response to a specific threat which eventually led to their murder. They also note that both gun ownership and homicide may be influenced by a third, unidentified factor (Kellermann et al. 1993, 1089). From those characteristics that were observed in this study, it is clear that the victims differed from the controls in a number of ways that may have contributed to their demise, and that may also have contributed to the likelihood that there was a gun in the house. In comparison with their controls, the cases or the people they lived with were more likely to have a criminal record, to use illicit drugs, and to have a drinking problem.

13. Kleck and Patterson (1993) assert that the intercity differences in the prevalence of gun ownership are influenced by crime rates. While this may explain some small part of the variance, it could not reasonably be considered the dominant explanation. For one thing, the vast majority of gun owners in the United States are sportsmen, for whom self-defense is a secondary purpose at most.

14. A recent comparison of victim survey estimates found that the U.S. robbery rate was substantially higher than that of England, Germany, Hungary, Hong Kong, Scotland, and Switzerland. On the other hand, Canada's robbery rate was nearly twice as high as that of the United States (Block 1993).

15. The notable exception is sex. Male victims predominate in both homicide and suicide.

16. This is true not just for law-abiding citizens but is felt even more keenly by drug dealers and other criminals who are frequently threatened by the bad company they keep (Wright and Rossi 1986).

17. Jefferson to Peter Carr, 19 August 1785, quoted in Kates (1992, 96).

18. William Van Alstyne (1994) argues that the Second Amendment has generated almost no useful body of law to date, substantially because of the Supreme Court's inertia on this subject. In his view, Second Amendment law is currently as undeveloped as First Amendment law was up until Holmes and Brandeis began taking it seriously in a series of opinions in the 1920s.

19. The idea that citizens have responsibility for their own self-defense is now widely embraced by police executives, and is central to the strategy known as "community policing," which seeks to establish a close working partnership between the police and the community. But the emphasis in this approach is on community-building activities such as the formation of block watches groups or neighborhood patrols, rather than on individual armaments.

20. The McClure-Volkmer Amendment of 1986 eased the restriction on out-of-state purchases of rifles and shotguns. Such purchases are now legal as long as they

comply with the regulations of both the buyer's state of residence and the state in which the sale occurs.

21. An important loophole allowed the import of parts of handguns that could not meet the "sporting purposes" test of the Gun Control Act. This loophole was closed by the McClure-Volkmer Amendment of 1986.

22. At the time this is written the federal tax on producers is 10 percent for handguns and 11 percent for long guns.

23. There is good evidence on other unsafe behaviors by youth. In particular, youthful consumption of cigarettes and beer has been shown to be highly responsive to price. It should be noted that there is a possibility that higher prices of guns will stimulate gun theft somewhat; if so, that may have the good effect of encouraging owners to store their guns more securely.

24. While federal law does not prohibit gun possession by youth, a number of states have placed limits on when youth can carry guns in public.

25. An example of this restrictive approach was until quite recently embodied in the North Carolina pistol permit requirement: permit applicants were required to satisfy their sheriff that they were of "good moral character" and needed the gun to defend their homes.

26. One distinction may be deemed important here. Drivers licenses are required only for operating a vehicle on the public highways, and not on one's own land. By analogy, a licensing requirement for guns could be limited to those who wish to carry the gun in public.

27. The Brady Bill, enacted in 1993, raised the three-year fee for obtaining a dealers license from $30 to $200. At the time of this writing (April 1994) it is not yet known how much effect the higher fee will have on the number of dealers.

28. A provision of the 1986 McClure-Volkmer Amendments to the Gun Control Act creates a federal criminal liability for individuals who transfer a gun to a person they know or have reasonable cause to believe fall into one of the seven high-risk categories specified in the act.

29. The annual average number of incidents in which at least one firearm was stolen can be estimated from the National Crime Victimization Survey. This average was 356,600 during the period 1987–1992 (personal communication from Charles Kinderman, Bureau of Justice Statistics, 28 March 1994). Of this total, 189,400 were handguns, and 167,200 were other types of guns. These numbers are underestimates because they exclude thefts from commercial places, and because the number of incidents understate the number of guns stolen.

30. In a poll conducted in fall 1993, 19 percent of gun owners said they carried guns on their person at times, while 26 percent carried guns in their vehicles for self-defense.

31. Surprisingly it is a *federal* crime (under the Gun-Free School Zones Act of 1990) for an individual to carry a gun in a school zone.

32. Upgrading criminal history files will of course have value in a variety of other law enforcement tasks as well.

References

Block, Richard. 1993. "A Cross-Section Comparison of the Victims of Crime: Victim Surveys of Twelve Countries." *International Review of Criminology* 2: 183–207.

Clotfelter, Charles T. 1993. "The Private Life of Public Economics." *Southern Economic Journal* 59 (4): 579–96.

Conklin, John E. 1972. *Robbery and the Criminal Justice System.* Philadelphia: Lippincott.

Cook, Philip J. 1976. "A Strategic Choice Analysis of Robbery." In *Sample Surveys of the Victims of Crimes,* ed. Wesley Skogan, 173–87. Cambridge, Mass.: Ballinger.

———. 1979. "The Effect of Gun Availability on Robbery and Robbery Murder: A Cross-Section Study of Fifty Cities." *Policy Studies Review Annual* 3. Beverly Hills: Sage.

———. 1980. "Reducing Injury and Death Rates in Robbery." *Policy Analysis,* Winter, 21–45.

———. 1981. "The Effect of Gun Availability on Violent Crime Patterns." *Annals of the American Academy of Political and Social Science* 455:63–79.

———. 1985. "The Case of the Missing Victims: Gunshot Woundings in the National Crime Survey." *Journal of Quantitative Criminology,* March, 91–102.

———. 1986. "The Relationship between Victim Resistance and Injury in Noncommercial Robbery." *Journal of Legal Studies* 15, no. 1 (June): 405–16.

———. 1987. "Robbery Violence." *Journal of Criminal Law and Criminology* 70 (2).

———. 1991. "The Technology of Personal Violence." In *Crime and Justice: A Review of Research,* ed. Michael H. Tonry, vol. 14. Chicago: University of Chicago Press.

———. 1993. "Notes on the Availability and Prevalence of Firearms." *American Journal of Preventive Medicine* 9 (Suppl. 1): 33–38.

Dabbs, Stuart. 1994. "How North Carolina Can Better Regulate Gun Dealers." Master's thesis, Sanford Institute of Public Policy, Duke University.

Deutsch, Stuart Jay. 1979. "Lies, Damn Lies, and Statistics: A Rejoinder to the Comment by Hay and McCleary." *Evaluation Quarterly* 3:315–28.

Fingerhut, L. A. 1993. "Firearm Mortality among Children, Youth, and Young Adults 1–34 Years of Age, Trends and Current Status: United States, 1985–90." *Advance Data from Vital and Health Statistics.* No. 231. Hyattsville, Md.: National Center for Health Statistics.

Halbrook, Stephen P. 1986. "What the Framers Intended: A Linguistic Analysis of the Right to 'Bear Arms.'" *Law and Contemporary Problems* 49, no. 1 (Winter): 151–62.

Jones, Edward D. III. 1981. "The District of Columbia's Firearms Control Regulations Act of 1975: The Toughest Handgun Control Law in the United States—or Is It?" *Annals of the American Academy of Political and Social Science* 455 (May): 138–49.

Kates, Don B., Jr. 1983. "Handgun Prohibition and the Original Meaning of the Second Amendment" *Michigan Law Review* 82, no. 2 (November): 204–73.

———. 1992. "The Second Amendment and the Ideology of Self-Protection." *Constitutional Commentary* 9, no. 1 (Winter): 87–104.

Kellermann, Arthur L., F. P. Rivara, N. B. Rushforth, J. G. Banton, D. T. Reay, J. T. Francisco, A. B. Locci, J. Prodzinski, B. B. Hackman, G. Somes. 1993. "Gun Ownership as a Risk Factor for Homicide in the Home" *New England Journal of Medicine* 329 (7 October): 1084–91.

Kellermann, Arthur L., F. P. Rivara, G. Somes, D. T. Reay, J. Francisco, J. G. Banton, J. Prodzinski, C. Fligner, and B. B. Hackman. 1992. "Suicide in the Home in

Relation to Gun Ownership" *New England Journal of Medicine* 327 (13 August): 467–72.

Killias, Martin. 1992. "Gun Ownership and Fatal Events: A Look on Suicide and Homicide from an International Perspective." University of Lausanne. Unpublished.

Kleck, Gary. 1984. "Handgun-only Control: A Policy Disaster in the Making." In *Firearms and Violence: Issues of Public Policy,* ed. Don B. Kates, Jr. Cambridge, Mass.: Ballinger.

———. 1988. "Crime Control through the Private Use of Armed Force." *Social Problems* 35:1–22.

———. 1991. *Point Blank: Guns and Violence in America.* New York: Aldine de Gruyter.

Kleck, Gary, and Karen McElrath. 1991. "The Effects of Weaponry on Human Violence." *Social Forces* 69:669–92.

Kleck, Gary, and E. Britt Patterson. 1993. "The Impact of Gun Control and Gun Ownership Levels on Violence Rates." *Journal of Quantitative Criminology* 9 (3): 249–87.

McDowall, David, Colin Loftin, and Brian Wiersema. 1992a. "A Comparative Study of the Preventive Effects of Mandatory Sentencing Laws for Gun Crimes" *Journal of Criminal Law and Criminology* 83, no. 2 (Summer): 378–94.

———. 1992. "The Incidence of Civilian Defensive Firearm Use." Discussion paper, Institute of Criminal Justice, University of Maryland, College Park.

Moore, Mark H. 1980. "Police and Weapons Offenses." *Annals of the American Academy of Political and Social Science* 452: 22–32.

———. 1981. "Keeping Handguns from Criminal Offenders." *Annals of the American Academy of Political and Social Science* 455: 92–109.

———. 1983. "The Bird in Hand: A Feasible Strategy for Gun Control" *Journal of Policy Analysis and Management* 2 (2): 185–95.

Pierce, Glenn L., and William J. Bowers. 1981. "The Bartley-Fox Gun Law's Short-Term Impact on Crime in Boston" *Annals of the American Academy of Political and Social Science,* No. 455, 120–37.

Pierce, Glenn L., and James Alan Fox. 1992. "Recent Trends in Violent Crime: A Closer Look." Northeastern University, Boston. Photocopy.

Polsby, Daniel D. 1993. "Equal Protection." *Reason,* October, 35–38.

Saltzman, L. E., J. A. Mercy, P. W. O'Carroll, M. L. Rosenberg, and P. H. Rhodes. 1992. "Weapon Involvement and Injury Outcomes in Family and Intimate Assaults." *Journal of the American Medical Association* 267, no. 22 (10 June): 3043–47.

Skogan, Wesley. 1978. "Weapon Use in Robbery: Patterns and Policy Implications." Center for Urban Affairs, Northwestern University. Unpublished.

Snyder, Jeffrey R. 1993. "A Nation of Cowards," *The Public Interest* 113 (Fall): 40–55.

Tennenbaum, Abraham N. 1993. "Justifiable Homicides by Civilians in the United States, 1976–1990: An Exploratory Analysis." Ph.D. dissertation, University of Maryland, College Park.

Teret, Stephen P. 1986. "Litigating for the Public's Health." *American Journal of Public Health* 76(8): 1027–29.

Teret, Stephen P., and Garen J. Wintemute. 1993. Policies to Prevent Firearm Injuries." *Health Affairs,* Winter, 96–108.

Van Alstyne, William. 1994. "The Second Amendment and the Personal Right to Arms." Durham, N.C.: Duke University School of Law.

Violence Policy Center. 1992. *More Gun Dealers Than Gas Stations.* Washington D.C.

Wolfgang, Marvin E. 1958. *Patterns in Criminal Homicide.* Philadelphia: University of Pennsylvania Press.

Wright, James D. 1981. "Public Opinion and Gun Control: A Comparison of Results from Two Recent National Surveys." *Annals of the American Academy of Political and Social Science* 455:24–39.

Wright, James D., and Peter H. Rossi. 1986. *The Armed Criminal in America: A Survey of Incarcerated Felons.* Hawthorne, N.Y.: Aldine.

Wright, James D., Peter H. Rossi, and Kathleen Daly. 1983. *Under the Gun: Weapons, Crime, and Violence in America.* Hawthorne, N.Y.: Aldine.

Wright, James D., Joseph F. Sheley, and M. Dwayne Smith. 1992. "Kids, Guns, and Killing Fields." *Society,* November/December, 84–89.

Zimring, Franklin E. 1968. "Is Gun Control Likely to Reduce Violent Killings?" *University of Chicago Law Review* 35:21–37.

———. 1972. "The Medium Is the Message: Firearm Calibre as a Determinant of Death from Assault." *Journal of Legal Studies* 1:97–124.

———. 1991. "Firearms, Violence and Public Policy." *Scientific American* 265, no. 5 (November): 48–54.

13. David Boyum and Mark A. R. Kleiman, "Alcohol and Other Drugs"

Notes

1. Alcohol, "Dutch courage" in the vernacular of the British Army, is sometimes referred to in America as "liquid courage."

2. Regarding drug use in the trade, it has been widely reported by ethnographers that more and more young drug dealers are abstaining from use. However, a recent study that interviewed 121 male youth several months after their release from the Rikers Island Adolescent Reception and Detention Center in New York City casts some doubt on this theory. Although almost two-thirds of them denied *ever* having used cocaine, hair testing indicated that 71 percent of the respondents had used cocaine in the past ninety days (Magura, Kang, and Shapiro 1993). Also, contrary to popular conception, many dealers sell drugs part-time, doing legitimate work as well (Reuter, MacCoun, and Murphy 1990). The work, however, tends to be sporadic and low-skilled.

3. Many studies support this view. See Anglin and Speckart (1986; 1988); Ball (1986); Ball et al. (1982); Ball, Shaffer, and Nurco (1983); Inciardi (1979; 1980); Inciardi, Horowitz, and Pottieger (1993); Johnson et al. (1985); McBride and McCoy (1982); Nurco et al. (1985); Nurco, Kinlock, and Balter (1993); Stephens and McBride (1976).

4. According to an analysis of 1990 data from the Drug Use Forecasting program (DUF), mean and median self-reported weekly expenditures on cocaine by heavy cocaine users were $430 and $217, respectively. Mean and median weekly expenditures on heroin by heavy heroin users were $519 and $216 (Rhodes et al. 1993).

5. By the same token, very high cigarette taxes, or even the prohibition of tobacco, might be well justified for the protection of the public health; but either one would necessarily increase, rather than decrease, crime, since cheap, legal nicotine does not seem to be criminogenic.

6. Model's finding (1994) that lower legal barriers to marijuana consumption tend to decrease homicide, though important on its own terms, does not fully answer the substitute/complement question. It is possible, for example, that marijuana is a substitute for alcohol, but a "gateway" for cocaine and heroin, and that in terms of homicides, the alcohol connection is far more significant that the cocaine or heroin connection. A reduction in alcohol use might also explain Model's observed reduction in emergency room visits involving cocaine, since a large proportion of cocaine "mentions" involve alcohol as well.

7. As a matter of law, most U.S. jurisdictions do not allow a "diminished capacity" defense for voluntary intoxication. As a practical matter, prosecutors, judges, and juries often see the issue differently.

References

Anderson, Elijah. 1994. The Code of the Streets. *Atlantic Monthly,* May, 80–94.

Anglin, M. Douglas, and Yih-Ing Hser. 1990. "Treatment of Drug Abuse." In *Drugs and Crime,* ed. Michael H. Tonry and James Q. Wilson, 393–460. Vol. 13 of *Crime and Justice: A Review of Research.* Chicago: University of Chicago Press.

Anglin, M. Douglas, and George Speckart. 1986. "Narcotics Use, Property Crime, and Dealing: Structural Dynamics Across the Addiction Career." *Journal of Quantitative Criminology* 2:355–75.

———. 1988. "Narcotics Use and Crime: A Multisample, Multimethod Analysis." *Criminology* 26:197–233.

Ball, John C. 1986. "The Hyper-criminal Opiate Addict." In *Crime Rates and Drug Abusing Offenders,* ed. Bruce D. Johnson and Eric Wish. New York: Narcotic and Drug Research, Inc.

Ball, John C., Lawrence Rosen, John A. Flueck, and David N. Nurco. 1981. "The Criminality of Heroin Addicts: When Addicted and When off Opiates." In *Drugs-Crime Connection,* ed. James A. Inciardi, 39–65. Beverly Hills: Sage.

———. 1982. "Lifetime Criminality of Heroin Addicts in the United States." *Journal of Drug Issues* 12:225–39.

Ball, John C., John W. Shaffer, and David N. Nurco. 1983. "The Day-to-Day Criminality of Heroin Addicts in Baltimore: A Study in the Continuity of Offense Rates." *Drug and Alcohol Dependence* 12:119–42.

Becker, Gary S., Michael Grossman, and Kevin Murphy. 1991. "Rational Addiction and the Effect of Price on Consumption." *American Economic Review* 81 (2): 237–41.

Bejerot, Nills. 1970. "A Comparison of the Effects of Cocaine and Synthetic Central Stimulants." *British Journal of Addiction* 65:35–37.

Blackstone, William. 1890. *Commentaries on the Laws of England.* San Francisco: Bancroft-Whitney. Reprint of 8th ed., 1778.

Block, Carolyn Rebecca, and Richard Block. 1993. *Street Gang Crime in Chicago.* National Institute of Justice, Research in Brief. Washington, D.C.: United States Department of Justice, December.

Blumstein, Alfred. 1993. "Making Rationality Relevant: The American Society of Criminology 1992 Presidential Address." *Criminology* 31 (1): 1–16.

BOTEC Analysis Corporation. 1990. *Program Evaluation: Santa Cruz Street Drug Reduction Program.* Cambridge, Mass.

Boyum, David. 1992. "Reflections on Economic Theory and Drug Enforcement." Ph.D. dissertation, Harvard University.

Brown, George. F., and Lester. P. Silverman. 1974. "The Retail Price of Heroin: Estimation and Applications." *Journal of the American Statistical Association* 69:595–606.

Cavanagh, David P., and Mark A. R. Kleiman. 1990. *A Cost-Benefit Analysis of Prison Cell Construction and Alternative Sanctions.* Cambridge, Mass.: BOTEC Analysis Corporation.

Chaiken, Jan M., and Marcia R. Chaiken. 1990. "Drugs and Predatory Crime." In *Drugs and Crime,* ed. Michael H. Tonry and James Q. Wilson, 203–39. Vol. 13 of *Crime and Justice: A Review of Research.* Chicago: University of Chicago Press.

Clayton, Richard R., and Harwin L. Voss. 1981. *Young Men and Drugs in Manhattan: A Causal Analysis.* NIDA Research Monograph No. 39. Rockville, Md.: Alcohol, Drug Abuse, and Mental Health Administration.

Cleary, Paul D., Jan L. Hitchcock, Norbert Semmer, Laura J. Flinchbaugh, and John M. Pinney. 1988. "Adolescent Smoking: Research and Health Policy." *Milbank Quarterly* 66 (1): 137–71.

Cohen, Jacqueline, and Daniel S. Nagin. 1993. "Criminal Careers of Drug Offenders: A Comparison." Paper presented at the annual meeting of the American Society of Criminology, Phoenix, 29 October.

Cook, Philip J. 1981. "Research in Criminal Deterrence: Laying the Groundwork for the Second Decade." In *Crime and Justice: A Review of Research,* ed. Michael H. Tonry and Norval Morris, 2:211–68. Chicago: University of Chicago Press.

———. 1986. "The Demand and Supply of Criminal Opportunities." In *Crime and Justice: A Review of Research,* ed. Michael H. Tonry and Norval Morris, 7:1–27. Chicago: University of Chicago Press.

Collins, James J., Robert L. Hubbard, and J. Valley Rachal. 1985. "Expensive Drug Use and Illegal Income: A Test of Explanatory Hypotheses." *Criminology* 23:743–64.

Dewey, W. L. 1986. Cannabinoid Pharmacology. *Pharmacology Review* 38:151–78.

DiNardo, John. 1991. "Are Marijuana and Alcohol Substitutes? The Effect of State Drinking Age Laws on the Marijuana Consumption of High School Seniors." Santa Monica, Calif.: Rand.

DuPont, Robert L., and Mark H. Greene. 1973. "The Dynamics of a Heroin Addiction Epidemic." *Science* 181:716–22.

DuPont, Robert L., and Eric D. Wish. 1992. "Operation Tripwire Revisited." *Annals of the American Academy of Political and Social Science* 521 (May): 91–111.

Fagan, Jeffrey. 1990. "Intoxication and Aggression." In *Drugs and Crime*, ed. Michael H. Tonry and James Q. Wilson, 241–320. Vol. 13 of *Crime and Justice: A Review of Research*. Chicago: University of Chicago Press.

———. 1992. "Drug Selling and Licit Income in Distressed Neighborhoods: The Economic Lives of Street-Level Drugs Users and Dealers." In *Drugs, Crime, and Social Isolation*, ed. Adele V. Harrell and George E. Peterson, 99–146. Washington, D.C.: Urban Institute Press.

Ferguson, Ronald. 1993. Personal communication with the authors. 14 December.

Gersh, Debra. 1988. "Some Newspapers Refuse to Run Anti-drug Ad, Object to Photo of a Man with a Gun Pointed up His Nose." *Editor and Publisher*, 23 January, 17.

Gerstein, Dean R., and Henrick J. Harwood, eds. 1990. *Treating Drug Problems*, vol. 1. Washington, D.C.: National Academy Press.

Goldman, Fred. 1976. "Drug Markets and Addict Consumption Behavior." In *Drug Use and Crime: Report of the Panel on Drug Use and Criminal Behavior*, ed. Robert Shellow, 273–96. Washington, D.C.: National Technical Information Service.

———. 1977. "Narcotics Users, Narcotics Prices, and Criminal Activity: An Economic Analysis." In *The Epidemiology of Heroin and Other Narcotics*, ed. J. Rittenhouse, 30–36. NIDA Research Monograph Series 16. Rockville, Md.: National Institute on Drug Abuse.

———. 1981. "Drug Abuse, Crime and Economics: The Dismal Limits of Social Choice." In *The Drugs-Crime Connection*, ed. James A. Inciardi, 155–82. Beverly Hills: Sage.

Goldstein, Paul J. 1985. The Drugs/Violence Nexus: A Tripartite Conceptual Framework. *Journal of Drug Issues* 15 (4): 493–506.

Goldstein, Paul J., and Henry H. Brownstein. 1987. *Drug Related Crime Analysis: Homicide*. Report to the National Institute of Justice Drugs, Alcohol, and Crime Program. Washington, D.C.: United States Department of Justice, July.

Goldstein, Paul J., Henry H. Brownstein, Patrick J. Ryan, and Patricia A. Bellucci. 1990. "Crack and Homicide in New York City, 1988: A Conceptually Based Event Analysis." *Contemporary Drug Problems* 16 (4): 651–87.

Grinspoon, Lester, and James B. Bakalar. 1985. *Cocaine: A Drug and Its Social Evolution*, rev. ed. New York: Basic Books.

Hamid, Ansley. 1990. "The Political Economy of Crack-Related Violence." *Contemporary Drug Problems* 17 (Spring): 31–78.

Heymann, Philip. 1994. Personal communication with Mark Kleiman.

Hser, Yih-Ing, Douglas Longshore, and M. Douglas Anglin. 1994. "Prevalence of Drug Use among Criminal Offender Populations: Implications for Control, Treatment, and Policy." In *Drugs and Crime: Evaluating Public Policy Initiatives*, ed. Doris Layton McKenzie and Craig D. Uchida, 18–41. Thousand Oaks, Calif.: Sage.

Horgan, John. 1990. "An Antidrug Message Gets Its Facts Wrong." *Scientific American* 262 (May): 36.

Hubbard, Robert L., Mary Ellen Marsden, J. Valley Rachal, Hendrick J. Harwood, Elizabeth R. Cavanaugh, and Harold M. Ginzburg. 1989. *Drug Abuse Treatment: A National Study of Effectiveness*. Chapel Hill: University of North Carolina Press.

Hyatt, Raymond, and William Rhodes. 1992. *Price and Purity of Cocaine: The Relationship to Emergency Room Visits and Deaths, and to Drug Use among Arrestees.* Report prepared for the Office of National Drug Control Policy, Washington, D.C.

Inciardi, James A. 1979. "Heroin Use and Street Crime." *Crime and Delinquency* 25 (July): 335–46.

———. 1980. "Youth, Drugs, and Street Crime." In *Drugs and the Youth Culture*, ed. Frank R. Scarpitti and Susan K. Datesman, 175–203. Beverly Hills: Sage.

Inciardi, James A., Ruth Horowitz, and Anne E. Pottieger. 1993. *Street Kids, Street Drugs, Street Crime: An Examination of Drug Use and Serious Delinquency in Miami.* Belmont, Calif.: Wadsworth.

Inciardi, James A., and Anne E. Pottieger. 1991. "Kids, Crack, and Crime." *Journal of Drug Issues* 21 (Spring): 257–70.

Johnson, Bruce D., Kevin Anderson, and Eric D. Wish. 1988. "A Day in the Life of 105 Drug Addicts and Abusers: Crimes Committed and How the Money Was Spent." *Sociology and Social Research* 72 (3): 185–91.

Johnson, Bruce D., Paul J. Goldstein, Edward Preble, James Schmeidler, Douglas S. Lipton, Barry Spunt, and Thomas Miller. 1985. *Taking Care of Business: The Economics of Crime by Heroin Users.* Lexington, Mass.: Lexington Books.

Kennedy, David M. 1993. "Closing the Market: Controlling the Drug Trade in Tampa, Florida." National Institute of Justice Program Focus, NCJ 139963. Washington, D.C.: United States Department of Justice, April.

———. 1994. "Can We Keep Guns away from Kids?" *The American Prospect.* Forthcoming.

Kleiman, Mark A. R. 1992a. *Against Excess: Drug Policy for Results.* New York: Basic Books.

———. 1992b. "Neither Prohibition nor Legalization: Grudging Toleration in Drug Control Policy." *Dœdalus* 12, no. 3 (Summer): 53–83.

Kleiman, Mark A. R., Christopher E. Putala, Rebecca M. Young, and David P. Cavanagh. 1988. "Heroin Crackdowns in Two Massachusetts Cities." Report prepared for the Office of the District Attorney for the Eastern District, Commonwealth of Massachusetts, Hon. Kevin M. Burke, under National Institute of Justice Grant no. 85-JJ-CX-0027.

Kushner, Jeffrey. 1993. "Salient and Consistent Sanctions: Oregon's Key to Reducing Drug Use." *Treatment Improvement Exchange Communiqué.* Washington, D.C.: Center for Substance Abuse Treatment, Spring.

MacIntyre, Alasdair. 1981. *After Virtue.* Notre Dame, Ind.: University of Notre Dame Press.

McBride, Duane C., and Clyde B. McCoy. 1982. "Crime and Drugs: The Issues and the Literature." *Journal of Drug Issues* 12 (Spring):137–52.

Magura, Stephen, Sung Yeon Kang, and Janet Shapiro. 1993. "Detecting Cocaine Use by Hair Analysis among Criminally Involved Youth." Paper presented at the annual meeting of the American Society of Criminology, Phoenix, 30 October.

Manning, Willard G., Emmet B. Keeler, Joseph P. Newhouse, Elizabeth M. Sloss, and Jeffrey M. Wasserman. 1989. "The Taxes of Sin: Do Smokers and Drinkers Pay Their Way?" *Journal of the American Medical Association* 261:1604–9.

Martin, W. R. 1983. "Pharmacology of Opioids." *Pharmacology Review* 35:283–323.

Mill, John Stuart. 1989. *On Liberty*. Cambridge: Cambridge University Press. First published 1859.

Model, Karyn. 1991. "The Effect of Marijuana Decriminalization on Hospital Emergency Room Drug Episodes: 1975–1987." Department of Economics, Harvard University. Unpublished paper.

———. 1994. Personal communication with Mark Kleiman.

Moore, Mark H. 1973. "Policies to Achieve Discrimination on the Effective Price of Heroin." *American Economic Review* 63:270–77.

———. 1979. "Limiting Supplies of Drugs to Illicit Markets." *Journal of Drug Issues* 9:291–308.

———. 1990. *An Analytic View of Drug Control Policies*. Working paper no. 90-01-19. Program on Criminal Justice Policy and Management, John F. Kennedy School of Government. Cambridge, Mass.: Harvard University.

———. 1991. "Drugs, the Criminal Law, and the Administration of Justice." *Milbank Quarterly* 69 (4): 529–60.

Nadelman, Ethan A. 1988. "The Case for Legalization." *The Public Interest* 92 (Summer): 3–31.

National Institute of Justice. 1993. *Drug Use Forecasting 1992 Annual Report*. Washington, D.C.: United States Department of Justice.

Nurco, David N., John C. Ball, John W. Shaffer, and Thomas F. Hanlon. 1985. "The Criminality of Narcotics Addicts." *Journal of Nervous and Mental Disease* 173:-94–102.

Nurco, David N., Thomas E. Hanlon, Timothy W. Kinlock, and Karen R. Duszynski. 1988. "Differential Criminal Patterns of Narcotic Addicts over an Addiction Career." *Criminology* 26:407–23.

Nurco, David N., Timothy Kinlock, and Mitchell B. Balter. 1993. "The Severity of Preaddiction Criminal Behavior among Urban, Male Narcotic Addicts and Two Nonaddicted Control Groups." *Journal of Research in Crime and Delinquency* 30 (3): 293–316.

Office of National Drug Control Policy. 1994. *National Drug Control Strategy*. Washington, D.C.: The White House.

Pindyck, Robert S. 1979. *The Structure of World Energy Demand*. Cambridge, Mass.: MIT Press.

Post, Robert M. 1975. "Cocaine Psychoses: A Continuum Model." *American Journal of Psychiatry* 132:225–31.

Reiss, Albert J., Jr., and Jeffrey A. Roth, eds. 1993. *Understanding and Preventing Violence*. Washington, D.C.: National Academy Press.

Reuter, Peter, and Mark A. R. Kleiman. 1986. "Risks and Prices." In *Crime and Justice: A Review of Research,* ed. Michael H. Tonry and Norval Morris, 7:289–340. Chicago: University of Chicago Press.

Reuter, Peter, Robert MacCoun, and Patrick Murphy. 1990. *Money from Crime: A Study of the Economics of Drug Dealing*. Santa Monica, Calif.: Rand.

Rhodes, William, Paul Scheiman, and Kenneth Carlson. 1993. *What America's Users Spend on Illegal Drugs, 1988–1991*. Washington, D.C.: Office of National Drug Control Policy.

Rocheleau, Ann Marie. 1994. Personal communication with David Boyum, 7 March.

Rocheleau, Ann Marie, and Mark A. R. Kleiman. 1993. *Measuring Heroin Availability: A Demonstration*. Washington, D.C.: Office of National Drug Control Policy.

Roth, Jeffrey A. 1994. *Psychoactive Substances and Violence.* National Institute of Justice, Research in Brief. Washington, D.C.: United States Department of Justice, February.

Sheley, Joseph F., and James D. Wright. 1993. *Gun Acquisition and Possession in Selected Juvenile Samples.* National Institute of Justice, Office of Juvenile Justice and Delinquency Prevention, Research in Brief. Washington, D.C.: United States Department of Justice, December.

Silverman, Lester P., and Nancy L. Spruill. 1977. "Urban Crime and the Price of Heroin." *Journal of Urban Economics* 4:80–103.

Stephens, Richard C., and Duane C. McBride. 1976. "Becoming a Street Addict." *Human Organization* 35:87–93.

Turner, David. 1991. "Pragmatic Incoherence: The Changing Face of British Drug Policy." In *Searching for Alternatives: Drug-Control Policy in the United States,* ed. Melvyn B. Krauss and Edward P. Lazear, 175–90. Stanford, Calif.: Hoover Institution Press.

Trebach, Arnold S., and James A. Inciardi. 1993. *Legalize It? Debating American Drug Policy.* Washington, D.C.: American University Press.

United States Department of Justice. 1988. *Profile of State Prison Inmates 1986.* Bureau of Justice Statistics. Special Report NCJ-109926. Washington, D.C.: U.S. Department of Justice, January.

———. 1991. *Profile of Jail Inmates, 1989.* Bureau of Justice Statistics. Special Report NCJ-129097. Washington, D.C., April.

———. 1992. *Drugs, Crime, and the Justice System.* Bureau of Justice Statistics, Washington, D.C.

Wasserman, Robert. 1993. Personal communication with the authors, 14 December.

Watters, John K., Craig Reinarman, and Jeffrey Fagan. 1985. "Causality, Context and Contingency: Relationship between Drug Abuse and Delinquency." *Contemporary Drug Problems* 12 (3): 351–373.

Weisman, J. C., S. W. Marr, and P. L. Katsampes. 1976. "Addiction and Criminal Behavior: A Continuing Examination of Criminal Addicts." *Journal of Drug Issues* 6:153–65.

Weiss, Roger D., and Steven M. Mirin. 1987. *Cocaine: The Human Danger, The Social Costs, The Treatment Alternatives.* New York: Ballantine Books.

Wilson, James Q. 1985. *Thinking about Crime,* rev. ed. New York: Vintage Books.

Wilson, James Q., and Richard J. Herrnstein. 1985. *Crime and Human Nature.* New York: Touchstone.

14. Lawrence W. Sherman, "The Police"

Notes

1. Russakoff 1994, A1, A25.

2. Crime Control Institute 1990 (unpublished survey).

3. Computed, by subtracting jail and court personnel from local Sheriff's agencies, from Reaves (1993).

4. Gottfredson and Hirschi 1990, 270.

5. Klockars 1983, 130.

6. Federal Bureau of Investigation 1993; also years 1989–1991.

7. Kelling et al. 1974.

8. One MIT professor estimated that police responses to calls in the "no patrol" area created as much patrol visibility as normal patrol (Larson 1976). Other scholars pointed out that the study had inadequate statistical power to detect any effects patrol may have had upon crime (Fienberg, Larntz, and Reiss 1976).

9. More detailed reviews of this evidence may be found in Sherman (1990 and 1992).

10. Klockars 1985.

11. Fielding 1751 and 1755.

12. Gurr, Grabosky, and Hula 1977, especially 64–69.

13. 1950.

14. Reiss 1972.

15. Sherman 1992, 192–93.

16. Sherman, Gartin, and Buerger 1989.

17. See Sherman (1992a).

18. Sherman, Gartin, and Buerger 1989.

19. See Barr and Pease (1990).

20. Sherman 1990.

21. Sherman and Weisburd 1992.

22. Koper 1992.

23. Personal interview with deputy commissioner, London Metropolitan Police, 24 October 1992.

24. Spelman and Brown 1981.

25. Sherman 1992, 338.

26. Reiss 1971; Smith and Visher 1981.

27. Bittner 1970.

28. Black 1982.

29. Pocock 1983.

30. Weisburd and Garner 1992.

31. Sherman and Berk 1984.

32. Petersilia 1987b. While much social science is condemned as irrelevant, this study was condemned as being too "relevant" by other scholars who thought the publicity was inappropriate. See Lempert (1989); Binder and Meeker (1993). See also Sherman (1993); Sherman and Cohn (1989).

33. Sherman 1992b.

34. Sherman and Smith 1992; Pate and Hamilton 1992; Berk et al. 1992.

35. Marciniak 1994.

36. Sherman 1992b; Pate and Hamilton 1992; Berk et al. 1992; Marciniak 1994.

37. Sampson and Cohen 1988; Wilson and Boland 1978.

38. Wilson and Kelling 1982.
39. Boydstun 1975.
40. See, for example, National Advisory Commission on Civil Disorders (1968).
41. *Wall Street Journal* 1994.
42. Reaves 1993, 3.
43. Moore 1992.
44. James Q. Wilson 1968.
45. Reiss and Roth 1993.
46. FBI 1993.
47. Sherman et al. 1989.
48. Shaw 1994.
49. United States Supreme Court 1968.
50. James Q. Wilson 1994.
51. Petersilia 1987a, 66–68.
52. Martin and Sherman 1986.
53. Spelman 1990.
54. Podmolik 1994.
55. Krauss 1994.
56. Banerjee 1994.
57. Banerjee 1994.
58. Kotlowitz 1991.
59. Goldstein 1979.
60. Jerry V. Wilson 1990; Reiss and Roth 1993.
61. Clarke 1992.
62. Landes 1978.
63. Chaiken, Lawless, and Stevenson 1974.
64. Pease 1991.
65. Scherdin 1986.
66. Buerger 1993.
67. Sherman, Schmidt, and Velke 1992.
68. *Security Law Newsletter* 1992.
69. Masters 1993.
70. Sherman 1991.
71. Sherman 1994.

References

Banerjee, Neela. 1994. "Curfews Spread, but Effects Are Still Not Clear." *Wall Street Journal,* 4 March, B1.

Barr, Robert, and Ken Pease. 1990. "Crime Placement, Displacement, and Deflection." In *Crime and Justice: A Review of Research,* ed. Michael H. Tonry and Norval Morris, vol. 12. Chicago: University of Chicago Press.

Berk, Richard A., Ruth Klap, Alec Campbell, and Bruce Western. 1992. "The Deterrent Effect of Arrest in Incidents of Domestic Violence: A Bayesian Analysis of Four Field Experiments." *American Sociological Review* 57:698–708.

Binder, Arnold, and James W. Meeker. 1993. "Implications of the Failure to Replicate the Minneapolis Experiment Findings." *American Sociological Review* 58:886–88.

Bittner, Egon. 1970. *The Functions of the Police in Modern Society*. Bethesda, Md.: National Institute of Mental Health.

Black, Donald. 1982. "Crime as Social Control." *American Sociological Review* 48:34–45.

Boydstun, John. 1975. *San Diego Field Interrogation Experiment: Final Report*. Washington, D.C.: The Police Foundation.

Buerger, Michael E. 1993. "Convincing the Recalcitrant: Reexamining the Minneapolis RECAP Experiment." Ph.D. dissertation, School of Criminal Justice, Rutgers University.

Chaiken, Jan M., Michael Lawless, and Keith A. Stevenson. 1974. *The Impact of Police Activity on Crime: Robberies on the New York City Subway System*. Santa Monica, Calif.: Rand.

Clarke, Ronald V., ed. 1992. *Situational Crime Prevention*. New York: Harrow and Heston.

Cook, Philip J. 1991. "The Technology of Personal Violence." In *Crime and Justice: A Review of Research*, ed. Michael H. Tonry and Norval Morris, vol. 14. Chicago: University of Chicago Press.

Federal Bureau of Investigation. 1993. *Crime in the US, 1992*. Washington, D.C.

Fielding, Henry. 1751. *An Enquiry into the Causes of the Late Increase of Robbers*. Reprint ed. Montclair, N.J.: Patterson-Smith, 1977.

———. 1755. Preface to *Journal of a Voyage to Lisbon*.

Feinberg, Stephen, Kinley Larntz, and Albert J. Reiss, Jr. 1976. "Redesigning the Kansas City Preventive Patrol Experiment." *Evaluation* 3:124–31.

Goldstein, Herman. 1979. "Improving Policing: A Problem-Oriented Approach." *Crime and Delinquency* 25:236–58.

Gottfredson, Michael R., and Travis Hirschi. 1990. *A General Theory of Crime*. Stanford, Calif.: Stanford University Press.

Gurr, Ted Robert, Peter N. Grabosky, and Richard C. Hula. 1977. *The Politics of Crime and Conflict: A Comparative History of Four Cities*. Beverly Hills: Sage.

Kelling, George L., Tony Pate, Duane Dieckman, and Charles Brown. 1974. *The Kansas City Preventive Patrol Experiment*. Washington, D.C.: The Police Foundation.

Klockars, Carl, ed. 1983. *Thinking about Police*. New York: McGraw-Hill.

———. 1985. *The Idea of Police*. Beverly Hills: Sage.

Koper, Christopher. 1992. "The Deterrent Effects of Police Patrol Presence upon Criminal and Disorderly Behavior at Hot Spots of Crime." M.A. thesis, Institute of Criminal Justice and Criminology, University of Maryland, College Park.

Kotlowitz, Alex. 1991. *There Are No Children Here*. New York: Doubleday.

Krauss, Clifford. 1994. "Reacting to Crime, New York City Is Planning to Round Up Truants." *New York Times*, 23 February, B3.

Landes, William N. 1978. "An Economic Study of U.S. Aircraft Hijacking, 1961–1976." *Journal of Law and Economics* 21:1–31.

Larson, Richard C. 1976. "What Happened to Patrol Operations in Kansas City?" *Evaluation* 3:117–23.

Lempert, Richard. 1989. "Humility Is a Virtue: On the Publicization of Policy-Relevant Research." *Law and Society Review* 23:146–61.

Marciniak, Elizabeth. 1994. "Community Policing of Domestic Violence: Neighborhood Differences in the Effect of Arrest." Ph.D. dissertation, Department of Criminal Justice and Criminology, University of Maryland.

Martin, Susan E., and Lawrence W. Sherman. 1986. "Selective Apprehension: A Police Strategy for Repeat Offenders." *Criminology* 25:155–73.

Masters, Brooke A. 1993. "Close Early to Cut Crime, D.C. Chief Tells Retailers." *Washington Post,* 19 November, A1.

Moore, Mark H. 1992. "Problem-Solving and Community Policing." In *Modern Policing,* ed. Michael H. Tonry and Norval Morris. Vol. 15 of *Crime and Justice: A Review of Research*. Chicago: University of Chicago Press.

National Advisory Commission on Civil Disorders. 1968. *Report*. Washington, D.C.: U.S. Government Printing Office.

Pate, Antony, and Edwin E. Hamilton. 1992. "Formal and Informal Deterrents to Domestic Violence: The Dade County Spouse Assault Experiment." *American Sociological Review* 57:691–97.

Pease, Ken. 1991. "The Kirkholt Project: Preventing Burglary on a British Public Housing Estate." *Security Journal* 2:73–77.

Petersilia, Joan. 1987a. *Expanding Options for Criminal Sentencing*. Santa Monica, Calif.: Rand, 1987.

———. 1987b. *The Influence of Criminal Justice Research*. Santa Monica, Calif.: Rand.

Pocock, Stuart J. 1983. *Clinical Trials: A Practical Approach*. London: Wiley.

Podmolik, Mary Ellen. 1994. "Attention, Shoppers: Security at Malls a Major Concern." *Chicago Sun-Times,* 21 March, 39.

Reaves, Brian A. 1993. *Census of State and Local Law Enforcement Agencies, 1992*. Washington, D.C.: Bureau of Justice Statistics.

Reiss, Albert J., Jr. 1971. *The Police and the Public*. New Haven: Yale University Press.

———. 1972. Remarks presented to the Law Enforcement Assistance Administration Conference on Innovation in Law Enforcement, Shoreham Hotel, Washington, D.C., May.

Reiss, Albert J., and Jeffrey Roth. 1993. *Understanding and Preventing Violence*. Washington, D.C.: National Academy of Sciences.

Russakoff, Dale. 1994. "Another Kind of Help." *Washington Post,* 20 March, A1, A25.

Sampson, Robert, and Jacqueline Cohen. 1988. "Deterrent Effects of Police on Crime: A Replication and Theoretical Extension." *Law and Society Review* 22: 163–89.

Scherdin, Mary J. 1986. "The Halo Effect: Psychological Deterrence of Electronic Security Systems." *Information Technology and Libraries,* September, 232–35.

Security Law Newsletter. 1992. (Crime Control Research Corp., Washington, D.C.) August.

Shaw, James W. 1994. "Community Policing against Crime: Violence and Firearms." Ph.D. dissertation, Department of Criminal Justice and Criminology, University of Maryland, College Park.

Sherman, Lawrence W. 1990. "Police Crackdowns: Initial and Residual Deterrence." In *Crime and Justice: A Review of Research*, ed. Michael H. Tonry and Norval Morris, vol. 12. Chicago: University of Chicago Press.

———. 1991. Review of Herman Goldstein, *Problem-Oriented Policing*. In *Journal of Criminal Law and Criminology* 82:690–707.

———. 1992a. "Attacking Crime: Police and Crime Control." In *Modern Policing*, ed. Michael H. Tonry and Norval Morris. Vol. 16 of *Crime and Justice: A Review of Research*. Chicago: University of Chicago Press.

———. 1992b. *Policing Domestic Violence: Experiments and Dilemmas*. New York: Free Press.

———. 1993. "Implications of a Failure to Read the Literature." American Sociological Review 58:888–89.

———. 1994. Memorandum to Stephen Goldsmith, mayor of Indianapolis, 29 April.

Sherman, Lawrence W., et al. 1989. "Stray Bullets and 'Mushrooms': Bystander Killings in Four U.S. Cities. *Journal of Quantitative Criminology* 5 (4):297–316.

Sherman, Lawrence W., and Richard A. Berk. 1984. "The Specific Deterrent Effects of Arrest for Domestic Assault." *American Sociological Review* 49:261–72.

Sherman, Lawrence W., and Ellen G. Cohn. 1989. "The Impact of Research on Legal Policy: The Minneapolis Domestic Violence Experiment." *Law and Society Review* 23:117–44.

Sherman, Lawrence W., Patrick R. Gartin, and Michael E. Buerger. 1989. "Hot Spots of Predatory Crime: Routine Activities and the Criminology of Place." *Criminology* 27:27–55.

Sherman, Lawrence W., Janell D. Schmidt, and Robert J. Velke. 1992. "High Crime Taverns: A RECAP Project in Problem-Oriented Policing." Crime Control Institute, final report to the National Institute of Justice, grant no. 89-IJ-CX-0058.

Sherman, Lawrence W., and Douglas A. Smith. 1992. "Crime, Punishment and Stake in Conformity: Legal and Informal Control of Domestic Violence." *American Sociological Review* 57:680–90.

Smith, Douglas A., and Christy A. Visher. 1981. "Street-Level Justice: Situational Determinants of Police Arrest Decisions." *Social Problems* 29:167–78.

Sherman, Lawrence W., and David Weisburd. 1992. "Does Police Patrol Prevent Crime? The Minneapolis Hot Spots Experiment." Paper presented to the International Society of Criminology, Conference on Urban Crime Prevention, Tokyo, April.

Spelman, William. 1990. *Repeat Offender Programs for Law Enforcement*. Washington, D.C.: Police Executive Research Forum.

Spelman, William, and Dale K. Brown. 1981. *Calling the Police: A Replication of the Citizen Reporting Component of the Kansas City Response Time Analysis*. Washington, D.C.: Police Executive Research Forum.

United States Supreme Court. 1968. 392 U.S. 1.

Wall Street Journal. 1994. 22 March, 1.

Weisburd, David, and Joel Garner. 1992. "Experimentation in Criminal Justice: Editor's Introduction." *Journal of Research in Crime and Delinquency* 29:3–6.

Wilson, O. W. 1950. *Police Administration*. Reprinted. New York: McGraw-Hill, 1963.

Wilson, James Q. 1968. *Varieties of Police Behavior.* Cambridge, Mass.: Harvard University Press.

———. 1994. "Just Take Away Their Guns: Forget Gun Control." *New York Times Magazine,* 20 March, 46–47.

Wilson, James Q., and Barbara Boland. 1978. "The Effect of Police on Crime. *Law and Society Review* 12:367–90.

Wilson, James Q., and George L. Kelling. 1982. "Broken Windows: The Police and Neighborhood Safety." *Atlantic Monthly,* March, 29–38.

Wilson, Jerry V. 1990. *Convenience Store Robberies: The Gainesville, Fla. 2-Clerk Law.* Washington, D.C.: Crime Control Research Corp.

15. Charles Murray, "The Physical Environment"

Notes

1. Jacobs 1961.

2. Newman 1972. Jeffrey (1971) antedated Newman along with Jacobs. He originated the acronym CPTED (Crime Prevention through Environmental Design) which has remained a common label in the technical literature but (for obvious reasons) never grabbed the public imagination in the way that "defensible space" did.

3. Coleman 1985.

4. "Territoriality," "natural surveillance," and "image and milieu" were the constructs used by Newman. Timothy Crowe, former head of the National Crime Prevention Institute, has proposed the "Three D's" as another framework: "Designation" refers to the assignment of functions to a given space, how well the space supports its actual and intended use, and conflicts between the two. "Definition" refers to the ownership of the space and the specifications of its use, both legal and through sociocultural signs, the clarity of the borders, and characteristics that demarcate the space. "Design" refers to the ways in which the physical design supports the intended function of the space (Ward and Brooks 1991). A more complex framework is proposed by Taylor and Gottfredson, consisting of an interaction between the objective characteristics of the neighborhood and the offender's perceptions of the neighborhood (Taylor and Gottfredson 1986).

5. Ardrey 1966.

6. Newman 1983, xii.

7. Kohn, Franck, and Fox 1975.

8. Fowler and Mangione 1982.

9. Tien et al. 1977.

10. Griswold 1984.

11. Skogan 1977.

12. Tien et al. 1977, exhibit 4.4.

13. Kohn, Franck, and Fox 1975.

14. Fowler and Mangione 1982, 123.

15. Poyner's 1983 review stated this conclusion confidently (Poyner 1983). Two earlier reviews of studies through the late 1970s (Taylor, Gottfredsen, and Brower 1980; Rubenstein et al. 1980) and Taylor and Gottfredson's 1986 review (Taylor and Gottfredson 1986) were less optimistic that improvements in natural surveillance had been identified as the causal factor, and emphasized the inconsistency of many of the results.

16. Jordan 1993.

17. Jordan 1993.

18. Jordan 1993, 35.

19. Wilson and Kelling 1982. The quotation is taken from the version in Wilson (1983, 79).

20. Skogan 1990.

21. Newman and Franck 1980 and 1982. The conclusions of these studies should be interpreted cautiously. See Rubenstein et al. (1980 2 [C]: 104–33).

22. Taylor, Schumaker, and Gottfredson 1985; Taylor and Gottfredson 1986.

23. Merry 1981a. See also Merry (1981b).

24. Merry 1981a, 419.

25. Merry 1981a, 418.

26. Atlas 1991.

27. Jordan 1993.

28. The term was coined in Brantingham and Brantingham (1981). The summary here draws extensively from Clarke (1992b and forthcoming).

29. Clarke 1992b, 10. Clarke associates this formulation specifically with "routine activity theory" (Cohen and Felson 1979).

30. See Cornish and Clarke (1986) for a collection of studies and Clarke (1992b) for citations of more recent studies. Much more work on this issue has been done in England and Europe than in the United States.

31. For an American study of residential burglary, see Repetto (1974).

32. Hunter and Jeffery 1992.

33. Bommer and Ford 1974. See also Scherdin (1992) and Tuller (1984).

34. Clarke 1992a. Caller ID is an optional service in which the phone number of the caller registers on a device in the recipient's home.

35. Chaiken, Lawless, and Stevenson 1974.

36. For a review of displacement relative to situational crime prevention, see Clarke (forthcoming).

References

Ardrey, Robert. 1966. *The Territorial Imperative*. New York: Atheneum.

Atlas, Randall. 1991. "The Other Side of CPTED." *Security Management* 35: 63–66.

Bommer, M., and B. Ford. 1974. "A Cost-Benefit Analysis for Determining the Value of an Electronic Security System." *College and Research Libraries* 35: 275.

Brantingham, P. J., and P. L. Brantingham. 1991. *Environmental Criminology*. Beverly Hills: Sage.

Chaiken, Jan, Michael W. Lawless, and Keith A. Stevenson 1974. *The Impact of Police Activity on Crime: Robberies on the New York Subway System.* Report P-4625. Santa Monica, Calif.: Rand Corporation.

Clarke, Ronald V. 1992a. "Deterring Obscene Phone Callers: the New Jersey Experience." In *Situational Crime Prevention: Successful Case Studies,* ed. Ronald V. Clarke, 124–32. New York: Harrow and Heston.

———, ed. 1992b. *Situational Crime Prevention: Successful Case Studies.* New York: Harrow and Heston.

———. Forthcoming "Situational Crime Prevention: Achievements and Challenges." In *Crime and Justice: A Review of Research,* ed. M. H. Tonry and D. P. Farrington. Chicago: University of Chicago Press.

Cohen, Lawrence E., and Marcus Felson. 1979. "Social Change and Crime Rate Trends: A Routine Activity Approach." *American Sociological Review* 44: 588–608.

Coleman, A. 1985. *Utopia on Trial: Vision and Reality in Planned Housing.* London: Hilary Shipman.

Cornish, Derek B., and Ronald V. Clarke, eds. 1986. *The Reasoning Criminal.* New York: Springer-Verlag.

Fowler, Floyd J., Jr., and Thomas W. Mangione. 1982 *Neighborhood Crime, Fear, and Social Control: A Second Look at the Hartford Program.* Washington, D.C.: United States Department of Justice.

Griswold, David B. 1984. "Crime Prevention and Commercial Burglary: A Time Series Analysis." *Journal of Criminal Justice* 12: 493–501.

Hunter, Ronald D., and C. Ray Jeffrey. 1992. "Preventing Convenience Store Robbery Through Environmental Design." In *Situational Crime Prevention: Successful Case Studies,* ed. Ronald V. Clarke, 194–204. New York: Harrow and Heston.

Jacobs, Jane. 1961. *The Death and Life of Great American Cities.* New York: Random House.

Jeffery, C. Ray. 1971 *Crime Prevention through Environmental Design.* Beverly Hills: Sage.

Jordan, Anne. 1993. "Walls that Unite." *Governing,* October, 32–35.

Kohn, I., Karen A. Franck, and S. A. Fox. 1975. "Defensible Space Modifications in Row House Communities." Unpublished report prepared for the National Science Foundation by the Institute for Community Design Analysis.

Merry, Sally E. 1981a "Defensible Space Undefended: Social Factors in Crime Control through Environmental Design." *Urban Affairs Quarterly* 16:397–422.

———. 1981b. *Urban Danger: Life in a Neighborhood of Strangers.* Philadelphia: Temple University Press.

Newman, Oscar. 1972. *Defensible Space: Crime Prevention through Urban Design.* New York: Macmillan.

———. 1983. *Architectural Design for Crime Prevention.* Washington, D.C.: United States Government Printing Office.

Newman, Oscar, and Karen A. Franck. 1980. *Factors Influencing Crime and Instability in Urban Housing Developments.* Washington, D.C.: United States Government Printing Office.

———. 1982. "The Effects of Building Size on Personal Crime and Fear of Crime." *Population and Environment* 5.

Poyner, B. 1983. *Design against Crime: Beyond Defensible Space*. Stoneham, Mass.: Butterworth-Heinemann.

Repetto, Thomas A. 1974. *Residential Crime*. Cambridge, Mass.: Ballinger.

Rubenstein, Herb, Charles A. Murray, Tetsuro Motoyama, and W. V. Rouse. 1980. *The Link between Crime and the Built Environment: The Current State of Knowledge*. American Institutes for Research.

Scherdin, Mary Jane. 1992. "The Halo Effect: Psychological Deterrence of Electronic Security Systems." In *Situational Crime Prevention: Successful Case Studies*, ed. Ronald V. Clarke, 133–38. New York: Harrow and Heston.

Skogan, Wesley G. 1977. "Public Policy and Fear of Crime in Large American Cities." In *Public Law and Public Policy*, ed. John A. Gardiner, 1–18. New York: Praeger.

———. 1990. *Disorder and Decline: Crime and the Spiral of Decay in American Neighborhoods*. New York: Free Press.

Taylor, Ralph B., and Stephen Gottfredson. 1986. "Environmental Design, Crime, and Prevention: An Examination of Community Dynamics." In *Communities and Crime*, ed. Albert J. Reiss, Jr., and Michael Tonry, 8. Chicago: University of Chicago Press.

Taylor, Ralph B., Stephen D. Gottfredson, and Sidney Brower. 1980. "The Defensibility of Defensible Space: A Critical Review and a Synthetic Framework for Future Research." In *Understanding Crime*, ed. Travis Hirschi and Michael Gottfredson, 64–75. Beverly Hills: Sage.

Taylor, R. B., S. A. Schumaker, and S. D. Gottfredson. 1985, "Neighborhood-level Link between Physical Features and Local Sentiments: Deterioration, Fear of Crime, and Confidence." *Journal of Architectural Planning and Research* 2: 261–75.

Tien, James M., et al. 1977. *Street Lighting Projects: National Evaluation Program, Phase I Final Report*. Cambridge, Mass.: Public Systems Evaluation, Inc.

Tuller, D. 1984 "Electronic Surveillance Systems in Bookstores." *Publishers Weekly*, 25 May, 46.

Ward, A. E. and W. B. Brooks. 1991. "Environmental Design at Work." *Security Management* 35:75–78.

Wilson, James Q. 1983. *Thinking about Crime*, rev. ed. New York: Basic Books.

Wilson, James Q., and George Kelling. 1982. "Broken Windows: Police and Neighborhood Safety." *Atlantic Monthly*, 29–38.

16. Brian Forst, "Prosecution and Sentencing"

Notes

The author wishes to thank Dierdre Golash, James Lynch, Candace McCoy, David Saari, Ronald Weiner, and the editors of this volume for their helpful comments on earlier drafts of this chapter.

1. Federal Bureau of Investigation 1993.

2. This is due largely to the effect of huge increases in imprisonments for felony drug offenses, typically reported only at the time of arrest. Total index crimes

for 1970 and 1989 were 8,098,000 and 14,251,000, respectively (FBI 1970 and 1989). Total admissions to federal and state prisons for the same years were 79,351 and 316,215 (Bureau of Justice Statistics 1991a and United States Bureau of the Census 1993, table 343).

3. The Bureau of Justice Statistics launched a series of reports on the outcomes of prosecution in the mid-1970s, conducted by the Institute for Law and Social Research until 1985, then by Abt Associates. The numbers in Figure 16.1 are derived from Boland, Mahanna, and Sones (1992); Lisefski and Manson (1988); and Langan (1989).

4. Some 690,000 were admitted to juvenile facilities in 1990 nationwide, over 80 percent to short-term confinement (Parent et al. 1994, 1). See also Dougherty (1988, 72–79); Snyder et al. (1987); Forst and Blomquist (1992); Allen-Hagen (1991); Bureau of Justice Statistics (1988).

5. Toborg 1982; Rhodes 1985; Bureau of Justice Statistics 1991b, 1.

6. The average case-processing time for felonies that go to trial is about one year (391 days for murder, 333 for rape and robbery, 259 for burglary, 248 for larceny); the numbers are somewhat higher in larger jurisdictions than in small ones (Solari 1992, 60).

7. Differences within Los Angeles County have been reported by Petersilia, Abrahamse, and Wilson (1990), and earlier by Greenwood et al. (1976). Differences between United States Attorney offices in adjacent federal districts were reported by Boland and Forst (1985).

8. Nationwide, the ratio of pleas to trials, based on felony arrests, is slightly less than 10 to 1. Three jurisdictions with extremely low rates are Washington, D.C. (5:1), New Orleans (4:1), and Portland (4:1); two with extremely high rates are Geneva, Illinois (37:1), and Littleton, Colorado (19:1) (Forst and Boland 1984, 2).

9. Boland and Forst 1985, 11–13. In Manhattan, where the plea-to-trial ratio is 24:1, only 3 percent of all felony arrests are rejected; the local crime unit in the U.S. Attorney's Washington, D.C., office, with a plea-to-trial ratio of 5:1, rejects 15 percent (Boland, Mahanna, and Sones 1992).

10. Legislative attempts to ban plea bargaining have been studied extensively, with conclusions that, while varied, are consistent in their generally negative assessments. For analyses of the effects of attempts to ban plea bargaining under the 1973 New York drug law see Joint Committee on the New York Drug Law (1979). Rubinstein and White (1979) reported the findings of their study of the effects of a sweeping 1975 ban on plea bargaining. A 1977 plea bargaining ban in Michigan firearm cases was analyzed by Loftin, Heumann, and McDowall (1983, 287). The 1982 attempt to better serve victims with California's Proposition 8 referendum substantially accelerated the plea negotiation process in that state, but appears to have done so in a manner that undermines both the due process of defendants and the concerns of victims to have their views aired in court and receive appropriate levels of attention; see McCoy (1993).

11. Boland, Mahanna, and Sones 1992.

12. Such findings were reported for Washington, D.C., by Forst, Lucianovic, and Cox (1977); for New York, similar findings were reported by the Vera Institute of Justice (1977); for New Orleans, such findings were reported by Forst et al. (1981).

13. For an in-depth analysis of the prosecutor's view of the witness problem, see Cannavale and Falcon (1976).

14. Forst, Lucianovic, and Cox (1977, 28). Similar findings were found for New York by the Vera Institute and for New Orleans by Forst et al. (1981).

15. Some researchers have found that violent offenders in the family are also more likely to assault nonfamily members (Hotaling and Straus 1989, 315–75).

16. Forst, Lucianovic, and Cox 1977; Brosi 1979; Boland, Mahanna, and Sones 1992.

17. This is not to suggest that the practice of aborting or retarding prosecution is an appropriate response to questionable police procedures of obtaining evidence. The 30,000 or so felony cases that are rejected annually in the United States because of such violations of rights to due process may be 30,000 too many from the public's point of view. I wish only to point out here that the problem is small from another perspective: for each case rejected because of an exclusionary rule violation, about 20 are rejected because the police failed to produce sufficient tangible or testimonial evidence.

18. Forst, Lucianovic, and Cox 1977; Forst et al. 1981.

19. This was found in Washington, D.C., by Forst, Lucianovic, and Cox (1977), and in seven jurisdictions by Forst et al. (1981). In the latter study, arrests made by about 10,000 police officers during 1977 and 1978 were examined; half of the convictions that followed those arrests were the product of a mere 12 percent of the officers. Nearly twice as many officers (22 percent) made arrests that failed to yield a single conviction. This pattern held up after the researchers accounted for the officer's assignment, the number of arrests made by the officer, the normal conviction rate associated with each officer's offense mix (e.g., the conviction rate for robbery is considerably higher than for assault), and randomness associated with the small number of arrests made by most of the officers. Similar differences in conviction rates were found in a study of arrests for robbery and burglary by twenty-five different police departments operating in Los Angeles County in the 1980s—some departments produced arrests that resulted in conviction at twice the rate as others (Petersilia, Abrahamse, and Wilson 1990, 23–38.

20. Reiss 1974.

21. Forst and Brosi 1977; U.S. Department of Justice 1977; Jacoby 1981; Feeney, Dill, and Weir 1983.

22. Chelimsky and Dahmann 1981.

23. The twelve special prosecutors from Archibald Cox in the Watergate scandal to Lawrence Walsh in the Iran-Contra affair have had a mixed record. According to Robert Bennett, counsel to former defense secretary Caspar Weinberger in the Iran-Contra indictment, "The trouble with independent counsels is that you give one case and enormous power to a single individual, and the pressures to find wrongdoing are overpowering. You don't get much credit saying that nothing wrong occurred" (Johnson 1993, 47). No one disputes that they are expensive. Walsh's team, which produced a largely inconclusive investigation, spent $35 million. More troublesome to many than the cost is the fact that the independent prosecutor "conflicts with the Constitution's creation of three and only three separate branches"—Will (1994) in arguing against a special prosecutor to investigate President Clinton's "Whitewater" matter.

24. Blumstein et al. 1983, 11–12.

25. Blumstein et al. 1983, 18.

26. Hogarth 1971; Diamond and Zeisel 1975; Forst and Wellford 1981. Consistent with this evidence is a summary statement by the National Academy of Sciences Panel on Sentencing Research: "Despite the number and diversity of factors investi-

gated as determinants of sentences, two-thirds or more of the variance in sentence outcomes remains unexplained" (Blumstein et al. 1983, 10).

27. Forst and Wellford 1981.

28. Bureau of Justice Statistics 1992a, 83.

29. Blumstein et al. 1983. Similar conclusions were derived by Joan Petersilia and Susan Turner following an investigation of sentencing guideline systems—although it is apparently inadvertent, sentencing criteria under many guideline systems do produce systematic racial differences in sentencing (Petersilia and Turner 1985).

In death penalty cases, racial effects in sentencing have revealed themselves more clearly by taking account of the race of both the offender and the victim. See Wolfgang and Riedel (1973); Baldus, Pulaski, and Woodworth (1983); Vito and Keil (1988).

30. Blumstein et al. 1983.

31. Rhodes and Conly 1981; Nagel and Hagan 1983; Blumstein et al. 1983; Simon 1993, 142.

32. Mean sentences are shorter in each of the eight categories of felony offenses for the nation's seventy-five largest counties than for the nation as a whole (Solari 1992, tables 4.4a and 4.4b, 49–50).

33. Restitution and rehabilitation are often proposed as alternatives to incarceration. Clearly, each can coexist with imprisonment, at least in principle; as a practical matter, however, restitution while in prison may be impossible for all but a few wealthy offenders, and rehabilitation has yet to demonstrate itself systematically as an achievable goal.

34. Samuel Walker likens these celebrated cases to the small top layer of a much larger wedding cake (Walker 1985).

35. In 1972, Marvin Wolfgang and his associates at the University of Pennsylvania reported that 18 percent of all boys born in Philadelphia in 1945 accounted for 52 percent of all the offenses committed by the group. See Wolfgang, Figlio, and Sellin (1972, 88). Then in 1976, Kristen Williams, analyzing PROMIS data from the District of Columbia for 1971–1975, found that 7 percent of the 46,000 different defendants arrested accounted for 24 percent of the 73,000 felony and serious misdemeanor cases handled by the prosecutor for that jurisdiction. Those findings appeared in a 1976 working paper by Williams and in a finished version, Williams (1979, 5–6).

36. Forst and Brosi 1977.

37. Chelimsky and Dahmann 1981; Rhodes 1985.

38. Wolfgang, Figlio, and Sellin 1972, 88; Williams 1979; Forst et al. 1982; Greenwood 1982; Chaiken and Chaiken 1982.

39. Four offices that have instituted such programs are the office of the state's attorney for Montgomery County, Maryland, and the offices of the district attorneys for Brooklyn, Milwaukee, and Portland. The Montgomery County and Brooklyn operations are discussed in Forst 1993, 291–302.

40. Peters and Waterman 1982.

41. Szanton 1972.

42. Blumstein et al. 1983; McCoy 1993.

43. See note 66, and accompanying text.

44. Martinson 1974, 22–54. These findings appeared later in a more extensive version (Lipton, Martinson, and Wilks 1975). Similar findings had been obtained a decade earlier in a survey of 100 rehabilitation programs (Bailey 1966).

45. See notes 25 and 26, and accompanying text. Evidence on disparity in federal sentencing practices was presented to the U.S. Senate Subcommittee on Criminal Law (Senator Edward Kennedy presiding), prior to the enactment of federal sentencing guidelines under the 1984 Federal Sentencing Reform Act. See testimony of Brian Forst and William Rhodes in U.S. Senate (1983, 1000–1004).

46. Tonry 1988, 267.

47. Frankel 1973.

48. Controlled experimentation, with random assignment of cases to experimental and control groups, is generally more difficult to administer in the case of special deterrence than in the case of rehabilitation. Experiments have been conducted to test the special deterrent effect of arrest for misdemeanor domestic assaults, with some evidence of effectiveness in cases involving unemployed and inner city offenders (Sherman 1992). For convicted offenders, however, such experimentation runs afoul of constitutional provisions ensuring equal treatment under law. And evidence from "natural experimentation" is invariably untrustworthy because of selection bias—offenders selected for incarceration tend to be rearrested and reconvicted at higher rates than those given terms of probation not necessarily because of the criminogenic effect of prison, but at least in part because they were more recidivistic to begin with, and were correctly perceived as such by the sentencing authorities.

49. Supporters of the "just deserts" concept of sentencing often distance themselves from conventional notions of retribution, arguing that fairness in sentencing—proportionality between the gravity of the crime and the severity of the sanction—need not have anything to do with archaic or cruel treatment. See von Hirsch (1992, 55–98).

50. Tonry 1988, 269.

51. Most sentencing systems appear to be based primarily on just deserts rather than utilitarian considerations. Average terms served for murder are about two to three times as long as average terms for robbery and more than five times longer than average terms for burglary, despite the fact that the average number of crimes committed per year free are highest for burglars and lowest for murderers. See Langan and Dawson (1990, 3).

52. What some see as a shift in discretionary authority from judge to prosecutor others may see as a net reduction in unwarranted disparity under sentencing guidelines with no absolute increase in prosecutorial discretion. Judges surely have less discretionary authority under the guidelines; but it is not evident that prosecutors have more, either in filing charges or reducing them, than they did before guidelines. I argued earlier for the need for prosecutorial guidelines to reduce such disparity (see the section "Unbridled Prosecutorial Discretion?"). In the meantime, prosecutorial discretion will continue to be somewhat structured, at least insofar as assistant district attorneys work for the D.A.; prior to guidelines and tight determinate sentencing laws, individual judges reported to no one in shaping sentences. If the issue is cast primarily as a problem of relative power between judge and prosecutor, it becomes tempting to find solutions that result in the return to disparate sentencing, with no less prosecutorial discretion.

53. A 1989 challenge to the constitutionality of federal guidelines designed by a sentencing commission under the 1984 SRA was rejected by eight to one in the Supreme Court. See U.S. Supreme Court (1989).

54. Bureau of Justice Statistics 1992b, tables 9 and 15. Much of the increase in federal prosecutions is attributable to a unilateral decision by federal prosecutors to accept cases that had previously been prosecuted at the state level. Coordination between federal and state/local prosecutors has been notoriously poor in many areas of the country (Hausner et al. 1982).

The increase has been attributed also to mandatory minimum sentencing, which, according to Supreme Court Chief Justice William Rehnquist, may have induced state and federal authorities to "funnel more and more of their drug cases into federal courts" (Rehnquist 1993).

55. Bureau of Justice Statistics 1992c.

56. Bureau of Justice Statistics 1992b, table 18. The expected prison term for each convicted drug trafficker, including those sentenced to terms of probation, increased by 67 percent, from 12.38 months in 1986 to 20.65 months in 1992.

57. In 1986, 10,336 persons were convicted for drug trafficking in federal courts, and 8,588 of those were incarcerated; in 1992, the corresponding numbers were 17,578 and 15,987 (Bureau of Justice Statistics 1992b, tables 9 and 15).

58. Blumstein 1992. See also the chapter by Blumstein in this volume (Chapter 17).

A 1992 study by the U.S. Sentencing Commission reported that blacks served more time on cocaine-related charges than whites because mandatory minimum sentences adopted by Congress in the 1980s for the sale of crack are more severe than sentences for selling comparable amounts of cocaine in powder form. More than 90 percent of the defendants are black in crack cocaine cases, while slightly more than 25 percent are black in cocaine cases involving powder (*New York Times* 1993).

59. For a fuller discussion of these issues, see Chapter 17 in this volume.

60. U.S. Sentencing Commission 1991a. Michael Tonry sees the evidence on disparity reduction attributable to the federal guidelines as inconclusive (Tonry 1992b).

61. Tonry 1992b, 138, 144, 176, 187. Tonry summarizes the evidence as follows: "Commissions have . . . managed to make sentencing more accountable, more consistent, and less disparate in its impact on minority group members, and those are not small achievements" (p. 180).

62. Tonry 1992b, 141.

63. Tonry 1992b, 140–41.

64. Blumstein et al 1983.

65. Schulhofer 1993; Tonry 1992a; U.S. Sentencing Commission 1991b; Bynum 1982; State of Massachusetts 1974. Washington (1993) and California (1994) were among the first states to enact the three-strikes-and-you're-out laws.

66. Alschuler 1993, 733.

67. A U.S. Sentencing Commission study found that trial rates were two and a half times greater (30 percent of all convictions) for offenses subject to mandatory penalties than for all offenses (12 percent). Even larger increases were found following enactment of the 1973 Rockefeller Drug Laws in New York State (U.S. Sentencing Commission 1991b).

68. Tonry finds something more charitable to say about legislators' motives: "Put positively, elected officials want to reassure the public generally that their fears have been noted and that the causes of their fears have been acted on. Put negatively, officials want to curry public favor and electoral support by pandering, by making

promises that the law can at best imperfectly and incompletely deliver" (Tonry 1992a, 265).

69. Reiss and Roth 1993, 6. Some of this increase may be attributable to an increase in average severity of violent episodes.

70. See the chapter by James Lynch in this volume (Chapter 2).

71. More explicitly, let S_i denote the sentence for offense/offender category i; N_i denote the number of offenses in that category; CA_i and CC_i denote costs attributable to each arrest and conviction respectively; CP_i denote the cost of each offense in category i incurred by the private sector; CI denote the cost of one year of imprisonment; and PA_i, PC_i, and PI_i denote the respective probabilities of arrest, conviction, and imprisonment. The sentence, S_i, that minimizes the total social cost of crime and punishment, TSC_i, will be determined by forming the function

$$TSC_i = (CA_i)(PA_i)(N_i) + (CC_i)(PC_i)(N_i) + (CI)(PI_i)(S_i)(N_i) + (CP_i)(N_i),$$

given the deterrent and incapacitative effects

$$N_i = f_i(PA_i, PC_i, PI_i, S_i, \ldots).$$

S_i is determined by combining these expressions, differentiating TSC_i with respect to S_i, and setting the resulting expression equal to zero. For further detail, see Forst, Rhodes, and Wellford (1979, 372–76).

72. A National Academy of Sciences panel recently estimated that a 50 percent increase in the probability of incarceration prevents about *twice* as much violent crime as does a 50 percent increase in the average term of incarceration (Reiss and Roth 1993, 6).

73. Snell and Morton 1992.

74. Langan and Cuniff found that financial restitution was stipulated in some 29 percent of all probation cases, averaging $3,400 per case (Langan and Cuniff 1992, 1). Restitution associated with victim-offender reconciliation programs, which emphasize emotional healing rather than restitution per se, tend to involve smaller payment amounts. Reconciliation programs are described in Pollack (1993).

75. Cole 1993.

76. In *Tate v. Short* the Supreme Court recognized that fines can discriminate against the poor (U.S. Supreme Court 1971). New York City has experimented with "day fines," amounts that are linked to the offender's net income. See *Criminal Justice Newsletter* 1988.

77. Morris and Tonry 1990.

78. Evidence obtained by Rhodes (1978) suggests that many defendants have indeed been induced to accept offers of excessively punitive terms from prosecutors in a pre-guideline environment.

79. Jeffrey Roth and Paul Wice estimated that by incorporating factors that had been found not to be used in the bail decision, such as illegal drug involvement, and discarding factors that had been used in the bail decision but were not found to be related to pretrial misconduct, such as whether the defendant has a local residence, jail populations could be reduced by about 20 percent without any increase in the rate of failure to appear, or by about 40 percent without any increase in the pretrial rearrest rate (Roth and Wice 1980).

80. It is frequently argued that statistical prediction should not be used as a basis for criminal justice decision making because of the false positives problem. In fact, nonstatistical assessment of dangerousness—the method preferred in most jurisdictions—has been found repeatedly to produce false positives at a *higher* rate than statistical assessments. See Monahan (1981); Steadman and Cocozza (1978, 226–31); Meehl (1954).

The legitimacy of prediction as a basis for criminal justice decisions has been generally well established. Judges routinely base bail decisions on the perceived risk of defendant misbehavior prior to trial. The exercise of discretion by prosecutors in filing charges and in targeting cases involving dangerous offenders for special prosecution, and by judges in making bail and sentencing decisions, has been subjected to challenge and reversal only very rarely.

81. Interviews with 180 police officers who made arrests in New York City and Washington, D.C., revealed that none of the officers (nor their immediate supervisors) routinely received information about the court outcomes of their arrests. Forst et al. 1981.

Fortunately, there are signs of improvement on this front. A recent survey of prosecutors revealed that the rate at which prosecutors notify police and victims of the outcomes of their cases more than doubled from 1974 to 1990 (Bureau of Justice Statistics 1992d).

References

Allen-Hagen, Barbara. 1991. *Children in Custody, 1989.* Washington, D.C.: Office of Juvenile Justice and Delinquency Prevention.

Alschuler, Albert W. 1993. "Monarch, Lackey, or Judge." *University of Colorado Law Review* 64:733.

Bailey, Walter C. 1966. "Correctional Outcome: An Evaluation of 100 Reports." *Journal of Criminal Law, Criminology, and Police Science* 57.

Baldus, David, C. Pulaski, and G. Woodworth. 1983. "Comparative Review of Death Sentences: An Empirical Study of the Georgia Experience." *Journal of Criminal Law and Criminology* 74:661–85.

Blumstein, Alfred. 1992. "Making Rationality Relevant: The American Society of Criminology 1992 Presidential Address." *Criminology* 31:1–16.

Blumstein, Alfred, Jacqueline Cohen, Susan E. Martin, and Michael H. Tonry, eds. 1983. *Research on Sentencing: The Search for Reform.* Washington, D.C.: National Academy Press.

Boland, Barbara, and Brian Forst. 1985. "Prosecutors Don't Always Aim to Please." *Federal Probation* 49 (June): 11

Boland, Barbara, Paul Mahanna, and Ronald Sones. 1992. *The Prosecution of Felony Arrests, 1988.* Washington, D.C.: Bureau of Justice Statistics.

Brosi, Kathleen. 1979. *A Cross-City Comparison of Felony Case Processing.* Washington, D.C.: Institute for Law and Social Research.

Bureau of Justice Statistics (BJS). 1988. *Survey of Youth in Custody, 1987.* Washington, D.C.: United States Department of Justice.

———. 1991a. *Correctional Populations in the United States.* Washington, D.C.: United States Department of Justice.

———. 1991b. *Pretrial Release of Felony Defendants, 1988*. Washington, D.C.: United States Government Printing Office, February.

———. 1992a. *Correctional Populations in the United States, 1990*. Washington, D.C.: United States Department of Justice.

———. 1992b. *Federal Criminal Case Processing, 1982–91, with Preliminary Data for 1992*. Washington, D.C.: United States Department of Justice.

———. 1992c. *Four Percent More Prisoners in First Half of 1992*. Washington, D.C.: United States Department of Justice.

———. 1992d. *Prosecutors in State Courts, 1990*. Washington, D.C.: United States Department of Justice.

Bynum, Timothy. 1982. "Prosecutorial Discretion and the Implementation of a Legislative Mandate." In *Implementing Criminal Justice Policies*, ed. Merry Morash. Beverly Hills: Sage.

Cannavale, Frank J., Jr., and William D. Falcon. 1976. *Witness Cooperation*. Lexington, Mass.: D. C. Heath.

Chaiken, Jan M., and Marcia R. Chaiken. 1982. *Varieties of Criminal Behavior*. Santa Monica, Calif.: Rand.

Chelimsky, Eleanor, and Judith Dahmann. 1981. *Career Criminal Program National Evaluation: Final Report*. Washington, D.C.: United States Department of Justice.

Cole, George. 1993. "Monetary Sanctions: The Problem of Compliance." In *Smart Sentencing: The Emergence of Intermediate Sanctions*, ed. James Byrne, Arthur Lurigio, and Joan Petersilia. Newbury Park, Calif.: Sage.

Criminal Justice Newsletter. 1988. " 'Day Fines' Being Tested in a New York City Court," 1 September, 4–5.

Diamond, Shari S., and Hans Zeisel. 1975. "Sentencing Councils: A Study of Sentence Disparity and Its Reduction." *University of Chicago Law Review* 43.

Dougherty, Joyce. 1988. "A Comparison of Adult Plea Bargaining and Juvenile Intake." *Federal Probation*, June, 72–79.

Federal Bureau of Investigation (FBI). 1970. *Uniform Crime Reports*. Washington, D.C.

———. 1989. *Uniform Crime Reports*. Washington, D.C.

———. 1993. *Uniform Crime Reports*. Washington, D.C.

Feeney, Floyd, Forrest Dill, and Adrianne Weir. 1983. *Arrests without Conviction: How Often They Occur and Why*. Washington, D.C.: National Institute of Justice.

Forst, Brian. 1993. "The Prosecutor and the Public." In *The Socio-Economics of Crime and Justice*. Armonk, N.Y.: M. E. Sharpe.

Forst, Brian, and Barbara Boland. 1984. "The Prevalence of Guilty Pleas." *Bureau of Justice Statistics Special Report*. Washington, D.C., December.

Forst, Brian, and Kathleen Brosi. 1977. "A Theoretical and Empirical Analysis of the Prosecutor." *Journal of Legal Studies* 6.

Forst, Brian, Frank Leahy, Jean Shirhall, Herbert Tyson, Eric Wish, and John Bartolomeo. 1981. *Arrest Convictability as a Measure of Police Performance*. Washington, D.C.: Institute for Law and Social Research.

Forst, Brian, Judith Lucianovic, and Sarah Cox. 1977. *What Happens after Arrest?* Washington, D.C.: Institute for Law and Social Research.

Forst, Brian, William Rhodes, James Dimm, Aruthur Gelman, and Barbara Mullin. 1982. *Targeting Federal Resources on Recidivists.* Washington, D.C.: Institute for Law and Social Research.

Forst, Brian, William Rhodes, and Charles Wellford. 1979. "Sentencing and Social Science: Research for the Formulation of Federal Sentencing Guidelines." *Hofstra Law Review* 7, no. 2 (Winter): 372–76.

Forst, Brian, and Charles Wellford. 1981. "Punishment and Sentencing: Developing Sentencing Guidelines Empirically from Principles of Punishment." *Rutgers Law Review* 33.

Forst, Martin, and Martha-Elin Blomquist. 1992. "Punishment, Accountability and the New Juvenile Justice." *Juvenile and Family Court* 43:1.

Frankel, Marvin E. 1973. *Criminal Sentences: Law without Order.* New York: Hill and Wang.

Gennaro, Vito, and Thomas Keil. 1988. "Capital Sentencing in Kentucky: An Analysis of the Factors Influencing Decision Making in the Post-Gregg Period." *Journal of Criminal Law and Criminology* 79:493–503.

Greenwood, Peter. 1982. *Selective Incapacitation.* Santa Monica, Calif.: Rand.

Greenwood, Peter, Sorrel Wildhorn, E. Poggio, M. Strumsasser, and P. Deleon. 1976. *Prosecution of Adult Felony Defendants in Los Angeles County.* Santa Monica, Calif.: Rand.

Hausner, Jack, Barbara Mullin, Amy Moorer, and Brian Forst. 1982. *The Investigation and Prosecution of Concurrent Jurisdiction Offenses.* Report prepared for the Office of Legal Policy, United States Department of Justice. Washington, D.C.: Institute for Law and Social Research.

Hogarth, John. 1971. *Sentencing as a Human Process.* Toronto: University of Toronto Press.

Hotaling, Gerald T., and Murray A. Straus. 1989. "Intrafamily Violence, and Crime and Violence outside the Family," with Alan J. Lincoln. In *Family Violence,* ed. Lloyd Ohlin and Michael Tonry. Chicago: University of Chicago Press.

Jacoby, Joan E. 1981. *Prosecutorial Decisionmaking: A National Study.* Washington, D.C.: Bureau of Social Science Research.

Johnson, Constance. 1993. "High Crimes and Special Prosecutors." *U.S. News and World Report,* 8 November, 47.

Joint Committee on the New York Drug Law. 1979. *The Nation's Toughest Drug Law: Evaluating the New York Experience.* Washington, D.C.: United States Government Printing Office.

Langan, Patrick. 1989. *Felony Sentences in State Courts.* Washington, D.C.: Bureau of Justice Statistics.

Langan, Patrick, and Mark Cuniff. 1992. *Recidivism of Felons on Probation, 1986–1989.* Washington, D.C.: Bureau of Justice Statistics.

Langan, Patrick, and John Dawson. 1990. *Felony Sentences in State Courts, 1988.* Washington, D.C.: Bureau of Justice Statistics.

Lipton, Douglas, Robert Martinson, and Judith Wilks. 1975. *The Effectiveness of Correctional Treatment.* New York: Praeger.

Lisefski, Edward, and Donald Manson. 1988. *Tracking Offenders.* Washington, D.C.: Bureau of Justice Statistics.

Loftin, Colin, Milton Heumann, and David McDowall. 1983. "Mandatory Sentencing and Firearm Violence." *Law and Society Review* 17:287.

Martinson, Robert. 1974. "What Works?—Questions and Answers about Prison Reform." *The Public Interest* 35 (Spring): 22–54.

McCoy, Candace. 1993. *Politics and Plea Bargaining: Victims' Rights in California*. Philadelphia: University of Pennsylvania Press.

Meehl, Paul E. 1954. *Clinical vs. Statistical Prediction*. Minneapolis: University of Minnesota Press.

Monahan, John. 1981. *Predicting Violent Behavior: An Assessment of Clinical Techniques*. Beverly Hills: Sage.

Morris, Norval, and Michael Tonry. 1990. *Between Prison and Probation: Intermediate Punishments in a Rational Sentencing System*. New York: Oxford University Press.

Nagel, Ilene H., and John Hagan. 1983. "Gender and Crime: Offense Patterns and Criminal Court Sanctions." In *Crime and Justice: A Review of Research,* ed. Michael H. Tonry and Norval Morris, vol. 4. Chicago: University of Chicago Press.

New York Times. 1993. "U.S. Appeals a Case Defying Sentence Guides," 29 August, 25.

Parent, Dale G., et al. 1994. *Conditions of Confinement: Juvenile Detention and Corrections Facilities*. Washington, D.C.: Office of Juvenile Justice and Delinquency Prevention.

Peters, Thomas J., and Robert H. Waterman. 1982. *In Search of Excellence: Lessons from America's Best-Run Companies*. New York: Harper and Row.

Petersilia, Joan, Allan Abrahamse, and James Q. Wilson. 1990a. *Police Performance and Case Attrition*. Santa Monica, Calif.: Rand.

———. 1990b. "The Relationship between Police Practice, Community Characteristics, and Case Attrition." *Policing and Society* 1:23–38.

Petersilia, Joan, and Susan Turner. 1985. *Guideline-Based Justice: The Implications for Racial Minorities*. Santa Monica, Calif.: Rand.

Pollack, Ellen Joan. 1993. "Victim-Perpetrator Reconciliations Grow in Popularity." *Wall Street Journal,* 28 October, B1 and B6.

Rehnquist, William (chief justice of the United States Supreme Court). 1993. Remarks at U. S. Sentencing Commission Symposium on Drugs and Violence in America, 18 June.

Reiss, Albert J., Jr. 1974. "Discretionary Justice in the United States." *International Journal of Criminology and Penology* 2.

Reiss, Albert J., Jr., and Jeffrey A. Roth, eds. 1993. *Understanding and Preventing Violence*. Washington, D.C.: National Academy of Sciences.

Rhodes, William 1978. *Plea Bragaining: Who Gains? Who Loses?* Washington, D.C.: Institute for Law and Social Research.

———. 1985. *Pretrial Release and Misconduct*. Washington, D.C.: Bureau of Justice Statistics.

Rhodes, William, and Catherine Conly. 1981. *Analysis of Federal Sentencing*. Washington, D.C.: Institute for Law and Social Research.

Roth, Jeffrey, and Paul Wice. 1980. *Pretrial Release and Misconduct in the District of Columbia*. Washington, D.C.: Institute for Law and Social Research.

Rubinstein, Michael L., and Teresa J. White. 1979. "Alaska's Ban on Plea Bargaining." *Law and Society Review* 13.

Schulhofer, Stephen J. 1993. "Rethinking Mandatory Minimums." *Wake Forest Law Review* 28.

Sherman, Lawrence W. 1992. *Policing Domestic Violence: Experiments and Dilemmas.* New York: Free Press.

Simon, Rita. 1993. "Women, Crime, and Justice." In *The Socio-Economics of Crime and Justice,* ed. Brian Forst. Armonk, N.Y.: M. E. Sharpe.

Snell, Tracy L., and Danielle C. Morton. 1992. *Prisoners in 1991.* Washington, D.C.: Bureau of Justice Statistics.

Snyder, Howard, Terrence A. Finnegan, Ellen Nimick, Melissa Sickmund, Dennis Sullivan, and Nancy Tierney. 1987. *Juvenile Court Statistics, 1984.* Pittsburgh: National Center of Juvenile Justice.

Solari, Richard. 1992. *National Judicial Reporting Program, 1988.* Washington, D.C.: Bureau of Justice Statistics.

State of Massachusetts. 1974. General Laws, Chapters 269 and 649, Acts of 1974.

Steadman, Henry J., and Joseph Cocozza. 1978. "Psychiatry, Dangerousness and the Repetitively Violent Offender." *Journal of Criminal Law and Criminology* 69:-226–31.

Szanton, Peter L. 1972. *Public Policy, Public Good, and the Law.* Washington, D.C.: Rand.

Toborg, Mary. 1982. *Pretrial Release: A National Evaluation of Practices and Outcomes.* Washington, D.C.: National Institute of Justice.

Tonry, Michael H. 1988. "Structuring Sentencing." In *Crime and Justice: A Review of Research,* ed. Michael H. Tonry and Norval Morris, vol. 10. Chicago: University of Chicago Press.

———. 1992a. "Mandatory Penalties." In *Crime and Justice: A Review of Research,* ed. Michael H. Tonry, 243–73. Chicago: University of Chicago Press.

———. 1992b. "Sentencing Commissions and Their Guidelines." *In Crime and Justice: A Review of Research,* ed. Michael H. Tonry. Chicago: University of Chicago Press.

United States Bureau of the Census. 1993. *Statistical Abstract of the United States.* Washington, D.C.

United States Department of Justice. 1977. *Justice Litigation Management.* Washington, D.C.: U.S. Government Printing Office.

United States Senate. 1983. Hearings before the Subcommittee on Criminal Law of the Committee on the Judiciary, First Session on S.829 (Comprehensive Crime Control Act of 1983), 23 May 1983. Serial no. J-98-37.

United States Sentencing Commission. 1991a. *The Federal Sentencing Guidelines: A Report on the Operation of the Guidelines System and Short-term Impacts on Disparity in Sentencing, Use of Incarceration, and Prosecutorial Discretion and Plea Bargaining.* Washington, D.C.

———. 1991b. *Mandatory Minimum Penalties in the Federal Criminal Justice System: A Special Report to Congress.* Washington, D.C.

United States Supreme Court. 1971. *Tate v. Short.* 401 U.S. 395, 91 S. Ct. 668, 28 L. Ed. 2d 130.

————. 1989. *Mistretta v. United States.* 488 U.S. 361.

Vera Institute of Justice. 1977. *Felony Arrests: Their Prosecution and Disposition in New York City's Courts.* New York.

von Hirsch, Andrew. 1992. "Proportionality in the Philosophy of Punishment. In *Crime and Justice: A Review of Research,* ed. Michael H. Tonry. Chicago: University of Chicago Press.

Walker, Samuel. 1985. *Sense and Nonsense about Crime.* Monterey, Calif.: Brooks/Cole.

Will, George F. 1994. "Fangs of the Independent Counsel. *Washington Post,* 7 January, A19.

Williams, Kristen. 1979. *The Scope and Prediction of Recidivism.* Washington, D.C.: Institute for Law and Social Research.

Wolfgang, Marvin E., Robert M. Figlio, and Thorstein Sellin. 1972. *Delinquency in a Birth Cohort.* Chicago: University of Chicago Press.

Wolfgang, Marvin E., and Marc Riedel. 1973. "Race, Judicial Discretion, and the Death Penalty." *Annals of the American Academy of Political and Social Science* 407: 119–33.

17. Alfred Blumstein, "Prisons"

Notes

1. Blumstein 1983.

2. Blumstein and Cohen 1973. Subsequent work with Dr. Cohen and others led to further tests and development of that theory. These included Blumstein, Cohen, and Nagin (1977) and Blumstein and Moitra (1979).

3. Gilliard and Beck 1994.

4. The reports are published annually by the FBI as *Crime in the United States: Uniform Crime Reports.*

5. In a survey of state prisoners conducted in 1991, murder accounted for 10.6 percent of inmates and robbery another 14.8 percent. Burglars make up another 12.4 percent and drug offenders 21.3 percent. These are the only groups that account for more than 10 percent of inmates (Beck et al. 1993, 4).

6. The trend line for the murder series has a slight negative slope of 0.03 murders per 100,000 per year, This slope is .28 percent of the mean value of the murder rate for the full period, and is not statistically significantly different from zero. For robbery, the slope of the upward trend line is also small, 3 robberies per 100,000 per year, or 1.36 percent of the mean value of the robbery rate for the full period.

7. Beck et al. 1993, 4.

8. Langan (1991) has demonstrated the increase in probability of incarceration, but has claimed that there has been no increase in observed average sentence of those sent to prison. In the face of the increased incarceration risk, this observation of no change in average sentence could result even if all sentences were increased, because many of the sentences that were formerly zero (i.e., probation or suspended sentences and not counted in the average time served of those sent to prison) are

converted to positive sentences, but generally below the previous average, thereby compensating for the increase in sentences for all others. The expected sentence per crime is more properly calculated as $Q_i S_i$, where Q_i is the probability that a crime of type i will result in a prison sentence, and S_i is the average time served on such a sentence when imposed. If one is interested in calculating the average time served for a particular crime type, then it is important to include the zeroes in order to be sensitive to the effects of a shift in Q_i.

9. Langan 1991; Cohen and Canela-Cacho 1994.

10. Golub 1992.

11. The rates reported here are based on the ages of the arrestees, which are typically used as proxy for the age of crime commission.

12. Gender is even more salient than age in distinguishing criminal activity, but the gender composition is reasonably stable, and so is less relevant as a factor contributing to change.

13. To smooth out the year-to-year fluctuations of the distribution, the figure presents at each age the average of the number of people of that age and of the year before and the year after (for example, $N_{13sm} = [N_{12} + N_{13} + N_{14}]/3$).

14. See, for example, Easterlin (1980).

15. Blumstein, Cohen, and Miller 1980.

16. Of course, other factors, such as changing economic conditions or sanction policies, could influence the crime rate and make it higher or lower than that projected based on demographic considerations alone.

17. There are separate institutions for juvenile offenders. In 1989, there were 93,945 juveniles in those institutions on a single day (United States Department of Justice 1992).

18. The most influential synthesis of these studies was Martinson (1974). This study was based on Lipton, Martinson, and Wilks (1975). The results were reexamined in a study by the National Research Council's Panel on Research on Rehabilitative Techniques (Sechrest, White, and Brown 1979). This review confirmed the previous findings of no net rehabilitative effect. More recent reviews of the literature, including some of the careful meta-analyses by Paul Gendreau (see, for example, Gendreau and Andrews [1990]) are generally more optimistic about the prospects of rehabilitative effectiveness under special conditions of inmate selection and focused treatment.

19. The major drugs include heroin, methadone, cocaine, PCP, and LSD.

20. BJS (1993, 650).

21. The assistance of Sharon Profiter in providing more recent Uniform Crime Reporting Program information for Figures 17.7 and 17.8 is much appreciated.

22. Beck et al. 1993, 4.

23. Barr 1992.

24. Logan 1989.

25. See Parkinson (1957), which suggests that, in any bureaucracy, the amount of work will expand to fill the time available.

26. Carlson et al. 1980.

27. Blumstein, Cohen, and Gooding 1983.

28. Morris and Tonry 1990.

29. See Petersilia and Turner (1993).

30. See, for example, Austin and Krisberg (1982).
31. For a review of the literature, see Nagin (1978).
32. See Blumstein, Cohen, and Hsieh (1982).
33. See Lemov (1994).
34. BJS 1993.
35. Aspects of this approach are developed in Blumstein and Kadane (1983).

References

Austin, James, and Barry Krisberg. 1982. "The Unmet Promise of Alternatives." *Crime and Delinquency* 28 (July): 374–409.

Barr, William P. 1992. *Combating Violent Crime: 24 Recommendations to Strengthen Criminal Justice*. Washington, D.C.: United States Department of Justice, Office of the Attorney General, July.

Beck, Allen, et al. 1993. *Survey of State Prison Inmates: 1991*. Report no. NCJ-136949. United States Department of Justice, Bureau of Justice Statistics, March.

Blumstein, Alfred. 1983. "Prisons: Population, Capacity, and Alternatives." In *Crime and Public Policy*, ed. James Q. Wilson. San Francisco: ICS Press.

Blumstein, Alfred, and Jacqueline Cohen. 1973. "A Theory of the Stability of Punishment." *Journal of Criminal Law and Criminology* 64 (Summer): 198–206.

Blumstein, Alfred, Jacqueline Cohen, and William Gooding. 1983. "The Influence of Capacity on Prison Population: A Critical Review of Some Recent Evidence." *Crime and Delinquency* 29 (January): 1–51.

Blumstein, Alfred, Jacqueline Cohen, and Paul Hsieh. 1982. *The Duration of Adult Criminal Careers*. Final Report to the National Institute of Justice. Pittsburgh, Pa.: Urban Systems Institute, Carnegie Mellon University.

Blumstein, Alfred, Jacqueline Cohen, and Harold Miller. 1980. "Demographically Disaggregated Projections of Prison Populations." *Journal of Criminal Justice* 8 (January): 1–26.

Blumstein, Alfred, Jacqueline Cohen, and Daniel Nagin. 1977. "The Dynamics of Homeostatic Punishment Process." *Journal of Criminal Law and Criminology* 67 (Fall): 317–34.

Blumstein, Alfred, and Joseph Kadane. 1983. "An Approach to the Allocation of Scarce Imprisonment Resources." *Crime and Delinquency* 29 (October): 546–60.

Blumstein, Alfred, and Soumyo Moitra. 1979. "An Analysis of the Time Series of the Imprisonment Rate in the States of the United States: A Further Test of the Stability of Punishment Hypothesis." *Journal of Criminal Law and Criminology* 70 (Fall): 376–90.

Bureau of Justice Statistics (BJS). 1993. *Sourcebook of Criminal Justice Statistics: 1992*. Report no. NCJ-143496. Washington, D.C.: United States Department of Justice.

Carlson, Kenneth, et al. 1980. *American Prisons and Jails*. Vol. 2, *Population Trends and Projections*. Washington, D.C.: National Institute of Justice, Abt Associates.

Cohen, Jacqueline, and Jose A. Canela-Cacho. 1994. "Incarceration and Violent Crime—1965–1988." In *Understanding and Preventing Violence: Consequences and Control*, ed. Albert J. Reiss, Jr., and Jeffrey A. Roth, vol. 4. Washington, D.C.: National Academy of Sciences.

Day, Jennifer Cheeseman. 1993. *Population Projections of the United States, by Age, Sex, Race, and Hispanic Origin: 1993 to 2050.* United States Bureau of the Census Series P25-1104. Washington, D.C.: U.S. Government Printing Office.

Easterlin, Richard A. 1980. *Birth and Fortune.* New York: Basic Books.

Federal Bureau of Investigation (FBI). Various years. *Crime in the United States: Uniform Crime Reports.* Washington, D.C.: U.S. Department of Justice.

———. 1990. *Age-Specific Arrest Rates and Race-Specific Arrest Rates for Selected Offenses, 1965–1988.* Washington, D.C.: Uniform Crime Reporting Program.

———. 1993. *Age-Specific Arrest Rates and Race-Specific Arrest Rates for Selected Offenses, 1965–1992.* Washington, D.C.: Uniform Crime Reporting Program, December.

Gendreau, Paul, and D. A. Andrews. 1990. "Tertiary Prevention: What the Meta-Analyses of the Offender Treatment Literature Tell Us about 'What Works.'" *Canadian Journal of Criminology* 32:173–84.

Gilliard, Darrell K., and Allen J. Beck. 1994. *Prisoners in 1993.* Report no. NCJ-147036. United States Department of Justice, Bureau of Justice Statistics, June.

Golub, Andrew. 1992. "The Termination Rate of Adult Criminal Careers." Dissertation, Carnegie Mellon University.

Langan, Patrick A. 1991. "America's Soaring Prison Population." *Science* 251 (March): 1568–73.

Lemov, Penelope. 1994. "Justice by the Grid." *Governing,* March, 27–30.

Lipton, D., R. Martinson, and J. Wilks. 1975. *The Effectiveness of Correctional Treatment: A Survey of Treatment Evaluation Studies.* New York: Praeger.

Logan, Charles H. 1989. "Proprietary Prisons." In *The American Prison: Issues in Research and Policy,* ed. Lynne Goodstein and Doris Layton MacKenzie. New York: Plenum Press.

Martinson, Robert. 1974. "What Works?—Questions and Answers about Prison Reform." *The Public Interest* 35:22–54.

Morris, Norval, and Michael Tonry. 1990. *Between Prison and Probation: Intermediate Punishments in a Rational Sentencing System.* New York: Oxford University Press.

Nagin, Daniel. 1978. "General Deterrence: A Review of the Empirical Evidence." In *Deterrence and Incapacitation: Estimating the Effects of the Crime Rates,* ed. Alfred Blumstein et al. Washington, D.C.: National Academy of Sciences.

Parkinson, C. Northcote. 1957. *Parkinson's Law, and Other Studies in Administration.* (Boston: Houghton Mifflin).

Petersilia, Joan, and Susan Turner. 1993. "Intensive Probation and Parole." in *Crime and Justice: A Review of Research,* ed. Michael H. Tonry. Chicago: University of Chicago Press.

Sechrest, Lee B., Susan O. White, and Elizabeth Brown, eds. 1979. *The Rehabilitation of Criminal Offenders: Problems and Prospects.* Panel on Research on Rehabilitative Techniques, National Research Council. Washington, D.C.: National Academy of Sciences.

United States Department of Justice. 1992. *National Juvenile Custody Trends: 1978–1989.* Washington, D.C.: Office of Juvenile Justice and Delinquency Prevention, March.

18. Todd R. Clear and Anthony A. Braga, "Community Corrections"

Notes

We would like to thank James Byrne for his comments and advice in the preparation of this chapter.

References

Allen, H., R. Seiter, E. Carlson, H. Bowman, J. Grandfield, and J. Beran. 1976. *National Evaluation Program Phase I: Residential Inmate Aftercare, the State of the Art Summary*. Columbus: Ohio State University.

Andrews, D., and J. Bonta. 1994. *The Psychology of Criminal Conduct*. Cincinnati: Anderson.

Andrews, D., I. Zinger, R. Hoge, J. Bonta, P. Gendreau, and F. Cullen. 1990. "Does Correctional Treatment Work? A Psychologically Informed Meta-Analysis." *Criminology* 28:369–404.

Austin, J. 1990. "America's Growing Correctional-Industrial Complex." *NCCD Focus*.

Austin, J., and P. Hardyman. 1991. "The Use of Early Parole with Electronic Monitoring to Control Prison Crowding: Evaluation of the Oklahoma Department of Corrections Pre-Parole Supervised Release with Electronic Monitoring." Unpublished report to the National Institute of Justice.

Austin, J., and R. Tillman. 1988. *Ranking the Nation's Most Punitive States*. San Francisco: National Council on Crime and Delinquency.

Baird, S. 1981. "Probation and Parole Classification: The Wisconsin Model." *Corrections Today* 43:36–41.

Baird, S., T. Clear, and P. Harris. 1986. "The Behavior Tools of Probation Officers: A Study of Probation Sanctions in Five Sites." Unpublished proposal to the National Institute of Justice.

Baird, S., R. Heinz, and B. Bemus. 1979. *The Wisconsin Case Classification/Staff Deployment Project: A Two Year Follow-Up Report*. Madison: Wisconsin Department of Health and Human Services.

Banks, J., A. Porter, P. Rardin, T. Silver, and V. Unger. 1977. *Evaluation of Intensive Special Probation Projects*. Washington, D.C.: United States Government Printing Office.

Baumer, T., and R. Mendelsohn. 1992. "Electronically Monitored Home Confinement: Does It Work? In *Smart Sentencing: The Emergence of Intermediate Sanctions*, ed. J. Byrne, A. Lurigio, and J. Petersilia. Newbury Park, Calif.: Sage.

Baumer, T., and R. Mendelsohn. 1990. *The Electronic Monitoring of Nonviolent Convicted Felons: An Experiment in Home Detention*. Final Report to the National Institute of Justice.

Bemus, B. and S. C. Baird. 1988. *Workload Measures in Probation and Parole*. Madison, Wis.: National Council on Crime and Delinquency.

Bureau of Justice Statistics (BJS). 1988. *Report to the Nation on Crime and Justice.* Washington, D.C.: United States Government Printing Office.

————. 1991. *Bulletin.* Washington, D.C.: United States Department of Justice.

————. 1992. *Correctional Populations in the United States, 1990.* Washington, D.C.: United States Department of Justice.

Burke, P., and L. Adams. 1991. *Classification of Women Offenders in State Correctional Facilities: A Handbook for Practitioners.* Washington, D.C.: National Institute of Corrections.

Byrne, J. 1989. "Re-integrating the Concept of Community into Community-Based Corrections." *Crime and Delinquency* 35:471–99.

————. 1990. "The Future of Intensive Supervision Probation." *Crime and Delinquency* 36:6–39.

Byrne, J., and M. Brewster. 1993. "Choosing the Future of American Corrections: Punishment or Reform?" *Federal Probation* 57:3–9.

Byrne, J., and L. Kelly. 1989. *Restructuring Probation as an Intermediate Sanction: An Evaluation of the Massachusetts Intensive Probation Supervision Program.* Final report to the National Institute of Justice.

Byrne, J., A. Lurigio, and S. C. Baird. 1989. "The Effectiveness of the 'New' Intensive Supervision Programs." *Research in Corrections* 5:1–70.

Byrne, J. and A. Pattavina. 1992. "The Effectiveness Issue: Assessing What Works in the Adult Community Corrections System." In *Smart Sentencing: The Emergence of Intermediate Sanctions,* ed. J. Byrne, A. Lurigio, and J. Petersilia. Newbury Park, Calif.: Sage.

Carter, R., and L. Wilkins. 1976. *Probation, Parole, and Community Corrections,* 2d ed. New York: Wiley.

Clear, T., and A. Braga. 1994. "Intensive Supervision—Why Bother?" In *Innovative Trends and Specialized Strategies in Community-Based Corrections,* ed. C. Fields. New York: Garland.

Clear, T., J. Byrne, and J. Dvoskin. 1993. "The Transition from Being an Inmate: Discharge Planning, Parole, and Community-Based Services for Mentally Ill Offenders." In *Mental Illness in America's Prisons,* ed. H. Steadman and J. Cocozza. Seattle: National Coalition for the Mentally Ill in the Criminal Justice System.

Clear, T., and G. Cole. 1994. *American Corrections,* 3d ed. Belmont, Calif.: Wadsworth.

Clear, T., and K. Gallagher. 1983. "Screening Devices in Probation and Parole: Management Problems." *Evaluation Review* 7:217–34.

————. 1985. "Probation and Parole Supervision: A Review of Current Classification Practices." *Crime and Delinquency* 31:423–43.

Clear, T., and V. O'Leary. 1983. *Controlling the Offender in the Community.* Lexington, Mass.: Lexington Books.

Cunniff, M., and M. Shilton. 1991. *Variations on Felony Probation: Persons under Supervision in 32 Urban and Suburban Counties.* Washington, D.C.: United States Department of Justice.

Dawson, J. 1990. *Felony Probation in State Courts.* Washington, D.C.: National Institute of Justice.

Dillingham, S. 1990. *National Corrections Reporting Program, 1985.* Washington, D.C.: National Institute of Justice.

Erwin, B. 1986. "Turning up the Heat on Probationers in Georgia." *Federal Probation* 50:17–29.

Florida Department of Corrections. 1989. "Boot Camp Evaluation and Boot Camp Commitment Rate." Unpublished report by the Bureau of Planning, Research, and Statistics.

Geerken, M., and H. Hayes. 1993. "Probation and Parole: Public Risks and the Future of Incarceration Alternatives." *Criminology* 31:549–64.

Gendreau, P., F. Cullen, and D. Bonta. 1994. "Intensive Rehabilitation Supervision: The Next Generation in Community Corrections?" *Federal Probation* 58:72–79.

Georgia Department of Corrections. 1989. "Georgia's Special Alternative Incarceration." Unpublished report to the Shock Incarceration Conference, Atlanta.

Gottfredson, S. D., and D. M. Gottfredson. 1992. *Incapacitation Strategies and the Criminal Career.* LEIC Monograph Series, no. 8. Sacramento: California Department of Justice, December.

Hillsman, S., and J. Greene. 1992. "The Use of Fines as an Intermediate Sanction." In *Smart Sentencing: The Emergence of Intermediate Sanctions,* ed. J. Byrne, A. Lurigio, and J. Petersilia. Newbury Park, Calif.: Sage.

Lab, S. P., and J. T. Whitehead. 1990. "From 'Nothing Works' to 'The Appropriate Works': The Latest Stop in the Search for the Secular Grail." *Criminology* 28: 405–17.

Langan, P. 1994. "Between Prison and Probation: Intermediate Sanctions." *Science* 264:791–93.

Langan, P., and M. Cunniff. 1992. "Recidivism of Felons on Probation, 1986–89." *Special Report.* Washington, D.C.: U.S. Department of Justice.

Latessa, E. and H. Allen. 1982. "Halfway Houses and Parole: A National Assessment." *Journal of Criminal Justice* 10:153–63.

Latessa, E., and L. Travis. 1992. "Residential Community Correctional Programs." In *Smart Sentencing: The Emergence of Intermediate Sanctions,* ed. J. Byrne, A. Lurigio, and J. Petersilia. Newbury Park, Calif.: Sage.

Lipsey, M. 1992. "Juvenile Delinquency Treatment: A Meta-analytic Inquiry into the Variability of Effects." In *Meta-Analysis for Explanation: A Casebook,* ed. Thomas Cook. New York: Sage.

Lipton, D., R. Martinson, and T. Wilks. 1975. *Effectiveness of Correctional Treatment: A Survey of Treatment Evaluation Studies.* Springfield, Mass.: Praeger.

Logan, C. H., and G. G. Gaes. 1993. "Meta-analysis and the Rehabilitation of Punishment." *Justice Quarterly* 10:245–64.

McDevitt, J., and R. Miliano. 1992. "Day Reporting Centers: An Innovative Concept in Intermediate Sanctions." In *Smart Sentencing: The Emergence of Intermediate Sanctions,* ed. J. Byrne, A. Lurigio, and J. Petersilia. Newbury Park, Calif.: Sage.

McDonald, D. 1986. *Punishment without Walls: Community Service Sentences in New York City.* New Brunswick, N.J.: Rutgers University Press.

———. 1989. "The Cost of Corrections." *Research in Corrections* 4:1–72.

———. 1992. "Punishing Labor: Unpaid Community Service as a Criminal Sentence." In *Smart Sentencing: The Emergence of Intermediate Sanctions,* ed. J. Byrne, A. Lurigio, and J. Petersilia. Newbury Park, Calif.: Sage.

MacKenzie, D. 1991. "The Parole Performance of Offenders Released From Shock Incarceration." *Journal of Quantitative Criminology* 7:213–36.

MacKenzie, D., and D. Parent. 1992. "Boot Camp Prisons for Young Offenders." In *Smart Sentencing: The Emergence of Intermediate Sanctions*, ed. J. Byrne, A. Lurigio, and J. Petersilia. Newbury Park, Calif.: Sage.

Markley, G., and M. Eisenberg. 1987. *Evaluation of the Texas Parole Classification and Case Management System.* Austin: Texas Board of Pardons and Paroles.

Matthews, T. 1991. *Survey of Probation Cost Considerations.* Lexington, Ky.: American Probation and Parole Association.

Morris, N., and M. Tonry. 1990. *Between Prison and Probation: Intermediate Punishments in a Rational Sentencing System.* New York: Oxford University Press.

National Institute of Corrections. 1981. *Model Probation and Parole Management Project Handbook.* Washington, D.C.

New York State Division of Parole. 1989. "Shock Incarceration: One Year Out." Unpublished report.

Nurco, D., T. Hanlan, and T. Kinlock. 1990. *Offenders, Drugs, and Treatment.* Washington, D.C.: United States Department of Justice.

O'Leary, V., and T. Clear. 1994. *Community Corrections into the 21st Century.* Washington, D.C.: National Institute of Corrections (forthcoming).

Palmer, T. 1992. *The Re-Emergence of Correctional Intervention.* Newbury Park, Calif.: Sage.

Parent, D. 1989. *Shock Incarceration: An Overview of Existing Programs.* Washington, D.C.: National Institute of Justice.

———. 1990. *Day Reporting Centers for Criminal Offenders: A Descriptive Analysis of Existing Programs.* Washington, D.C.: National Institute of Justice.

Pearson, F., and A. Harper. 1990. "Contingent Intermediate Sentences: New Jersey's Intensive Supervision Program." *Crime and Delinquency* 36:75–86.

Petersilia, J. 1987. *Expanding Options for Criminal Sentencing.* Santa Monica, Calif.: Rand.

———. 1994. "What Punishes? Inmates Rank the Severity of Prison vs. Intermediate Sanctions." *Federal Probation* 58 (1).

Petersilia, J., and E. Deschenes. 1994. "Perceptions of Punishment: Inmates and Staff Rank the Severity of Prison versus Intermediate Sanctions." *Prison Journal* 73, no. 3 (September).

Petersilia, J., J. Peterson, and S. Turner. 1992. *Intensive Probation and Parole: Research Findings and Policy Implications.* Santa Monica, Calif.: Rand.

Petersilia, J., and S. Turner. 1993. "Intensive Probation and Parole." In *Crime and Justice: A Review of Research*, ed. M. H. Tonry and N. Morris, vol. 19. Chicago: University of Chicago Press.

Petersilia, J., S. Turner, J. Kahan, and J. Peterson. 1985. *Granting Felons Probation: Public Risks and Alternatives.* Santa Monica, Calif.: Rand.

Reiss, A., and J. Roth. eds. 1993. *Understanding and Preventing Violence.* Washington, D.C.: National Academy Press.

Renzema, M. 1992. "Home Confinement Programs: Development, Implementation, and Impact." In *Smart Sentencing: The Emergence of Intermediate Sanctions*, ed. J. Byrne, A. Lurigio, and J. Petersilia. Newbury Park, Calif.: Sage.

Renzema, M., and D. Skelton. 1990. *The Use of Electronic Monitoring by Criminal Justice Agencies in 1989.* Final report to the National Institute Of Justice.

Robison, J., and P. Takagi. 1976. "The Parole Violator as Organizational Reject." In *Probation, Parole and Community Corrections*, ed. R. Carter and L. Wilkins. New York: Wiley.

Ross, R., and E. Fabiano. 1985. *Time to Think: A Cognitive Model for Delinquency Prevention and Offender Rehabilitation.* Johnson City: Institute of Social Science and Arts.

Spelman, W. 1994. *Criminal Incapacitation.* New York: Plenum.

Taxman, F., and J. Byrne. 1994. "Punishment, Probation, and the Problem of Community Control: A Randomized Field Experiment on Absconder Location Strategies." In *Innovative Trends and Specialized Strategies in Community-Based Corrections*, ed. C. Fields. New York: Garland.

Tonry, M. 1990. "Stated and Latent Features of ISP." *Crime and Delinquency* 36:174–91.

Turner, S., J. Petersilia, and E. Deschenes. 1994. "The Implementation and Effectiveness of Drug Testing in Community Supervision: Results of an Experimental Evaluation." In *Drugs and Crime: Evaluating Public Policy Initiatives*, ed. D. MacKenzie and C. Uchida. Thousand Oaks, Calif.: Sage.

United States General Accounting Office (GAO). 1990. *Intermediate Sanctions: Their Impacts on Prison Crowding, Costs, and Recidivism.* Washington, D.C.

Vito, G. 1986. "Felony Probation and Recidivism: Replication and Response." *Federal Probation* 50:17–25.

von Hirsch, A., M. Wasik, and J. Greene. 1989. "Punishments in the Community and the Principles of Desert." *Rutgers Law Journal,* 20:595–618.

19. John J. DiIulio, Jr., Steven K. Smith, and Aaron J. Saiger, "The Federal Role in Crime Control"

Notes

The views expressed herein are solely those of the authors and do not represent those of the United States Government or the United States Department of Justice.

1. Weaver and Rockman 1993a.

2. DiIulio, Garvey, and Kettl 1993, 39. Also see Kettl (1993).

3. Weaver and Rockman 1993b, 459.

4. For example, see Martha Derthick's study (1972) of a federal community development program; also see Jeffrey L. Pressman and Aaron Wildavsky's study of the U.S. Economic Development Administration's public works project (1973).

5. Osborne 1993, 243.

6. For a general analysis, see Rivlin, (1992). For examples related to national health reform, see DiIulio and Nathan (1994). In this context, it is worth noting that

a recent blueprint for national governance identified criminal justice both as an area that should be left entirely to the states and localities, and as an area that merited new and expanded national government action; compare Osborne (1993) and Kilgore (1993).

7. Lindgren, 1992; Bureau of Justice Statistics (BJS) 1993a; Langan and Solari, 1993; Gilliard 1993.

8. BJS 1993a.

9. Federal Bureau of Investigation (FBI) 1992.

10. For examples, see Bayley (1985 and 1991) and Nadelmann (1993). It should be noted, however, that Nadelmann (see especially chapter 8) has found that, beginning in the 1970s, the American "war on drugs" triggered a "transformation of U.S. international law enforcement" which, over two decades, brought the criminal justice systems (investigation procedures, prosecution practices) of several contemporary European and Latin American democracies more in line with U.S. norms.

11. *Washington Post*/ABC News 1994.

12. National Women's Political Caucus 1987.

13. One of the most influential of these studies was Millsbaugh (1936).

14. President's Commission on Law Enforcement and Administration of Justice 1967, 285.

15. Diamond and Alligood 1971; DiIulio 1992.

16. Keve 1991.

17. Morrison 1992.

18. Mayer 1992, 19–20.

19. McKelvey 1977; Friedman 1993.

20. For example, in a typical survey, 22 percent of respondents volunteered "both" when asked whether government should rely more heavily on "much stricter law enforcement and severer punishments" on the one hand or "comprehensive programs that get at the root of the problems that cause people to commit crimes" on the other. Forty-four percent favored the former alone, 31 percent the latter (BJS 1993b, 195).

21. DiIulio 1991, chap. 7.

22. *PS: Political Science and Politics* 1994.

23. One of the few works on the subject remains Nagel et al. (1983).

24. Mayer 1992.

25. Between 1971 and 1987, the number of sworn officers per 1,000 resident population in fifty-nine big-city police departments fell from 2.4 to 2.3; see Maguire and Flanagan (1991, 35, 46). Also see the estimates of number of officers actually on the streets in several big cities at any given time in DiIulio (1993, sec. 3). In 1989 about 4 million persons were under correctional supervision, 17 percent in prison, 10 percent in jail, 62 percent on probation, and 11 percent on parole; see BJS (1991, 5). On time served in prison, see the following: Langan 1991, 1568–73; BJS 1987; Perez 1987; and BJS 1994b, 23.

26. After proponents tried and failed to place a three-strikes-and-you're-out initiative on the ballot in 1992, the initiative was placed on the 1993 ballot with almost 300,000 signatures and was passed in November 1993 with 76 percent of the vote. The initiative campaign was orchestrated by an assault victim turned activist and was

passed despite substantial opposition from the criminal justice system establishment in Washington. See Lewis (1993 and 1993). A California initiative patterned on the Washington initiative has gained support (Gross 1993).

27. Advisory Commission on Intergovernmental Relations (ACIR) 1993, 207.

28. The LEAA and its programs have spawned a substantial historical and evaluative literature. The most comprehensive empirical review of the early years of LEAA is ACIR (1977). Important evaluative studies include: Twentieth Century Fund Task Force on the Law Enforcement Assistance Administration (1976), which includes a background paper by Darrel Paster and Victor Navasky; Feely and Sarat (1980); and Hudzik (1984). A useful review article is Diegelman (1982).

29. Office of Law Enforcement Assistance 1968.

30. Omnibus Crime Control and Safe Streets Act 1968, Title I, Law Enforcement Assistance.

31. Title I, Part C, Sec. 307 of the Safe Streets Act designates projects dealing with "prevention, detection, and control of organized crime and of riots" as areas for special emphasis.

32. As cited in *Attorney General's First Annual Report* (1972, 37).

33. Law Enforcement Assistance Administration (LEAA) 1980, 97.

34. As quoted in Hucker (1979, 366).

35. Maguire and Flanagan 1991, 353.

36. For related discussion see Anton (1989, 115–19).

37. *Congressional Quarterly Weekly Report* 1982.

38. Office of National Drug Control Policy (ONDCP) 1992a, 141 and 1992b, 3.

39. BJS 1993a.

40. BJS 1992, 195.

41. FBI 1992, 212.

42. Innes 1988; Beck et al. 1993.

43. Stutman and Esposito 1992; Kleiman 1992.

44. A typical survey found that "crime is the number one specific issue according to 33% of voters in the country." See Tarrance Group (1994, 3).

45. DiIulio, Kettl, and Garvey 1994.

46. Primary source material on the BJA grants-making process, with particular emphasis on the role of the state planning agency, can be found in Dunworth and Saiger (1992).

47. Dunworth and Saiger 1992, 47–48.

48. Sec. 501 of the Omnibus Crime Control and Safe Streets Act 1968, as amended.

49. Bureau of Justice Assistance 1993, 5.

50. Bureau of Justice Assistance 1993, 5.

51. Bureau of Justice Assistance 1994, 3.

52. Kettl refers to "double" discretion (1983, 57). A model of this discretion in terms of "principal agent" theory is provided in Chubb (1985, 994–1015).

53. BJS 1994, 55.

54. BJS 1994, 12; Snell 1993, 61.

55. BJS 1994, 23.
56. Bayley 1993.
57. Reaves 1993, 2.
58. See BJS (1994).
59. See Moore and Alpert (1993); see also BJS (1994).
60. DiIulio, Garvey, and Kettl 1994.

References

Advisory Commission on Intergovernmental Relations (ACIR). 1977. *Safe Streets Reconsidered: The Block Grant Experience 1968–1975*. Washington, D.C.

———. 1993. *The Role of General Government Elected Officials in Criminal Justice.* Washington, D.C., May.

Anton, Thomas J. 1989. *American Federalism and Public Policy.* New York: Random House.

Attorney General's First Annual Report: Federal Law Enforcement and Criminal Justice Assistance Activities. 1972. Washington, D.C.: United States Government Printing Office, September.

Bayley, David. 1985. *Patterns of Policing: An International Comparative Perspective.* New Brunswick, N.J.: Rutgers University Press.

———. 1991. *Forces of Order: Policing Modern Japan.* Berkeley and Los Angeles: University of California Press.

———. 1993. "The Cop Fallacy." *New York Times,* 16 August, A17.

Beck, Allen, et al. 1993. *Survey of State Prison Inmates, 1991.* Washington, D.C.: Bureau of Justice Statistics, March.

Bureau of Justice Assistance. 1993. *Fiscal Year 1993 Review of State Formula Grant Strategies.* Fact Sheet. Washington, D.C., November.

———. 1994. *Edward Byrne Memorial State and Local Law Enforcement Assistance.* Fact Sheet. Washington, D.C., January.

Bureau of Justice Statistics (BJS). 1987. *Sentencing and Time Served.* Washington, D.C.: United States Department of Justice.

———. 1991. *Correctional Populations in the United States, 1989.* Washington, D.C.: U.S. Department of Justice, October.

———. 1992. *Drugs, Crime, and the Justice System: A Report to the Nation.* Washington, D.C..

———. 1993a. *Federal Criminal Case Processing, 1982–91.* Washington, D.C., November.

———. 1993b. *Sourcebook of Criminal Justice Statistics 1992.* Washington, D.C.: United States Department of Justice.

———. 1994a. *Bureau of Justice Statistics/Princeton University Working Group on Community Policing Evaluation.* Washington, D.C.: Brookings, 28 January.

———. 1994b. *National Corrections Reporting Program, 1991.* Washington, D.C., February.

Chubb, John E. 1985. "The Political Economy of Federalism." *American Political Science Review* 79:994–1015.

Congressional Quarterly Weekly Report. 1982. "Administration of Justice Escapes Deep Spending Cuts in New Reagan Budget Plan," 13 February, 275.

Derthick, Martha. 1972. *New Towns In-Town: Why a Federal Program Failed.* Washington, D.C.: Urban Institute.

Diamond, Robert A., and Arlene Alligood, eds. 1971. *Crime and the Law: The Fight by Federal Forces to Control Public Problem Number One in America.* Washington, D.C.: Congressional Quarterly.

Diegelman, Robert F. 1982. "Federal Financial Assistance for Crime Control: Lessons of the LEAA Experience." *Journal of Criminal Law and Criminology* 73 (3): 994–1011.

DiIulio, John J., Jr. 1991. *No Escape: The Future of American Corrections.* New York: Basic Books.

———. 1992. "Crime." In *Setting Domestic Priorities: What Can Government Do?* ed. Henry J. Aaron and Charles L. Schultze, chap. 4. Washington, D.C.: Brookings.

———. 1993. *Community Policing in Wisconsin: Can It Cut Crime?* Milwaukee: Wisconsin Policy Research Institute.

DiIulio, John J., Jr., Gerald J. Garvey, and Donald F. Kettl. 1993. *Improving Government Performance: An Owner's Manual.* Washington, D.C.: Brookings.

DiIulio, John J., Jr., Donald F. Kettl, and Gerald J. Garvey. 1994. "An Ounce of Implementation Is Worth a Pound of Policy." In *Making Health Reform Work: The View from the States,* ed. John J. DiIulio, Jr., and Richard P. Nathan. Washington, D.C.: Brookings.

DiIulio, John J., Jr., and Richard P. Nathan, eds. 1994. *Making Health Reform Work: The View from the States.* Washington, D.C.: Brookings.

Dunworth, Terence, and Aaron Saiger. 1992. *State Strategic Planning under the Drug Formula Grant Program.* Washington, D.C.: National Institute of Justice.

Federal Bureau of Investigation (FBI). 1992. *Crime in the United States 1991.* Washington, D.C., August.

Feeley, Malcolm M., and Austin D. Sarat. 1980. *The Policy Dilemma: Federal Crime Policy and the Law Enforcement Assistance Administration.* Minneapolis: University of Minnesota Press.

Friedman, Lawrence. 1993. Crime and Punishment in American History. New York: Basic Books.

Gilliard, Darrell K. 1993. *Prisoners in 1992.* Washington, D.C.: Bureau of Justice Statistics, May.

Gross, Jane. 1993. "Drive to Keep Repeat Felons in Prison Gains in California." *New York Times,* 26 December, A1.

Hucker, Charles W. 1979. "LEAA Funding Controversy Deciding Agency's Future." *Congressional Quarterly Weekly Report.* 3 March, 366.

Hudzik, John K. 1984. *Federal Aid to Criminal Justice: Rhetoric, Results, Lessons.* Washington, D.C.: National Criminal Justice Association.

Innes, Christopher A. 1988. *Profile of State Prison Inmates, 1986.* Washington, D.C.: Bureau of Justice Statistics, January.

Kettl, Donald F. 1983. *The Regulation of American Federalism.* Baton Rouge: Louisiana State University Press.

———. 1993. *Sharing Power: Public Governance and Private Markets.* Washington, D.C.: Brookings.

Keve, Paul W. 1991. *Prisons and the American Conscience: A History of U.S. Federal Corrections*. Carbondale: Southern Illinois University Press.

Kilgore, Ed. 1993. "Safe Streets and Neighborhoods." In *Manadate for Change*, ed. Will Marshall and Martin Schramm. New York: Berkeley Books.

Kleiman, Mark A. R. 1992. *Against Excess: Drug Policy for Results*. New York: Basic Books.

Langan, Patrick. 1991. "America's Soaring Prison Population." *Science*, 29 March, 1568–73.

Langan, Patrick A., and Richard Solari. 1993. *National Judicial Reporting Program, 1990*. Washington, D.C.: Bureau of Justice Statistics, December.

Law Enforcement Assistance Administration (LEAA). 1980. *LEAA Eleventh Annual Report, Fiscal Year 1979*. Washington, D.C.: United States Department of Justice.

———. 1993. "I-593 Backers Open to Law's Fine-Tuning: Some Suggest Narrowing Scope of 'Three Strikes You're Out'." *Seattle Times*, 5 November, B4.

Lewis, Peter. 1993. " 'Three Strikes' Initiative Gains Strength, Takes Aim at Felons— But Opponents Say Measure Will Be Drain on Taxpayers." *Seattle Times*, 31 August, A1.

Lindgren, Sue A. 1992. *Justice Expenditure and Employment, 1990*. Washington, D.C.: Bureau of Justice Statistics, September.

Maguire, Kathleen, and Timothy J. Flanagan, eds. 1991. *Sourcebook of Criminal Justice Statistics. 1990*. Washington, D.C.: Bureau of Justice Statistics.

Mayer, William G. 1992. *The Changing American Mind*. Ann Arbort: University of Michigan Press.

McKelvey, Blake. 1977. *American Prisons: A History of Good Intentions*. Montclair, N.J. Patterson-Smith.

Millsbaugh, Arthur C. 1936. *Local Democracy and Crime Control*. Washington, D.C.: Brookings.

Moore, Mark H., and Geoffrey Alpert. 1993. "Measuring Police Performance in the New Paradigm of Policing." *Performance Measures for the Criminal Justice System*. Discussion Papers from the BJS-Princeton Project. Washington, D.C.: United States Department of Justice, October.

Morrison, David C. 1992. "Police Action." *National Journal*, February, 267–70.

Nadelmann, Ethan. 1993. *Cops across Borders: The Internationalization of U.S. Criminal Law Enforcement.*" University Park: Pennsylvania State University Press.

Nagel, Stuart, et al., eds. 1983. *The Political Science of Criminal Justice*. Springfield, Ill.: Charles C. Thomas.

National Drug Control Strategy. 1992. Washington, D.C.: United States Government Printing Office, January.

National Women's Political Caucus. 1987. Poll conducted 26 May.

Office of Law Enforcement Assistance. 1968. *LEAA Grants and Contracts, Fiscal 1966–1968*. Washington, D.C.: United States Department of Justice.

Office of National Drug Control Policy (ONDCP). 1992a. *National Drug Control Strategy: A Nation Responds to Drug Use*. Washington, D.C., January.

———. 1992b. *The War on Drugs: A Progress Report*. ONDCP Bulletin no. 4. Washington, D.C., February.

Omnibus Crime Control and Safe Streets Act. 1968. P.L. 90-351.

Osborne, David. 1993. "A New Federal Compact." In *Mandate for Change,* ed. Will Marshall and Martin Schramm. New York: Berkeley Books.

Perez, Jacob. 1987. *Tracking Offenders, 1987.* Washington, D.C.: Bureau of Justice Statistics, October.

President's Commission on Law Enforcement and Administration of Justice. 1967. *The Challenge of Crime in a Free Society.* Washington, D.C.: United States Government Printing Office.

Pressman, Jeffrey L., and Aaron Wildavsky. 1973. *Implementation.* Berkeley: University of California Press.

PS: Political Science and Politics. 1994. "Forum: Public Opinion, Institutions, and Policy Making" 27, no. 1 (March): 5–38.

Reaves, Brian A. 1993. *Census of State and local Law Enforcement Agencies, 1992.* Washington, D.C.: Bureau of Justice Statistics, July.

Rivlin, Alice M. 1992. *Reviving the American Dream: The Economy, the States and the Federal Government.* Washington, D.C.: Brookings.

Snell, Tracy L. 1993. *Correctional Populations in the United States, 1991.* Washington, D.C.: Bureau of Justice Statistics, August.

Stutman, Robert M., and Richard J. Esposito. 1992. *Dead on Delivery: Inside the Drug Wars, Straight from the Street.* New York: Warner Books.

Tarrance Group. 1994. *The 1994 Mid-Term Elections: An Issues Perspective.*

Twentieth Century Fund Task Force on the Law Enforcement Assistance Administration. 1976. *Law Enforcement: The Federal Role.* New York: McGraw Hill.

United States General Accounting Office. 1993. *War on Drugs: Federal Assistance to State and Local Drug Enforcement.* GAO/GGD-93-86. Washington, D.C., April.

Washington Post/ABC News. 1994. Poll conducted 24–27 February.

Weaver, R. Kent, and Bert A. Rockman, eds. 1993a. *Do Institutions Matter? Government Capabilities in the United States and Abroad.* Washington, D.C.: Brookings.

Weaver, R. Kent, and Bert A. Rockman. 1993b. "When and Where Do Institutions Matter?" In *Do Institutions Matter? Government Capabilities in the United States and Abroad,* ed. R. Kent Weaver and Bert A. Rockman. Washington, D.C.: Brookings.

20. Alfred Blumstein and Joan Petersilia, "Investing in Criminal Justice Research"

Chapter 20 is not annotated.

References

Ellickson, Phyllis. 1992. "Helping Urban Teenagers Avoid High-Risk Behavior: What We've Learned from Prevention Research." In *Urban America.* Santa Monica, Calif.: Rand.

New York Times. 1994. "The Nation's Changing Concerns." 23 April.

Petersilia, Joan, and Susan Turner. 1993. "Intensive Probation and Parole." In *Crime and Justice: A Review of Research,* ed. Michael H. Tonry 17:281–335. Chicago: University of Chicago Press.

Wilson, James Q., ed. 1983. *Crime and Public Policy.* San Francisco: ICS Press.

21. James Q. Wilson, "Crime and Public Policy"

Notes

This chapter draws on the essays appearing in this book but is neither a complete summary of them nor always in agreement with them. I have benefited greatly from the writings of the authors who have contributed to this book, but many of them will disagree with some of the inferences I have drawn (as they will disagree with what other contributors have written).

1. These comparisons depend on official police statistics. There are of course errors in such data. But essentially the same pattern emerges from comparing nations on the basis of victimization surveys.

2. Female high rate offenders are *much* less common than male ones, but to the extent they exist they display most of these traits.

3. A summary of what we know about the certainty of punishment can be found in Wilson (1983, chap. 7). I cannot recall any good studies of the effect of the swiftness of penalties on crime; as criminologist H. Laurence Ross put it, "celerity is the orphan variable in deterrence research."

4. Many individual programs involve so few subjects that a good evaluation will reveal no positive effect even if one exists. By a technique called meta-analysis, scores of individual studies can be pooled into one mega-evaluation; because there are now hundreds or thousands of subjects, even small gains can be identified. The best of these meta-analyses, such as the one by Mark Lipsey (1991), suggest modest positive effects.

5. In Charleston, South Carolina, the police pay this reward to anyone identifying a student carrying a weapon to school or to some school event. Because many boys carry guns to school in order to display or brag about them, the motive to carry disappears once any display alerts a potential informer.

6. I take these cost calculations from Kleiman et al. (1988).

7. I anticipate that at this point some readers will call for legalizing or decriminalizing drugs as the "solution" to this problem. Before telling me this, I hope they will read my argument against it in Wilson (1990). I have not changed my mind.

8. It is not clear why manganese has this effect; but we know that it effects the availability of a precursor of serotonin, a neurotransmitter, and low levels of serotonin are now strongly linked to violent and impulsive behavior.

References

Blumstein, Alfred, Jacqueline Cohen, and Paul Hsieh. 1982. "The Duration of Adult Criminal Careers." Carnegie Mellon University School of Urban and Public Affairs. Unpublished.

Cavanagh, David P., and Mark A. R. Kleiman. 1990. *A Cost-Benefit Analysis of Prison Cell Construction and Alternative Sanctions*. Cambridge, Mass.: BOTEC Analysis Corporation.

Dawson, Deborah A. 1991. "Family Structure and Children's Health: United States, 1988." *Vital and Health Statistics,* series 10, no. 178 (June).

DiIulio, John J., Jr., and Anne Morrison Piehl. 1991. "Does Prison Pay?" *Brookings Review,* Fall.

Driscoll, Connie. 1993. "Chicago's House of Hope." *Policy Review,* Summer, 50–54.

Farrington, David P. 1991. "Explaining the Beginning, Progress, and Ending of Anti-social Behavior from Birth to Adulthood." In *Advances in Criminological Theory,* ed. Joan McCord, vol. 3. New Brunswick, N.J.: Transaction.

Farrington, David P., and Patrick A. Langan. 1992. "Changes in Crime and Punishment in England and America in the 1980s." *Justice Quarterly* 9 (March): 5–46.

Farrington, David P., Lloyd E. Ohlin, and James Q. Wilson. 1986. *Understanding and Controlling Crime.* New York: Springer-Verlag.

Farrington, David P. and Per-Olof H. Wikstrom. 1993. "Changes in Crime and Punishment in England and Sweden in the 1980s." *Studies on Crime and Prevention* 2:142–70.

Fishbein, Diana, and Susan Pease. 1988. "The Effects of Diet on Behavior: Implications for Criminology and Corrections." *Research in Corrections* 1 (June).

Furstenberg, Frank, et al. 1989. "Teen-Age Pregnancy and Child-Bearing." *American Psychologist* 44:313–20.

Gottschalk, Louis A., et al. 1991. "Abnormalities in Hair Trace Elements as Indicators of Aberrant Behavior." *Comprehensive Psychiatry* 28:212–23.

Kalish, Carol B. 1988. *International Crime Rates.* Bureau of Justice Statistics Special Report. Washington, D.C., May.

Kleiman, Mark, et al. 1988. "Imprisonment-to-Offense Ratios." Kennedy School of Government Working Paper 89-06-02, Harvard University, August 5.

Kurz, Gwen A., and Louis E. Moore. 1994. *The Eight Percent Problem: Chronic Juvenile Offender Recidivism.* Santa Ana, Calif.: Orange County Probation Department, March.

Langan, Patrick A. 1991. "America's Soaring Prison Population." *Science* 251 (29 March): 1568–73.

———. 1994. "Between Prison and Probation." *Science* 254:791–93.

Lipsey, Mark W. 1991. "Juvenile Delinquency Treatment: A Meta-Analytic Inquiry into the Variability of Effects." In *Meta-Analysis for Explanation: A Casebook.* New York: Sage.

McLanahan, Sara, and Gary Sandefur. 1994. *Growing Up with a Single Parent: What Hurts, What Helps.* Cambridge, Mass.: Harvard University Press, forthcoming.

Petersilia, Joan, and Susan Turner. 1993. *Evaluating Intensive Supervised Probation/ Parole: Results of a Nationwide Experiment.* National Institute of Justice Research in Brief. Washington, D.C., May.

Wilson, James Q. 1983. *Thinking about Crime,* rev. ed. New York: Basic Books.

———. 1990. "Against the Legalization of Drugs." *Commentary,* February, 21–28.

———. 1993. "The Family-Values Debate." *Commentary,* April, 24–31.

———. 1994. "Just Take Away Their Guns." *New York Times Magazine,* 20 March.

Wilson, James Q., and Richard J. Herrnstein. 1985. *Crime and Human Nature.* New York: Simon and Schuster.

Yoshikawa, Hirokazu. 1994. "Prevention as Cumulative Protection: Effects of Early Family Support and Education on Chronic Delinquency and Its Risks." *Psychological Bulletin* 115:28–54.

CONTRIBUTORS

Alfred Blumstein is J. Erik Jonsson University Professor of Urban Systems and Operations Research at the H. John Heinz III School of Public Policy and Management, Carnegie Mellon University, where he also served as dean from 1986 to 1993. Dr. Blumstein was the 1991–92 president of the American Society of Criminology and in 1987 received the society's Edwin H. Sutherland Award for his contributions to research.

David Boyum is senior research analyst at BOTEC Analysis Corporation and research fellow in drug policy in the Department of Neurobiology, Harvard Medical School. Dr. Boyum has been an adjunct lecturer at Harvard's John F. Kennedy School of Government, a visiting scholar at the Yale School of Organization and Management, and a postdoctoral fellow at the University of Texas Health Science Center at Houston.

Anthony A. Braga is a doctoral candidate in the School of Criminal Justice, Rutgers University, and research associate at the Center for Crime Prevention Studies there. He is field research director for a project funded by the National Institute of Justice to implement problem-oriented policing in Jersey City, New Jersey.

Patricia A. Brennan is research associate at the Social Science Research Institute, University of Southern California, where she has most recently been principal investigator for a research project on psychopathology and criminal violence, carried out under a 1992-1994 grant from the Harry Frank Guggenheim Foundation. Dr. Brennan also teaches in USC's Department of Psychology.

Todd R. Clear is professor in the School of Criminal Justice, Rutgers University, and has received the Cincinnati Award of the American Probation and Parole Association for his research on supervision technologies. Two of Dr. Clear's recent books are *Controlling the Offender in the Community: American Corrections* and *Harm in American Penology.*

Philip J. Cook is the ITT/Terry Sanford Professor of Public Policy and professor of economics and sociology at Duke University. In addition to numerous journal articles and chapters in scholarly books, Dr. Cook's publications include *Selling Hope: State Lotteries in America* (with Charles T. Clotfelter) and a forthcoming book (with Robert H. Frank) *The Winner Take All Society.*

615

John J. DiIulio, Jr. is professor of politics and public affairs at Princeton University, founding director of the Brookings Institution Center for Public Management, and a member of the National Commission on the State and Local Public Service. Dr. DiIulio has received the American Political Science Association's Leonard D. White Award in public administration. The author or volume editor of many books, he is coauthor (with James Q. Wilson) of *American Government: Institutions and Policies.*

Edward Donnerstein is professor of communication and psychology at the University of California, Santa Barbara, and a member of the American Psychological Association's Commission on Violence and Youth. Dr. Donnerstein's many scientific articles and books include *Big World, Small Screen: The Role of Television in American Society,* winner of the American Psychological Association's Division 46 Award for distinguished contribution to psychology and media.

Brian Forst is associate professor in the Department of Justice, Law, and Society, School of Public Affairs, the American University. Dr. Forst is a member of the American Board of Forensic Examiners and of the Governor's Committee on Prison and Jail Population Forecasting of the state of Virginia. He is coauthor of *What Happens after Arrest?* and volume editor of *The Socio-Economics of Crime and Justice.*

Richard B. Freeman is Herbert Ascherman Professor of Economics at Harvard University, program director for labor studies at the National Bureau of Economic Research, and faculty cochair of the Harvard University Trade Union Program. Dr. Freeman is the author or editor of many books, including the newly published volume *Working under Different Rules.*

Peter W. Greenwood is director of the Rand Corporation's Criminal Justice Program and is currently directing several evaluations of preventive and correctional interventions for high-risk juveniles. Dr. Greenwood has published extensively on police investigation practices, prosecution policy, criminal careers, selective incapacitation, juvenile justice, and corrections. His works include *Selective Incapacitation.*

R. J. Herrnstein was Edgar Pierce Professor of Psychology at Harvard University and a member of the American Academy of Arts and Sciences. Among his books are *I.Q. in the Meritocracy, Crime and Human Nature* (with James Q. Wilson), and the new study *The Bell Curve: Intelligence and Class Structure in American Life* (with Charles Murray). Professor Herrnstein died on September 13, 1994.

Travis Hirschi is a Regents Professor at the University of Arizona. A past president of the American Society of Criminology, Professor Hirschi is a recipient of that society's Edwin H. Sutherland Award. He is the author of numerous articles and books, notably *Causes of Delinquency* and *Measuring Delinquency* (with Michael Hindelang and Joseph Weiss) and *A General Theory of Crime* and *The Generality of Deviance* (both with Michael Gottfredson).

Mark A. R. Kleiman is associate professor of public policy at the John F. Kennedy School of Government, Harvard University. He was formerly head of the Office of Policy and Management Analysis of the Criminal Division of the U.S. Department of Justice. Among Dr. Kleiman's publications are *Against Excess: Drug Policy for Results* and *Marijuana: Costs of Control.*

Malcolm W. Klein is professor of sociology and director of the Social Science Research Institute, which he founded, at the University of Southern California. Dr. Klein is a past president of the California Association of Criminal Justice Research and a recipient of the Edwin H. Sutherland Award, the highest honor of the American Society of Criminology. He is the author of many publications, including the forthcoming book *The American Street Gang*.

Daniel Linz is professor of communication and psychology and director of the Law and Society Program at the University of California, Santa Barbara. Dr. Linz has published extensively on mass media effects (particularly those concerning sex and violence), policy, and law. His most recent books include *The Question of Pornography: Research Findings and Policy Implications* (with Edward Donnerstein and Steven Penrod) and *Pornography* (with Neil Malamuth).

James Lynch is associate professor in the Department of Justice, Law, and Society, School of Public Affairs, the American University. A former research associate at the Bureau of Social Science Research and a member of the Office for Improvements in the Administration of Justice in the U.S. Department of Justice, he is coauthor (with Albert Biderman) of *Understanding Crime Incidence Statistics: Why the UCR Diverges from the NCS*.

Sarnoff A. Mednick is professor of psychology at the University of Southern California and research professor at USC's Social Science Research Institute. Dr. Mednick's extensive research in psychiatry and psychology is reflected in a large number of publications, including the forthcoming volumes *Neural Development and Schizophrenia* (with J. M. Hollister) and *Schizotypal Personality Disorder* (with A. Raine and T. Lencz).

Mark H. Moore is the Guggenheim Professor of Criminal Justice Policy and Management at the John F. Kennedy School of Government, Harvard University, and faculty chairman of the Kennedy School's Program in Criminal Justice Policy and Management. Among Dr. Moore's many publications are the books *Buy and Bust: The Effective Regulation of an Illicit Market in Heroin* and *Dangerous Offenders: Elusive Targets of Justice*, as well as *Beyond 911: A New Era for Policing*.

Charles Murray is the Bradley Fellow at the American Enterprise Institute. Widely published and a frequent contributor to televised commentary and debate on policy issues, Dr. Murray is best known as an author for *Losing Ground* and *In Pursuit of Happiness and Good Government*. His latest book, written with the late R. J. Herrnstein, is the new work on the effect of intellectual ability, *The Bell Curve: Intelligence and Class Structure in American Life*.

Joan Petersilia is professor of criminology, law, and society in the School of Social Ecology, University of California, Irvine, and former director of the Rand Corporation's Criminal Justice Program, to which she now acts as a consultant. Dr. Petersilia has served as president of the California Association for Criminal Justice Research and president of the American Society of Criminology. She is the 1994 recipient of the ASC's August Vollmer Award for her distinguished contributions to criminal justice policy.

Aaron J. Saiger is a doctoral candidate in public affairs at the Woodrow Wilson School of Public and International Affairs, Princeton University, where he is a National Science Foundation Predoctoral Fellow. He was formerly a resident consultant in the Criminal Justice Program of the Rand Corporation.

Robert J. Sampson is professor of sociology at the University of Chicago and re-search fellow at the American Bar Foundation. Dr. Sampson's extensive publications on crime and community include *The Social Ecology of Crime* (edited with J. Byrne) and his most recent book (coauthored with John H. Laub), *Crime in the Making: Pathways and Turning Points through Life.*

Lawrence W. Sherman is professor of criminology at the University of Maryland and president of the Crime Control Institute. He is also chief criminologist of the In-dianapolis Police Department and director of gun crime policy for the mayor of Indianapolis. Dr. Sherman's book *Policing Domestic Violence: Experiments and Dilemmas* received the 1993-94 American Sociological Association Distinguished Scholarship Award in Crime, Law, and Deviance.

Steven K. Smith is an associate director with the Bureau of Justice Statistics, in Washington, D.C. Dr. Smith has worked as an analyst at the U.S. Information Agency and the U.S. Department of Housing and Urban Development and has held several university faculty positions.

Jackson Toby is professor of sociology at Rutgers University. For twenty-five years he was director of the Institute for Criminological Research at Rutgers and conducted research on school violence, on intermediate punishment (such as boot camp pro-grams) to control crime, and on factors causing dropouts from high school and possible ways to deal with this problem. Professor Toby's opinion pieces on crime and education appear in the *Wall Street Journal*, the *New York Times*, and other newspapers.

Jan Volavka is professor of psychiatry at the New York University School of Medi-cine, director of research at the Manhattan Psychiatric Center, and chief of the Clinical Research Division, Nathan S. Kline Institute for Psychiatric Research. Dr. Volavka has also taught or conducted research at a number of other institutions, including the Max Planck Institute for Psychiatry, Munich. He has published extensively over a long career and is the author of the forthcoming book *Psychobiology of Violence*.

James Q. Wilson is James A. Collins Professor of Management at the John E. Ander-son Graduate School of Management, University of California, Los Angeles. Since the 1960s, Dr. Wilson has chaired or served on a great number of commissions, task forces, advisory panels, and governing boards, in both the public and private sectors. He is a past president of the American Political Science Association and a recipient of that association's James Madison Award for distinguished scholarship. He is well known as the author or editor of many works on crime, including *Thinking about Crime, Crime and Human Nature* (with R. J. Herrnstein), and *Crime and Public Policy* (published by ICS Press in 1983).

INDEX

Abuse
  characterization of, 125–26
  child, 97, 114
  See also Domestic violence; Drug
    abuse
Accountability
  contemporary systems of, 382–84
  modification of juvenile laws for,
    106–7
  of prosecutors, 374–75
Adolescence
  beginnings of criminal behavior in,
    47
  criminogenic traits in, 40–41
Aggravated assault, 273–74
Aggressive behavior
  caused by drugs, 297
  caused by media violence, 242–45
  long-term effects of television
    violence on (New York study),
    253–56
  predictions of childhood, 43–45, 48
  related to television violence,
    246–50
Alcohol
  crimes committed under influence
    of, 302, 315
  effects of, 297
  legal status of, 304–6
  link to crime, 345
  pricing of, 315
American Broadcasting Corporation
  (CBS), 260
American Psychological Association
  (APA), 238

Commission on Youth and Violence,
  248–49
Amphetamines, effect of, 298
Anonymity, 196
Anti–Drug Abuse Acts (1986, 1988),
  451, 455–56
Antisocial behavior
  adoption studies of, 71–75
  childhood aggression predicts, 45
  evident at early age, 138
  family studies of, 67–68
  neurochemical and
    psychophysiological factors in,
    82–87
  neuropsychological factors in,
    78–80, 88
  perinatal and neurodevelopmental
    influences on, 76–78
  twin studies of, 68–71
Appearance, physical
  minor anomalies in, 77–78
  of offenders, 56–57
Arrest rates
  effects of, 335–36
  trends in juvenile, 95–99
Arrests
  deterrent effect of, 337
  disposition of felony, 363–64, 366–70
  for drug offenses, 399
  ethnic orientation of drug, 399
  probable cause and trial-worthiness
    of, 365
  screening for prosecution, 364–65
    365
  See also House arrest programs

ATM locations, 346
Auto theft, cross-national comparison
    of, 16

Bartley-Fox Amendment (1974),
    Massachusetts, 378
Behavior. *See* Aggressive behavior;
    Antisocial behavior; Childhood
    behavior; Criminal behavior;
    Parental behavior; Violent
    behavior
Biological factors
    as influence on crime, 65–67
    interacting with adverse social
    environments, 87–88
Boot camps
    effectiveness of, 92–93
    as intermediate programs, 430,
    435–36
    for juvenile and young adult
    offenders, 110–11
Boston Youth Survey (1989), 190
Brain dysfunction
    frontal lobe, 78–79, 80, 82
    left fronto-temporal, 79
    neuropsychological measures of, 80
Brain-imaging techniques, 80–81
Bureau of Alcohol, Tobacco, and
    Firearms (BATF), 287
Bureau of Justice Assistance (BJA),
    458–59
Bureau of Justice Statistics (BJS), 425
Bush administration, 456
Byrne Program, 457–59

Cambridge Study of Delinquent
    Development, 43–47
Career criminal
    predictors, 93
    programs, 372–73
    research in description of, 472–73
Centers for Disease Control (CDC), 238
Center for Intentional Injury
    Research, 467
Centerwall study of television violence,
    250–53
Childhood behavior
    associated with becoming adult
    burglar, 45–47
    in relation to adult behavior, 43–49
    in relation to criminal behavior,
    54–55
Child-rearing practices, 127

Oregon Social Learning Center
    model of, 138
Children
    deviant behavior in, 126–27
    neglected, 125
    perception of violence in, 239
    resemblance in behavior of natural
    parents and, 55–56
    of single parents underrepresented
    in samples, 136
    See also Juvenile crime; Juveniles
Civil rights (school setting), 153
Cocaine
    effects of, 297–98, 303
    legalizing, 307–9
    legal status of, 304–6
    pricing of, 314
    in relation to crime, 303–4, 307–9
    users, 323
Columbia Broadcasting System (CBS),
    261
Community
    as focus of proposed policy, 214–16
    isolation from school, 152–53
    policing, 338–43
    service, 381, 406, 428, 437
Community Development Corporations
    (CDCs), 211
Community structure
    effect of crime on, 202–4
    related to gangs, 234–35
    with social disorganization, 198–201
Community Youth Gang Services
    (CYGS), 224–25
Computerized tomography (CT), 80–81
Conflict, 125
Constitution, the (Second
    Amendment), 281
Control
    in community policing concept,
    338–43
    of community when no one cares,
    150
    with social organization and
    disorganization, 198–201
    and tracking of convicts, 341
    weakened social and cultural,
    152–58
    See also Crime control; Drug abuse
    control policy; Gun control; Risk
    control; Schools; Self-control
    concept
Control theory, 114

Correction programs,
    community-based, 382
    effectiveness of, 430–38
    removal of offenders from, 438–39
    residential, 437
    solutions offered by, 440–44
Correction programs, juvenile
    commitments to public and private,
        110
    evaluations of, 111–12
    short-term challenge programs as,
        110–11
    types and facilities of, 108–10
Court intervention, 403
Crack trade, 303
Crime
    alcohol-related, 315, 317–19
    attributable to juveniles, 95–96
    children's exposure to, 121–22
    cross-national differences in, 15–26
    cross-section area studies of, 180–83
    definition and measurement of, 3
    as destiny, 66
    effect of labor market on, 178
    effect on labor market outcomes,
        187–90
    federal research programs on, 467–68
    increased propensity for, 175–78
    learning theory of, 122–27
    link to drugs, 296–304, 307
    link to heroin prices, 312
    link to labor market incentives,
        183–87
    link to unemployment, 171, 178–86
    perinatal factors in, 87
    and physical environment, 349–61
    proposed research on social
        environment's effect on, 480–82
    proposed research on justice
        system's effects on, 476–78
    resulting in prison sentences, 175
    time series analyses of, 178–80
    See also Domestic violence; Drug
        crimes; Gun crimes; Index crimes;
        Juvenile crime; Property crime;
        School crime; Violent crime
Crime control
    Crime Control Act (1990) and, 458
    federal government measures for, 451
    research, 472–73
Crime rates
    age-specific, 392, 394
    cross-national data on, 15

demographic shifts and, 392–95
determining prevalence across
    nations for, 15–22
    differences in cross-national, 17–22
    differences in cross-national
        interpretation of, 22–26
    economic incentives in determining,
        184–86
    effect of increased police presence
        on, 329–30
    growth of, 389–91
    in relation to poverty, 194–95
Criminal behavior
    causes of, 62–63
    childhood aggression predicts, 45
    continuity of, 41–42
    criminogenic variables determining,
        40
    neuropsychological factors in,
        78–80, 88
    psychology of, 49–55
    in relation to childhood behavior,
        43–49
    in relation to IQ, 50–53
    transmitted from parent to child,
        67–68, 87
Criminality
    adoption studies of, 71–75
    family studies of, 67–68
    twin studies of, 68–71
Criminal justice research program,
    472–83
Criminal justice system
    in comparison of similar nations,
        12–13
    resources diverted by drug trade,
        300
    identification of drug offenders
        under jurisdiction of, 323–25
    men under supervision of (1993),
        172
    role of federal government in,
        447–51
    transfer of discretion within, 397–98
Criminal records, as predictors of
    crime, 121
Criminals
    characteristics of, 184
    proposed research on careers of,
        472–75
    self-employed status of, 189–90
    stages in lives of, 40–49
    See also Career criminal

Criminogenic traits
  of Arthur Shawcross, 61
  defined, 39
Criminology, environmental, 358
Crisis Intervention Network (CIN), 224
Curfews, 342–43

Darwinism, social, 65
Data sources
  for cross-national crime incidence,
    15
  limitations of country, 17–21
  newly available for cross-national
    crime data, 25–26
  for effect of labor market on crime,
    178, 180
Decriminalization of drugs, 304–5
Defensible space theory
  applications of, 351–55
  principles of, 349–51, 356
Delinquency
  effect of population turnover on, 195
  family reduction of, 128–31
  learning theory of, 122–27
  link to child-rearing practices,
    124–28
  predictors, 97–98, 113–14
  rates in black and foreign-born
    areas, 195–96
  in relation to family size, 137
  strain, control, and social learning
    theories of, 114
  See also Self-control concept
Demoralization, 137
Detention, pretrial, 28
Detention centers (juvenile offenders),
    109
Deterrence
  effective, 408–9
  as rationale for sanctions, 400
Deterrence theory
  general, 375, 400
  in relation to gangs, 235
  in relation to intoxication, 318–19
  special, 375
Discipline, student, 153–54
Disobedience, 45–47
Disorder
  amelioration of, 160
  effect of social, 208
  effect on well-designed physical
    environment, 357–58
  neighborhood, 150

potential for school, 152
  proposed strategies to reduce, 208–9
  school, 149–50
  symptoms of school, 155–56
  teachers as cause of school, 156
Disorders, behavior, 76–78, 87
Disruptive behavior. See Antisocial
    behavior
District attorneys, 372
Domestic violence
  and assault crimes within families,
    366
  effect of arrests on incidence of,
    335–36
Dopamine, 82
Drug abuse
  attitude changes influencing, 320–25
  control policy, 304–25
  treatment programs, 322–23
  See also Drug use
Drug crimes
  imprisonment for, 378–79
  mandatory minimum sentences for,
    399
Drug markets
  crime related to, 298–300
  disruption strategy toward, 316–17
  dual, 314
  guns as tools of trade in, 412
  proposed research to study, 479
  punitive attacks in, 399, 401
  selling as crime of juveniles in, 97
  selling by gangs in, 227–28
Drugs
  differences in pharmacologic effects
    of, 303–4
  legal and illegal status of, 304–5
  linked to crime, 296–304, 307
  reducing demand for, 320–25
  See also Alcohol; Amphetamines,
    effect of; Cocaine; Heroin;
    Marijuana; PCP
Drug use
  coerced abstinence from, 323–25
  effect of raising prices on, 309–17
  as factor in juvenile crime, 98
  by gangs, 227
  interdrug substitution in, 313–14
  by probationers, 426
  in relation to crime, 301–3
  and sanctions for intoxication,
    317–19
  tough sanctions and , 370

Earnings from crime, 189–90
Education, public, 383
Electroencephalograms (EEGs), 86–87
Electronic monitoring, 434–35
Employment
  differences between criminals and
    noncriminals in rates of, 188
  effect of imprisonment on, 189
  See also Labor market;
    Unemployment
Enforcement
  to decrease drug availability,
    315–17
  effect of increased, 337
  police crackdowns and
    displacements in, 332–33
  truancy and curfew, 342–43
Environment, physical, 357–58
Environmental criminology, 358
Evidence, insufficient, 366

Family
  activities to reduce delinquency,
    128–31
  intervention program, 138
  present-day functions of, 131–32
  and proposed parent management
    training programs, 139
  as source of crime, 122–124
  structurally weak, 132–135
  structure and crime, 197–198
  traditional functions of, 131
  See also Parent, single; Unmarried
    parenthood; Self-control concept
Father, absent, 138
Fear of crime, 351–55
Federalism, 446–49
Felony Firearm Statute (1977),
  Michigan, 377
Film industry, 260–61
Fines, 380, 428, 437–38
Forfeiture, 380, 428
Fourth Amendment exclusionary rule,
  366

Gang cities, 226, 229–30, 233
Gang cycles
  defined, 221–22
  illusory, 225–26
  variation in, 222–25, 231–33
Gangs
  Asian, 218–19, 230
  as business enterprises, 186–87

characteristics of, 218, 230
as development from groups, 198
drug, 219–20, 227–28, 230
drug use and distribution by, 227–28
effect of social disorganization on,
  198–201
entrepreneurial, 220–21, 227–28
proliferation of, 226–27, 229–31
street, 219–220, 229–231
structure of, 220
white supremacist or skinhead, 231
Gang violence, 231–33
In re Gault (1967), 153
Gender
  in relation to property crime, 72
  representation in prison population,
    369–70
Genetic factors
  in criminal behavior, 55–58, 41–49
  in differences between men and
    women, 57–58
  and XYY chromosomes in males, 58,
    63
Goss v. Lopez (1975), 154, 165
Government
  actions related to media violence,
    261–62
  gun control roles of federal, state,
    and local, 291–94
  role of federal, 447–51
  strategies to deal with crime, 451–52
Group homes, 109
Groups, 198
Gun control
  community policing for, 339–41
  policy proposals for, 282–94
  proposed and adopted policy for,
    282–90
  rights and responsibilities in policy
    for, 280–82
  welfare economics in policy for,
    278–79
Gun Control Act (1968), 282
Gun crimes, fatal and nonfatal, 270–71
Gun markets
  dealers in, 287–88
  legal and illegal, 288–89
  regulation of, 287–88
Gun ownership patterns, 268–70
Guns
  availability and supply of, 275–78,
    284–89
  black and grey markets for, 288–89

Guns *(continued)*
  as cause of death in United States, 267
  as crime instrument, 273–75
  in gang-related homicides, 232
  high rates of U.S. homicides involving, 22–23
  licensing system for 287
  personalized, 286
  used in self-defense, 271–72, 275
  used against people, 270–72
  and value to users, 278
  See also Handguns

Halstead-Reitan Neuropsychological Test Battery, 79
Handguns
  as percentage of all guns used in crime, 271
  as risk factor, 339–41
Health care programs
  to prevent perinatal-related injury, 88–89, 214
Heart rate, resting, 85
Hereditary influences
  on resemblances between parents and children, 121–22
  transmitted from parent to child, 67–68, 87
  twin studies of, 68–71
Heroin
  effects of, 297
  legal status of, 304–6
  pricing of, 311–14
  in relation to crime, 303–4
  users, 323
Home confinement programs, 434–35
Homicides
  change in age-specific rates for, 411–12
  cross-national comparisons of, 16, 22–23
  drug-related, 298
  gang-related, 221, 231–32,
  by gunshot, 279
  and incidence in United States (1992), 238
  juvenile arrest rates for, 96
  victims and perpetrators of, 270
House arrest programs, 406, 429, 434–35
Housing

defensible space applications for public, 351–54
and effect of density on crime, 196–97
and proposed housing-based neighborhood stability, 210–11
proposed scattering of public, 211–12

ICS. *See* International Crime Survey (ICS)
Illegitimacy, 132–34
Imprisonment
  for drug and violent crimes, 380
  effect on employment, 188–89
  for index crimes, 380
  policy shifts related to, 395–98
  See also Incarceration
Incapacitation, 376, 379–80, 385, 409
Incarceration
  alternatives to, 381–82
  comparing levels and lengths of, 31–36
  cross-country comparison of prevalence of, 32–36
  defining , 27–28
  increase in probability of, 391–92
  of men as percentage of labor force (1993), 172
  propensity in United States, 11
  under war on drugs program, 457
Incarceration rates
  criticisms of comparing, 30
  cross-national comparisons of, 26–38
  distorted, 29–30
  Minnesota, 410
  per capita in United States, 26
  rise in (1980–1991), 172–73, 175
  for specific crimes, 30–31
  in United States (1924–1993), 387–88
Income
  delinquency related to mobility and low, 194–95
  in relation to property crime, 182–83
Index crimes
  identified, 363
  imprisonment for, 364, 380
Indianapolis Model of Police Accountability for Community Targets (IMPACT), 347
Inequality, ecological, 201–2

Information
    prosecution and sentencing role of,
        382–84
    sources of juvenile crime, 94
Information systems
    with police mobile data terminals,
        341
    and problem-solving attempts in
        Indianapolis, 347
    used by prosecutors, 374
Inmate surveys
    by Rand Corporation, 190
    by U.S. Department of Justice, 190
Intelligence
    of offenders, 49–53
    in relation to criminal behavior,
        49–54
Intensive supervision programs (ISPs),
    406–7, 426, 428–29, 431, 433–34,
    440, 442–43, 497
Intermediate programs
    boot camp/shock incarceration,
        430
    day reporting centers, 429–30, 436
    house arrest, 429
    intensive supervision programs as,
        428–29
Intermediate punishment,
    community-based, 406–7, 422,
    424–25
International Crime Survey (ICS)
    analyses of, 23–25
    data sample sizes in, 26
    as data source, 15
Interpol, 15
Intervention programs, 438
    gang-related, 234–35
    proposed gang-related, 235–36
Intoxication sanctions, 317–19
Invention theory of crime, 123

Judges
    sentencing decision role of, 369–70
    sentencing incentives for, 371–74
Juvenile court
    attention to rights of children in, 153
    changes in law to permit
        accountability to, 106–7
    criticism of, 100
    features of proceedings in, 101–2
    legislative restrictions on, 153–54
    operation and characteristics of,
        100–101

    principles and function of, 99–100
    reduced confidentiality of records in,
        107
    waiving jurisdiction of, 105–6
Juvenile crime
    approaches for early prevention of,
        112–17
    perception of, 92
    as predictor of adult crime, 98–99
    Rand Corporation study of, 103
    and treatment of repeat offenders,
        106
    trends, 93–99
Juvenile justice system, 99–108
Juveniles
    drug arrests of, 399
    homicide rates among, 411–12
    police control of, 342–43
    See also Correction programs,
        juvenile

Kelly v. R. G. Industries, 292

Labor market
    effect of crime on outcomes in,
        187–89
    effect on crime, 178
    incentives related to crime, 183–87
    link to crime, 181–83, 190–91
Law Enforcement Assistance
        Administration (LEAA), 372
    funding and grants, 453–54
    provisions and functions of, 452–53
Learning theory of crime and
        delinquency, 122–27, 130–31
Legislation
    on carrying a gun without a license,
        277
    proposed and adopted gun control,
        282–90
    restricting access to guns, 286
    See also Three-strikes law
Legislation, proposed
    for crime bill with federal role
        (1994), 459–62
    related to television violence,
        261–64
    for study of television violence,
        261–64
Legitimacy, 132–33
Liquor sales, 345
Louis Harris–MetLife survey (1993),
        143, 147–48

Luria-Nebraska Neuropsychological
    battery, 78–79
Lying, 46–47

Mandatory sentencing, 377–79
    See also Three-strikes law
Manganese, 82
Marijuana
    decriminalization of, 314
    effects of, 297, 303
    legalizing, 306
    markets, 303
    pricing of, 314
Media violence
    access to, 239–42
    in mass media, 238–39
    public opinion on, 238–39
    in stimulation of violent behavior,
        237, 242–45
    and theories related to aggression,
        256–60
    See also Television violence
Minneapolis Hot Spots Patrol
    Experiment, 333–34
Minnesota Sentencing Guidelines
    Commission, 409
Minor physical anomalies (MPAs),
    77–78
Morality, family, 132–35
Motion Picture Association of America,
    260
MPAs. See Minor physical anomalies
    (MPAs)
Municipal services, proposed, 212–13

National Commission on the Causes
    and Prevention of Violence
    (1972), 262
National Crime Survey, 143, 147–48
National Crime Victimization Survey,
    5–6, 173, 175
National Firearms Act (1934), 283
National Institute of Corrections, 427
National Institute of Education report
    (1978), 142–44
National Institute of Justice (NIJ),
    467–75
National Institute of Mental Health
    (NIMH), 247
    Violence and Traumatic Stress
        Research Branch, 467
National Science Foundation, Law and
    Social Science Program, 467

Neglect, 125–26
Neighborhoods
    cleanup of, 208–9
    defensible space applications in,
        352–57
    family structure influence on,
        197–98
    identification of high-crime, 207–8
    physical conditions in, 355–58
    proposed housing-based
        stabilization for, 210–11
    proposed policy to identify and
        patrol "hot spots" in, 207–8
Networks, neighborhood and
    community, 198–201
Neurochemical factors, 82–83, 88
Neurodevelopmental influences,
    76–78
Neuropsychological factors, 78–80, 88
Neurotransmitters
    in antisocial populations, 82–83
    defined, 82
Norepinephrine, 82–83

Offenders
    deterrence theory related to, 376
    drug-related, 300
    incapacitation of, 376, 379, 380
    intelligence of, 49–53
    mandatory sentences for, 377–79
    neurological factors related to
        behavior of, 80–82
    physical appearance of, 56–57
    proportion of men to women
        among, 57
    serious habitual, 42–45
    traits of average, 39
    typical, 40–41
    violating sentence conditions,
        438–39
Offenders, juvenile
    in juvenile court system, 100–105
    and suggested reforms in juvenile
        court system, 105–8
    See also Juvenile crime
Office of Juvenile Justice and
    Delinquency Prevention, 107
Omnibus Crime Control Act (1970),
    454
Omnibus Crime Control and Safe
    Streets Act (1968), 452
Operation Cul-de-Sac, Los Angeles,
    354

Order
  with presence of adult students,
    168–69
  school, 158–59
  See also Disorder
Oregon Social Learning Center, 138
Overcrowding
  avoiding, 407
  effect of prison, 402–5
  response to prison, 406–11

Parent, single
  and delinquency of child, 138
  as risk factor, 97
  unmarried, 132–35
  See also Children
Parental behavior
  criminal, 55
  deviant behavior and attitudes,
    126–27
  as predictors of chronic offending,
    48
  in relation to offspring, 67–68
Parenting, poor, and delinquency, 114
  See also Child-rearing practices
Parents
  deviant behavior and attitudes of,
    126
  and prevention of delinquency, 128
  See also Unmarried parenthood
Parolee release, 341
Parole system, federal, 377
PCP, 306–7
Perinatal factors, 76–78
Personality traits, 53–55
Phillips study of television violence,
    252–53
Physical traits, 56–57
Plea bargaining, 365–66
Police
  attention to crime risk factors, 327
  constraints on problem solving by,
    344–45
  effect of rapid response by, 334–35
  monitoring of parolees and
    probationers, 341
  repeat offender units, 341
  role in family problems, 139
Police presence
  in control of handguns, 339–41
  for crackdowns and displacement,
    332–33
  and effect on crime rate, 329–30

estimated current and proposed
    increase in, 328–29
  history of, 330–31
  for hot spot visibility, 331–34, 340
  Kansas City Patrol Experiment and,
    332, 340
  in relation to arrest rates, 335–36
  strikes decrease, 331
Policing, problem-oriented, 343–47
Policy interventions, community-based,
    210–14
Policy proposals
  for drug use prevention, 321–25
  for drug-related sentencing, 319–20
  implications of, 325–26
  for intoxication sanctions, 317–19
  politicization of, 413–16
Political factors
  in crime policy, 413–16
  related to imprisonment policies,
    397
  in response to drug wars, 399
Population concentration, 196–97
Population growth. See Prison
    population
Positron emission tomography (PET),
    80–81
Poverty
  as cause of delinquency, 113
  as factor in crime rate, 194–95
  percentage of youth raised in,
    113–14
  proposals to lower concentration of,
    211–12
  in relation to unmarried parenthood,
    133
  as risk factor, 97
Prevention
  approaches for early, 112–17
  police role in, 347–48
  situational, 358–60
  through police problem solving,
    343–47
Prevention programs
  community-level, 206–7
  delinquency, 115
  dropout, 151
  proposed drug-related, 321–25
Prison population
  black people's representation in,
    370
  factors in growth of, 389–95,
    397–401

Prison population *(continued)*
  growth under federal sentencing
    guidelines, 377
  political factors in, 397
  related to drug arrests, 398–401
  responses to growth of, 401–11
  strategies to control, 407–11
  See also Overcrowding
Prisons
  construction of new, 403–5
  overcrowded, 402–3
  privatization of, 404–5
  rationed space proposal for, 410–11
  state and local funding of, 423
  strategy for use of, 416–19
Probation
  community programs of, 426
  as crime control strategy, 430–31
  intensive supervision in, 382, 406–7,
    431, 433
  in split sentencing, 423–424
  state and local funding of, 423
Probationers
  behavior of, 430–31
  characteristics of, 425
  misbehavior by, 426
Problems
  family moral, 132–37
  solutions to crime, 344
  in toddlerhood, 47–48
Programs. *See* Correction programs,
    community-based; Correction
    programs, juvenile; Family
    intervention program; Home
    confinement programs;
    Intermediate programs;
    Intervention programs; Prevention
    programs; Prosecution programs,
    community-oriented; Research
    programs; Treatment programs;
    Youth programs
Prohibition (of drug use), 305
Property crime
  adoption studies related to, 72–75
  cross-national comparison of, 16–17,
    24–25
  juvenile arrest rates for, 95
Prosecution
  determinants of, 365–68
  effective use of information in,
    382–84
  reform of practices in, 374
  screening arrests for, 364

Prosecution programs,
    community-oriented, 373
Prosecutors
  and career criminal programs,
    372–73
  discretion transferred to, 397–98
  and incentives to prosecute, 371–74
Psychological traits, 57–58
Psychophysiological factors, 83–88
Public opinion, 450–51
Public policy
  alternatives for federal government,
    451–52
  for children with perinatal
    complications, 213–14
  community-oriented implications of,
    207–14
  for prenatal health care to mothers,
    214
  proposals for gun control, 283–94
  related to gun control, 282–83
Punishment
  cross-national characterization of, 27
  intermediate , 406–7
  See also Intermediate punishment;
    Sanctions
Punishment, physical, 125–26
  See also Abuse
Punitiveness
  increased, 401–2
  of United States, 36–37

Rand Corporation juvenile crime study,
    103
Randomized control trial, 336–38
Reagan administration, 455
Recidivism
  and employment, 189
  of federal prisoners, 460
  genetic factors in, 74
  of incarcerated individuals, 189
  with intensive probation
    supervision, 406–7, 432–33
  linked to perinatal and neurological
    factors, 77
  parolees' rate of, 341
Recreation, supervised, 343
Reforms, procedural, 105–8
Regional cerebral blood flow (RCBF),
    80–81
Regulation
  of drugs, 304–6
  of gun dealers, 287–88

for gun purchases, 287–88
by police in crime prevention,
345–47
Repeat offender units, 341
Research
bias in, 469–70
on communities and crime, 204–7
important areas of, 472–83
legal profession's perception of,
471–72
proposals for additional federal,
483–87
skepticism toward, 470–71
topics requiring, 465–67
Research programs
federal, 467–72
randomized controlled trial design
in, 336–37
Residential placements, 109–10
Restitution, 381, 428
Retribution, 66, 376
Rhodes v. Chapman, 403
Risk assessment
applied to policing, 344
in reduction of prison population,
407
Risk control, 344
Risk factors
contributing to juvenile delinquency,
97–98
handguns as, 339–41
juveniles as, 343
of parents with criminal behavior,
55–57
police attention to, 327–28
security guard control of, 338–39
Robbery, 273–75, 278
Rockefeller Drug Law (1973), New
York, 378

Safe School Study survey (1976),
143–47, 148, 149 156–58, 160
Sanctions
in drug cases, 371
intermediate, 422, 424–25
for intoxication, 317–19
with mandatory sentences, 378–79
See also Punishment
School crime
incidence and scope of, 144–47
1978 report of, 142–43
Schools
disorder in, 149–58

effect of weakened controls in,
152–58
and isolation from community,
152–53
strengthening adult control in, 168–70
School violence, 141–42
dealing with, 170
disorder and, 149–58
strategies to deal with, 160–70
against students, 147–49
surveys, 143
against teachers, 147
Second Amendment, 280–81
Security guards, 338–39
Self-control concept, 122–23, 135, 137
Sentences
for drug crimes, 300
expansion of mandatory, 378–79
federal appellate review of, 377–78
split, 423–44
Sentencing
change from indeterminate, 375–79
deterrence theory of, 376
effective use of information in,
382–84
factors in decisions on, 368–70
under federal guidelines, 377
under federal and state laws, 460
indeterminate, 375–76
just and effective system of, 379
just-deserts basis for, 379–80, 383, 397
rates for split, 425–26
role of judge in, 370–71
truth in, 460
utilitarian system of, 380
See also Sentences; Sentencing,
mandatory; Sentencing
commissions; Sentencing
guidelines; Sentencing laws;
Shock probation or split sentence
Sentencing, mandatory
incidence of, 424
in reduction of homicides, 274
Sentencing commissions, 398
Sentencing guidelines
acceptance of, 384
federal, 377–78, 384
intermediate punishment in, 407
and Minnesota Sentencing
Guidelines Commission, 398,
409–10
state-level systems of, 374–78, 385,
399

Sentencing laws
  proposed additional policy reforms
    in, 385
  reforms in, 374–75
  state-level statutory determinate,
    376, 378–79
Sentencing Reform Act (1984), 377
Serotonin, 82
Sexual activity, 45–46
Shock probation or split sentence, 382,
  423–24, 430
Single parent. See Parent, single
Situational crime prevention, 358–60
Skin conductance response tests,
  83–85, 87
Social capital
  concept of, 199–200, 209–10
  proposed policy to build, 209–10
Social disorganization, 198–201
  See also Disorder
Social learning theory, 114
Social networks
  as informal social control , 209–10
  social capital embodied in,
    199–201
Social service system, 139
Strain theory, 114
Street closure, 354–55, 358
Street-lighting projects, 353
Street work programs, gang-related,
  234–35
Students
  adults as high school, 168–69
  ensuring willing, 161–68
  strengthening adult control over,
    168–70
  subcultures of, 152
Suicide, 279
Supervision
  changes in programs for community,
    426–30
  community-based, 460
  as intensive probation supervision,
    382, 406–7, 431, 433–34
  mandatory, 423–24
  men under (1993), 172
  parental, 128
Surgeon General's Report (1972), 247,
  260

Taverns, 345
Teachers
  as cause of school disorder, 155–56
  disciplinary role of, 156–58
  violence against, 147
Television industry, 260–61
Television violence
  and aggressive behavior, 246–50
  Centerwall and Phillips studies of,
    250–53
  and effect on violent crime, 250–53
  measurement of, 245–46
  and study of youth in Columbia
    County, New York, 253–56
Temperament, 53–55
Terry v. Ohio (1968), 340
Thievery, 46–47
Three-strikes law, 300, 413–16
Time served, United States, 11
Toddlerhood, 47–48
Training schools, for juvenile
  offenders, 109–10
Traits
  criminogenic, 39, 40–41, 61
  individual, 39
  personality, 53–55
  physical, 56–57
Treatment Outcome Prospective Study
  (TOPS), 322
Treatment programs
  drug-related, 322–23
  parent management training
    included in, 138–39
Truancy
  laws, 342
  related to adult burglary, 46–47
Twin criminality, 68–71

UCR. See Uniform Crime Reports
Unemployment, 178–84
Uniform Crime Rate
  levels of (1947–1992), 173–75
  propensity for crime revealed in,
    175–78
Uniform Crime Reports (UCR), 5–6, 94,
  173, 389
U.S. General Accounting Office (GAO),
  433–34
Unmarried parenthood, 132–35
  See also Illegitimacy

Vandalism, school-related, 147
Victimization
  conditions favoring, 197–98
  by gun use, 273
  of juveniles, 98

in neighborhoods with high
mobility, 195
rate of criminal (1973–1992),
173–77
in schools, 142–49
Victim surveys, 5–6, 18, 94
Violence
among drug dealers, 298–300
comparison of (Canada, South
Africa, United States), 250–52
defining, 240–42
drug-related, 302–3
in mass media, 238–42
measurement of television, 245–46
proposed research on juvenile,
475–76
street gang, 231–32
in taverns, 345
urban, 299
by young people, 411–13
See also Aggressive behavior;
Domestic violence; Media
violence; School violence;
Television violence
Violent behavior
caused by media violence,
242–45
neurochemical and

psychophysiological factors in,
82–87, 88
by victims of abuse or neglect, 114
Violent crime
adoption studies related to, 76
correlated with media events,
252–53
cross-national comparisons of,
15–16
effect of television violence on,
250–53
imprisonment for, 380
juvenile arrest rates for, 95–96, 104
outcomes for juvenile and adult
cases of, 103–4

War on drugs (1982–1993)
criticism of, 457
and differences from LEAA era, 455
federal government's role in, 456–59

XYY chromosomes, 58, 61, 63

Youth advocacy lobby, 100
Youth programs
Community Youth Gang Services,
224–25
in conjunction with curfews, 343